THE
GUINNESS
GUIDE TO

THE
GUINNESS
GUIDE TO
CLASSICAL
COMPOSERS

Keith Shadwick

GUINNESS PUBLISHING

ACKNOWLEDGMENTS

Thanks are due to the following, all of whom played a role in this book taking the form it has: Bill Holland, Becky Stevenson, Lucy Maxwell-Stewart, John Jones and Liam Toner at Polygram Classics; Kate Jones at Collins and at Philips and just—well, generally; Barry McCánn and Kathryn Howard at EMI Classics; Harriet Capaldi and Tara Guha at Warner Classics; Carol Lowry at Sony Classical and Decca—remember?; Paul Wescott at Chandos; Michael Deacon, Richard Wenn and Ann Cater at BMG; Jo Carpenter and Alexander Spicer at Select; Celia Ballantyne at Hyperion; Mike Wilpizeski at New Albion; Victoria Bevan at Harmonia Mundi; Roger Mills at Auvidis; Ivor Fuell and Jeremy Elliot at Complete; Tom Norden in his various capacities, and the good people at ASV, Cala, Priory and Carlton.

Reprint 10 9 8 7 6 5 4 3 2 1 0

Published in Great Britain by Guinness Publishing Ltd, 338 Euston Road, London, NW1 3BD.

'Guinness' is a registered trademark of Guinness Publishing Ltd.

Printed and bound in Great Britain by The Bath Press.

Project Manager:	Helen Weller
Editor:	Caroline Chapman
Design & Page Make-up:	Keith Jackson
Cover Design:	
Picture Research:	Richard Philpott
Publishing Director:	Ian Castello-Cortes

A catalogue record for this book is available from The British Library

ISBN 0-85112-605-7

CONTENTS

Acknowledgments 2
Preface by Stephen Jones 3
Contents 5
Introduction 7

Part I: 1000–1500 8

Hildegard von Bingen 12
Guillaume de Machaut 14
Guillaume Dufay 15
Johannes Ockeghem 16
Josquin Desprez 17
Clément Janequin 19
John Taverner 20

Part II: 1500–1600 22

Thomas Tallis 24
Giovanni Pierluigi da Palestrina 25
Orlande de Lassus 28
William Byrd 31
Tomás Luis de Victoria 33
Giovanni Gabrieli 35
Carlo Gesualdo 37
John Dowland 38
Claudio Monteverdi 40
Girolamo Frescobaldi 44
Orlando Gibbons 45
Heinrich Schütz 47

Part III: 1600–1700 50

Pietro Francesco Cavalli 52
Jean-Baptiste Lully 53
Marc-Antoine Charpentier . .56
Arcangelo Corelli 58
Johann Pachelbel 60
Marin Marais 61
Henry Purcell 62
Alessandro Scarlatti 65
François Couperin 67
Tomaso Albinoni 69
Antonio Vivaldi 71
Georg Philipp Telemann 74
Jean-Philippe Rameau 77
Johann Sebastian Bach 79
Georg Frideric Handel 83
Domenico Scarlatti 86

Giuseppe Tartini 88

Part IV: 1700–1800 90

Giovanni Pergolesi 92
Carl Philipp Emanuel Bach . .93
Christoph Willibald Gluck . . .96
Franz Joseph Haydn 99
Luigi Boccherini 102
Wolfgang Amadeus Mozart .104
Ludwig van Beethoven 110
Niccolò Paganini 114
Carl Maria von Weber 116
Giacomo Meyerbeer 119
Gioacchino Rossini 122
Gaetano Donizetti 124
Franz Schubert 127

Part V: 1800–1825 132

Vincenzo Bellini 134
Hector Berlioz 136
Mikhail Glinka 139
Felix Mendelssohn 141
Frédéric Chopin 144
Robert Schumann 146
Franz Liszt 149
Giuseppe Verdi 153
Richard Wagner 156
Charles Gounod 160
Jacques Offenbach 161
César Franck 164
Bedřich Smetana 166
Anton Bruckner 169

Part VI: 1825–1849 172

Johann Strauss II 174
Alexander Borodin 176
Johannes Brahms 179
Camille Saint-Saëns 182
Léo Delibes 185
Georges Bizet 187
Max Bruch 190
Modeste Mussorgsky 192
Pyotr Tchaikovsky 194
Emmanuel Chabrier 198
Antonín Dvořák 200
Jules Massenet 203

Edvard Grieg 206
Nicolai Rimsky-Korsakov . . .208
Gabriel Fauré 211

Part VII: 1850–1875 214

Leos Janáček 216
Edward Elgar 219
Ruggiero Leoncavallo 221
Giacomo Puccini 223
Isaac Albéniz 227
Gustav Mahler 228
Hugo Wolf 232
Claude Debussy 235
Frederick Delius 238
Pietro Mascagni 240
Richard Strauss 242
Alexander Glazunov 245
Carl Nielsen 248
Jean Sibelius 250
Erik Satie 253
Enrique Granados 255
Franz Lehár 256
Alexander Zemlinsky 259
Alexander Scriabin 260
Ralph Vaughan Williams . . .263
Sergei Rachmaninov 266
Gustav Holst 270
Charles Ives 273
Arnold Schoenberg 275

Part VIII: 1875–1900 . . .280

Maurice Ravel 282
Manuel de Falla 286
Ottorino Respighi 288
Béla Bartók 290
Zoltán Kodály 294
Igor Stravinsky 296
Edgard Varèse 300
Anton Webern 302
Alban Berg 304
Heitor Villa-Lobos 308
Frank Martin 310
Bohuslav Martinů 312
Sergei Prokofiev 314
Arthur Honegger 318

Darius Milhaud 321
Paul Hindemith 324
Carl Orff 327
George Gershwin 328
Francis Poulenc 331

Part IX: 1900–1925 334

Aaron Copland 336
Kurt Weill 339
Joaquín Rodrigo 341
William Walton 343
Aram Khachaturian 346
Michael Tippett 347
Dmitri Shostakovich 350
Olivier Messiaen 354
Samuel Barber 356
John Cage 358
Benjamin Britten 361
Witold Lutosławski 365
Alberto Ginastera 367
Leonard Bernstein 368
György Ligeti 371
Luigi Nono 372

Part X: 1925–PRESENT . . .374

Luciano Berio 376
Pierre Boulez 377
Hans Werner Henze 379
Karlheinz Stockhausen 381
Henryk Górecki 384
Krzysztof Penderecki 385
Harrison Birtwistle 386
Peter Maxwell Davies 387
Arvo Pärt 389
Steve Reich 390
Philip Glass 392
John Tavener 394
John Adams 395

The Orchestra 398
Glossary 399
Index 404
Bibliography 415
Picture credits 416

INTRODUCTION

It is something of an irony that the early history of what has commonly become known as Classical music contains precious few composers' names; until the 12th century, when Hildegard von Bingen became internationally fêted for her musical and literary achievements, church music had been composed—largely anonymously—for over 500 years. It was only with the slow advance of humanist thought during the Middle Ages, and a gradual acceptance that serious music could be pleasurable as well as serve the spiritual and ceremonial needs of the Western Church, that individual figures came to be routinely named and eventually revered for their talents. By the time the French 'ars nova' and the latter Renaissance had arrived in Italy and Northern Europe, the process had begun which, by the mid-19th century, raised composers from their position as paid servants and established them as charismatic icons in their own right. Since that relatively recent occurrence little has changed, apart from the fascination developed by many lesser mid-20th century composers for scaring away potential admirers of their music by making it as unapproachable as possible. Meanwhile, great creative talents such as Stravinsky, Bartók, Britten, Copland, Shostakovich and Berg strove to write music which had something urgent to communicate to the world.

This book, covering 150 composers and their creations over the last 900 years, was written with the intention of communicating to its readers the nature of each composer's achievement and the way in which it relates to that person's life and character. After all, composers have always been just as intensely human and as prey to life's pitfalls, prizes, illusions and realities as the rest of us; their brilliance with music often belies their ability to deal with life's wider challenges. Their uniqueness lies in how they transformed these circumstances through their dedication and artistry into works of art which continue to bewitch and fascinate each succeeding generation. For this reason, particular stress has been given to the social and personal context of each composer's life. A proper identification of their outstanding works and an attempt, on occasion, to explain why a particular work is outstanding in a composer's output is also central to the usefulness of this volume.

These parameters will supply a ready answer to those wondering why I have not listed the composers in alphabetical order. A grouping according to chronology allows assumptions common to a particular age to become clear and the interconnections between composers, countries and styles easier to follow. Most people with an interest in music beyond that of youthful excursions into the Top 40 are aware of names like Bach and Vivaldi, Haydn, Mozart and Beethoven, Liszt and Wagner, Tchaikovsky and Debussy; this book enables the common reader to discover not only the unique quality of each composer, but their similarities and differences, even the individual way they reacted to the same external events; for example, it is of more than passing interest that Haydn was a friend of both Mozart and Beethoven, and that Schubert was a pallbearer at Beethoven's funeral. The connections, personal and musical, continue to spiral out from there.

Every effort has been made to ease the reader's way through a mass of information and opinion. For example, if a reader simply needs a quick reminder of a particular composer's most representative work they need only refer to the 'Don't Miss' box to be put on the right track. However, attentive readers will be able to find their way with confidence through the most significant Western Classical music of the past 900 years and identify what they would like to listen to and why. If this object is attained, I shall have succeeded in my aims.

People who have been greatly instrumental in making this book as good as it is and helping me over many hurdles—in so doing winning my undying gratitude—include the following: Caroline Chapman, my editor, whose precision and perspicacity averted many a bear-trap; Richard Milbank, who commissioned the book in the first place; Helen Weller, who guided the project through with unerring deftness and civility; and my family, who reminded me that at all times in life a sense of humour helps.

1000-1500

As with art of every age, the music of this period gradually evolved from the forms of the past, both recent and antique. The trouvères and troubadours notwithstanding, the main body of composed music existed to serve the purposes of the Christian Church. This music had evolved directly from the plainchant tradition, which in turn had evolved from the gradual codification of numerous different regional chant practices. This codification is usually credited to Pope Gregory I (pope from 590-604)—hence the name Gregorian Chant—but such a massive undertaking was probably completed by a body of church scholars working under both his and others' jurisdiction.

Prior to such regulation, the church music of both the Western and the Eastern Empires (Rome and Byzantium) could trace its roots back to the musical practices and theories of the Greeks, Romans and inhabitants of Asia Minor in particular, especially the organization of note sequences into modes. Byzantium continued to preserve its own Eastern-based religio/musical traditions until its eventual eclipse in 1453. A fundamental fact has to be observed when investigating the nature of written/notated music at this time: the church regarded music's primary function to be that of aiding people to praise God and strengthen their relationship with him. Music which drew attention to itself for its own sake was largely frowned upon for it was failing in its prime purpose. The intense visions to be found in the

music and writings of Hildegard von Bingen, couched in the monophonic idiom, hold fast to this approach.

During 1000-1400 the monody of plainchant slowly gave way to the delights and disciplines of polyphony. By the 11th century, the medieval modal system was fully evolved, there being eight modes in all. At the same time the invention of the staff as an aid to writing down music was a key moment in the evolution of Western music, allowing the accurate notation of pitch and melody. The beginnings of polyphony are to be found in *organum* and *conductus*. *Organum* was exclusively liturgical in nature, and invariably based on pre-existing material, usually an earlier plainsong; it was nearly always a setting of liturgical prose. *Conductus* was set to poetry (usually original), the melody typically being a new invention, with the parts all moving together in the same rhythm. Both types alternated stretches of monody with stretches of polyphony. This 'singing together' was the kernel of polyphony, and it was the added intricacies of *organum*—the slower and faster parts, the held tones—which were particularly appropriate for development. The two most noted exponents of these early forms came from the French 'Notre Dame' school of the late 12th and early 13th centuries, Léonin (c. 1159–c. 1201) and Pérotin (c. 1170–c. 1236). From these two masters also evolved a form which was to become beloved of all polyphonic composers, the motet, originally a distinct descant section of

A musician playing bells from the 13th century Velisslavovy manuscript

an *organum* but latterly a separate and distinct form by which to set Latin and French verse. This separate form was thriving by the later 13th century, and was beginning to admit secular as well as sacred texts.

In Paris during the 14th century there was such an explosion of new artistic energy across all the arts that it was dubbed by the writer and composer Philippe de Vitry the 'new art', or 'ars nova'. Based on a further development of rhythmic values which gave composers greater freedom and subjectivity, especially in their secular and satiric compositions, it reflected the turbulence and change of a very uncertain century, but one which was crucial in its laying of the foundations of new art, writing and music—from Petrarch, Boccaccio, Dante and Chaucer to de Machaut, de Vitry, Lescurel and Jehan des Murs to Giotto, Simone Martini and Duccio. In Italy the foundations of later music traditions were being laid by composers such as Jacopo de Bologna (active c. 1340—1360) and Francesco Landini (c. 1325—97), with their development of the madrigal and *ballata* styles respectively. As these separate developments gathered momentum, the previously distinct Italian and French compositional styles began to converge, while at the end of this period the influx of music from other centres, including Britain and Wallonia, would prove of fundamental importance in the subsequent century.

The developments which occurred during the lifetimes of the composers born in the 15th century had a far-reaching impact on the religious and courtly music of the two centuries that followed. The first 50 years saw a continual evolution of musical theory and practice along the lines of the immediate past, with only gradual changes. These changes included the increased proliferation of the motet and its progressively wider definition so that it became not merely French-origin polyphonic devotional Latin-text work exhibiting plainsong characteristics, but virtually any polyphonic composition using Latin which was not composed as part of the Ordinary in the Christian service. This allowed a rapid expansion of creative ideas to take place within its form and prepared it to be a key creative vessel for such brilliant musicians as Ockeghem, Obrecht, Josquin Desprez and Dufay. It is no surprise that all these compositional giants came from the Burgundian or Hainault/Wallonian regions, for the flourishing of the arts and humanities under the Burgundian and French Courts in this century was virtually unparalleled elsewhere, especially in its cosmopolitan nature and in its leadership of artistic and musical fashion; many of its brightest creative lights, including Josquin, were later tempted away to the greatest of the Renaissance Italian Courts. The Burgundian composers were to the fore in developing the new unifying architectural elements for the music of the Mass, especially the use of the *cantus firmus* where a previously extant plainchant or melodic motif is used as an underpinning of the polyphonic structure, much as the keel holds a ship together.

During this period the importance and brilliance of the devotional music being written in Britain was recognized for the first time; throughout the Continent, Britain was generally acknowledged as providing the impetus for the proliferation of what became known as fauxbourden, a compositional technique which used two voices singing in parallel sixths, using octave cadences which allowed an unwritten third voice to be added, normally set at the interval of a fourth below the lead voice which was usually the treble. This led in the latter part of

A Concert *by Lorenzo Costa,* c. *1488*

the century to a more evenly balanced polyphony where all three voices often moved together, the upper voice leading the melody. An emerging strain of this type of writing is preserved in the *Old Hall Manuscript* of around 1420.

The practitioners working during the second half of the 15th century and into the 16th also absorbed the impact of two tremendously exciting developments: the application of the printing press (first used by Gutenberg in 1450) for the dissemination of music in manuscript form from the mid-1470s onwards, and the rapid transferral westwards of refugees from Byzantium (which fell to the Turks in 1453) bringing with them a flood of antique knowledge. In the realms of music, this meant access to the original Greek and Roman modes and their concomitant music theory leading in turn to a new realization that further codification of harmony, pitch and tuning was needed to take their own music on to the next stage. The ramifications of all this would keep composers occupied until well into the following century.

HILDEGARD VON BINGEN

1098–1179

Hildegard von Bingen was one of the most famous and brilliant women of the Middle Ages; a correspondent with popes and potentates, a gifted poetess and seer and the intensely practical head of her own convent. She was also an extraordinary composer and musical performer.

Born into a wealthy Rheinhessen family, Hildegard von Bingen was marked down from birth as destined to become a nun. Initially accepted at the age of eight into the Benedictine monastery of Disibodenberg, a mixed (male and female) establishment near Bingen, she was immediately recognized as possessing special gifts and thenceforth came under the personal tuition of the Abbess, Jutta von Spanheim. Her development in administrative, spiritual and artistic matters was such that by the time of Jutta's death in 1136, the 38-year-old Hildegard acceded to the position of magister of the convent. The increased duties and responsibilities of this position did nothing to slow her personal development, although she was a lifelong victim of ill-health.

In 1141 she experienced a series of religious visions, culminating in a visitation of tongues of fire from heaven. From then on she began recording her visions and insights in a series of manuscripts collected into the

Frontispiece to Hildegard's Scivias (Know the Ways)

book *Scivias* (Know the Ways). Work on this extensive opus lasted well into the 1160s; one of the most important

manuscripts, the Rupertsberger Codex, complete with beautiful illuminated miniatures, was finished in 1165. At the same time, and much against the wishes of the Disibodenberg abbot she set about founding an independent Benedictine convent in Rupertsberg, near Bingen. However, his objections were overcome and by 1152, the new buildings (which housed 50 women) were completed under her personal supervision.

During the 1140s Hildegard also experienced a period of intense musical creativity; during the following decade she spent much of her time gathering her music into a coherent cycle, as well as writing new tracts and songs designed to complete this extensive body of work. By 1158 the cycle had been delineated to her satisfaction, and was given the title *Symphoniae harmoniae a celestium revelationum* (The Symphony of the Harmony of Celestial Revelations). Though the original edition of this work contained over 60 antiphons, responsories, hymns and sequences—some of extraordinary length and complexity—Hildegard continued to enlarge this collection throughout the 1160s.

Hildegard von Bingen composed in the monophonic (single-line) style prevalent during her lifetime. This style made great use of plainchant modes and methods of musical organization which had roots, via Pope Gregory and St Augustine, in the earliest musical culture of the Christian Church, and hence in the Roman and Byzantine periods. Her life coincided with a rebirth of economic and cultural life unparalleled prior to the Italian Renaissance of three

centuries later, while just 40 years before her birth the final split between the churches of Constantinople and Rome had taken place, thus acknowledging the dissolution of the last vestiges of Rome's political and cultural legacy. She also began her career in music at a time when composition was gaining ground over improvization as the customary way of making music within religious circles. She used the plainchant tradition and its harmonic horizons, but was a great deal more ambitious and imaginative in the use to which she put her music. Her best works avoid being simply functional music written for everyday services, and are wholly caught up in the spiritual message carried by the words. In this she was the first great *known* setter of words (her own) in Western music— a tradition which continues to the present day. That she was a brilliant wordsmith clearly adds substantially to the originality and impact of her achievement, but above all her music contains great beauty and intense spirituality.

During this same 20 years Hildegard von Bingen began a large and varied correspondence with the leading religious and political figures of her

day, writing as far afield as France and Italy. As a result, she was the most famous—and certainly the most influential—woman of her time, and much honoured while she was alive.

One other major work involving music was completed: the *Ordo Virtutum*, a morality play with words and music wholly composed by Hildegard. The *Ordo* is bound by subject and allusion to the earlier cycle, giving allegorical life to the spiritual forces of the universe first depicted in the *Symphoniae*. This extraordinary work, takes as its main subject Hildegard's own soul; the story revolves around this soul's struggle to reach immortality and reject the tawdry pleasures proffered by the devil, and predates any other work in this form by more than 100 years.

Abbess Hildegard von Bingen completed one last major work before her death, the cosmology *Liber divinorum operum* (1163–73). In the next century her name was put forward more than once for canonization, but this ultimate recognition was not forthcoming. Yet the very fact that she was considered for it by at least two popes is a measure of her importance to 12th-century culture and history.

DON'T MISS

▶ **Ordo Virtutum**
▶ **Symphoniae harmoniae a celestium revelationum**
▶ **Liber divinorum operum**
▶ **Scivias (Know the Ways)**

GUILLAUME DE MACHAUT

c. 1300–1377

Together with his contemporary Philippe de Vitry (1291–1351) and the slightly earlier (and decidedly more obscure) Jehan de Lescurel (?1275–1304), Machaut brought to a peak the exciting innovations and developments associated with the Ars Nova movement which swept through France, bringing with it a concentration on secular rather than religious music.

It was de Vitry, the accomplished poet, musician and diplomat, who coined the term Ars Nova in a treatise of that name circulated in 1323 (although by that date the movement had already been in flower for a quarter of a century) which had been assembled in the famous satirical collection, *La Roman de Fauvel*, a work which contains all the extant music of de Lescurel who was hanged as a thief and a murderer in 1304.

Machaut managed to avoid any such fate, enjoying not only a relatively long life for the period, but also one of luxury and privilege. Born in the Champagne region, he was prepared for holy orders as was customary at the time. Due to his skills as a poet and musician he was much sought after by kings and potentates. While continuing his religious duties at Rheims Cathedral he entered the service of John, King of Bohemia and Duke of Luxembourg, remaining with him until the King's death at the battle of Crécy in 1346. Three years at the Normandy Court of the King's daughter were followed by

periods of valuable service with Charles de Navarre, King Charles V and the Due du Berry. That de Machaut's services were both appreciated and well rewarded is clear from the substantial house in Rheims where he lived until his death. The opulence and luxury of the house fits the overall image cultivated by Machaut, an image perpetuated by the lavish style of his surviving manuscripts; using only the finest materials, these were beautifully produced and often contained glorious illuminated illustrations and fine calligraphy.

Machaut was a central figure in the Ars Nova movement. His style combined traditional elements of organization—in his religious motets, for example, which adhered to the liturgical pattern already in use—with a new complexity of rhythm and polyphony. His religious works made great use of the concept of isorhythm, a method of unifying ever-longer compositions through skilfully repeated and juxtaposed melodic and rhythmic units of differing note-values. With texts which did not lend themselves to this treatment, a more traditional method was employed where irregular verbal patterns were mirrored in the music, only occasionally being interrupted by a flourish which could be used as a punctuation or as a type of cadence. In all, he composed a Mass and more than 20 motets for use in church.

Machaut was also instrumental in the formation of the *ballade* style. Indeed, most of his creative effort was in the

secular area, his *Messe de Notre Dame* being the exception rather than the rule. In this he is typical of his time, a period when the Church was in temporary political eclipse and increasingly inclined to reject the newer musical ideas which religious authorities felt (quite rightly, as it happens!) were directing people's attention to the music rather than to the religious impulse and ritual behind it. Machaut was breaking new ground by creating his own musical accompaniment for his song melodies, and was the last poet of his day to create the music for his own lyrics, thus again combining tradition with innovation.

He composed a substantial amount of secular music in which the monophonic traditions of the French *trouvères* of previous periods were for the most part upheld, though with a new emphasis on rhythmic subtlety and melodic grace. Over 45 *ballades* and more than 20 rondeaus are extant today, as well as

---

DON'T MISS

▶ **Messe de Notre Dame**

▶ **Foy porter, honneur garder**

▶ **Quant je sui mis au retour**

▶ **Comment qu'a moy lonteinne**

▶ **Dame, de qui toute ma joie vient**

nearly 50 other secular pieces. In the eight polyphonic virelays he composed, his Ars Nova credentials are at their

most notable: he not only exploits the angularity and occasional dissonance associated with past centuries, but the

sweeter and more ordered harmony of the new music, plus an ongoing fascination with rhythm applied to lyrics.

GUILLAUME DUFAY
c. 1400–1474

Dufay was one of the greatest French composers of any period, and the dominant musical personality between de Machaut and Desprez. His reputation is possibly founded more on his religious music—Masses and motets—than on his secular compositions, but there is much to admire and enjoy about the relative musical freedoms he finds in either genre.

Dufay used current polyphonic techniques in his masses and his 'occasional' motets. His work clearly shows the influence of the English composers whose music was known in the Burgundy region due to English political influence and the musical pre-eminence of John Dunstable (c. 1390–1453). Dufay continued the polyphonic tradition, deepening its contrapuntal complexity and reaching new subtleties of melodic and rhythmic line as well as introducing novel intervals learned from England into his part-writing, in keeping with general contemporary trends. There was increased freedom and embellishment in the melodic solo treble voice, while the tenor line was kept recognizably close to the Gregorian original on which a particular Mass or motet may be based.

Guillaume Dufay (left) and Gilles Binchois.

Born probably in the Hainault region near Cambrai, by the age of eight Dufay was a choirboy at Cambrai Cathedral. There are indications that he spent some of his time in Paris, but by 1420 he had moved to Pésaro in Italy to join the Malatesta Court—as an occasional piece, *Vasilissa, ergo gaude*, marking the late summer departure that year of Cleofe Malatesta to Byzantium, attests. A similar celebratory piece from 1423 marks the marriage of Carlo Malatesti and Vittoria di Lorenzo Colonna (a niece

of the presiding pope). After close on a decade with the Malatestas, either in Pésaro or Rimini, in 1428 Dufay moved to Rome to serve in the choir of the Papal Chapel where he remained (apart from a two year interval in the service of the Duke of Savoy) until 1437. During this time he moved with the Papal Court to both Florence and Bologna.

At about this time Dufay was made canon of Cambrai by Pope Eugène IV, and shortly afterwards he added a Mons canonry to his credentials, although it was not until the end of the decade that he removed himself from the Savoy circle. For some time prior to Dufay's association, Cambrai had enjoyed a high reputation as an ecclesiastical centre, and during his lifetime had also become renowned for its musical excellence. In the late 1430s Dufay gained his degrees of *Magister in artibus* and *Baccalaureus in decretis* at the Sorbonne in Paris, completing both in time to take a position as music tutor to the son of Philip le Bon, Duke of Burgundy, in 1442. In addition to his Sorbonne qualifications, he also had a law degree from the University of Bologna, proving his exceptional breadth of knowledge and education. Dufay remained based in Cambrai (apart from one last stint in service as choirmaster to the Duke of Savoy, 1452–58) until his death.

Dufay's secular works, or *chansons*, were built on the same foundations as his religious and liturgical music, using polyphonic techniques to embellish occasional and lyric texts, and to render them in a style suited to courtly ceremony or entertainment. Both

religious and secular settings could also have instrumental accompaniment, often from an organ, a stringed instrument, trumpets or a recorder. There are eight complete Masses extant, three of which are believed to be relatively early works: of these, *Missa sine nomine* is entirely representative. A later Mass, *Missa 'Se la face ay pale'*, illustrates Dufay's later *cantus firmus* approach, where a *cantus firmus* vocal line is repeated from beginning to end of the Mass (although it can, in practice, be interrupted). This device gives a unity to otherwise disparate parts of the same Mass.

Dufay's motets are fascinating, both intellectually and emotionally: one, the four-part *Nuper rosarum flores*, has been shown to correspond exactly to the proportions of Florence's Duomo, designed by Filippo Brunelleschi on ancient musical values and proportions. The composer's *chansons* are written to texts in Latin, French and Italian. The latter date from his time in Italy, and *Vergene bella*, a piece which combines both chanson and sacred processes, demonstrates the wealth of imagination Dufay could bring to what was

becoming an increasingly conservative form of musical composition.

Dufay's will still exists, its terms demonstrating both his wide-ranging interests and his generosity. He gave some of his best books (gifts from the Duke of Burgundy's son) to a friend, a portrait of Louis XI to another, and sundry other possessions to a range of friends. He also made clear stipulations as to what should happen when he was read his last rites: he wanted eight choristers from the Cathedral very quietly to sing a favourite hymn, followed by his own motet, *Ave regina celorum*. This request was observed, after a fashion: the music was sung, but only after his death, in the presence of his corpse in the Cathedral chapel itself.

DON'T MISS

▶ **Vasilissa, ergo gaude**

▶ **Missa sine nomine**

▶ **Missa 'Se la face ay pale'**

▶ **Nuper rosarum flores**

▶ **Flos florum**

JOHANNES OCKEGHEM

c. 1420–1497

The uniformly high quality of Ockeghem's religious music ensured his place as the dominant composer of the day. He was also a fine teacher, yet he created no school, and few composers who succeeded him

were able to utilize the elements of his creative craft.

As with so many 15th- and 16th-century composers, few details of Ockeghem's life survive. It is known that he was born in Flanders, and that by the early

1440s he was a chorister in Antwerp Cathedral. In 1444 he relinquished this position to go into service with Duke Charles I of Bourbon. Clearly highly regarded by his patron, Ockeghem prospered at Court and in 1452 entered the Chapelle Royale, becoming premier chaplin two years later and head of the Chapel by the time Charles VII died. Thus, by early middle age Ockeghem had achieved a comfortable niche in exalted circles and could play and compose in whatever way he saw fit.

Ockeghem seems to have enjoyed high favour with Charles VII's successor, Louis XI. One of his rewards was the appointment as Treasurer of St Martin's in Tours, a position which afforded him a comfortable lifestyle. He remained on good terms with Charles VIII, who succeeded Louis, retaining both the Tours Treasury and the Chapelle Royale positions until his retirement a year prior to his death when he was well into his eighties. On his death, Josquin Desprez penned the famous motet *Déploration sur le trépas de Jean Ockeghem*, with its lines: 'Clothe yourselves in mourning/ Josquin, Pierson, Brumel, Compère/and weep great tears from your eyes/for you have lost your good father'.

Compositionally, Ockeghem was a law unto himself: he disregarded its rules at will (sometimes not troubling to create a *cantus firmus)*, avoided cadences, or dispensed with imitation if it did not suit his purpose. There is general agreement that he was a deeply religious man and a highly serious composer of religious works, but the impression his music conveys is of an inward spirituality rather than of a great theological outpouring: Ockeghem is making his own private compact with God and mortality. That he was a skilled and often daring composer can be detected in any number of his works. His use of the canon, often masked and hidden in a proliferation of varieties, shows his delight at using basic structural devices in novel and surreptitious ways; his decision to dictate that his *Missa cuisvis toni* could be sung in any mode simply by reading the music in different clef combinations demonstrates a virtuoso's enjoyment of concealed artifice.

Ockeghem concerned himself almost exclusively with church music, having little interest in the *chanson* or song forms, pouring his creative energies into liturgical music of great solemnity. It could be said that the prevailing tone of his music is mystical, something often emphasized by the apparent simplicity of many of his church compositions, but this would not be entirely true as Ockeghem was no ascetic: he also enjoyed the finer things of life. It is perhaps more accurate to say that his music projected something of the introspection which must have been at the core of his being, and which drove him to take such an impressive individual path which few were able to sustain after his death.

DON'T MISS

▶ Missa' 'Mi–Mi'
▶ Missa cuisvis toni
▶ Missa Ecce ancilla Domini
▶ Requiem
▶ Se vostre cuer eslongne

JOSQUIN DESPREZ
c. 1440–1521

Josquin Desprez was the greatest composer of his age, and arguably one of the greatest of all time. As no composer of comparable stature preceded him, he could justly be called the first giant of Western music. He composed over 18 Masses, nearly 100 motets and scores of *chansons*, and these works show

him to be, like Mozart and Bach, a supreme synthesizer of the various forms and styles which existed before and during his lifetime.

Probably born in Condé, Hainault (from whence came de Machaut a century earlier), Josquin received his earliest musical education at the church of St Quentin (some claim Ockeghem was his teacher), but by 1459 he was in Italy, singing in Milan Cathedral and employed in the Sforzas' chapel. Serving until 1486 under both the notorious Galeazzo Sforza, and later Ascanio Sforza, Josquin spent nearly 30 years in Milan, with the period between 1486 and 1494 spent at the Papal Chapel in Rome (echoing the earlier experience of Dufay).

Josquin Desprez

this inventiveness was at its peak, both in the musical ingenuity and the setting of the words; given the fresh challenges of new texts, as opposed to the unvarying words of the Mass, Josquin revealed the great variety of expression he could encompass. A work such as the *Miserere*, set to Psalm 51 and written for Ercole I prior to 1505, is made up of three sections and constructed around a very simple *cantus firmus*, but the architecture he builds upon it is exceedingly ingenious and unfailingly eloquent. Josquin's remarkable feeling for words enabled him to select their most apposite musical setting. In this he was aided by the current interest in the effect of harmony on the colour and shades of meaning available from the text being set. Martin Luther's famous observation that Josquin was the "master of the notes...while other composers must do what the notes dictate" arises, at least in part, from these qualities.

Josquin's abilities in the area of *chanson* and other secular works rival those displayed in his motets. With the motets he often took earlier *chanson* forms, such as repetition schemes, and then invested them with such freshness and variety that he virtually reinvented them. He was also capable of following the meaning of a text to the point of creating strophic pieces with no exact repetition, or using any number of cunningly disguised musical schemes to achieve a wonderful balance between formal symmetry and the appearance of spontaneous effort. Josquin often took as a starting point a 'sample' or piece of melody from either folk material or from an earlier composer, but would then reveal his mastery in what new variants he could invent from that sample.

Josquin began the 16th century with three years in a French court, possibly Louis XII's. He returned to Italy around 1503 and took up the position of *maestro di cappella* with Ercole I's Court in Ferrara, but this lasted only one year: not wishing to risk death from the plague, which reached Ferrara in 1504, Josquin returned to France. That same year he is recorded in the register of chorists at Notre Dame, Condé, followed by an appointment there as provost. This position, and the canonship of St Gudule's in Brussels, were combined with a further period at Louis XII's Court which continued until the King's death in 1515.

Now in his mid-seventies, Josquin spent his remaining years in and around the area of his birthplace, and it is likely that he was buried in St Gudule's. Epitaphs to him in the Condé and Brussels churches indicate the high esteem in which he was held. His fame was such that it has been suggested that Leonardo da Vinci painted the composer's portrait during his time in Italy.

A composer who created music with consummate ease, Josquin was able to adapt his muse to suit the occasion. Thus he composed Masses which are duly conservative in form and musical vocabulary, but which are so brilliantly conceived and full of such wonderful invention within those forms that he not only wrote the greatest Masses of his day but also opened up new compositional possibilities within the old forms for later composers to explore. His skill in weaving contrapuntal polyphony so that it sounds the most natural thing in the world seemed to his contemporaries little short of miraculous. In his motets

Josquin's virtuosity was not only allowed free reign in the pursuit of sober musical goals; there are a number of anecdotes which show him capable of subtle and not-so-subtle musical and verbal jokes, anagrams and even blatant cajoling of patrons through his words and music. His motet on the 119th Psalm, written (it appears) at Louis XII's request, contains a plea for monies owed to him by the King, the plea relentelssly repeated in his rendering of the first line of the second section, '*memor esto verbi tui*' (remember to keep your word). When he heard this motet performed, Louis managed to find the money his composer so urgently required!

Josquin's position in history, though obscured for many years, is now unassailable. His ability to combine the grace and melodicism of his native French music with the intellectual and creative ebullience of the contemporary Italian style alone makes him a major influence on the way music developed in the years after his death. His fame was such that even in his own lifetime, and in the years after his death, many works were attributed to him in an attempt to lend them distinction. Three volumes of his works appeared in 1502, 1505 and 1514, a rare honour as most composers were lucky to have one complete volume to themselves. The demand was such that the first two books went into reprint.

DON'T MISS

▶ **Missa 'Ave maris stella'**
▶ **Missa 'De beata virgine'**
▶ **Salve Regina (4vv)**
▶ **Mille regretz**
▶ **Miserere mei, Deus**
▶ **Je ne me puis tenir d'aimer**
▶ **La déploration sur le trépas de Johannes Ockeghem**

CLÉMENT JANEQUIN
c. 1485–1558

Janequin was a highly unusual figure for his day: instead of following the conventional path of a musician/composer—choirboy, chorister, master of the choir, organist and composer—he relied mainly on the attractions of his secular *chansons* to make his living. He was one of the principal recipients of Josquin Desprez's musical legacy and his compositions made him one of the most famous men of his age.

Little is known about Janequin's early years beyond the fact that he was born in Châtellerault, a town situated between Poitiers and Tours. By 1505, when he was around 30 years old, he was in Bordeaux where he worked for an official of the Bordeaux Parliament, Lancelot du Fau. With the death of du Fau in 1523, he passed into the service of Jean de Foix, the Bishop of Bordeaux, where he served in various musical capacities at St Emilion and St Michel de Rieufret. It was during this time that his fame as a composer became apparent through the offices of Pierre Attaingnant, a Parisian publisher who published in 1528 a collection of Janequin's *chansons*. These proved sufficiently popular for regular subsequent volumes to appear.

Following in the wake of both Josquin and his disciple Nicolas Gombert (c. 1495–c. 1560), Janequin often used imitations of various creatures and natural effects in his songs; in *La Guerre 'La battaile de Marignan'* he even imitates the songs and cries heard on a battlefield. The extreme facility, taste and charm with which he could accomplish such effects made him immensely popular in his own country, and many of his *chansons* were repeatedly republished by Attaingnant during his lifetime. *La Guerre* and a work such as *Le Chant des oyseaux* (1547) also demonstrate Janequin's ease in sustaining longer forms for the chanson (six minutes or more) than virtually anyone else at the time. Janequin was often able to unify his works not only by motivic devices but through the employment of popular dance rhythms of the day, set to unusual verses. The subject-matter of many of his chansons was an important ingredient in his success, being often amorous or wickedly satirical, but the settings were so skilful and seemingly devoid of solemnity that the songs engendered delight, not outrage.

Janequin's reputation rests firmly on his chansons, but he also created a small body of church music of which only two Masses remain extant: La Bataille (1532) and L'Aveuglé Dieu (1554), both of which make no attempt to conceal the chanson composer lurking within. With the former Mass,

Janequin even manages to transform a battle song into a song of reconciliation during the course of the work, evoking an intensely human and immediate quality which was rare in such liturgical music at the time. This was no doubt due in part to Janequin's extreme sensitivity to texts and his mastery in the art of subtle word settings, an ability growing from his chanson experience but also from the legacy of Josquin.

Janequin was only once in charge of a church choir: from 1534–37 he directed the choir at Angers Cathedral. He relinquished the role but remained contentedly in Angers until 1549, by which time he was in his sixties and looking for some form of permanent recognition and stability. He settled in Paris and continued to compose,

hoping for official favour from the royal court. This was not forthcoming until 1554 when he was appointed the new chantre ordinaire du roi to the Chapelle Royale. He did not have long to enjoy this official recognition, nor the honorary title he received in 1558—compositeur ordinaire du roi— for he died in the early spring of that year.

JOHN TAVERNER
c. 1490–1545

Taverner was perhaps the greatest English composer of his age, and although he wrote in a more antique style, certainly equal to the majority of his European contemporaries. His grace and lucidity, and his careful construction on clear musical principles, were a source of inspiration to the next generation of English composers, many of whom had to cope with the schism brought about by Henry VIII's break with Rome.

Taverner was one of the second generation of musicians and composers

which flowered after the Wars of the Roses. He followed Robert Fairfax (1464–1521) and was a contemporary, though slightly younger, of Nicholas Ludford (c. 1485–1557), a composer who prospered in London while Taverner made his way in Oxford. With the glories of the Eton Choirbook (in which Fairfax was represented) by then consigned to history, Taverner wrote his music for liturgical use and within the florid English tradition where polyphony and counterpoint were lavishly developed but strictly applied, and where the occasional held chord was used for punctuation rather than as a basic musical building-block.

Taverner was born and raised in or near Tattershall in Lincolnshire, a small village which nonetheless possessed a fine manor and a first-class collegiate church. Although no records place him there in boyhood, it is known that his brother William Taverner lived in the village, and records of a Taverner family in the area at the close of the 15th century would seem to confirm it. Tattershall—both manor and village— had been in the possession of the Cromwell family since 1367, and by Taverner's day was a possession of the Crown. A series of enlightened patrons kept its artistic and scholarly leanings thriving.

Although it is likely that Taverner spent some years in London, he was closely associated in his early years with the manor and church of Tattershall (where he later became a clerk-fellow) and was a fine singer. In 1526 he was recommended by the Bishop of Lincoln for a post at the new College in Oxford founded by Cardinal Wolsey, and by November of that year he was in place at Cardinal's College as *informator choristorum*. His duties included Master of the Choristers at St Frideswide's, the chapel for the college, where he was required to play the organ for service. His annual salary was a princely £10 plus a further £5 for clothing and the like. This position lasted barely three years.

In late 1527 Taverner became involved—involuntarily—in a sequence of events which led to the interrogation for heresy of several of the fellows of Cardinal's College. It was discovered that Taverner, no doubt sympathetic to the Lollard cause and the Lutheran teachings that inspired it, had looked after some books belonging to one of the prime Lollard conspirators, and for a while a shadow hung over him. This was finally removed in 1528 by one of Cardinal Wolsey's officers who commented in his report: 'Taverner and Radley, they be unlearned, and not to be regarded'. Such is a musician's lot...

By the summer of the same year Taverner was delivering books of music to Wolsey at Hampton Court, his position clearly retrieved. Taverner was now at the height of his musical and personal influence, being a trusted and brilliant member of the Oxford musical circle which Wolsey valued so highly. With Wolsey's fall in October 1529, this

all changed: Cardinal's College was then at the mercy of Henry VIII and its future in doubt. Many of Wolsey's possessions had been forfeited, suppressed or dissolved, and the College was fully expected to meet a similar fate. Taverner, deciding not to linger, left by the spring, disappearing from the records until some seven years later when he finally comes to light in Boston, not far from his old village of Tattershall.

In Boston Taverner not only continued his musical career, but also acted as one of Thomas Cromwell's agents in the suppression of the friaries. Taverner's loyalty to both Cromwell and the Crown ensured his steady rise, and by 1545 he was described in contemporary documents as a 'gentleman'. Cromwell's fall in 1540 did not affect Taverner's position within the Boston community: he had exercised his powers as Cromwell's agent with discretion and relative humanity. In 1541 he became Treasurer of the Guild of Corpus Christi, followed four years later by his appointment as an alderman of the borough of Boston. Records relating to his death reveal that soon after leaving Oxford he had married (possibly for a second time) a widower with two daughters by a previous marriage. He had also become a substantial freeholder of lands in and around the

town. Taverner died in October 1545, and was buried (according to some sources) under the bell-tower at St Botolph's Church, a singular honour possibly awarded for the music he had composed for its choir over the previous decade.

Taverner was able to write for larger vocal ensembles than the majority of his contemporaries, skilfully adapting the music to suit the choirs or groups for whom he was writing. Of particular interest is his *Mass 'Western Wynde'*, as the 'Western Wind' melody he took as the basis for the work was also set by Christopher Tye and John Sheppard. Thus within a short period of English history, three outstanding works come from a common musical basis. Taverner also wrote Masses which omit parts of the text (as in *Missa sine nomine* and *Missa O Michael*), and often used simple juxtaposition techniques such as alternating plainsong and polyphonic writing for different parts of the same service or Mass. His music perhaps sounds more austere than his Continental counterparts, but the rigor of his intellect meant that what may seem at first glance to be a following of convention is in fact a significant development of that convention into new areas of compositional interest.

DON'T MISS

▶ **Mass 'Western Wynde'**

▶ **Missa sine nomine**

▶ **Missa O Michael**

▶ **Dum transisset Sabbatum I and II**

▶ **Te Deum laudamus**

PART II

1500-1600

The period of time encompassed by the composers born in this century was notable initially for the rapid flowering of national musical traits, styles and forms across much of Western Europe. Countries such as Flanders, England, Italy, France, Germany and Spain were all evolving distinct national attributes, aided by the compositional genius of men like Gibbons, Tye and Byrd in England; de Rore, Palestrina, Monteverdi, Gesualdo and Frescobaldi in Italy; Janequin and Le Jeune in France; Lassus and Schütz in Germany; Gombert in Flanders and del Encina, de Morales, Milán and Victoria in Spain.

The century was important for the gradual rise to pre-eminence of the Italians, chiefly through their development and perfection of a new secular form—the madrigal—and the new interest in purely instrumental music as instruments such as the viol, lute, clavichord and various woodwinds were increasingly played in domestic as well as courtly and devotional settings. Much of the music being written and published for these instruments took the form of dance styles, such as the *galliard*, *pavane* and *saltarello*. There was also a marked concentration on both the French *chanson* and its Italian equivalent, the *canzona*, by composers writing secular vocal music.

The madrigal had evolved steadily over the previous 200 years from a song-form which used a set refrain and fixed structural formulas into a piece of through-composed vocal music which generally used only the most elevating texts of the highest quality. Petrarch was one of the favoured poets throughout this period, and the developing sophistication of the madrigal can be traced through settings of his work by musicians such as de Rore, de Wert and, crucially, the brilliant Orlande de Lassus. The supreme inventiveness of these and other composers, plus the secular issues addressed in the texts, gave Italy the lead in music for the first time. It would be another 150 years before that impetus faded in the face of the emerging Classical forms of France and Austria/Germany.

Elsewhere, the impact of Luther's Reformation in northern European countries had a particular relevance to the eventually distinct shape of devotional music composed for the new Protestant services, and the separate traditions evolved in both Germany and England were born in this period. Luther's actions even had a profound impact on Catholic liturgy as a result of the Counter-Reformation's actions during the Council of Trent, some of which had a direct bearing on musical practice in Catholic churches. It fell to Palestrina to gradually effect the purification and realignment of musical composition to comply with the new religious attitudes, and although the work was not completed until decades after his death, the newly-evolved devotional style continued to be closely identified with his name.

Detail of marble statue of Orpheus by the Italian sculptor Antonio Canova; before 1822

THOMAS TALLIS

c. 1505–1585

Thomas Tallis and Christopher Tye were the dominant Tudor composers of the mid-to-late 16th century. Traditionally credited with being the 'Father of English Cathedral Music', the relative lack of dates for most of Tallis' works makes this contention difficult to prove.

That Tallis' name has been more prominent than Tye's during the present century is due in part to the interest shown in his achievements by English composers such as Benjamin Britten and Vaughan Williams—particularly the latter who wrote his famous *Fantasia on a Theme of Thomas Tallis* based on 'Why fumeth in fight?', one of the nine tunes contributed by Tallis to Archbishop Parker's Metrical Psalter of 1567.

Thomas Tallis

Tallis was born in south-east England, his ties with the county of Essex indicated by his early appointment as organist at the Abbey of the Holy Cross in Waltham. Tallis was a confirmed Catholic throughout his life, a fact which speaks volumes about his character as he lived during the reigns of no fewer than five Tudor monarchs— a period when the country's religious affiliations caused the most fundamental upheavals. Tallis seems to have stayed at Waltham Abbey, either as organist or chorister, until its dissolution by Henry VIII in 1540, and it is conceivable that he became known to the monarch earlier as the King was a regular visitor to the Abbey prior to his final schism with Rome. This is borne

out by the compensation Tallis received on the Abbey's dissolution and also by the fact that at about this time Tallis became a Gentleman of the Chapel Royal, the musical establishment maintained for the monarch's personal needs. By then Tallis was approaching middle age; he did not marry until 1552, when he was nearly 50.

At the funeral of Henry VIII in 1547 Tallis was one of 20 members of the King's household to receive a livery, and was also present at Edward VI's coronation, so his position within the Chapel Royal was by that time secure. Perhaps Henry's own musical leanings explains his appreciation of Tallis'

extraordinary musical gifts, despite the composer's Catholicism. Tallis continued in royal service throughout the brief and turbulent reigns of Edward VI and Queen Mary: from the Queen he and the Chapel's Master of the Children, Richard Bowyer, jointly received a 21-year lease on Minster Manor on the Isle of Thanet. These signs of royal favour did not cease with the accession of Elizabeth: in the first year of her reign Tallis was granted a gratuity.

With the arrival at the Chapel Royal in 1570 of the young composer, William Byrd (born 1543), a productive and long-standing friendship developed between the two composers, perhaps sparked initially by their commitment to Catholicism. By 1575 the two men, now joint organists in the Chapel Royal, had not only published a collection of motets, *Cantiones Sacrae* (34 in all, divided roughly equally between them), but had also been granted a licence which gave them the sole right for 21 years to print music and music manuscript paper in England. Oddly enough, this extraordinary monopoly profited them little initially, for by 1577 they had presented a petition to Elizabeth asking her to grant them a lease by way of compensation for the losses they maintained they had suffered over the previous 24 months. The petition referred to Tallis as 'now very aged', having served at Court 'these fortie yeres and hadd as yet never anie manner of preferment except onely one lease...' Elizabeth granted the new 21-year lease, which gave the men £40 per annum.

Tallis and Byrd continued close friends, Tallis becoming godfather to Byrd's second son, Thomas, while in 1583 Byrd was appointed as an 'overseer' of his will.

Tallis' title of 'Father of English Cathedral Music' contains a grain of truth: although both Tye and Byrd have claims to such a title, Tallis was certainly among the first to set music to English texts to be used with the rites of the newly-established English Church. Pieces composed for these occasions include the *Benedictus* and the brief but exquisite anthem *If ye love me,* as well as a number of equally effective psalm settings. His compositional style remains essentially medieval, concentrating on polyphonic settings of occasional texts. The sensitivity with which he achieved this can readily be appreciated in the masterful *Lamentations of Jeremiah,* where grand polyphonic passages open each section before the more subtle telling of the texts' stories are interwoven. His technique descends from Taverner and Fayrfax, relying on multiple divisions and a large number of changes in vocal registration, as well as the intense counterpoint which so occupied Taverner. This can be heard to great effect in the motet *In jejunio et fletu.* Tallis was a great employer of canon and imitation, as his motet *Spem in alium,* and his two motet settings of *Salvator mundi* demonstrate: in *Spem in alium* he establishes no less than two sets of 20 voices working separately in imitation on two themes.

DON'T MISS

▶ **Salvator mundi I & II**

▶ **O sacrum convivium**

▶ **Lamentations of Jeremiah**

▶ **Purge me, O Lord**

▶ **Spem in alium**

▶ **Blessed are those that be undefiled**

GIOVANNI PIERLUIGI DA **PALESTRINA**
c. 1525–1594

Palestrina possessed the genius to combine at will elements of the immediate and distant past with contemporary practices, accomplishing the synthesis at such a high level that nearly four centuries later Claude

Debussy could hear Palestrina's music in a church in Rome and at once recognize his 'divine spark'.

Palestrina always strove for complete clarity in his music, and was not afraid to express emotion by the simplest of means. This explains his wide contemporary appeal, and why his reputation remained intact in the centuries after his death. His part-writing became the standard study for music students from the 18th century

Giovanni Pierluigi da Palestrina

During the seven years he spent in Palestrina, the composer evidently laid the foundations of his own compositional style and expertise, as well as establishing his position in life. In 1547 he married a local woman, Lucrezia Gori, who bore him three sons. Pierluigi continued undisturbed in Palestrina until the town's bishop Cardinal del Monte, was elected Pope Julius III. Before the close of the following year the composer was installed as choirmaster at the Capella Giulia in Rome, the nursery chapel for the Vatican's own choir, giving rise to the belief that the Cardinal must have been a great supporter of the young man if not his outright patron. His patronage was soon made clear: in 1554 Palestrina published his first book of Masses with an illustrated frontispiece containing a flattering dedication to Julius III. This book contains four four-voice Masses and one five-voice Mass, and even at this early stage it demonstrates not only his dexterity but the breadth of his abilities. It also shows that he was very much of his age in using material from earlier Masses to create new works. This practice was officially encouraged, the resultant Mass being called a 'parody mass', although it is misleading to take this literally as no humour was intended; a composer was expected to show his virtuosity by the brilliance of his variations from the original.

The 1554 collection may have been groundbreaking, but it was only the start of what became a steady flow of published music. Palestrina was clearly flourishing under the Pope's patronage. In early 1555 the Pope created a controversy by appointing Palestrina to

onwards after the rehabilitation of polyphony. Like Josquin Desprez, he was able to take old forms—fauxburden, *cantus firmus*, imitation and the rest— and make such a personal combination of their attributes, as well as a transparent use of the techniques of polyphony, plainchant and simple chordal singing, that they overwhelmed the listener by their sheer natural musicality.

Giovanni Pierluigi was born in 1525, probably in Palestrina, a small town in the hills to the east of Rome. The town's name became a useful way of differentiating him from other Giovanni Pierluigis.

Palestrina's childhood and early youth appear to have been spent in Rome, where he is listed among the choir of Santa Maria Maggiore in 1537. That he received his earliest musical training there appears beyond doubt, though the extent of his tuition at this early age is undocumented. Indeed, it has been suggested that Palestrina only took up serious musical and compositional studies in Rome from 1540 onwards, and that these studies were continued until his departure in 1544 for Palestrina, where he was engaged as organist and choirmaster at the Cathedral.

DON'T MISS

▶ Missa Assumpta est Maria

▶ Stabat Mater

▶ Missa Papae Marcelli
  (1567)

▶ Missa brevis (1570)

▶ Tu es Petrus (1572)

his own chapel, the Cappella Sistina, overriding the usual selection procedure by refusing to consult the pre-existing members and ignoring the stricture that married men were barred from membership. Thus Palestrina was obliged to resign his sinecure in the Cappella Giulia to effect his advancement. Unfortunately for the composer, the Pope died two months later and his successor, Marcellus II, lasted only three weeks before he too died. That Marcellus also looked kindly on Palestrina would seem logical in the light of the composition of the memorial Mass, *Missa Papae Marcelli*, which, though not published for some 12 years, may have been written at the time of Marcellus' death.

However, 1555 ended badly for Palestrina: despite publishing his second collection, this time of 22 madrigals, the summer election of the new pope, Paul IV, quickly led to a pronouncement that the three married members of the Sistine Chapel singers were to be dismissed with only a small pension as compensation. By October he was again employed, this time in the prestigious but poorly endowed musical chapel of St John Lateran. It was this inadequate funding which drove him to resign his post five years later.

Thus, in 1561, Palestrina returned to the church where he first began his musical education, Santa Maria Maggiore. In 1559, the publication of his *Good Friday Improperia* led to a request by the new pope, Pius IV, for a copy to be made available for performance in Palestrina's old place of employment, the Sistine Chapel. Further works were presented to the Chapel in 1561, and were copied into the Chapel book, but the 35-year-old composer had to wait another decade before being recalled to the Sistine.

Meanwhile, the less demanding nature of his position at Santa Maria (1561–66), and a later position serving Cardinal Ippolito II d'Este (1567–71), gave him more time for other commissions; a regular stream of compositions were published during the 1560s, including the first book of four-voice motets (1563), the second book of Masses (1567), the first book of five-voice motets (1570) and a third book of Masses (1570). It is no coincidence that his position as the premier living composer in Italy was secured during this decade.

His rehabilitation finally took place in 1571 on the death of the incumbent master, Paolo Animuccia, and Palestrina was once again within the embrace of

St Peter's Church in Rome where he remained until his death. During this final period, offers from Santa Maria Maggiore (1575) and the Gonzagas of Mantua (1583) were reluctantly declined. Certainly Duke Giugliemo Gonzaga was a long-time admirer and correspondent of the composer's, even at one stage offering his own compositions to Palestrina for criticism. This friendship lasted until the Duke's death in 1587, and was the source of a number of important commissions (the second book of motets in 1572 was dedicated to him). That the Duke was not alone in his affections is borne out by the 1575 dedication of the third book of motets to the Duke of Ferrara, Alfonso II d'Este.

Yet all did not go well in this decade: in 1572 his son Rodolfo died from the plague, while the same pestilence took his brother the following year. After a year's respite, the plague returned in 1575 to claim his second son, Angelo. Finally, his wife Lucrezia died in 1580. Only his third son would outlive him. By the close of 1580, now 55 and buffeted by life, he seriously considered joining the priesthood, yet by late February 1581 he had remarried—a good match which permanently relieved him of financial worries. The rest of his life was spent dividing his time between his wife's business

DON'T MISS

▶ Motets, Book 4 (1584)

▶ Magnificat Primi Toni (1591)

▶ Missa pro defunctis (1591)

▶ Missa Hodie Christus natus est

interests, composing and his duties for the Sistine Chapel. In 1584 he published his settings of the Psalms of David, dedicated to Pope Gregory XIII, and these were to become some of his most celebrated pieces.

Palestrina lived to receive universal acknowledgement as the supreme composer of his day, this acknowledgment coming in 1592 in the tangible form of an anthology of psalms written by his peers and dedicated to him in the frontispiece. He wrote more than 100 Masses, most of them in the 'parody' or imitative tradition, the great majority of which have fallen into undeserved obscurity. However, the most famous Masses

receive regular performances, 'live' and on CD. These include the *Missa Papae Marcelli* and the *Missa brevis,* the latter published in 1570. Other Masses exceptional for their supremely skilful impression of apparent simplicity and great beauty of line and proportion include *Missa Aeterna Christi munera* and *Missa Assumpta est Maria.* An apparently early Mass, the *Missa Benedicta es,* gives a clear indication of the type of development Palestrina underwent in this musical form.

His Masses notwithstanding, it is arguable that his most famous—and most admired—works fall outside this description. The *Cantico Canticorum Salomons* (Song of Songs) of 1584

contains 29 motets or madrigals which are unique for that period in their combination of intimate musicality and unity of purpose. These compositions make no attempt to hide the erotic nature of Solomon's inspiration, and are quite clearly inspired by similar thoughts. These points aside, the level of creativity is uniformly high, and this intoxicating combination has kept this set of works at the forefront of Palestrina's reputation ever since their first appearance. The *Lamentations of Jeremiah,* published in 1588 and dedicated to Pope Sixtus V, are set for four or five voices; again, the depth of religious feeling has consistently won it admirers among composers and general music-lovers alike.

ORLANDE DE LASSUS
1532–1594 (Orlando di Lasso)

Lassus was the equal of any composer of a generation which included Palestrina and William Byrd, and a key influence on the music of future generations. Skilled in every contemporary musical form, he was fêted throughout Europe for his genius. Beset by illness during his later years, he descended into a state of melancholy which pervades every note of his last great works.

Lassus (also known as Roland de Lassus) was born in the town of Mons

in the Burgundian province of Hainault, an area also responsible for such key composers as Dufay and Josquin a century earlier. His musical life possibly began when he became a chorister at the church of St Nicholas. His earliest biographer, Samuel Quickelberg, a contemporary of the composer, relates unlikely tales of Lassus being thrice abducted as a boy owing to the beauty of his singing voice, but however apocryphal these stories may be, they illustrate the remarkable musical talent of the young Orlande. It is possible that these 'abductions' were in fact invitations to Orlande by foreign

noblemen to enter their service. In any case, at the age of 12 his parents agreed that Orlande should go to Italy to enter the service of Ferdinand Gonzaga, Viceroy of Sicily.

DON'T MISS
▶ First Book of Madrigals (1555)
▶ Salve Regina misericordiae (1573)
▶ 6 Chansons françaises nouvelles (1573)

This appointment gave Lassus his first taste of foreign climes, and he spent six years in Gonzaga's service. In 1550, at the age of 18, he moved to Naples to serve the Marquis of Terza. Three years later he arrived in Rome and was appointed choirmaster at the church of St John Lateran.

Lassus's first published compositions appeared in 1555. There is speculation that he began his real vocation during his stay in Naples, yet the *villanelles* which made up the first collection were published in Antwerp, and he had already returned to Hainault the year before on hearing that his parents were mortally ill. He arrived too late to see them alive, but did not return to Italy, preferring to drift to Antwerp where he soon became a member of the town's artistic circle. Yet Italy had not forgotten him: in 1555 his first book of madrigals was printed in Venice, thus confirming his growing reputation. This sudden appearance of good-quality works was sustained in 1556 by a second Antwerp publication, this time of motets. In the space of 12 months Lassus had demonstrated his expertise in three different musical disciplines, thus firmly staking his creative claim.

One potentate impressed by all this activity was Duke Albrecht V of Bavaria, who invited Lassus to join his Court at Munich. The invitation was readily accepted and Lassus arrived together with a number of other Flemish singers and musicians employed by Albrecht to give a cosmopolitan flavour to his somewhat provincial Court. Within a few years Orlande was recognized as the pre-eminent musician of the group and promoted accordingly.

Orlande de Lassus

In 1558, at the age of 26, Lassus married Regina Wecklinger, the daughter of a Court family. This was the foundation of what proved to be a lifelong relationship with the Munich Court. Any journeys he made after this date, such as those to Ferrara and Venice in 1567, were made for specific reasons and were never more than visits. That he and his music were appreciated throughout Europe is demonstrated by the honours he received: Emperor Maximilian II ennobled him in 1570; the French king Charles IX invited him to his Court in 1573; in 1574 Pope Gregory XIII made him a Knight of the Golden Spur.

That Lassus enjoyed a relationship of rare civility with his employer is surely at the root of both his loyalty to

Munich and his uninterrupted creative flow. He was an artist appreciated in his own time, and the favour in which he was held by Albrecht and his son and heir, Wilhelm, allowed for the most relaxed of relationships. Albrecht also gave Lassus a written undertaking that he would be paid his salary as long as Orlande lived, and Wilhelm was to honour this agreement after his father's death in 1579. Wilhelm and Orlande had become close friends, and the only surviving letters by Lassus are all addressed to him. Full of jokes and a wonderful verbal dexterity, they offer a fascinating picture of a man completely at ease in exalted company. His interests were wide-ranging, his humour engaging, and his enthusiasms sincere.

The relationship remained intact despite Wilhelm's substantial reduction of his musical establishment. By then, the composer was approaching 50 and feeling the need to pace himself. His son Ferdinand began to take on some of his Court duties, while Orlande took the opportunity to travel once again to Italy where he heard some of the newer trends in musical composition. These he treated with impatience as his own tastes tended towards an innate conservatism.

During the 1580s Lassus slowed his activities considerably: he suffered from intermittent illness and became seriously depressed by his condition. By the early 1590s a state of melancholia had settled upon him, and even the understanding Wilhelm was hard-pressed to maintain the usual close relations, although he responded to Orlande's complaints about his salary by increasing the payments to him and his three sons. Though his output was reduced, he continued to publish volumes from his vast reserves of material as well as new works. In 1592 he completed a book of Cantiones sacrae which he admitted in the dedicatory preface were more concerned with serious thoughts than had been the works of his youth. Though not an old man (he had just turned 60), Lassus seems to have been preparing for his own demise. His last work, the extraordinary Lagrime di San Pietro, was published in 1593 and dedicated to Pope Clement VIII. Made up of 20 spiritual madrigals, it was published in June 1594, one month after its creator's death. In his will, among other bequests, Lassus left alms to the poor of Munich hospital.

Lassus was a prolific composer, with over 1,250 accredited compositions. Within this grouping, his motets are perhaps the most remarkable. Neither a ground-breaking nor a revolutionary composer, in his youth he was nevertheless at the forefront of current styles (having been deeply influenced by Italian models during his period of service with Gonzaga). His 150 chansons and his vast collection of motets attest to his irrepressible playfulness, both verbal and musical: endless hidden references, double meanings and puns were carefully woven into the works as a kind of delightful game for the listener to play. The chansons Margot labouréz les vignes, Le temps pent bien and Las, voulez vous, all demonstrate various aspects of his artistry, but the general level of sophistication and the integration of words with music, whether solemn, humorous or even burlesque, is astonishing. His was a true and all-encompassing virtuosity.

His Masses are much less numerous, and although they are every bit as skilful, they tend to be conservative, as if the formality of the occasion for which they were written precluded the full expression of his musical personality. This is certainly not the case in the motets—probably his crowning achievement—where the drama and variety of the texts allowed unlimited freedom for his expressive talents. In this, Lassus was following the Italian trends of his youth, which were to make the text clearer to the listener and to depict its emotions and images in music as precisely and colourfully as possible. Lassus was happy to pursue this to its logical conclusion, which was to become more deeply interested in

the chordal and harmonic movement of the music than in the polyphonic movement of the different vocal lines. Chordal composition is particularly evident in the motet Heroum soboles, while Musica Dei Donum and Lauda Sion salvatorum reveal his close attention to meaning. For a good example of what Lassus achieved in his Masses, the Missa puisque i'ay perdu, a typical parody mass, will suffice. In it, Lassus not only combines a whole raft of styles and techniques, but achieves considerable charm in an area of music where he is usually considered to be Palestrina's inferior.

It is also worth mentioning the Penitential Psalms, the St Matthew Passion, Hieremiae prophetae lamentationes (The Lamentations of Jeremiah), and his last work, the moving Lagrime di San Pietro, (Tears of St Peter), a cycle of spiritual madrigals which for Lassus is unusual in many ways, both musically and personally as it is based extensively around the numeral seven. A motet added to the cycle, Vide homo quae pro te patior, was his last completed composition and is a personal expression of suffering through the words of Christ: 'Behold, man, what I suffer for you'.

DON'T MISS

▶ **Psalmi Davidis poenitentiales (1581)**

▶ **Cantiones sacrae (1592)**

▶ **Lagrime di San Pietro (1593)**

▶ **Missa Bell'Amfitrit'altera (1610)**

WILLIAM BYRD

1543–1623

Byrd had the good fortune to be taken under the wing of the pre-eminent English composer of his youth, Thomas Tallis, but then proceeded to outshine both Tallis and his own contemporaries by composing the greatest English religious music up to that time.

Byrd's musical ability was recognized early, and he was appointed organist at Lincoln Cathedral before his twentieth birthday. The key factor governing Byrd's creative life is that he was born into a Catholic family at a time of great religious change in England, and that he held steadfastly to his religious convictions regardless of the prevailing political currents. It is significant that his openly-held beliefs did not appear to affect his career, for by the age of 27 he was appointed to the position of Gentleman of the Chapel Royal under the patronage of Elizabeth I.

Byrd shared the Chapel's organ duties with Thomas Tallis, and the two composers developed a close friendship. Tallis is sometimes regarded as Byrd's mentor, but is more likely to have been an enthusiastic companion since Byrd was already sufficiently recognized as a musician to be elevated to the Chapel Royal. From this point on Byrd ran parallel careers as a composer: he wrote major pieces in English for the newly established Anglican church services while secretly composing to the old Latin texts for the private Catholic services still

William Byrd

being held by those unwilling to bend with the Elizabethan political and ecclesiastical wind. That Byrd took risks in so doing is clear: his three great Catholic Masses (for *Five voices*, *Four voices* and *Three voices*) were all published anonymously during the 1590s, without so much as a title page between them; they were breaking the law by their very existence.

By 1575 Byrd and Tallis were sufficiently confident of each other's abilities to co-publish a collection of 34 motets. This publication was the first fruit of the unusual favour shown them by Elizabeth: she had

given them an exclusive 21-year patent for printing and selling music and music manuscript paper. The two men may not have seen it as such a business opportunity at that time— the music publishing industry being minuscule—as they claimed two years later to have made a substantial loss and petitioned the Queen to accept a lease on their patent which would furnish them with an annual income of £40. By then Tallis was an old man, but Byrd was in his early thirties and at the peak of his powers, yet he claimed in the petition to be in a parlous financial state: 'By reason of his daily attendance in the Queen's service he is letted reaping such

DON'T MISS

▶ **O Lord make thy servant—anthem**

▶ **Sellinger's Round—variations (1570s)**

▶ **Cantiones, quae ab argumento sacrae vocantur (1575)**

▶ **Psalmes, Sonets and Songs (1588)**

The composer Thomas Morley (a pupil of Byrd's) wrote of him in 1603 that he was 'never without reverence to be named of the musicians'.

Byrd's long career saw him rise rapidly to prominence in the British Isles; by the time he reached the Chapel Royal he was set to become the pre-eminent composer for an entire generation. He also became increasingly old-fashioned. His compositions for both Anglican and Catholic services remained central to his musical achievement, the Anglican compositions becoming definitive during his lifetime. Oddly enough, he never took steps to publish his largest and most overpowering work, the *Great Service in F*. Hence it can only be conjectured as to when this fine work in the Anglican tradition, (established by Tallis and Tye) was composed, although the forces involved, the maturity of the part-writing and the ample conception, would suggest that it is not an early work. Byrd's three famous Latin Masses (mentioned above) show the more intimate and devotional side of his religious work and also demonstrate his readiness to take the form and style of the work most emotionally resonant to him to carve out new approaches to liturgical music.

commodity by teaching as heretofore he did'. It seems the Queen granted their petition.

By 1577 Byrd and his family had moved to Harlington in Middlesex where he added to his duties at the Chapel Royal by taking on extra work, including teaching music. Byrd was clearly an ambitious and capable man: his handling of the publishing monopoly in the years after Tallis's death in 1585 shows acumen and determination. He wrote for a great variety of commissions, including one for St John's College, Cambridge and (probably) for the Lady Nevell to whom he dedicated his collection of 42 keyboard pieces.

His connections at Court enabled him to take advantage of the misfortune of another Roman Catholic: in 1583 one William Shelley was condemned to death for his alleged part in a so-called Popish plot, and confined to the Tower of London. In 1593 Byrd obtained the remainder of a lease on Shelley's farm of over 200 acres at Stondon Place in Essex. Two years later the property was sequestered and Byrd now enjoyed a Crown lease on it which would expire only on the death of his children.

Yet Byrd had a less than easy passage through the latter part of his life. The composer went through a long period of creative silence at the close of the 16th century, broken only by renewed activity in 1603. His will, dated 1622, reveals upheavals and bitterness within his own family, for his eldest son Christopher was cut out of the will's provisions entirely, all Byrd's legacy being left to his wife and three surviving younger children.

The final 20 years of Byrd's long life were not particularly prolific, the last of his compositions to be published in his lifetime—four anthems—appearing in 1614. He was clearly a man who devoted as much energy to his daily life and family commitments as to his music. But he was not without rewards in his own lifetime: he not only had the unbroken patronage of Elizabeth and James I, but the admiration of his musical colleagues.

DON'T MISS

▶ **Mass for 4 Voices (1592–3)**

▶ **Mass for 3 Voices (1593–4)**

▶ **Mass for 5 Voices (1595)**

▶ **Ave verum corpus 1605)**

Byrd set himself apart from his contemporaries by declining to borrow plainchant bases or use the common building-blocks of polyphonic writing, and instead concentrated on free composition which allowed him to get as close to the meaning of the text being set as was possible. In this way Byrd made the words 'come alive' for his audience, and it is this quality that keeps them so singularly attractive more than 400 years after their creation.

Byrd also composed a good deal of instrumental music, both for a consort of viols and for various keyboards—the virginal, the harpsichord and the chamber organ. *My Lady Nevell's Booke* (1591) is a collection of 42 galliards, grounds, pavanes, variations and fantasias meant for playing at the keyboard. Byrd cast his net wide for models for these pieces, using traditional English song as well as Italianate practices in an attempt to compose

in as diverse a manner as possible. This diversity alone keeps the collection continually interesting. Byrd also composed many songs to be sung on a variety of occasions. In these he again showed his preference for older forms, repeatedly ignoring the newer madrigal and English anthem and choosing instead the consort song as his vehicle of expression. His later pioneering use of the verse anthem is a logical step forward from the consort song.

TOMÁS LUIS DE VICTORIA
1548–1611

Victoria was the greatest Spanish composer of 16th-century polyphony and a highly organized and efficient promoter of his own compositions. Though he spent much time in Italy, he came to be venerated in his own country and passed the last 25 years of his life faithfully serving his patroness, the Dowager Empress Maria.

Born in Avila into a large and vigorous family (he was the seventh of 11 children), Victoria had uncles who were variously naval commanders, missionaries, priests and Florentine merchants. Although his father died before Tomás Luis was 10, his training as a choirboy in Avila Cathedral

continued throughout the 1550s and the early 1560s, while his more general education was conducted at the Jesuit school of S Gil in Avila.

By 1565, aged 17, Victoria was given a grant by King Philip II to attend the Jesuit Collegium Germanicum in Rome where the devout Victoria availed himself of the opportunity to perfect his Latin and develop his new-found interest in composition. It is often speculated that Victoria at this time received lessons from Palestrina, then working at the nearby Seminario Romano. Certainly, Victoria's knowledge of Palestrina's works and compositional methods more than hints at some form of personal contact. Victoria left the Collegium Germanicum in 1569 to begin a series of paid appointments in

Rome, including eventually returning to teach at the Collegium. When the Collegium was reorganized in 1573 into two separate wings, he became *maestro di cappella* of the German wing. Victoria continued his religious studies and in 1575 was ordained a priest. Before spring 1577, he had left the Collegium, briefly joining a new community of lay priests before finally settling as chaplain to S Girolamo della Carita.

Meanwhile Victoria had not been slow to get his early compositions into print: in 1572 a 'book' containing the majority of what was to be his output of motets was published in Venice. There was a nine year gap before the next collections were published, two appearing in 1581 in the lavish style later to be closely associated with him. Victoria kept the S Girolamo appointment until 1585, boosting his income by combining this post with numerous others. Yet a work written in 1583 for Philip II, *Missarum libri duo*, carried a dedication to the King expressing his desire to return to Spain, thereby putting to an end 'my labour of composing, to rest for a time in honest leisure and to be able to compose my soul in honest contemplation, as befits a priest'.

Philip recognized in Victoria just the type of person he needed to become chaplain to the Dowager Empress Maria of Austria, his sister and the widow of Maximilian II. He offered Victoria the post and the musician-priest remained in her service from about 1584–85 to her death in 1603. Maria was a highly-cultured woman with a sophisticated enjoyment of the liberal arts and a devout Catholic who, on the death of her husband, had retired to a convent in Madrid.

In 1603 Victoria wrote the *Officium defunctorum*, the Requiem Mass for the deceased Dowager Empress which was performed at her lying-in-state. It is this Mass for which he is most famous today. The following year Victoria, now in his mid-fifties, was given the less demanding duties of organist for the convent, a post he held until his death seven years later. Life at the convent suited him admirably, allowing him leave to go to Italy on a number of occasions, including the funeral of Palestrina in 1594 and the performance

the year before of his motet *Surge Debora et loquere canticum* at the Collegium Germanicum to celebrate the Spanish victory against the Turks. Victoria's last years were peaceful, his works attaining an international popularity quite staggering for the time; even in Mexico the demand for his works outstripped local production techniques. The composer, still living near the convent he had served for over 25 years, died in 1611 and was buried in the convent itself.

Victoria was not especially prolific, but he was both a perfectionist and an astute publisher of his works, encouraging their acquisition by ensuring that they were presented with the greatest accuracy and opulence, even making arduous journeys to Italy to oversee the printing of each volume and publishing corrections in later volumes.

Victoria combined a highly-sophisticated appreciation of the polyphony of Palestrina with an outgoing and forceful personality which expressed itself clearly in his music. He was prepared to take chances with his

melodic lines and go for bolder cadences, but his work was not so concerned with the subtleties of textual illumination as that of Orlande de Lassus. He wrote no madrigals, and his main efforts were directed towards the area of Masses and motets. Of his 20 Masses, 11 are parody works set to lines from his own motets, while his 16 Magnificat settings seem for the most part to be earlier works, all of them published by 1581. Although there is no doubt that the *Officium defunctorum* written for Empress Maria and published in 1605 is the best place to start with an appreciation of his work, other Masses are equally rewarding, including the brilliantly polyphonic *Missa Gaudeamus* and the later *Missa pro Victoria* (1600), one of his rare secular works and a Mass which points to the embryonic Baroque style with its heavier reliance on chordal movement in the vocal lines. For an example of a parody Mass built on the basis of one of his own motets, *Missa Trahe me post te* (1592) is based on the 1585 motet of the same name, the original being set to the first chapter of the 'Song of Solomon'.

DON'T MISS

▶ **O magnum mysterium (1572)**

▶ **O quam gloriosum (1572)**

▶ **Missa O quam gloriosum (1583)**

▶ **Officium Hebdomadae Sanctae—Tenebrae Responsories and Lamentations of Jeremiah (1585)**

▶ **Officium defunctorum (1605)**

GIOVANNI GABRIELI

1557–1612

Together with his uncle, Andrea Gabrieli (c. 1520–1586), Giovanni was an important member of the Venetian school of music which enjoyed a spectacular flowering during the 16th century, especially in the realm of sacred vocal music. Indeed, he is often regarded as the peak of that particular school's achievement.

Giovanni came from a line of Gabrielis involved in music: his uncle Andrea was an internationally renowned composer in his own right, and one of a number of composers concerned with moving towards a stable form of monodony after the long ascendancy of polyphony in serious European music. It was this tendency which would soon point to the later Baroque and Classical styles and the development of opera. His nephew Giovanni would see the triumph of Monteverdi's great operas in Venice and the dawning of the new tradition.

Giovanni was born in Venice and took his first music lessons from Andrea. He also followed his uncle's example by travelling to Munich to be with the great Orlande de Lassus. It is possible that the young man, who was with Lassus between 1576 and 1580—from his teens into early manhood—took a course of tuition from the great master; his first mature compositions were written at the Munich Court, and laid the foundations of his later reputation.

Title page to Gabrieli's Concerti for voices and instruments, 1587

After a number of insecure years, Giovanni returned to Venice where he accepted the post of temporary organist at St Mark's. In 1585 he took the position of second organist (his uncle Andrea became first organist), and continued in this position until his death 27 years later. Never a spectacular player, he nonetheless quickly built a reputation as a composer and teacher, even attracting foreign pupils such as Heinrich Schütz and Michael Praetorius. Both Gabrielis composed music for use at St Mark's

DON'T MISS

▶ O magnum mysterium (1587)

▶ Intonationi (1593)

▶ Symphoniae sacrae—8, 10 and 12 instruments (1597)

▶ Symphoniae sacrae for various voices (1597)

▶ Symphoniae sacrae, liber secundus (1615)

(which until the 19th century was the private chapel of the Doge rather than a public place of worship), though it was only after Andrea's death that Giovanni became the principal supplier of ceremonial and liturgical music, much of it proving to be sumptuous in the extreme. Gabrieli rarely left Venice, yet his musical presence continued to be widely felt, even after his death, especially in Germany where his pupil Schütz continued to hold his ideals in high esteem and to apply many of his methods .

Gabrieli's compositions, especially those specifically written for the magnificent religious celebrations at St Mark's, demonstrate high levels of skill at marshalling large vocal and instrumental forces. Using the *chori spezzati* technique, he often deployed his choral forces into separate groups, using monodic melody of phrases with each group but having such an active dialogue between groups as to create a rich musical experience for the listener. He was one of the first composers to develop the idea of the *basso continuo*, a device in music by which the upper melodic line and the chordal

movement is underpinned by an unchanging bass pattern—an important step on the way to Baroque musical practices. He also wrote purely instrumental pieces, combining brass and string instruments such as violins and sackbutts.

Gabrieli's famous publication, *Symphoniae sacrae* (both collections 1 and 2 of 1597 and 1615), demonstrates his pivotal position between the older polyphonic tradition and the newer monodic ideas. They are masterpieces of contrapuntal interweaving, with up to 16 or 19 voices being a common occurrence. Both these compositions and the 1587 *concerti* were published in such a way as to give the impression that purely vocal performances were intended, but close examination of the demands made on the vocalists suggest that many of the vocal lines were supported by instruments as well. Thus Gabrieli used instruments in otherwise vocal compositions which experienced—for those days—such radical harmonic modulations as to raise serious doubts about Gabrieli's consideration of the poor singers' lot. Without instrumental accompaniment

in such passages, it is likely that a contemporary performance of some of the *Symphoniae sacrae* would have degenerated into chaos. An observer at a San Rocco performance of one of his works, Thomas Coryat, commented: "When they sung, the instrumentall musitians played also. Sometimes sixteene played together on their instruments...sometimes there sung sixteene or twenty men together, having their master or moderator to keepe them in order". Gabrieli also helped to promote the relatively novel idea of having contrasting solo voices singing against the full choir, thus presaging the later deployment of solo instruments in this role as the instrumental Venetian concerto developed to its Baroque apotheosis in the hands of Corelli, Albinoni and Vivaldi.

Gabrieli's output is dominated by church music, especially that written for ceremonial occasions, but as his early compositions written while he was at Munich demonstrate, he was also adept at madrigals. The magnificence of his settings, his love of instrumental and vocal colour, and his concern with creating a music which is simple of line and clear of texture—while not losing any of its power to impress—echoes the independent Venetian musical developments which preceded him, and also points to where music in Venice was to lead. This would in turn have important effects on the subsequent development of music in the Baroque era, both in Italy and Germany.

CARLO GESUALDO
1560–1613

Gesualdo was an important if somewhat isolated figure. His harmonic thinking was far ahead of its time in the way in which it outstripped the modal basis of the music of his predecessors and many of his contemporaries. His music comes at the beginning of the era of codified laws for harmony, so his highly individual solutions to harmonic questions often surprise even today's listener.

Born in Naples, Don Carlo was the Prince of Venosa and an altogether extraordinary nobleman. The son of Don Fabrizio Gesualdo—who had set up a musical academy which employed some of the leading contemporary musicians—and the nephew of Alfonso Gesualdo, Archbishop of Naples, from an early age Carlo was surrounded by both learning and privilege. As a teenager he was instructed in the art of playing the lute and in general musical theory, and was soon recognized throughout Italy as an outstanding lutenist. As the second son, Carlo spent his youth and early manhood unburdened by the need to assume the responsibilities of power, pursuing instead his all-consuming interest in music. A rich man, he was able to develop his tastes and creative requirements free of any constraints imposed by a demanding patron.

In 1585 his life changed irrevocably: his elder brother died leaving Carlo at the age of 25 with the necessity of marrying and bearing children to ensure the continuity of the Gesualdo line. His choice proved unfortunate: Donna Maria d'Avalos, just 21 years old, was not only his first cousin but had already twice been married. Nevertheless she and Don Carlo were wed in 1586. An unhappy union turned rancorous when Carlo established that Donna Maria was having an affair with the Duke of Andria. The birth of a boy to Maria apparently precipitated Gesualdo's subsequent action: unable to believe that the child was his, Gesualdo had the two lovers brought before him, together with the child, and had all three murdered in his presence. In a final act of barbarism, he ordered the lovers' corpses to be put on public display. The Kingdom of Naples was shaken by these events which caused outrage throughout Italy. Yet Gesualdo was never brought to trial, remaining free to pursue his normal lifestyle. Gesualdo himself felt that he inhabited the moral high ground in the situation, having dispensed summary justice to an adulterous wife.

Evidence that he was not ostracized for this act came four years later in the northern Court of Ferrara—then nearing the end of its glittering ascendancy in the arts under Duke Alfonso II d'Este, the last in his line. Gesualdo had gone to Ferrara in search of artistic and musical stimulation, and had been very active since his arrival, the first two of his books of madrigals being published in Ferrara in 1594. The summer of that year saw the marriage of Gesualdo to Donna Eleonore d'Este, a union which cemented Gesualdo's ties with the ruling family. These ties remained close until the death in 1597 of Alfonso. The Duke's demise led to the dissolution of the fabulous d'Este Court, and soon afterwards Gesualdo returned to Naples with his wife.

The second marriage, however, proved little better than the first; there were reports that Eleonore had made several

---

DON'T MISS

▶ **Gagliarda de Principe di Venosa**

▶ **Sospirava il mio core (1595)**

▶ **Assumpta est Maria (1603)**

▶ **Illumina nos misericordiarum (1603)**

▶ **Sacrarum cantionum (1603)**

▶ **Responsoria et alia ad Officum Hebdonadae Sanctae spectantia (1611)**

attempts to secure a divorce through her powerful contacts in the Vatican, but without success. The couple eventually led virtually separate lives, Gesualdo immersing himself in his music and withdrawing from society. There were rumours that his mind was deranged, but this is unlikely: he was simply acting in his usual arrogant and autocratic fashion, pursuing his own interests exclusively. These included the building of a Capucin convent where in his last years he attempted, through penitence, to come to terms with his 'dark soul'. He continued to live a singular and increasingly remote life until his death at the age of 53.

By then he had published six books of madrigals (another was to appear posthumously) and a set of *Sacrae Cantiones* for both 5 and 6 voices, thus securing his future reputation.

Gesualdo concentrated on the madrigal genre, and his first four books, published in the space of three years (1594–96) when he was in his mid-thirties, probably account for his earlier output as well as more up-to-date

compositions. For the most part they do not deviate from the prevalent style, being well constructed, mindful of the texts being set and concerned with expressing the depth of feeling contained therein. It is only with the fifth book of madrigals that the originality—which was to secure Gesualdo an eminent place among the composers of his day—began to win through. He was content at first to use contrapuntal techniques, thus following the lead of his contemporaries. With the fifth and sixth books (both published in 1611) his music suddenly takes a dramatic turn into fresh and utterly personal territory. Gesualdo's concern to place himself in relation to God and the rest of creation fuels a compulsion for risk-taking in terms of chromaticism and harmony which has no contemporary parallel. His madrigals seek out texts which illuminate his own dark thoughts and the music exists not so much to communicate with the listener but for the altogether more private purpose of self-discovery and penitential brooding. Often his works are like the whispers of intimate conversations overheard, full of

darkness and doubt, the subject-matter removed from the world and bound up in religious notions of guilt, sin and absolution.

The first book of *Sacrarum Cantionum* (1603) continues this process: the motet writing is profoundly personal, frequently taking abrupt leaps, using chromatic sequences in unexpected contexts, often embracing dissonance in a curiously unresolved way and, where there is polyphony, expounding the different voices in such an individualistic and unorthodox manner as to question Gesualdo's intentions. Yet his basic competence is beyond reproach. Thus the only tenable conclusion is that Gesualdo was using music as an intensely personal language, somewhat in the way Mannerist painters represented familiar forms in exaggerated and distorted ways. It is therefore not surprising to find his reputation re-appraised this century, with composers like Stravinsky finding in Gesualdo a deep musical *thinker* with a message for today's equally barbaric and frightening world.

JOHN DOWLAND
1563–1626

For many, John Dowland represents the apogee of English Renaissance musicians. Writing consort music, lute music and ayres for a largely secular audience, he occupied

a position close to the seat of power in England for much of his adult life. He was universally recognized as the greatest lutenist of his time, and his services were much

in demand at Court. Yet this is only part of a more complex and troubled story.

Dowland was probably born in London. Little is known of his early years beyond

DON'T MISS

▶ Lord Essex, his Galliard

▶ Melancholy Galliard

▶ The Whole Booke of Psalmes (1592)

▶ First Booke of Songs (1597)

▶ Lachrimae, or Seven Teares (1604)

▶ A Pilgrimes Solace (1612)

the fact that he entered the service of Sir Henry Cobham while still a teenager, and that after 1579 he was employed as a lutenist by Cobham in Paris when Cobham became English Ambassador to France. It was in Paris that the young Dowland's problems began: he came in contact with a number of expatriate Englishmen fleeing from religious persecution and they persuaded him to become a Roman Catholic. This conversion was not a problem while he remained in France; indeed, he was retained by the new ambassador, Sir Edward Stafford, after Cobham's recall in 1583, leaving Stafford only when it was time to marry.

In 1588 Dowland took a music degree at Oxford. He was later to repeat this process at Cambridge, thus obtaining music degrees from both universities. These achievements should have qualified him for a glittering career at Court, and in 1594 he applied to join Queen Elizabeth's retinue as a musician. On the grounds of musicianship and reputation he would have been a natural choice, yet his petition was refused. He was convinced that the only reason for his rejection was his conversion to Catholicism, commenting in a letter some years later, 'my religion was my hindrance'. Already accustomed to foreign climes, an appointment

abroad seemed a natural solution to this impasse, and when the Duke of Brunswick invited Dowland to join his Court, Dowland obtained from the Earl of Essex and Sir Robert Cecil the necessary licence to go abroad.

Fêted at the German court (and later at the court of the Landgrave of Hessen), Dowland nevertheless did not remain long at either place, having determined to travel to Italy to meet a composer for whom he had the greatest admiration, Luca Marenzio. Marenzio was based in Rome, and Dowland travelled south, visiting Venice (where he met Giovanni Croce) and then Florence. Florence was to be the furthest extent of his Italian journey (he never met Marenzio), for there Dowland found himself beguiled by a group of English Catholic expatriates who were actively advocating sedition against Queen Elizabeth. Alarmed by the severely compromised position in which he found himself, Dowland resolved to return at once to England, presaging his return by a letter to Sir Robert Cecil in which he recounted his travels and detailed the treasonable activities he had encountered in Florence. He also announced that he had abandoned Catholicism, and 'wept

heartily to see my fortune so hard that I should become servant to the greatest enemy of my prince, country, wife, children, and friends, for want'.

The letter appears to have made it possible for Dowland to return to England without official harrassment, and he spent the next year in London putting his affairs in order. This led to the publication of his *First Booke of Songes*, which proved so successful that it was followed by a series of reprints totalling five by 1613. His star seemed in the ascendant both at home and abroad, but still he lacked a royal appointment. When Christian IV of Denmark asked him to become his lutenist at the extraordinary salary of 500 dalers a year (equivalent to the salary of a senior Court dignitary) Dowland quickly accepted. His time at Elsinore was generally successful, his musical abilities sustaining his position despite his inability to deal with his private finances. Christian showed him particular favour, giving him extra funds and occasional gifts, and tolerating his frequently lengthy absences in England. By late 1605, however, the Court had finally tired of him, and in February 1606 he was dismissed. He returned to London where he rejoined his wife and family in their house in Fetter Lane.

Dowland had not neglected his English reputation during his time in Denmark: his *Second* and *Third and Last Booke of Songes* had been published in 1600 and 1603 respectively, while early spring 1604 saw publication of his *Lachrymae, or Seven Teares*. This was a collation of consort dance music of the type which had gained great popularity in both English and German-speaking countries in the last decade or so of the 16th century.

With James I's accession to the throne, Dowland attempted to ingratiate himself with the new administration. Failing once again, for a time he had to shift for himself until he was employed by Lord Walden, heir to the earldom of Suffolk. During this period he wrote and translated musical treatises (such as *A Short Treatise on Lute-Playing*), and also prepared his final work, *A Pilgrimes Solace*, for publication. It appeared in 1612 and was dedicated to Lord Walden, although Dowland describes himself in the preface as being 'long obscured from your sight, because I received a kingly entertainment in a forraigne climate'.

Dowland's uneasy relationship with the upper echelons of English life was finally resolved in 1612 when he was created second lutenist of the King's

Musicians. The following year Dowland's son Robert joined his father at Court. Both men remained in royal employ for the rest of their lives: Robert, appointed in 1626 by Charles I to his father's old post, died in 1641 at the age of 55. John Dowland published nothing of great moment in his last decade, seemingly content that his reputation and position were secure.

The greatest lutenist of his age, Dowland wrote extensively for his preferred instrument but oversaw only a small fraction of it for publication in his son Robert's *Varietie of Lute-Lessons* (1610). The reason for his reluctance to publish his lute works may lie in his own improvisatory brilliance as well as a fear of committing his compositional secrets to print for all to copy.

Dowland's contribution to music is perhaps at its most influential in his songs. Although composers such as Milan and Byrd were active in the

area of art-song long before Dowland, his concentration on the form and his development of the top line into a dominant melody—with the other lines being subsidiary and assigned to instruments such as the lute and bass viol—was a decisive artistic step. The lute's harmonic role in these songs also aided the progress of music towards later forms. Dowland's concentration on secular music, far removed from the great religious music of the day, was typical of English musicians at the time, but unusual in Europe where even a composer as wide-ranging as de Lassus combined his skill with the *villanelle* and madrigal with mastery of the motet and Mass. There are a number of psalms and sacred settings by Dowland, but they constitute a minor part of his achievement. His lute music is every bit as arresting and inventive as his songs, and his unflagging melodic genius leads the listener through his often fascinating and unusual harmonic choices and progressions.

CLAUDIO MONTEVERDI
1567–1643

Monteverdi's name will be forever associated with the birth of Italian opera, but his roots are firmly in the Italian Renaissance music of his youth. In Monteverdi's works and career it is possible to see the progress from High Renaissance/

Mannerist music into mature Baroque concepts. He also ranks as one of the great composers of any age.

Monteverdi was born in Cremona, a small town some 40 miles from Milan. It seems that he was born into

a comfortably-off and musical family; his father was a type of apothecary who somehow contrived to have three wives (Claudio was born to the third). Claudio showed sufficient musical talent to study at Cremona Cathedral under the *maestro di cappella*, Marc'Antonio

Ingegneri, a composer of church music and a man of conservative musical tastes.

Monteverdi was clearly something of a prodigy and responded admirably to his tutor. By 1583, when he was just 16, his first works, *Madrigali spirituali,* were published in Brescia. In the following year his *Canzonette a tre voci* were made available by a Venetian printer. These early works exhibited youthful charm, facility and a vacillation between the style of his teacher and his own more modernist leanings. Though they only hint at the music to come, they are impressive for the work of such a young man. This success convinced him that his career was in music, and he began writing more earnestly and looking for paid work as a violinist. His search for a professional position was rewarded in 1589 with his appointment to the Mantuan Court of the Gonzagas, where he was a violinist and also studied under the Flemish-born composer Giaches de Wert, the Court's musical director.

With little but music and the entertainment of his patrons to concern him, Monteverdi so consolidated his instrumental and compositional prowess that when Duke Vincenzo I went to the aid of Emperor Rudolf II against the Turks in Hungary in 1595, the Duke took Monteverdi with him. The reasons for this preference are not difficult to find in the superb second book of madrigals, published in 1590, and the third, in 1592. With these two books Monteverdi, now in his mid-twenties, broke decisively with the forms of his teachers and ventured out with a

mature and striking style of his own. In 1599 Monteverdi once again accompanied Duke Vincenzo when he visited Spa in Flanders: clearly he was a valued member of the Duke's conspicuously impressive Court, where the display of wealth and talent had, in Vincenzo's eyes, become as important as the possession of it.

Monteverdi was clearly at ease in this atmosphere, and this was confirmed by his marriage to one of the Court's outstanding singers, Claudia Cattaneo. The marriage proved an unusually close one, producing three children in quick succession. Monteverdi's life continued to progress satisfactorily: on the resignation in 1601 of the *maestro di cappella,* he was given the top musical position in the Mantuan Court. The following year the Duke created him a citizen of Mantua. His elevated position made him both an object of envy and a target for bitter criticism; his madrigals had made him enemies who now lost little time in criticizing what they saw as his 'unmusical' methods of composition and harmonic progression. Monteverdi sought to answer such charges by publishing, in 1603 and 1605 respectively, his fourth and fifth books of madrigals, the latter

containing a preface in which he defended his methodology, relating it to the Classical Greek search for 'truth' in art and music.

None of this notoriety did him any harm, and his position as one of the leading composers in Europe was assured. But personal reverses were to put earthly fame into perspective: in October 1607, seven months after the première of his opera *L'Orfeo,* Monteverdi's much-loved wife Claudia died. This affected him spiritually, emotionally and physically, the intense loss remaining with him for years, his health suffering in consequence. He began to find the multiple duties of his position onerous. Although the opera *L'Arianna* (written to celebrate the wedding of the Duke's son in 1608) was a triumph, in the *Lamento d'Arianna* (the only part of the opera to survive today) Monteverdi is clearly unburdening a heart full of grief.

The Duke's pressing demands for new works, allied to the relatively low pay, led to Monteverdi's repeated requests to relinquish his position as *maestro di cappella,* but his requests were always refused. In March of 1608 another blow fell: Monteverdi's star singing pupil,

Venice, braving an attack by bandits to arrive there during August 1613.

From this point on his life became more settled. His sixth book of madrigals, published in Venice in 1614, was the most personal of all his books. It included a five-voice version of the *Lamento d'Arianna*, but the main thrust of the collection was towards a greater declamation of emotion, further simplifying and redeploying of counterpoint, and an acceleration of the movement towards a story-telling and character-painting mode of madrigal writing which would finally bring about its own demise and the birth of the art-song.

Monteverdi flourished in the cosmopolitan atmosphere of Venice, where the size of the musical ensembles allowed him free reign to compose. Both religious and secular works were written and performed, while the excellent salary and working conditions allowed him to take stock of his life and career. He now actively embarked on writing for the theatre, combining full length operas and opera-ballets with shorter theatre pieces. Each work was commissioned, the commissions ranging from Parma to his old Court at Mantua, where he seemed in greater demand since his departure.

Claudio Monteverdi

Caterina Martinelli, died at the age of 18. In the space of four months, Monteverdi had lost his wife and his best singer. Over the next two years he composed the music for the *Vespro della Beata Vergine* of 1610, and it would seem that this great work was partly inspired by his changing view on life and partly by a desire to demonstrate his primacy in religious music—which he was not encouraged to pursue by his patron who was always greedy for new secular music—to a potential new employer.

Monteverdi's wish for freedom was finally granted in 1612, though not in a way he would have wanted: his patron Vincenzo Gonzaga died and Monteverdi, now aged 45 and increasingly unsettled, was dismissed. Plainly surprised by this development, Monteverdi was forced to return to his father's house in Cremona and seek a new position. This came from an unlikely direction: he was invited by St. Mark's in Venice to become its new *maesto di cappella*. He accepted with alacrity and moved his family to

Perhaps the peak of these productions, however, came with *Il Combattimento di Tancredi e Clorinda* (1624), a setting of part of Torquato Tasso's *Gerusaleme liberata* and premièred at the Venetian Palace of Girolamo Mocenigo (who was also to finance the first performance in 1630 of the opera *Proserpina rapita*). This work is in the form of a secular cantata and is avowedly dramatic; it is in many ways more fully operatic than *L'Orfeo,* by then almost 20 years old. In this work Monteverdi's idea of the *stile concitato*—a style devised to depict more fully the warring and harmonious nature of human relationships—is at a peak, combining action and words in a newly dramatic manner.

Two operas from the latter part of the 1620s are now lost, and the next major event in Monteverdi's life was not of an artistic nature: the plague arrived in Venice in 1630, causing massive disruption. Monteverdi (now in his early sixties) and his immediate family seem to have escaped unharmed, but he again used a cataclysmic event to reassess his life. The next few years were spent putting his musical affairs in order and training for the priesthood. His induction took place in 1633, and five years later the massive eighth book of madrigals was produced. This, his first since the seventh book in 1623, contained an enormous variety of works which Monteverdi himself subtitled *Madrigals of Love and War.* In addition, there were larger works which could 'serve as intermissions between the madrigals without action'. *Il Combattimento* was included in this category. Equally massive in size and scope was his collection of religious works, *Selva morale e spirituale,* published in 1640–41. With these two collections the composer clearly felt he was preserving his output for posterity and making his artistic claim.

Yet more was to come. In 1637 Venice had finally acquired a public opera house, the Teatro San Cassiano, and before the end of the decade Monteverdi

had written the now lost *Adone* for performance there, while his 1608 opera *L'Arianna* was dusted down for a new production. In 1642 two new operas were premièred in the Teatro: *Il Ritorno d'Ulisse in Patria* and *L'Incoronazione di Poppea.* These operas show the immense amount of stylistic development which had taken place in the 35 years since *L'Orfeo.* By this time the Baroque period of music was under way and Monteverdi's own operatic compositional principles were fully developed. In both these works all his efforts are concentrated on giving primacy to the words and action. The music is there only to emphasize and delineate these two crucial aspects. Thus there are no arias, and the events intertwine seamlessly to give a complete dramatic experience to the audience as well as convincing characterizations with which they can identify, while the orchestra is given an entirely subservient role, its liberty to interpolate sinfonias and other such instrumental interruptions being severely curtailed.

By now Monteverdi was in his mid-seventies and aware of his failing strength. He spent the first part of 1643 revisiting his birthplace Cremona and also returned to Mantua, where he was duly fêted. Returning to Venice in the autumn, he died in late November. In 1650 two posthumous collections, a spiritual and a secular one, were published, thus completing all the material which has been handed down to future generations.

Monteverdi's position in Western music is a key one: he presided over one of the crucial shifts of emphasis which allowed music to develop the

modern characteristics it still exhibits today. Thoroughly grounded in the immediate and more distant past, he was able to seize the moment and make decisive moves in his music; in *L'Orfeo,* acknowledged as the first stage work which can justify the title 'opera', Monteverdi took modern practices—in terms of treatment of text and characterization as well as dramatic consistency—and brought them to a logical but new state of development. This he achieved while still working within pre-existing forms of musical entertainment and expression. Thus his break with the past was radical but not immediately apparent. The weight of intent he brought to both his madrigals and his religious works gave the listener a direct line into the prescribed text. Monteverdi's work in refining and simplifying the orchestra—making it paradoxically more malleable and subtle in its responses to the singers—was also of inestimable value to future composers. His knowledge of harmony, and his ability to use it in novel but still logical and deeply moving ways, again pointed to the future systematic development of harmony as the supreme indicator of states of being.

DON'T MISS

▶ **L'Orfeo (1607)**

▶ **Vespro della Beata Vergine (1610)**

▶ **Il sesto libro de madrigali (1614)**

▶ **Lamento d'Arianna (1623)**

GIROLAMO FRESCOBALDI

1583–1643

Frescobaldi was not only the pre-eminent organist of 17th-century Italy, but a fine singer and lutenist who composed music of equal merit for all three genres. He was one of the most important composers of the so-called *seconda prattica*, the movement away from the *stile antico*—with its emphasis on the beauty of polyphony—towards the *stile moderno*, where new methods of declamation and an emphasis on the single line gradually evolved.

Girolamo Frescobaldi

Girolamo was born into a Ferrarese family with musical traditions, studying organ and music theory with the Ferrara Cathedral musician, Luzzasco Luzzaschi. As a boy he possessed an exceptionally beautiful voice and was constantly in demand for the performance of church music in and around Ferrara. He was also on call as a keyboardist (he played harpsichord and organ) and as a lutenist. By his early twenties his reputation had spread far enough beyond Ferrara for him to enjoy a short-term appointment as organist at Santa Maria in Trastevere, Rome. He then moved to Antwerp, where his first book of music, a set of five-part madrigals, was published in 1608. A second book, this time of instrumental compositions, was published in Milan before the end of the year, but it is unclear whether Frescobaldi was present to see it through the presses. What is beyond doubt, however, is his

assumption of the organist's chair in St Peter's, Rome, in November of that year, an appearance alleged to have attracted an audience of some 30,000. He was to remain there for 20 years, carving for himself an awesome reputation during that time. By 1612 he was a father, and in the following year married the boy's mother.

Frescobaldi's first publication of keyboard music was the 1615 collection, *Il primo libro di Ricercari e*

canzoni francesci, followed by a second book in 1627, this time of *toccatas*, *canzoni* and various other types. These came at the beginning of his most intense period of composition and publication, during which time appeared vocal and instrumental works such as *Il Primo libro di canzone a 1, 2, 3, 4 voci* (1623–28), *Fiori musicali* (1635), *Arie musicali per cantari*, books 1 and 2 (1630) and *Il primo libro di Toccata, Partite, Corrente, Belleti,* etc (1637).

This body of work showed Frescobaldi gradually transforming the genres within which he was working, using a variety of *cantus firmus* for the architectural underpinning of his larger works as well as demonstrating wide contrapuntal accomplishments. His development of these individual forms, valuable in their own right for his own music, became more precious in the decades after his death when many of his ideas and practices were developed by the new German school of organ composers. This newly-evolving style pointed directly to the development of

DON'T MISS

▶ **Il Primo libro delle canzoni (1628)**

▶ **Toccata per Spinettina e Violino (1628)**

▶ **Arie musicali, primo et secondo libri (1630)**

▶ **Fiori musicali (1635)**

▶ **Canzoni alla francese in partitura, Libro quarto (1645)**

what became known as the Baroque period of Italian music. It is perhaps due to the continuing development of vocal music away from Frescobaldi's

rather narrower stylistic range that his music for voices, often highly distinguished in its own right, has fallen into relative neglect.

ORLANDO GIBBONS

1583–1625

Gibbons has won his place in musical history due to the quality of his religious compositions. Still a teenager when Queen Elizabeth died, he eschewed the Latin texts and wrote exclusively for the English Church, suffering none of the religious crises which many of his predecessors found so challenging.

Gibbons was born in Cambridge. As a teenager he was a member of King's College choir; his father, William, was admitted as a Cambridge 'wait', which implies a considerable degree of instrumental skill. His older brother, Ellis, was a composer and an organist, who had two of his madrigals included in Thomas Morley's collection *The Triumphes of Oriana*.

It was Orlando, however, who was to outshine both brother and father. Sharing choral duties at first with his brother at King's College, he matriculated in 1598 and by 1602–03 he was receiving payment from the College for commissioned compositions. At the unusually young age of 21 he was made organist in the Chapel Royal, and the following year he received the degree of Bachelor of Music at the University. Apparently feeling the need to settle down, he married Elizabeth Patten, daughter of a Yeoman of the Vestry of the Chapel Royal.

During the next decade or more Gibbons continued to receive indications of royal favour, including incremental positions and payment for specially commissioned services. He

also kept up his studies, receiving a Bachelor of Music degree at Oxford to add to his Cambridge one. On his father-in-law's death in 1623, Gibbons was given the older man's position as organist at Westminster Abbey. It was Gibbons who played and conducted the music at King James's funeral in 1625. In the summer of the same year, while attending Charles I's Court in Canterbury in preparation for the arrival of Queen Henrietta Maria from France, Gibbons died of an apoplectic fit. He was buried in Canterbury Cathedral.

Gibbons' musical style combines a thorough knowledge and use of polyphony with a fast-developing expertise in the deployment of solo voice against elaborate instrumental backgrounds. His verse anthems are often pointed to as the source for the later developments of the form by Purcell and Blow; only two of the verse anthems were published during his lifetime, but Barnard's 1641 edition of the *First Book of Selected Church Musick* contained five anthems, a number of psalms and the two services Gibbons wrote and which have survived. This constituted the religious music which was to have the greatest impact on subsequent generations. Later, Boyce's anthology of *Cathedral Music* narrowed this selection still further, but added the perennially popular anthem 'O clap your hands'. Nearly 40 further anthems remained in manuscript for subsequent centuries to rediscover. Of these, less than half are written in the older polyphonic style which had been in vogue during the Tudor years, while the rest are written for chorus with solo verse (the solo being supported by instrumental accompaniment). Gibbons so concentrated on the verse anthem and brought his own individual technique and ideas to bear upon it that, his predecessors notwithstanding, he can truly claim a pivotal role in its subsequent development.

The madrigals are a different matter; in 1612 Gibbons himself published a

Orlando Gibbons

collection called *Madrigals and Mottets of 5 Parts: apt for Viols and Voyces*. In fact, the motets described are not written in the strict motet form, but denote madrigals of a serious nature and content. There are 13 complete compositions in the collection, written in the polyphonic style, and demonstrate Gibbons's complete mastery of the madrigal

form. Of the 13, the most famous is undoubtedly 'The Silver Swan', while 'What Is Our Life' offers a glimpse of what Gibbons held to be the more forbidding motet form. Both approaches reveal a wealth of genuine inspiration and close attention to the text being set. Gibbons also constructed an elaborate fantasia on a plain song base of the 'Cries of London'. A small selection of keyboard music, ostensibly for the virginal but some no doubt intended initially for the organ, was included in the 1611 publication, *Parthenia,* the first published English compilation of keyboard work. In addition, a set of nine fantasies for strings were published: these were the first such publications 'in copper' in England.

DON'T MISS

▶ **Almighty and everlasting God—anthem**
▶ **Madrigals and Mottets of 5 parts (1612)**
▶ **O clap your hands—anthem**
▶ **Pavan and Galliard in A minor, 'Lord Salisbury'**
▶ **This is the record of John—anthem**

HEINRICH SCHÜTZ

1585–1672

Schütz was Germany's most respected composer prior to the advent of J. S. Bach. He provides a link between Orlande de Lassus, still alive at the time of Schütz's birth, and the Baroque period of which Bach is the pre-eminent German representative. Schütz is often called 'the father of German music', yet all three greats learned from contemporary developments in Italy.

Schütz was a native of Saxony where his family had for generations enjoyed a good social standing. His entry at the age of 14 into the choir of Landgraf Maurice of Hesse-Cassel's chapel gave him not only the musical experience but the education to study law at the University of Marburg, as his parents had wished. Yet his patron, Landgraf Maurice, had noted Schutz's early musical promise, and the following year offered the young man a scholarship to study composition with the composer-teacher Giovanni Gabrieli. Schütz saw this as fate pointing him in the direction of music; his family's concerns overcome, he left Marburg for Venice. The four years he spent in Venice laid the foundation for his mature musical personality, for he not only became thoroughly grounded in methods of composition and musical theory (as applied by the latest generation of Italian musicians), but he also became an admirer of Italian culture in general. In particular, the

prevalent idea that music should closely follow the arguments and images of the text it was illustrating was to have a long-term resonance in his work.

A quick learner, by 1611 Schütz had published his first volume, a collection of 5-part madrigals dedicated to Landgraf Maurice. In these works Schütz shows his grasp of the lessons taught him by Gabrieli, and also an awareness of contemporaneous work by other Italian composers, principally Monteverdi, whose own publications from earlier in the decade had been very influential in Venice. Gabrieli died in 1612, prompting Schütz to return to Cassel to take up the role of organist. He also pondered resuming his law career. Luckily for music, in 1614 he received an invitation to become Musical Director of the Elector of Saxony's Kapelle in Dresden. After two years 'on loan' from a reluctant Landgraf Maurice, he eventually obtained permission to make the move to Dresden permanent. His initial work in Dresden was to mould its music on the Italian model of concerted music, both instrumental and vocal: in his endeavours to encourage the Italianate approach he even sent some of his musicians to Italy to experience the new Italian approach at first-hand.

Two major events occurred in 1619: his marriage to Magdalene Wildeck (she was to die in 1625 after bearing

him two daughters) and the publication of his first significant work, the *Psalmen Davids*, a setting of 26 psalms which clearly indicates his mastery of the contemporary Italian monodic style. His next major achievement came in 1623 when the *Easter Historia* (the first of two such *Historiae)* was published. In this piece Schütz demonstrated how he could balance a feeling for the past with a passion for the present. He used the *Easter Historia* text from one of his Dresden predecessors, Antonio Scandello, as well as some of the music. This was common practice at the time, and was indeed expected of most composers; it is what Schütz does with this basic material which makes the new work so compelling even today. Schütz unites dramatic expression with a careful observance of religious tradition, the contrast heightening the effect of both elements.

In 1625 his famous *Geistliche Chormusik* was published. In 1627, two years after his wife's death, Schütz was commissioned by Johann Georg I of Saxony to produce what eventually became the first German-language opera, *Dafne*. Based on the opera of the same name by Jacopo Peri, the music had to be rewritten by Schütz once it became clear that the German translation would not fit Peri's original music. Unfortunately, Schütz's music is now lost. This remained his only attempt at theatre music. The following year, while still recovering from the grief caused by his wife's death, he undertook simple resetting of some of the Psalms of David, and then set off to visit Italy. He arrived in 1629 and found the Venetian musical scene, now under the spell of Monteverdi's ideas, greatly altered since his visit 17 years earlier. The heightened expressivity of the vocal line and the richer and more varied instrumental accompaniment made a deep impression on him, and traces of this style can be found, combined with his earlier polyphonic technique, in works written after his Venetian sojourn (the *Symphoniae sacrae* of 1629, for example).

His return to Dresden did not remain long undisturbed: the outbreak of the Thirty Years' War in 1631 soon spread discord and turmoil throughout large areas of Germany, including Dresden, and the Elector no longer had time to concern himself with the regular payment of his Kapelle musicians. Schütz found himself working under intolerable stresses; unable to reconcile his loyalty to the Elector with his concerns for his own musicians, he gained temporary leave to take up a position at Christian IV's Court in Copenhagen. Between 1633 and 1641 he vacillated between the two courts, neither of them giving him the stability he needed. After 1641 the Elector insisted on him remaining in Dresden. Schütz, however, continued to battle against the odds, and in 1645 produced a work of lasting worth, a new setting of *The Seven Last Words from the Cross* which included some novel elements which later became standard for such a work. In 1648 another key work emerged: the

Musicalia ad Chorum sacrum, in which for the first time the composer shows a decided reaction against contemporary trends, preferring the more traditional manner of composition such as the use of strict contrapuntal writing in the old style.

The reasons for this shift were not entirely aesthetic in origin. By 1648 Schütz had tired of the constant sacrifices he was making to sustain the Dresden Kapelle, often paying the musicians out of his own pocket. The new Italian style, now represented at Dresden by the young G. A. Bontempi, manifested a distaste for high art and a relish for more frivolous entertainment, and this could only provoke a serious-minded composer like Schütz. From then until the mid-1650s Schütz repeatedly requested to be released from his Dresden commitments, but the Elector refused all his attempted resignations. Schütz was now nearly 70 years old and exhausted by the constant battles at Court. He remained at Dresden, however, and by the end of the decade the Elector allowed him more freedom to pursue his private life. He moved to his sister's home in

Wessenfels and worked on various revisions and requests made to him by his employer.

The slower pace of life suited him, though the work was often tedious, and Schütz felt that time squandered on his patron's whims would be better spent on completing his own projects. Nonetheless, major works were premièred in the 1660s, including *The Christmas Story*. After this, Schütz managed just one major work, dating from 1655–56, which related the Passion as told by the four gospels, which was published posthumously. This remains a monumental achievement and was undoubtedly his swan song. Now old and quite frail, with failing hearing and an unwillingness to become embroiled in Dresden Kapelle politics, Schütz remained employed by the Elector but increasingly housebound in Wessenfels. His chief pastime, apart from tidying up his musical legacy, was the reading of the scriptures. He died in Dresden in November 1672, a month after his 87th birthday. By then his position in German music was secure for all time.

DON'T MISS

▶ **Il Primo libro di madrigali (1611)**

▶ **Psalmen Davids sampt etlichen Moteten und Concerten (1619)**

▶ **Cantiones sacrae (1625)**

▶ **Symphoniae sacrae (1629)**

▶ **Musicalisches Exequien (1636)**

▶ **Geistliche Chormusik (1648)**

Schütz was important not only in the music he bequeathed to posterity, but in the lessons he left for others to learn. That his music remained so important to so many, despite his concentration on religious music when others were diversifying into newer secular forms, says much for the power of what he wrote. His use of the older polyphonic style, combined adroitly with the earlier innovations of a composer like Monteverdi, enabled him to succeed brilliantly in most forms he attempted. It also pointed the way for later composers like Bach and Handel. It has been said that all the elements of their music can be found in embryo in Schütz, and while it is important that Schütz's work is not downgraded by being regarded purely as a precursor for what came after, it is a mark of the depth and breadth of Schütz's achievement that such a statement can be made. Schütz's skilful use of soloist and choir in juxtaposition to each other, his careful addressing of text and meaning, his brilliantly resourceful use of instrumental forces, all would mark him out as a consummate composer in any period. That he was putting these pieces together often for the first time and formulating much of what was to be developed later, and writing such beautiful and finely-wrought music at the same time, proves conclusively the stature of this key transitional composer.

PART III

1600-1700

Composers born during the course of this century were to witness the rise and ultimate triumph of the new Italianate style of composition which in time came to be known as the Baroque, named after the equally ornate and flamboyant art and architecture of the same period. That the seeds of the mature Baroque style were sown in various parts of Italy, but especially in Venice, is beyond dispute; that it ultimately took many forms, with distinct national styles developing especially in France and Germany, is also a historical fact. During Monteverdi's primacy in Venice in the early part of the century, he made the point that there were two approaches being taken in Italian vocal music of the time—the *prima prattica*, which continued the polyphonic traditions of earlier styles, and *seconda prattica*, where the modern concern with bringing expressive life to the set text was of prime importance. Monteverdi himself was of the latter persuasion, as was his operatic successor, Cavalli.

These divisions quickly broadened into three approaches when chamber music—containing a much greater emphasis on non-vocal music—began to make larger demands on composers' time and creativity. From this chamber music emerged the concept of instrumental accompaniment, especially in the form of *basso continuo*, designed to suggest the harmonic context for the melodic parts above. This pointed the way to a new approach to counterpoint which was eventually to lead to both

Vivaldi and, in Germany, to Johann Sebastian Bach.

Venice continued to take the lead in music, first through the emerging sinfonia and concerto forms which were given definitive shape by men such as Albinoni and Corelli, and later through the brilliance of younger Italian Baroque composers such as Vivaldi and Domenico Scarlatti, the latter an important formulator of what would in time become known as the early Classical style through his extraordinary keyboard sonatas. Further afield, Handel, Telemann and Bach took elements of the Italianate style (Handel even writing a series of successful Italian-language operas before later switching to oratorios), combined it with Germanic musical practice— much of it inherited from Heinrich Schütz—and forged a truly distinctive Germanic Baroque variant. Much the same happened in France through men such as Marais, Rameau, Charpentier and the Couperins, although there is a certain irony in the fact that the man who presided over the incredible flowering of French music and theatre in the latter half of the 17th century, Jean-Baptiste Lully, was an Italian. Meanwhile, the great British musical flowering, which had largely begun with John Dunstable some 250 years earlier, came to a premature end in 1695 with the death of Henry Purcell. Handel aside, another two centuries would pass before comparable music would again be written in Britain.

PIETRO FRANCESCO CAVALLI
1602–1676

Though not blessed with the genius of his mentor, Monteverdi, Cavalli nonetheless played an extremely important role in the crystallization of the opera form during the 17th century, and contributed a number of first-class operatic productions to the burgeoning tradition.

Cavalli was the son of Gian Battista Caletti-Bruni, director of the choir of the cathedral in Crema, a town in northern Italy. Caletti-Bruni held the position for 40 years and gave his son his early musical tuition. The boy's exceptional singing came to the attention of the local Venetian governor, Federigo Cavalli, who became his patron and enabled him to study in Venice. This aid to his career resulted in Pietro Francesco adopting his benefactor's surname. By 1617 he had become a singer at St Mark's under Monteverdi and soon after became organist at the church of SS Giovanni e Paolo. For the next decade he was content with his reputation as one of the best Venetian tenors and with studying composition under Monteverdi. Cavalli's works at this time were limited to a number of motets and other church music.

With the opening of the first public opera houses in Venice in 1638, this situation altered radically. Until then opera had been a courtly entertainment and Cavalli had remained outside the circle of composers commissioned to provide music for such occasions. Like his teacher Monteverdi, who composed no operas for Venice until the opening of the public theatres, Cavalli had concentrated on other genres. The advent of paying audiences and impresarios had an immediate and drastic impact, creating a demand for musical theatre of a new kind, partially dictated by monetary constraints (the new, commercially-based opera companies could only afford a fraction of what the courts could spend on productions) and partly by the different tastes of the new audiences. The stories and characters of the operas gradually became more down-to-earth, the librettos full of low-life humour and irony as well as grandiloquence and pathos, and the relationship between the music and the text became more complex. In all these areas, but especially in the latter, Cavalli played an important part.

Cavalli was instrumental in forging the new balance between music and words, reducing the incidence of purely declamatory passages and increasing the number of set pieces and the closed forms of arias and songs, while his recitative is as flexible and striking as Monteverdi's. Due to the demise of the opera chorus at this time and the need for a dramatically satisfying substitute, Cavalli soon discovered a natural facility for melody and character delineation which he was only too pleased to develop. This was still in the future for him, however, when he received his first operatic commission, in 1638, for the production of *Le Nozze*

di Teti e di Peleo . This was a success, and Cavalli quickly became in demand as an operatic composer, writing for all five opera houses in the city. In the next 30 years he wrote over 30 operas, mainly for first productions in Venice, though his fame soon spread to France and Austria and his works were duly staged in Paris and Vienna.

Meanwhile Cavalli continued to maintain his religious connections in music, holding the positions of second, then first, organist at St Mark's, and in 1665 he became the *maestro di cappella*. During this long period he wrote a great number of festive and solemn occasional works for use in St Mark's as well as for other religious institutions in Venice, though little of it has survived—a Magnificat, several pieces for Vespers, a few motets, a Requiem written specifically for his own funeral service, and the *Musiche Sacrae* which was clearly modelled on Monteverdi's 1610 collection by the same name. Cavalli's was published in 1656 and remained his only religious work to be published during his lifetime; its purpose was to provide a selection of different forms of religious music suitable for a variety of ceremonies and liturgical functions. His extensive operatic experience is demonstrated throughout by his attention to the shape and beauty of his melodic line.

Recently, a new generation of performers exploring the beginnings of the operatic form have begun to reexamine Cavalli's operas; as the composer spent much of the last few years of his life making new manuscript copies of them, many have survived. Of the early works, *L'Egisto* (1643) and *Giasone* (1649) are good examples, though they contain relatively few true arias but much expressive recitative. *La Calisto* (1652) comes at Cavalli's creative peak and strikes a wonderful balance between the earlier dominance of words and the later tendency for more formal vocal elaboration, brought about by the audience's demands for ever more astounding vocal feats from the main characters—as demonstrated by *Xerse* (1654). Another of Cavalli's stage works, *L'Ercole amante* (1662), was commissioned in 1659 by the opera-loving Cardinal Mazarin of France, then preparing for the wedding of Louis XIV to the Spanish Infanta Maria Theresa the following year. Ever since the 1646 production of his opera *L'Egisto,* Cavalli's reputation in Paris had been immense, and though he was reluctant to travel, a large sum of

money finally persauded him to accept the commission. But in Paris Cavalli found that everything was not going according to plan: the new theatre—which was to be opened by his opera in front of the newly-married royal couple—was far from ready while the scenery and costumes had not even been contemplated. A change of plan was required, and the ten-year-old production of *Xerse* was revived at the Louvre, creating few ripples.

L'Ercole amante had to wait until 1662 for its première at the new Salle des Machines in the Tuilleries, and by then its sponsor Mazarin was dead. The opera was very long and Cavalli had written it to an Italian libretto which few of his audience could understand. Although Louis was flattered by an elaborate allegorical prologue, the work was pronounced boring by the vast majority in attendance, who talked all the way through, only stopping for the (purely instrumental) ballet music written for the opera by Jean-Baptiste

Lully. *L'Ercole amante* was deemed a flop and Cavalli quit Paris in high dudgeon, leaving the field of French opera to Lully, who wasted little time in fashioning his own characteristic marriage of Italian and French operatic forms and traditions. Cavalli continued to produce operas in Venice (*Scipione affricano* appeared in 1664, followed by *Mutio scevola* and *Pompeo Magno* in successive years), as well as religious music, living on into his seventies. By this time he was moderately rich and could afford to take a sanguine view of his life and work. He died on 17 January 1676, famous throughout Europe.

DON'T MISS
▶ Canzoni (Musiche Sacrae)
▶ Salve Regina
▶ L'Ormindo (1644)
▶ La Calisto (1652)
▶ Xerse (1654)

JEAN-BAPTISTE LULLY
1632–1687

Lully's pre-eminence in French music during the reign of Louis XIV is undisputed, as is the extent of his posthumous influence over subsequent generations of French composers and musicians. That his life and career exhibit a relentless consistency of good fortune can not simply be put down to chance: Lully is one man who

can be said to have 'made his own luck'.

Born into a Florentine miller's family, while still a boy Jean-Baptiste showed an aptitude for playing musical instruments. Contrary to Lully's later claim that his parents were of noble birth, they were humble artisans and clearly had neither the time nor money to train the boy;

he was lucky enough to find a local shoemaker who taught him the rudiments of music and guitar playing. A combination of chance and charm set in motion the chain of events which led to Lully's career in France. The Chevalier de Guise, returning to France from Malta, encountered Lully and struck by his impishness and amenability, suggested that the youth might be the ideal

Jean-Baptiste Lully

and of the King's favoured forms of entertainment, concentrated on more elaborate *chansons* with a prominent instrumental accompaniment, and on dance music, of which the King was inordinately fond.

Success and celebrity had their attendant problems, not least the fact that Lully, now in his early twenties and hoping to consolidate his position at Court, felt keenly his lack of any formal musical training. He attempted to alleviate this lack with a succession of teachers, the last of whom, Nicholas Gigault, was a superior organist and composer in his own right. Not content with his position as foremost musician, Lully coveted a still more glorious situation: to a keen mind and undoubted talent were added vanity and an almost total lack of scruples in achieving his ambitions—ideal attributes for his social, musical and professional advancement. Yet Lully succeeded by more than mere guile and intrigue: he was clearly a charming and engaging companion when he chose, and never failed to please the King, a formula which was to keep him firmly in the ascendant throughout his career.

After his dance music had won Louis's favour, in 1653 Lully was appointed *compositeur de la musique instrumentale*. By 1658 his ballet *Alcidiane* had been a success, and the 1660 performance of *Xerse* by the Italian composer Pietro Cavalli (1602–1676) had been a triumph for Lully when his instrumental ballet music drew more praise from the royal audience than Cavalli's opera itself (this was to be repeated in 1662 with Cavalli's *L'Ercole amante*). Lully's success can be explained in part by the

'joli petit Italien' required by his niece, Mlle de Montpensier, to teach her Italian.

The boy was taken to France and put to work as a scullery boy. His notion of entertaining himself in his spare time by singing and playing popular airs on the violin brought him to the notice of the Comte de Nocent, who suggested to Mlle de Montpensier that the boy might be better employed. She responded by promoting him to her ensemble at the Palais d'Orléans; Lully soon confirmed the wisdom of her choice by rapidly outshining his peers. However, in one of his rare slips, Lully allowed the mischievous side of his nature to lead him astray and one of his *chansons* lampooning Mademoiselle

was played within her hearing. Lully was summarily dismissed.

Clearly there was more to this story for Lully (on whose testimony all the above is based) was immediately taken into the service of the 15-year-old Louis XIV, who had been 'impressed' by his musical skills when visiting Mlle de Montpensier. Lully became a member of the King's famous '24 Violons du Roi'. Only just out of his teens, Lully charmed his new master with his outstanding violin skills and his entertaining patter. Within a short time the King became convinced that his young Italian needed his own violin troupe, and assembled the Petits Violons for Lully to train and lead. Lully, well aware of his own musical abilities fact that Cavalli was writing for small instrumental forces while Lully could afford more sumptuous arrangements for his sections of the work.

Not that Lully treated Cavalli's works with disdain: indeed, what Cavalli's music taught Lully about the nascent opera movement proved highly significant. Cavalli had been the pupil of Monteverdi and was his natural successor in the field of opera; noting the developments in early 17th-century Venice which had allowed opera to become a public event subsidized solely by paying audiences rather than by artistocratic benefactors, he developed not only the music given to the arias and set pieces but also kept the action moving and the plot unified by the formulaic application of recitative. In Cavalli's work Lully saw the way ahead for himself in formulating a French opera.

In 1661 Jean de Cambefort, holder of the important position of *Surintendant de la musique de la chambre du roi*, died, and Lully was appointed in his place. Before the year was out Lully had been granted French citizenship by Louis XIV which stifled any future complaints about top jobs going to foreigners. By the summer of 1662 Lully was once again favoured by the King: he was given the title *La charge de maître de musique de la famille royale* and his income increased in line with his new roles. He was now just 30 years old. By 1664 he had married the daughter of the *maître de la musique de la cour*, Michel Lambert; the marriage was to produce three sons and three daughters.

That same year Lully struck up a close—and artistically very important—

friendship with the dramatist Molière. The relationship soon became a professional one, Molière working in partnership with Lully on nearly 30 ballets over the next seven years. Today, by far the most famous of these is *Le Bourgeois Gentilhomme* (1670), a comedy with appropriate dance episodes which was a great success with the King and his Court. But this marked the high tide of Molière's career, both with Lully and with the King: within three years Lully would be actively suppressing his colleague's productions.

The reasons for this shift are obscure, although there remains the possibility that Lully saw Molière's theatrical genius as a threat to his own supremacy when, in 1672, Lully saw the chance to become the *éminence grise* of the bourgeoning French opera industry. In 1669 Louis XIV had awarded a licence to Robert Cambert (1628–1677) and Abbé Pierre Perrin to establish an 'Académie Royale de Musique' which was to be concerned primarily with presenting musical theatre in various guises and to concentrate increasingly on opera. Lully had noted with mounting concern the success of Robert Cambert's musical comedies and pastorales, culminating in one of the very first French operas, the five-act *Pomone* of 1671. A period of intense intrigue slowly prised Perrin's grasp from the royal licence, and when he found himself temporarily in a debtor's prison (due to the unsavoury business practices of his creditors), Lully approached Perrin with an offer he could hardly refuse—the purchase of the royal patent. Thus equipped, Lully lost no time in sending Cambert packing (quite literally, for Cambert

took flight to London, where he was to spend the rest of his declining career) and applying to Louis for a series of savagely restrictive patents and proclamations which gave Lully control over the use of music in any Parisian theatrical production. It was this drive for total control which ended his working relationship with Molière as Lully quickly deprived the playwright of all but the barest musical accessories to his productions.

Meanwhile, the composer struck up a new creative relationship, this time with a man as docile and unthreatening to his position as Molière had been excitable and challenging—the poet Philippe Quinault. Lully and Quinault embarked on a remarkable series of some 20 operas, thus establishing the French operatic tradition through the *tragédie-lyrique* genre. They began with the pastiche *Les Fêtes de l'Amour et de Bacchus* (1672), followed six months later by *Cadmus et Hermione*, reaching artistic heights with *Alceste* (1674), *Atys* (1676), *Armide* (1686) and *Acis et Galatée*. Whatever Lully's methods for gaining his prominence, his artistic merits at least justify his ruthlessness for there is no doubting the quality of what he produced. He was a composer who synthesized much of what already

DON'T MISS

▶ **Le Bourgeois Gentilhomme (1670)**

▶ **Alceste (1674)**

▶ **Te Deum (1677)**

▶ **Armide (1686)**

▶ **Le Carousel du Roy (1688)**

existed, taking the forms established by Cavalli, Rossi and Carissimi to establish a definitive format for his airs, and substituting lively dances and allegros for the slower, more stately ballet numbers previously associated with the theatre, again taking the lead over his French contemporaries. He was such a master of these forms that they continue to satisfy today. His insistence on accompanied recitative, and the variety of pacing he created for it showed the astuteness of his insight into how theatre actually interacts with its audience.

Now at the peak of his power and influence, Lully never once relaxed his grip on the Paris he dominated; indeed, he still aspired to more honours and loftier positions. In 1681 he was granted his *Lettres de noblesse* and, more importantly, was installed as one of the *Secrétaires du Roi*. This last post was official confirmation of the easy intimacy which had long existed between the monarch and himself, and also virtually placed him alongside the country's nobility. For Lully this was no empty honour as can be seen by the

1784 decree from Louis that no opera was to be played anywhere in the kingdom without the express permission of Lully: an extraordinary state of affairs given Lully's still active opera-composing career. By the time of his death Lully had become a rich man. He died in a most bizarre way: conducting a Te Deum to celebrate the recovery of the King from a serious illness, he struck himself on the leg or foot with his baton. The minor wound festered and Lully died from the infection. His family erected an impressive statue in commemoration in a church near the Place des Victoires. The King remained true to his friend by appointing two of Lully's sons to succeed him in his old position as *Surintendant de la musique*. His musical legacy, however, has kept his name alive without the prompting of visual or familial memorials.

Although Lully occupies a central position in France's musical development, his work consisted more of the consolidation and codifying of a disparate number of musical inclinations, traditions and trends

rather than a radical striking out into previously uncharted territory. Looked at from another perspective, Lully was instrumental in the success of new ventures such as the French *tragédie-lyrique*. His genius for clarity, and the progressive simplifying of the forms he moulded together, aided his quest for a flexible music which would deliver dignity, grandeur and profundity as well as drama and excitement. His passion for dance led him to update and codify many of the dance forms and patterns which until then had been allowed either to ossify or to escape the net of compositional patronage. His dramatic genius and gift for melody, as well as his utter domination of the music of his time, led to a long period of artistic hegemony in France after his death, where his models were held up well into the 18th century as the 'true way' for a composer to advance. Even in religious music, an area in which Lully was successful but for which he hardly saved his most ardent music, the balance he achieved between dramatic unity and musical piety was seen as a worthy goal to pursue for generations to come.

MARC-ANTOINE CHARPENTIER
1643–1704

Charpentier may have been overshadowed in his lifetime by the dominant musical and political figure of Lully, but his importance as a composer, especially in the realm of devotional and occasional religious pieces, has meant

a major restoration of his reputation in recent times.

Charpentier was a Parisian by birth, and the latest addition to a family of sculptors and painters. In his youth he was torn between continuing the family's fine art traditions or branching

out into music. This dilemma was not finally resolved until he made a trip to Rome in the 1660s where he came under the influence of contemporary Italian musical style, studying for several years under the eminent composer Giacomo Carissimi, a musician of great imagination and originality and one of the first to bring the sacred cantata to perfection. Carissimi's influence on Charpentier's musical thinking was profound, giving him great insight into the construction of sound choral writing for church use while at the same time helping him to acquire a daringly human quality to his music which served him well in his later dramatic compositions.

On his return to Paris in 1670 Charpentier became a member of the household of the pious Duchesse de Guise. He remained in her service until 1687, writing and performing music, but his duties were not so onerous as to preclude his collaborations— beginning around 1672—with the brilliant playwright Molière who had recently fallen out of favour with the autocratic Lully. One of their first ventures was Le Malade imaginaire (1673). After the playwright's death Charpentier continued working occasionally for the company, writing songs, overtures and pieces of incidental music. Yet he was unable to establish himself in royal favour, although his brilliance was acknowledged by Louis XIV; the pre-eminence of Lully and Michel-Richard de Lalande at Court precluded any permanent position for Charpentier, although he did manage to secure the indulgence of the Dauphin, becoming his chapel composer in 1680. An application for a position within the Chapelle Royale failed and he was finally obliged to look for work elsewhere.

In 1684, at the age of 41, Charpentier became maître de musique at the most important Parisian Jesuit church, St Louis, also assuming the duties of music teacher at the Jesuit college of Louis-le-Grand. These important appointments were to determine the nature of much of the music he composed from then on; by the end of the century Charpentier was widely regarded as its most important composer of French sacred music. His early Italian training—a distinct disadvantage in his music for the theatre where his Italianate style was much out of favour—proved an invaluable aid.

Charpentier wrote extensively for a great many occasions, introducing, for example, the genre of the sacred oratorio which he had learned in Rome (some 35 such works survive). Charpentier's exquisite musicality and his ability to retain the utmost clarity in his choral works, whatever the forces employed (at times he uses up to four or five separate vocal ensembles), justifies his elevated reputation even today when his work is still largely neglected. In recent years there has been a concerted attempt to revive his stage works, with the sacred opera David et Jonathas (1688) and the short but intensely lyrical opera La Descente d'Orphée aux enfers (1687) both receiving deserved attention. The most important restoration to the stage, however, has been what is generally acknowledged as Charpentier's masterpiece, and the one work which drew a favourable commment from Louis XIV at the time of its first performance in 1693. Médée was created within the French operatic form brought to a peak by Lully, but constantly subverted that form through the Italianate passion of the melodies, the warmth of the musical inspiration, and the constant dramatic touches which, through skilful orchestration and brilliant occasional use of polyphony, sustain the audience's attention through a long and intense depiction of the great Greek tragedy.

Although it initially met with royal approval, and the score was printed in 1694, Médée achieved just one more production in its complete state before it vanished from the stage for nearly 300 years. Charpentier continued to work for the Jesuits at St Louis, and from 1692 onwards was involved with Duke Philippe of Orléans, first as his composition instructor and from 1698 onwards as maître de musique des enfants at Sainte-Chapelle. He continued to teach, direct choirs and compose until his death. By then, his position with regard to contemporary religious music in France was supreme.

ARCANGELO CORELLI

1653–1713

Corelli was the composer of many charming chamber works in the burgeoning Italian Baroque style, and was fundamental to the way in which that style developed. A modest and unostentatious man, he was a formidable performer on the violin, using his knowledge of the instrument to write music perfectly suited to its musical character.

Corelli was born in Fusignano, a village between Bologna and Ravenna. It is thought that he came from a prosperous professional family, well supplied with doctors and lawyers, but his leanings towards music remain unexplained by genealogy. His early aptitude for music was not ignored by the family, who obtained training for him from local priests. When Corelli wished to move to Bologna to obtain better tuition, no-one stood in his way. In fact, his admittance into the Accademica Filarmonica in Bologna in 1670 at the age of 17 suggests strong support from the family.

His history before his move to Rome in 1675 is little documented, but older traditions suggest a period in Munich spent at the same Court—the Elector of Bavaria's—as de Lassus some 100 years earlier. In 1675 Corelli was happily ensconced in the ensemble of the church of S Luigi dei Francesi, as well as playing in theatres. Within a few years he was directing the church orchestra, and from 1679 onwards,

leading the Teatro Capranica's orchestra, thus sustaining a balance between spiritual and temporal life. By this time Corelli's reputation as a violin virtuoso of the highest quality was becoming widespread and this helped him to propagate his own music. The progress he was making in Rome is attested by the publication in 1681 of his Opus 1, a set of Trio Sonatas. This book carried a dedication to Queen Christina of Sweden, who was an occasional frequenter of the S Luigi church. Corelli liaised closely with the Queen in 1687 when she organized a festival at the church when it seemed likely that James II would return to England and into the embrace of the Roman Catholic Church.

Corelli's talents were also appreciated by prestigious personages closer to home. In 1687 he was appointed music master to Cardinal Panfili and given apartments in his palazzo. Two years later Alexander VIII's election as Pope placed his nephew, Cardinal Pietro Ottoboni, in a powerful position. The Cardinal, a great enthusiast for the best of the music being performed and written in Italy at the time, was a close friend and admirer of Corelli. He immediately moved to prevent Corelli from taking up a position offered him in Modena by engaging him at considerable expense to become director of the music of his household. This was no mere rag-bag of musicians: Corelli had not only a high class ensemble at his disposal, but also elegant apartments and a considerable staff.

Corelli's reputation continued to expand and by early 1690 it had spread abroad; students and musical enthusiasts came from Scandinavia, Britain and the German states to learn from him; his pupils included Geminiani, Locatelli and Castrucci. The King of Naples made repeated attempts to lure him from Rome to join forces with no less a talent than Alessandro Scarlatti, but Corelli, a humble and modest man, who, according to contemporary sources, never sought out prestige or ostentation for the sake of it, felt no need to move from the comfort and security of his Roman position. He did not neglect his composing, however: between 1689 and 1700 he published four books of trio sonatas and one set of solo violin with continuo. These sonatas and his *Concerti Grossi* would eventually secure his reputation up to the present day.

As his 50th birthday approached, there was evidence that Corelli's desire for new musical knowledge had withered as the younger generation overtook him in technical prowess and other compositional and playing styles became fashionable. There is a famous story of Corelli's first visit to Naples in 1702: the Roman had come expecting to find a provincial orchestra in need of rigorous rehearsal to enable it to meet the challenge of playing his music, but was astounded to find it capable of near-perfect readings of his concertos from the score (he was moved to exclaim: "They can play in Naples!"), discovering in the process that Scarlatti

Arcangelo Corelli

although it is true that the piece made use of violin positions and florid patterns never used by Corelli in his own concertos.

Corelli spent the rest of his career in Rome, still fêted and admired, but by 1710 his health had begun to deteriorate. During 1712, before his health gave way entirely, he prepared his final compositions for publication: the famous and immensely influential *12 Concerti Grossi*, Op. 6 (finally printed in 1714). This set of concertos was dedicated to another friend and long-time admirer, the Prince Palatine John William of the Rhine. Corelli himself did not live to see its great success, dying in early 1713 after making a will which left a sizeable fortune and all his considerable effects to Cardinal Ottoboni. The Cardinal, hardly in need himself, kept only the superb picture collection and distributed the money between surviving members of Corelli's family. The Cardinal also saw to it that his dear friend was buried in the Pantheon and that a suitable marble monument was erected to his memory.

was a superior technician to himself. At a concert where Corelli conducted his own work the King of Naples announced to all within earshot that he found Corelli's music "boring" and left before the concert was over. Further problems in later concerts led him to leave Naples under something of a cloud, cowed by his own technical frailties and Scarlatti's brilliance. He never returned.

Another encounter with someone with talents equal to his own again showed him in a less than flattering light: in 1707 Handel, then aged 22 and full of ambition, came to Rome and made

Corelli's acquaintence. He found Corelli set in his ways and quite out of touch with international developments. At a concert rehearsal Handel was attempting to guide Corelli and his orchestra through one of his compositions, but Corelli was unable to execute certain passages to Handel's liking. Handel took the violin from Corelli and played the passage himself, whereupon the ever-polite Corelli remarked: "But, caro Sassone (dear Saxon), this is in the French style, with which I am entirely unfamiliar". That the piece was written by Handel with Corelli in mind must have seemed doubly ironic to the younger man,

Corelli's first claim to lasting fame was his excellence as a violinist. His playing seems to have been admirably direct and lacking in affectation, as well as completely assured within the bounds he chose for himself. Although most of his works were for chamber groups of varying sizes, and left blueprints for the development of all subsequent solo violin sonatas, the most influential music came in the form of concertos. His *Concerti Grossi* virtually founded the genre and were pivotal in the development of this form and thus a significant part of the concertante form of music

DON'T MISS

▶ 12 Trio sonatas, Op. 1 (1681)

▶ 12 Sonatas, Op. 5 (1700)

▶ 12 Concerti Grossi, Op. 6 (1714)

in the 18th century, Italian and otherwise. Corelli profoundly understood the characteristics of his favourite instrument, the violin, and his music reflected his love of its ability to sustain long, emotive phrases and melodies, thereby communicating intimate emotions. Corelli had an innate sense of balance and beauty, accompanied by an admirable ability to express himself simply and concisely, and these qualities are the hallmarks of his compositional style throughout his relatively small oeuvre. The 12 Sonatas for Violin, Op. 5 and *12 Concerti Grossi,* Op. 6 summarize his overall contribution admirably.

JOHANN PACHELBEL
1653–1706

Pachelbel is overwhelmingly identified with the canon section of his *Canon and Gigue in D*, now principally performed by a string orchestra. In his own day, however, he would have been known mainly for his organ playing and the compositions he wrote for organ and other keyboard instruments.

Pachelbel was born in Nuremburg, then one of the so-called 'free' imperial cities and a great centre of learning and culture, and took instruction from Heinrich Schwemmer. After leaving school in 1669 he spent a year in Altdorf before moving to Regensburg where he began to make important contacts with musicians associated with the Austrian Court in Vienna. By 1673 he was living in Vienna, where he was deputy organist at St Stephen's Cathedral and took music lessons with Johann Kaspar Kerll, who fashioned Pachelbel's mature organ style. The younger man often deputized for Kerll on the organ of the Predigerkirche.

In 1677 Pachelbel left Vienna and began a peripatetic period in his life where he held the organ position in churches in many towns across the central and southern German states, including Eisenach and Erfurt (where he came into contact with the Bach family, including Ambrosius Bach, J. S. Bach's father), Stuttgart and Gotha. He remained in Gotha from 1692–95, then returned to his home city of Nuremburg, this time on a substantially different footing than when he had left it; Pachelbel was by now a famous and influential figure in the world of music, his especial skill in composition—his infinitely inventive creation of chorale variations stressing the importance of cantabile and clarity of line—proving especially popular and definitive in the world of organ music at that time. His many pupils included J. S. Bach's elder brother Johann Christoph, who was one of many to digest his methodology and carry his compositional message to others.

Pachelbel had returned to Nuremburg to succeed his old teacher Georg Kaspar Wecker at the church of St Sebaldus, a position he retained until his death at the age of 52. Most of his music was written for the organ, but some of his earliest surviving works are a set of motets including *Nun danket alle Gott* and *Der Herr ist König*, written during his time in Erfurt, which are models of clarity and tunefulness. His greatest compositional achievement is generally recognized to be the *Hexachordum Apollinis* of 1699, six sets of keyboard variations on various airs, but other worthy efforts include the *Musikalische Sterbens-Gedanken* of 1683 and the *Musicalische Ergötzung* (1695), a series of dance suites written for string trio which were meant for the type of

DON'T MISS

▶ Canon and Gigue in D

▶ Magnificat

▶ Musicalische Ergötzung (1695)

▶ Hexachordum Apollinis (1699)

domestic entertainment at court or among musical colleagues supplied in a later generation by Telemann's *Tafelmusik*. It would seem that the famed *Canon and Gigue* for three violins and bass continuo was probably written for a similar Hausmusik function; its orchestration only occurred at a much later stage.

MARIN MARAIS
1656–1727

The older contemporary of François Couperin, Marais was an important composer and musician at the Court of Louis XIV. He first came to prominence during the ascendancy of Lully, but managed to avoid the ill-fortune of Lully's ruthless competitiveness.

Marais was one of the few composers to be both born and become famous in Paris. His early training began while a member of the choir of Sainte-Chapelle. Before his teenage years were over he had been taught the viol to a high degree of competence by Hautmann and Sainte-Colombe. In 1680 Marais was appointed as *Ordinaire de la Chambre du Roy pour la viole* and soon inspired praise for his skill. By then he had married Catherine Damicourt and they had begun the process of producing no less than 19 children. By the mid-1680s he joined the orchestra of the Académie Royale du Musique, where he came under the wing of the great Jean-Baptiste Lully himself who personally supervised his compositional studies.

By 1686 the 30-year-old Marais had published his First Book of music 'for two viols', which was appropriately dedicated to Lully, and in the same year had a minor theatrical piece performed at Court. By the time of Lully's unfortunate death in 1687, Marais was the coming man. When three of his sons proved musical, he was able to train them up sufficiently to appear in concert at Louis XIV's Court, while a fourth turned the pages of the music. Marais' viol playing became renowned throughout Europe, and his compositions for the instrument show a profound understanding of the two contemporary schools, the simple melodic approach and the style whereby the melody is more subtly interwoven with the accompanying harmony.

In 1692 he published a collection of trio sonatas (usually performed with recorders or transverse flutes), and the following year collaborated with Louis de Lully (son of the great composer) on a new setting of de la Motte's opera *Alcide* and a court entertainment. Still in demand, Marais wrote an opera based on a new version of the myth of Ariane and Bacchus, with words by Saint-Jean. His last two stage works were *Alcyone* (1706)—the dramatic storm scene was a hit—and *Sémélé* (1709). By then two more collections of music for viols had been published, both in 1701, making up the two halves of the Second Book. He repeated this kind of division in 1711, when Parts One and Two of the Third Book appeared. By 1717, when he published the two halves of the Fourth Book (the second being considerably more difficult to execute, many of the pieces being in unusual and taxing keys as well as having deliberate technical complexities to challenge the practised player), Marais was over 60 and beginning to feel the pace of life at Court. For a long time he had been a keen horticulturalist, and when in 1725 the opportunity came for him to retire to a Parisian house with a garden large enough to satisfy his desires, he took it with alacrity. He spent the last three years of his life alternating between his enjoyment of a semi-retirement spent mainly in his garden, and giving lessons on the viol. A Fifth and last book of viol pieces appeared in 1725.

DON'T MISS

▶ **Variations on 'Les Folies d'Espagne'**

▶ **Pièces de viole, Livre 1 (1685)**

▶ **Alcyone (1706)**

▶ **Pièces de viole, Livre 3 (1711)**

HENRY PURCELL

1659–1695

Purcell's importance to the history of English music has long been acknowledged, but the recent tercentenary of his death and the resultant interest in his works has made it possible to properly assess him in the wider European context.

Considering his eminence during his own lifetime and after, it is extraordinary just how little is actually known about Purcell. It is clear that he came from a musical family for Henry Purcell the elder is named by Pepys in 1659 as Master of Musique, and it may be the same Henry Purcell who appeared in William Davenant's *The Siege of Rhodes* in 1656. In 1660 Henry Purcell the elder was appointed one of the Gentlemen of the newly re-established Chapel Royal, and also became Master of Choristers at Westminster Abbey. He died in 1664, when young Henry was just five years old, leaving three sons and a wife. The elder Henry's brother Thomas, also a musician in the Chapel Royal, took on the responsibility of rearing the children.

England at this time was only six years away from Cromwell's Protectorate with its blanket ban on all theatrical performances, and at the Restoration Charles II found the Exchequer to be virtually bankrupt. These were difficult times for musicians for even though the King restituted many musical institutions and employed a great number of people, few of them were paid regularly. Brought up against a

background of the Great Plague of 1665 and the Great Fire of 1666, young Henry's childhood certainly did not lack incident.

Purcell's first appearance in connection with music was his entry into the Children's Choir of the Chapel Royal, directed by Captain Henry Cooke, an ex-boy chorister in the Chapel Royal in the reign of Charles I. Cooke had built up an excellent choir which contained boys of the quality of William Turner and John Blow. Purcell's interest in composition was awoken early, his first attested composition being a Birthday Address to the King in 1670 when the boy could have been no more than 11 years old. Cooke was conversant with the Italianate style, especially in the area of vocal music, and this, combined with the newly fashionable French leanings of his 1672 successor and son-in-law, Pelham Humfrey, a composer in his own right, would have given Purcell a valuable breadth as well as depth of stylistic models.

In 1673 Purcell's precocious talents won practical recognition when he was made Assistant Keeper of the King's instruments, a valuable position for an aspiring composer. At the age of 14, a year after his voice had broken, he wrote the catch 'Here's that will challenge all the Fair'. This was followed at regular intervals during the 1670s by airs which appeared in various anthologies. That he was also writing anthems is confirmed by letters from musicians employed to sing them.

In 1674 Humfrey died at the early age of 27, and was succeeded by the composer John Blow who had been organist at Westminster Abbey. Blow was to remain head of the Children of the Chapel Royal until his death in 1708. He was just 6 years older than Purcell but proved an excellent tutor. Due to the death in 1677 of his friend and mentor, the composer Matthew Locke, Purcell was appointed to Locke's position of 'composer ordinary with fee for the violin to His Majesty'. Purcell's personal grief at the loss of Locke was recorded in his published air 'On the death of his worthy friend, Matthew Locke'. By 1679 Purcell had become organist at Westminster Abbey.

This moved the young man further into the mainstream of English musical life, and within a year he began his long series of compositions for the burgeoning London theatre world (beginning with a number of songs for Nathaniel Lee's *Theodosius*), as well as composing during the fine summer of 1680 his famous set of Fantasias for Strings. These pieces were possibly written while Purcell was at Windsor with the King's retinue, thus explaining the unusual intensity and productiveness of this set of some 12 pieces. By this date, as the fantasia had fallen out of favour in Restoration England, these compositions were written purely for Purcell's own enjoyment, remaining in manuscript until edited and published by Philip Heseltine (Peter Warlock) in 1927.

They have since been acknowledged as contrapuntal music of the very highest calibre.

Purcell began writing his long series of odes and welcome songs for the royal family in 1680, a year so packed with progress on virtually every front that it could almost be termed his *annus mirabilis*. It can certainly be pointed to with confidence as being the year when he demonstrated an absolute maturity of compositional thought. The year was equally memorable on a private level, for in September he married Frances Peters and they moved to a house in Westminster, close to the Abbey. It is possible that 1681 also saw the composition of the famous *Chaconne in F* for recorders. A number of deaths the following year substantially altered the composer's life once more: in July the Chapel Royal organist Edward Lowe died, and Purcell was appointed in his stead; later that month his uncle, Thomas Purcell, also passed away; three months later his second son—the first having died soon after he was born—also died.

Nevertheless, the following year saw Purcell's first published music advertised in the London Gazette: *12 Sonatas of III Parts, for two violins and bass, to the harpsichord or organ*. These works were dedicated to Charles II and prefaced by a portrait of the composer 'Aetat: suae 24'. The written preface, composed either by Purcell himself or by the publisher Playford, stresses the point that Purcell is here endeavouring 'a just imitation of the most fam'd Italian Masters; principally, to bring the seriousness and gravity of that sort of Musick in vogue'.

Henry Purcell

The first odes for St Cecilia's day were written in 1683. In December John Hingston, Purcell's superior as keeper and repairer of the King's instruments, died and Purcell was promoted to his position. The year 1685 saw the death of Charles II and the coronation of James II, his Catholic brother. Apart from writing music for the coronation, Purcell had a thin time of it during the four years of James's ultimately disastrous reign. James and his wife were fundamentally uninterested in music and the arts in general; when they had to commission music for state or court occasions they chose foreign composers—Italians and French—who were not only Catholic but fashionable in the great European cities, especially

the Paris of Louis XIV. Purcell lost two of his most prestigious positions—composer ordinary and organist to the Chapel Royal—to Catholic rivals. Yet he was still expected to compose music for royal occasions.

In the midst of these humbling circumstances, in 1686 the Purcells had another child, Thomas, which did not survive. The wholesale rearrangement and standardization of musicians' salaries at Court (which involved clearing Charles II's debts) did not affect Purcell, but the year was not financially rewarding, and when a fourth child died after just three months of life, Purcell was under pressure from every quarter. However,

DON'T MISS

▶ Bess of Bedlam 'From silent shades', Z370

▶ Birthday Ode, 'Come ye sons of art away', Z323

▶ Chaconne for Strings in G minor, Z730

▶ Fantasia in F, 'Upon one note', Z745

▶ Funeral sentences for the death of Queen Mary (1695)

he continued to work and when Playford's *Harmonia Sacra* was published in 1687 it contained several Purcell works of high quality.

The following year, 1688, witnessed the Glorious Revolution and the accession of William and Mary to the throne. It also ushered in the first child born to the Purcells which survived into adulthood and produced descendants—a daughter named Frances. The accession of the new monarchs did not improve Purcell's situatiion, William and Mary being as uninterested in music as James. It was clear that Purcell and his colleagues would have to find other ways to earn a satisfactory living. The development of a close friendship between Purcell and the poet/playwright John Dryden in 1689 was not the only good news that year: the first recorded performance of Purcell's operatic masterpiece, *Dido and Aeneas* took place at a girls' boarding school in Chelsea. There is no real consensus as to whether *Dido* was especially written by Purcell and his librettist Nahum Tate for this occasion, or whether it had been written in the first half of the 1680s and adapted specifically, with a new prologue and epilogue, for the performance. Certainly, the artistic parallels with John Blow's *Venus and Adonis*—which appeared in 1682—are too many to be coincidental.

Purcell's earlier compositional practices also appear too often for the work to be comfortably given 1689 as its year of gestation.

Meanwhile, Purcell's relationship with Dryden was fast developing into one of real significance: a Dryden adaptation of John Fletcher's *Dioclesian* had music added by Purcell and was sufficiently successful for the pair to move on to a project wholly their own, *King Arthur* (first produced in Dorset Garden in 1691). This work is a step back from the unity of *Dido*, with the music (including the wonderful 'frost' scene) and spoken text existing side by side rather than as an integrated whole—a throwback to the masques and earlier forms of English musical entertainments rather than a real attempt to create an Italian-style operatic piece.

Seen as part of a conscious move by Purcell into the realm of music for public theatre, *King Arthur* was a good career move, and was followed by numerous other occasions when music was required to aid the dramatic realization of a range of new plays and revivals. That it was begun at around the same time as Purcell produced the third of his birthday odes for Queen Mary emphasizes the composer's willingness to serve any client to the best of his ability. His major success in

1692, *The Fairy Queen*, was another Dorset Garden production, costing over £3,000 to mount and using over 100 performers. Again Purcell provided instrumental music for the masques and music for a number of airs. Only a selection of the work's songs were published during the composer's lifetime, and the original score was lost to the world until discovered in the library at the Royal Academy of Music in 1901.

In 1692 Purcell composed the wonderful ode, *Hail, bright Cecilia*, celebrating St Cecilia's Day; Purcell himself sang the second stanza at its first performance. He celebrated the February 1693 birthday of Queen Mary with one of his most famous pieces, *Come ye sons of art away*. At the death of the Queen in December 1694, Purcell took part in the elaborate funeral arrangements, his music becoming one of the emotional focal points of the occasion. By May 1695 he was making final preparations for the première of the operatic version of a play first mounted in London in 1694, *The Indian Queen*, written by Dryden and Sir Richard Howard. This was to be his last major theatrical work, although in the same year he wrote the incidental music for a number of new ventures, including *Timon of Athens* and *Don Quixote, Part III*, as well as a last (and most beautiful) ode for the royal family, *Who can from joy refrain*.

Purcell died on November 21, the eve of St Cecilia's day. The cause of death was not recorded, although contemporaries made allusions to him composing songs 'in his sicknesse', thus conveying the impression that it was not a precipitous collapse. Purcell was mourned by his fellow-musicians, and some of the music he had written for Queen Mary's funeral 10 months earlier was played at his own service. He was interred in Westminster Abbey.

Purcell straddled old and new forms with ease. His love of the older English composers, especially the Tudors, is evident in his use of musical forms which by his day were regarded by most as archaic—the fantasia, the air, and so on. Yet he was well aware of contemporary developments in Italy and elsewhere, and indeed was happy to use Gabrieli as a model on which to fashion his Te Deum of 1693. It is

possible to regard his occasional music as Baroque, but it would be more accurate thus to describe the composers he influenced—such as Handel—rather than Purcell himself. Like Mozart a century later, Purcell was cut down in his prime before he could

address himself to the larger forms then rapidly emerging—such as opera and the Reformation style of oratorio—and just before the major shift in musical and theatrical sensibilities which would launch the mature Baroque style.

DON'T MISS

▶ **If music be the food of love, Z379/1**

▶ **Dido and Aeneas, Z626, (1689)**

▶ **The Fairy Queen, Z629, (1692)**

▶ **St Cecilia's Day Ode 'Hail, bright Cecilia', Z328 (1692)**

▶ **Lord, what is man?, Z192 (1693)**

ALESSANDRO SCARLATTI
1660–1725

Scarlatti was one of the great formative composers from the beginning of the Baroque period. Unjustly neglected today, he was a prolific creator, completing over 700 cantatas, more than 60 operas, a series of *concerti* and *concerti grossi*, as well as various occasional works and instrumental pieces. Of this vast output, only a tiny fraction is currently available on record and few of his stage works have been revived in recent years.

Though born in Palermo, Sicily, there are suggestions that Scarlatti's family moved to Rome in 1672, and that for a short time Alessandro studied with the composer Giacomo Carissimi. Little more is known about his early life,

although he was *maestro di capella* at Rome's San Giacomo degli Incurabili in 1678, and the records of another church show that he was commissioned in 1679 to write an oratorio. The previous year he had married Antonia Anzalone and they had started what became a large family.

By 1679 Scarlatti had studied and worked in music circles sufficiently to receive his first opera commission which was performed in Rome. He also received the endorsement of patrons such as Christina of Sweden and Cardinal Pamphili. His connection with Queen Christina proved of great value while he was still in Rome, and by the following year he was her *maestro di cappella* as well as the successful writer of a second opera. In 1683 his

first *opera seria*, called *Il Pompeo*, was produced; two years later he collaborated with Cardinal Pamphili on the oratorio *Maddalena*, a large and important work which also had the good fortune to remain consistently popular for the next two decades.

This work was performed in Florence, Lucca, Modena and Vienna, but its Rome performance took place (in March 1685) just as Scarlatti was preparing to take up residence in Naples as *maestro di cappella* to the Viceroy of Naples. He remained in Naples until 1702, composing operas for the royal palace or the royal theatre of San Bartolomeo, but gradually became disillusioned by the lack of opportunities to write music which had to appeal to the lowest common denominator, and by the

Alessandro Scarlatti

There is evidence that his commitment to Naples was sporadic until as late as 1713, when the Viceroy confirmed his position as *Maestro da Real Cappella* at an increased salary. The next few years saw him producing consistently brilliant works, both oratorios and operas, and his talents were publicly recognized in 1716 when he was made a Cavaliere (knight) of the city and also received the Order of the Golden Spur from the Pope (the latter distinction presumably due to Scarlatti's composition of the *Messa Clementina II* for Pope Clement XI and naming it after him).

Another move away from Naples occurred around 1719, for the opera *Cambise* proved to be his last to be produced in the city during his lifetime and followed the artistic triumphs of *Telemaco* (1718) and *Marco Attilo Regolo* (1719) in Rome. Scarlatti retained his *maestro*'s title in the Viceroy's court, but his stipend was no longer paid to him, and it seems certain that he once again made his way back to Rome. His last opera, *Griselda,* was performed there in 1721, the year of Clement XI's death, and in November of that year he was commissioned to write a pastorale for the incoming Pontiff's formal accession—perhaps the last work he wrote for the city. He appears to have finally left Rome the following year, travelling about Italy for a while before returning to Naples. There he was virtually forgotten, thought of (if at all) as an old and rather bad-tempered remnant from a past era. He died there in 1725 and was buried in the church of Montesanto, his epitaph written by that true friend and believer, Cardinal Ottoboni.

relatively poor pay and conditions. In 1702 Scarlatti at last gained temporary leave from his Neapolitan duties, and taking his 17-year-old son, the composer Domenico, left for Florence; he had long-harboured an ambition to work in the Medici household. Although Scarlatti composed several operas for Ferdinand de Medici, a permanent appointment was not forthcoming, so he moved on to Rome where a consistent admirer of his music, Cardinal Ottoboni (the great champion of Corelli), procured him two minor posts which gave him a small income.

The lack of opportunities to write opera in a Rome obsessed with the Counter-Reformation and public morality, and his relative poverty, were enough to

give Scarlatti a poor impression of the Eternal City. Recognition, however, was not in short supply: in 1706 he was elected, together with Corelli and Pasquini, as a member of the Arcadian Academy. He was also composing at a consistently high level, both in chamber music and motets, and other church music. In 1707, despite the offer of a position at Santa Maria Maggiore and the successful production of two of his best operas in Venice, he returned to Naples. Considering the quality of the two Venetian operas (which he travelled to Venice to direct), *Mitridate Eupatore* and *Il trionfo della libertà* (*Mitridate* being one of his greatest works), and the increased scale of their musical and dramatic ambitions, his return to Naples was especially ironic.

Scarlatti's operas and cantatas contain his most deeply-felt and rigorously-constructed music. His music is central to the development of the full Baroque style which, in turn, led to the Classicism of Haydn and Beethoven. He devoted himself to the clarifying and systematizing of the monodic system of composing, which was still in its infancy when he began his career, and he was instrumental in standardizing a style based on the tonal system which was to serve as the basis of Western music for the next 200 years.

His operas developed features which became pivotal to the Italian style, with the 'Italian' overture becoming a fixture, as much as the *da capo* form of aria (which Scarlatti did not invent but by the sheer force of his example was established as the only aria form to use) and the first use of accompanied recitative (in the opera *Olimpia vendicata*, 1686). Scarlatti, not willing to entrust such a sensitive and exposed position to the strings in an opera orchestra of the 18th century—the standard of playing was wildly variable—awarded that role to the fixed-pitch harpsichord, an instrument less likely to leave the singers and audience up in the air. This became standard operatic practice for most of the century, until recitative itself was finally sidelined in favour of unbroken dramatic and melodic action.

DON'T MISS

▶ Il Pompeo (1683)

▶ Messa di Santa Cecilia (1720)

▶ 12 Sinfonie di concerto grosso (1720)

▶ Sonatas for Flute and Strings (1725)

▶ 6 Concerti Grossi (publ. 1740)

FRANÇOIS COUPERIN
1668–1733

Couperin was one of the key figures in the formulation of what came to be perceived as a characteristically French approach to composing for the keyboard. His ability to bring imagination and flair to the simplest of pieces has kept his reputation and influence alive until the present day.

François Couperin is commonly referred to in France as 'le Grand' in order to differentiate him from the other members of a famous musical dynasty. He was the son of Charles Couperin (1638–1679), one of three brothers (the other two being Louis [1626–1661] and François [1631–1701]). The family was established in Chaumes. Louis moved to Paris, becoming in time the organist at

St Gervais, a post he held until his death, as well as playing the violin in court orchestras and composing keyboard music which has maintained a high reputation up to the present day. François was taught music by his father and by the King's Chapel organist, Jacques-Denis Thomelin, who was well-versed in the harpsichord repertoire and the art of counterpoint. Charles had inherited the organist's chair at St Gervais after the death of his brother Louis: in turn, young François inherited the position on his father's death, although he did not take up the post until after his eigtheenth birthday in 1685. His reputation as a keyboard composer was not, however, to be centred around the organ; his preferred instrument was the harpsichord.

In 1689, aged 21, he married Marie-Anne Ansault, and in time they had two daughters. (The second, Marguerite-Antoinette [1705–1778], was a gifted harpsichordist who taught Louis XV's daughters and eventually succeeded her ageing father as harpsichordist to the King.) François made his first move into the royal household in 1693 when he was appointed Thomelin's successor at the Chapel Royal. He thereafter became a trusted teacher to the royal children as well as to other nobles such as the Comte de Toulouse and the Duc de Burgundy. Just prior to his royal appointments, Couperin had taken the unusual step of publishing the first of a series of Italianate trios under a pseudonym–an Italianized anagram of his name: Pernucio. In his 1726 Preface to *Les Nations* (his first publication of

François Couperin

dance pieces and non-dance items. His understanding of the instrument enabled him to write beautifully to its strengths, emphasizing, as he expressed it, its "precision, clarity, brilliance and compass".

The second *Livre de pièces de clavecin* was published between the two editions (1716–1717) of his famous and important treatise on harpsichord technique, *L'Art de toucher le clavecin*, and with this second volume Couperin moved into a more thoroughly individualistic style and formula, abandoning the dance suite and adopting instead the idea of a collection of character pieces. This period was an important one professionally for Couperin for in March 1717 the office of *Ordinaire de la Musique du Roy pour le clavecin*, held until then by d'Anglebert's son Jean-Baptiste-Henri, reverted to him, while he maintained his Versailles position as organist to the Royal Chapel until after Louis XIV's death in 1715 and the removal of the Court to Paris.

these works under his own name), Couperin admits to practising this deception because he feared the French were not ready for the new Italian style if proffered by a Frenchman; "Charmed by the sonatas of Signor Corelli, whose works I shall love as long as I live, just as I do the French works of Monsieur de Lulli (Lully), I attempted to compose one myself, which I then arranged to have performed at the concert series where I had heard those of Corelli... The sonata was eagerly devoured, and I...was encouraged by this. I wrote others, and my Italianized name brought me, in disguise, considerable applause".

Couperin's contentment with obscurity meant that while many of his works were common property at the turn of the century, and he was universally acknowledged as the greatest living French composer, he did not publish any of his keyboard music under his own name until as late as 1713 when he was already 45 years old and had been in royal service for 20 years. This enormous volume, *Premier Livre de pièces de clavecin*, shows Couperin using the notion of the suite in the direct tradition of Jean-Henri d'Anglebert, with its more vigorous dances–*allemande*, *courante*, *sarabande*–combined with delicate

The pattern established by the second *Livre*, giving elusive titles to characters portrayed in each harpsichord piece, was continued and elaborated upon in 1722 and 1730 when the *Troisième* and *Quatrième Livres* appeared. Birds as well as people became the subject of some pieces, while others may well relate to paintings executed by his contemporary, Watteau. By the time of the fourth book's publication Couperin had just three years to live and was already experiencing a general failure in health. Yet his harpsichord music had long taken on a life of its own, becoming, in the composer Louis Claude Daquin's words, one of France's "national delicacies". The music, together with his Treatise of 1716, was to form one of the most stable and comprehensive foundations in the art of keyboard music for succeeding generations to be found in any country. Couperin clearly had faith that his music would long outlive him, writing in the Preface to the 1730 *Livre*: "I hope that my family will find among my papers matter which will cause them to regret my death". However, his family did not treat his unpublished legacy with much consideration, some of his chamber music lying unheard and unseen in private hands until the present century.

That Couperin's reputation lies almost exclusively in the world of instrumental music has as much to do with the King's lack of interest in long religious ceremonies as it has with the composer's own artistic inclinations. Ironically, the first of his music Couperin had printed (in 1703–05 and,

most notably, 1713–15, with the *Leçons de Tenèbres*) was a series of motets written for the King. These are typical of his vocal output, being for small forces, and although Titon du Tillet (an early chronicler of the composer) claimed that Couperin wrote 12 large-scale motets for choir and instrumental accompaniment, none of them were published in his lifetime, and none have come down to us today. The motets are models of grace and understatement, combining an Italianate grace and subtlety with a French dignity and clarity.

Couperin's reputation rests squarely on his four harpsichord books. These show such a deep understanding of the instrument, combined with a subtle and brilliant grasp of form, as well as an intuitive flair for portraiture of any kind which has inspired the imagination and respect of every generation of musician and composer since. It is no accident that Maurice Ravel, some two centuries later, was to write a suite entitled *Le Tombeau de Couperin*, and that Debussy was to use Couperin as one of his models when he turned to his late style in his last chamber works.

DON'T MISS

▶ Victoria! Christo resurgenti
▶ Premier Livre de pièces de clavecin, Ordres 1–5 (1713)
▶ 3 Leçons de ténèbres (1713–17)
▶ Concerts royaux (1722)
▶ Les Nations (1726)

TOMASO ALBINONI
1671–1751

Albinoni was one of the group of Venetian composers called the *Scuola veneziana* which first made its presence felt at the close of the 17th century and was dominating the Italian musical scene by the first decades of the 18th. He was an important figure in the formation of the Italian Baroque period, but his innate conservatism led to a prolonged neglect of his work before and after his death.

Albinoni was born into a wealthy Venetian family who had made their money out of the manufacture of paper and playing-cards. Unlike the majority of his antecedents and contemporaries, he was not obliged to work for a living. At first he regarded his music only as a serious hobby, describing himself as a dilettante and specializing in singing and playing the violin. In 1694, at the age of 23, his first opera *Zenobia, regina di Palmieri* appeared and a collection of Trio Sonatas, Op. 1 was published. His Opus 2 of 1700, however, was more influential, being 6 Concerti combined with 6 Sonatas. It claims the distinction of being the first publication by a Venetian in the new genre. Written for a string ensemble with a principal

Tomaso Albinoni (far left), with his colleagues Egizio and Colla

violin part, and exhibiting all the liveliness, melodic grace and brilliance of sound to be expected from strings, it established Albinoni at the forefront of the younger generation of Venetian composers, together with Caldara, Gasparini, Marcello and Vivaldi. Albinoni's championing of the three-movement concerto (fast-slow-fast) was to have a lasting effect.

Albinoni further cemented his position with the publication of *12 Concerti a cinque*, Op. 5 in 1707, in which he showed himself to be less concerned with solo violin lines accompanied by an ensemble, preferring instead the richer sounds made by the five voices of a concerted ensemble. His gift for melody is nowhere more pronounced than in this set of concerti, a gift which seems to owe much to his preoccupation with the voice and the natural melodic lines both a voice and a violin can sustain.

Indeed, this set of works can be seen as a high point in his career. From then on he became increasingly disinclined to alter his format or style to accommodate the newer concerto ideas being developed by composers such as Marcello and Vivaldi. Within a decade, Albinoni was perceived as a force for conservatism in everything regarding musical matters. Perhaps his fascination with opera enabled him to simply ignore developments in the other genre: in the year of Opus 5's publication, no fewer than four Albinoni operas made their Venetian débuts (he was to complete 80 in his lifetime).

With the death of his father in 1709, Albinoni's material circumstances changed: at the age of 38 he felt he had discharged his obligations to the family business, so he left it to his two younger brothers and became a full-time composer and musician. Within a

few years, however, Albinoni was being overtaken by the more brilliant and fiery work of Vivaldi whose *Estro armonico*, Op. 3 of 1711 set a new pace and style for Venetian concerted music. Albinoni was publicly dismissive of the new ideas; in fact his style changed very little from this period onwards, and although he occasionally attempted to incorporate some of the superficial stylistic traits with which Vivaldi had attracted so much attention, he made no attempt to go deeper into his rival's music and restructure his own compositional thinking.

From then on Albinoni's 'firsts' were restricted to such things as being the first into print with concertos written for oboe (his Op. 7 and 9 containing four such concertos each), although it is certain that other composers had previously written concertos for the instrument but had not yet published them. It was not until 1735 that Albinoni published another set of concertos, his 12 Concerti, Op. 10, which show his style to have hardened and, even then, become for the most part anachronistic, although there are some attempts to cast the solo instrument in the nascent Classical style. The intervening years had been taken up principally with the writing and staging of operas, but by 1735 the taste for Venetian operatic style was waning and the more vigorous Neapolitan school, personified by such as Hasse, Leo and Porpora, had taken over the Venetian stages. On the instrumental front, the two sexagenarians, Vivaldi and Albinoni, found their positions challenged by the Paduan, Giuseppe Tartini, and Pietro Locatelli from Bergamo, both of whom moved to Venice and impressed Ventian audiences with their brilliant virtuoso writing and playing.

Vivaldi just managed to survive the influx of new music, but Albinoni's last decade was spent in complete obscurity and it is doubtful whether any compositions later than his Opus 10 currently exist. After his death in 1751 his music had to wait more than two centuries before it was restored to its former levels of appreciation.

It is a curious fact that Albinoni is best-known for a work not actually written by him: the famous *Adagio* is a concoction by the 20th-century Italian scholar, Roberto Giazotto (born 1910), based on a fragment by Albinoni. A cursory acquaintance with genuine concertos or adagios by Albinoni will establish the considerable stylistic gulf

between the two. Of his bona fide output, it is difficult to recommend any of his operas to the general listener because so few are even available in published form. Only *Pimpinone*, a fine short work, has gained any sort of reputation in this century, and has been occasionally staged, both inside and outside Italy, as well as recorded.

The concertos are a different matter, his Opus 2, 5, 7, 9 and 10 concertos all containing a great deal of memorable and melodic music. These are often given in recitals or performed as a complete opus number, and are now the subject of study by authentic instrument groups as well as performers using modern instruments. The Opus 7 and 9 concertos are divided more or less equally between works for oboe and those for violin; many of the oboe

pieces have become popular in their own right. Albinoni published an Opus 4 of 12 Cantatas in 1702, but his real inclinations in vocal music lay within opera. There was no economic necessity for him to compose religious music, which remains a relatively minor part of his overall output and achievement.

DON'T MISS

▶ **Adagio in G minor (spurious)**

▶ **12 Trio sonatas, Op. 1 (1704)**

▶ **12 Concerti a cinque, Op. 5 (1707)**

▶ **12 Concerti a cinque, Op. 7 (1719)**

▶ **12 Concerti a cinque, Op. 9 (1722)**

ANTONIO VIVALDI
1678–1741

For such an outstanding composer, relatively little is known about Vivaldi's life beyond the fact that he was born and raised in Venice. This is ironic, considering this great Baroque composer's close association in the public's mind with everything Venetian—an association only bettered by Canaletto.

Vivaldi's father was a violinist at St. Mark's, and there are indications that Antonio received his early musical schooling from within the family. He is understood to have trained as a priest,

and was ordained in 1703. With this achieved, Vivaldi gave up any pretence to a life of the cloth and instead concentrated on his musical career. The same year he was appointed as *maestro di violino* by the Ospedale della Pietà, a charitable religious foundation for the education and upbringing of female orphans. His relationship with the Pietà was to last for the rest of his life, a central pivot around which his musical activities could revolve.

Thus began the career of the man known to all as 'Il Prete Rosso' (the Red Priest) on account of his extraordinary

shock of red hair. It is worth conjecturing that Vivaldi's decision to join the priesthood solved the problem of how to support himself while he practised the art which obsessed him. It is clear that his family was not well-to-do, unable to support him in the manner of Albinoni who remained a dilaettante composer until well into his thirties. That Vivaldi's appointment was made—in part at least—because of his composing abilities seems assured by the fact that his superior at the Pietà was Francesco Gasparini who had been a pupil of Corelli and was a capable operatic composer.

Vivaldi's skill as a violinist and his organizational abilities made him an ideal man for the role. The instrumental ensembles of the Pietà—already acknowledged as unusually high in achievement—eventually became a source of public admiration, their Sunday concerts often attended by capacity crowds. Vivaldi's role enabled him to experiment with his compositional ideas and techniques, and by 1705 he had earned enough of a reputation to publish his Opus 1, a series of Trio Sonatas. Three years later his Opus 2, a set of Violin Sonatas, appeared. It is clear, however, that some of his concertos were already in private circulation, and that the publication of L'Estro Armonico, Op. 3 publicly confirmed what a number of Venetians had begun to grasp: that here was a genius who was bringing the Baroque concerto form to a peak of perfection while simultaneously initiating a new approach to the idea of instrumental musical expression.

What Vivaldi achieved with this vastly important collection was the definitive organization of musical material into a unified and highly expressive form which allowed for a hitherto unimagined freedom of invention, as well as enormous scope for drama and surprise. He aimed at simplicity and clarity at all times, avoiding the bombastic and portentous and concentrating on the telling phrase and the expressive sweep of a single melody perfectly accompanied by flawless harmony transparently scored. L'Estro Armonico was a revelation to his contemporaries, rendering obsolete all that came before it in the genre. After this there was nothing more for other Italian composers to do but try to beat Vivaldi at his own game. Few came close, for Vivaldi had such a wonderful combination of passion and imagination, elegance and poise. It is no accident that the young J. S. Bach came to know and revere this set of concerti, using it as his model for composing. As his early biographer Forkel commented: "He listened to them often, with great attention, and finally conceived the idea of transcribing them for his own keyboard. It was in this way that he learned the logic of musical ideas, their sequence, the correct succession for modulations, and many other things...he learned to think in music...(and)...borrow his musical ideas not from his fingers, but from his imagination".

Vivaldi, however, did not rest on his laurels; he was intensely interested in opera, and 1713 saw his debut with Ottone in Villa. This heralded a new stage in his compositional life; increasing amounts of time were spent either composing, sourcing, overseeing or producing his (and other composers') operas. Another important watershed in his professional life occurred with the departure in 1714 of Gasparini, his superior at the Pietà, for Rome. Vivaldi now had to supply regular musical material for the Pietà's choir, in addition to his usual outpouring of instrumental and operatic music. By the end of the following year, Vivaldi was being praised by the Pietà's governors for already delivering a Mass, an oratorio, more than 30 motets and a Vespers. In 1714 Vivaldi published his Op. 4, La Stravaganza, which made further advances in the evolution of the concerto genre. Time and again he excites the anticipation of the audience through his clever musical constructions, only to overturn it by the most imaginative and capricious means at his disposal. This, however, should not give the impression that these concertos were any less rigorously organized than the former series; they are every bit as formally perfect, and the underlying musical forms which Vivaldi took for new development point, in part, to concerti grossi models as well as to the solo concerto in which he specialized.

After this series of artistic triumphs, Vivaldi increasingly applied for leave of absence to travel extensively in Italy and further abroad. There was a period of time (estimated to be about four years, although the actual dates vary from between 1707 to 1721) when he was in the service of Philip von Hessen (of Hesse-Darmstadt), the Governor of Mantua. While in Mantua he met a singer, Anna Giraud, who later appeared as the soprano lead in many of his operas. Their relationship

---

DON'T MISS

▶ Ottone in Villa (1713)

▶ Tito Manlio (1720)

▶ 12 Concerti 'Il cimento dell'armonia e dell'inventione', Op. 8 (includes 'Le quattro stagioni') (1725)

▶ 6 Concerti for Flute and Strings, Op. 10 (1728)

---

remained close and Anna, together with her sister, often acted as his travelling companions.

His concertos continued to be published in Amsterdam, with Opus 7 appearing in 1716. His crowning glory, Opus 8, appeared in 1725, although the music had probably been composed from 1720 onwards. This set of 8 concerti, entitled *Il cimento dell'armonia e dell'inventione*, included the now universally acclaimed sub-set of four concerti called *Le quattro stagione* (The Four Seasons), which were accompanied by brief poems describing the seasonal pictures Vivaldi wished to echo in his music. The second section included the famous *La tempesta di mare* (Storm at Sea) and *La Caccia* (The Hunt), violin concertos which were every bit as pictorial as the former four works. These works were all dedicated to the Bohemian Count Wenzel von Morzin, a Habsburg potentate with whom Vivaldi was regularly associated.

Antonio Vivaldi

The composer, meanwhile, had been to Rome in 1723–4, where he was given the opportunity to impress the Pope, playing before him to sustained applause. By 1727 he was ready to publish his last great set of concerti, *La Cetra* (The Lyre), Op. 9. This was dedicated to the Austrian Emperor, Charles VI, with whom Vivaldi seems to have become acquainted in Vienna during the mid-1720s. The Emperor, a great music enthusiast, a keen amateur composer and keyboard player, could not have failed to be impressed by Vivaldi. This is born out by a report of their later meeting in Trieste in 1728: 'The Emperor conversed for a long time with Vivaldi about music; they say that he talked longer to him in private in 15

days than he talks to his ministers in two years'. It is interesting to note that there exists a second set of 12 concertos entitled *La Cetra* and dedicated to the Emperor which contains just one work common to both sets and remained in manuscript during Vivaldi's lifetime. The music in this later set is every bit as compelling and inventive as earlier collections, with the quality of the writing uniformly high.

With this work and the corresponding operas of the late 1720s and early 1730s, Vivaldi passed from the peak of his profession into a long decline. New composers and new styles of Italian opera and chamber music were pressing for the public's attention, especially

those from Naples. Vivaldi, now in his mid-fifties, was beginning to be taken for granted by his audience. His absences from Venice and the Pietà also told against him as the tide of public fashion turned, and when his great patron Philip von Hessen died in 1736 the church authorities lost little time making him feel uncomfortable in Venice. In 1737 his operas were banned on the pretext that he was to be regarded as a lapsed priest due to his association with Anna Giraud, and the following year the governors of the Pietà used similar reasoning in their decision not to renew his contract. By 1740, tired and increasingly isolated, Vivaldi left Venice once more and travelled to Vienna, perhaps in the hope of gaining a position there. Like Mozart 40 years later, he was disappointed; his great friend, Emperor Charles VI, had died just prior to his arrival and the new rulers were already plunged into what became the War of Austrian Succession. Vivaldi spent the winter in Vienna hoping for an upturn in his fortunes but nothing transpired. By the spring he was weak and ailing, and in July, at the height of summer, he died. He was buried—again like Mozart—in a pauper's grave.

With a catalogue of works which include nearly 500 concertos alone, and considering that Vivaldi himself only published—in the collections detailed above—close to 100 concertos, there is a vast amount which is not in any way conveniently collected and are only identifiable by instruments, keys employed and RV numbers. The most famous sets of concertos—Opus 3 and Opus 8, the latter including the *Four Seasons* —contain the richness and freshness of Vivaldi's invention at its early and middle peaks. The Opus 3

L'Estro Armonico concertos are greatly varied in terms of the combination of solo instrumentation (there are also a number in the *concerti grossi* style), while Opus 8 reflects a peak in terms of Vivaldi's marvellous ear for the sounds of nature, as well as his ability to convert what he sees around him into musical phrases. Apart from concertos written for one, two or three violins, there are over 20 'cello concertos, close to 50 bassoon concertos, 20 for the relatively new instrument, the oboe, plus concertos for what was then a very new instrument, the clarinet, concertos for mandolins, and the ravishing Opus 10 flute concertos.

As with the concertos, Vivaldi's sacred music is usually represented by his Glorias, RV 589 and 588, but there is a great deal more very beautiful and often moving music written for religious settings, including a *Stabat Mater* RV 621 and over 20 cantatas. There is no doubt that Vivaldi set great store by his stage works, claiming to have produced close to 100 of them in

the 28 years between his first and last operas. This can no longer be authenticated, although nearly 50 can be accounted for. Unfortunately, nowhere near that number of scores have been located, and only a minority of the operas to have survived have received professional productions in modern times. Vivaldi wrote in the *opera seria* style, as well as completing a number of the more *opera buffo*-type intermezzi before the end of his career. The latter is well represented by *La Senna Festeggiante* (1728), while his operatic style can be accurately surmised from the 1735 production, *Catone in Utica*.

DON'T MISS

▶ Gloria in D, RV589
▶ Mandolin Concerto in C, RV425
▶ Stabat Mater in F, RV621
▶ 12 Violin Sonatas ('Manchester Sonatas')

GEORG PHILIPP TELEMANN
1681–1767

Although regularly undervalued as a composer and influence in the present century, Telemann in his own lifetime was the single most famous and honoured of contemporary German composers, and seen as a model musician whose example young composers aspired to.

Telemann, the son of a pastor, was born in Magdeburg, a town lying between Berlin and Hannover. It is claimed that the boy became proficient on the flute, violin and zither while still attending primary school. At this stage he was entirely self-taught, and read not a note of music, but entertained his family and friends with impromptu recitals.

Telemann received his education in Magdeburg and Hildesheim, but continued to build on his musical knowledge almost entirely through his own efforts, in particular studying the scores of such formal perfectionists as Lully and Campra. By 1701 he was accepted at Leipzig University where he studied languages and science but also became involved in the Leipzig music scene, which included being appointed as organist at the Neukirche in 1704. He also founded a musical society for the university students. Even prior to his Neukirche appointment he had begun writing operas, many of which were produced at the Leipzig Theatre. In 1704 he received his first court appointment as *Hofkapellmeister* to Count Erdman von Promnitz in Sorau, and over the course of the next two decades held a number of court posts, including *Kapellmeister* to the Prince of Bayreuth.

Telemann was always keenly aware of the music of his contemporaries, showing a willingness to work in the styles favoured by his employers. Von Promnitz, for example, was a devotee of French musical styles, and this gave Telemann the opportunity to explore the French manner of instrumental writing with his patron's approval. This most cosmopolitan of German composers constantly used French and Italian devices in his writing, especially in his characteristic employment of short, clear and distinctive themes which always had a winning elegance and charm. This facility with such melodies has led to a constant denigration of his achievements, as if such musical goals were below a German composer's dignity, but this is to penalize Telemann for one of his greatest merits. A close scrutiny of the composer's work will show that, contrary to expectation, the variety, intricacy and skill found in his work is exceptional.

At the age of 40, Telemann became cantor of Hamburg's Johanneum as well as Music Director of the principal

Georg Philipp Telemann

Hamburg church. These two moves proved decisive for him, and although he continued to travel in Germany (with a visit to Paris in 1737), he held the Hamburg posts until his death. Telemann was one of the first composers to combine musical and business talents, and his brilliant organizational abilities are clearly displayed during the period he spent as Frankfurt's municipal Director of Music between 1712 and 1716. Dissatisfied with the musical forces at his disposal, he struck up a friendship with Christoph Graupner, *Kapellmeister* at the music-loving Landgrave of Hesse's Court in Darmstadt. Within a short time the two composers were regularly borrowing members of each others' orchestras so as to have larger forces with which to perform their grander compositions. Even after his departure

from Frankfurt, Telemann kept in touch with Darmstadt, and as late as 1765 he dedicated newly published works to the incumbent Landgrave.

In his private life, Telemann had need to be financially astute for his wife Maria Katherina was conspicuous in her consumption of his earnings, and before she finally left him in the 1740s for a Swedish army officer she had done serious damage to his finances.

Within a year of his Hamburg appointment, he had successfully lobbied to have himself appointed Music Director of the Hamburg Opera, a position which left him free to mount productions of his own theatrical works. This and his other official posts kept him happily centred in Hamburg for the rest of his long life.

▶ **Overture-Suite in A minor for recorder and strings**

▶ **Trumpet Concerto in D**

▶ **Musique de table (Tafelmusik) (1723)**

Telemann also established the first musical periodical: in 1728–29 he published 25 'lessons', in 25 issues of *Der Getreue Music-Meister* (The Constant Music Master), which were sold by subscription, each issue containing at least one outstanding composition, instrumental or vocal. These were certainly not all his own compositions for he actively solicited them from other musicians, and in fact published works by a long list of people including J. S. Bach, J. G. Pisandel and J. D. Zelenka. He was astute enough to know that the secret of a periodical's success lies in retaining its clients, so he cleverly published works in successive issues—a part or a movement per issue.

Such enterprise brought success: during his lifetime Telemann was the most famous and sought after German composer. This level of popularity was sustained for some time after his death and his combination of formal clarity and grace is to be found in the work of composers of the Classical period right up to the end of the 18th century. Thereafter his reputation took a tumble from which it has never really recovered. There is no doubt that the incredibly prolific Telemann—of whom the young Handel once said: "He could write an eight-part motet as easily as anyone else could write a letter"—is currently under-estimated, and that the breadth of his accomplishments, which

included over 40 operas (most of them now lost) and many religious works, as well as his famous series of *Hausmusik* and orchestral suites, is only now being looked at in a sympathetic light. The old charge against him—that he lacked originality—is no longer seen in such a perjorative light, and a more balanced assessment of his real achievements is becoming yearly more feasible.

Telemann composed in a style which suited his gregarious and easy-going personality. He was a lifelong admirer of both the Italian and French musical traditions of his youth, and combined the forms and proportions of French compositions with the natural ebullience and grace of Italian invention. Other important considerations are his love for and understanding of many of the folk forms he witnessed in his travels around Germany and its spheres of influence. Thus he could express admiration for the 'barbaric beauty' of the folk music he discovered in Moravia at a time when most composers would have had little or no time for the folk tradition of any country. The rhythmic thrust of such music had an ever-present place in Telemann's mature style, and helps give him his distinctive voice. The fact that his music was perceived by his contemporaries as a high point of the Baroque style would indicate that a proper assessment of his approach would be one of synthesis: he takes elements from many sources and transforms them through judicious combinations into a distinctive and urbane style.

With an output as vast and as yet relatively unexplored as Telemann's, there are many starting-points for an appreciation of his music, perhaps the

easiest way being to begin with a selection of his concertos, including those for violin, flute, oboe, recorder and trumpet, as well as various combinations of the above. Equally, his so-called 'Darmstadt Overtures', which are in reality a set of dance suites modelled on the French style of Lully, offer the listener a varied and fascinating panorama of his approach to orchestral writing. They were written between 1712 and 1721, and number around 80 separate compositions. There are many recordings of selections of these lively and characteristic pieces.

Equally enjoyable are the *Paris* Quartets. These, like his *Der Getreue Music-Meister,* were offered on subscription, the quartets being sold in specially engraved editions. These were published in Paris in 1738 and were the result of Telemann's trip to the French capital the year before where he obtained a 20-year guarantee of publishing rights from the King. These quartets again exhibit the nature of dance suites, each with six movements. The transparency of texture, the specially written virtuoso passages created by Telemann to highlight the dexterity of his Parisian friends, and the pleasing balance of melody and dance, have kept this music in the public eye since its first appearance. There is also the *Musique de table* (Banquet Music of Tafelmusik). This production was advertised by Telemann in 1732, soliciting subscriptions: its success was immediate and impressive. Subscribers from all over Europe sent in their requests, not least amongst them the composer Handel, an old friend of Telemann and then at the peak of his powers in London. The *Banquet Music* is entirely instrumental, and is divided into three 'Productions', as Telemann termed them, which have identical layouts but infinitely varied and subtle details which create such a wealth of interest that the music never becomes boring or monotonous.

Telemann also composed a great deal of vocal music, including a few score of cantatas and a *St Matthew Passion*. He has not been given a place amongst the choral greats, but his work, contrary to received opinion, exhibits a sincerity and integrity which belies the attractiveness of the style in which he worked. His

operas are something of an unknown quantity, few of them having been graced with a 20th-century production. His Intermezzo from 1725, *Pimpinone* (given its first performance as the Intermezzo performed to accompany the German première of Handel's *Julius Caesar*), shows his astute combination of French and Italian style with his dextrous use of dance well to the fore, as is his ability to inject humour into the music and action—an absolute prerequisite for the Intermezzo, which functioned as a low-life 'entertainment'

in the interludes between acts of *opera seria* productions, and later evolved into the genre of *opera buffa*.

DON'T MISS
▶ **Der Getreue Music-Meister (1728–29)**
▶ **Pimpinone (1728)**
▶ **12 Paris Quartets (1730/38)**
▶ **St Matthew Passion (1746)**

JEAN-PHILIPPE RAMEAU
1683–1764

Rameau, the younger contemporary of François Couperin, became the pre-eminent French composer of his day. A maverick in both theory and compositional practice, Rameau was particularly important in his development of the Lullian model for French grand opera.

Rameau was born in Dijon into the family of organist Jean Rameau, the seventh of 11 children. He stubbornly resisted his father's wish that he should become a lawyer, dedicating himself single-mindedly to the pursuit of music. Something of a child prodigy, he played the harpsichord and read music fluently at the age of seven. While studying at Dijon Jesuit College he neglected his other studies and was generally so obnoxious that he was expelled. From then on he gave himself wholly to his musical interests, quickly becoming

adept at a number of instruments and teaching himself musical theory. Entirely self-motivated, he only learned correct spelling and punctuation when he fell in love with a young widow and was so embarrassed by the crudeness of his love-letters that he temporarily threw all his energies into the perfecting of his verbal skills.

His success at wooing the widow prompted his father to send him to Italy for further musical studies. After visiting Milan, he took up temporary musical positions in various French provincial cities, but by 1706 he had settled in Paris. In the same year he published his *Premier Livre de pièces de clavecin* and accepted the position of organist at both the Jesuit convent and the Chapel of the Pères de la Merci. Rameau remained in Paris until his father's death in 1709, returning to Dijon that year to take up his father's

old position as organist at Dijon's Notre Dame. However, such a provincial appointment was never going satisfy the ambitions of such a strong-minded man, and in 1714, at the age of 31, he moved to Lyon. A year later he became organist at the cathedral at Clermont-Ferrand where he remained until 1722. During this time he completed his first treatise, *Traité de l'harmonie*, a work he set great store by; Rameau generally considered his theoretical work to be of equal value as his compositions. Rameau planned to go to Paris to arrange its publication but met with stern resistance from the church fathers, his organ improvisations being very popular with the congregation. He finally won his freedom and in 1722 Paris became his home once more; this time it was to be permanent.

Typically, Rameau quickly advanced on more than one front: his treatise was

Jean-Philippe Rameau

published and in 1723 he began a collaboration with the dramatist Alexis Piron on what became a string of 'entertainments' for the Théâtre de la Foire. In 1724 Rameau won the right to publish various cantatas and instrumental compositions. The year 1726 was a pivotal one, containing both the publication of his second major theoretical work, *Nouveau système de musique théorique*, and his marriage. The former event caused both controversy and excitement amongst other musicians, for while Rameau's ideas were logical and novel, and his discovery of the principle of chord inversions was important, there were many flaws in his perceptions of the basis of harmony, and his insistence on deriving all theory from the major or minor triad led him up numerous harmonic cul-de-sacs.

However, he did have the intellect and the good grace to modify his views over the succeeding years, as indicated by the string of modifications which he continued to publish until the 1750s.

His marriage to 18-year-old Marie-Louise Mangot, the daughter of a Court musician (Rameau was aged 43) appears to have been a happy one, and was certainly fertile, producing four children. Marie-Louise was herself a musician and singer. The late 1720s were spent in tandem with his patron Joseph Le Riche de la Pouplinière attempting to find the appropriate librettist and text with which to launch Rameau's operatic career (at one point Voltaire was a likely candidate), but no real progress was made until 1732 when the Abbé Pellegrin provided a libretto (based on

Racine's *Phèdre*): *Hippolyte et Aricie* received its first private production in April 1733, and a public one in October. *Hippolyte* was an important step for Rameau: it was his first serious theatrical piece and a success, and it marked his entry into the latter part of his career when the theatre became his primary source of musical inspiration. The 1730s proved a controversial period for Rameau, as his string of major productions—including *Les Indes galantes* (1735), *Castor et Pollux* (1737) and *Les Fêtes d'Hébé* (739)—established him as the most important theatre composer since Lully, but also provoked fierce divisions amongst pundits, with many damning his new ideas.

Confident that this type of reaction proved the validity of his approach, Rameau pressed on, even diversifying into opera-ballets such as *La Princesse de Navarre* (1745, with Voltaire), various other forms of ballets without words, and *divertissements* such as *La Rose* (1744). The King made him composer of his chamber music in 1745, and his patent of nobility was registered. He went on to write works for the Court, including *Anacréon* (1754) and *La naissance d'Osiris* (1753). His output was prodigious, and during the five years (1740–45) when he was given no commissions by the Opéra, he filled in his spare time by publishing his *Nouvelles suites de pièces de clavecin* and the *Pièces de clavecin en concert avec un violon et une flûte* (1741). He also became the conductor of the Opéra-Comique.

Yet universal acclaim for his operas—either in France or beyond—eluded him in a way that his predecessor Lully would never have allowed. Rameau himself recognized the problem as being a fundemntal one: he was more interested in the music itself and its eventual resolution than the drama taking place. Consequently, he often set inferior texts and rarely took the trouble to radically alter a plot for the better—as a man of impeccable theatrical instincts like Lully would have done. Rameau was content with what he had; "After 60 one cannnot change. Experience points plainly enough the best course, but the mind refuses to obey". His last important opera, *Zoroastre*, was produced in 1749.

In his declining years Rameau produced little music, but did not go without honour in his own country: he was accorded a pension by the Opéra and was given an ovation whenever he attended a performance, and was also made a member of the Dijon Académie in 1761. He and his family were even exempted from paying taxes for life. Rameau died at the age of 81. His

funeral was one of the largest in Paris at that time.

Rameau today is chiefly remembered and enjoyed for the operas and other theatrical music he composed in the latter half of his career, yet his approach to music and his basic style were cemented during his early years in Dijon and Paris, when he wrote instrumental and chamber pieces, progressing in the 1720s to the seven known chamber cantatas, such as *Le Berger fidèle*, which were carefully balanced works using both French and Italian stylistic sources.

Pre operatic works of note include the four extant grand motets, which continue the tradition laid down in Louis XIV's reign by the composer Delalande and extended by his successor, Mondonville. But it is on his stage works that Rameau's reputation mainly rests. He wrote works which were full of musical invention and developed the French tradition of Lully

by combining it more exactly with musical developments in Italy after Lully's death. Rameau's florid style lent itself well to the demands of French grand opera, and his energetic approach to dance in all his music makes his ballet-operas especially enjoyable. *Castor et Pollux* is often seen as his greatest operatic triumph, but the late piece *Zoroastre* saw him moving onto new ground by abandoning Lullian structure and adopting a five-act architecture which also jettisoned the usual prologue.

DON'T MISS

▶ **Premier Livre de pièces de clavecin (1706)**

▶ **Théris (1718)**

▶ **Les Indes galantes (1735–61)**

▶ **Pygmalion (1748)**

▶ **Castor et Pollux (1754)**

JOHANN SEBASTIAN BACH

1685-1750

Johann Sebastian Bach has long been regarded—with justification—as equal in his musical genius to any other composer of Classical music. His delight in the subtleties of counterpoint, allied to his deep religiosity, were the parameters within which he worked his muse to the enrichment of every musical generation which followed.

Bach came from a family with demonstrable musical talents documented at least as far back as the mid-16th century; of the seven generations of Bachs—beginning with the first-known professional musician, Veit Bach (died 1619) and ending with William Friedrich Ernst Bach (died 1845)—less than 10 of them chose a profession other than music. The Bach family's identification with music is

unparalleled in Western music, as is the genius of Johann Sebastian.

He was the youngest child in the family; by the age of 10 his father had died and many members of the household were dispersed to other more financially stable branches of the family. Bach himself, together with his brother Jakob, moved from Eisenach to live with his eldest brother Johann Christoph in Ohrdruf. In early adolescence Johann

Johann Sebastian Bach

Sebastain suffered from poor health which led to an erratic attendance at school, but his outstanding boy soprano voice won him admiration and at the age of 15 he was recommended for a position in the choir of Michaelis-Kirche in Lüneburg, a town more than 200 miles away. There, remote from his family, he struck up a friendship with the composer-organist Georg Böhm, a man 20 years older than himself and willing to give him material and artistic guidance. Bach's musical education was aided by his passion (which proved lifelong) for studying other composers' music in manuscript and drawing his own musical lessons from what he discovered. His interests were unusually wide, and he found as much pleasure and inspiration in Couperin as he did in German or Italian composers.

This intense study eventually produced the young Bach's first efforts at composition, a set of variations; with his first organ appointment at Arnstadt's Bonifacius-Kirche in 1703–04, he wrote his first cantatas and a number of preludes and fugues. These early works show him already in the possession of unusual melodic inventiveness within the strict forms he used. Church work was for Bach the ideal form of employment, for it combined his intense religiosity with the opportunity to create music for voice and organ in particular, the organ being his first and final fascination.

In autumn 1705 he took leave of absence from Arnstadt and travelled on foot to Lübeck where Dietrich Buxtehude, universally recognized as the foremost living German musician and composer, had long been in residence as organist at the Marien-Kirche. Bach remained in Lübeck for four months, studying with the old man, returning to Arnstadt in January 1706. His prolonged absence provoked an official reprimand from the church authorities, and when his young cousin, Maria Barbara (later his wife), was found to be singing in the church choir at Bach's behest, he found himself in further trouble. Within a few months he resigned and moved to a more prestigious position at the Blasius-Kirche, Mühlhausen. In October 1707 he and Maria Barbara were married; they had their first baby, a daughter, the following year. Yet the appointment at Mühlhausen proved unsatisfactory both financially and theologically. Early in 1708 he accepted an appointment as *Hof-Organist* and *Kammer-Musikus* to Duke William Ernst of Weimar. This was hardly the top position within the Court's musical circles, but it was preferable to the situation at Mühlhausen.

Until 1714, when he was finally promoted to be *Konzertmeister,* his chief duty was to play the church organ, and the intervening years were notable principally for the outpouring of organ masterpieces, including the *Passacaglia and Fugue in C minor,* BWV 582 and the *Orgel-Büchlein.* His performance of these and other works earned him a reputation far beyond the environs of Weimar. After promotion, his tasks became more specific (including the monthly delivery of new cantatas) and his duties more onerous. Bach felt his situation to be intolerable; he now had four children and was dissatisfied with his family's standard of living. He seemed to lack the courtier's ability to deal advantageously with such situations, and when he was passed over in 1716 he took the opportunity to move on, this time to become *Kapellmeister* in the newly-established household of the Duke of Weimar's son, Duke Ernst August, who had married and moved to Cöthen, where the bride's father, Prince Leopold, was a great music-lover.

However, Duke Wilhelm August did not give Bach up without some unpleasantness: determined to humble the proud and plain-speaking musician, he refused to give Bach permission to leave his employ, actually keeping the composer under arrest for over a month before finally relenting and allowing him to move to Cöthen. There, the demand was for chamber music in which Prince Leopold could play an active role. Thus Bach composed a series of suites, overtures and concertos as well as sonatas and other small ensemble pieces. These were to include the four orchestral suites, the *Brandenburg Concertos* (so-called because they were dedicated to Duke Christian Ludwig of Brandenburg) and the beautiful Violin Concertos, BWV 1041/2/3, 1064/5, which were modelled on works by Italian composers (such as Vivaldi) whom he so admired.

These were relatively stable, happy years for Bach and his family, but obliged to accompany the Prince on a trip to Carlsbad in 1720, he found on his return

that his wife had died and was already in her grave. From then on his desire to leave the Court became steadily more urgent, especially when in 1721 his patron married a young woman with little musical inclination and a determination to lead her husband into other diversions. Bach himself had remarried: his new wife Anna Magdalena was just 20 (Bach was now 36) and required to act as step-mother to Bach's children whose education was proving problematic in a town where the best school was Calvinist.

This situation made the post as Cantor of the Thomasschule in Leipzig very appealing when it fell vacant in 1722. Bach was not first or even second choice for the position—both Christoph Graupner and Telemann were offered it but had to decline. Nearly a year after the appointment was originally advertised, Bach took up the position, pledging in his contract not to supply music which was 'too theatrical' or 'too operatic'. Bach's new responsibilites included teaching various groups of scholars at the school, composing music for two churches (St Thomas and St Nicholas) and providing the occasional piece of music for the local university. He also had to ask permission from the Council if he wished to absent himself from Leipzig

for any reason. The situation must have been very bad at Cöthen for Bach to accede to these conditions.

Yet he was to remain in this post for the rest of his life, and although his pride and sense of self-worth led him into regular and bruising contact with the various authorities to whom he was responsible, he never became disenchanted enough to resign. Despite endless arguments between himself and the Thomasschule appointees over whose empire ended where, Bach continued to produce his sublime music throughout the decades he was in Leipzig, and his eminence was recognized by various admirers, including the King-Elector of Poland-Saxony, who in 1736 awarded him the coveted title *Königlicher Hof-Componist*. His son Carl Philipp Emanuel, then 26, became attached to the Court of the music-loving (and amateur flautist) Frederick the Great of Prussia in 1740. In 1741 Bach visited his son in Berlin, Frederick's capital, and six years later he was invited to attend on Frederick at Potsdam. Thus, in May 1747 'Old Bach', as Frederick fondly called him, arrived and was presented to the King. The meeting was a complete success, Bach overwhelming Frederick with his ability to extemporize at the keyboard on demand. On his return to Leipzig, Bach

---

DON'T MISS

▶ **Brandenburg Concertos, BWV 1046–51 (1708–21)**

▶ **Fantasia and Fugue in G minor, BWV 542 (1708–23)**

▶ **Orchestral Suites, BWV 1066–9 (1717–23)**

▶ **Violin Concertos, BWV 1080 (1717–23)**

▶ **The Well-tempered Clavier, Books 1 & 2, BWV 846–893 (1722/1738–42)**

DON'T MISS

▶ Cantata No. 82 'Ich habe genug', BWV 82 (1727)
▶ St Matthew Passion, BWV 244 (1727)
▶ Christmas Oratorio, BWV 248 (1734)
▶ Goldberg Variations, BWV 988 (1741–42)
▶ The Art of the Fugue, BWV 1080 (1745–50)

took one of Frederick's own themes used during the meeting and developed it into the famous *A Musical Offering*, dedicated (in June 1747) to 'a monarch admired in music as in all the other sciences of war and peace'.

Bach was now in his sixties, and his general health had begun to follow the course of his eyesight, which had been damaged irreparably by the years of studying music by candlelight. By 1749 he was completely blind. The advent of blindness greatly hindered his efforts to complete the works he felt to be his last, and among the many pieces left incomplete at his death (although heavily revised) was the famous *Die Kunst der Fuge*, a set of fugal pieces which has fascinated musicians and commentators ever since. The great man, only 66 when he died, was buried in an unmarked grave near the south door of Leipzig's Johanneskirche. In the late 19th century his grave was rediscovered during building work. His ashes were moved inside the church where they are now marked by the somewhat undemonstrative words, 'Johann Sebastian Bach, 1685–1750'.

In Bach, Baroque polyphony reached its apotheosis and—at least to the succeeding generation—its point of exhaustion, for by the time of his death his music had already fallen a long way behind the forefront of musical fashion.

His achievements were to languish in obscurity for close to 100 years before the efforts of others, particularly Mendelssohn, revealed Bach's genius to a wider world. Bach was no innovator and no iconoclast: what he revered above all was musical truth and beauty, and he was ready to appreciate these wherever he came across them—from the manuscripts of older Italian masters to the extemporizations of fellow Germans. His musicality was complete and all-embracing, and only his temperament and his natural inclination to regard music as an adjunct to his religion restrained him from composing for the theatre (as did his contemporary Handel). His oratorios demonstrate his complete grasp of what is required to write convincingly for voices and orchestra. The connection between religion and music cannot be overstressed: Bach invariably added homilies to God or Jesus at the beginning or end of his scores, even when they were modest chamber pieces or exercises for his children and students. Bach's music is a colossal summation of the traditions in Western music which led to his mature style: his genius allowed him the perfect synthesizing power to create the multitude of masterpieces which came from his pen.

In a body of work which is so crammed with significant achievements, the selection of key works means that many fine or important pieces of music will go unremarked, but this leaves much for the reader to explore after initial contact. Perhaps the most instructive and entertaining place to start is at the keyboard. *Das Wohltemperierte Klavier* (The Well-Tempered Clavier) contains two books of 48 preludes and fugues which are an object lesson in what Bach set out to achieve in his music. The use of a single instrument also helps the listener to follow more closely the musical imagination at work. A subsequent keboard piece with equal rewards is the *Goldberg Variations*, BWV 988, completed in the early 1740s at much the same time as the second book of *Das Wohltemperierte Klavier*. The great mass of organ works can be approached through such pieces as the Toccata and Fugue in D minor, BWV 565, Toccata and Adagio in C, BWV 564, Fantasia and Fugue in G minor, BWV 542, Passacaglia and Fugue in C minor, BWV 582 and the Preludes and Fugues in A minor and C, BWV 543 and 545. The *Orgel-Büchlein*, BWV 599–644, contains 48 pieces which explore a wide range of the organ's sonic and musical repertoire. In terms of solo instrumental music, the other key works are the astonishing and very beautiful 6 Suites (Sonatas) for Cello, BWV 1007–12.

Apart from the 295 cantatas Bach wrote during his lifetime, of which there are numerous favourites, his *St John* and *St Matthew* Passions are deeply-felt recountings of the gospels which cannot fail to move the listener, while the *Christmas Oratorio* and Mass in B minor, BWV 232 demonstrate Bach's ability to deal profoundly with such occasional pieces.

GEORG FRIDERIC HANDEL
1685–1759

A man of immense musical talent, Handel presided over one of the richest periods of British music, supplying an unbroken stream of theatrical and quasi-theatrical vocal compositions, be they Italianate operas or the great oratorios of his later career.

Handel matured from being a German composer using a provincial style into a complete musician by using the contemporary Italianate base he acquired during his stay in Italy as a foundation for a style which was as practical as it was attractive. He had a virtually limitless gift for musical creation, and was as fond of extemporising as of actually composing. He consistently wrote his music at breakneck speed, often finishing whole operas or oratorios in two to three weeks; the quality of his talent and inspiration shows in the fact that these works have often been regarded by posterity as great masterpieces. Another characteristic of his work is plagiarism, but he not only took from other composers (invariably improving upon the original) but also from himself, reusing whole sections from earlier works in new settings. Handel was not in any real sense an innovator, and towards the end of his career he abandoned any pretence at following current fashions, but his innate sense of proportion and his breathtaking invention, as well as a natural talent for musical drama, made his music initially accessible, and latterly loved, by all who came into contact with it.

Georg Frideric Handel

Born in Halle, Saxony, to a 63-year-old father, also named Georg, and a parson's daughter, Handel was brought up strictly to the older man's exacting standards. Young Georg showed an early inclination towards music but was consistently prevented from pursuing this interest, being groomed instead for a career in the law. During a fortuitous visit in 1693 with his father (who was a barber-surgeon) to Saxe-Weissenfels, the Duke noticed Georg's impromptu excursions on the chapel organ and suggested the boy should be given music lessons. It was a suggestion his father could not ignore and Handel began his training under F. W. Zachau, the organist at St Michael's Church in Halle. From then on he combined the pursuit of a general education, hopefully leading to a degree in law at Halle University (although when his father died in 1695 he left after just one year), with a burgeoning career as a musician.

At first his musical activities centred around playing church organs (he became organist at Halle Cathedral in 1702), but after meeting Telemann he abandoned Halle for Hamburg, quickly gaining employment in the orchestra of the Opera. There he had the good fortune to meet the young composer Johann Mattheson with whom he quickly struck up a friendship, and who appears to have helped Handel to find some pupils to ease his financial position. The two friends travelled together to Lübeck where a competition was being held to replace the venerable Dietrich Buxtehude who was retiring as organist at the cathedral. In the event, neither took up the post, and both settled once more into the somewhat loose-living mode of life offered at the Opera in Hamburg, but due to Handel's insistence on directing one of Mattheson's operas, he and Mattheson quarrelled. Mattheson's recollection of the event included a duel in which Handel's life was saved from the outraged composer's sword by a particularly obdurate metal button.

That Mattheson actively helped Handel mount his first opera, *Almira*, suggests the breach was not permanent, although when a second opera, *Nerone*, proved unsuccessful, Handel decided to leave Hamburg for Italy, perhaps in order to perfect his training. By the summer of 1706 he was at the palace of Ferdinand de Medici in Florence where he composed a series of cantatas based on the Italian models of Alessandro Scarlatti, Carissimi and others. By 1708 he was sufficiently accepted as a musician to be duetting in friendly rivalry with Domenico Scarlatti at Cardinal Ottoboni's palace in Rome, as well as being on familiar terms with Alessandro Scarlatti (Domenico's father), Corelli and Pasquini. Further travels in Italy took him to Venice and Naples, but Rome remained his focal point. Important works written during his Italian sojourn included the serenata *Aci, Galatea e Polifemo* and the opera *Agrippina*, as well as some cantatas and the oratorios *La Resurrezione di Nostro Signor Gesù Cristo* and *Il Trionfo del Tempo e del Disinganno*. The Italian experience, which was terminated in 1710 by Handel's appointment as *Kapellmeister* to the Elector George of Hannover, was an artistically vital one as it came at a time when the composer—extraordinarily adept at assimilating new musical idioms—was ready to form a mature and individual style of his own. Always with an eye to commercial success, Handel rarely strayed far from the prevalent musical taste.

Handel had barely arrived in Hannover before he received an invitation to visit London. Having moved to Hannover with the proviso that he be granted time for a London visit should an invitation be forthcoming, Handel lost no time in heading for the English capital. His arrival could hardly have been better timed: London was in the grip of 'Italian fever' and society was hungry for operas in the latest Italian style. With the death of Purcell some 15 years earlier, the musical community was leaderless. Within a month of his arrival Handel was hurrying to complete his opera *Rinaldo,* which was produced at the Queen's Theatre, Haymarket, in 1711. His British reputation was made by the overwhelming success of this production, and he was in such demand that his summer return to Hannover was doomed to be brief. Unable to resist the siren call of fame in London, he arranged another leave of absence, much against his employer's wishes, and returned there in 1712, overstaying his leave long enough for his German master to become the new king of England, George I. There was now no need for him to prevaricate about his country of choice, although it was not for another two years that he and George I were reconciled. Posterity has cause to be grateful to the King for this reconciliation: soon after he commissioned Handel to write some occasional music to accompany the royal boat party on the Thames in 1717. The King was so pleased with the result that according to a first-hand report, 'he caused the music to be repeated three times in all, although each performance lasted an hour'. The *Water Music* was not

---

DON'T MISS

▶ **The Water Music (1715–17)**

▶ **Giulio Cesare (1724)**

▶ **Coronation Anthems (1727)**

▶ **Organ Concertos, Op. 4 (1735)**

▶ **Serse (Xerxes) (1738)**

published until 1740 and was made up of various pieces written at different times.

The years 1719–20 were important ones for Handel: in 1719 he was appointed composer-in-residence at Cannons, the residence of the Duke of Chandos, and this led directly to the composition of the *Chandos Anthems*. The following year, at the King's request, he formed an Italian opera company which would be based at the King's Theatre in Haymarket, and would be called the Royal Academy of Music. The triumphant success of his operas *Radamisto, Floridante* and *Giulio Cesare*, was soured, however, by rival factions setting up the composer Bononcini in competition with Handel. This, plus the huge fees demanded by the major singers and endless petty disputes, made the Academy a troubled place. Although the operas *Tamerlano, Rodelinda, Scipione* and *Alessandro* were all produced, the King's death in 1727, followed by the triumph of John Gay's *Beggar's Opera*—a work which introduced an entirely new audience to musical theatre—were two developments which helped plunge the company into bankruptcy. Yet 1727 was also the year that Handel completed the process of naturalisation as a British subject, as well as supplying four magnificent Coronation anthems for George II, one of which was the perennial *Zadok the Priest*.

For once wrongfooted by a younger composer and a newer style, Handel continued to place his trust in Italian opera, and although he also began regular presentation of English-text oratorios, he and his rival Bononcini

re-convened hostilites in separate opera companies in the Italian style, both of them to dwindling popular returns. Indeed, his greatest success of the 1730s came with the oratorio *Alexander's Feast* (1736), and by 1737, suffering from persistent illness and harried by debts, his company once again went bankrupt. After a 'cure' at Aix-la-Chapelle to restore his health, Handel returned to opera, completing *Serse* (which contains the famous aria 'Ombra mai fu'), and also composing music for Queen Caroline's funeral in November. Still gravely in debt, he held a benefit in the spring of 1738 which enabled him to repay all his creditors, and then settled down to write the two works which pointed the way forward for him: *Saul* and *Israel in Egypt*, performed in 1738 and 1739 respectively.

Curiously enough, his greatest popular triumph, *Messiah,* got off to an unsteady start. Although it was an instant favourite at its Dublin première in 1743, its first London showing, after a string of successful mountings of his earlier oratorio *Samson*, was a failure. Not until its massive success at the Foundlings' Hospital in 1750 did Handel find the British public prepared to embrace it wholeheartedly. This came as a welcome relief after

another period of financial insolvency and failing health; although he had written music to commemorate George II's victory at the Battle of Dettingen in 1743 and the Aix-la-Chapelle peace accord (for which he composed *Musick for the Royal Fireworks*), as well as the 1745 Jacobean uprising (*Judas Maccabaeus* was written after the Battle of Culloden), all of which proved instantly popular, his return to financial stability and national reverence was slow and difficult.

He was now in his sixties and constantly in poor health (his failing eyesight had progressed to total blindness by 1753), but he continued to compose. During the 1750s he led a long series of concerts of his music from the organ, and his annual charity performance of *Messiah* at the Foundlings' Hospital, of which he was a governor, was unfailingly popular. It was after a Covent Garden performance of this work in April 1759, which Handel had directed from the organ, that he was taken ill and confined to his bed in Brook Street. Eight days later he died. His state funeral at Westminster Abbey was attended by over 3,000 people, and a monument was erected to him in the Abbey.

DON'T MISS

▶ **Concerti Grossi, Op. 6 (1739)**
▶ **L'Allegro, il penseroso ed il moderato (1740)**
▶ **Messiah (1742)**
▶ **Judas Maccabaeus (1747)**
▶ **Musick for the Royal Fireworks (1749)**

GIUSEPPI DOMENICO SCARLATTI

1685–1757

Like his father Alessandro, Domenico Scarlatti was a well-trained and professional composer able to write successfully for a number of genres. Unlike his father, he found keyboard composition sufficiently challenging and inspirational for him to be content with supplying his patroness with over 500 such works, a project which fully occupied his last two decades. These extraordinary works form the basis of his present-day fame.

Domenico Scarlatti brought an original compositional approach to his harpsichord works, which stand at the centre of his artistic achievement. Apart from technical advances, such as the novel idea of crossing the hands on the keyboard which was to be taken up by piano composers such as Liszt and Mendelssohn, Scarlatti used simple musical forms within which he found endless variety of expression. His harpsichord pieces, invariably short and to the point, use a vast array of rhythms and expressive devices, and range from the most formidably challenging to the simplest and purest of melodies and chord sequences. His constant search for freshness of expression led him to employ unusual and exciting harmonic patterns and voicings. Although he wrote for an instrument which was later to be supplanted by the piano, the fecundity of his inspiration and the directness of his message makes itself felt to the

Giuseppi Domenico Scarlatti

listener whether it is played by Horowitz on a modern grand or Scott Ross on an authentic instrument from Scarlatti's day.

Domenico was the sixth son of the famous Alessandro Scarlatti. Brought up in a household dedicated to music, it is no surprise that he showed his musical leanings early in life. He was taught first by his father, but before he was 20, Alessandro recognized that his son's fascination with the harpsichord would need nurturing in an artistic

climate more kindly disposed towards keyboard virtuosity than late 17th-century Naples, where the organ was considered the prime instrument. Domenico was organist in the royal chapel where his father was *maestro di cappella* and travelled with Alessandro to Florence and Rome before returning alone to Naples where three of his operas were produced, the last, *Irene*, in 1704.

Yet he felt unfulfilled, and his father encouraged him to explore as far north as Venice in search of a sinecure which would give him the creative recognition he sought. A letter from Alessandro to Ferdinando de Medici in 1705 craves the Duke's indulgence with regard to his son when it comes to 'opportunities...for making himself known—opportunities for which it is hopeless to wait in Rome nowadays', but there was no opening in Florence, so Domenico pressed on to Venice in the company of the Neapolitan composer and musician, Nicolino. There he had more luck, for he remained in Venice for about three years, learning much from teachers such as Francesco Gasparini and gaining the friendship of a number of young composers. Among them was the English harpsichordist Thomas Roseingrave, who (according to Dr Burney) regarded Scarlatti as exhibiting "every degree of perfection to which he thought it possible he should ever arrive, that, if he had been in sight of any instrument with which to have done the deed, he would have cut off his own fingers". Roseingrave carried the news of Scarlatti's excellence back to England, in so doing laying the foundations for a long-lasting Scarlatti influence in English keyboard practices. While in Venice Domenico also became a friend of Handel's whose excellence as a harpsichordist matched Scarlatti's, although Handel surpassed him as an organist, a fact Scarlatti was happy to concede, commenting that he had never conceived the existence of such organ playing. The two men remained in touch for the rest of their lives, and always spoke of each other's gifts with admiration.

In 1709 Scarlatti and Handel left Venice for Rome, where they visited Cardinal Ottoboni's Accademie Poetico Musicali.

Scarlatti then entered the service of the Queen of Poland, Marie Casimire. He wrote eight operas between 1709 and 1715, all except the final one (an early setting of *Amleto*), composed for the Queen's private theatre. Further positions in Rome followed, including that of *maestro di cappella* at St Peter's. In 1717 he gained legal independence from his father, and two years later left Rome, ostensibly for London, where his opera *Narciso* was performed in 1720, although his actual presence in London at that time is impossible to verify. His next confirmed sighting was in Lisbon later the same year, where he became *maestro* to the royal chapel and tutored the King's younger brother and daughter.

By now approaching his thirtieth year, Domenico was still unable to settle down, despite his great popularity at Court, and is known to have visited Naples and Rome during the course of 1724–25. At the age of 33, Scarlatti married Maria Catalina Gentili who bore him five children. Domenico and his wife returned to Portugal from Rome in time to be taken as members of the newly-married Princess Maria Barbara's entourage to her new home in Madrid. Scarlatti was to serve the new Queen of Spain faithfully for the rest of his life.

This fidelity was rewarded by a Spanish knighthood in 1738. On the Queen's death he was left 2,000 doubloons as a mark of appreciation for his 'great diligence and loyalty'. That the Queen had also frequently helped him out of financial difficulties caused by his inveterate gambling shows the extent of her indulgence. Scarlatti's wife died in 1739, but he remarried in the early

1740s. Although now in his mid-fifties, he sired a further four children. Like his father he was regarded as a modest and charming man, unlikely to resort to arrogance or displays of petulance, and this no doubt endeared him to the Queen and other composers. That he had no great ambition apart from creating his music is demonstrated by the fact that although he wrote nearly a dozen operas, many religious works and over 500 harpsichord sonatas, only 30 of the sonatas were published in his lifetime (under the title *Essercizi per Gravicembalo* and dedicated to the King of Portugal) in London in 1738. The remainder, apart from a collection of 42 suites printed under the auspices of Thomas Roseingrave, remained in the possession of the Portuguese royal family for whose sole pleasure they were composed. They were kept in 15 morocco-bound gold-inlaid volumes, and comprise the heart of Scarlatti's posthumous keyboard reputation.

Scarlatti lived out the rest of his life at the Spanish Court, continuing to supply new compositions until just prior to his death. The single-voice *Salve Regina* is generally thought to be his last composition. He died at the age of 72 and was buried in the Convent of San Norberto in Madrid.

DON'T MISS

▶ **Keyboard Sonatas, K1–555**

▶ **Salve Regina**

▶ **17 Sinfonias for oboe, strings and continuo**

▶ **Stabat Mater in C minor**

GIUSEPPI TARTINI

1692–1770

Tartini remains principally associated with important advances in the arts of making, playing and composing for the violin, his own choice of instrument and one which was at the heart of the development of classical music, especially in Italy.

Tartini was born in Padua, the first son of a wealthy and respected Florentine businessman who had moved to the city in the 1680s. Giuseppi was well educated at various religious institutions and began learning the rudiments of music and violin-playing while at the school of Capo d'Istria. In 1709 his studies in Padua ended and Bishop Naldini secured a place for him at Padua University. After a tempestuous struggle with his father, who wished him to become a priest, Tartini was allowed to enrol as a law student.

Now 17 and full of spirit, he became a first-class swordsman and even planned to support himself as a fencing teacher should his musical career not succeed financially. He also fell passionately in love with Elizabetta Premazone, one of his private music pupils. It would seem that his violent feelings were reciprocated, for they eloped and married, thus upsetting Tartini's family and incurring the wrath of the local cardinal, Giorgio Cornaro, who regarded himself as the girl's guardian. On their return to Padua, Giuseppi found the Cardinal

had ordered his arrest and that his family had cut him off from all dependency. He had no choice but to abandon Padua in a monk's habit while his wife remained behind.

Giuseppi found refuge in a monastery in Assisi, and for the next few years occupied himself in musical studies. He made significant strides in his understanding and control of the violin, making advances on the models of method and practice left by Corelli, his inspiration. Among these advances was the use of thicker gut strings; a lighter bow with a straight stick; a more secure place for holding the stick; and a discovery of the sympathetic tones (resultant tones), or harmonics, which arise from the bowing of a string, and the use to which these can be put in the tuning and playing of the instrument. He expounded this in a 1745 treatise on harmony, claiming that he had made his discoveries in 1714 during time spent in Ancona subsequent to his Assisi training. There is reason to believe that the famous *Devil's Trill* Sonata in G minor for violin and continuo, which exploits so many of the violin's inherent qualities, dates from this time. Described by Tartini as having come to him in a dream, for many years the work stood as a by-word for the *ne plus ultra* of violin playing.

However, Tartini was soon pining for his native Padua and his abandoned wife. He timed his appeal for clemency

to coincide with the annual pilgrimage to the tomb of St Francis and the Day of Forgiveness, and was eventually allowed to return to Padua and to his wife. By 1721 he had been offered the post of first violin at St Anthony's basilica at an annual stipend of 150 florins. He was also allowed to perform elsewhere—a considerable privilege at a period more noted for treating musicians as chattels than as persons of intrinsic interest. Taking advantage of this, Tartini visited Prague in 1723, staying three years at the behest of the music-loving Chancellor of Bohemia, Count Kinsky, but eventually family and financial constraints at home forced him to return to Padua.

By 1728 Tartini had satisfied a long-held ambition to establish a school for violin playing in Padua. By now his reputation as a technician and violin player was second to none, his dexterity and his extraordinary ability to give *cantabile* to the humblest melodic line winning him the respect of all musicians. A humility and generosity towards others made him a popular teacher and as the years passed, his popularity matured into a respect for his abilities and methods which spread throughout Europe. He wrote a number of treatises on violin playing, some of which were published during his lifetime; the others (six books in all) were entrusted to his friend Professor Colombo for posthumous publication, but were tragically lost due to Colombo's death soon after Tartini's. Tartini devoted most of his energies to the successful running of his school and to his family and although he received a stream of requests to travel abroad over the next 40 years, he refused virtually all of them. "Although not rich", he told an English admirer in 1730, "my wife and I have sufficient and do not need for more".

The majority of Tartini's compositions are concentrated in the concerto and sonata forms, many of his works being written to or inspired by poetic and literary texts. He also showed a great liking for the folk and popular music of his native country. His *Sonate del Tasso*, dating from the 1740s, has settings of an aria from a Tasso poem, 'Combattimento fra Tancredi e Clorinda', while the basic inspiration for his melodic content came from the songs of Venetian gondoliers. These sonatas were never published in his lifetime, though his first published works, Opus 1, were a set of sonatas for five or six instruments from 1734. Many of Tartini's concertos have poetic texts from Metastasio accompanying various different movements; others are said to be based on passages from Petrarch which Tartini kept in mind as he composed, and this poetic inspiration underlines the lyrical nature of Tartini's slow movements in particular. He wrote over 130

concertos, many of which have remained in manuscript until the present century, and these works confirm his advance on Corelli, both in terms of the soloist's technical accomplishment and individuality of expression. Many of his manuscripts are headed by written inscriptions which provide the key to the feelings expressed in the piece, as well as the source of the work's inspiration. Similarly, close to 50 sonatas have survived, mostly for violin. In addition, a handful of vocal works are known to exist, such as the *Miserere* Tartini wrote for Pope Clement XII and which was performed in the Sistine Chapel in 1740, and a *Salve Regina,* the manuscript of which bears an inscription from a third party describing it as his last composition. There are also a small number of *canzone.*

Tartini continued to enjoy a peaceful and celebrated existence, spending

his days teaching, composing and writing, and his evenings either with his family or with the great men of the day who lived in, or travelled through, Italy; many came to Padua expressly to meet the great man. Tartini was of the generation after Vivaldi and Albinoni, outliving them both and becoming the senior Italian composer of his day. He remained active and full of creative energy well into his seventies, finally succumbing in 1768 to what was probably a stroke which left him partially paralysed for six months. His slow recovery from this physical setback was curtailed by the onset of cancer, and when he finally died he was buried in the church of St Catherine of Padua, accompanied by a Requiem composed by his old colleague Francesco Vallotti, while a number of his former pupils accompanied the body to its final resting place.

DON'T MISS

▶ **Violin Concerto in A (D 96)**
▶ **12 Sonatas. Op. 1 (1734)**
▶ **Miserere (1740)**
▶ **Le sonate del Tasso (c. 1750)**
▶ **'Devil's Trill' Violin Concerto in G minor (1750)**

PART IV

1700-1800

The changes in music which came about during the lives of the composers born in this century were unprecedented, both in their number and in their underlying effect on the nature of all serious music composed since. During this period not only was *opera seria*—with its concentration on the set-piece aria—brought to an early peak by Pergolesi, but it was also reformed later in the century by Gluck who provided proper plots, character development, and what he felt was a 'natural' singing style. Meanwhile, from humble Italian theatrical beginnings an overwhelmingly popular strain, *opera buffa*, developed which by the early decades of the 19th century and through the good offices of Rossini, eventually banished the formal elegance and stiltedness of *opera seria* and its German cousin, *Singspiel*, from European stages.

Triumphal arch, Vienna.
Engraving, c. 1721

Developments of equal importance were taking place in other genres: the sonata, symphony, concerto, string quartet and German *Lied* all took on their characteristic forms. While the creative drive which propelled opera into a new era was initiated in Italy (and followed up enthusiastically elsewhere), much of the groundwork for these crucial formulations was being prepared in the music of Austrian and German composers, starting with J. S. Bach's sons, J. C. and C. P. E. Bach, and continuing through Joseph Haydn and (in the case of the concerto) Mozart, arriving finally at the protean form of

Beethoven. The concerto, brought to an early peak by the Italians and later progressed in that country by composers such as Boccherini, was further developed and extended by Haydn and his German-speaking successors so that by the time Paganini came to write his own spectacular concertos in the early 19th century (simultaneously ushering in the age of the virtuoso), he adopted the developed Germanic model on which to embroider his dexterity.

It is arguable that the diversity of this period's creative endeavour, its far reaching and fundamental nature and the longevity of its impact, derives from the thoroughly modern spirit in which it was undertaken. All these composers lived through the so-called Age of Enlightenment, when traditional, religiously based assumptions about the world and man's place within it were debunked, and the cults of nature, rationality and intellectual inquiry were established in their place. This ascendancy of reason and belief in the individual's capacity for enlightenment and progress would, in turn, lead via the Gothic novel and the ideas of Goethe, Byron and his contemporaries, to full-blown musical Romanticism. While Beethoven was a seminal figure in both the apotheosis of Classicism and the initial formulation of a Romantic sensibility in music, younger men such as Schubert and Weber would be its first fully-fledged exponents.

GIOVANNI PERGOLESI
1710–1736

Pergolesi's short life was full of incident and achievement as well as romantic dalliances. His lively and charismatic character inspired no less than two operas by other composers which purport to tell his life story, both written over 100 years after his death.

Pergolesi was born in Jesi, near the Italian town of Ancona, the only child of a surveyor by the name of Draghi. Draghi and his wife had previously lived in Pergola, and following the custom of the time, when they arrived in Jesi they took the descriptive name of Pergolesi. Showing a remarkable natural aptitude for music, Giovanni studied in Jesi, taking violin lessons from Francesco Mondini until he was sent to Naples at the age of 16 to study music at the Conservatorio dei Poveri di Gesu Cristo. His fees were paid by a local Jesi aristocrat who had taken an interest in the young man. Pergolesi's technical prowess on the violin and his ability to improvise his own florid passages was noted by his teachers at the Conservatorio. In 1727 he suffered a double blow when his mother died and her dowry went missing. When his father suffered a loss of income, the small family entered a difficult period.

Early in his time at the Conservatorio, Pergolesi began composing, possibly the chamber music and concerti for violins which have never been assigned definite dates and were mostly published posthumously. The first work

Giovanni Pergolesi

to attract attention was his 'sacred drama', *La Conversione di San Guglieme d'Aquitania* (1731), given its first performance by his fellow students at a Naples monastery. Also performed at this time was Pergolesi's humorous little intermezzo, *Il maestro di musica*, which was a considerable success and brought him to the attention of three men who became his patrons: the Viceroy of Naples' equerry, the Prince of Stigliano, the Prince of Avellino and the Duke of Maddaloni.

With such powerful allies, Pergolesi was invited to repeat his theatrical success at the Naples Court, and composed the opera *La Sallustia*, accompanied by a new comic intermezzo, *Nerino e Nibbia*; the opera pleased but the intermezzo failed. The following year was not a happy one: his beloved father died and his latest theatrical ventures, the opera *Ricimero* and its intermezzo *Il geloso schernito* suffered a dismal reception. Deciding to retreat and re-group, Pergolesi switched to instrumental

DON'T MISS

▶ La Serva Padrona (1733)
▶ Salve Regina in A minor (1736)
▶ Stabat Mater (1736)

music, producing more than 30 sonatas for violin and bass for the Prince of Stigliano (24 of these were printed in London long after the composer's death). Pergolesi also wrote some religious music at this time, including a Mass to commemorate the legacy of the earthquake which had devastated Naples in the spring of 1731; it won high praise at the time but has since been lost.

In an attempt to restore his theatrical fortunes, Pergolesi returned to *opera buffa* in 1732 with the deliberately Neapolitan-flavoured work *Lo frate 'nnamorato*, which met with rousing approval. A year later the *opera seria, Il prigionier* appeared, accompanied by its comic intermezzo *La Serva Padrona*. Both were again successful, but *La Serva*

has long since been detatched from its original position in support of the serious work, and to this day enjoys an audience of its own. These two years of gradual consolidation were crowned by Pergolesi entering the service of the Duke of Maddaloni. Pergolesi travelled to Rome with his new master in 1734, where he enjoyed the privilege of having his Mass in F performed. Back in Naples by mid-summer, he met with another *opera seria* failure when *Adriano in Siria* was premièred, although the two intermezzi, *Tracollo* and *Livietta*, fared reasonably well. The following year saw two theatre productions, the first a disastrous Rome première of the *opera seria, L'Olimpiade*, which so displeased the crowd that an orange was lobbed at Pergolesi's head. He responded by placing his next production in Naples, where he met with success with the *opera buffa* entitled *Il Flaminio*. By now Pergolesi was aware of something seriously wrong with his health, and his remaining time was spent attempting to put his affairs in order. Years of fast and reckless living had weakened his resistance to infection, and he was now in the grip of consumption.

His patron allowed him to become a house guest at Pozzuoli in the early months of 1736, and Pergolesi left Naples having instructed his aunt to take possession of any property he left behind; he clearly did not expect to return to Naples. He died in Pozzuoli in March 1736. Not until after his death did his most famous composition, the *Stabat Mater*, come to light and achieve publication, together with three *Salve Reginas*, in A minor, C minor and F minor, also published in 1736. The *Stabat Mater*, possibly written as far back as 1729, was quickly recognized as something out of the ordinary and achieved an international reputation. Many arrangements were made of it, J. S. Bach transforming it into his motet *Tilge, Höchster, meine Sünden*. It has attracted its critics as well as its passionate admirers, and shows the operatic background of the man who composed it, but as one of its later re-arrangers, John Adam Hiller, commented: "The man who could remain cold and unmoved when hearing it does not deserve to be called a human being".

CARL PHILIPP EMANUEL BACH
1714–1788

Together with his brother, Johann Christian Bach (1735–1782), who was a significant influence on the young Mozart, C. P. E. Bach was a key composer in the transition between the Baroque and Classical styles, and possibly the single most important composer of the generation between his father and Haydn.

Carl Philipp, the second son of Johann Sebastian's first marriage to Maria Barbara, was born in Weimar. His musical proclivities were exhibited at an early age, and he was properly schooled at the keyboard and in theory (mainly by his father), excelled in his studies at the Thomasschule in Leipzig and then attended Frankfurt University. Carl Philipp was left-handed and took a particular delight in playing the supportive role on the keyboard, often playing with his father. Even at the age of 11 he was a brilliant sight-reader and could play his father's works effortlessly from manuscript.

His time at university was accompanied by intense activity within the city's musical circles, and by 1737 he was sufficiently admired to be invited to play his own compositions for Friedrich Wilhelm I of Prussia and his son, Markgraf Friedrich Wilhelm. Given a warm welcome, especially by the Crown Prince, C. P. E. was disappointed to find that no summons to the Prussian Court was forthcoming. He had to wait until 1740, when the old King died, for the newly-crowned Friedrich to appoint him cembalist at his *Kapelle*. This post gave Bach direct access to the monarch (Frederick the Great) who was an enthusiastic flute player and amateur composer. There would be many times in the coming years when Bach would play in concert with the King.

Carl Philipp Emanuel Bach

This privilege was to be as much a burden as an advantage, given Frederick's innate musical conservatism, his tendency to be wayward in rhythm in his own playing, and his utterly authoritarian attitude to his fellow-musicians, all of whom had to take their lead from him. To a man such as Bach, this soon became wearisome, and within a few years he was longing to get away, especially when it became clear that Frederick preferred the conservative style of his other musical employees, Carl Heinrich Graun and J. J. Quantz, the latter being the King's flute teacher and a particular favourite. Even the visit of Bach's esteemed father

Johann Sebastian in 1747 only temporarily alleviated C. P. E's disillusionment, and by the time of Johann Sebastian's death in 1750 he was desperate enough to apply for his father's old position as cantor at Leipzig's Thomasschule, but was passed over. Having married Johanna Maria Danneman, the daughter of a Berlin wine merchant in 1744, C. P. E. was in the curious position of being a free Saxon married to a Prussian who needed the King's permission to leave Berlin. Despite the rise of C. F. C. Fasch in the 1750s to become the new Court

favourite, Frederick—who was well aware of Bach's abilities and eminence—still would not allow C. P. E. to move on. Bach derived some consolation from his teaching of the clavier to the royal family, as well as his friendship with Frederick's sister-in-law, Princess Amalia. From this relationship evolved the two-part instructive publication *Versuch über die wahre Art das Klavier zu spielen*. This, the first such book of its kind, was enormously influential in establishing keyboard technique, and the form of the music written for it for the next 100 years,

DON'T MISS

▶ Trio Sonata, H571 (1731)

▶ Magnificat, H772 (1749)

▶ Flute Concerto, H445 (1755)

▶ Oboe Concerto, H468 (1765)

▶ Sinfonias, H657–662 (1773)

claiming among its adherents Hummel and Mozart, the latter commenting: "He is the father, we are the children". Haydn was also galvanized by its publication, making it an urgent priority to master the book's contents.

In the summer of 1767 Bach was finally granted the freedom he craved, brought about, ironically, by the death of his godfather, Telemann, who had long reigned supreme in Hamburg as a composer and holder of important musical posts. Bach moved to Hamburg before the year was out, and remained in place there, attending the Johanneum (the musical directorship of Hamburg's five principal churches) for the rest of his life. Hamburg was no longer the opera-loving city of Handel and Mattheson, but was quick to embrace the series of concerts mounted by Carl Philipp to which he introduced much of the repertoire he had written during his stay in Berlin. His cello concertos, for example (which also exist in versions for harpsichord), though written in the early 1750s, were in the fashionable new style, while his works for keyboard continued pre-eminent. Bach also shared his father's gift for long and intricate extemporisation; Reichart observed him improvising in 1774 and commented:

"Bach would become lost for hours in new ideas... His eyes swam as though in some delectable dream. His lower lip drooped over his chin, his body and face bowed, seemingly lifeless, over the keyboard".

Bach led a relatively untroubled existence in Hamburg, free to compose and concertize as well as to fulfil his church duties. His new lease of life was attested to by Dr Burney who met him in 1772 and described him as having "a very animated countenance, and...a cheerful and lively disposition". In 1778 his second son, Johann Sebastian, an aspiring painter, died at the age of 30. After an illness which affected his chest, Bach himself died in late 1788. The regard in which he was held manifested itself in a glowing obituary in the local newspaper, in which Bach was described as one of the greatest musicians of his time and a man of considerable humour and wit. In 1795 Joseph Haydn visited Hamburg on his way from England to Vienna, expressly to pay his respects to Bach, only to find that his daughter was the last member of the family still alive, her mother having died that summer; the news of the composer's death had not penetrated beyond northern Germany.

C. P. E. Bach had emphatically rejected the delight with counterpoint and polyphony which had so engaged his father's creative faculties, turning instead to the embryonic sonata form and the concerto which he caught in transition, somewhere between the old Vivaldian model and its expanded and developed later Classical form. Bach developed the centrality of the solo role as well as helping to clarify and lighten the orchestral textures around and behind the soloist. His work with the outer movements of the concerto form, built around thematic patterns, also prefigured the massive developments it was to undergo in the following 50 years. He composed over 50 concertos for a variety of instruments, although every one of them also exists in a keyboard version.

Concertos were certainly not all: Bach left a legacy of over 700 works which include songs, cantatas, two Passions (St Matthew and St Luke) and a variety of chamber works. He was also prolific in his solo keyboard output, especially for his favourite instrument, the harpsichord (of which the *Prussian Sonatas* of 1742 and the later *Württemburg Sonatas* are key examples), although he certainly did not neglect his father's favourite, the organ. Although regarded mainly as a transitional figure, his work stands by itself as worthy of close investigation, and there are many delights to be found by the diligent. He was instrumental in laying the theoretical and compositional groundwork for the later flowering of not only Haydn's Classical style but also the early romanticism of Beethoven and beyond.

CHRISTOPH WILLIBALD GLUCK
1714–1787

Today Gluck is remembered as a key figure in the 18th-century rejuvenation and revival of opera, a music form which had become vitiated and enfeebled by the malpractice of singers and composers alike. But he is not simply a figure in history, for his greatest operas— including *Orfeo ed Euridice*— are a core part of the performing repertoire of the greatest opera houses today.

Gluck was born in the village of Erasbach in the far east of Germany. His father was a huntsman, his mother a member of Prince Lobkowitz's household at Eisenberg. By the time Christoph was of kindergarten age the family had moved to Neuschloss in Bohemia, the home of Count Kaunitz. His father moved from one Bohemian court to another, but there is a tradition that Gluck spent the years 1726–28 at the Jesuit school in Komotau, where he presumably gained a good grounding in classics and music. It is possible that he spent the rest of his adolescence in Bohemia, but it is known that he was in Prague by 1732 and probably started at the university in the same year.

By the time Gluck moved to Vienna in 1736 his father had returned to the service of Prince Lobkowitz. Gluck took up a position in Lobkowitz's chamber orchestra in his Viennese household where he was fortunate to meet Prince Melzi, an Austrian diplomat based in Milan who was so impressed with the 23-year-old that he engaged him in his own band and took him back with him to Milan. Gluck prospered in the northern Italian city, studying with Giuseppi Sammartini for three years and wholeheartedly embracing opera as his chosen field of composition. By 1741 he had written and produced his first opera, *Artaserse*, which proved a success. Eight operas followed in the next four years, premièred across northern Italy, from Turin to Venice.

This success prompted the Haymarket Theatre in London to invite Gluck to write a new work for them. Gluck arrived in London with his old patron, Prince Lobkowitz, late in 1745, and wrote a *pasticcio*, entitled *La caduta de' Giganti*. Produced in January 1746, it was a dismal flop, as was another work produced in the spring. This sobering experience, plus the lessons learned in Paris en route to Italy— where Gluck studied Rameau's operas in performance—led him to conclude that the current Italian operatic form would no longer suffice: it must be reconstituted so that each element— plot, music and lyrics—had an equal opportunity to impress and involve the audience.

Gluck did not settle on his solutions to the questions posed by such a novel balance overnight: while working as a conductor with an Italian travelling opera company for the three years he had a number of works produced which indicate how his ideas were developing. That year he settled once more in Vienna, attracted by the daughter of a rich merchant, Marianna Pergin whom he married in 1750. The marriage was to be a happy but childless one, and Marianna's considerable inheritance eased Gluck's fears regarding his future financial security.

During the following decade Gluck remained in Vienna. He accepted a post as conductor for Prince Hildburghausen, which led him to becoming a regular at Empress Maria Theresa's summer Court in Schlosshof. In 1745 Gluck scored a notable success with his opera, *Le Cinesi* written to a text by the leading librettist in Vienna, Pietro Metastasio. From this triumph came many important developments in Gluck's career, and not before time for he was now 40 years old and only just breaking through to the first rank. He was engaged as Emperor Francis I's composer of ballets and French comic operas as well as being responsible for court concerts. Soon after he was appointed General Director of Music at a salary double that of before.

Much of this preferment came about through his success with the Emperor and Empress, but its continuance was largely due to Gluck's happy professional relationship with the

Christoph Willibald Gluck

Gluck took his time in consolidating the artistic gains of *Orfeo*, even going back to writing slight and occasional works with Metastasio in 1763 and 1764. Although he resigned his Court appointment (as did Durazzo) in 1764, he continued to fulfil various commitments to the royal household, even giving regular singing lessons to Marie Antoinette until her departure for France to marry the Dauphin, later Louis XVI. His next major operatic step was quite deliberate: the successful Viennese production of *Alceste* in 1767 led to a printed version of the score with a preface by Gluck in which he put forward his ideas on reforming opera. 'I resolved to avoid all those abuses which had crept into Italian opera through the mistaken vanity of singers and the unwise compliance of composers, and which had rendered it wearisome and ridiculous... I endeavoured to reduce music to its proper function, that of...enforcing the expression of the sentiment, and the interest of the situations, without interrupting the action, or weakening it by superfluous ornament'. Gluck had made a thorough study of every part of an opera, and even the overture was to be reformed: 'The overture ought to indicate the subject and prepare the spectators for the character of the piece they are about to see'. Previously, overtures were more likely to be used by a composer to gain the audience's attention and impress them by their cleverness and novelty—two things Gluck was specifically not seeking. 'My chief endeavour should be to attain a grand simplicity... consequently, I have avoided a parade of difficulties at the cost of cleverness'.

Director of Imperial Theatres, Count Durazzo. Durazzo was keen to reform court opera in the same way envisaged by Gluck: unifying the action along French lines and dispensing with *castrati* whose pre-eminence to the exclusion of operatic commonsense he had grown to detest. By 1761, with the arrival of Ranieri Calzabigi in Vienna (the presiding librettist Metastasio was firmly of the old school and opposed to change), Gluck and Durazzo had found the librettist they needed to bring their ideas to fruition. In October of the following year Gluck's great

masterpiece, *Orfeo ed Euridice*, was premièred. Its clarity of plot and character, plus its concentration on a single continuity of event through both music and text, overcame the more traditional elements such as the casting of a *castrato* in the lead role, and the opera struck its first audiences as something truly novel. Within a short while the opera had premièred in Paris and Frankfurt, and was finally published in complete score—the first of Gluck's operas to be so treated—thus making its treasures available to all.

DON'T MISS

▶ **Don Juan (1761)**

▶ **Orfeo ed Euridice (1762)**

▶ **Iphigénie en Aulide (1774)**

▶ **Alceste (1776)**

▶ **Iphigénie en Tauride (1779)**

Gluck's follow-up, *Paride ed Elena* (1770), confirmed this new approach. The simple but revolutionary idea of an opera with a continuity of plot, action and characters, and in which the performers related to each other in a true ensemble way, created a tremendous stir, with pro- and con-camps quickly springing up—a sure sign of success. Yet Gluck was tiring of the constant battle to establish his ideas; this period found him writing trivial *divertissements* along the old lines for wealthy patrons willing to pay well, and though Gluck himself was now a wealthy man—so much so that he and his wife felt able to adopt a daughter—he longed for a more sophisticated and appreciative audience. This was not long in coming.

In Marie Antoinette, Gluck had a powerful friend at the French Court, and through her encouragement and the blandishments of one of the French diplomats in Vienna, the Bailly du Roullet, Gluck was persuaded that his ideas could find a successful outlet on the opera stages of Paris. The French capital had been without artistic input in the operatic field since

the death of Rameau and French opera was in a moribund state. Du Roullet had already prepared a libretto from Racine's *Iphigénie* which Gluck accepted enthusiastically: *Iphigénie en Aulide* was the result. Gluck's first opera in French, it was produced in April 1774 after a tryout in Vienna, and aroused a storm of controversy. Indeed, if it were not for Gluck's assiduous courting of influential figures such as Rousseau and the very active support of Marie Antoinette, it is possible that the opera would have failed, such was the animosity felt towards it by the traditionalists. Yet Gluck won the day convincingly, and by August had prepared a new French-language version of *Orfeo*, now called *Orfée et Eurydice*, which was again a singular success. A similar French adaptation of 1767's *Alceste* was premièred in 1776 and confirmed the complete triumph of Gluck's new method in France, despite the competition from the Italian composer Piccini.

In 1776 Gluck's adopted daughter, who had embarked on a fine operatic career, fell ill and died. Devastated, Gluck persevered with his operatic work, premièring *Armide* in 1778 and perhaps his most perfect work, *Iphigénie en Tauride*, in 1779. But his active career was drawing to a close. A slight work, *Echo et Narcisse*, failed the same year, while *Les Danaides* was in progress when his first heart seizure compelled him to suspend all work and hand the incomplete manuscript to his favourite pupil, Antonio Salieri, for the latter to finish. He returned to a more sedate life in Vienna, where he

watched with pleasure the advancement of Salieri in court circles, just as he enjoyed a special performance of Mozart's *Seraglio*, mounted for his benefit in 1782. For the next five years he passed his time contentedly until his second stroke from which he did not recover.

Gluck wrote over a score of operas, but just half a dozen works ensure his immortality. With *Orfeo*, *Alceste*, the two *Iphigénies*, *Paride ed Elena* and *Armide*, Gluck not only reformed operatic compositions and gave a blueprint for all opera for the next 100 years or more, but he created a series of masterpieces which have the ability to move modern audiences just as they did Gluck's contemporaries. His elegance and simplicity transformed opera into a vehicle for eloquent and dignified expression of the human condition through allegory and history. Opera was no longer a mere entertainment or diversion.

Gluck was fully conscious of what he had achieved and of its relative importance. He was willing to curry favour with royalty when it came to patronage and support, but when it came to mounting a correct and fully competent production, then he was even prepared to delay an opening night—as he did in Paris with *Iphigénie en Aulide*—and risk the wrath of the royal family in order to bring the opera up to the desired level of performance. In this he was of a new breed of musician and composer, a breed which was in time to blossom into the fully-fledged Romanticism of Schumann, Liszt and Wagner.

FRANZ JOSEPH HAYDN

1732–1809

Haydn was a pivotal figure in the development of Classicism: without him the Germanic music of the following century would have taken a very different path. His evolutionary contribution to the symphony, the string quartet and instrumental sonata was immense. He was a creative spirit whose music was both sophisticated yet utterly simple; his most complex music was never far removed from the elements of dance and folk song at its root. It is this common touch which makes him so immensely likeable to such a wide range of listeners.

Franz Joseph Haydn

Haydn was born into a Croat community in the Lower Austrian village of Rohrau. Both his parents and grandparents appear to have been Croatian in origin, giving Haydn a Slav rather than a Teutonic background. Franz Joseph, the second of 12 children, showed an early aptitude for music. His father, a wheelwright, wanted Joseph to follow in his footsteps, while his mother wanted him to become a priest. A cousin, Johann Franck, suggested that Joseph should receive a musical training, and took him to live with him in Hainburg. Franck himself taught Joseph, combining strictness with a real ability to impart knowledge to the boy, for which Haydn remained grateful for the rest of his life.

By the age of eight Haydn was relatively well tutored. Following a chance meeting with the visiting *Kapellmeister* of St Stephen's Cathedral, Vienna, Haydn became a chorister at the cathedral. In Vienna he completed his studies, becoming a proficient violinist and keyboardist as well as a featured singer in the choir, but was eclipsed by his younger brother Michael who had the sweeter voice and joined the choir in 1745, just as Joseph's voice broke. Haydn was dismissed from the choir and entered a period of real deprivation, only surviving by the occasional tutoring. But he did not waste his time: he studied the

compositions of C. P. E. Bach, read theory and was fortunate enough to receive a few lessons from the composer Nicola Porpora.

During the 1750s Haydn made progress with a range of compositions, including operas, masses and various pieces of chamber music. He also wrote his first quartets and symphonies, in which he showed a deep understanding of C. P. E. Bach's methods. By the end of the decade he had gained enough of a reputation in Vienna to be recommended to Count Morzin, who engaged him as *Musikdirektor* and *Kammercompositor* for his small orchestra at Lucaveč, near

DON'T MISS

▶ **Symphony No. 45
  (Farewell) (1772)**

▶ **String Quartets, Op. 33
  (1781)**

▶ **Cello Concerto in D
  (1783)**

▶ **Symphony No. 94
  (Surprise) (1791)**

▶ **String Quartets, Op. 76
  (1793)**

Plzeň. It was his first full-time position. In 1760 he married Maria Anna Keller, who was not only three years older but utterly unsuited to him both temperamentally and in outlook; the marriage remained childless.

Soon after the wedding, Count Morzin dismissed his entire musical staff. Fortunately for Haydn, an admirer, Prince Paul Esterházy, engaged him as his second *Kapellmeister*, and in May 1761 Haydn and his wife travelled to Eisenstadt, Esterházy's country seat. He remained based there for nearly 30 years, becoming first *Kapellmeister* in 1765. His success at building the Eisenstadt musical unit into a flexible and ever-expanding aggregation was closely tied to his relationship with Prince Paul, followed after Paul's death in 1762 by his son, Nicholas Esterházy, a generous and kind hearted potentate with a genuine love of the arts. Esterházy appreciated the enthusiasm and simple grace Haydn brought to his position, the constant improvements he made in instrumental standards and the strides he made in his compositional development. All this made for a lively and inspired cultural environment, considerably enhanced when the Prince

converted an old hunting lodge into a new palace called Esterház—described by visitors as rivalling Versailles in magnificence. Its buildings included an opera theatre, a marionette theatre—for which Haydn particularly enjoyed composing music—and two concert halls. Haydn's orchestra was regularly supplemented by bands of strolling musicians who entertained Esterházy's constant stream of guests.

The only real burden for the musicians was the rule that, with few exceptions, they were not allowed to have their wives and families with them. For Haydn, this was probably a blessing in disguise: 'I...was in a position to improve, alter, make additions or omissions, and be as bold as I pleased: I was cut off from the world, there was no-one to confuse or to torment me, and I was forced to become original'. Yet his isolation at Esterház did not prevent his reputation from becoming first national, and then international. By the end of the 1760s he was being referred to in the Austrian newspapers as a national treasure, while his symphonies and chamber music were being published in Paris, London and Amsterdam. His opera *Lo Speziale* was performed in Vienna in 1769 during a visit there by the Esterházy household, followed in 1771-2 by a *Stabat Mater*, a *Salve Regina* and the *Cäcilienmesse* in C. An even greater honour awaited him: in the autumn of 1773 the Empress Maria Theresa visited Esterház and was entertained by the first performance of Symphony No. 48—subsequently subtitled the *Maria Theresia*—and a production of one of his best operas, *L'infedeltà delusa*, together with a marionette piece, *Philemon und Baucis*.

In 1779 the Esterház theatre was destroyed by fire, curtailing the season and obliging the Prince to go to Paris while the rebuilding was completed. The year was also a difficult one for Haydn: he became enamoured of the wife of a recent arrival in the violin section and she took advantage of the situation by constantly asking him for money and other material favours. She even managed to get herself written into his will (although he later removed this codicil) and for a time her second son was believed to be Haydn's, though he left the boy nothing in his will, which would seem to indicate no actual paternity.

The 1780s were years of continuing triumph for the composer, now in his fifties and ready to taste the fruits of fame. He entered into long-term business partnerships with publishers in London, Amsterdam and Paris, and his operas were performed in various European centres. In early 1782 he met Mozart, whose genius he was quick to recognize. The admiration was mutual, and the influence of both composers on each other is readily discernible. Mozart even dedicated his set of six string quartets, published in 1785, to Haydn. Though subsequently the two rarely had a chance to meet—Mozart was in Vienna and Haydn in Esterház—the relationship remained cordial, at times bordering on the filial. Haydn's famous statement to Mozart's father: "Your son is the greatest composer I have ever heard: he has taste, and possesses the most complete knowledge possible of the art of composition", says as much for Haydn's generosity of spirit as for Mozart's talent.

In 1785 Haydn received an urgent invitation from the London promoter, Johann Peter Salomon, to visit London, but Haydn's ties with Esterház were still too close for him to accept. Five years later, however, everything had changed: Prince Nicholas died and Haydn's life was radically altered. The exceptionally close relationship between the two men left Haydn emotionally bereaved, and although well-looked after in the Prince's will (his successor actually increased Haydn's annual pension by half as much again), the Esterház troupe of musicians were dismissed *en masse*, leaving Haydn with no ensemble to write for or direct. He moved to Vienna but was soon confronted by a visitor at his door: Salomon had heard of Prince Nicholas's death and hurried to Vienna to renew his entreaties to the composer to make the journey to England. At the same time he commissioned Haydn to write six new symphonies. Haydn finally agreed. After spending the evening before his departure in convivial conversation with Mozart, in mid-December Haydn left with Salomon for England, arriving at Dover on New Year's Day 1791.

In London he was fêted on all sides, and the series of subscription concerts offered by Salomon were an unprecedented success. Haydn settled in Lisson Grove, north of Marylebone, and enjoyed the fuss being made of him. Oxford University awarded him an honorary Doctorate of Music, and the Prince of Wales introduced him to his brother, the Duke of York, who had just married the 17-year-old Princess of Prussia; at a private concert the Princess and Haydn together performed the master's work.

Haydn's stay in London was uniformly successful. At a performance of Handel's *Messiah* in Westminster Abbey he was reported to have ended the concert in tears, exclaiming: "He is the master of us all". Haydn remained in London until the summer of 1792. On his way back to Vienna he stopped at Bonn where he met Beethoven, then aged 22, who sought Haydn's opinion on some of his early pieces. Haydn's approval quickly matured into a willingness to help the young composer, and when Beethoven moved to Vienna, Haydn gave him regular lessons until his own return to London in 1794. Beethoven always remained a great admirer of Haydn's gifts and was genuinely grateful for his unselfish help.

The 1794 trip to London was no less successful than the first. Haydn was warmly welcomed by the royal family, and even invited to spend the summer at Windsor, but declined, wishing to return to the new Prince Esterházy who was reconstituting a musical aggregation at Esterház. His second trip had also contained a romantic involvement: this time there were tangible fruits from his passionate friendship with Anne Hunter, a poetess who contributed lyrics for a series of songs Haydn composed and published.

On his return to Austria Haydn was fêted as never before. In 1797 he was approached by a number of noblemen to write an oratorio for which they would underwrite the expenses. The result was *Die Schöpfung* (The Creation), a work for which Haydn "knelt down every day and prayed to God to strengthen me for my work". The private première was given in 1798,

the public one the year after: barely a member of the audience was left unmoved. The pious Haydn was shocked by the depths of emotion provoked in himself by his own music, commenting: "More than once I was afraid I would have a seizure". This overwhelming success led to the immediate commissioning of the oratorio, *Die Jahreszeiten* (The Seasons) which was premièred in 1801.

The effort required for two such vast undertakings virtually put an end to his public life; he was exhausted, and turned down all subsequent commissions, even declining an invitation to conduct *Die Schöpfung* at Eisenstadt in 1803 on grounds of infirmity. He was now in his late sixties, and his body began to fail him. Often confined to his room, he received a steady stream of visitors which included Cherubini, the Weber family (from whence Carl Maria later emerged), Esterházy family members and even Mozart's widow. His last public appearance was at a performance of *The Creation* at Vienna University in 1808; he was carried in on a chair and placed with the royal family, but was so agitated by his own

DON'T MISS

▶ **Sonata for Keyboard No. 60 in C (1794-95)**

▶ **Symphony No. 104 (London) (1795)**

▶ **The Creation (1796-98)**

▶ **Nelsonmesse (1796)**

▶ **Trumpet Concerto in E (1796)**

▶ **The Seasons (1799-1801)**

music that he had to be escorted from the hall. As he left, Beethoven kissed his hand and forehead. From then on he was confined to his house, dying on the last day of May 1809. After his death memorial services were held in his honour all over Europe.

Although Haydn was immensely proud of his many operas, today, due to their antiquated form, they are looked upon as curiosities rather than works for the general music-lover. His reputation rests squarely on his two great oratorios *Die Schöpfung* and *Die Jahreszeiten*, his sacred music and the orchestral, chamber and instrumental works. He was in at the beginning of string quartets, and although he did not invent the symphony, as is often claimed, he certainly did more than anyone else to develop its potential and expand its architecture so that it

could become the prime mode of Austro-German musical expression for the following century, the concerto form notwithstanding. Of the symphonies, the series of 12 late works known popularly as the *London* Symphonies (Nos. 93–104) include such favourites as the *Clock*, the *Surprise*, the *Miracle*, the *Military* and *Drum Roll*. as well as the *London* itself. Earlier symphonies of particular note include No. 22 *The Philosopher*, Symphony No. 45 *The Farewell*, Symphonies 48 and 49, *Maria Theresia* and *La Passione*.

Haydn's string quartets have incredible variety and span a large portion of his creative life, but the six Op. 33, the six comprising the later Op. 76, and the *Sun* Quartets of Op. 20 (these last dating from early in his career and closer to the *divertimento*) give a clear

and fascinating picture of what Haydn was capable of in this new 18th-century form. Haydn also wrote a mass of keyboard sonatas, the final numbers of which (Nos. 45 onwards, from 1776 up to the mid-1790s) are exceptionally fine works with great complexity, dramatic expression and subtlety. Being a devout man, he gave of his best when it came to writing Masses, and of these, the *Theresienmesse* of 1799, the *Nelsonmesse* of 1798 and the dramatic *Missa in tempore belli* give a clear indication of his arresting invention and deep sincerity. The oratorio, *The Seven Last Words* of 1795 is uniquely available as both an oratorio and as scored for string quartet, both versions executed by Haydn himself. Of his concertos, the two for cello and orchestra have deservedly held their place in the repertoire.

LUIGI BOCCHERINI
1743–1805

As with most composers of his day, Boccherini was skilled at more than one genre of music, being an expert composer of operatic, orchestral, vocal and chamber music. Today it is the latter which is most often heard and which forms the largest single group of compositions. Yet there is much more to discover about his charming and graceful music, and perhaps future musical researchers will establish the true scope of his overall achievement.

Boccherini was born in the northern Italian town of Lucca, thus sharing his birthplace with the Puccini family. While still very young, Luigi was taught the cello by his father, but when he outstripped his father's expertise, he was delivered into the hands of Abbé Vannucci, a composer who was *maestro di cappella* to Lucca's Archbishop. Vannucci was so impressed by the boy's progress that at the age of 14 he was sent to Rome to be taught by Giovanni Batista Costanzi, a former pupil of Tartini's. From Costanzi, Boccherini learned a playing tradition

which reached back to Corelli, and was also much impressed by Costanzi's own compositions which were mostly operatic and taught young Luigi the value of a good voice-like melody.

Boccherini's first efforts at composition were in chamber music; of these, his early cello sonatas are the most frequently heard today. Never catalogued by Boccherini (who kept a reasonably accurate account of his compositions from 1760 onwards), they contain the hallmarks of Boccherini's style—charm, grace, an understanding

Luigi Boccherini

persuaded him to stay in Madrid as his *compositore e virtuoso di camera*. The musical needs of Don Luis's household were for the most part small-scale—chamber music, concertos and symphonies—and although Boccherini also wrote song settings, operas were not required of him.

This was certainly no bar to his continuing creativity, for he was prolific even by the standards of the day; one observer compared his output to a flow of water which could be turned on or off at will according to the needs of the day. If this sounds today like a slur, it was seen as a great compliment at the time for this is also what was expected of composers such as Bach, Telemann, Vivaldi and Haydn, and every one of them obliged. In the early 1770s Boccherini began writing symphonies for Don Luis (he completed over 20 before his death). In his view, these were concertos written for orchestra, and have the liveliness and grace of the concerto form, eschewing any Germanic tendency to portentous musical statements. Boccherini also continued his remarkable run of chamber music written for a wide range of instrumental combinations, and did much to establish—together with Haydn—the string quartet form, finally completing no less than 120 such works. He also wrote the opera *La Clementina* (1786) for the Infanta's daughter. He continued in the service of Don Luis until the latter's death in 1786, by which time he had settled with his family in Madrid. The Infanta's death put the composer in a difficult position as there was little appreciation of his remarkable musical talents outside Don Luis's establishment. However, he quickly canvassed a

of the instrument being written for and a real flair for memorable melody—and belong firmly to the chamber tradition favoured by Tartini and Vivaldi.

By the early 1760s Boccherini was composing wholly characteristic concertos, mainly for the cello, which exploited the gloriously mellow, human timbre of the instrument and gave it a joyous expressivity which has eluded many other composers. By 1764 Boccherini was dividing his time between Lucca, where he worked as a musician in the theatre orchestra, and Vienna, where he enjoyed a number of minor posts associated with the Court orchestra and where his early trios for two violins and cello were much admired. During this period he also completed oratorios and other vocal music, including at least one opera. By

1766 he was sufficiently confident of his new stature to travel through northern Italy and parts of France on a concert tour with the violinist and Tartini scholar, Filippo Manfredi. By 1768 they had reached Paris, where the young Boccherini's music became all the rage.

To achieve celebrity in Paris, which in the mid-18th century was the musical capital of Europe, did not go unnoticed, and Boccherini and Manfredi were invited to Madrid by the Spanish ambassador in Paris, who promised them a rapturous reception from the heir to the throne, Prince Asturias. But their arrival at the Spanish Court in early 1769 was greeted coldly by Prince and King alike. The situation was saved by the music-loving brother of the King, Infante Don Luis, who became Boccherini's patron and

DON'T MISS

▶ Cello Concerto No. 7, G480 (1770)

▶ Cello Concerto No. 10 (1782)

▶ String Quintets, G236–241 (op. 53) (1796)

▶ Guitar Quintets, G445–453 (1798)

▶ Stabat Mater, G532 (1800)

number of options among the royal courts of Europe, and a new composition dedicated to King Friedrich Wilhelm of Prussia was successful; by 1787 Boccherini was appointed chamber-composer to the Prussian monarch.

This appointment has often given rise to the assumption that Boccherini spent much of his time in Berlin, but it would seem from recent research that the relationship was almost entirely conducted by letter and written submission. For the next decade Boccherini not only wrote for Friedrich Wilhelm alone, but agreed to abide by a condition of employment which banned him from publishing any composition accepted by the Prussian monarch. This condition ultimately proved damaging for a composer now well into middle-age

and living on the periphery of the larger European cultural confluence. Until this time regular publication of his new works in Paris, London and Amsterdam had kept his name before the music-loving and music-playing public. Now, and for a period of 10 years, Boccherini's opportunities to publish were severely limited. The death of Friedrich in 1797 released him from this condition, and his new patron—a Spanish dignitary, the Marquis Benavente—had no desire to curtail Boccherini's activities.

Unfortunately, ill-health (he was now suffering from a pulmonary condition) and a series of domestic upheavals led to him suspending his playing career, driving him further from the public eye even in his adopted country. In addition, the Marquis was appointed Spanish ambassador to Vienna and

dispensed with Boccherini's services. A pension from the Royal Chapel of Madrid helped defray some of his medical expenses, but at the turn of the century Boccherini was experiencing hard times. The new French ambassador to Spain, Lucien Bonaparte, a music-lover and appreciative of Boccherini's talents, gave him some respite from his financial troubles, receiving the dedication of the String Quintets Opp. 60 and 62 (1801–02) in return.

In 1801 Bonaparte also received the dedication of a *Stabat Mater*, published that year in Paris, and other works published prior to and after Boccherini's death indicate a renewed French interest in his late work, but the composer's last three years were a battle against encroaching illness and mounting financial pressures in a city in which he had become an anachronism. His death in 1805 released him from his earthly cares and his fame promptly evaporated, but despite the travails of the last years, his music—as the late quintets amply demonstrate—retained all the grace, verve and optimism for which he was prized and honoured in the heady days of his early career.

WOLFGANG AMADEUS MOZART
1756–1791

Like J. S. Bach, Mozart had little interest in establishing new forms within Classical music: he was more committed to the idea of synthesis and the perfection of forms already in existence. Thus

it is only in the area of the concerto that he could be said to have moved the music forward in any substantial way. However, again like Bach, the supreme quality he brought to previously

defined forms places him in the front rank of musical geniuses.

Mozart was the seventh-born child of a musically gifted and personally ambitious father, Leopold, the son of an Augsburg bookbinder. By dint of his determined character, Leopold eventually attained the positions of Court composer and vice-*Kapellmeister* to the Salzburg establishment of Count Thurn und Taxis, Canon of Salzburg. Leopold was an able composer, and his *Toy* Symphony is still regularly performed, but the accomplishment most admired during his lifetime was a treatise on violin playing published in 1756, the year of Wolfgang's birth.

Both Wolfgang and his elder sister, Maria Anna (nicknamed Nannerl), were child prodigies. Wolfgang was given lessons by his father from the age of four, and within a year he was not only duetting with his sister, but composing little minuets in imitation of the pieces his father set him. His annual progress continued to be prodigious and by early 1762 Leopold believed the two children were ready to be shown to the world. All three Mozarts were presented at the Court of the Elector of Munich and later in the same year their burgeoning reputations led to an appearance at the Emperor's Viennese Court at Schönbrunn, where little Wolfgang's talent and artless behaviour (which included jumping into the Empress's lap and kissing her) made him the object of everyone's indulgence.

Over the next few years the Mozart family followed a pattern of increasingly ambitious tours to various cities throughout Europe, including Paris, London, Amsterdam, Utrecht and Munich, as well as giving concerts to the aristocracy of Salzburg and Vienna. Another pattern which emerged from the tours, however, was not so

Wolfgang Amadeus Mozart

propitious: the regular illnesses suffered by all the family, but by the two children in particular. It has since been speculated that these illnesses had a generally weakening effect on the boy's constitution, leaving him vulnerable in later life, although Nannerl outlived Wolfgang by 28 years.

In 1768, and by imperial command, Wolfgang composed a full-length opera, *La finta semplice* (K51) to words by Coltellini, and also saw a private production of his short operatic work *Bastien und Bastienne* (K50). He was now aged 12. An extended tour of Italy (1769–71) by father and son met with unprecedented success: Wolfgang was given a private audience with the Pope

in Rome and was awarded the Order of the Golden Spur. In Bologna he was admitted to the ranks of *compositore* by the Accademica Filarmonica—a position normally denied to anyone under 20. At this stage Wolfgang was still very much a child, writing to his sister from Milan: 'Lest you should think I am unwell I am sending you these few lines. I kiss Mamma's hand. My greetings to all our good friends. I have seen four rascals hanged here in the Piazza del Duomo. They hang them just as they do in Lyon. Wolfgang'. Less than a year after their return to Salzburg (where Wolfgang was again seriously ill) the Mozarts were back in Milan where the opera *Lucio Silla* (K135) was completed. Austria

DON'T MISS

▶ Exsultate, Jubilate, K165 (1773)

▶ Violin Concerto No. 3, K216 (1775)

▶ Flute Concerto, K622 (1791)

▶ Coronation Mass, K317 (1779)

▶ Gran Partita, K361 (1781–84)

beckoned once more, and a Viennese visit in the late spring of 1773 brought Mozart into contact with the work of Joseph Haydn, specifically his String Quartets Op. 20, the so-called *Sun Quartets*, from which Mozart later claimed to have learned vital lessons in form and development.

The Munich Carnival of 1775 prompted a commission for a new opera; the result was *La finta giardiniera* (K196), which made a deep impression on the German composer Christian Schubart, a wild and dissipated man but a great judge of musical talent, who commented: "Unless Mozart should prove to be a mere overgrown product of the forcing-house, he will be the greatest composer that ever lived".

Now approaching the end of his teenage years, Mozart was committed to composing in the fashionable style of the time, the 'gallant' style, which emphasized brilliance and display. and which would keep him enthralled for at least the next two years. He was also kicking at the boundaries of life in Salzburg, a city which, for all its pride in its cultural accomplishments, was deeply parochial. For Mozart, who had already seen the most sophisticated cities in Europe, this must have been doubly hard to bear, especially when

his father's employer at the Cathedral, Archbishop Colloredo, was utterly out of sympathy with his aims and outlook on life.

In September 1777 Mozart left for Paris with his mother, leaving Leopold and Nannerl in Salzburg: the tour was to be financed solely by fees earned while travelling. The pair had reached Mannheim when an event occurred which decisively shaped his future: Wolfgang fell in love with Aloysia, the second daughter of the impecunious prompter and copyist, Fridolin Weber. As the girl, who was a talented singer, returned his affections, Mozart hatched a hare-brained scheme to take her to Italy and make her a prima donna. He wrote to his father to inform him but Leopold saw only catastrophe ahead; after a series of bullying and wheedling letters, he eventually persuaded Wolfgang out of the idea.

Mozart and his mother finally arrived in Paris in March 1778, but she was ill on arrival; her condition worsened and in early July she died in Mozart's arms. The distraught son remained sensitive to his father's feelings throughout this terrible experience, asking a mutual friend to prepare Leopold for bad news before writing to him himself. In a letter to a friend, Mozart wrote: 'She

was constantly delirious, and today at twenty-one minutes past five o'clock the death agony began and she lost all sensation and consciousness. I pressed her hand and spoke to her, but she did not see me, did not hear me and all feeling was gone'. He left Paris soon after, travelling back via Munich, now the home of the Weber family, but Aloysia had married and affected to retain no feelings for him. By January 1779 he was back in Salzburg where he took up the position of *Konzertmeister* to the Court and Cathedral. His life had irreversibly altered.

A brief and pleasant interlude in Munich, which included the première at the 1781 Munich Carnival of *Idomeneo, Rè di Creta* (K367)—one of his greatest *opera serias*—was brought to a close by an urgent summons from the Salzburg Archibishop for Wolfgang to join his party in Vienna. He was treated by the Archbishop as a possession, shown off to the aristocracy of Vienna but made to eat and live with the domestic servants. Mozart's anger over his employer's arrogant attitude led to a row and subsequently to Mozart being literally kicked out of the Archibishop's residence, pursued by a string of expletives from his secretary, Count Arco. Braving his father's anger, Wolfgang refused to attempt a reconciliation, knowing that the time for such things was past. He had high hopes for an independent career in Vienna.

Leopold's anger turned to paroxyms of rage when Wolfgang moved into lodgings in Vienna with the Weber family with whom he had had such curious relations in Mannheim a few years previously. Herr Weber had died, leaving the family relatively poor. Wolfgang now fell for the third sister, Constanze. Young and still gullible, he was put under pressure by Constanze's mother and agreed to sign a marriage contract of intent. This nearly drove Leopold to distraction, but by now his son's mind was fixed. Amidst the chaos of his personal life, Mozart enjoyed the successful première of *Die Entführung aus dem Serail* (K384), and in all probability met Haydn for the first time in the late autumn of 1781, when the older man was visiting Vienna. From the beginning the admiration between the two composers was mutual. Mozart was only 26 while Haydn was nearly 50, but both learned a good deal from each other, Mozart in the realm of structure and expressive dignity, Haydn in colourization and richer melody.

The year 1782 began with a series of subscription concerts for which Mozart often prepared new piano concertos or symphonies, and which were regularly attended by the Austrian nobility, but the hoped-for Court appointments failed to materialize. When he and Constanze finally married late that summer (against the wishes of his father and sister), the newly-married couple looked forward to a precarious existence, sustained in part by private music lessons, for which Mozart was singularly ill-suited. The first child arrived the following summer, and in 1783 Mozart and his wife visited Leopold in Salzburg. But the relationship between father and son could never be the same, even though Leopold returned the visit in 1785. This was to be their last meeting, and was fortunately a happy one; Leopold met Mozart's friend Haydn and was told by the older composer that Wolfgang had "the most

consummate knowledge of the art of composition". The father's return to Salzburg was accompanied by ill-health, and he was dead within two years.

Another major development in Mozart's life began when he joined the Freemasons, a powerful secret society. This was no passing fancy on Mozart's part, as was demonstrated by the constant undertone of Masonic thought which can be traced in so many of the works composed in his remaining years. A more artistically important event occurred in 1785 when Mozart became acquainted with the newly-appointed Imperial Court Poet, the Jewish Italian Lorenzo da Ponte. He invited da Ponte to compose a libretto, and together they created *Le nozze di Figaro* (K492) based on Beaumarchais' anti-establishment satire. Produced in Vienna on the first day of May 1786, after surviving vicious Court intrigues against it, the opera became the hit of the season. A subsequent production in Prague (to which Mozart was invited) was an even greater success, and Mozart wrote to a friend: 'Here they talk about nothing but *Figaro*. Nothing is played, sung or whistled but *Figaro*. No opera is drawing like *Figaro*. Nothing, nothing but *Figaro*. Certainly a great honour for me!'

Before leaving Prague Mozart was commissioned by a local entrepreneur to provide a new opera for the following season: the result was his next collaboration with da Ponte, *Don Giovanni* (K527). This was given its première in Prague in October 1787 and was a fantastic success; Mozart was given a trumpet fanfare even as he arrived at the theatre. But even with such public acclaim, the composer was by no means financially secure; as copyright did not yet exist in the theatre, he had nothing to show for his operatic triumphs but the initial fee paid to him. Compounded by their unworldly approach to domestic economy, the Mozarts were constantly on the edge of a financial crisis, alleviated only by the generosity of friends or the occasional windfall of some profitable concert or commission.

The composer Gluck's death in November 1787 cleared the way for a long-overdue appointment to the Emperor's Court, although only as *Kammercompositor*, which came with a paltry salary; Mozart could hardly conceal his contempt when writing to accept the offer. Around the same time his letters reveal that he was borrowing consistently from a Masonic colleague, the wealthy merchant Michael Puchberg. Despite being in desperate

---

DON'T MISS

▶ **Symphony No. 36, K425 (Linz) (1783)**
▶ **String Quartet No. 17, K458 (Hunt) (1784)**
▶ **Piano Concerto, K467 (1785)**
▶ **Kegelstatt Trio, K498 (1786)**
▶ **Le nozze di Figaro, K492 (1786)**

financial need, the quality of Mozart's artistic output is staggeringly consistent—it was at this time that he completed his last three symphonies, including the most famous of all, the *Jupiter* (K551).

With no alleviation of his condition, in 1788 he accepted the invitation of his friend and pupil Prince Karl Lichnowsky to travel with him to Berlin with the object of playing at the Court of Frederick William II. The tour was a considerable success, with Mozart being well-received in towns along the route. He also managed to please the King enough to be commissioned to write a series of quartets. Yet he returned to Vienna in early summer with little money, and was immediately plunged back into the familiar cycle of penury and his wife's constant ill-health (perhaps resulting from her almost perpetual state of pregnancy). The Emperor commissioned a new opera, for which Mozart once again collaborated with da Ponte; the result, *Così fan tutte* (K588), had a short but successful run in 1790 before being suspended due to the death of the Emperor. The bad timing which had dogged Mozart for so much of the 1780s seemed set to continue. The new Emperor, Leopold II, cared little for music or for the advancement of an

insignificant commoner like Mozart. Wolfgang's attempts to improve his position at Court only resulted in an agreement that he should become *Kapellmeister* at St Stephen's Cathedral on the death of the incumbent, Hoffman. Needless to say, Hoffman outlived him.

A tour of parts of Germany in autumn 1790 was Mozart's last (he had consistently turned down offers of tours in England), and he had to pawn the family silver to mount it. In Munich, he appeared at the Elector's Court before the King of Naples, who was a member of the Hapsburg dynasty—a cruel irony for Mozart who had been denied the opportunity of playing to the King in Vienna. As he commented: "It is greatly to the credit of the Viennese Court that the King has to hear me in a foreign country".

By now Mozart was showing signs of fatigue and illness which proved permanent. His phenomenal rate of composition had slowed markedly in 1790, and it was only through a supreme effort of will that he raised his creative tempo again in 1791. A commission from an old friend, Emmanuel Schikaneder, to write music to a libretto of his, gradually evolved into the sublime *Die*

Zauberflöte (K620), a work with strong Masonic imagery throughout as well as an undending supply of immortal melodies. It was premièred at a theatre in the grounds of Prince Starhemberg's house in the Viennese suburb of Wieden in the same month that his last *opera seria*, *La Clemenza di Tito* (K621), was given its première at the National Theatre in Prague on the eve of the coronation of the new emperor.

Mozart's last months were spent in a spiral of increasing illness, financial worries and a rising fear that he would not complete his final commission—his Requiem (K626). This had been requested by a messenger who refused to divulge either his own name or that of the patron who wanted the work. Mozart became convinced that the messenger had been other-worldly, and that he was composing his own requiem. The truth was more prosaic: the Viennese nobleman who had commissioned it was in the practice of commissioning works from established composers and then passing them off as his own to his friends. This was not to be the case with Mozart, as he left the work uncompleted at his death, his last days largely taken up with detailed instructions to his friend and acolyte Süssmayer as to how it should be completed after his death.

Mozart died in December 1791, aged just 36, his funeral service held in the open air at St Stephen's Cathedral. With a violent snowstorm raging, the coffin was taken in the pallbearer's wagon unaccompanied to a common graveyard, where Mozart's body was consigned to an unmarked pauper's grave: a fitting epitaph to his life in Vienna.

DON'T MISS

▶ **Piano Concerto, K488 (1786)**

▶ **Don Giovanni, K527 (1787)**

▶ **Serenade, K525 'Eine kleine Nachtmusik' (1787)**

▶ **String Quintets, K515/6 (1787)**

▶ **Divertimento, K563 (1788)**

During his short life, Mozart wrote sublimely for every known musical form, creating a vast array of masterpieces both great and small. Of the 23 original piano concertos (the first four are arrangements of works by other composers), the works from 1782 Concerto No. II in F (K413) onwards are generally regarded as completely mature, exhibiting a wholly remarkable balance between melody and harmony, soloist and orchestra. The soloist is a leader amongst equals and the listener can be forgiven for feeling he is in a musical heaven when these works are played by the right musicians.

The flute/oboe concertos (K313/314) have been particularly popular in recent years, as has been the Concerto for Flute and Harp (K299), and the four bravura horn concertos—written, it would seem, with the intent of testing the soloist—have never ceased to be in demand. But perhaps the most fully-realized of all the wind concertos is the late Concerto for Clarinet in A (K622), written in 1791 and exhibiting Mozart's deep love of the instrument. It explores the instrument's range and tonal qualities so successfully as to be a complete exposition of its musical qualities within the Classical style. The five violin concertos come from his Salzburg period and, while offering plenty to enjoy, lack the depth of his later concertos.

As far as the symphony is concerned, there is little reason initially to go beyond the last four (Nos. 38–41), all written in 1788, to find the perfect introduction to all the greatest qualities his symphonies can exhibit. Each is written in a contrasting manner and mood to the other, and each in its own

DON'T MISS

▶ **Symphony No. 41, K551 (Jupiter) (1788)**
▶ **Così fan tutte, K588 (1790)**
▶ **Clarinet Concerto, K622 (1791)**
▶ **Die Zauberflöte, K620 (1791)**
▶ **Piano Concerto, K595 (1791)**
▶ **Requiem, K626 (1791)**

way represents a summation of style and content which repays years of study. Of the numerous serenades, nocturnes, dances and marches, the former group represent the most substantial musical contribution, but each grouping brings its own felicities; the dances and marches, for example, have such a degree of élan and skill that they give much pleasure to the listener not looking for the utmost profundity. The two famous serenades, *Eine kleine Nachtmusik* (K525) and *Gran Partita* (K361) are irresistible.

Mozart's achievement in every area of classical music is staggering; it would be unwise, therefore, to overlook either his chamber music or his keyboard music, although no-one would claim for the keyboard sonatas the pre-eminent place enjoyed by his successor, Beethoven, in this field. Of the chamber music, the two marvellous String Quintets, (K515 and 516), are unsurpassable in their own very different ways, while the Clarinet Quintet (K581) has the warmth and dexterity of its concerted equivalent plus a special intimacy endemic to the smaller forces. Of the string quartets, those dedicated to Haydn (the six quartets K387, 421, 428, 458 *Hunt*, 464 and *Dissonance* 465), written between

1783 and 1785, are the most famous and frequently performed. They show both his great debt to Haydn and his complete ease with the quartet format.

Finally, the vocal works: of a vast quantity written for religious occasions, the unfinished Requiem (K626) is by far the most famous, and stands as one of his supreme creations. Also eternally popular are the *Coronation* Mass (K317) and the C minor Mass *(Great)* (K427), while the beautiful *Exsultate, jubilate* (K165) and *Ave verum corpus* (K618) are a favourite with every singer and represent Mozart at his most affecting. Also not to be overlooked is the aptly named *Vesperae solennes de confessore* (K339). Of the operas, the essential works if a listener is to grasp the range and depth of Mozart's theatrical genius would have to include all three da Ponte operas (*Le nozze di Figaro, Don Giovanni* and *Così fan tutte), Die Zauberflöte* and quite probably the delightful *Die Entführung aus dem Serail*. Some would also claim a place for *Idomeneo* and *La Clemenza di Tito*, but these fine examples of the *opera seria* form are something of an acquired taste for a modern audience. They are best arrived at after a thorough assimilation of the five mentioned above.

LUDWIG VAN BEETHOVEN

1770–1827

Beethoven's name is synonymous with Classical music: it is his name which invariably first comes to mind when people are asked to name the archetypal composer. The reason for this is his unique combination of innovative genius, moral rectitude and high seriousness.

Beethoven was born into a Bonn family of Flemish descent. Both his father Johann and his grandfather Ludwig were musicians at the Court of the Elector of Cologne which was based in Bonn. His father, a severe man who turned to drink as his career failed to blossom, married Maria Magdalena Keverich in 1767 and Ludwig was the first of their children to survive infancy.

The young Ludwig was taught music by his father but by the age of nine he had already outstripped his father's musical knowledge and was taken under the wing of Christian Neefe, organist at the Bonn Court, who gave him a conservative but thorough musical training. In 1783 Neefe became director of both sacred and secular music at Court and Ludwig was appointed cembalist-in-orchestra, an unpaid post which gave him responsibility for rehearsing and conducting the opera band. The death of the Elector Max Friedrich in 1784 led to a thorough reappraisal of the Elector's establishment by his successor, Max Franz, and Beethoven received a small stipend for his work (together with his father, who was still in the choir), while Neefe's salary was halved.

Ludwig van Beethoven

Beethoven was already composing small works and beginning to come to terms with the demands of writing music. In 1787 he made a short trip to Vienna, probably at the invitation of one of the nobles who admired Beethoven's work and who had good connections in the Austrian capital, for while there Beethoven not only met and played for Mozart, but also for Emperor Joseph II. Whether Mozart uttered the famous phrase: "Pay attention to him: he will make a noise in the world some day or other", it is now impossible to say, but it is likely that the 16-year-old Beethoven made a considerable impression as Haydn refers

to a 'Ludwig' in a letter to a friend in Vienna in June 1787 asking him what all the fuss was about.

But 1787 was memorable for Ludwig in more chilling ways: in July his much-loved mother died of consumption, the illness accelerated by her escalating alcoholism. In November of the same year his young sister died. During the following two years Ludwig broadened his circle of friends to include Count Waldstein, a music-loving nobleman eager to help the young composer financially and spiritually, and the Countess of Hatzfield, the recipient of Ludwig's dedication in his variations on

Vincenzo Righini's *Venni Amore*. In 1788 the Elector Max Franz reorganized his musical establisment, appointing Anton Reicha as its director and moving Neefe to the position of pianist and stage manager. Beethoven played second violin as well as keeping up his duties as organist. The new company performed most of the best operas of the day, including Mozart's. Son now overtook father both within the family and the Court: with Johann now an alcoholic and his singing voice gone, the family was so poverty-stricken that the Elector decided to pay the greater part of Johann's salary to young Ludwig, thus ensuring that the family would at least eat and be clothed. At the age of 17 Ludwig had become the sole reliable source of income for the Beethoven family. The only other event of note between then and Beethoven's departure for Vienna in 1792 was a visit by Haydn on his return from London, during which Ludwig presented his *Funeral Cantata*, which was duly praised by the great man.

In 1792, for reasons which remain obscure, the Elector decided to finance Beethoven's removal to Vienna, there to study at Bonn's expense. By this time Beethoven had a group of nobles convinced of his musical worth, (including Count Waldstein) who— perhaps encouraged by Haydn's praise— had helped inform the Elector's decision. In November Beethoven departed for the Austrian capital, speeded on his journey by the entry by Waldstein in his Leaving Album: 'Dear Beethoven, you are travelling to Vienna in fulfilment of your long-standing wish... Labour assiduously and receive Mozart's spirit from the hands of Haydn'. Within weeks of his arrival, his

DON'T MISS

▶ **Archduke Trio, Op. 97**
▶ **Piano Sonata No. 8 (Pathétique) Op. 13 (1798)**
▶ **Sonata for Violin and Piano No. 9 (Kreutzer) Op. 24 (1803)**
▶ **String Quartet No. 7 (Rasumovsky) Op. 59/1 (1805-06)**
▶ **Violin Concerto, Op. 61 (1806)**

father died, and Beethoven, his roots in Bonn withering, brought his younger brothers to Vienna to join him.

Beethoven took regular lessons from Haydn, even accompanying him to Eisenstadt in 1793, but was clearly dissatisfied with Haydn's level of involvement, and when the composer left for London in 1794, Ludwig transferred to Albrechtsberger who, though diligent in his teaching, thought Beethoven a hopeless case: "He has learnt nothing, and will never do anything in decent style", he commented to a colleague. Beethoven also took lessons on operatic points from Antonio Salieri. In the month that Haydn went to London, however, the Elector of Bonn visited Vienna, and two months later, Beethoven's small allowance was stopped. He was on his own.

Due to the relative frequency with which Beethoven was engaged by the nobility to give recitals in their houses, this situation did not prove as taxing as it might have done. Prince Lichnowksy and his wife, both former pupils of Mozart, invited him to live at their Viennese house; it is a measure of Beethoven's rapid acceptance in Viennese aristocratic circles that such an offer was made to a young man with much still to prove. For the next

few years he made his way by his skill as a performer and by the strength of his personality, a magnetic and charismatic one whose brutal side had quite as compelling a quality as did its philosophical and charming one. In 1796 his First Piano Concerto appeared, and in 1797, with Napoleon on the rampage through Europe, Beethoven produced one of his first thoroughly original works, Sonata for Piano in E-flat, Op. 7. Between then and spring 1800 Beethoven's most impressive music was written for the piano, his Op. 10 and Op. 14 sonatas being outstanding, while the Op. 12 sonatas for violin and piano showed his mastery of composition for both instruments. A major step into more adventurous composition came in 1800 with his First Symphony receiving publication, together with the septet and the first six string quartets (Op. 18). Later the same year his Concerto for Piano and Orchestra No. 3 appeared. Beethoven now turned from performance to concentrate on composition. He moved from Prince Lichnowsky's and took his first summer holiday in the country—a practice which was to become increasingly important to him in the future.

The next five years contained the most extraordinary outpouring of masterpieces: his Second Symphony

DON'T MISS

▶ Symphony No. 5, Op. 67 (1807)

▶ Piano Concerto No. 5, Op. 73 (1809)

▶ Symphony No. 6, Op. 92 (1812)

▶ Fidelio, Op. 72 (1814)

was published in 1804, but by then the *Eroica* was well under way (he had been mulling it over since 1798), while his ballet *Prometheus* and the oratorio *Christ on the Mount of Olives* had been premièred in 1801 and 1803 respectively. By this time Beethoven had also experienced the vicissitudes of getting his music published in an accurate and acceptable form: his rages, brought on by the number of mistakes he found at proofing stage, became legendary, particularly when, in 1803, he found that one Zurich publisher had not only amended idiosyncracies in one of his piano sonatas, but had had the effrontery to add four bars to make one passage more palatable to a conservative ear. One later printed work that Beethoven corrected received this tirade: "I have passed the whole morning today—and yesterday afternoon—in correcting these two pieces, and am quite hoarse with stamping and swearing".

In early 1804 the Third Symphony was being prepared for publication. It had always privately been known as the 'Napoléon Bonaparte' symphony—Beethoven saw the great Corsican as a force for freedom and the emancipation of the common man—but in May news filtered through to Vienna of Bonaparte's coronation as Emperor.

Disgusted beyond measure, Beethoven tore the title-page from his fair copy and substituted instead *Sinfonia eroica per festeggiare il souvenire d'un gran uomo*. Prince Lobkowitz having received the dedication and exclusive rights to its use, Symphony No.3, Op. 55 ("*Eroica*") was to remain unpublished until 1806.

It was characteristic of Beethoven to be engaged upon more than one composition at a time. His restless creative energy would continually spill from one idea to another, one form of expression to another, so it is no surprise to find him working next on the opera *Fidelio* and its possible production (1806, but destined to be shelved for the best part of a decade) as well as the beautiful Fourth Piano Concerto, the Violin Concerto, the Fourth Symphony and the beginning of the Fifth Symphony. Yet all this was only the beginning of his ascendancy in the world of Classical music, for there was much to come of equal merit.

By this time Beethoven was already aware of the distressing rate at which his hearing was deteriorating. In 1802 he wrote a statement—later dubbed the Heiligenstadt Testament—to his two brothers, Karl and Johann, in which he detailed his physical frailty and his attitude towards the death which he saw as alarmingly close, although in reality he still had 25 years to live. His hearing was long thought to be a casualty of hereditary syphilis, but more recent research has come down on the side of other non-venereal diseases of which Beethoven himself had no knowledge and over which he had no control. By 1807, when in one concert he premièred Symphonies 1, 2, 3 and 4,

(the programme lasted over two and a half hours), Beethoven had difficulty in hearing the music. The following year's concert in Vienna premièred the Fifth and Sixth Symphonies, the *Choral Fantasia*, plus the last-minute addition of Concerto for Piano No. 4, and a couple of arias. Beethoven himself was at the piano, but his deafness had reached the point where he could no longer properly follow the orchestra's tempo. The concert was given in December, the hall was bitterly cold and the performance so ragged as to be almost bizarre in places. Yet his will prevailed: all the music was played, and he remained at the keyboard throughout.

In 1809, with Austrian exertions against Napoleon at fever-pitch, Beethoven intimated that he would leave Vienna for better-paid work elsewhere. The general consternation caused Archduke Rudolph, Prince Lobkowitz and Prince Kinsky to club together to pay Beethoven a small but helpful annuity. Though the composer made it clear that he would have preferred to have been made imperial *Kapellmeister*, he remained in Vienna. He not only stayed, but when the French bombarded the city in the autumn, he completed the composition of his Fifth and last piano concerto, the *Emperor*. He also wrote a piano sonata which he named *Les Adieux* when Archduke Rudolf (a close friend as well as a patron) left the besieged capital.

The disastrous effect of the Napoleonic wars on the Austrian economy meant that by the end of 1810 the true value of Beethoven's annuity had shrunk to a tenth of its value. A reorganization of the Austrian currency only made the position worse, but Archduke Rudolf continued to support Beethoven, as did Lobkowitz. But with Kinsky he was less fortunate: the Prince had removed to Prague, dying in 1812 before making arrangements for Beethoven's revised payments. Undeterred, Beethoven sued Kinsky's heirs, and after three years of dogged legal action, secured not only a proper restitution of his annuity, but also payment in arrears. This success followed a year of triumphs, for 1814 had been in many ways a public culmination of Beethoven's career: *Fidelio* finally saw the light of day, his Seventh Symphony was premièred, and he was commissioned to write new music and mount concerts for the Congress of Vienna. Two concerts were held, and Beethoven was presented by the Archduke to all the visiting royalty and potentates, including the Empress of Russia.

From this point on his problems multiplied. A confirmed bachelor and a difficult man—who frequently fell out with friends and patrons—he nevertheless retained strong family feelings. When his brother Karl died in 1815, leaving his nine-year-old son (also named Karl) in Ludwig's care, the composer entered into a long and vexatious dispute with the boy's mother, whom he detested. Unfortunately, the boy held his mother in too great esteem to ever permanently take sides with Beethoven. Uncle Ludwig spent the best part of three years in suits and counter-suits and in making arrangements for the education of the child—who proved a very ordinary boy—and it is no surprise that the sum total of his compositions during this period of stress was the three piano sonatas, Op. 106, Op. 109

and Op. 110, plus a number of songs and arrangements. His finances strained (Prince Lobkowitz's share of his annuity had ceased with the Prince's death in 1816), his nerves in tatters, Beethoven was prematurely aged by the exigencies of these years.

Nonetheless, by 1819 he had completed a commission to supply a Mass for the installation of Archduke Rudolf as Archbishop of Olmütz: this was his great *Missa Solemnis*. In the next few years he took up the task of completing a symphony in D minor which he had actually started in 1812: as late as 1822 he finally came up with the idea of including Schiller's *Ode to Joy* in a choral final movement. His Ninth Symphony, *Choral* was at last taking on its final shape, and was completed in the summer of 1823. Beethoven had orginally planned to première it in Berlin, but disgusted by the lack of interest in his new music occasioned by the 'Rossini-fever' then sweeping Austria, premièred it instead in Vienna. It was sufficiently successful to produce a second concert, but neither made a great deal of money after the substantial costs had been defrayed. Beethoven was now anxious to make more money on account of the needs of his nephew, and his anxiety to take his fair share, or perhaps more than his fair share, led to conflicts with his erstwhile friends.

That this anxiety was well-founded was borne out by the series of disasters perpetrated by nephew Karl: in late 1824 he joined Vienna University, but soon dropped out and moved to a polytechnic with the intention of learning a trade. By the end of 1825 this idea had also foundered and, seemingly without a path to tread, the young man tried to

shoot himself. He even failed to do this properly, and was arrested by the police as an attempted suicide. Within a few days he had been ordered out of Vienna, joining the army soon after. He spent the latter part of 1826 with his Uncle Ludwig at the house of Uncle Johann, but this broke up in a series of ugly scenes and in December Ludwig and Karl returned to Vienna. The journey was made in haste in the freezing cold and precipitated Beethoven's final illness. He languished for four months, scarcely aided by the attentions of one of the few doctors in Vienna still prepared to visit the rude and grumpy old man.

Composing was now beyond him, and although in 1824-25 he had written the last three string quartets—the famous Op. 127, Op. 130, Op. 132 and *Grosse Fuge*, Op. 133—and had sketched out, in his mind at least, his Tenth Symphony (requested by the Philharmonic Society of London), there was to be no more music from his pen. On his death-bed just days before the end, a particulary offensive acquaintance told him: "Your new quartet did not please". By now resigned to approaching death, Beethoven replied "It will please them some day."

DON'T MISS

▶ Piano Sonata No. 29 (Hammerklavier) Op. 106 (1818)

▶ Missa Solemnis, Op. 123 (1818–23)

▶ Symphony No. 9 (Choral) Op. 125 (1822–24)

▶ String Quartet No. 13, Op. 130 (1825–26)

NICCOLÒ PAGANINI

1782-1840

The Italian virtuoso was a charismatic and profoundly influential figure in musical history. Not only did he considerably advance the frontiers of violin technique, both in performance and in composition, but he was one of the first great virtuosi whose impact has not been diluted by time. This is due to the high quality of the compositions he bequeathed to posterity as well as the model he left for younger musicians to emulate.

Born into a family in the Genoese shipping business, Paganini was the first of the astonishing 19th-century virtuosi whose reputations survive today. His father was a gifted amateur musician and quick to recognize Niccolò's unusual musical talent. His rudimentary violin lessons were delivered with a severity which would have extinguished the ardour of a lesser spirit, but the boy, aided by his mother's unwavering belief in him, stuck to his task and quickly exhausted his father's knowledge. Two professional teachers brought him up to a sufficiently high standard for the 11-year-old to make his public début at a concert in 1793 at Genoa's main theatre at which he played his own variations on a French patriotic song, 'La Carmagnole'. Soon after, his father arranged for young Niccolò to play in the local church, a routine which required the boy to rehearse new pieces every week. In later life Niccolò

always spoke of this enforced discipline as an ideal training for his career.

By the time he was 13, Paganini had outstripped his peers in Genoa and needed to move on. A benefit concert raised the required sum for him to travel to Parma and take up studies with the local virtuoso, Alessandro Rolla. These soon progressed to lessons from Gasparo Ghiretti, under whose tutelage Paganini composed 24 fugues and studied orchestration and the characteristics of various instruments.

After two years in Parma, Paganini and his father embarked on a tour of the principal towns in Lombardy. Within a few months he was touring further abroad, venturing to Lucca and Pisa. This signalled the end of his father's direct influence over his life; by the time of his triumph in Pisa, Niccolò was looking after his own affairs. Still only 16, the temptations for indulgence were hard to resist, and he soon succumbed to most of them: drinking and gambling became compulsive. Once, after a particularly severe loss at cards, he was offered a substantial sum for his Guarneri violin, a gift from an admirer. Chancing his arm on one last card game, he won sufficient funds to stave off immediate penury and the need to sell his violin, but swore that from then on he would give up gambling. Yet alcohol and the delights of carnal love continued to fascinate and exhaust him; by the time he was 19, his peers

took the view that he would be lucky to reach 21.

According to the later testimony of Paganini himself, his fortunes were restored in 1801 by the intervention of a Tuscan lady of aristocratic rank whose identity has never been established. Paganini lived in her palazzo for three years, devoting his time to her and to the study of the guitar, an instrument he later affected to dislike but for which he composed over 100 pieces and which undoubtedly helped him work out many of the details of his startling violin compositions. A move back to Genoa during 1804 presaged a set of quartets for violin, viola, 'cello and guitar which were inspired by close study of the innovative violin techniques of Pietro Locatelli. The following year he resumed his public career with a tour of the northern states.

His playing powers were clearly undiminished for the tour was a triumph and resulted in him being pressed to accept the position of director of private music for the Princess Elisa of Lucca and Piombo (Napoleon's sister). Clearly enamoured of Paganini, she also made him conductor of the Court orchestra and a Captain of the Royal Bodyguard, the latter position admitting him to all Court functions.

What was it about Paganini that exerted such fascination over his contemporaries? His violin technique was unequalled, but this in itself is not enought to sustain a career. Others before him had at least attempted most of the innovations with which he was later credited: extensive double-stopping, pizzicato left-hand passages, playing melodies constructed from the harmonics available from the violin strings, and so on. But Paganini was the first to construct a complete approach to playing from all these disparate techniques, and he also had the inestimable gift of being able to write memorable melodies. The last but certainly not the least part of the equation was his undoubted charisma. A thin, strange figure, with long, unruly hair and a remote manner bordering on arrogance, he mesmerized his audiences not only by his playing but by his sheer presence. He had an arsenal of tricks, some musical, some extra-musical—such as deliberately breaking violin strings and continuing to play when clearly exhausted—which kept the audience in a perpetual state of thrilled expectation. This, allied to his unerring technique and the brilliance of the music he elected to play, meant that every concert he gave was a memorable experience. He was to be the first of many to tread the route of the charismatic virtuoso in the next 100 years.

Within a short time of his return to the public arena he was a rich man. Obtaining leave from Princess Elisa in 1808, he resumed his touring, in 1809 meeting 17-year-old Rossini in Bologna with whom he formed a long-term friendship. His touring was now extensive and exhausting, his fees considerable. In 1815 he brought before his public his First Violin Concerto, which remained a constant favourite throughout his career, although,

Niccolò Paganini

jealously guarding what he saw as his compositional secrets, he never published it or any of his other six concertos. That same year he met the dancer Antonia Bianchi, already a star in her own right, and plunged into a relationship with her which changed his life in many ways. For the next decade their careers and explosive personal lives ran parallel to each other. In 1817 he met the great Count Metternich who invited him to Vienna, but Paganini's poor health prevented him from making the long journey: indeed his health was so bad that for a while he was close to death. Staging a recovery, in 1826 he sired a son, Achillino, by Antonia Bianchi. Two years later Bianchi's violent jealousy and possessiveness provoked a separation which proved final. A settlement gave Bianchi a generous lump sum in return for her renouncing all rights to the

child, to whom Paganini was passionately devoted. It was Achillino who was to publish Paganini's First and Second Violin Concertos shortly after his father's death.

In 1831 Paganini embarked on a tour of England, Scotland and Ireland. Arriving in London, he was mobbed wherever he went. He finally left the country in the summer of 1832 having earned over £16,000, an incredible sum for that time. The following year found him in Paris where he commissioned a work for viola and orchestra from his friend Berlioz: the result was *Harold en Italie*, which he premièred at the Paris Conservatoire in 1834.

In 1836 he made a disastrous attempt to marry his old passion for gambling with his latter-day accumulation of wealth: he became involved in a new casino, the Casino Paganini in Paris. Never granted a licence by the government, it was forced to close and Paganini lost a sizeable fortune. In an attempt to regroup he moved to Marseilles, but by 1839 his health, never stable, had seriously deteriorated. He returned to Genoa, only to find the climate adversely affected his condition. A further move to Nice merely delayed what was now inevitable, and he died of a throat and chest complaint in June 1840. He was a millionaire at his death, and provided generously for his entire family, including Antonia Bianchi, in his will.

Paganini's style was an easy combination of the elegance of classicism and the tunefulness and virtuosity of Italian music. Most of his orchestral compositions are designed specifically to show off the violinist's role, but the Third and Fourth Concertos in particular have more than mere superficial flashiness to recommend them. His other compositions include many works for guitar and violin, as well as quartets and quintets for various combinations of stringed instruments. The *24 Caprices for Violin* were for a long time a benchmark in technical bravura and elegance, and today his violin concertos (of which there are six extant) receive regular performances and recordings. The fact

DON'T MISS

▶ **24 Caprices, Op. 1 (1801–07)**
▶ **Violin Concerto No. 1, Op. 6 (1817)**
▶ **Violin Concerto No. 2, Op. 7 (1826)**
▶ **Moto perpetuo in C, Op. 11**
▶ **Grand Sonata for Violin and Guitar, Op. posth.**

that Schumann, Liszt, Brahms and Rachmaninov all used his themes for sets of variations show that his work

has consistently been studied and enjoyed by some of the best composers of subsequent generations.

CARL MARIA VON WEBER
1786-1826

Weber was one of the first composers to respond emotionally and intellectually to the darker forces in mankind as portrayed by the Gothic and German romantic writers. His highly-charged, at times terrifying, treatment of the supernatural levels of action in his opera *Der Freischütz* could hardly be more distant from the balance and gentle humour Mozart brought to those in *Die Zauberflöte*.

Carl Maria came from a musically gifted family; his father was the brother of Fridolin Weber, father of the Constanze who married Mozart. Carl Maria's father, director of the band of Eutin, near Lübeck, where Carl Maria was born, was determined that he should have a child prodigy like Mozart, but none of his children fulfilled such a quixotic wish. In 1787 the father became director of a

travelling dramatic company, in which he was joined by his wife, a talented singer. Thus Carl Maria spent his first years experiencing the life of a travelling player. As his father's music lessons proved inadequate, he was taught by a man called Heuschkel in Hildburghausen who gave him a thorough grounding in keyboard technique and the art of composition. Weber never forgot this early training, writing many years later of his gratitude to this thorough and painstaking man who, to a pupil who already possessed an affinity for the theatre unparalleled by any other composer, gave an unusually sound theoretical base.

Before a year was out, however, the family had moved on again; although Weber enjoyed a brief period in Salzburg under the tutelage of Michael Haydn (Joseph's highly gifted brother), when his mother died of consumption the Weber family moved first to

Munich and then to Freiburg. In Freiburg his father procured a commission from a theatre company for Carl Maria (now aged 13) to write music for a libretto, *Das Waldmädchen*. The work was staged by the company in Vienna, Chemnitz, Prague and St Petersburg, and caused a stir. Carl Maria's remarkable gift for the stage is clearly demonstrated, even in such an immature work.

Another opera followed but met with little success. Weber, feeling the need for further musical training, met up with the great musicologist Abbé Vogler in Vienna in 1803 and spent the next two years "in diligent study of the various works of the great masters, whose method of construction, treatment of ideas, and use of means, we dissected together..." His studies with Vogler completed, he obtained a position as *Kapellmeister* at Breslau, a post he held until 1807 when Napoleon's defeat of the Prussians brought great insecurity to the region and led to the dismissal of the entire orchestra. He moved to Stuttgart where he became private sectretary to Duke Ludwig, the degenerate and corrupt brother of Frederic of Würtemberg. Still only an innocent of 21, Weber fell into the dissolute life of his employer and for a time lost sight of his musical ambitions. Yet his talents did not go unnoticed and he became music teacher to the Duke's children, also forming a close friendship with the *Kapellmeister* Franz Danzi, a talented composer. In 1810 the inevitable fall from grace occurred: the Duke's chicanery rebounded on his secretary; Weber was made a scapegoat and banished from

Würtemberg by the King. Weber saw this downfall as retribution for three wasted and dissolute years.

He was helped by Danzi, who gave him an introduction to the Mannheim *Kapellmeister,* Gottfried Weber (no relation). The latter arranged concerts of the young composer's music, including his first completed symphony. Further work as a pianist, composer and music critic followed, and in 1811 he was commissioned to write the music for the short comic opera *Abu Hassan.* It was at this time that he began his concert tours throughout the German-speaking lands, making many friends and useful contacts in the process. While in Berlin in 1812 he learned of

the death of his father in Mannheim, an event which for a time increased his sense of rootlessness and isolation. The following year he was appointed *Kapellmeister* to the music theatre in Prague. In his new role he proved himself to be a fine conductor, setting new standards for orchestral playing in the city and showing an instinctive understanding of dramatic pacing.

But Weber quickly realized there was a limit to what he could achieve in a provincial capital like Prague. He also had a personal reason for wanting to move on: he had long conducted a quixotic relationship with a young German operatic singer, Caroline Brandt, and wished to bring matters to a head. She was in Germany, unsure of her own feelings; he was in Prague. In the autumn of 1816 she and Weber travelled together to Berlin where they were both engaged to perform; they were married the following year. While working hard at various compositions, Weber heard that he had been appointed by the King of Saxony as *Kapellmeister* to the Dresden Court Opera, where he was to remain until his untimely death.

It was during this last period that Weber composed the works which made him such a profound influence on subsequent musical developments. He had always known that it was not in the type of music written by Haydn or Beethoven where his own genius lay, however much he might admire their achievements. His muse was more wayward, more idiosyncratic, more personalized. His deep love of drama and music for the stage, and his commitment to forms of musical composition which would allow his

Carl Maria von Weber

DON'T MISS

▶ Clarinet Concertos 1 & 2 (1811)

▶ Clarinet Quintet, Op. 34 (1815)

▶ Invitation to the Dance, Op. 34 (1815)

▶ Der Freischütz (1821)

▶ Oberon (1826)

muse room for expression, led him away from forms such as the sonata and the concept of absolute music. His attraction was towards music which told a story and dramas which contained elements of the fantastic, picturesque or grotesque.

In many ways Weber's new position in Dresden was ideal for it gave him daily experience of the best way to go about productions, tell stories and coax the maximum out of singers and musicians. Weber's greatest single work, the opera *Der Freischütz*, had been occupying his thoughts from the early days of his arrival in Dresden. He and his librettist friend, Johann Friedrich Kind, adapted Apel's gothic novel of the same name, completing the libretto in less than two weeks. The composition, however, was written over years, with a pattern emerging of intense work on the opera followed by long lay-offs when Weber was embroiled in activities for the Dresden Opera. The work was completed in the late spring of 1820. The previous summer he had taken time out to write one of his most delightful pieces, *Invitation to the Dance*, Op. 65. Following the completion of *Freischütz*, Weber accepted a commission for incidental music to a play, *Preciosa*. He also commenced work on a comic opera, *Die drei Pintos*, which was to remain uncompleted at his death.

The première of *Der Freischütz* took place in June 1821 in Berlin and it immediately became the centre of controversy. Nevertheless, the opera was a triumph, news of its success spreading rapidly throughout Germany and Austria. At a production in Vienna in March 1822, Weber took the podium, writing later in his diary: 'Greater enthusiasm there cannot be, and I tremble to think of the future, for it is scarcely possible to rise higher than this'.

Weber had just cause to be concerned about his future: stung by criticism from some conservative quarters that *Freischütz* lacked proper operatic form, he was determined to write a grand opera to silence such insinuations, and accepted an invitation to write one for the Kärntnertor Theatre in Vienna. With the librettist, Helmina von Chézy, he chose the subject of Euryanthe. The bulk of the opera was written during the summer of 1823 and premièred in Vienna in September. It did not succeed, due mainly to the incoherent plot and to Weber's decidedly innovative approach to the musical accompaniment in which his ideas of grand opera took a tangential curve away from those of previous generations, producing a more seamless and flowing drama which highlighted the libretto's weaknesses rather than disguised them.

By this time Weber's health was failing. Märschner, the composer of the gothic opera *Der Vampyr*, visited him in 1821 after settling in Dresden and the two men became friends. Märschner's record of their first meeting makes explicit reference to Weber's physical condition: 'The disease which was to carry him off had made its mark...the projecting cheek-bones, the general emaciation, told their own tale'. It was consumption, the same disease that had killed his mother. The failure of *Euryanthe* plunged him into a depression which further weakened him, and for a period in the summer of 1824 he lost all appetite, even for music.

A commission from Charles Kemble, the lessee of the Covent Garden Theatre (one of three London theatres to have success with *Freischütz*) to write an opera in English proved the catalyst which rekindled Weber's spirit. Aware of the cause of his physical decline, and realizing that he had months rather than years in which to secure the financial future of his wife and family, Weber agreed to write an opera on the subject of Oberon, and struck a particularly hard bargain over his fee: £1,000. On this basis the 37-year-old invalid set to work learning English— proving remarkably adept at the language—and spending the majority of his free time in Dresden and the spa at Ems composing the music to the libretto as it arrived from London. A meeting with the great poet Goethe during his journey to Ems was a great disappointment: Goethe completely failed to appreciate Weber's genius, and the two did not part friends. Weber had enjoyed more luck with Beethoven, however, and his Dresden production of *Fidelio* in 1823 had been the bridge to a cordial understanding between the two great composers.

Weber left Dresden for London in February 1826, travelling via Paris, where he was fêted by all and met the composer Cherubini. The *Oberon* première in April 1826 was a success, but as with *Euryanthe* the success did not last. There was no doubting the beauty of the music, but an unwieldy production and a skittish plot robbed the audience of the *Freischütz*-like thrills they were seeking. Weber lingered in London, exhausted by overseeing the opera's production and trying to gather enough strength for the journey back to Dresden and his family. It was not to be: he died during the night of 4 June 1826. He was buried in the graveyard at Moorfields Chapel with an enormous crowd in attendance and the music of Mozart's Requiem reverently performed by a

small band. It took 18 years for his body to be removed to Germany where it was at last interred in the family vault in Dresden. Richard Wagner gave the graveside oratory.

Weber's output was not vast in comparison with Bach, Beethoven or Mozart, and the key works are easily listed, with *Der Freischütz* at the top. But it is worth stressing the quality of his works for the clarinet, an instrument for which he had a great love. His three concerted works for clarinet and orchestra—the two Clarinet Concertos, Opp. 73 and 74, and the *Concertino for Clarinet,* Op. 26—were all written in 1811 as a result of a meeting in Munich with the brilliant clarinettist Heinrich Bärmann. These works are often mentioned, together with Mozart's late masterpiece, as the greatest concertos written for the instrument. Weber was equally inspired with his chamber music

for the instrument, the Clarinet Quintet, Op. 34 (1815) residing with those of Brahms and Mozart at the pinnacle of quintets written with the clarinet as lead.

Weber's two symphonies are less interesting, being early works (both dating from 1807) and both written out of necessity and a sense that he ought at least try the symphonic form. Even if he had never turned his attention to opera , there is no doubt that his orchestral, chamber and instrumental work would have been held in sufficient regard for his name to be venerated today, but it is his operatic achievement which made his name in his own lifetime and which placed him firmly at the centre of the embryonic Romantic movement in Western art-music. The heroic and the ghastly, the battles between good and evil, would all strike a chord in Richard Wagner's soul for he was to be the direct beneficiary of Weber's pioneering music.

GIACOMO MEYERBEER
1791–1864

Meyerbeer's cosmopolitanism was often referred to by his critics and detractors as a reason for the so-called inadequacies of his musical output. Far from being superficial, this broad outlook lay at the heart of his creative character. Born Jakob Liebmann Beer, the eldest son of a prosperous Jewish Berlin banking family, he was to spend time in Italy, change his first name to Giacomo, then live and

experience unparalleled success in Paris.

Jakob appears to have inherited his innate musicality from his mother, Amalie Wulf, who was said to possess exceptional mental and intellectual powers. As the eldest son, Jakob was able to choose his own career and was given piano lessons at an early age; before his tenth birthday he was recognized as a prodigy. His maternal grandfather, Liebmann Meyer Wulf, granted his grandson an income of

300,000 francs for life to free him to pursue his musical career, with one stipulation—that Jakob add 'Meyer' to his name; thus he became Jakob Meyer-Beer.

Jacob was tutored by a succession of musicians, spending from 1810 to 1813 in the Darmstadt household of the famed Abbé Vogler. Carl Maria von Weber was a fellow student and the two became lifelong friends. By 1813 two of Meyerbeer's early operas had been produced: *Jephthas Gelübde* (a rather dry and overly formal work which failed in Munich) and a comic opera, *Alimelek*, which made little impact at its Viennese première. His ability was recognized, however, by professionals in the Austrian capital who saw in him a great pianistic talent. Antonio Salieri felt Meyerbeer only needed to come to terms with the human voice to write great operas, and advised a period in Italy. Meyerbeer duly travelled to Venice where his first Rossini opera utterly bewitched him. So completely did he fall under Rossini's spell that all the operas Meyerbeer completed between 1816 and 1824 were little more than neatly turned but slavish imitations of the Rossini style.

However, in 1816, entranced by the soprano Hélène Harlas and the virtuosity of the clarinettist Heinrich Bärmann, he composed an unusual cantata, *Gli Amori di Teolinda*, with soprano and clarinet solo roles, which demonstrated his ability to construct original compositions. The last of the series of Rossini-inspired operas, *Il Crociato in Egitto* (Venice, 1824), easily the most substantial up to then, enjoyed productions in Munich and London before being staged in Paris by Rossini himself in 1826. While in Paris Meyerbeer met the librettist and playwright Eugène Scribe; from the first they hit it off artistically and

DON'T MISS

▶ Robert le Diable (1831)
▶ Les Huguenots (1836)
▶ Le Prophète (1849)
▶ L'Etoile du nord (1854)
▶ L'Africaine (1865)

personally, and when Meyerbeer had to return to Berlin to attend to his family's affairs after the sudden death of his father, it was with a libretto by Scribe in his luggage.

The year 1826 proved a pivotal one for the young composer for not only did he become the head of his immediate family, but he also married his cousin, Minna Mosson and settled in Berlin to start a family and ruminate on the type of opera he would next produce. With the loss of two children who died in infancy, between 1826 and 1831 no work was produced. But convinced that his future lay in Paris, Meyerbeer began a systematic study of earlier French opera—as far back as Lully—and of French literature, until he felt ready to embark upon a French subject. He also maintained close contact with operatic developments abroad, especially when Rossini delivered his late masterpiece, *Guillaume Tell* (1829). By early 1830 he was ready to try out his ideas for a new type of French opera. The result was *Robert le Diable*, written to a Scribe libretto. It was produced in Paris in 1831 and with it came the virtual birth of 19th-century French grand opera, the genre which brought an integrated work in five acts plus ballet to the stage and treated the audience to an overwhelming spectacle of fast-moving scenes played out against a dramatic historical background. Once the work had been accepted at the Opéra, and with no financial constraints to hinder him, Meyerbeer rehearsed the cast for five months in order to achieve exactly the opera he and Scribe had envisaged. The result was a spectacular triumph and the birth of a new operatic era in France, one which today would be called a multi-media event, utilizing

and drawing together in one work every level of audience appreciation then available.

Within a few years *Robert le Diable* had introduced Meyerbeer's name and style of opera throughout the world. Never ones to change a winning formula, Meyerbeer and Scribe chose the period of the persecution of the Huguenots to create *Les Huguenots* (1836), a work huge in scale and effect, dwelling on the wonderful contrasts between the two utterly opposed worlds of the Protestant Hugenots and the colourful, charismatic standard-bearers of French Catholicism. Perhaps musically superior to its predecessor and more skilfully interwoven on every level, *Les Huguenots* took a little while to triumph in Paris, but was soon acknowledged worldwide to be Meyerbeer's best opera yet.

Meyerbeer did not take his popularity for granted: for him each new production was a make-or-break situation, and his excessive nervousness compelled him to check and recheck every little detail of an operatic work, from the lighting to the auditorium layout, until there was nothing left to chance. This may indicate an underlying lack of confidence in his abilities; it may also hint at a perfectionist and a neurotic who, being both a Jew and a German at work in Paris, felt twice the outsider and therefore twice the anxiety to succeed.

Meyerbeer's next undertaking with Scribe, *L'Africaine* (begun in 1838), finally came to grief through Meyerbeer's inability to control his compulsion to rewrite scenes and to demand libretto rewrites of rewrites. By

1842 the opera was all but complete, yet Meyerbeer persisted in tinkering until Scribe withdrew his—by now—unrecognisable libretto, leaving Meyerbeer with nothing to show for four years' work. Undaunted, Meyerbeer offered Scribe a new opportunity with the story of true and false prophets, *Le Prophète*; such was their joint enthusiasm for the project that it was completed within a year, and its short gestation period certainly helped to create one of Meyerbeer's most impressively unified and sustained dramatic works where his mastery of vocal and orchestral forces reached a new peak.

By this stage Meyerbeer's influence on other opera composers was as considerable as Rossini's had been when he was at his zenith. Both Wagner and Verdi found in Meyerbeer's work models for their own very different operatic methodologies. Meyerbeer had elevated spectacle and entertainment to a new level and, while his characters had little real emotional or psychological depths, that had never been his intention. His role, as he saw it, was to create a wholly convincing and entertaining evening of music drama.

With *Le Prophète*, Meyerbeer's career climaxed; the year before its composition he had been made Music Director to the King's Court in Berlin, a post he held until 1849, the year *Le Prophète* was premièred. The opera was successful, but took some time to win audiences around the world. By the beginning of the new decade his health was showing signs of breaking down. In a quest for quicker results (there had been a 13-year gap between the

Giacomo Meyerbeer

premières of *Les Huguenots* and *Le Prophète*), he decided to exert himself in a new direction, producing in 1854 a charming and deliberately lightweight opera, *L'Etoile du nord*. The work was generally successful in Paris and led to a follow-up, *Le Pardon de Ploermel* (1859). Yet the opera he had originated with Scribe in 1838, *L'Africaine*, dominated his thoughts, and he spent the first three years of the 1860s preparing it for production and trying to assemble the perfect cast.

Finally he had all the elements in place to his satisfaction, and a production was scheduled for 1864.

With rehearsals under way, his always unsteady health finally gave way and in May 1864 he died. *L'Africaine* was given its début performance, lasting no less than six hours, at the Opéra in April 1865, receiving a muted welcome. Subsequent productions have regularly made cuts, which have added little to the coherence of the plot or characters, and it is only in very recent times that any kind of attempt has been made to revert to Meyerbeer's full-length score. With the general level of acceptance of grand opera rising after an abeyence, the time for a full reappraisal of Meyerbeer's final work—indeed his entire output—is fast approaching.

GIOACCHINO ROSSINI

1792–1868

Rossini's achievement in launching the world-wide popularity of the updated *opera buffa* genre caused reverberations which have continued up to the present day. His fine dramatic judgement, allied to an inexhaustible musical vitality and hard-headed pragmatism, gave him virtually unbroken operatic success between 1813 and 1829, and made Italian opera the envy of the world.

Rossini was born in Pésaro, the only child of Giuseppi, the town trumpeter (and apparently its inspector of slaughterhouses), and Anna, a talented singer. His mother's talent proved fortunate when Giuseppi was gaoled in 1800 for expressing his political opinions; taking four-year-old Gioacchino with her, Anna secured a *prima buffa* singing role in Bologna where Giuseppi joined them on his release from prison.

While in Bologna Gioacchino received his first music lessons. By the age of 10 he was able to carry out musical tasks such as accompaniment and church music. When his mother's voice deteriorated and she was unable to find work, young Rossini's earnings became essential. He earned more than money, however: a well-meaning patron by the name of Chevalier Giusti showed his admiration for the boy's talent by taking him under his wing and preparing him for a more formal

Gioacchino Rossini

musical education. By the time he was 15, Gioacchino was ready to enter Bologna's Liceo Communale, where he was put in Padre Stanislao Mattei's counterpoint class. Rossini and Mattei never saw eye to eye; strictly of the old school, Mattei insisted upon the delights of counterpoint while Rossini wanted to learn just enough to enable him to begin composing operas. At the age of 18, Rossini finished his studies at the Liceo and was commissioned to write a one-act *opera buffa*. The result, *La cambiale di matrimonio*, was premièred in Venice and was

sufficiently successful for him to write some six more one-acters over the next 12 months, capped by his first La Scala production in late autumn 1812, the two-acter *La pietra del paragone*. Rossini was on the verge of stardom.

This was to come with his next two operas, *Tancredi* and *L'Italiana in Algeri*, both produced in Venice in 1813 to overwhelming acclaim. Rossini's melodic gifts and wonderful dramatic sense, allied to his irrepressible humour and the sheer impetus of his operas had a powerful impact on his audience. An invitation to compose for Milan confirmed his widening popularity, although the operas written for production there (which included *Il Turco in Italia*) were not immediate successes, and he had to wait until 1815 and Naples for his next triumph. This was for the *opera seria, Elisabetta, Regina d'Inghilterra*, a work occasionally revived today, and which is notable in Rossini's oeuvre for being the first for which he wrote out the vocal ornamentation, thus removing the opportunity for prima donnas to introduce their own set-pieces into his music and destroy its unity. *Elisabetta* was also an opera from which Rossini made a number of borrowings for his most famous work, written (according to Rossini in less than a fortnight) for Rome's Teatro Argentina, *Il Barbiere di Siviglia*. It is worth pointing out, however, that parts of *Elisabetta* had been lifted from *Aureliano*, one of the Milan disappointments of 1814: in this, Rossini was only confirming a habit practised by many composers, great and mediocre, of self-plagiarism.

Certainly the borrowing did not adversely affect *Il Barbiere*, which remains today one of the jewels of the opera stage, an ever amusing, beautifully paced and genuinely comical opera whose good-humoured and delicious absurdities, wrapped in the most energetic and melodious music, never fail to please. Not that the first-night audience in Rome agreed; they were still loyal to the opera of the same name written by Paisiello, and only grudgingly gave their support, but by the second performance, all resistance was swept away by Rossini fever.

His connection with Naples grew in significance as the operas continued to come. While he was writing witty and entertaining *opera buffas* for other Italian cities, for Naples between 1815 and 1822 he was serving up an unbroken line of *opera seria* which, although not so popular today, served to make him the idol of the Neapolitans. During this time he was not only composing for the Naples impresario Domenico Barbaia, but working as musical and artistic director for the same theatres. His taste, then, became paramount. His taste in women also became artistically important, as he and the prima donna Isabella Colbran began an affair which was to culminate in marriage in Bologna in 1822. He wrote music to suit her florid, dramatic style of singing all the years he was based in Naples, and this is a distinguishing trait of his *opera seria*. Of the operas written for Naples during this time, *Otello* (1817) stands out as a key work, especially in the third act where Rossini handles Desdemona's doom with utter authority. *Armida* (1817) and *Ermione* (1819) demonstrated Rossini's ability to retain a tight grip on the drama without abandoning his dedication to his fertile production of musical ideas.

Outside Naples, Rossini still had an audience eager for more *opera buffa*, especially in the wake of *Il Barbiere*. The follow-up, *La Cenerentola* (modelled on the Cinderella story, but stripped of all supernatural elements), was a massive early-1817 success in Rome, and today is second perhaps only to *Il Barbiere* in popularity. As usual, it borrowed from earlier works, especially *La Gazzetta* and *Il Turco in Italia*, and this occasionally mars its overall

impact, but the characterization and plot is mature and satisfying. *La Gazza ladra* (The Thieving Magpie), which contains one of Rossini's most famous overtures, is a pot boiler of an opera with copious padding, and shifts uneasily between the comic and the serious, but it was a hit in Milan.

Meanwhile in Naples, Rossini was taking musical strides with works such as *La Donna del lago* (1819), *Zelmira* and the superb *Semiramide* (Venice, 1823). Within these works he was pushing *opera seria* to new boundaries and making decisive moves away from his first mature style into an openly more Romantic approach to his subjects and their settings.

The 1820s were the years when Rossini's reputation became international, from London to St Petersburg. Two visits to Vienna in 1822, where *Cenerentola* was given in February, were followed by a series of cantatas for the Congress of Vienna which proved beyond doubt that his music was truly international in appeal. A trip to London via Paris in 1823 was illuminating and flattering, and laid the foundations of his return to Paris in the late summer as musical director of the Théâtre Italien. Once ensconced he introduced some vibrant new singers and musicians to revitalise the company, including Hérold and Meyerbeer (Rossini staged *Crociato,* the first Meyerbeer opera to be heard in Paris). He also gave productions of his own operas which had yet to receive Paris premières and wrote a new opera for the 1825 season, *Il viaggio a Reims,* timed to celebrate the coronation of King Charles X. Withdrawn by the composer after the festivities had ended, the work was plundered heavily by Rossini for *Le Comte Ory,* his 1828 French-language comic opera, and forgotten for 150 years until its rediscovery in the 1980s.

Rossini's position in Paris was elevated still higher in 1826 when a new contract allowed him to write for the Paris Opéra, and the government awarded him the titles *Premier compositeur du Roi* and *Inspecteur général du chant en France.* In this guise he presented his late masterpiece in the heroic mould, *Guillaume Tell* (1829). This work, a long and often misunderstood epic opera (with a ridiculously famous overture), was originally conceived as the first of five new works for Paris. But events overtook Rossini's intentions: his mother died in 1827, leaving his father

alone and Rossini began to feel that his place was in Bologna with what little family remained. His decision was eased by the French government's overthrow and Charles X's abdication in July 1830. Rossini, then in Bologna, resolved to return to Paris to settle his affairs and then move to Italy. Law suits to retrieve the money owed him kept him in Paris until 1836, but no more operas were written.

Rossini spent the rest of his life in leisured retirement from opera composing. A lavish entertainer of his friends and a fine cook, he even wrote a recipe book which was circulated amongst a favoured few. His travels were extensive, especially after his separation from his wife Isabella. He refused all offers to write further operas, and as time passed and Bellini, Donizetti and Verdi came on the scene, his compositional style became more remote from what was fashionable, so his judgement may well have been astute. In 1845 Isabella died, and Rossini, now 53, married his Parisian mistress, the celebrated beauty Olympe Pélissier.

Middle age proved difficult for him and for a time he suffered considerable mental anguish. A move back to Paris in 1855 was the start of a personal rehabilitation for the composer, and in the 1860s he even began composing small piano pieces—works he described as 'trifles' and which he called *Sins of Old Age.* In 1864 came the misleadingly titled *Petite Messe Solennelle,* a choral work of considerable length and no little wit. In 1867 he wrote a cantata for the Exposition Universelle, but by now his physical health was no longer sound: in November 1868, after a short but painful illness, he died aged 76. His funeral at the Church of the Trinité was virtually a state occasion.

GAETANO DONIZETTI
1797–1848

Donizetti was the master of the *bel canto* style of opera, which allowed for florid vocal writing married to a clear and attractive melody. His music called for an extraordinary vocal agility on the part of his lead singers, especially his sopranos and mezzos, as well as a degree of

technical accuracy rarely called for previously.

Born into a large family in the north Italian town of Bergamo, Donizetti showed his musical talents early. He attended the Bergamo Musical Institute, where he was tutored by the Bavarian, Johann Mayr. Mayr was a

successful Italian-language operatic composer, and undoubtedly awoke a love for opera in his young pupil. In 1814 Donizetti went to the Liceo Filarmonico in Bologna, recently attended by Rossini, where he was taught by Rossini's old counterpoint master, Padre Mattei. Again like Rossini, Donizetti experienced a divergence of

Gaetano Donizetti

Barbaia as well as accepting commissions from Milan, Rome and Genoa. This situation continued until 1830, and although his operatic technique matured in these years—his own melodic voice emerging as distinct from Rossini's, who still remained the dominant influence in Italian opera—none of these early works have survived in terms of regular (or even isolated) performances today. His private life, meanwhile, continued to flourish, and in 1828 he married Virginia Vasselli—a good match, as she came from a prosperous family.

His first major success came in 1830. This was *Anna Bolena*, one of five operas produced by Donizetti that year. It was premièred in Milan, starring big names such as Pasta and Rubini, and introducing Lablache. Within three years it had triumphed in London, Paris, Vienna and Madrid, decisively establishing his international reputation—together with Bellini—as the heir to Rossini's operatic legacy. With *Anna Bolena* he had risen beyond the *opera buffa* and farces of his previous years, and composed a fine romantic opera utilizing the still-evolving *bel canto* style of singing and presentation. His characterization was vivid, his pacing superb. Although he took another two years to find another opera libretto worthy of his talents (*L'Elisir d'amore*, Milan 1832), *Anna Bolena* had given him a permanent place at opera's high table.

The remainder of the decade was packed with events: for every new triumph (*Lucretia Borgia,* Milan 1833, based on Victor Hugo's play), there was at least one failure, usually due to intransigent singers or capricious and

views with the old man, and was relieved to return in 1817 to Bergamo. With Mayr's help, he was commissioned by the Venetian impresario Paolo Zancla to write a series of operas; none of these works have survived in Donizetti's repertoire—nor do they really justify a revival, being works which betray an immature hand. At this stage of his career Donizetti was prepared to write anything to commission, composing orchestral, instrumental and choral music—often a piece a day—utilizing his famous intensity of concentration to accomplish such prodigious feats. Other characteristics were also fast becoming notable: his charm, and his attraction for the opposite sex.

It was to be another four years before Donizetti achieved his major breakthrough, and once again it was Mayr who brought it about. By turning over to his acolyte a commission from Rome's Teatro Argentina, Mayr presented Donizetti with an ideal opportunity to make a splash with the opera *Zoraide di Granata*. Donizetti did not disappoint: the Romans took to the opera wholeheartedly. Returning from one performance, his carriage was illuminated by a torchlight procession as a mark of approbation. *Zoraide's* success led directly to Donizetti being offered a role in Naples similar to the one just vacated by Rossini: he was to write between two and five operas a year for the Neapolitan impresario over-sensitive censors. *Maria Stuarda*, with its regicidal ending, fell foul of both types of interference in 1834–5, and it was only much later that its true worth came to be appreciated. Similarly, *Poliuto* (1838) was banned outright by the censors due to its depiction of a saint's martyrdom. Considering that in Naples Donizetti had no control over the subject-matter of his operas (chosen, as stipulated in his contract, by the theatre), this state of affairs was absurd and insufferable. It proved to be the spur for Donizetti to leave a city which had lost its appeal when, in 1837, two events occurred which shattered his equanamity: a victim of perennial intrigues, he was passed over for the post of Director of Naples Conservatoire. This was followed by a much more personal loss: the death of his wife during a cholera epidemic. Donizetti was devastated.

But work had always been his salvation. Disenchanted with Naples he decided to go to Paris, arriving there in October 1838. His diligence, industry and talent quickly won him a dedicated audience. With a ready supply of Italian-language operas, all he had to do was translate them into French, and by 1840 he had

DON'T MISS

▶ Anna Bolena (1830)
▶ L'Elisir d'amore (1832)
▶ Lucia di Lammermoor (1835)
▶ La Favorita (1840)
▶ La Fille du régiment (1840)
▶ Don Pasquale (1843)

Poliuto (now entitled *Les Martyrs*), *La Favorita* and *La Fille du régiment* all in production, with only *Les Martyrs* not garnering the success he had hoped for.

With Paris at his feet and Italian operatic style triumphant, Donizetti felt that after a few more years of hard work he could plan for a long retirement. With this in mind he plunged into writing a new series of operas and undertook a great deal of travelling. He was in Rome for the 1841 première of *Adelia*; in Milan for the first night of the dramatic opera *Maria Padilla*; and in Vienna for the April 1842 opening of *Linda di Chamounix*, a romantic work which proved an unqualified success. A mark of this success came with his appointment as *Kapellmeister* to the Austrian Emperor, while the previous month his *Stabat Mater* had been given its Italian première in Bologna. But Donizetti saved his best work for Paris: in February 1843 came the marvellous *opera buffa* entitled *Don Pasquale*, premièred at the Théâtre-Italien. This perfectly judged comic work has been irresistible since its first night, and has rarely been absent from the footlights in one major city or another. It stands beside *Falstaff* and *Barbiere* as a supreme example of 19th-century Italian comic opera.

More was to come, but the rest of his life was lived under the shadow of increasing physical and mental stress brought on by the advent of tertiary syphilis. Just three more operas remained to be written by a composer who had managed close to 60 up to that point in his life, and was previously capable of turning out five operas a year. The next to be written

(but the last to be produced) was *Caterina Cornaro*, premièred in Naples in 1844. *Maria di Rohan* opened in Vienna in 1843, and was a typical Donizetti melodrama, showing little sign of any failing control of his musical materials. *Dom Sebastien* was his last new work for Paris, and was first seen in November 1843, receiving mixed reviews. The Paris rehearsals had been more than usually taxing, Donizetti having to referee in a feud between the soprano and baritone leads. At one point the exhausted composer threw his score on the floor and left the theatre, shaking with anger and so unsteady on his feet that he had to be guided to his carriage. He never completely regained his former balance. This last work, dragged out of himself through sheer determination and against a backdrop of increasing difficulties with concentration and bouts of melancholia, is as inconsistent as one would expect, and not helped by a leaden and patchy libretto.

After this the composer's compositional pen was silenced by his illness, and his letters, once so prolific, to his friends and family, tailed off. Final visits to Austria and Italy left him drained, and he sank into an irreversible state. His brother sent one of his sons to care for him, and the son, André, found him in a shocking state of physical decline and mental disorder, including constant delusions of being robbed. A medical report from January 1846 recommended that he should be hospitalized for his own good, and a suitable place was found in Ivry. Donizetti's fear and grief were immense, and he sent a stream of heartbreaking letters to friends and acquaintances, pleading with them to rescue him.

His decline was swift, and confinement no longer necessary. He was taken back to Bergamo, where an aristocratic family cared for him. He was visited by many of his old friends and colleagues, but showed no sign of comprehension, even when they sang or played his own music. He died after a short fever on 8 April 1848.

The famous 'mad scene' in *Lucia di Lammermoor* (an opera based on Sir Walter Scott's *The Bride of Lammermoor*) is one of the classic examples of quintessential Donizetti operatic style, with its heightened emotions, vocal dominance of all other musical matters, and its extreme changes of melodic and dramatic approach—from a scream to a whisper, indeed. Yet there is nothing ugly in Donizetti's music: his rhythm is as balanced and elegant as his melodies, and the vocal sounds remain *dolce* even at their most extreme. Excelling in many types of opera, including farce, *opera buffa* and melodrama, Donizetti generally managed a superb example of each genre, with *Don Pasquale* a wonderful comic opera and *Anna Bolena* a marvellous tragic work. Donizetti has often been dismissed, together with Bellini, as a transitional figure between Rossini and Verdi, although lacking Rossini's theatrical surety and Verdi's humanity. But this is to seriously undervalue him, and his best works stand as some of the great high points of 19th-Italian opera of any school.

FRANZ SCHUBERT

1797–1828

Schubert's life is the quintessential example of the Romantic notion of the neglected genius who dies in obscurity. Even Mozart, who probably had a harsher life and greater obstacles to overcome, was at least accorded a modicum of recognition in his own lifetime. For Schubert, an entire generation had to pass before his most substantial achievements saw the light of day.

Franz Schubert is the one 'Viennese' composer who was truly Viennese born and bred. One of five children out of nine who survived infancy he came from a modest schoolmaster's family living in Vienna's Lichtenthal district. His father, Franz Theodor, was a keen amateur musician and quickly detected his son's talent, giving him violin lessons while the oldest brother taught him piano. After a short interlude with a private teacher, Franz was accepted as a choir-boy in the Court chapel which automatically admitted him as a pupil to the Imperial and Royal City College. There he benefitted greatly from contact with men such as Salieri and Phillip Körner, and wrote his first compositions. Schubert achieved satisfactory results in all subjects, but his musical abilities were recognized by all as exceptional. In 1812 his mother died: his father remarried the following year. Always close to his father, Franz grew to love his stepmother Anna, who in later years helped him with loans of money. While at the College Schubert experienced his first opera performances, and also discovered the music of Beethoven and Mozart. He held the latter in the greatest awe: 'O Mozart, immortal Mozart!' he wrote in 1816, 'what numberless consoling images of a better, brighter world have you engraved upon our souls!'

When he left the College in 1814, Schubert taught at his father's school, though this had little effect on his enthusiasm for composition. Indeed, that autumn his *Mass No. 1 in F* was performed to great acclaim, also his first *lieder* masterpiece, 'Gretchen am Spinnrade' (to words from Goethe's *Faust*); he was just 17. The following year was even more impressive: symphonies, operas (no less than four attempted in one year), chamber music and nearly 150 songs spilled from his pen, all written out of a determination to earn money from his music so that he could escape the need for earning it through his detested teaching. Of the songs, the Goethe setting, 'Der Erlkönig', is the most remarkable and most famous. A friend sent this and 30 other Goethe settings to the great man

Franz Schubert

noticeably when he returned to the hated teaching. The following summer he became music master to the children of Count Johann Esterházy in Zseliz (in Hungary, hundreds of miles from Vienna), and broke forever his ties with schoolteaching. After a fitful summer at the Zseliz residence, Schubert returned to Vienna with the Esterházy family, but took up lodgings with his poet friend Mayrhofer. He continued to teach the Esterházy children while 'living out'.

Schubert's life remained uneventful until the summer of 1819 when he joined Vogl on a trip to the country, spending three of the happiest months of his life discovering countryside which he thought 'inconceivably lovely'. This trip had a beneficial effect on his creative juices, the wonderful *Trout* Quintet being conceived and begun at this time. Inspiration remained with Schubert all through the following autumn and winter in Vienna, compositions coming thick and fast. During his time with Mayrhofer, Schubert would often sleep in his clothes, or leave his glasses on overnight, indulging in typical bachelor behaviour and using the time-worn excuse that 'it saved time and trouble' when asked why he was so slovenly. He certainly was not lazy when it came to composing, commenting: "I compose every morning, and when one piece is done I begin another". The spring of 1819 had been spent writing the music for a third-rate one-act libretto, *Die Zwillingsbrüder*, which was staged in 1820 with Vogl taking both twin-brother roles. This relative failure (only five performances) led to a further commission for music for a three-act play, *Die Zauberharfe*. This was no

himself in Weimar. They were returned unaccompanied by any offer of help; Goethe did not appreciate Schubert's attempts to heighten the poet's words through his musical commentary.

'Der Erlkönig' was published in all the German-speaking territories and made Schubert famous outside his native city, and this led directly to a meeting with a young law student, Franz von Schober. Schober had come across 'Erlkönig' and the song had made such a deep impression on him that he determined to meet its creator. He suggested to Schubert that they take lodgings together at Schober's expense. With his father's consent, the 19-year-

old Franz moved in to rooms in Schober's mother's house. While there he was introduced to the baritone Johann Michael Vogl, a successful operatic singer, who was so excited by Schubert's songs that within a few weeks the pair were performing concerts for Viennese society.

In 1817 Schubert branched out into piano sonatas and before the end of the year he had also written three more of his most famous songs: 'Der Tod und das Mädchen', 'An die Musik' and 'Die Forelle'. By then, however, he had been obliged to move back to his family home—the Schober idyll was over and his work rate slackened better than the one-acter which preceded it, but Schubert's music shone out: the overture, for example, was later reused in *Rosamunde*, and thus gained immortality. Schubert's reputation in Vienna was hardly well-served by such failures, and he was never to see another presentation of his theatrical music.

Schubert moved from Mayrhofer's rooms to the house of a new friend, the amateur painter Moritz von Schwind, and was soon at work on one of his most striking Goethe compositions, a setting for four tenors and four basses, with string accompaniment, 'Gesang der Geister über den Wassern' (D714), the work's mystical element holding great significance for him. Schubert's songs were now receiving fairly regular performances by his friends and colleagues in Vienna, and it is singular that he consistently failed to have them accepted for publication by local publishers. Frustrated by this intransigence, his supporters funded a sponsored publication of 'Erlkönig' by the Viennese firm Cappi & Diabelli. This and seven other sponsored publications did so well that Cappi & Diabelli afterwards published Schubert direct and at their own risk. Schubert also managed to raise some much needed income by dedicating these pieces to wealthy patrons.

The ambition to compose weightier material continued to haunt him, and in August 1821 he attempted his Symphony No. 7 in E (D729), but this was only completed in full score up to the 110th bar; the rest was left marked down on a single line, accompanied by detailed annotation as to how the missing parts would be completed later

which, of course, never happened. In recent years this and the other unfinished symphonies (Schubert only completed one of his many symphonic projects) have been given orchestral 'realizations' which enable the music-lover to hear brilliant and exploratory works otherwise condemned to perpetual obscurity.

Schubert had returned to live at Schober's house, but was now immersed in a triangular friendship of great intimacy with Moritz von Schwind and a young playwright, Eduard Bauernfeld. The composer meanwhile persisted with his attempts to mount a successful opera, and in 1822 completed *Alfonso und Estrella* (D732). It was never produced, the libretto (by Schober) falling foul of Vogl's censure and therefore not receiving his influential backing. Three other events made this a pivotal year in Schubert's life. In April he met Beethoven, a meeting achieved by the presentation of his *Variations on a French Air, Op. 10* (with a fulsome dedication) to Beethoven by a mutual friend. Accounts of the meeting are unrealiable, but there is reason to believe that Beethoven enjoyed the *Variations* enough to keep the music in his possession. The second event was

the writing—and abandonment—of the famous Eighth Symphony (*Unfinished*), although by now Schubert had a number of unfinished symphonies to his name. The multiplicity of reasons advanced for the abandonment of this sublime two-movement torso tend to prove that no-one really knows why Schubert stopped writing it. What is beyond dispute is that he presented the manuscript the following year to his friend Anselm Hüttenbrenner. The work disappeared until 1865, when Hüttenbrenner allowed it to be performed in one of the Viennese Gesellschaft concerts and published the following year. This work was a clear statement from Schubert that he had found his own original approach to symphonic form.

The third event of 1822 was a tragic one: Schubert discovered that he had contracted syphilis. This discovery, and the illness which accompanied its initial onset, forced Schubert to return to the parental home. Until late spring 1823 he was too ill to leave the house, and this frightening collapse in one so young (he was just 25) led to a near-suicidal depression. A spell in Vienna General Hospital seems to have helped, and he composed all through this dark period of suffering,

DON'T MISS

▶ An die Musik, D547 (1819)
▶ Piano Quintet in A (Trout) D667 (1819)
▶ Symphony No. 8 (Unfinished) D759 (1822)
▶ Die schöne Müllerin, D795 (1823)
▶ Piano Sonata No. 14, D784 (1823)
▶ String Quartet No. 14, (Death and the Maiden) D810 (1824)

completing the Piano Sonata in A minor (D784) and another one-act opera, *Die Verschworenen*. During the summer he left hospital and travelled to Linz and Steyr, beginning yet another doomed opera, *Fierrabras* (D796), set to yet another poor libretto, and composing the first songs of the immortal cycle, *Die schöne Müllerin*. His health remained pracarious throughout the year, only stabilizing as winter took hold and the *Müllerin* cycle was completed.

It is possible that Schubert felt he had overcome his affliction, but the disease had only entered its second phase. From this time on his previously carefree and sunny disposition became more troubled, his moods unpredictable. The year 1823 closed with yet another theatre-music failure, this time the play *Rosamunde*, written by Helmina von Chézy. It managed just two performances, then vanished into oblivion. The orchestral music Schubert mustered for this play eventually proved to be some of his most popular. In spring 1824 Schubert turned to chamber music: among the masterpieces to emerge was the quartet *Der Tod und das Mädchen*, which used variations on the song of the same name. The magnificent Octet in F (D803) followed soon after. This, plus the publication of the first part of *Die schöne Müllerin*, made this a special spring. Yet Schubert's mood was dark. He wrote to a friend at this time: 'Think of a man whose health can never be restored, and who from sheer despair makes matters worse instead of better. Think of a man...to whom love and friendship are a torture... every night I go to sleep hoping never to wake again...'

Schubert spent much of 1824 once again with the Esterházys in Zseliz; the slow pace of life seems to have been beneficial, although he chafed at having to teach again. The following year was notable for the steady increase in the number of his songs being published and the resultant spread of his reputation beyond Vienna. A summer holiday with Vogl in the country gave him the happiness and peace of mind which had been so conspicuously absent the previous spring. Here he began work on his Symphony No. 9 (*Great*) in C, the first to be completed in more than six years. His return to Vienna in September initiated a twelve month period of great conviviality in and around Vienna with the famous musical evenings among his friends and admirers—known as the Schubertiads—standing out in the memory of all who attended them. Schubert and Schwind remained particularly close during this time, sharing lodgings, food, clothes and money. To Schubert, Schwind was 'seine Geliebte' (his beloved).

Early 1827 was memorable for Schubert's commencement of the first songs in *Die Winterreise* and for the death of Beethoven. Schubert had visited the fading genius shortly before his death, and was one of the torchbearers in his funeral procession. Notices of Schubert's numerous *lieder* publications at this time continued to multiply and spread across the German-speaking countries, yet his major instrumental achievements were hardly known outside his circle of close friends. He completed *Winterreise* by the end of 1827, the emotional profundity of the music echoing the bleak depths of the verses being set. His health was again poor, with random headaches and dizziness; his moods were clearly reflected in his songs. The complexities of the *Impromptus* written at around this time are perhaps a prism through which his melancholia can be glimpsed.

In March 1828 a concert was organized in one of the Vienna Gesellschaft's private rooms which was a first-ever Schubert-only event. It was sold-out and filled with Schubert's friends, patrons and admirers. The programme was exclusively made up of *lieder* and chamber music. Schubert completed his Symphony No. 9 (*Great*) in C and for a time hoped it would receive a performance in Vienna, but this came to nothing. In September he moved in with his brother Ferdinand. Now suffering from regular headaches and nausea, he composed his last three Piano Sonatas, D 958, 959 and 960, as well as the famous song 'Der Hirt auf dem Felsen' (with clarinet obbligato). By now he was close to exhaustion, and a short walking tour confined him to bed. The syphilis was now claiming him, and on 19 November he died in his brother's bed. The funeral was a modest affair, his coffin borne by students to St Margaret's Church, and from thence to the Währing cemetery.

Ferdinand went to every conceivable effort to see his brother's music published (mostly by Diabelli & Co), but it was 1835 before a visit by Robert Schumann, by then an influential critic and budding composer, discovered the symphony manuscripts in Ferdinand's house and wrote about Schubert's genius after reading the score of the Ninth Symphony. He then arranged for its world première and a complete re-evaluation of Schubert's achievements paved the way for his true musical worth to at last reach a wider audience. A complete edition of his works appeared for the first time between 1884 and 1897.

PART V

1800-1825

A glance at the list of this period's composers is enough to confirm that the Romantic era of music had begun in earnest. In this it would be only right to include the Italian opera composers, for their attitudes and story lines—often extracted from Romantic novels such as those of Sir Walter Scott—were invariably steeped in Romanticism. Rossini's remarkable popularity had prepared European and American audiences for the feast of *cantilena* melody and vocal fireworks to be found in the *bel canto* operas of Donizetti and Bellini, together with their frequently melodramatic plots and characterization. Yet it took a genius of Verdi's dimensions to take Italian opera on to its next great stage of development. The world proved even more unprepared for Wagner's genius before at length capitulating so completely that no Western European composer of the century's final quarter could escape his influence, either by imitating it or by rejecting it outright.

Poster for Offenbach's four-act opera buffo Les Brigands, *1805*

Away from opera, in Germany the world of romance held sway, whether by Schumann's espousal of the cause of the recently deceased Schubert in bringing his own music forward, or whether it was the brilliant prodigy Mendelssohn launching confidently into virtually every musical genre. In Austria, Bruckner was a forerunner in the spiritual and artistic quest in music which later followers of Wagner would have to deal with in order to find their own distinct voices. France, as usual, found its own path through the Romantic thicket, with generous contributions from Eastern and Central Europen expatriates such as Chopin, Liszt and Offenbach (the latter with his tongue firmly in cheek), while indigenous talent such as Gounod helped define and redefine French Grand Opera (as originally rendered by Rossini and Meyerbeer), and Berlioz and Franck dragged French orchestral music into the modern era with works such as *Harold in Italy, Symphonie Fantastique* and *Symphonic Variations*.

This period also ushered in the first generation of musical nationalists—which should include Liszt—who would be touchstones for the later outburst of creativity in their native countries. Both Smetana in Bohemia and Glinka in Russia would become honoured as the virtual 'fathers' of their nations' modern musical cultures.

VINCENZO BELLINI

1801–1835

Bellini is often seen as the epitome of *bel canto* opera. This operatic genre is often associated with flimsy plots and a lack of characterization, but Bellini was gifted with the ability to paint a character in a few eloquent phrases, scrupulously avoiding mawkishness or excessive melodrama. As a link between Rossini and Verdi, he stands equally with Donizetti as a necessary stepping stone, while his operas are brilliant enough in themselves to pass scrutiny without the support of an historical context.

Bellini was born in Catania in Sicily, the son of an organist. At the age of five he was playing the piano fluently and writing his first compositions at the age of six. A Sicilian nobleman who enjoyed the boy's recitals in Catania paid for his further musical education. In June 1819, Vincenzo went to Naples where he studied at the Conservatoire under Niccolo Zingarelli. His training was thorough in both vocal and instrumental music, and his wedding cantata of 1824 shows the diligence of his studies. In 1825, having completed his course with honour, he was given the opportunity to compose an opera which would be staged in the Conservatoire's theatre. The result, *Adelson e Salvini*, was sufficiently impressive for him to be given a

Vincenzo Bellini

commission by the Teatro San Carlo's manager, Domenico Barbaia. Vincenzo's opera, *Bianca e Fernando*, was performed in May 1826 and was received well enough for Barbaia to entrust the 24-year-old with a commission for a new work to be given at La Scala in Milan.

The new opera, *Il Pirata,* was ready by October 1827. With a libretto written by Felice Romani, a superior writer with whom Bellini forged a formidable creative partnership, the opera's simple melodic elegance and dramatic unity was something fresh and different to an audience weaned on the colour, spectacle and elaboration of a Rossini opera. The clarity of line stressed by Bellini in his work was embraced wholeheartedly by the great tenor Rubini, who would be an important champion of subsequent Bellini operas. *Il Pirata* made Bellini's reputation far beyond Italy's borders; over the next few years it was performed in all the great centres, including Vienna, Paris and London.

As Milan had proved a lucky city for Bellini, he took up residence there and acquired two new operatic commissions: *La Straniera,* a limited success, and *Zaira,* a failure. He also took a mistress, Giuditta Turina, with whom he had a passionate but informal relationship for the next five years. Bellini was now making a comfortable living from the proceeds of his operas, and his reputation was such that he was in demand for new works throughout Italy. His next work, *I Capuleti ed i Montecchi,* was premièred at the Teatro La Fenice in Venice in 1830 and was wildly successful. After a summer holiday recovering from a serious attack of gastroenteritis, Bellini wrote *La Sonnambula,* the first of a string of operas which would make his name immortal in opera circles. It was

premièred in March 1831 at the Teatro Carcano in Milan. The pastoral story and its gentle pathos suited Bellini's style of melody and simple eloquence to perfection, and the work had an immediate and lasting effect on its audiences. In a letter to a friend after the first night Bellini commented: 'Rubini and Pasta are two angels who enraptured the entire audience to the verge of madness'.

The next opera to appear on Milan's stages (this time at La Scala) is generally regarded as Bellini's masterpiece; this was *Norma,* the dramatic story of a Druid priestess. Forever associated in each generation with a string of charismatic female leads, this work is a tragedy which has a perfect dramatic shape and music which avoids bathos while stirring the emotions of the audience to a level of keen sympathy.

A failure with *Beatrice di Tenda* in Venice early in 1833 did nothing to dent Bellini's confidence, either in his own talent or in the intrinsic worth of *Beatrice,* whose time, he felt sure, would come. Today this dramatic work is still not granted the approval accorded *Norma,* or his next (and last) work, *I Puritani,* but it has been recorded and is regularly staged. Perhaps the libretto, not one of Romani's best (they had quarrelled over it), was below standard, but the music was fine enough. In 1833 Bellini took the path once trodden by Rossini: signing a contract to direct one of his operas in London, he travelled via Paris and, after his stay

in the English capital was over, returned to Paris. There he concluded protracted negotiations for his next opera which was to be at the Théâtre Italien. Bellini enjoyed life in Paris, becoming good friends with Chopin, while Rossini himself took him under his wing and helped him establish himself in the city.

In the spring of 1834 Bellini started work on Count Carlo Pepoli's libretto for *I Puritani:* it was finished in time to be given a triumphant Parisian première in January 1835. Within a few months he had been made a Chevalier of the Légion d'honneur, and his position in Parisian operatic circles was second only to Rossini's. The world was at his feet, and with Rossini in retirement and Donizetti (whom he knew and admired) his only serious rival—albeit in a different style to his own—Bellini could look forward to a glittering future. Alas, it was not to be: complications from a further bout of gastroenteritis led to a fatal inflammation of the bowel and liver. Bellini died in Paris at the age of 33. The funeral was well-attended, with Rossini and Cherubini among the official mourners. In 1876 his remains were transferred to his home town of Catania.

DON'T MISS

▶ **Il Pirata (1827)**

▶ **La Sonnambula (1831)**

▶ **Norma (1831)**

▶ **Beatrice di Tenda (1833)**

▶ **I Puritani (1835)**

HECTOR BERLIOZ
1803–1869

For many Berlioz is the archetypal Romantic composer, inspired primarily by literature, legend and romance, given to expansive musical statements expressed by gigantic orchestral forces. His concern with Classical form marked him as typical of his time in France, but in most other ways—from his thoroughly original approach to scoring to his violent and flamboyant use of instrumental colour—he was an isolated figure.

Berlioz was born in the small town of La Côte-Saint-André, near Grenoble, the son of a free-thinking doctor and a devoutly Catholic mother. He was joined later by three sisters, but remained the only boy in the family. From the outset his character was formed by the religious and emotional schisms within his own family. A career in medicine was planned for him, although he never showed any interest in the subject. His earliest leanings were towards music, but his parents found this an impossible course for any son of theirs, and he received only the most rudimentary musical education, becoming moderately proficient on the guitar and flute but failing to get to grips with the piano. His father ensured the boy had a thorough classical education so that by the time he went to Paris in late 1821 he was admitted without difficulty to the Medical School. Disgusted with the studies expected of him—which included the dissection of corpses—and already

taken by the attractions of the Opéra and the library of the Conservatoire, Berlioz spent little time at the school. An all-out battle developed between Berlioz and his parents, won eventually by the son: he dropped out of school, was cut off by his father, and had to make ends meet by various means while attempting to gain admission to the Paris Conservatoire. This came in 1823 through the good offices of Lesueur, one of the Conservatoire professors who had taught him privately for a time.

For such a determined character the Conservatoire promised to be a rough ride; Berlioz fell out with everyone, Lesueur excepted, from the Director, Cherubini, downwards. His inability to disguise his contempt for the Classical models and methods favoured by his teachers entailed continual confrontation and no preferment. His determination to win the Prix de Rome led to the prolongation of this conflict at every level. Between 1823 and 1827 Berlioz suffered serious deprivation, keeping body and soul together by singing in the chorus at popular theatres, but he never abandoned his principles or his pursuit of the musical expression which he saw as his prime reason for existing.

During these years, however, he encountered works by those he perceived to be 'like souls', such as Beethoven and Shakespeare. For the latter he developed a lifelong enthusiasm, and a number of his works

were directly inspired by the playwright. Finally, his father restored his allowance, thus removing the necessity for Berlioz to sing in the theatres. But Shakespeare had another, completely unforseen, effect on his life: at a performance of *Hamlet* he fell violently in love with the Irish actress playing Ophelia, Harriet Smithson. Going backstage, he loudly declared his passion, scaring the poor girl out of her wits. Now free to compose music day and night and dream of Harriet, in the summer of 1828 he even organized a concert of his own music, much against Cherubini's wishes, with the sole intention of impressing the actress. The gambit failed—she remained unaware that it had taken place. Berlioz continued to pursue her, writing letters to her regularly until she instructed her maid not to accept them. He determined that the only way to win her attention was to compose something too large and too good for her to ignore. All of 1829 and part of 1830 was spent writing the work which would encapsulate his feelings towards her. This, his most famous orchestral work, was the *Symphonie fantastique*, written as an autobiographical piece describing the sufferings and dreams of an artist in

DON'T MISS

▶ **Symphonie fantastique, Op. 14 (1830)**

▶ **Harold in Italy, Op. 16 (1834)**

▶ **Les nuits d'été, Op. 7 (1840–1)**

pursuit of his beloved. It ends in the middle of a witches' sabbath where his beloved appears after he thought he had killed her. She joins in the obscene orgy and he witnesses the witches' triumph amidst the sounding of the *Dies Irae*. The *Symphonie* introduced Berlioz's notion of the musical *idée fixe*, the recurring theme, by which he constructed the entire musical architecture of the piece, and this remained one of his most enduring contributions to musical development. A second work, *Lélio, ou le Retour à la Vie*, was written, depicting the artist's return to sanity and normal life, and was originally planned to be played in conjunction with the *Symphonie* (although it rarely is). In the summer of 1830 he finally won the Prix de Rome for which he had tried unsuccessfully for five years; this gave him financial security for a further five years as long as he travelled abroad for no less than two of those five.

A new woman now came into his life, Camille Moke. When warned by a friend of Berlioz's insane passion for Smithson and that he would never fall for her, she determined to prove otherwise and soon had Berlioz hopelessly in love with her. Before the end of the year they were engaged. Berlioz contrived to delay his departure to Italy under the terms of the Prix de Rome, even arranging for a performance in December at the Conservatoire of the *Symphonie fantastique*. Franz Liszt was in the audience and the generous and astute Hungarian became a friend and ally for life.

Berlioz finally departed for Rome, but by late March 1831, with no word from his fiancée, he bolted for Paris. In Florence he received a letter from her informing

Hector Berlioz

him that she had married Ignaz Pleyel, the rich piano manufacturer. His melodramatic reaction was to contemplate double murder and suicide—he even bought guns for the purpose—but eventually he cooled down and returned to Rome. His musical response was the overture to *King Lear*—another man, in Berlioz's eyes, deceived by evil women. The rest of his time in Rome was uneventful if constructive, and he received special dispensation to return to Paris six months early. He took an apartment in Rue Neuve-Saint-Marc, only to find that it had been vacated the previous day by Harriet Smithson, then appearing at the Théâtre Italien.

For him this was fate: "If I went to the theatre...the old delirium tremens would inevitably seize me... I would first give my concert...[and then]...give myself up to the destiny which seemed to pursue me..." Berlioz's surrender to fate was carefully stagemanaged. The 'concert' referred to was to mark his return to the Conservatoire; his *Symphonie fantastique* and *Lélio* were played, with Harriet Smithson—by special invitation—ensconced in a box. The following day they were formally introduced. The romance between composer and the by now impoverished and fading actress blossomed and in October 1833 they were married.

In the last days of 1833, following a concert which included the *King Lear* overture, Berlioz met Paganini. Within weeks a firm friendship was formed and in January 1834 Paganini commissioned Berlioz to write *Harold in Italy*. (Paganini was never to play the work, although he did pay for it.) Berlioz's next two major compositions were his Requiem (1837) and his first opera, *Benvenuto Cellini* (1838). The latter had a disastrous concert première, although some good came of it, for Paganini had attended the concert with his son, who claimed "never in all his life to have been so affected". Two days later a commision arrived from the great Italian for any work Berlioz felt like composing, accompanied by 20,000 francs, a fortune which eradicated years of debt and put Berlioz on a secure financial footing. Ironically, soon afterwards his marriage, put under intense strain by his erratic nature and his wife's increasing alcoholism, disintegrated. Berlioz moved in with his mistress, the opera singer Marie Récio, leaving his 5-year-old son in his wife's care.

Berlioz continued to compose, frequently going on tour which was beneficial both to his career and his finances. At the beginning of the 1840s

DON'T MISS

▶ Le Carnaval romain, Op. 9 (1844)

▶ Les Troyans (1853)

▶ La Damnation de Faust, Op. 24 (1854–6)

▶ Béatrice et Bénédict (1862)

he completed the orchestral songs *Les nuits d'été* as well as *Symphonie funèbre et triomphale*. Travel and the composition of *La Damnation de Faust* took up much of the early 1840s, the latter's failure in Paris in 1846 being a dark moment for the composer who had to take on numerous conducting engagements abroad in order to recoup his financial losses. Late-1847 to mid-1848 was spent in London, conducting and writing a new opera for Drury Lane, but although Berlioz won the undoubted admiration of the music-loving English public, he made little money. He did, however, avoid the 1848 Paris revolution.

Berlioz returned to France in July 1848 to discover that his father had died just days earlier. After a period of mourning and settling his father's affairs, he arrived in a Paris still shattered by the revolution. In 1850 he was made president and chief conductor of the Société Philharmonique, but this only lasted until March 1851 and he was reduced once more to music journalism. In 1854 his wife Harriet died, leaving him obliged to marry his mistress Marie Récio. He attempted to relocate his career abroad, and for a time enjoyed success in Weimar and London, even conducting the première of Liszt's Concerto for Piano in E flat in Weimar. In 1855 he had met Richard Wagner in London, and had the signal honour of impressing the egocentric composer to the extent that Wagner jotted in his journal: "On the whole I think I am happier than Berlioz". But Berlioz's heart remained in Paris: once he had established himself internationally and was satisfied that there was a demand for his music, he returned to his native city.

In 1855 he was awarded a gold medal by Louis Napoléon, and settled down to write his last great works, the opera *Les Troyens* (The Trojans), which was based on Virgil's *Aeneid*, and *Béatrice et Bénédict* (1863). The idea for *Les Troyens*, an enormous project (the complete opera runs for around 5 hours), came from Princess Sayn-Wittgenstein, who had informed Berlioz of Wagner's plans for his massive *Ring* cycle. Work on the opera began in 1856 and was completed in 1858. Aware of the faint chance of getting such a massive work produced in Paris, Berlioz divided it in two: only the concluding part, *Les Troyens à Carthage*, which contains Dido's lament, was given during Berlioz's lifetime, in November 1863. The full opera was heard for the first time in Karlsruhe in 1890, more than 20 years after the composer's death; as a final irony, it was sung in German. The opera combines the Classical tradition so adored by Berlioz and symbolized by Gluck with the romantic pomp and grandeur of the contemporaneous Meyerbeer school of French grand opera, sometimes falling between the two stools. However, its power and passion is undeniable, as is its scope.

By now Berlioz was in his sixties and attempting to enjoy what years were left to him. His second wife, Marie, had died of a heart attack in the summer of 1862, and though their relationship had not been any happier than his first marriage, the loneliness now became almost unbearable. A commission from Baden-Baden for a comic opera gave him the motivation to complete the charming and delightfully light-hearted *Béatrice et Bénédict* in time for an 1863 production; it proved to be his last completed musical project. He spent the next three years finishing his memoirs which were printed at his own expense in 1865. The previous year, attempting to relieve his isolation and complete the circle of his own life, he re-established contact with his first love, Estelle Duboef, now a middle-aged woman with six children. They were to correspond until the time of his death. In 1867, however, he suffered the cruellest blow yet when his beloved seafaring son Louis (his child by Harriet Smithson) died of yellow fever while in Havana. There now seemed little reason to live, and after being confined to bed in January 1869, he sank into a coma and died in March the same year. He was buried in Montmartre cemetery.

MIKHAIL GLINKA
1804–1857

Considered by all subsequent Russian composers as the father of modern Russian music, Glinka was something of an unlikely hero. An aristocrat and a dilettante, he became a determined reformer of Russian music through his passion for Italian and French culture. His operas, though Russian in subject, used Italian and French operatic practice and forms as models on which to build.

Glinka was born in Novospasskoye in the district of Smolensk, and spent much of his early childhood living with his maternal grandmother whose smothering affection seems to have aggravated the boy's already sensitive nature. From infancy Glinka demonstrated a remarkable affinity for musical sounds; living on his father's estate he developed a love for the local folk music which remained with him for life. Such music would often send him into long reveries—'possessed by delicious languor' as he described it.

As a child of the aristocracy, Glinka received a private education. His governess, Fräulein Klammer, taught him the piano. At the exclusive St Petersburg school to which he was dispatched in 1817 he continued private piano tuition, employing the Irish composer John Field to teach him. A later teacher was Karl Meyer, while Theodore Böhm gave him violin lessons. Glinka began trying to compose in 1822, with very little formal theoretical training to guide him, but none of his early compositions deviate markedly from the prevailing German and Italian models.

During the early 1820s Glinka travelled around Russia; in typical Romantic style, he was impressed by the scenery, especially the mountains of the Caucasus. In 1824, after spending some months on the family estate studying Classical masters, he joined the Ministry of Ways and Communication in St Petersburg. Though financially secure, he clearly felt the need of more direction in his life and found the society of St Petersburg entertaining and diverting. A natural dilettante, Glinka indulged in an endless series of dalliances with pretty young girls, hardly pausing to marry one of them before resuming where he left off. During the remainder of the decade he continued his desultory composing and music study with a variety of teachers.

The period in St Petersburg was vital in forming his intellectual outlook; he was moving in distinguished literary circles which included men like Pushkin and Theodore Tolstoy, and meeting eminent musical practitioners. By 1828 he had tired of working for the Ministry; pleading ill-health, he resigned and took himself off to Italy for three years. There he fell in love with Italian culture, became a friend of Donizetti and Bellini, and for a while wrote pieces drenched in the Italianate style of the period. This great passion proved to be the final part of the formative process which eventually bore fruit in his operas. During the latter part of his stay in Italy he began to yearn for the melodies of his native land, resolving to create an opera which would contain a specifically Russian sensibility, just as Donizetti's and Bellini's were quintessentially Italian.

DON'T MISS

▶ Sextet in E flat (1832)

▶ A Life for the Tsar (1836)

▶ A Farewell to
   St Petersburg (1840)

▶ Ruslan and Lyudmila
   (1842)

▶ Kamarinskaya (1848)

In 1833 Glinka moved to Berlin where he took his first serious course of study in music theory under Siegfried Dehn— an enlightened choice. Dehn was a musical scholar of the highest calibre and conducted his own rigorous researches into such disparate and unlikely subjects as the then unfashionable J. S. Bach and the virtually forgotten Orlande de Lassus. Dehn set about systematizing Glinka's already substantial but uncoordinated musical knowledge. On Glinka's return to Russia the following year due to his father's death, he was well enough equipped musically to attempt a national opera along the lines he had envisaged.

When the poet Jukovsky suggested the historical story of Ivan Susanin's heroic sacrifice to save the Tsar during war with Poland, Glinka saw an opportunity to introduce music from both Poland and Russia as the basic materials with which he could mould a truly Russian opera. This became A Life for the Tsar, and although much of the forms, especially when vocal set-pieces were involved, were borrowed from French and Italian opera, Glinka went far beyond his models in using novel musical means (including the pioneering use of

leitmotifs) to bring a real musical and dramatic unity to the opera. It was premièred in the presence of the Imperial family in November 1836, two years after its completion, and was an immediate success. This led to his appointment as choirmaster to the Imperial Chapel (1836–39) on whose behalf he visited Little Russia to look for new voices for the choir. This visit inspired him to make further studies of the region's music and sowed the seed of his later choral pieces.

The follow-up to A Life for the Tsar took some time to write, partly because of Glinka's natural tendency to laziness, partly because of his inability to get a satisfactory libretto completed, and partly because his health proved frail during a time when his marriage was disintegrating. His wife finally left him to marry another man—without bothering to divorce him first. During these years he spent much time in the countryside, and composed a set of 12 songs with the collective title of A Farewell to St Petersburg, which dealt with the thorny problems of his private life. Finally, in November 1842, Ruslan and Lyudmila was ready for production. All St Petersburg's society attended the opening. Glinka used very similar compositional methods in Ruslan to A Life for the Tsar, although the results were quite different, in part due to the different nature of the plot (taken from Pushkin), and partly because the models he used to contrast with the native Russian style were taken not from Poland, but from Persia, Turkey and states bordering Russia. This exoticism fazed the audience, and the plot, which reflects Pushkin's idea

of the rulers-to-be having to endure severe trials before attaining their thrones, caused the Tsar's party to leave early. Under these circumstances, it is hardly surprising that Ruslan failed to please. Its more adventurous musical nature, beautiful in its own right and perfectly in tune with the fantasy element of the story, later supplied much musical food for thought to composers such as Mussorgsky, Rimsky-Korsakov and Borodin. However, Glinka's sense of undeserved failure left him a bitterly disappointed man.

Now deprived of domestic stability and with a monumental operatic flop on his hands, Glinka resolved to travel and forget, and spent much of the rest of his life wandering from one European cultural centre to another, to France and Spain in particular. He became a friend and ally of Berlioz, whose music he tried to promote in Russia, and composed the occasional orchestral concert piece, such as Jota aragonesa—Spanish overture No. 1 (1845) and the Kamarinskaya (1848), but little else was attempted. He tried a few choral works in the 1850s, and the orchestral A Night in Madrid (1851), but a symphonic poem based on Gogol's Taras Bulba remained unfinished at his death. The following year, on the trail of the roots of Western harmony in the old modes, he returned to Berlin to study with Dehn once more. Shortly after his arrival he suffered a seizure and died. Hě was buried in Berlin; four months later his remains were moved to St Petersburg for reinterment, the ceremony presided over by the dignitaries who had ignored him and his music for over a decade.

FELIX MENDELSSOHN

1809–1847

Like Mozart, Mendelssohn was a rarity in that his precociousness led later in life to mature music of real and lasting worth. A man of unusually wide interests and culture, unfailingly polite and at ease in the presence of royalty and commoner alike, he was revered during his lifetime as few other composers have been.

A brief look at Mendelssohn's life and career will be enough to confirm that here was a man who was singularly blessed in both his astonishing talent and the happy circumstances of his family life. He was born in Hamburg into a prosperous and remarkably close German Jewish family. From the age of seven Felix received music lessons together with an excellent liberal education. Having converted to Protestant Christianity when the children were born, the family left Hamburg when Felix was three years old, spending time in both Berlin and Paris before they settled once more in Berlin in 1816. Within two years Felix was not only composing but had made his Berlin début in a concert at which he played the piano part in a trio for piano and two horns. At about this time he also had the good fortune to meet the poet Goethe, who was impressed by his manners and his precosity. By the age of 12 young Felix had profited from his studies with Carl Friedrich Zelter to the extent that he had a secure grip on the principles of canons and fugues, as well as counterpoint in two and three parts. Not only is this a tribute to his

Felix Mendelssohn

teacher and Mendelssohn's innate talent, but also to the naturally disciplined and structured way in which he approached his studies.

Immediately after this period the adolescent composer wrote the first of his series of String Symphonies, 12 of which were to be completed between 1821 and December 1823 (a thirteenth survives only as one movement). These remarkable works, which progress from

little more than exercises to fully developed little symphonies with added instrument parts, were lost for well over a century until they were found in East Berlin in 1950. They are invaluable in casting light on the young man's developing capacities as well as his models—Mozart, Handel and Haydn in particular.

To achieve such high standards, Felix and his sister Fanny followed a strict

DON'T MISS

▶ Octet for strings, Op. 20 (1825)

▶ Songs Without Words, Books 1–8 (1825–45)

▶ A Midsummer Night's Dream, Op. 21 & 61 (1826–42)

regime; Felix commented in later life how much they used to enjoy Sundays, the only day they were not required to rise at 5 am in order to fulfil their duties. Soon Felix and his siblings were performing to invited audiences which included some of Berlin's most important cultural heavyweights. In 1822–23 the family went on a tour of Switzerland and Germany, and Felix again met Goethe; on one occasion the poet was astonished to hear the 14-year-old extemporise at length on a favourite Bach fugue. He continued to make great strides in his compositions, and by 1825 had written his first indisputable masterpiece, the Octet, Op. 20. Written entirely for strings, it emphasizes the symphonic conception Mendelssohn planned—giving each part responsibility for delivering a truly ensemble performance, rather than allowing latitude for idiosyncratic interpretations. The previous year had included his first 'official' symphony, while the following year, 1826, witnessed his wonderful overture to *A Midsummer Night's Dream*, composed fittingly enough during the glorious summer of that year in the family's Berlin garden and as a result of Mendelssohn's delighted discovery of Shakespeare. On a visit to Paris in 1825 he had made the acquaintence of several older composers, including the

Conservatoire Director, Cherubini, but this overture, when performed to the Berlin public in 1827 confirmed his arrival on the wider cultural stage at the age of 18.

Felix finished his education at Berlin University, completing his classical studies, studying Geography and Philosophy, the latter under the great philosopher Hegel. He also became a proficient swimmer and horseman, and mastered the popular dance steps which he would enjoy on dancefloors throughout Europe for the rest of his life. No longer in any sense a student of composition, he continued to produce a stream of memorable works, including in 1828 the evocative response to Goethe's poem, 'Calm Sea and Prosperous Voyage', an overture designed to fall naturally into two parts. The following spring was a great occasion: at the Berlin Singakademie, Mendelssohn conducted Bach's great *St Matthew Passion*, the first occasion since Bach's death that his masterpiece had been heard. According to reports, more than 1,000 people had to be turned away, and a wildly enthusiastic reaction from those lucky enough to get seats inside assured a rebirth of interest in the great Baroque composer. Mendelssohn himself remained a Bach devotee for the rest of his life.

Just prior to this key occasion, Felix's sister Fanny, a gifted pianist and distinguished composer in her own right, became engaged to William Hensel. Fanny and Felix being unusually close (Fanny enjoying an uncanny insight into Felix's creative processes), this event was marked by a great celebration. Brother and sister were to remain close despite Fanny's happy if

conventional marriage to Hensel (she gave up composition immediately after her wedding).

In spring Felix went to England and greatly appreciated the warmth of his welcome, especially when his First Symphony, performed under his baton in the Argyll Rooms, was met with such approbation. Felix went on an extensive tour of Scotland, visiting Edinburgh and travelling as far as the Hebrides. This visit was tremendously stimulating to Mendelssohn, who jotted down the theme to *Fingal's Cave* while in the boat observing the great natural cavity, and also came up with the main theme for his *Scottish* symphony.

In May 1830 Mendelssohn embarked on a Grand Tour of Europe, visiting no less than six countries. Italy in particular had a great effect on him, and it is no coincidence that his next completed work was the *Italian* symphony. After a miserable time in Paris where his *Reformation* symphony was refused a performance and he suffered an attack of cholera, the tour finished in London in 1832. There he occupied the same rooms in Great Portland Street as he had in 1828, commenting: "That smoky nest is fated to be forever my favourite residence; my heart swells when I think of it!" While in London he completed the first book of his piano pieces, *Lieder ohne Wörte* (Songs without Words), destined to become some of his most frequently played music in the salons of Europe. The *Italian* symphony was premièred in London in 1833 and was an immediate success: its sunny nature and comprehensive brilliance of construction and scoring made it his most completely satisfying symphonic effort to date. And 'effort' was the right word, for he struggled uncharacteristically to get the work into a shape which pleased him.

Conducting appointments now gave him an opportunity to embark on an energetic new career, firstly in Düsseldorf where he ran all the town's musical activities, including church music (1833–35), and latterly in Leipzig (1835–47). If Düsseldorf revealed the extent of his resourcefulness in establishing a repertoire and a performance standard, Leipzig was where he felt most comfortable, and although he was engaged on endless musical activities away from the city, he was careful to conserve his energies for what he saw as his most congenial public position right up to his death. That he left Düsseldorf on good terms is reflected by the première there of his first oratorio, St Paul, in 1836, a year after his removal to Leipzig. At Frankfurt he was persuaded to conduct the choir in Handel's Samson and also met his future wife, Cécile Jeanrenaud, the daughter of a well-connected clergyman. They were married in the spring of 1837. There is every sign of it having been a love match; the marriage produced five children in just 10 years.

Over the next few years the pattern of his life changed little. He was required to stretch himself to the full to meet the enormous scope of public and private commitments which came his way. By the beginning of the 1870s he was not only a tremendously popular figure throughout Germany (in 1841 he was given the position of Kapellmeister in Berlin through the personal intervention of Frederick William IV) but he became the unchallenged leader of his generation of composers and

conductors in Britain, obliged to give concerts to Victoria and Albert on every visit he made there. But it was always on music and his family that the thoughts of this remarkably kind and able man were focussed. In 1843 he was instrumental in founding the Leipzig Conservatory, a task in which he was aided by Robert and Clara Schumann.

At this time his marvellously evocative incidental music for A Midsummer Night's Dream was completed and premièred (in a German adaptation) in Berlin, while in 1844 one of the most famous and favourite of all violin concertos was written, receiving its première in Leipzig. The most substantial composition of these last years was his second great oratorio, Elijah. This received its première in Birmingham in 1847 after months of preparation, much of it while travelling in Europe, and a tremendous last-ditch effort in the summer to finish the work to his satisfaction. It was during this stressful time that his friends and family first noted the exhaustion which overwhelmed him after intense work. Nevertheless, the Birmingham première was a triumph, with no less than eight sections of the oratorio being encored. Not content to rest now that the work was before his public, the composer revised it, improving it in countless small ways.

A return to Leipzig for the winter gave him only partial relief from his exertions, and he was back in England the following April, giving a private concert at Buckingham Palace. By May he was looking tired and drawn; a British acquaintance noticed he was looking old beyond his years (he was still only 38), like someone entering middle-age. In this weakened state he received the shocking news that his beloved sister Fanny had died suddenly in Berlin. His mother and father had both died recently and this third death was more than he could bear. He fainted on hearing the news and took to his bed for days afterwards. After returning to Germany and taking medical advice, he and his entire family retired to Switzerland until September, Felix attempting to stabilize his health and his emotional state. Still in shock, suffering from headaches and dizziness as well as outbursts of shattering grief, this equanamity was a long time in coming. He was incapable of writing new music during this time, and the String Quartet, Op. 80, his first completed work after his collapse, is a desperately sad and troubled piece, utterly at odds with the music which had gone before.

The family returned to Leipzig in late September, with Felix resolved to retire from public life and concentrate

DON'T MISS

▶ **The Hebrides, 'Fingal's Cave' – Overture, Op. 26 (1830)**
▶ **Symphony No. 3 (Italian) Op. 90 (1833)**
▶ **Violin Concerto, Op. 64 (1844)**
▶ **Elijah (1846)**

entirely on composing and his family. Yet his health was now broken, and a steady decline through October was ended by his untimely death, in his sleep, on 4 November 1847. The shocked musical world was plunged into universal mourning: Leipzig grieved openly, and a service in the presence of the coffin in the Pauliner Church was attended by every stratum of Leipzig society. The body was taken by train to Berlin, where a massive funeral was held and Mendelssohn laid to rest in the family plot in the Dreifaltigheits Kirchhof.

FRÉDÉRIC CHOPIN
1810–1849

Chopin is remembered today as the composer of some of the most challenging and subjective music in the whole of the keyboard repertoire. A Pole who spent his mature years in France, he brought to his music a keen interest in his native musical forms and was a precursor of the 'nationalist' composers who did so much to bring new life to Classical music during the course of the 19th century.

Chopin was another of the blighted Romantic generation who was doomed to die young through physical infirmity; in his case it was not the syphilis which claimed Schubert and Schumann, but the tuberculosis which also killed Weber. Frédéric was the only boy of four children born to Nicholas Chopin, a professor of French at Warsaw Lyceum, and his wife Justine. His father taught him until he was old enough to go to the Lyceum, but his musical proclivities manifested themselves early and at the age of seven he began piano lessons with Adalbert Zywny. The lessons were so successful that the young boy played at a public concert before he was nine. He also wrote a little march for the Russian Grand Duke Constantine, who

Frédéric Chopin

not only accepted the dedication but had the work scored for military band.

At the age of 16 Chopin entered Warsaw Conservatory where he was taught by the composer Joseph Elsener.

Elsener was helpful in a number of ways, but two in particular: he taught Chopin the value of sheer hard work, and ignited in him a passionate interest in the music and culture of Poland; the latter was to become especially significant to Chopin later in life. By 1828 his student days were over and he departed for Berlin, where he heard a series of new operas and also caught glimpses of musical personalities such as Spontini (then very fashionable) and Mendelssohn (only 20 at the time but already making his way). Duly inspired, he travelled to Vienna where a Count Gallenberg, apprised of his abilities, had organized two concerts. These went well, and this early success was enough to convince Chopin that he could earn his living as a travelling virtuoso.

Returning to Warsaw, Chopin lost his heart to a Conservatory student, Constantia Gladkowska. It is believed that his feelings for her inspired the beautiful slow movement of the F minor Piano Concerto (called No. 2, although written prior to No. 1). Whatever the emotional reasons for this work, it is true to say that both concertos were written to satisfy the young virtuoso's need for concert works to play while establishing himself as an international performer. In late 1830 he embarked on an extensive tour which took him to various German towns, then on to Prague, Vienna, Munich and finally to Paris, where he arrived in 1831. The tour had not been financially rewarding, but it had at least kept him away from the ferment of the Polish uprising of 1831 which at one point he was tempted to join, but the brutal Russian response persuaded him to keep clear of his homeland for a while.

In his music he poured out his reaction to what was happening to Poland, especially in the Etude in C minor, Op. 10, No 12. Paris was receptive to a gifted Pole at such a time, and Chopin quickly met the cream of Parisian

musical life, including Cherubini, Meyerbeer and Liszt. At his first concert, at which he played his Concerto for Piano in F minor, Mendelssohn led the way by applauding with great enthusiasm. But Chopin's style of playing was not generally delivered with sufficient bravura to set the Parisian audiences alight. It was not until the intervention of the Rothschild family, offering him tutoring work and engagements for private functions, that he earned sufficient income to spend the majority of his time composing. In the year that followed he gradually began to acquire a reputation in both France and Germany, and his works—waltzes, mazurkas, études and preludes, as well as other keyboard pieces—began to receive regular publication.

Chopin remained single, although an affair with Marie, daughter of Count Wodzinski, was terminated by her parents only after a prolonged attempt by the couple to win them over. One of the Wodzinski's reasons for discouraging the match was Chopin's already poor state of health. In July 1837 he visited England to obtain professional advice on his condition; the prognosis was not good, and Chopin returned to Paris with a good idea of what ailed him: he had consumption.

Prior to his London visit, Chopin had been introduced by Liszt to the fashionable and free-thinking novelist George Sand, a woman of generally gargantuan appetites. On Chopin's return to Paris the two began an affair which would last for a decade and was characterized by violent emotional storms and constant jealousy on Chopin's part. A woman of resource and

experience, Sand had already been married and separated, and for her Chopin was the latest affair. In late 1839 she persuaded him to escape Paris with her and winter in Majorca. While this adventure began happily enough, things began to unravel as winter arrived in earnest and Chopin fell seriously ill. Due to Chopin's illness, they were asked to leave their comfortable apartments, finding refuge in a damp, cold monastery. Sand, with a family of her own to support, tended to the sick composer and managed to get him back to Marseilles, where she arranged for the best doctors available to aid his recovery. From Marseilles they moved to Sand's country house at Nohant, where Chopin put the finishing touches to his 24 Preludes and the famous Sonata for Piano No. 2 in B flat minor into which he interpolated an earlier funeral march; such was his state of mind at the time.

For the next few years Chopin's life revolved around George Sand and the company she kept: whether they were in Paris or spending their summers at Nohant, Chopin either composed or spent as much time with Sand as she was prepared to give him. This should have sounded warning bells to the increasingly dependent Chopin, but if they tolled, he did not hear them. Sand

DON'T MISS

▶ Piano Sonata No. 2, Op. 39 (1839)
▶ Nocturnes
▶ Polonaises
▶ Waltzes

was bound to tire of such dependency, and by the mid-1840s the danger signs were multiplying. Sand wanted her freedom once more, and although she still admired him, he no longer stimulated her. He never felt completely at ease with her children, and grew increasingly unwilling to share her with them. One of the characters in her novel *Lucrezia Floriani* was a Polish prince by the name of Karol; a thinly-disguised portrait of Chopin, it was almost entirely unflattering, and gave the distinct impression that Sand was looking for an excuse to break with Chopin long before the series of quarrels in 1847 which finally drove them apart. The novel was published soon after their separation, causing the ailing man considerable distress.

Such turmoil did not improve his state of health; when his Sonata for Cello and Piano Op. 65 was published, it was not hard to believe that it would be the last work published in his lifetime. The following February he gave what proved to be his final Paris concert. With the outbreak of the revolution in 1848, he hastily left for London. Although a tour of Britain was organized for him with every good intention, it clearly overtaxed his waning strength, and when he reached Scotland in October, he collapsed and took to his bed. He was tended closely by friends and admirers, and his journey back to Paris was arranged with every consideration. He arrived in the French capital in November, low in spirits and unable to rally his strength. Although he continued to plan new works, he no longer had the strength to compose the music which had given his life its shape and meaning. He survived into the summer of 1849, but the arrival of autumn and the cold weather brought about the final collapse, and he died that October. At his funeral in the Chapelle de la Madeleine, Mozart's Requiem was performed, as he had requested.

Chopin's legacy consists almost entirely of works for the piano. The instrument was everything to him, and he found previously undreamt of levels of subtlety and expression within its keys. He was acknowledged as a virtuoso, but one who had a very distinctive style, concentrating on delicacy of touch and extreme variations of dynamics and colour. He was singularly gifted in the realm of melody, and was also a key figure in the popularizing of the polonaise, mazurka and other dance rhythms which was to lead many other composers to listen closely to the music of their own countries. Chopin's music is mercurial, and can move from the dreaminess of the nocturnes to the fire and spirit of the ballades and polonaises, the elegance and dash of his waltzes to the brutal emotional realism of his sonatas. His output was relatively slim, and of his orchestral works only the two piano concertos have held their place in the popular repertoire, but the diversity and variety of his keyboard achievements, and the phenomenal technical challenges set by his solo pieces, have given him a special place in the development of music.

ROBERT SCHUMANN
1810–1856

Schumann was the arch-Romantic composer, thoroughly committed intellectually and emotionally to the idea of music being composed to register the feelings, thoughts and impressions garnered by a sensitive spirit on its journey through life.

Robert was born into a devoted family based in Zwickau, 40 miles south of Leipzig. His musical and literary leanings were encouraged by his father who secured a tutor for him; although the lessons were rudimentary, the boy was composing little pieces by the age of seven. He entered Zwickau Gymnasium aged 10, matriculating in 1828; the latter part of his time there was increasingly spent writing, especially poetry. While at the Gymnasium his beloved father died, leaving his mother with no alternative but to place Robert under the guardianship of a family friend. It was decided that Robert should study law at Leipzig University, which he joined in 1828.

From the first, Robert neglected his law studies, plunging instead into the musical and artistic life of Leipzig. Clearly a romantic and impressionable young man, he was not sparing in his affections towards women, apparently smitten by every pretty girl he encountered. But it was not all play; when he became acquainted with Friedrich Wieck, an outstanding piano teacher (whose daughter Clara was already a remarkable pianist), he arranged to take lessons with him. After two years in Leipzig, Schumann persuaded his mother to allow him to continue his studies at Heidelberg University. Again, he neglected his law studies, and in the summer of 1830 wrote to his mother begging her to allow him to take up music full-time. After consulting Wieck, a deeply conservative man whose judgement she felt she could trust, it was agreed that Robert should move into Wieck's house and submit himself to a year of Wieck's rigorous teaching methods. Wieck's intention was to make Robert into a concert pianist, but Schumann's obsession with the development of his finger technique led to his damaging the muscles in his third finger so badly that it remained useless for the rest of his life. He turned, instead, to composition. At this time Schumann also suffered an undisclosed crisis with his health which worried him deeply (he even made out his will). This could possibly have been the first signs of the syphilis which ultimately killed him.

With the publication of his earliest successful piano compositions, such as *Papillons*, Op. 2 and the *Paganini*

Robert Schumann

Caprices, Op. 3, Schumann began to appreciate more clearly the interpretative abilities of 13-year-old Clara Wieck, describing her to one friend as 'perfection'. The adolescent girl naturally idolized the handsome and romantic 22-year-old. But deeper bonds were in the future: first came the launch of the *Neue Zeitschrift für Musik*, a weekly magazine initiated by a group of Leipzig musicians and writers with the express intention of countering the crushingly conservative orientation of Leipzig's music critics. This was to prove a vital outlet for Schumann's writings, and he was sufficiently committed to it to become its proprieter in 1835. In the magazine he made many astute observations and

championed the recently deceased and almost forgotten Schubert, whose music he did so much to establish in Germany and beyond. It also carried his famous pronouncement on Chopin after encountering the composer's Opus 2: 'Hats off, gentlemen! A genius!'.

The years 1834–35 were also a turning point in his emotional life; he became engaged to another of Wieck's students, Ernestine von Fricken—not the most obvious match he could have made, considering her lack of intelligence and her aristocratic background. This announcement led to Clara displaying her first signs of a strong emotional involvement with Schumann. As he began to cool towards Ernestine by late

DON'T MISS

▶ Carnaval, Op. 9
   (1833–35)

▶ Kinderszenen, Op. 15
   (1838)

▶ Dichterliebe, Op. 48
   (1840)

▶ Frauenliebe und leben,
   Op. 42 (1840)

▶ Liederkreis, Op. 24/39
   (1840)

1835, he and Clara acknowledged their mutual attraction. When Wieck became aware of the situation, to Robert's surprise he violently opposed it. An all-out war for the affections of Clara, which provoked staggering depths of vituperation from Herr Wieck, ended in a lawsuit. Wieck lost, which enabled Clara and Robert to marry in September 1840. The following day Clara turned 21.

Throughout this period Schumann had composed almost exclusively for the piano. Now there was a tremendous outburst of *lieder*, and the following year, much to the approval of the ambitious Clara, Schumann buckled down to compose his first symphony. Their close working relationship, and the arrival of their first child in 1841 (they produced seven in all), meant that Clara's career had to suffer. Although she continued her concert tours (they needed the money), she willingly suspended her musical activities. The marriage at this time was blissfully happy. In the spring of 1841 Robert's *Spring Symphony* was premièred. By the following year Clara was on tour again: as women did not travel alone at that time, Robert had to accompany her. Deeply insecure away from domestic

routine, his health deteriorated and he began to resent his wife's addiction to the pleasures of concert-giving.

His professional career was still in the ascendant, and in 1843, when Mendelssohn provided the impetus for the founding of the Leipzig Conservatory, he also insisted that Schumann be given a teaching role there. Robert, however, proved to be a diffident teacher; unable to communicate his ideas, he would often sit through an entire lesson without saying a word to his students. He resigned his post in 1844. By then his bouts of depression (he called them 'melancholy') were more severe and more prolonged.

However, he was still composing prolifically, and in 1843 his choral work *Das Paradies und die Peri* was premièred, Schumann himself conducting. It was an immediate success in Leipzig and also received a warm welcome in Dresden. Yet 1844 brought more problems: a Russian tour by Clara, accompanied by Robert, was a tremendous financial success and both artists were treated with enormous respect. But Robert experienced frightening physical distress, including temporary blindness and frequent vertigo. He became so deeply depressed that he was often unable to engage in the most basic conversation. One observer noted: 'Schumann sat mostly in a corner near the piano...with a sunken head, his hair was hanging in his face, he had a pensive expression, as if he were about to whistle to himself... Clara Schumann was a little more talkative; she answered all the questions for her husband...but one could hardly characterize her as a gracious or sympathetic woman".

Sympathetic or not, Clara soon had to face a full-scale collapse by Schumann. Resigning his *Neue Zeitschrift* editorship, by the end of the summer, he was reduced to a pathetic condition, too weak to walk, often trembling for hours and frequently bursting into tears. Sleep eluded him. The two went to Dresden, where Clara's family lived, and experienced "eight terrible days", according to Clara; Robert failed to sleep, had terrifying hallucinations, and, in her words, "gave up completely". In a decision which smacks of panic, the Schumanns decided to move to Dresden, then something of a quaint backwater, where they felt Robert's health might be restored. The slower pace of life helped initially and the compositions flowed from his pen with renewed vigour: in their first year at Dresden he completed his only Piano Concerto and the Second Symphony. Both were coolly received at their Dresden première, and afterwards Clara could not disguise her bitterness, but Robert replied: "Calm yourself, dear Clara. In 10 years it will all be different".

Schumann became acquainted with another Dresden resident, Richard Wagner, whose ardent commitment to his own operatic genius inspired Robert to compose an opera himself. The result was *Genoveva*, premièred after many delays, to a mixed reception in June 1850. A move to Düsseldorf came that same year when Schumann accepted the position of Director of Music. The post demanded organization and man-management skills, both of which Schumann conspicuously lacked. After a heartening beginning, things deteriorated rapidly. After many absences through illness and a general inability to perform adequately, even with Clara's repeated interventions, he was forced to resign in 1853 and began composing at such a frenzied pace that she was concerned for his health. Before the year was out, a young composer from Hamburg, Johannes Brahms, called on the Schumanns, and Robert was sufficiently in control of his faculties to write in his notebook: 'Visit from Brahms, a genius'. For the first time in a decade he also wrote an article for the *Neue Zeitschrift,* declaring to the world that a majesterial talent had arrived in the shape of his new friend.

This was one of Schumann's last acts of clarity: by early 1852 he had lapsed into insanity. Clara remained with him day and night, but after a fortnight, he himself asked to be placed in an asylum "as he could no longer control his own mind and could not know what he might do next". In late February he attempted suicide, but failed. Soon after he entered Endenich asylum near Bonn. In an attempt to stabilize his condition, Clara was kept away from him and her letters intercepted: it would be over

two years before she saw her husband again. Their last child was born several months after he was committed. His last years were anguished and degrading; when he died in July 1856, after being fed wine and gelée at the asylum by Clara, she and their friends considered it a blessed release.

Schumann's early piano works, many of them dedicated to Clara, are wonderful distillations of a wide range of sensibilities, with *Kinderszenen,* Op. 15 (1838) painting glorious miniature pictures of the life of children, while *Album für die Jugend,* Op. 66 (1832–45) collated a long series of pieces meant to be heard and appreciated by children. Equally, his *Carnaval,* Op. 9 (1833–35) and *Waldszenen,* Op. 82 (1848–49) illustrated ideas and scenes from life, often taking as their inspiration—as did so much of his piano work—a literary source.

Another form of music much favoured by Schumann—also taking its inspiration directly from literature—was *lieder.* The vast bulk were written

between 1840 and 1849, and included such Romantic masterpieces as *Liederkreis* (two books, Op. 24 and 39), *Frauenliebe und leben,* Op. 42 (1840), and the four books of *Lieder und Gesänge* (1840–50). This is a treasure-trove of wonderful settings, and shows Schumann as a worthy successor to Schubert in this field. His four symphonies have been popular since his own day, and that popularity shows no sign of abating, while of the concertos (cello, violin, piano), the latter, Op. 54 (1841–45) has become one of the best-loved piano concertos in the repertoire.

DON'T MISS

▶ Piano Concerto, Op. 54 (1841–5)

▶ Symphony No. 1 (Spring) Op. 38 (1841)

▶ Symphony No. 4, Op. 120 (1841–51)

▶ Waldszenen, Op. 82 (1848–9)

▶ Genoveva, Op. 81 (1850)

FRANZ LISZT

1811–1886

Liszt was a major figure in 19th-century music, an innovator in the way he combined a fierce and unquenchable creative fire with a fully developed connoisseur's appreciation of both the music of contemporary composers and of giant figures from the past.

The only child of Adam and Anna Liszt, Franz was born in Raiding, Hungary. The small town came under the administrative aegis of the Esterházy family who employed Adam as a steward. Franz showed musical promise early, beginning lessons with his father before he was six; by the age of seven he was writing music. Three years later

the boy was ready to make his concert début in the nearby town of Sopron. This was followed by two more concerts performed before the cream of Austrian society. As a direct result, young Franz was given an annual stipend for six years to enable him to concentrate solely on a musical career. His father secured Karl Czerny, an ex-pupil of

Franz Liszt

stream of juvenile works, few of which have survived in their original form. By the summer of 1827 Franz, still only 16, was exhausted and took to his bed in Paris. Doctors recommended a cure at the baths in Boulogne, to which both father and son repaired. Shortly after their arrival, Franz's father, aged 51, died from typhoid.

This shocking event forced Liszt to re-evaluate his existence. Already deeply disaffected with the life of a touring virtuoso, he found the prospect of prolonging it repugnant. For him, music was a noble calling; being "a musician in the employ of the rich, who patronized me and paid me like an itinerant entertainer" he felt to be degrading. Arranging for his mother to join him in Paris, he earned a living by teaching piano to the children of the rich and influential, falling deeply in love with the 16-year-old daughter of a cabinet minister. Though his feelings were reciprocated, her father objected and the girl was quickly married off to a socially acceptable suitor. Liszt never forgot her, even making provision for her in his will. For several years he withdrew from the world, and even considered entering a seminary. He had lost the way forward. It took the 1830 revolution in France to present him with a solution.

For a young man with a passionate commitment to social equality and democracy, the overthrow of an autocratic monarch was profoundly inspiring: he immediately planned a *Revolutionary* symphony to express his sentiments, and although he never progressed very far with the idea, it had the effect of bringing him out into the world again. A series of musical events

Beethoven, as Franz's piano teacher, while Antonio Salieri taught him theory. As both Czerny and Salieri lived in Vienna, the family moved there in 1821.

During his time in Vienna Liszt had the good fortune to meet Beethoven, who although profoundly deaf, attended one of his concerts and bestowed his blessing on the boy. Franz's reputation spread quickly, and before the end of 1821 he had been chosen as one of 50 composers (others included Beethoven, Czerny and Salieri) to write a set of variations to a waltz written by the composer/publisher Diabelli. By the

autumn of 1823 Franz's father decided it was time to widen his son's audience and moved the family to Paris. Liszt took the Parisians by storm. He also completed his musical education by taking private lessons from Anton Reicha and Ferdinando Paer.

A visit to London in 1824 was a triumph, crowned by a private concert before George IV. By late 1825 Franz had even composed a one-act opera, *Don Sanche*, which was premièred in Paris to a mixed reaction. The next two years brought constant travel through much of Europe, financial rewards and the premières of a in 1830–31 cemented his renewed ties with humanity and confirmed the form his artistic voice would take. Attending the first performance of Berlioz's *Symphonie fantastique*, Liszt was overwhelmed by the vivid expression of such turbulent ideas and emotions. He applauded wildly according to Berlioz, dragging him off "for dinner at his house and overwhelming me with his enthusiasm". The two became friends, Liszt learning a great deal from Berlioz about scoring for an orchestra. Three months later he was in the audience at Paganini's Paris début. Once again he was overwhelmed, this time by the sheer demonic pitch of Paganini's virtuosity, and his charismatic presence. Soon after the concert, he began work on the first *Etudes d'exécution transcendante d'après Paganini,* works long regarded as a set of impossibly difficult piano pieces.

At the end of 1831 Frédéric Chopin (then aged 21) arrived in Paris and held his first concert. Liszt was again present and, true to his open nature, immediately declared his belief in Chopin's genius, a belief which was never shaken. All these composers helped define the approach Liszt took towards his own compositional wizardry and helped him to mould his talents until his audiences became as possessed by his music as himself. But it required one more event to put all these encounters into perspective: in 1833 Liszt, still only 22, fell in love with Countess Marie d'Agoult, a married woman of 28. The impact was mutual. Marie recorded her feelings for him: "With passion he uttered thoughts and opinions totally strange to ears like mine, accustomed as they were to hearing only banal, conventional views".

Although deeply moved, Marie delayed for over a year. They finally eloped to Switzerland, where for the next four years they lived together, Marie producing two daughters (Blandine and Cosima) and one son (Daniel), and Franz composing and enlarging his intellectual horizons. He also gave the occasional concert. By 1838 Liszt was travelling more widely; his ardour for Marie had cooled. By the end of 1839 they were living apart, Marie in Paris while Liszt continued to develop his concert career. Liszt's mother took over the education of the children—against Marie's wishes.

For the next 10 years Liszt continued to build his already towering reputation and by the late 1840s he was unchallenged as the greatest virtuoso of his day. It was his pre-eminence which ushered in the solo 'recital' whereby a single artist would mostly perform for an entire programme. In Liszt's case, the recital's music usually consisted of his own compositions. These recitals were given throughout Europe, including satellites such as Britain, Turkey and Russia. The money which these tours engendered forced Liszt to take on a personal manager, thus freeing him to conduct his personal life as he saw fit. This inevitably meant affairs—many of them notorious—with leading female personalities of the day. In his travels

he also met many musicians and composers, from the Schumanns in Leipzig to Glinka in Moscow and Wagner (then penniless and virtually unknown) in Weimar. The connection with Weimar was to grow in significance; in 1842 he was given a largely honorary conducting position by Grand Duke Carl Alexander (holding his first concert in Weimar in 1844), and over the next few years he became increasingly involved in the planning of the city's cultural development. This would inevitably involve Liszt in Wagner's rise to fame.

The event which finally decided him to move to Weimar was his meeting while on tour in Kiev with Princess Carolyne von Sayn-Wittgenstein, an immensely rich Polish aristocrat already separated from her German husband, a member of the Tsar's military élite. Their decision to marry entailed Carolyne, a devout Catholic, obtaining a divorce which required special permission from the Tsar. The Princess's belief in the spiritual nature of Liszt's artistic calling helped him decide to abandon his largely frustrating (although very lucrative) concert career. By the spring of 1848 they were settling into life in Weimar. This was harder for the Princess than for Liszt; living openly with him, she was snubbed by Weimar society and her estate in the Ukraine sequestered by the Russian state as

---

DON'T MISS

▶ **Années de Pèlerinage, années 1–3, S160/1/3 (1844–77)**
▶ **10 Hungarian Rhapsodies, S244 (1846–65)**
▶ **Les Préludes, S97 (1848)**
▶ **Piano Concertos 1 & 2, S124/125 (1849–39)**

DON'T MISS

▶ Piano Sonata in B minor, S178 (1852–3)

▶ A Faust Symphony, S106 (1854–7)

▶ A Dante Symphony, S109 (1855–6)

part of the eventual secular divorce settlement in 1852.

Despite these obstacles, the Princess's rented house in Weimar became a major centre for artists, musicians and writers. During this settled period Liszt began composing his first orchestral works, initiating the series of tone poems which would remain one of his most distinctive compositional legacies—*Tasso* and *Les Préludes* for example—and planning his Weimar musical seasons. Looming large in his plans was a production of Wagner's *Lohengrin*. (Wagner attended the rehearsals while on the run from the authorities in Dresden for his part in the 1848–49 uprisings all over Europe.) Liszt personally arranged for Wagner's flight to Switzerland. Wagner was not the only beneficiary of Liszt's generosity in Weimar: in the years before his 1859 resignation, Liszt mounted no fewer than 11 new productions of contemporary operas, including three from Wagner, Berlioz's *Benvenuto Cellini*, Meyerbeer's *Les Huguenots*, Verdi's *Ernani*, Schumann's *Genoveva* and Schubert's neglected *Alfonso und Estrella*.

Virtually everyone made the pilgrimage to Weimar, some remaining close to Liszt (von Bülow marrying Cosima Liszt in 1857), others, like Brahms, only fleetingly held in awe by the great

man's talent. Even good friends like the Schumanns found Liszt's compositions too much, as Clara commented after a visit from the pianist in the early 1850s: "Oh! What terrible compositions! If a youngster were to write such stuff, one might forgive him, but what can one say when a full-grown man is so deluded?". The critic Eduard Hanslick called his challenging B-flat sonata 'a brazen concatenation of utterly disparate elements...anybody who has heard this thing and liked it is beyond hope'.

The 1860s brought a series of disasters, presaged by the death in 1859 of Liszt's gifted only son, Daniel, from consumption; in 1861 the Pope refused to spiritually sanction the Princess's legal annulment; in 1862 his beloved daughter, Blandine, died; in 1863 his second daughter, Cosima, abandoned her husband Hans von Bülow, and eloped with none other than Richard Wagner, to Liszt's chagrin. The breach between father and daughter was never healed. Tired of the strife in Weimar, Liszt joined the Princess who was already in Rome on a pilgrimage, and devoted himself exclusively to religious music, even taking the four minor orders which allowed him to assume the title of abbé. The death in 1861 of the Princess's husband had left the way clear for a new attempt to marry, but neither had the will for it any more. After 1864 they were not to meet again.

By the end of the decade Liszt had written a series of devotional works, including *The Legend of Saint Elizabeth*, and had permanently adopted the wearing of a cassock. He was also invited back to Weimar to give a series of master-class demonstrations; these

were to continue for the rest of his life, Liszt spending part of each year in Weimar. He also developed his relationship with Budapest, nurturing his love for his homeland, and in 1870 was appointed President of Budapest's music academy. He now divided each year between Weimar, Budapest and Rome. In 1872 he came to a reconciliation of sorts with Cosima and Richard Wagner, now married and well advanced with their dream of building the Bayreuth theatre. Liszt's last great oratorio, *Christus*, was premièred at Weimar in 1873, with Wagner and Cosima present.

Liszt remained a focal point for the best young talents of the day, and as his attachment to Rome receded, his involvement in their developing careers increased. In 1876 his old lover, Countess Marie d'Agoult, died in France, but he was left unmoved. Later that year, the Bayreuth première of Wagner's *Ring* cycle gave him more to be moved by, as did the acclamation he received at the 1878 Universal Exhibition in Paris, when his old enemy Eduard Hanslick proposed that he should be made honorary president of the Exhibition's musical jury.

Yet the pattern of his life—Weimar-Budapest-Rome, with the occasional sortie to Bayreuth—did little to relieve his weariness. His rootlessness and the gradual deterioration of his health led to the diminution of his powers, while a series of piano works written in his last decade, most of them filled with a deep melancholy, leaving the impression of a troubled soul. In particular, four pieces written close to the time of Wagner's death in 1883 have an existential angst which is deeply disturbing.

By his last years Liszt and the Princess had drifted apart entirely; she refused to leave Rome and he was increasingly loath to go there. His health was giving out and he tended to remain within reach of the Wagners, and was deeply touched by Wagner's dedication of *Parsifal* to him. Yet with Wagner's death, Cosima pushed him away. His chief pleasure now was teaching the piano to his young pupils. With his eyesight considerably impaired and his energy gone, he rarely played in public. By the summer of 1886 he was virtually blind, his body invaded by dropsy. He returned, ailing, to Weimar where he had a devoted young companion, Lina Schmallhausen, to comfort him. He died from pneumonia in July, and was buried in Bayreuth during the festival.

Central to Liszt's achievement was his prodigious keyboard virtuosity, his inventiveness and his ability to devise new ways of playing which revolutionized the public's and other musicians' approach to the instrument. Thus it may be held that his copious solo piano output is the most crucial part of his legacy, including the B flat Sonata, his *Années de Pèlerinage* and the *études*. But his orchestral tone poems—the so-called programme music—are in a real sense his most permanent imaginative achievement. The *Dante* and *Faust* symphonies are both major testaments to a concern with literal and philosophical truths expressed in music, and as such are central to the 19th-century Romantic tradition. They are also clear examples of the sometimes demoniacal energies to be found in his music. Liszt has also often been cited as important in these works in his coining and development of the idea of theme transformation, rather than the more traditional ideas of Classical development. This approach perhaps reached its apotheosis in Wagner.

GIUSEPPE VERDI
1813–1901

Born in the same year as Wagner, but in many ways the operatic antithesis of the German giant, Verdi brought to his greatest works such brilliant dramatic and musical gifts and such a deep understanding of the human experience that they remain universally popular among opera lovers to this day.

Verdi was born in the village of Le Roncole near Parma. From early infancy he showed a powerful reaction to any music played near him. His father bought the family a spinet and allowed Giuseppe to learn music from the local priest. At the age of 10 he was sent to the nearby town of Busseto, where a local merchant provided accommodation and paid for musical tuition. Verdi responded to this kindness with dedicated hard work and was soon writing small pieces for the local Philharmonic Society. Busseto took pride in the fast-developing adolescent and by the time Verdi was 18, funds were provided for him to move to Milan where he hoped to study at the Conservatory. This hope was frustrated by the board of examiners, and Verdi had to arrange for private tuition.

After two years of intensive study he returned to Busseto where he became Director of the Philharmonic Society and fell in love with Margherita, the daughter of his benefactor Antonio Barezzi; they were married in 1836. By the time Verdi moved back to Milan in late 1838, he was 24 years old and on the threshold of his real vocation; his first opera, *Oberto*, had been accepted by the theatre's impresario, Bartolomeo Merelli, for production at La Scala. However, the young composer suffered a series of fatal blows: that November his daughter died of fever; the following summer, while he was at work on his second opera, the comic opera *Un giorno di regno*, his son died. *Oberto* had been sufficiently popular with the Scala audience at its November 1839 première for Verdi to hope his career was under way when a third tragedy befell him: his wife was suddenly taken ill with encephalitis and died. Utterly grief-stricken, Verdi completed *Un giorno* and watched it fail at its première at La Scala.

Verdi remained for ever grateful that Merelli refused to let him succumb to

Giuseppe Verdi

endless interference of the political censors who contrived to find hidden meanings in every theatrical production. As the social and political impetus for the Risorgimento began to gain ground, Verdi's coded political views contained within the operas gained him a following as much with patriots as with opera fans. His political stance was most blatant in *La battaglia di Legnano,* a melodramatic potboiler produced in 1849 which echoed the aspirations of the failed rebellions of the previous year.

Since the devastating loss of his family, Verdi had focused on his work, but in 1847 he met an old acquaintance, the opera singer Giuseppina Strepponi; their meeting in Paris ignited a passion which took them both by surprise: Verdi hastily rearranged his Italian obligations and spent the next two years in Paris where Strepponi was working as a singing teacher. Within a year they were living together—as they would until her death in 1897. While preparing for his eventual return to Italy, Verdi bought Villa Sant' Agata in the countryside near Busseto. This was to be his home base until his death, and gave him the peace and privacy he now craved.

grief by pressing on him a new operatic libretto. This eventually became *Nabucco.* After the première in 1842 Verdi commented: "My career as a composer may rightly be said to have begun; and though it is true that I had to fight against a great many difficulties, it is no less true that *Nabucco* was born under a very good star".

Over the next few years Verdi, like Donizetti and Rossini before him, became a one-man opera factory, composing around two a year, a process which continued until the March 1851 production of *Rigoletto.* Although many of the plots and the majority of the characters that throng the early operas are stock vehicles to make Verdi's operas tick along in the appropriate manner, his feeling for drama and unfailing ability

to highlight an action or emotion, however crude, make all his operas worth revisiting. In *Ernani* (1844), *Giovanna d'Arco* (1845), *Macbeth* (1847) and *Luisa Miller* (1849), he created works which would remain popular on stages throughout the opera-loving world up to the present day, though none of them could hope to supplant the trio of operas he was about to write: *Rigoletto, Il Trovatore* and *La Traviata* (1853). *Les Vêpres Siciliennes* was the last gasp of this creative spurt; it was given its Paris première in June 1855, two years after *Traviata.* After that he allowed himself a two year break.

Wholly bound up with his operas during this period, Verdi mixed for the most part with his professional peers and developed a healthy distaste for the

The fact that *Rigoletto, Trovatore, Traviata* and *Vêpres Siciliennes* all followed the establishment of a settled private life shows that Verdi knew what was right for him. He now had the creative space to put all the lessons of the earlier operas to good effect and produce a string of masterpieces (despite the weak *Vêpres* libretto, the music is superb). Each work has its own strong character, and demonstrates Verdi's complete dramatic and musical mastery: the vengeful tragedy of

Rigoletto, the broad-stroked, swashbuckling vigour of the romantic *Trovatore,* and the domestic pathos of the dying libertine mistakenly rejected by her lover in *Traviata,* all receive maximum deployment under Verdi's inspired scoring. He uses his melodic gifts to bring to life a wide range of characters and situations, creating immortal melodies which haunt the memory of every opera-lover and crystallize key dramatic moments in the scores.

After a lengthy break from composing, Verdi began to plan *Un ballo in maschera,* but quickly switched his attention to *Simon Boccanegra.* Though one of Verdi's personal favourites, it failed to excite the public's imagination; like *La Traviata,* it was initially a failure. Even today it is rarely given, due as much to the inadequacies of the plot as to any musical weakness.

In 1859 Verdi finally married Giuseppina. He also completed his most sophisticated and beautifully balanced opera to date, the previously abandoned *Un ballo in maschera,* where the new subtlety of the music matched the development of character and emotional range he now allowed himself. But 1859 also demonstrated another aspect of Verdi: he had always taken an intense interest in Italian politics and was a staunch nationalist. He was also an admirer of the Italian statesman Cavour, and when Italy's first free elections took place in 1860, Cavour persuaded a reluctant Verdi to stand: he was duly elected as Busseto's representative. At first he was actively involved in plans for music under the new constitution, but Cavour's premature death in 1861 effectively ended Verdi's direct interest

in politics. Deeply upset by his idol's death, he resigned his seat in 1865 and remained a spectator of politics for the rest of his life.

Three years after the production of *Ballo,* the Imperial Theatre in St Petersburg commissioned him to write his next opera. This time he chose a melodramatic story of a Spanish vendetta, thus defining at a single stroke both the style and the limits of the work. *La forza del destino* was premièred in St Petersburg in 1862, and Verdi and Giuseppina travelled there for the first night. Giuseppina wrote to a friend: '*La forza* has been produced with great success. A good performance by everyone, singers, chorus and orchestra... Verdi received the royal order of St Stanislaus, and that without any suggestion from outside...' A Madrid première soon after was equally successful.

After this there was another hiatus in terms of new operas (a revised *Macbeth* was offered in Paris in 1865) until the French opera, *Don Carlos,* first staged in Paris in 1867. For this work, Verdi made some concessions to the country where it was premièred; the formal designs of Meyerbeerian grand opera were adopted, but the melodic vivacity and the striking orchestral colours, as well as the vigorous characterizations, are all quintessentially Verdian. The period of *Don Carlos's* composition had included the deaths of both Verdi's natural father and his father-in-law and original patron, Antonio Barezzi. Verdi was devastated; of the latter he wrote to a friend: 'I have known many men, but none better than he. He loved me as one of his own sons, and I loved him as much as my father'.

The following year Rossini died, and Verdi led an attempt to create a requiem for the great man written by all the most eminent Italian composers of the day. It eventually came to nothing, the elements being too disparate, but in 1873 Verdi was to take up his own contribution on hearing of the death of the great Italian novelist Manzoni, and expand his thoughts into a complete Requiem of his own. In 1869 Verdi had been approached by an agent of the Egyptian Government to write a grand opera for the opening of the Cairo Opera House. After rejecting the offer several times, he finally read the libretto and changed his mind. Within weeks he was working on what was to become *Aida.* Its eventual Cairo opening took place amidst incredible scenes of splendour (Verdi, caught up in rehearsals for the Milan première, was unable to attend) and was a great success. With its combination of private anguish and public remonstrance, its contrasts of enormous scale and intense intimacy, the work has remained universally popular ever since.

After this period of concentrated work, Verdi retired to Sant' Agata to tend to his farm. Whether he was happy during this period is debatable; his letters are often full of complaints, one ending: 'We pass the time here quietly and, if not happily, well enough'. The 1870s

---

DON'T MISS

▶ **Nabucco (1842)**
▶ **Macbeth (1847)**
▶ **Rigoletto (1851)**
▶ **Il Trovatore (1853)**
▶ **La Traviata (1853)**

were a period of personal unrest for Verdi: now in his sixties, he fell prey to melancholy and increasingly mourned his lost youth. There is evidence that for a time he became infatuated with the young singer Teresa Stolz, his preferred soprano for many of his operas and a friend of Giuseppina's, and this caused his wife great pain. By the

---

DON'T MISS

▶ La forza del destino (1862)

▶ Aida (1871)

▶ Requiem Mass (1874)

▶ Otello (1887)

▶ Falstaff (1893)

---

end of the decade, however, he seems to have adjusted back to his old pattern of life with Giuseppina.

After a long campaign by his publisher Ricordi, in the early 1880s he was persuaded to write another opera. The subject was Shakespeare's *Othello,* a clever choice considering Verdi's love for the British dramatist's work. The composer/librettist Arrigo Boito wrote the adaptation; Verdi, now fired with enthusiasm, completed his great tragedy in time for a Milanese première in 1887. This and *Falstaff* (again Shakespeare, via Boito, but this time a genuine comic opera—something Verdi had long been accused of being incapable of writing), premièred at La Scala in 1893, were his last great

outpourings of creativity. By now he was entering his ninth decade and wished for nothing more than to enjoy his remaining years in peace. He had become the most famous and admired man in Italy and a living symbol of Italian opera. Giuseppina died in 1897, a victim of progressive disease, and Verdi became intensely lonely. His final years were busy as he involved himself in a number of special charitable projects, but since Giuseppina's death his own health had been poor and he knew he was simply marking time. The end came in Milan in January 1901 from a heart attack. His funeral was one of the largest ever held in Italy, and he was buried next to Giuseppina in Milan's Home for Musicians, as he had requested.

RICHARD WAGNER

1813–1883

In a career replete with ironies, perhaps the greatest is that such an unpleasant and self-aggrandising man, with a fascination for himself verging on the obsessive, should have created music which has been an inspiration to thousands looking for an understanding of the deeper wells of human existence.

Wagner was born in Leipzig during the chaotic final years of the Napoleonic wars. For over a century his paternity has been a subject of intense debate, a matter of little importance had Wagner not been rabidly anti-Semitic and had

he not suspected that his father's friend, Ludwig Geyer, was in fact his natural father and that Geyer was at least partly Jewish. Following his father's death, Richard's mother married Ludwig; thus Wagner became and remained Richard Geyer until 1828. Legitimacy apart, Wagner grew up in a loving environment at Geyer's house in Dresden, together with his mother, brother and three sisters, and Geyer ensured that he received a good education.

By the time Richard was in his mid-teens he was sufficiently interested in music to take secret lessons from a Leipzig teacher, and by 1830 was

ready to enter the Leipzig Thomas Schule where, among other subjects, he learned to play the violin tolerably well. He joined Leipzig University in 1831, extended his music lessons to take theory from Christian Weinlig and enjoyed the usual period of undergraduate dissipation. By then he had grown into a rather unprepossessing-looking young man, with a head too big for his short body (he was 5 ft 6 ins), a forceful jaw and high forehead.

He began his career as a composer with a series of instrumental and orchestral pieces which betrayed their debt to Mozart, Haydn and

Beethoven, his youthful Symphony in C receiving a Prague première in 1832. But with university over it was time for him to earn a living. His brother Albert, who had contacts in the theatrical world, secured him a rehearser's position at the theatre in Würzburg where Wagner gained valuable practical experience of many aspects of mounting operas. It also gave him direct knowledge of some of the most popular operas of the day, including Marschner's *Der Vampyr* and Meyerbeer's *Robert le Diable*. By then Wagner had already tried his hand at opera (*Die Hochzeit* and *Die Feen*), writing his own libretti, but his sister disapproved of the results and he suppressed the former work while the latter had to wait until after his death for its first performance. He had higher hopes for his next attempt, *Das Liebesverbot* (The Love Ban), a work based loosely on Shakespeare's *Measure for Measure* and described by the composer as a 'grand comic opera'. After being appointed as conductor in Magdeburg in 1834, he finally mounted a performance of it there in 1836, but the production company collapsed before a second performance could be mounted.

Richard Wagner

The summer of 1834 found Wagner in Lauchstädt in the throes of his first major love affair with Minna Planer, a young actress with the Magdeburg company. His passion for her reached obsessive levels. For a time she kept him at arms' length, but after he had pursued her from Lauchstädt to Königsberg, she finally accepted his offer of marriage. Wagner was already establishing a pattern of behaviour which he was to repeat many times over, and his flight to Königsberg was

prompted as much by his debts in Lauchstädt as by his love for Minna. After his marriage he proceeded to run up new debts in Königsberg and within a short time Minna was sufficiently fearful of the future to escape to her family in Dresden. Wagner effected a reconciliation, but the marriage remained troubled.

After an abortive season in Riga conducting light opera, Wagner fled the city under cover of darkness to

avoid his creditors and made for Paris, where he hoped for a production of his new opera, *Rienzi*. Through an introduction fortuitously gained from two travelling companions he and Minna met on their way to France, Wagner called on Meyerbeer on his arrival in Paris and the composer gave Wagner what advice he could for success in Paris. Operatic success eluded him, yet he managed considerable success as a critic while he was there, publishing a string of

DON'T MISS

▶ Tristan und Isolde (1865)

▶ Die Meistersinger von Nürnberg (1868)

▶ Der Ring des Nibelungen—
  1 Das Rheingold (1869)
  2 Die Walküre (1856)
  3 Siegfried (1876)
  4 Götterdämmerung (1876)

articles in several journals. In later years this was remembered as a humiliation, and his way of repaying Meyerbeer for his kindness was to publish anonymously a grossly anti-Semitic essay, 'Jewishness in Music', which specifically attacked Meyerbeer's operas. Wagner also blamed Meyerbeer, groundlessly, for his travails in Paris.

Wagner left Paris for Germany in 1842, Meyerbeer having helped him obtain a production of *Rienzi* in Dresden in 1841, and a production of *Der fliegende Holländer* in Berlin in 1843. *Rienzi* shows the influence of Meyerbeer in the way in which Wagner set and conceived his musical drama, and it is possible that, in his obsession with crediting only himself and Beethoven for all his creative developments (he similarly obscured the impact of Berlioz's music on his writing at this time), he deliberately attacked Meyerbeer and his music as the best form of defending his own unique genius to posterity.

The post of *Kapellmeister* at the Dresden Court fell vacant soon after the successful première of *Holländer,* and Wagner was persuaded to take the position. He remained there six years, during which time he engaged in a sustained campaign to jolt the

provincial Court out of its deeply conservative tastes. He continued to live well beyond his means and provoked criticism on a personal as well as a professional level. Nevertheless, during this time he completed *Tannhäuser* and it was premièred in Dresden in 1845 under his own baton. Indeed, many of his productions at Dresden were far-sighted and merit applause (his adherence to Gluck, for example). All this was brought to an end, however, by the 1849 revolution in Dresden. Wagner had backed the insurgents, writing inflammatory articles and helping to organize resistance to the Prussian troops. After the collapse of the insurrection, Wagner was lucky to evade arrest and made his way to Weimar where he threw himself on the mercy of Franz Liszt, a friend since his early days in Dresden. Liszt, then engrossed in preparing *Tannhäuser* for its Weimar debut, arranged for Wagner's safe passage to Switzerland.

Anxious to commence earning an income outside Germany, Wagner moved to Paris, but failure to obtain a production of any of his operas, a fraught affair with a friend's wife and the triumph of Meyerbeer's *Le Prophète* drove him back to Switzerland

in a bitter frame of mind. Liszt, however, went ahead with a first production of *Lohengrin* in Weimar in 1850, thereby declaring his loyalty to a composer he believed to hold the key to the future of music. Over the next two years Wagner completed the librettos for the entire *Ring* cycle. His Swiss exile was a great hardship for him, but he certainly employed the time profitably, writing *Das Rheingold*, (1854), *Die Walküre* (1856) and two acts of *Siegfried* (1857).

During these years his reputation continued to grow through the performance of excerpts from his operas, (he called them, graphically, 'bleeding chunks') such as those heard by Queen Victoria and Prince Albert (including the *Tannhäuser* Overture) in London in 1855 under Wagner's own direction. His intense and sustained burst of work on *The Ring* was interrupted by his sudden switch to the story of *Tristan und Isolde*, which engaged his full attention after he and Minna moved to a cottage near Zurich provided by his friend and patron, the rich businessman Otto Wesendonck, who lived nearby. The reason for this sudden change was the onset of a passionate affair between the composer and Wesendonck's wife, Mathilde. Wagner long suppressed his feelings towards this woman, but now the close proximity led him to press his suit, and Mathilde responded. The fast-appearing tragedy of *Tristan* was clearly being composed as a corollary to their doomed passion.

Minna discovered Wagner's liaison with Mathilde, and although Wagner was to finish *Tristan*—his opera dedicated to his doomed affair with Mathilde—as well as the beautiful *Wesendonck Lieder* (settings of poems by Mathilde), the affair was ended by Wesendonck removing his wife to Italy. Wagner completed *Tristan* before the close of 1859, producing an opera which was to prove as influential as any other written during the 19th century. There are few areas of Classical music the harmonies of Tristan did not reach in the next 50 years, and the deep neurosis of the work, embracing love and death as two sides of the same coin, admirably suited the *fin de siècle* sensibilities of the time.

For the next few years Wagner led a calmer but peripatetic life, even advancing plans for a grand comic opera which was to become *Die Meistersinger von Nürnberg*. By early 1862 he and Minna had agreed to a final separation and she moved back to Dresden. An 1863 concert tour in Russia brought him a financial windfall which enabled him to live extravagantly in Austria until he ran up debts which threatened his imprisonment. In 1864 he was still rootless and looking for somewhere to settle when he was summoned to Munich by Ludwig II, the new 18-year-old King of Bavaria.

His relationship with Ludwig II was remarkable in many ways, not least because the two men rarely met, preferring to communicate by letter even though Wagner was in the same city. The composer was given very generous terms over the years of Ludwig's patronage, being paid large sums of money, some of which he latterly used to save his Bayreuth project from collapse. But Wagner's conspicuous consumption of Ludwig's

money, allied to a transparent contempt for the local aristocrats, precipitated a move from Munich to Lake Lucerne in 1865. By this time he had begun an affair with Hans von Bülow's wife, Cosima (née Liszt), and his first child by her, Isolde, was born in 1865. Afraid that Ludwig would throw him out, Wagner and Cosima refused to admit to the child's illegitimacy, though Wagner's domestic situation eased somewhat with the death of his wife Minna in 1866.

In the following years Wagner balanced his demands for total artistic and financial freedom with Ludwig's demands to see results for his generous patronage. Against the composer's wishes, the first two operas of The Ring (*Das Rheingold* and *Die Walküre*) were premièred in Munich between 1869 and 1871, and Ludwig pressed Wagner continuously for *Siegfried* to be completed and staged there as well. But Wagner had found in the village of Bayreuth the ideal setting for the realisation of his ideals of German opera for the future, and was determined to press ahead with his plans to build an opera house to his specifications. Cosima moved there in 1868 and after her divorce from von Bülow in 1869, she and Wagner were married. By 1874 *Götterdämmerung* had been completed. So, too, had Wagner's own house in Bayreuth, Wahnfried, into which he moved Cosima and the children. But the theatre project came close to collapse as funds ran out and new investors proved hard to find. At this point Ludwig saved the project with financial aid: his reward was the manuscripts of many of Wagner's operas. He also came to the 1876 dress rehearsals for The

Ring (the first season): it was his first meeting with Wagner in eight years. Two years later, when the entire festival organization was close to bankruptcy, Ludwig again interceded and all debts were liquidated.

True to form, Wagner put the blame for the poor attendance during the first years of Bayreuth onto those groups he had spent most of his life berating, writing articles and essays excoriating the so-called elements in German life—Jews, radicals and so on—which prevented true Germans from appreciating his music. Certainly his last opera, *Parsifal*, is a spiritual expression of many of these debatable viewpoints, and although it is perhaps his greatest and most completely realized musical creation, there has never been general agreement on the exact nature of the Christian message at the heart of the opera. There have also been suggestions that this great spiritual work was initially inspired by his passionate and illicit love for another woman, this time Judith Gautier (daughter of the French writer Théophile Gautier), whom he had met in 1869. It was premièred at Bayreuth in 1882, by which time Bayreuth had become an annual place of pilgrimage for many of the most radical spirits in European culture.

In early 1883 Wagner went with Cosima to Venice to rest and plan for the future, but succumbed to a heart attack on 13th February. His body was transported back to Wahnfried and buried in the grounds nearby. Cosima lived until 1930, effectively shaping the posthumous reputation of her husband through her own highly selective interpretation of his legacy and life.

CHARLES GOUNOD

1818–1893

A major figure in 19th-century French music, whose influence was also deeply felt in Britain, Gounod's reputation has faded in more recent times. His great operatic masterpiece *Faust* apart, his music has largely been found wanting in both dramatic and intellectual interest, and though France has remained loyal to his music, he awaits rehabilitation elsewhere.

Gounod's Eyes *by the French photographer Nadar*

Gounod was that rare thing, a native Parisian who became famous in the city of his birth. His mother, a talented pianist and daughter of a Conservatoire professor, gave the boy his first musical lessons. In 1836, at the age of 18, he entered the Conservatoire; the following year he won the second Prix de Rome with a cantata, *Marie Stuart et Rizzio*. Two years later he won the First Prix de Rome and, following the stipulations of the prize, went to Rome where he was immensely moved by a series of musical and artistic experiences, especially the discovery of Palestrina's music. While in Rome, he made the acquaintence of young Fanny Mendelssohn which led to a meeting with Felix Mendelssohn in Berlin in 1842. He also heard Schumann's music for the first time.

Returning to Paris once more, he became organist and choirmaster at the church of the Missions Etrangères where he attempted to introduce some of his Roman discoveries into the staple diet of sentimental occasional music

then in fashion. That his religious impulses were sincere there is no doubt, for in 1846 he became an external student at Saint Sulpice seminary. By the dawning of the 1850s, however, his professional and private life had undergone a considerable revolution: guided by a close friendship with the influential and intelligent singer Pauline Viardot, he turned his creative hand to opera and by 1851 witnessed the Paris première of his first, *Sapho*, with Viardot in the leading role. From this time until the 1870s, although he kept up a continuous flow of choral compositions, opera became his bread and butter.

His crowning moment came in 1859 with the staging of *Faust*, a beautifully balanced and unpretentious rendering of a subject crying out for the overblown treatment which the grand

opera style would have normally demanded. But Gounod's talents always lay with melody and a certain simplicity and transparency of texture, and these gifts, as well as a genuine sense of pacing and continuity, made it a tremendous success with the opera-going public which welcomed this break with the then dominant heavyweight grand opera style. *Faust* remains his only opera which is regularly staged outside France.

His next real success was *Mireille* in 1864, a five-acter which Gounod eventually trimmed to three, and which again stresses the melodic gifts of the composer rather than his penchant for dramatic confrontation and action. Three years later, *Roméo et Juliette* (1867) again demonstrated his winsome talents in a version of the old Shakespearean story which remained remarkably faithful to the content and spirit of the play. After *Faust* it is decidedly his most popular opera, and is still given (and recorded) on a regular basis in France, and occasionally dusted down for performance elsewhere in the world.

In 1870, while on holiday with his wife (they had married in 1864), Gounod was shocked to learn of the outbreak of the Franco-Prussian war. Together with a number of friends, he decided to leave for England, and although most of them returned to France within a relatively short time, Gounod elected to stay in London, where he remained for five years. There were various reasons for this, chief among them being his dalliance with an eccentric but talented and strong-willed woman, Augusta Weldon. It was her influence, as well as the sound of English choirs he heard and conducted, which gradually turned him away from the operatic medium. By the mid-seventies he was ready to return to Paris (and abandon Augusta

Weldon), but he remained faithful to the new musical direction she had indicated for him. A string of liturgical pieces were premièred in the years that followed, crowned by two oratorios in the early 1880s, *La Rédemption* and *Mors et Vita*. These sincere works, written with the usual fineness of touch one associates with Gounod, have failed to find a regular audience, and their frequent lapses into what could only be termed sentimentality and cheap spiritualism do not help their cause, however attractive the occasional turn of melody or felicitous part-writing may be. His much-repeated claim that he wanted to represent only the best things that simplicity in music could provide often seemed in his later works to be an excuse for simple-minded and lax music-making.

At this stage Gounod's private life became somewhat stormy: he found to his cost that Augusta Weldon was not a woman to give up easily. She

insisted that his place was at her side, even filing a lawsuit against him for the alleged misuse of material she claimed to have rights to. As Gounod was—to all intents and purposes—a happily married and God-fearing man, this series of events was a continual embarrassment. Now approaching old age, Gounod increasingly withdrew from public life, and although he remained a much honoured figure, it was for his past rather than his present achievements. Increasingly taken up by religious mysticism in his declining years, he died in Saint-Cloud in 1893.

DON'T MISS

▶ **Sapho (1851)**
▶ **Ave Maria (1853)**
▶ **Faust (1859)**
▶ **Mireille (1864)**
▶ **Roméo et Juliette (1867)**
▶ **Mors et Vita (1885)**

JACQUES OFFENBACH
1819–1880

Though seen as a musical embodiment of the frothiness and extravagance of Louis Naploeon's mid-century France, Offenbach was a brilliant and hard working composer with an uncanny ability to give his audiences not just what they thought they wanted but what he perceived they needed.

Jacques Offenbach was born the son of Isaac Juda Eberst, the Cantor of Cologne synagogue. When Isaac moved to Cologne from the village of Offenbach-an-Maine, he was known as 'Der Offenbacher' amongst Cologne's Jewish population. With the wry humour typical of him, Isaac decided he would simplify matters by adopting the name Offenbach as his own. His second

son Jakob (and seventh child in all) proved to be highly talented from an early age. His father decided that he and his older brother Julius would have a better start in life if they studied music in Paris, and engineered their acceptance at the Conservatoire. Jakob's chosen instrument was the 'cello (he was later to compose extensively for it). His formal studies only lasted a year,

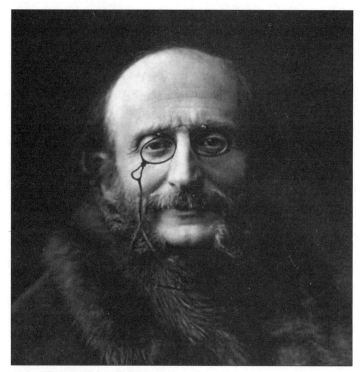

Jacques Offenbach

lyrical theatrical pieces turned down by the Comédie Française. Their success encouraged him to look for larger premises and within a year he had established the Bouffes-Parisiens in the Rue Choiseul and mounted the one-acter (most of the early works were one-acters) *Ba-ta-Clan*, for which his friend Ludovic Halévy wrote the script. Before the season was over, Louis-Napoléon requested Offenbach's company to stage a private performance for him at the Tuileries, and this put the seal on the Bouffes-Parisiens' success. Offenbach had hit upon a formula of witty, irreverent music, delivered with the help of rising star Hortense Schneider, plus first-rate librettos from his collaborations with such people as Halévy and the writer Henri Meilhac.

By the summer of 1858, however, Offenbach's rudimentary understanding of economics had brought him to the point of bankruptcy, and he needed two things in a hurry: a palpable 'hit' and a larger venue in which to mount it. To mull things over, and to escape his creditors, he went to Bad Ems to take a cure. From this period came the idea for his version of the Orpheus myth, *Orphée aux enfers*. The libretto was written by Halévy in collaboration with Offenbach himself and Henri Crémieux. After frantic preparations, *Orphée* was premièred in October 1858, and was doing steady business outraging refined Classical sensibilities when an attack by a particularly pompous critic, Jules Janin, brought it welcome publicity; before long the operetta was a roaring success. A command performance was attended by Louis-Napoléon in December 1859, shortly after the Emperor had insisted that Offenbach should officially be made a French

but by 1837 he was speaking French fluently, had changed his name to Jacques, and was a 'cellist in the orchestra pit of the Opéra-Comique, an ideal training ground for an intelligent, observant young musician. An informal apprenticeship with Friedrich Flotow was also useful, and the two men wrote two series of 'cello pieces together.

Offenbach was nothing if not resourceful; by the end of the decade he had impressed sufficient people with his 'cello playing to be invited while on tour in England to play for Queen Victoria and Prince Albert at Windsor. This tour was a turning-point, giving him the financial security to enable him to return to Paris and concentrate on his first love, composition. Having decided to convert to Catholicism, in 1840 he

was able to marry the woman of his choice, a Spaniard by the name of Hermine de Alcain. He spent several years writing theatrical works and songs but made little progress until after the revolutionary year of 1848 when the following spring he was offered the post of conductor at the Comédie Française. There he gained valuable experience and also supplied his own pieces for some of the plays, several of which became well known around Paris.

Offenbach remained at the theatre for five years, building up his connections and practical expertise to the point where he felt able to run his own theatre. After failing to persuade the Comédie Française to produce some of his compositions, in 1855 he leased the intimate Champs-Elysées theatre and began producing the short, funny and citizen. *Orphée* went on to become a European phenomenon, not only because foreign audiences were aware of contemporary French politics or laughed at Offenbach's word plays, but because the plot was genuinely funny. Offenbach's music, often juxtaposed with absurd reversals of so-called serious dramatic situations, was enormously tuneful and full of an exhilarating energy.

Offenbach and his company made enormous profits from the *Orphée* production (which was only finally taken off due to the exhaustion of the cast), but the composer was a notorious spendthrift, dandy and lavish entertainer. He once commented to a friend: "I have two—no, three—passions: cigars, women and gambling". His family—to which he was devoted—now numbered four daughters, thus he was driven by necessity and personal ambition to continue writing hit operettas.

His next few works were not successes, although a light-hearted jab at Wagner, *Le Musicien de l'avenir*, appearing in 1860 when Wagner was in Paris enduring the controversy engendered by *Tannhäuser's* première, was popular while it retained its topicality. True to form, Wagner never forgave the insult and wrote with childish vituperation about Offenbach over a decade later. Offenbach's talent for writing dance music—comic or serious—was so exceptional that it is no surprise that his next major success in France, *Le Papillon*, was a ballet.

By the summer of 1861 the proceeds from *Orphée* and its successors enabled Offenbach to build a holiday home, Villa Orphée, in Etrétat, a small village

on the Normandy coast. He also set to work on further operettas and what he termed '*opéra-comiques*', and his next success, *Les Bavards*, appeared early in 1863. This farce, based on an old Cervantes play, climaxes with a match where the vanquished woman marries her victorious chattering suitor. It progressed throughout Europe before going on to make people laugh in America and Russia.

After a triumphant visit to Vienna in 1863, Offenbach began work with Halévy and Meilhac on *La Belle Hélène*, the brilliant follow-up skit on the world of the Ancients, this time reducing the story of Helen of Troy and Paris to a rigged beauty contest and bedroom farce. The work was an immediate success, confirming Offenbach's complete domination of the world of operetta. Soon its melodies were being sung in theatres and cafés all over Europe.

Not long before this, Offenbach had embarked upon the most serious affair of his married life—with a petite young singer, Zulma Bouffar. The affair lasted well over a decade, Bouffar starring in many of his farces, including *La Vie Parisienne*, his next major hit. *La Vie* was produced in 1866 at a new venue for Offenbach, the Palais-Royale, and against even librettist Halévy's expectations, it was a riotous success from the first night onwards. Detailing the comings and goings of a gallery of rogues, madames and confidence tricksters—all facets of modern-day Paris—it had the first-night audience in stitches; in the following year, with thousands of tourists flocking to Paris for the 1867 Universal Exhibition, it played to packed houses. That same year

the political satire *La Grande-Duchesse de Gérolstein* gained a notable triumph, evading the delicate sensibilities of the censors by being resolutely light-hearted. The Emperor attended twice, laughing with everyone else at the caricatures of military grandees and high-ranking ministers. Count von Bismarck also laughed when he attended performances and left convinced that the incompetence displayed by the French army was real; he was to be proved right three years later.

The Franco-Prussian War of 1870 was a personal disaster for Offenbach: at the beginning of the year he had four productions running simultaneously in Paris, but by the time the war came, he was being attacked as a German sympathiser. For their part the German press lambasted him in turn for being a renegade. With the capitulation of the French army and the capture of the Emperor, Offenbach decided to move his family to Austria until things calmed down. From there he wrote to a friend: 'I feel sorry for those dear colleagues who hope, because I've had a lot of success, to harm me by saying that I'm a German, when they know very well that I'm French to the very marrow...'

DON'T MISS

▶ Orphée aux enfers (1858)

▶ La Belle Hélène (1864)

▶ Barbe-Bleue (1866)

▶ La Grande-Duchesse de Gérolstein (1867)

▶ La Périchole (1868)

▶ Les Contes d'Hoffmann (1881)

With the War and the Commune over, Offenbach returned in 1871 to a greatly changed France. He quickly decided to remain at his Etrétat villa while he was being publicly accused in print of every sin imaginable, including cowardice. In the past, his method of disarming criticism had been to work non-stop towards the next triumph; for the time being he was becalmed, looking for a new direction. This he decided he had found in the huge Théâtre de la Gaieté, which he leased in 1873 for his own productions. Now middle-aged and in poor health, he still had the energy to refurbish the place and write new works. Yet Offenbach repeated his past mistakes, throwing away the profits he made from revivals of old hits on production costs for new ones which proved less popular. By now in constant pain from rheumatism and gout, his only diversions were work and self-indulgence. Within three years of taking the lease and losing vast sums of money, Offenbach sold the theatre to one of his partners. He failed to clear his own debts from the sale with the result that even future royalties were

sequestered to satisfy his many creditors. Villa Orphée also had to be let to recoup money. That year Offenbach invaded the Paris theatres with new works and revivals in an attempt to make an inroad on his debts and to assuage his ever-present demon of creative energy, sick though he was.

In the post-1870 climate in France, composers like Lecocq and Johann Strauss II became the most fêted operetta writers, and Offenbach, though he fought against it, was falling out of fashion. Only an invitation to travel to America in 1876 to join the Centenary celebrations gave him the boost he needed. On the other side of the Atlantic his star was still in the ascendant and he was fêted in New York and Philadelphia. although he left America no better off financially.

On his return to a determinedly bemused Paris, he continued to pour forth new works with amazing fortitude; at last, in 1878, he achieved success with two works, *Madame Favart* (an 18th-century-style pastiche)

and *La fille du tambour-major*, the latter being his biggest success since the collapse of the Empire. During the course of that year he took up the completed libretto of *Les Contes d'Hoffmann*, his final work and one of the few serious theatrical pieces he ever attempted, and began writing the music for it. It was one of the few times that this most fecund and facile of composers (he often wrote a new work in a week) spent arduous days and months on a work in an attempt to bring to it everything he had. A five-act opera, it was all but finished at his death in late 1880. His last two years had been consumed by it. Typically, the theatre which mounted the posthumous first production butchered it, leaving out a whole act (Act II), and it is only relatively recently that audiences have come to know the work as Offenbach intended it. Some of the set arias and musical pieces have become famous, but the entire work deserves to stand with his greatest operettas such as *Orphée* and *Hélène* as part of his crowning achievement.

CÉSAR FRANCK

1822–1890

Like Berlioz, Franck developed an entirely individual and instantly recognizable compositional style. This arose initially from his childhood keyboard and theory studies, but matured into music of a deeply contemplative nature. Like many others, he was largely dismissed

as a composer during his lifetime, his gifts widely appreciated only after his death.

Franck was born in Liège. As early as the 16th century, his ancestors had displayed strong artistic inclinations, and both César and his brother Joseph showed musical ability at a young age. These

were seized upon by their father, who insisted they enter Liège Conservatoire. Still only 11, César emerged from the Conservatoire with honours, ready to embark on a career as an adolescent keyboard virtuoso, together with the older brother who was a fine violinist. After provincial tours, the father moved the entire family to Paris so that both boys could attend the Paris Conservatoire. César progressed rapidly and was ready to attempt the Prix de Rome when his father withdrew him so that he and his brother could go on tour and earn money. By this time, César was composing prolifically (chiefly to provide himself and his brother music to perform) and by the age of 12 had already completed at least two piano concertos. Even at this stage his compositions showed a command of form and technique rare at that time and in one so young, hinting at the perfection that his mature works would achieve.

By 1846 Franck was tiring of the life of a professional pianist, despite his father's attempts to drive him on. Now in his mid-twenties, he was ready to assert his independence. He became engaged to the daughter of a well-known actress and the two were married in 1848 during the chaos of the revolution. His family was scandalized by the marriage, but César settled with his wife in Paris where he earned a living as an organist, choirmaster and private tutor while continuing to compose. It was only after 20 years of such toil that he received in 1872 the appointment as organ professor at the Paris Conservatoire. An entirely unworldly and straightforward man, Franck's lack of cunning and inability to ingratiate himself with those in power were probably responsible for such a long delay in the recognition of his undoubted talents.

By 1873 he was busy composing the oratorio *Les Béatitudes,* the first of his mature works which is still regularly performed today. His teaching career continued uninterrupted and in time he

César Franck

came to be more highly regarded by talented pupils such as Vincent d'Indy, Ernest Chausson and Pierre de Breville than any other teacher at the Conservatoire; although he was nominally in charge of organ lessons only, his broad interest in music and deep understanding of composition equipped him to impart more information to talented and inquisitive students than their own backward-looking composition professors.

Yet Franck gained little or no recognition for the stream of mature compositions now issuing from his pen. A private concert at his home in 1879 was virtually ignored by his peers. During the 1880s he composed his greatest orchestral masterpieces, including the two symphonic poems, *Le Chasseur maudit* (1882) and *Les Djinns* (1884), his famous *Symphonic*

Variations (1885), the Symphony in D minor (1886–8) and *Psyché* (1887–8), as well as the brilliant Violin Sonata in A (1886), but none of this music was performed until another private concert in 1887, which was organized by his students in an effort to publicize their mentor's talents. The ill-rehearsed concert was a failure. Similarly, when his symphony received a première in 1889 from the Société des Concerts du Conservatoire, it was doomed before it was even played: the orchestra had no interest in the music and performed it badly, and the subscribers who supported the Société's events expressed little desire to hear the work.

In 1890 he achieved an unexpected success: the Ysaÿe Quartet performed his String Quartet in D and it received positive reviews—the first of his long career as a composer. Yet he was to

DON'T MISS

▶ Panis angelicus (1872)

▶ Symphonic Variations (1885)

▶ Symphony in D minor (1886–8)

▶ Violin Sonata in A (1886)

▶ 3 Organ Chorales (1890)

achieve no more, for in the spring of that year he was knocked down by an omnibus in Paris, receiving injuries to his side. After a short period of recuperation he declared himself fit and returned to work. However, his injuries were clearly not repaired and a few months later he developed pleurisy, quickly succumbing in his weakened state. At his death he remained still largely unrecognized, many of his greatest late works unperformed and unknown to all but his closest friends and loyal students. It was a former student of his, Charles Bordes, who wrote a compelling biography of his mentor which did much to turn the tide of public opinion in Franck's favour.

The mature works of his last two decades display the kind of melodic shape, harmonic construction and overall atmosphere which can be traced back to his long employment as organist/composer for St Clothilde's church in Paris. Franck was one of the first composers to aim at creating music which sustains a meditative mood without being histrionic or melodramatic: this is best exemplified by his masterpiece, the *Symphonic Variations*, in which the listener can virtually hear the composer improvising his variations at a church organ, especially at the crucial shift from major to minor midway through the piece. Such a strong individualist either creates a broad school of imitators and acolytes, or stands apart from the mainstream; Franck's music, though widely admired in the decades after his death, led to no school, as 'Debussyism' was to do within 10 years of Franck's demise.

Apart from the works already mentioned, his organ music demands attention, partly for the clue it gives to his overall output, but also for the special nature of the late compositions. Franck's organ music appeared at a time when organ music in France was becalmed and of little interest; his raising of its standards left a legacy built on later by Frenchmen such as Widor and Messiaen. His *Six Pieces* (1862) contained in embryo many of the musical ideas he later developed, while the *Three Pieces* (1878) and his last completed compositions, *Three Organ Chorales* (1890), are masterly expositions, the chorales for the most part using the variation form to excellent effect and exuding a wonderfully mystic, almost transcendental air. They are masterpieces which should be placed alongside his better-known pieces in any summary of his best work.

BEDŘICH SMETANA

1824–1884

One of the first of the great 19th-century 'nationalist' composers, Smetana gave his beloved Bohemia a central role in his two most famous works, the orchestral suite *Má Vlast* and the opera *The Bartered Bride*. Utterly devoid of bombast or jingoism, these allusions only serve to deepen a listener's appreciation of Smetana's music.

Smetana's creative career was bound up with the struggles of his native Bohemia to assert its basic right to exist. He was born into the family of an amateur musician and brewer on the Litomyšl estate of Count Waldstein and by the age of five was playing violin in a performance of a Haydn quartet. The following year, 1830, he made his début as a pianist, playing the overture to Auber's *La Musette de Portici*; aged eight he was happily composing folk and dance tunes. Yet his parents had neither the foresight nor the discipline to enforce his formal musical training, and while he had plenty of ambition—writing in his diary in 1840 that he wanted to become 'a Mozart in composition and a Liszt in technique'—he went on to complete a general education only at a school in Pilsen.

Pilsen played an important part in Smetana's life, for here he was reacquainted with Kateřina Kolár with whom he used to play piano duets in his boyhood. The 19-year-old Smetana fell hopelessly in love with her and she repaid him in a way which earned her his lifetime gratitude: at this time she was studying piano in Prague with the venerable teacher Josef Proksch, and through persistence and charm she persuaded Proksch to accept the impoverished Smetana as a student in composition and theory, allowing him to defer payment until he could afford it. This brought Smetana to Prague with at least some prospects. The connections which opened up led to the Director of Prague Conservatoire recommending Smetana to the family of Count Leopold Thun as their resident music master and piano tutor. Thus the newly employed Smetana combined extended stays in the country with the family during the summer with periods in town attending the Prague social 'season'.

In the succeeding years Smetana gradually shifted his ambition from being a virtuoso in the Lisztian manner to being a composer with a strong personality of his own. Even early piano pieces, such as *Bagatelles and Impromptus* (1844) had a charm and simple sincerity which contained his unmistakable stamp. They also reflected the trials and tribulations of his on-off affair with Kateřina Kolár.

In the build up to the turbulence of the 1848 revolutions in Europe, Smetana began to feel the limitations of his service in the Thun household; by 1847 he had decided to start his own music school in Prague. One of

Bedřich Smetana

those he applied to for financial help was Franz Liszt who saw the worth of some piano compositions Smetana had sent him and wrote encouragingly to the young Bohemian, even offering to find him a publisher for his music. Suitably enthused, and with the outbreak of the 1848 insurrections (to which he felt passionately committed), Smetana left the employ of the Thun family. Careful not to burn his bridges, he arranged for Kateřina to succeed him as Thun's music master. The music school opened in 1848, and in the following year Smetana and Kateřina were married.

However, the Smetanas found themselves constantly on the edge of financial precipices as they struggled to make the music school pay its way, and a series of childbirths resulted in only one infant, Zofie, surviving past early childhood. Although Smetana was widening his circle of musical friendships—meeting Clara and Robert Schumann and keeping in touch with Berlioz, whom he had met in 1847—Prague refused to be conquered by his achievements. In 1855 his beloved Kateřina began to show signs of consumption, and when Smetana accepted an offer from the Göteborg

DON'T MISS

▶ The Bartered Bride (1866)

▶ Dalibor (1868)

▶ Má Vlast (1872–9)

▶ Libuše (1881)

▶ The Devil's Wall (1882)

Harmoniska Sallskapet in Sweden to become their conductor, it enabled the Smetanas to escape Prague's vicious political intrigues. They remained in Sweden until 1861, Smetana developing his approach to orchestral composition, taking as his models the Lisztian and Wagnerian ideals of programmatic music, where a work is given its unity by thematic and motific means and by the subject matter itself. Curiously, his absence from Prague did not bring on a wave of creative nostalgia, and the works composed while in Sweden, including *Wallenstein's Camp* and *Richard III* (he was a fervent admirer of Shakespeare's plays) show him reacting to more cosmopolitan stimuli.

In 1857 Kateřina died, her illness hastened by the harshness of the Scandinavian winters. Smetana proved unable to cope with the loneliness, turning in his grief to Bettina Ferdinandová, the sister-in-law of his brother, Karl, marrying her a year after Kateřina's death. In 1861 Smetana and Bettina returned to Prague. Within a year of his arrival, the Provisional Theatre, dedicated to Czech language plays and operas, was opened, and Smetana became a leading light in the battle to establish it on a firm footing. This was achieved despite considerable opposition from the conservative elements within Prague's cultural

society, who did not appreciate an ardent supporter of Wagner and Liszt, those arch-modernists, leading the way in Prague.

It was at this time that Smetana's thoughts turned to creating musical dramas and orchestral pieces which celebrated the popular culture and history of the Czech people. By 1863 he had completed his first opera, *The Brandenburgers in Bohemia*. This patriotic work which deals with Bohemia's political history and a wholesale uprising, proved initially very popular and its warm reception inspired Smetana to look for a production of his already completed subsequent work. *The Bartered Bride*, as it came to be known, was produced at the Provisional Theatre. Smetana was now the Theatre's conductor, and all looked set for success. However, the Austro-Prussian War intervened, and although the *Bride* had a happy première, it was only after military manoeuvres were over that a less unnerved public took *The Bartered Bride* to its collective heart. The opera became such a runaway success that its position as the most popular Czech opera has remained unassailed ever since, despite the later triumphs of Janáček. *The Bride* was blessed with a strong, simple plot, a first-rate libretto, well-conceived characters and music which was endlessly charming—in short, its poise and balance were truly Mozartian. Smetana spent the rest of his life as an operatic composer trying to recreate this level of popular acclaim.

A combination of public expectation and Smetana's increasing inclination to take a more progressive musical stance led to his next opera, *Dalibor*, being

coolly received. This is not to assume that the work itself, a stern assessment of a key figure in Czech history, is poor; it is a fine piece, and is often performed in its homeland today, but Smetana had outdistanced his public. Undaunted, he chose an equally ambitious subject for his next opera, *Libuše*, which more closely reflected Bohemian political and national aspirations, combining legend and moral lessons in a sober prophecy of the eventual triumph of the Czech people. Smetana himself realised the 'occasional' nature of this opera, declaring it fit to be presented only "during festivals which touch the whole Czech nation". For this reason if none other he waited until the grand opening of the new National Theatre in Prague in 1881 for it to be premièred, more than eight years after its completion.

The operas which appeared between *Dalibor* and *Libuše* show the diversity of subject and mood, as well as sureness of touch, of the now fully mature and confident composer. *The Two Widows* (1874) was a comedy with French origins which is unfailingly light in mood and technique, while *The Kiss* (1876) and *The Secret* (1878) were both inspired by stories set in the Bohemian countryside.

Not content with celebrating his country's beauty and importance in opera, Smetana also took the earlier lessons he had learned from Liszt, Berlioz and Wagner with regard to extended orchestral works and turned them to bear on various aspects of Bohemia. In 1874, Smetana began work on the cycle of symphonic poems which would eventually form the six-part *Má Vlast* (My Country). At the same time the first signs of the physical disintegration which would kill him manifested themselves, and Smetana realised he was going deaf. *Má Vlast* is made up of individual movements, some of which have become world-famous in their own right. Certainly the second one, *Vltava* (The Moldau) is often played as a distinct entity, its wonderful storyline brought to life by the composer's deft melodic and rhythmic invention. The other exceptionally popular section is *From Bohemia's Woods and Fields*, and this glorious musical depiction of the Bohemian countryside has a magic all its own.

Smetana completed *Má Vlast* in 1878–9, although the complete cycle was not performed until 1882. By then

Smetana was aware that his deafness precluded any thought of him conducting the première. He had withdrawn from public life as his infirmities—caused it seems by hereditary syphillis— increasingly incapacitated him and his conservative enemies in Prague continued their attempts to undermine his position. Smetana completed one further opera, *The Devil's Wall*, which he described as 'comic-romantic' and which, despite a plot which lacks the usual lucidity of Smetana's other operas, has held its place on Czech stages. Smetana wrote it in the face of the most terrible physical and mental sufferings, all symptoms of the impending collapse. Despite his known condition and his courage in completing the work and its general public approval, its première

was marred by heartless criticism from his enemies.

A testament to his unending courage was the fact that Smetana embarked upon writing the opera *Viola* in 1883, based on Shakespeare's *Twelfth Night*, and in fact managed to complete a whole act before his final mental collapse in April 1884, just weeks after a Prague concert held in his honour. In mid-May he died. Smetana's happy disposition and endlessly brave optimism in the face of the most terrible private pain, as well as his unquenchable faith in the future of his nation, has given his music a unique place in Czech life, placing it apart from the humourlessness and gloom of much of the so-called serious music of his century.

ANTON BRUCKNER
1824–1896

Shy, naïve and deeply religious, Bruckner composed some of the most ambitious and challenging symphonic music of the 19th century—as far removed from the programme-music ideas for orchestral music of Wagner and Liszt as they were from the symphonic language of his other great contemporary, the so-called 'conservative' Brahms. A constant prey to self-doubt, he nonetheless had a major impact on those who followed him, from Mahler onwards.

Bruckner was born in Ansfelden in north eastern Austria, the son of the village schoolmaster. Little Anton was expected to follow in his father's footsteps, but the father died in 1837 and Anton was sent to school in the village of St Florian, where he also became a chorister at the monastery and received his first lessons on a variety of instruments, including the organ. After a period of further education in Linz, he returned to the school in St Florian as assistant teacher. In 1848 he became organist at St Florian's Institute, and for the next few years his exacting duties allowed

him little time to develop as a composer, although he was already attempting organ and choral works.

This unhappy state of affairs continued until his appointment as organist at Linz Cathedral in 1848. At a stroke he was freed from his schoolmaster's duties and, though the position was hardly lucrative, he was able to support himself and still find time for composition and for yearly stints in Vienna studying theory with Simon Sechter. He later studied composition with Otto Kitzler; a fine teacher, Kitzler's oft-expressed enthusiasm for

Matters took a turn for the better the following year when, through the influence of a good friend who was *Hofkapellmeister* in Vienna, Bruckner was given the post of counterpoint and organ teacher at Vienna Conservatoire; he was later promoted to Professor. This was augmented in 1875 by a lectureship at Vienna University. He also accepted the post of deputy librarian and assistant singing teacher to the Court chapel, as well as taking the service every Sunday.

His composing continued apace; in 1871 he completed his Symphony No. 2 in C minor, and the Third Symphony (dedicated to Wagner, who himself suggested the dedication on perusing the score) followed in 1873. The Second Symphony received a successful première in 1873. The only distractions from his regular pattern of existence were occasional trips abroad in order to demonstrate his organ-playing prowess. Audiences, from London to Paris and beyond, were impressed, especially by his powers of improvisation. Bruckner made great personal strides between his First and Third Symphonies, and it was an occasion of the utmost importance when a reluctant Vienna Philharmonic agreed to première his Third Symphony in 1877. By now he was identified in Vienna as belonging to the progressive camp of Wagner and Liszt, and this brought him powerful enemies, such as the famous critic, Eduard Hanslick. The première evolved into a disaster of epic proportions: the orchestra hardly gave of its best, and even before the first movement was over, sections of the audience began filing out of the hall while cat-calls interrupted the

Anton Bruckner

Wagner sparked Bruckner's own fascination with the controversial German's music. By the early 1860s Bruckner was deeply immersed in his studies of Wagner's scores, and finally attempted ambitious works of his own: a symphony in F minor (later rejected by him as 'schoolwork') and a Mass.

By the middle of the 1860s Bruckner, now nearly 40, was at last close to completing his first published symphony in C minor (1865–6), after having set aside the so-called Symphony No. 0 *(Nulte)* in D (1863–4),

which lay unpublished and unknown until after his death. In 1865 he travelled to Munich for the première of Wagner's *Tristan und Isolde*, which he found profoundly moving and which prompted the usually retiring Bruckner to introduce himself to Wagner and worship at the great man's shrine. These intense experiences, however, did nothing to dispel his underlying lack of belief in himself, and during 1867, when his bouts of depression reached suicidal levels, he suffered a complete nervous breakdown and was forced to convalesce in Bad Kreuzen to regain his equilibrium.

concentration of those who remained. By the end, only his faithful students and a smattering of friends were still present. This verdict was shattering to a character as sensitive as Bruckner.

It was 1880 before he finished another symphony, but in the years 1880–81 he completed the Fourth, Fifth and Sixth Symphonies, all works with their distinct character and all begun during the 1870s. His ability to handle large forms and huge orchestral forces continually developed, as did his highly individual ideas of contrast and dynamics in a work or movement where sudden change or transmutation—whether of the setting or of the principal material—is the norm rather than the exception. Yet at this time the practice of interference by his friends and colleagues began: sections of his new works would be reorchestrated or revised, often with his approval but sometimes without it. This showed both Bruckner's lack of faith in his own abilities as well as the level of humility he brought to his dealings with the outside world. It has taken until the present day for many of the distortions of his then-unfashionable orchestral practices to be stripped away and his original versions restored.

In 1881 the Fourth Symphony, conducted by Richter in Vienna, was well-received, but it was outside the Austrian capital that Bruckner's reputation began to take hold. His Seventh Symphony was premièred in Leipzig in 1884 under the famous Arthur Nikisch, and was given a rapturous welcome by audience and critics alike. After this, there was a

considerable wait for the Eighth, a massive work with the finale alone lasting as long as an average Mozart piano concerto. Once again Bruckner's insecurities got the better of him and the work was extensively revised, even though the composer himself felt the revisions unnecessary. Whatever Bruckner's misgivings (and he believed that all the cuts and revisions should, in the fullness of time, be rescinded), he was rewarded with another success in 1892 when the Eighth Symphony was first performed. This was to be the last symphony premièred in his lifetime: the Ninth remained incomplete at the time of his death, with three movements finished to his satisfaction but the finale unwritten.

Bruckner was a lonely and retiring man, almost unworldly in his dealings with everyday life and intensely involved in his devotion to the Catholic dogma. His mature Masses—in D minor, E minor and F minor—and much of his later choral music, such as the marvellous *Te Deum,* are substantial musical statements as well as being impressive personal testaments to an unerring faith. There was little beyond religion and music which interested him; he showed no inclination to embrace the wider culture of his times and the written word, with the exception of the Bible, left him untouched. His emotional attachments appear to have been adolescent in their nature—from his hero worship of Wagner to his undue affection for adolescent girls. He expended much of his energy—outside of composing—on the furtherance of his pupils' careers and musical knowledge and expounding on the genius of his beloved Wagner.

As Bruckner entered the last few years of his life, he found the tide of creative opinion in Vienna shifting towards him, with younger composers such as Hugo Wolf and Ferdinand Löwe becoming enthusiasts. In 1891 he was given an honorary Doctorate (in Philosophy) by Vienna Conservatoire. That same year he was invited by Emperor Franz Joseph to take up private rooms in the Belvedere Palace, at the Emperor's expense, and resigned from his position at the Conservatoire. He died from a combination of old age and relentless hard work, but even on his deathbed he worked on his final symphony until his last conscious minute. This obsession with work must be seen as a consolation against the larger background of his life; he died a well-known and largely respected figure in Austria and Germany, but until the following century he remained largely unknown in the world beyond. In recent times, following Mahler's lead, his star has risen higher internationally, but the inherent difficulties of his symphonic style, as well as the sheer proportions of his works, will be forever a stumbling block to mass popularity.

DON'T MISS

▶ **Ave Maria in F (1861)**

▶ **Symphony No. 4 (Romantic) (1874)**

▶ **Symphony No. 7 (1881–3)**

▶ **Te Deum in C (1881–4)**

▶ **Symphony No. 8 (1884–7)**

PART VI

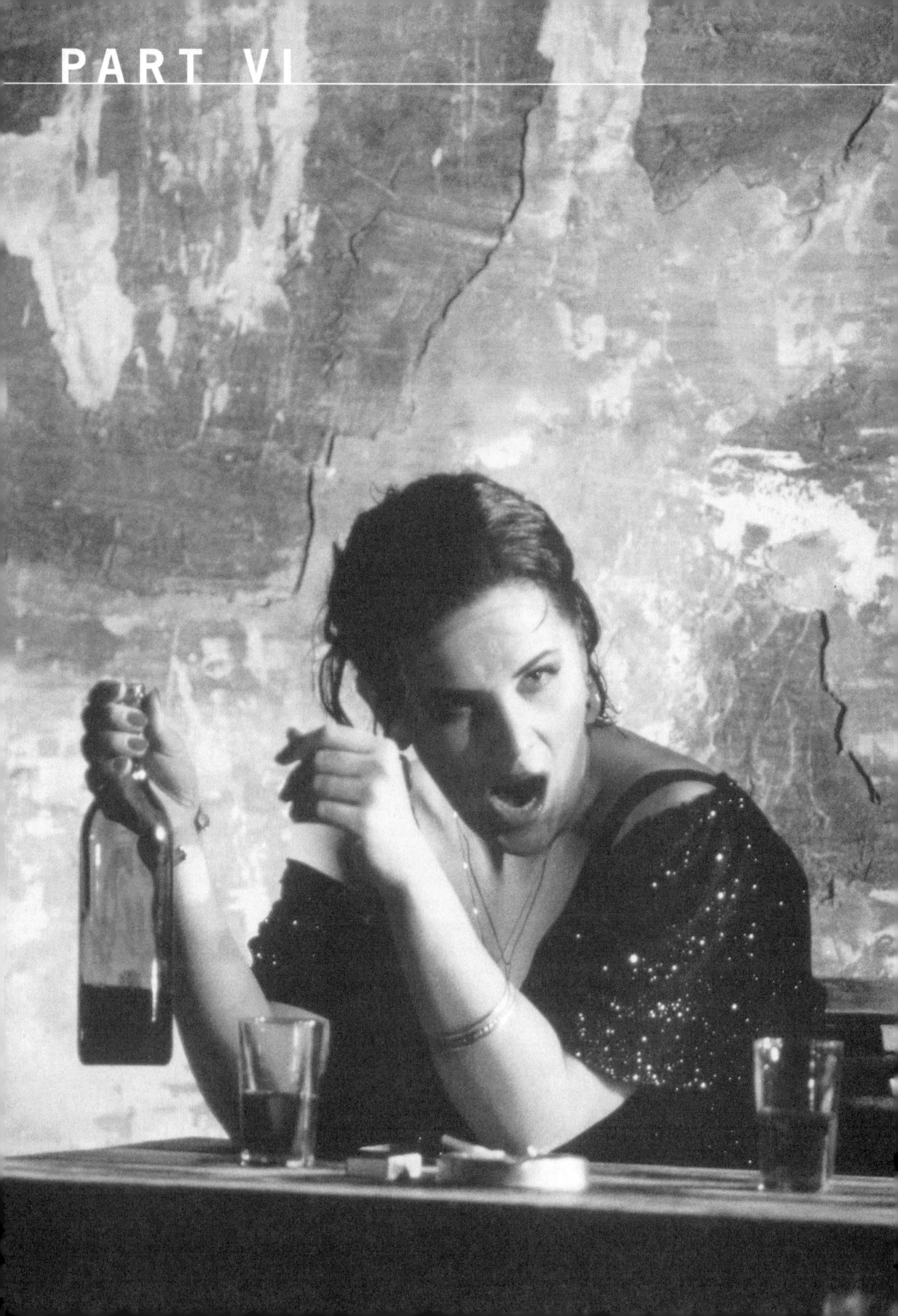

1825-1850

If the composers who were born in this period and achieved maturity in the second half of the 19th century are taken as a group, a decided shift in the national patterns is discernible. Only two composers from Germany and Austria—Brahms and Johann Strauss II—achieved a level of eminence equal to that of their predecessors, with Bruch managing at least one masterpiece in his First Violin Concerto. It is arguable that this relative decline in high quality music is attributable to the massive influence in Germany of Wagner during these years, and the difficulties encountered by other composers in forging themselves a separate creative identity. Certainly both Brahms and Strauss achieved it; Brahms by concentrating on musical forms largely untouched by Wagner, Strauss by restricting himself to waltzes, polkas and 'galops', or by refining the delicious ingredients of operetta as defined by Offenbach, then bringing his own Viennese elements in to play.

Elsewhere a more vigorous growth of musical life was being nurtured, with the emergence of the great French exoticists Bizet, Delibes and Chabrier (all of whom found rich inspiration in subjects and music from other lands), while both Delibes and Chabrier joined the facile and elegant Saint-Saëns in creating delightful comic fantasies for stage and salon, including *L'Etoile, Le Roi l'a dit* and *Carnival of the Animals* (the latter appearing long after its

Louise Winter performs in Carmen *with the English National Opera, London 1995*

creation). Delibes was also responsible for re-establishing standards of excellence in French ballet with his *Coppélia* and *Sylvia*. But the ruler of the French opera stage in this generation was Massenet, creator of *Manon* and heir to the legacy of Meyerbeer. Fauré, although he composed the remarkable opera *Pénélope* and the moving Requiem, largely adhered to French mélodie, chamber music and less ambitious orchestral works.

While France overflowed with creative energy, Edvard Grieg was striking rich veins of inspiration through his determination to bring the music and folklore of his native Norway into his compositions. Equally, Dvořák's incredible melodic gifts and formal expertise, allied to his keen ear for the native music of countries like his own and America, brought many new gems into the common repertoire. Further east, perhaps the most significant event in terms of the future of music was the rise to prominence of members of Russia's 'mighty five', Mussorgsky, Balakirev, Borodin, Cui and Rimsky-Korsakov. Apart from the tremendous freshness and dynamism of their own masterpieces, their impact was equally crucial in enabling later composers such as Debussy and Stravinsky to circumvent the artistic dilemmas posed by Wagner's legacy. Yet overshadowing everything in late 19th-century Russia was Tchaikovsky, who combined artistic integrity with an ability to write music in every genre which has remained

JOHANN STRAUSS II

1825-1899

Johann Strauss's genius lay in his ability to take the popular salon music of Vienna in the early decades of the 19th century—with its clear emphasis on melody and dance rhythms—and convert it into music which not only became fashionable but which in time evolved into high art. His own conducting talents (and that of his father's before him) were clearly of prime importance in achieving these aims.

Johann Strauss Jr was born into a musical dynasty of just one generation. His father, Johann Sr came from a desperately unhappy Viennese family; the mother died when he was seven and the drunken innkeeper father committed suicide. Johann Sr's behaviour to his own family was little better; by the time he was in his late twenties he was being openly unfaithful to his wife, by whom he had six children. Johann Jr saw little of his father who set up house in a dingy flat in Vienna with his mistress, by whom he proceeded to have five more children, all born out of wedlock. Although Strauss Sr was by then internationally famous as a composer of superior dance music (played by his own orchestra), he banned any of his own children from following in his footsteps, considering it too risky and fragile an occupation.

His three legitimate sons ignored his advice. Johann Jr was the oldest, and although he conscientiously completed

Johann Strauss II

his education at the Gymnasium and Polytechnic, advancing to the position of clerk in a savings bank, his mother had long encouraged his secret musical ambitions. By the time he was a teenager, he was an accomplished violinist and showed flair for leading ensembles, leading his own (in direct competition with his father's) by the time he was 19. He had also begun composing at a very early age, although in his first years as a musician he kept strictly to the type of music

already coined by his father and other contemporaries.

In 1849 Johann Strauss Sr died of scarlet fever in the apartment of his mistress. She decamped, leaving the body and little else. Within a short time Johann Jr had merged the two rival orchestras. Thus equipped, he quickly became the unchallenged leader of the Viennese dance scene, occupying several important posts in the capital's ballrooms and touring Austria, Germany and Poland. He had the rare combination of an artist's talent and an impresario's ability to exploit to the maximum the main chance, using a formidable network of contacts for the purpose. This he did so successfully that several times he collapsed through sheer exhaustion, his brother Josef taking over leadership of the family orchestra until Johann recovered. In 1856 Johann was commissioned to supply a set of autumn concerts in St Petersburg as part of a campaign by Russian industrial magnates to bring the fashionable set to the city. Strauss was paid handsomely to run these concerts, the orchestra playing a combination of popular classics and Strauss' own compositions. This lucrative connection lasted for a decade, while Johann Jr steadily amassed a considerable fortune.

At the beginning of the 1860s Johann met an old acquaintance, Henrietta (Jetty) Chalupetzky, a retired mezzo-soprano who was independently wealthy, a good 10 years older than Johann and the mother of five illegitimate children. They were married in late 1862, Jetty taking over the task (done until then by Johann's mother) of running the Strauss music-making business. By 1864 the Strauss family machine was working in top gear. When the reigning operetta king, Jacques Offenbach, made a visit to Vienna, Johann saw an opportunity to extract maximum publicity: he was contracted to supply a waltz for the 'Concordia' Ball in the Sofienbad Saal, and hearing that Offenbach had also been commissioned, he prevailed upon the critic Eduard Hanslick to ask Offenbach for permission to publish both waltzes through his new publishing partner, Spina. Offenbach

agreed, and the Strauss Orchestra performed first Strauss's *Morgenblätter* at the ball, followed by Offenbach's *Abendblätter*. This friendly contest gave Strauss not only a national boost but an international profile. It is often alleged that Offenbach suggested to Strauss that, considering his gifts for melody, he should seriously consider writing operetta. Ten years later Strauss would score a notable success by doing exactly that.

Meanwhile, the wonderful waltzes and polkas kept appearing, with the most famous of all, *An der schönen, blauen Donau* (Blue Danube) appearing in 1867, curiously enough to a muted response, many of the audience wondering whether this masterpiece had overstretched the genre for which it was written. *Blue Danube* and other favourites were played during an exhausting trip to America in 1872, and were phenomenally successful. On his return to Vienna, Johann began developing ideas for an operetta which eventually became *Der Carneval in Rom*. It was premièred in Vienna in 1873; although not a sensation, it was sufficiently popular to encourage Strauss to continue in this vein.

It was the director of Vienna's Carl-Theater, Franz Jauner, who suggested to librettist Richard Genée that he make

an operetta book of the successful French play, *Le Réveillon*, written by Offenbach's librettists Meilhac and Halévy. On seeing Genée's work, Strauss was immediately convinced that it was a suitable vehicle for his talents, and in the fall of 1873 set to work on the music. It soon took shape as *Die Fledermaus*. The April 1874 production was a roaring success and within three months a production had opened in Berlin. By the end of the decade it had been performed in countries as far apart as America and Australia, and was Strauss's most successful operetta of all, perhaps even in time eclipsing Offenbach's *Orphée*. From now on Strauss's creative life was firmly divided between his instrumental and his operatic ventures.

Strauss had unfortunately inherited his father's proclivity for indulging in extra-marital affairs; Jetty managed to bear this with dignity for many years, but by the time of *Fledermaus*, the marriage was in tatters. The impasse was only resolved by Jetty's death from a heart attack in April 1878. Strauss promptly remarried an actress, Angela (Lili) Dietrich, but the age difference (she was 27, he was 52), and his compulsive work patterns soon drove a wedge between them. Frustrated by his long absences and her dull life, she began an affair with

---

DON'T MISS

▶ **An der schönen, blauen Donau, Op. 314 (1867)**
▶ **Tales from the Vienna Woods, Op. 325 (1868)**
▶ **Kaiser–waltz, Op. 437 (1889)**
▶ **Morgenblätter, Op. 279 (1864)**
▶ **Perpetuum mobile, Op. 257 (1862)**

DON'T MISS

▶ Wiener Blut, Op. 354
  (1873)

▶ Unter Donner und Blitz
  Polka, Op. 324 (1868)

▶ Die Fledermaus (1874)

▶ Eine Nacht in Venedig
  (1883)

▶ Der Zigeunerbaron
  (1885)

theatre director George Steiner, eventually eloping with him. An uncontested divorce was granted in 1882. Strauss immediately took up with a 26-year-old widow, Adele Deutsch, and the two were soon living together in Vienna.

The spring of 1883 saw the first performance of the famous waltz *Frühlingsstimmen* (Voices of Spring) initially with text sung by a coloratura soprano, but then in the purely instrumental version which remains popular today. His opera *Eine Nacht in Venedig* was premièred in Berlin in the same year; the mediocrity of the libretto damaged its initial reception, but much work was done to improve it and by the time of the Viennese première it was a complete triumph.

A summer 1884 cure in Franzensbad left Strauss recharged and impatient to start the music for his next operetta, one on which he and his new librettist, Ignatz Schnitzer, lavished more care than on any other in the composer's career. This was *Der Zigeunerbaron* (The Gipsy Baron), arguably Strauss's greatest operatic achievement, even if it has not achieved the overall popularity of *Die Fledermaus*. This work, begun in early summer 1884, was not finally finished until late 1885—an unheard-of gestation period for someone like Strauss—but the first-night applause convinced Strauss that it had been worth the effort.

Two years later, convinced that in Adele he had finally found the right partner, Strauss arranged for a release from his Austrian citizenship and was then accepted as a citizen of the small German dukedom, Saxe-Coburg-Gotha. He also left the Catholic church and became a Lutheran Protestant, thus avoiding the papal intransigence which had ensnared the devoutly Catholic Liszt's attempts to remarry. He and Adele were married in 1887. His last decade was relatively content, Adele giving him the energy and support he required. She also brought him a new circle of friends, one of them being Johannes Brahms, an admirer who in time became one of Johann's most valued friends. Johann was deeply moved by Brahms's death in 1897, and took a long time to regain anything like his former vigour. By early 1899 he was preparing for the première of his ballet *Aschenbrödel* (Cinderella). Sadly, he was not to live to complete the full score, or see it performed: in May 1899 he fell prey to a chill which quickly developed into pneumonia. The years of punishing hard work had destroyed his powers of resistance and he died on 3 June 1899. He was laid to rest in Vienna Central Cemetery near the tombs of Brahms, Beethoven and Schubert.

Where Strauss differed from the rest of his family was the point at which he combined the Viennese dance tradition with the Parisian operetta forms largely devised and developed by Offenbach. Today it is widely agreed that *Die Fledermaus* and *Der Zigeunerbaron* are the greatest of all German-language operettas, and stand comparison with the best from the other opera genres of the time.

ALEXANDER BORODIN
1833–1887

Borodin was of great importance in that he showed the way forward for many composers, Russian and otherwise, who wished to follow **neither Wagner nor Brahms but to create music which reflected the character and history of their own countries.**

Borodin was born in St Petersburg, the illegitimate offspring of a liaison between Prince Luka Stepanovich Gedianishvili from Georgia and the sister of a distinguished civil servant.

Alexander Borodin

his first symphony, completed by 1866 and performed in 1869, by which time he had tried his hand at two operas, *The Valiant Knights* and *The Tsar's Bride*, neither of which were completed to his satisfaction.

He did, however, write an array of fine songs during this decade, but his second symphony, the first which had a truly Russian musical soul, took longer. He completed the piano score by 1871, but the orchestration, undertaken by someone who only composed on Sundays or on holiday, took another seven years. He dedicated the symphony to his wife, Yekaterina Sergeyevna, a good pianist and excellent musician, whom he had married in 1863. The first performance was given in 1877 in St Petersburg. Liszt, who had greatly admired Borodin's first symphony and was instrumental in the establishment of Borodin's international reputation, on being given the score of the second said to the composer: "They say there is nothing new under the moon, but this—this is completely new!... Yesterday a certain German came to see me and brought me his third symphony. I told him 'We Germans have a long way to go', and showed him your second".

Borodin never visited Georgia and was almost entirely raised by his mother, who denied him nothing. After completing a general education, he elected to study medicine in Heidelberg. While in Germany he discovered his other great passion in life—music. It was only natural that his first love was for German composers such as Mendelssohn and Schumann.

He returned to Russia in 1862 and was appointed assistant professor of chemistry at the St Petersburg Medico-Surgical Academy. Here he met Mily Balakirev and César Cui, later to be identified as formative members of the 'mighty handful', the five Russian nationalist composers whose works would revolutionize Russian Classical music. Balakirev in particular realized the extent of Borodin's hidden musicality, and encouraged him not only to study music but to begin composing. His interest fully awakened, Borodin became a fervent music student while pursuing a parallel career in the sciences. Under Balakirev's direct supervision he wrote

Borodin's professional career had taken a step forward in 1872 when he was given a professorship at the Academy; his commitments there further restricted his free time. His opera *Prince Igor* (left uncompleted at his death), which had already been laid aside once for the second symphony, remained at the back of his mind as a project for the future. During the 1870s he worked fitfully on parts of it, including the *Polovtsian Dances* (which had a

DON'T MISS

▶ Prince Igor (1890)

▶ In the Steppes of Central Asia (1880)

▶ Symphony No. 2 (1869–76)

▶ String Quartet No. 1 (1875–78)

▶ String Quartet No. 2 (1885)

separate performance in February 1879), but it was another orchestral project, *In the Steppes of Central Asia*, which was finished next. Dedicated to Franz Liszt, it was in the tradition of Liszt's own tone poems, and was first performed in 1880.

Between 1877 and 1881 Borodin also produced his two incomparably beautiful string quartets in which the glorious melody and exoticism of his style was given free reign within an intimate musical setting. These quartets have become two of the most beloved by performers and audiences in Borodin's entire repertoire. His last completed work was composed in the winter of 1884–85, a *Petite Suite* of seven salon-like piano pieces, dedicated to a Belgian aristocrat, Comtesse Louise de Mercy-Argentau. The Comtesse returned the compliment by inviting Borodin and César Cui to Belgium, and the success of the first trip in 1885 led to another in 1886, when his two symphonies and *In the Steppes of Central Asia* were performed and received favourable reviews, thus beginning the process of spreading his reputation in French-speaking countries.

Borodin's private life revolved around his family, the household cats (of which there were many), his scientific career and a number of other projects, only some of them musical. As Rimsky-Korsakov recorded, Borodin was easy prey to anyone wanting a willing pair of hands for an array of societies and charities. This left him little time to complete his various musical projects. As he wrote to a friend: 'I can only compose when I am too unwell to give my lectures. So my friends, reversing the usual custom, never say to me "I hope you are well", but "I do hope you are ill"'.

The musical projects included a Third Symphony (which he had completed in his own mind before he died, but for which he only found time to write the first two movements) and a third String Quartet for which he had written the scherzo. But by far the largest of the uncompleted projects was *Prince Igor*. This he worked on during holidays or in rare breaks from his usual routine, often jotting down ideas and adding them, higgledy-piggledy, to the pile relating to the libretto—the latter also created by him in parallel with the music. What Borodin might have achieved with all this material can only be speculated upon for in February 1887, while hosting a party in St Petersburg, he collapsed suddenly and died, a victim of a ruptured artery in the heart.

His closest musical colleagues, Rimsky-Korsakov and Glazunov, quickly set to work to try to bring some order to his unfinished works; within a year they had conjured up a 'complete' *Prince Igor*, with many parts orchestrated, reorchestrated or reordered by Rimsky-Korsakov, with Glazunov actually composing ('from memory', he claimed, of Borodin's own recitals) the Prologue. They also managed a similar feat for the third symphony, of which Borodin had scored two movements; here again Glazunov's memory of Borodin's pianistic run-throughs of later movements aided in the completion, while the scherzo from the incomplete Third String Quartet was pressed into service in the symphony. Glazunov also managed a sensitive and charming orchestral scoring for the *Petite Suite*.

These two colleagues did more than anyone to bring Borodin's music to a wider audience, and what they achieved with *Igor* enabled it to become what it is today—a Russian operatic institution and a work which must be included on any list of great operas. In recent years, much research has been done into the music by Borodin which Rimsky-Korsakov and Glazunov left *out* of the opera in order to produce a finished version, and today there is an intense debate about what constitutes an 'authentic' performance. Indeed, Borodin's insistence on turning east rather than to Europe for a truly Russian musical identity is more clearly grasped in the versions shorn of the alterations and accretions of his colleagues.

JOHANNES BRAHMS
1833–1897

To many the embodiment of Germanic rectitude and conservatism, Brahms was in fact a deeply romantic and highly sensitive man who, although prickly and acerbic in his everyday dealings with people, flooded his greatest works with an overwhelming depth of emotion.

Johannes was born into a happy but relatively humble family. His father Jakob, though the son of an innkeeper, was passionate about music and by dint of sheer determination managed to secure himself a position in a Hamburg theatre orchestra. There he met and married Johanna, a woman 17 years his senior. Brahms benefitted from his father's musical ambitions: when he and his younger brother Fritz showed musical talent, the money was found for them to attend Grammar school and take piano lessons. When Johannes was 10, he appeared at a concert arranged for him, impressing both his teacher and an American impresario, who wanted him to tour the US as a prodigy. To save him from this fate, it was arranged that he should embark on a course of study with Edward Marxsen, a teacher of theory and instrumental technique. It was Marxsen who first noted the boy's aptitude for composition and began his comprehensive musical studies. He also helped develop Brahms's already voracious appetite for books.

Johannes Brahms

During the late 1840s the Brahms family became too poor to continue without financial assistance from their children; Johannes made some extra money by playing the piano in bars, but his health suffered from the long hours and smoke-filled rooms. He continued his studies with Marxsen, refining his compositional techniques and trying out a number of piano and choral works. The concerts he gave in September 1848, May 1849 and April 1850 demonstrated his growing stature

as a pianist. In 1853 he paired up with a Hungaran violinist by the name of Edward Reményi and together they began a programme of recitals for violin and piano in Hamburg which were sufficiently well received for them to undertake a tour to other centres.

In Hannover, one of the tour venues, Brahms made the acquaintance of the 23-year-old violinist Joseph Joachim, already *Konzertmeister* to King George and destined to become one of

DON'T MISS

▶ Piano Concerto, No. 1, Op. 15 (1854–58)

▶ Piano Concerto, No. 2, Op. 83 (1878–81)

▶ Violin Concerto, Op. 77 (1878)

▶ Symphony, No. 3, Op. 90 (1883)

▶ Symphony, No. 4, Op. 98 (1884–85)

Brahms's greatest interpreters and champions. Joachim was inordinately impressed by the shy young man, and suggested they might play together in the future: as a gesture of friendship, he gave Brahms letters of introduction to Liszt in Weimar and Schumann in Düsseldorf. Brahms and Reményi travelled on to Weimar where they met Liszt, then living with Princess Caroline von Sayn-Wittgenstein. Though ill at ease in this sophisticated environment, Brahms came to like Liszt as a man (although not his works) and Liszt was perceptive enough to admire the youthful piano pieces Brahms showed him. Reményi, in his element, remained in Weimar while Brahms travelled on alone to Göttingen to meet up with Joachim who was studying at the University.

Encouraged by Joachim, Brahms finally called on the Schumanns in Düsseldorf. The night before his visit, Schumann entered in his diary: 'Herr Brahms, from Hamburg'. The following day he wrote: 'Visit from Brahms, a genius'. Brahms, just 20, found himself immediately in sympathy with people as deeply involved in the same romantic but highly structured approach to music which he himself preferred. He was completely entranced by Schumann's works, and Schumann returned the compliment, introducing him to

musician friends and writing an article for his journal, *Neue Zeitschrift für Musik*, proclaiming the arrival of a brilliant young talent to lead the coming generation of German composers. He also provided introductions to the cream of Leipzig musical society, which led not only to Brahms performing there but also entering into publishing agreements with two different Leipzig companies. In the new year his Piano Sonata, Op. 1, his F sharp Sonata, Op. 2, a group of Op. 3 songs and his Scherzo in E flat minor, Op. 4 were published by Breitkopf & Härtel, while his F minor Piano Sonata, Op. 5 and the songs, Op. 6, were published by Senff. By the time he returned to his parents in Hamburg, Brahms had, in seven months, become established throughout Germany as a name to be reckoned with.

In early 1854 Brahms received a letter from Joachim informing him of Schumann's mental collapse and suicide attempt. Brahms immediately rushed to Düsseldorf to help Clara, then heavily pregnant with her eighth child. Brahms helped around the house and spent hours entertaining the Schumann children. When Clara was not on tour raising funds for the family, Brahms became an almost constant presence, and before Clara realised what had happened, her friendship with Brahms

had turned into love—she was 35, he was 21—while his love for her bordered on adoration. When she was away, he managed her affairs, even visiting Robert at the sanitarium. He also continued to compose, attempting to write a symphony, two movements of which he later adapted for his First Piano Concerto. The four Ballades, Op. 10 were also written around this time.

Brahms realised that he must still earn a living, and began picking up the threads of a concert career. By early 1856 Clara had reorganized her life sufficiently for Brahms to feel able to move to Bonn, where he was close enough to Düsseldorf for emergencies, but far enough away to lead a separate existence. After Robert Schumann's death in July 1856, Brahms took the decision to distance himself and recommence his composing, while Clara threw herself into her concert career. The two were to remain emotionally dependent on each other for the rest of their lives (they died just one year apart), but there was never any question of them living together.

Back in Hamburg, Brahms taught and composed. In spring 1857, he was invited by the Court of Detmold to take up residence during the three autumn months and give lessons, play at Court and conduct the choral society. This arrangement left him free to do as he wished for the other nine months of the year; it continued until the end of 1859. In 1858 Brahms fell in love with a girl he met in Göttingen, Agathe von Siebold; they became secretly engaged, but Brahms suddenly withdrew, writing to her that he could not commit himself to anyone. She was broken-hearted, and his friends were furious with him.

In 1859 no less than three performances of his Concerto for Piano No. 1 took place, arousing controversy in Leipzig, Hamburg and Hannover. On a more convivial level, Brahms became the occasional conductor of the Hamburg Ladies' Choir; in future years he would try out his many new choral works on them. The following year his two charming Serenades, Opp. 11 & 16, were published, but the year was more memorable for the unfortunate manifesto organized by Brahms and Joachim attacking the pretensions of the so-called New German School of Liszt and Wagner. This poorly thought through attack collapsed in a welter of recrimination, especially against Brahms. The young composer, still only 27, contrived henceforth to keep his opinions on musical matters private, even when directly vilified by Wagner and his acolytes in later years.

Brahms now discovered the delights of Vienna, gradually spending more time each year in the city, in 1863 becoming conductor of the Wiener Singakademie. But more personal matters were pressing in on him; his parents separated, and Brahms made financial provision for each of them, but in February his beloved mother died of a stroke. Over the next year, the *Deutsches Requiem* slowly formulated in his mind, and it is entirely credible that at least part of the inspiration for this work came from his mother's death. On a happier note, he formed a friendship with a beautiful and bright young woman pupil, Elisabeth von Stockhausen. In time, Elizabeth married, and she and her husband, Heinrich von Herzogenberg, became two of his closest confidants.

In 1868 his *Deutsches Requiem* received a great welcome at its première in Bremen Cathedral before an audience of distinguished guests from all over Europe. The previous year his father had remarried, which relieved Brahms from any obligation to remain in Germany, and by Christmas 1869 he was in Vienna with every intention of making the move permanent. One of the first fruits of this move was the charming set of *Liebeslieder Waltzer*, Op. 52, a sure indication of his empathy with Viennese life. His next work—the 1870 masterpiece *Alt-Rhapsody*, Op. 53, set to words from Goethe—was of a darker hue, coloured by his private distress that Clara Schumann's third daughter, Julie, had opted for a husband other than himself. After the German defeat of France in the Franco-Prussian war, Brahms expressed his patriotism with the *Triumphlied*, Op. 55. That same year he moved into an apartment in Vienna, where he was to remain for the rest of his life. This was conveniently close to the Gesellschaft der Musikfreunde when he became their artistic adviser in 1872.

A man of simple tastes, Brahms channelled his increased earnings into projects to help his family. When that same year his father died of cancer,

Brahms not only continued to remain friendly with his stepmother, but also materially helped members of his step-family when required. His own life became progressively less eventful; he resolutely remained a bachelor, his time taken up with composition and his voracious desire for knowledge as well as regular trips abroad, especially to Italy, which he had grown to love. As the 1870s progressed he became more confident in his handling of orchestral forces; by 1876 he had completed both the String Quartets, Op. 51 and his First Symphony in C minor, a work written in the shadow of many previous composers, but especially of Beethoven. After the first symphony, the second, a more lyrical and relaxed work, came more easily; it was ready for its first performance in December 1877 under Hans Richter. This was a more universally welcomed symphony, and did much to put Brahms at the forefront of modern symphonic music. The conservative Viennese critic, Eduard Hanslick, was now happy to present Brahms as the example of where progressives such as Wagner and Liszt had 'gone wrong'.

Honours now began to be proffered from many corners of Europe; Brahms,

---

DON'T MISS

▶ **Haydn Variations, Op. 56a (1873)**
▶ **Clarinet Quintet, Op. 115 (1891)**
▶ **3 Pieces for Piano, Op. 117 (1892)**
▶ **6 Pieces for Piano, Op. 118 (1892)**
▶ **Ein Deutsches Requiem, Op. 45 (1857-68)**
▶ **4 Ernste Gesänge, Op. 121 (1896)**
▶ **Alt-Rhapsody, Op. 53 (1869)**

still an intensely private man who valued his friends and family above everything, spent his time refusing all the trappings which went with musical fame. For long an admirer of Johann Strauss II's music, Brahms' move to Vienna brought him in touch with the latest Straussian developments. A strong friendship sprang up between the two men, based on admiration of their respective talents (in a visiting-book Brahms scribbled the opening bars of the *Blue Danube* melody, then signed the book with the comment 'unfortunately not by—Johannes Brahms'), and Brahms spent many happy times with Strauss, either in Vienna or in the country. The untroubled nature of this relationship, however, was not repeated with many of his other friends, who were often flayed by fierce sarcasm and a Germanic clumsiness which he occasionally failed to control. Even Clara Schumann suffered on occasion.

The year 1878 saw the completion of the Violin Concerto, Op. 77, written specifically for Joachim to play: the première was given in Leipzig on New Year's Day, 1879. The Second Piano Concerto, Op 83, was written in 1881 and dedicated to Edouard Marxsen, his old Hamburg teacher. Brahms wrote the Third Symphony in Wiesbaden in 1883. There he met a young soprano, Hermine Spies, who while acknowledging his obvious fondness for her, accepted that the 50-year-old Brahms was too set in his ways to develop the relationship any further. The Third Symphony was premièred in 1884, while the Fourth, Op. 90, was completed in time for an 1886 performance in Meiningen, conducted by Brahms himself. This was his most ambitious exercise—and his last—in the symphonic form. From now on, apart from the *Concerto for Violin, Cello and Orchestra,* Op 102 of 1887, he

concentrated on chamber music, piano works and his beloved choral pieces. Many of his admirers regard these late works as his deepest and most moving: they include the exquisite *Quintet for Clarinet and Strings,* Op. 115, the two Clarinet Sonatas, Op. 120, and the superb sets of piano intermezzi and rhapsodies, Opp. 166-119.

As with all his other works, he sent these first to Clara Schumann, valuing her opinion more than any other. Her stroke in April 1896 prompted him to write *Vier ernste Gesänge,* Op. 121 for her, dark works much preoccupied with death. Her death in May, after a physically and emotionally punishing life, left him bereft. Within a few months, after a lifetime of rude health, he himself was taken seriously ill, dying of cancer of the liver in April 1897, less than a year after Clara Schumann. He was just 64.

CAMILLE SAINT-SAËNS

1835–1921

Living a long and full public life, Saint-Saëns experienced a wide range of reaction to his music, from admiration of his youthful talents to rejection of his early operas and finally exasperation at the extreme conservatism of his old age. Oddly enough, the work which was to make him most famous, *The Carnival of the Animals,* was never played publicly during his lifetime.

Saint-Saëns was unusual in that he was actually born in Paris, rather than

arriving there to seek his fortune. As his musical and intellectual gifts manifested themselves early, he was given his first lessons by his great-aunt, Charlotte Mason. At the age of seven he was taught piano by Camille Stamaty and theory by Pierre Maledon; the latter were essential as the boy had already begun to compose. In that same year he gave his first concert, playing the piano part in a Beethoven violin sonata. A recital by the 11-year-old at the Salle Pleyel preceded his induction into the Paris Conservatoire, where he initially studied organ, moving onto

Halévy's composition class in 1850. It was at this point that he came to the attention of many older musicians associated with the Conservatoire and also met Liszt, whose personality and music made a great impression on him. In the next few years he was a regular in Rossini's famous Paris salon, where he met many influential people in the music world. His extreme musical facility—he could play all of Beethoven's piano sonatas from memory and his compositions were produced with little apparent effort—was a passport to later fame, but it also became a handicap,

preventing him from progressing
to more profound musical levels later
in life.

Saint-Saëns failed to win the Prix de
Rome but decided against a compulsive
pursuit of the award, accepting instead
the position of organist at the Church
Saint-Merry. He remained there for four
years before becoming organist at the
Madeleine in 1857. By then he had
already written, and had performed, his
first and second symphonies, works
which demonstrated his complete ease
with symphonic form and tradition
without being dramatically original in
content. His remarkable piano playing,
which demonstrated a due concern
with musical structure and articulation
as well as a remarkable fluidity of
phrasing and a lucid tone, was not long
neglected by his compositional
activities; the First Piano Concerto, Op
17, appeared in 1858, and the first two
violin concertos quickly followed, but as
yet he could not devote himself entirely
to composition. In addition to his organ
duties, he became piano professor at
the Ecole Niedermeyer between 1861
and 1865: his two most famous pupils
were Fauré and the operetta composer,
Messager. In due course, Fauré became
a close and lifelong friend.

Camille Saint-Saëns

After a second and last failure with the
Prix de Rome in 1864, Saint-Saëns
turned his creative attentions to opera,
and with the help of Daniel François
Auber he obtained a serviceable
libretto: the resultant opera, *Le Timbre
d'argent* (1864–5) languished in
manuscript until 1877. The second
opera, *La princesse jaune* was written
and premièred in 1872, receiving little
reaction. His third opera, *Samson et
Dalila,* which was first given in Weimar

under the sponsorship of Franz Liszt,
had to wait until 1892 for its Paris
début. The fourth, given in Lyons in
1879, was coolly received and was not
given a Paris performance.

Saint-Saëns's operatic career was
severely hampered by the aversion of
both opera audiences and critics to
progressive music with which Saint-
Saëns had become identified through
his admiration for Wagner's operas. It

was a different story in orchestral and
instrumental music; by the end of the
1860s Saint-Saëns had created such a
favourable impression that in 1868 he
was awarded the Légion d'honneur. The
same year his second piano concerto
appeared and has remained one of his
most popular orchestral pieces. The
third followed in 1869, and this
winning sequence was only broken by
the outbreak of the Franco-Prussian
War in 1870. Saint-Saëns, as one of

France's most famous musicians, was regarded as particularly vulnerable, but he remained in Paris until the chaos of the Commune when he succumbed to parental pressure to leave the city. He went to London until Paris was sufficiently settled to ensure personal safety once more.

During the 1870s he began the series of European concert tours which brought him and his music into greater international prominence than any other French composer of his generation. It also brought him many distinctions and honours. Apart from his operas, he had a sure success with Danse macabre in 1874, while his superb First Cello Concerto, Op. 33, was premièred in 1873 and the fourth piano concerto in 1875, with the composer playing the soloist's part. Saint-Saëns, however, was no mere musical automaton, reluctantly churning out new works. As well as being a first-rate scholar and editor of manuscripts (he undertook a mammoth edition of all Rameau's works), he was an enthusiastic archaeologist and a dedicated traveller, not just in Europe but in Africa (especially Algiers), the Middle and Far East, Russia and even South America. He was also an active writer, able to produce plays as well as poetry and stories. Later in life he turned his hand to effective, if chauvinistic, journalism.

Despite all this activity, and the continued success of his music, Saint-Saëns was gradually becoming something of a misanthrope and a musical reactionary. The turning point in his life came in 1875: always deeply attached to his mother, at the age of 40 he had a whirlwind romance with the 19-year-old Marie-Laure Truffot, marrying her against his mother's wishes. From the outset the marriage was troubled, and although two sons were produced in quick succession, two domestic tragedies virtually sealed its fate: firstly, in an horrific accident, one son was killed when he fell from a fourth floor window; no more than six weeks later the second boy died of an infection from which he had been expected to recover. Devastated, and no doubt influenced by his mother, Saint-Saëns blamed Marie-Laure. The breaking point came for the composer while the couple were on holiday in 1881: he simply disappeared from their hotel and from that day on severed all connections with her. With normal relations restored with his mother, Saint-Saëns lived alone. Within a few years he had become an active homosexual: many of his overseas trips, especially those to Algiers where the availability of young boys was an open secret, were in part at least a form of sexual tourism.

The 1880s were productive years for the composer: his election to the French Institute in 1881 gave him entrée to all the Paris theatres, and in the next 20 years no less than nine new operas were premièred. The second violin concerto appeared in 1880, while the famous Havanaise, Op. 83 (for violin) was published in 1887. His sense of humour and his love of many avenues of knowledge may have enabled him to write the gallery of amusing musical portraits which made up Le Carnaval des Animaux (1886), but he barred any performance of the work (except 'Le Cygne') during his lifetime, afraid that his public image as a serious composer might suffer from this creative chink in his armour. Ironically, it is now his most popular work. His Symphony No. 3, Organ, in C minor, Op. 78 was completed in the same year as the Carnaval, while his Violin Sonata No. 1, Op 75, had appeared the year before, thus his mature years had produced his most popular works. His last piano concerto, premièred in 1896 and subtitled the Egyptian, is a perfect illustration of the pleasant exoticism he could bring to orchestral music, its slow movement being a shimmering, almost motionless series of arabesques sketching an indolent afternoon in the Egyptian heat.

The remainder of Saint-Saëns's long career was equally active. He gradually became identified with the most reactionary element of the conservative musical establishment in Paris, being one of the most vociferous denouncers of Debussy and his followers. He also became progressively more xenophobic: during WWI he published essays arguing that all German music should be banned from public performance in France. But this late fallibility in judgement does not alter his position as one of the key figures in the revival of French music in the latter half of the 19th Century.

LÉO DELIBES

1836–1891

With little interest in pursuing progressive musical tendencies, Delibes is given scant credit for his achievements, but he blessed the world with two of its most glorious ballet scores, while in the famous flower duet from *Lakmé* he wrote one of the best loved operatic passages in the world today.

Delibes was born in Saint-Germain-du-Val, a village on a tributary of the Loire. His family was musical, his mother an amateur pianist who taught Léo music. By the age of 12 the boy entered the solfège class at Paris Conservatoire where Adolphe Adam, the renowned operatic and ballet composer, became his composition teacher. In 1850 Delibes won a Conservatoire prize, and while his studies continued he took occasional jobs singing in choirs and playing the organ in various Parisian churches. At the age of 17, with the help of Adam, he obtained two useful positions: accompanist at the Théâtre Lyrique and organist at the church of St Pierre de Chaillot. For the next 10 years these two positions supported him financially while he attempted to write stage works in his spare time.

The first such work was a one-act farce entitled *Deux sous de charbon* (1855), which was staged by the Théâtre des Folies-Nouvelles. The welcome this received encouraged Delibes to continue in this vein, and he wrote a mixture of farces, short comic operas and little operettas for the Folies-Nouvelles, the Théâtre Lyrique and Offenbach's 'opposition' house, Bouffes Parisiens. No fewer than a dozen such works were successfully brought to the stage during the period up to 1863, and by this time Delibes had carved a small reputation for himself as a slight but engaging composer of amiable theatrical romps.

This was never going to be enough to slake the ambition of a man convinced of his own worth and prepared to work hard for real success. Delibes had also taken a position as a school inspector for the district of St Denis and Sceaux and written serious devotional music (including a Mass), some of it specifically designed for performance by the children in his inspectorate. By 1863 his work at the Théâtre Lyrique had become wearisome, and when he was offered similar work at the Opéra, he saw it as a means of furthering his career. He quickly assumed the roles of

second chorus master and assistant conductor at the Opéra, positions he would retain until 1872 when he no longer needed such work.

Delibes continued to compose for both stage and church, receiving a boost in 1865 when his cantata *Alger* was performed. He finally achieved a major breathrough when he was commissioned to work alongside the Polish composer Minkus to create a ballet, *La Source*, for the Opéra. At its première in November 1866, it became clear that all the ballet's best melodies had been written by Delibes, and he was promptly commissioned to supply new music for a revival of Adam's *Le Corsaire*. Its success in 1867 was rewarded by a commission—not before time—for a ballet written entirely by him. The result, *Coppélia*, which was premièred at the Opéra with Napoléon III in attendance, developed classical ballet in important ways, for the first time bringing to it an entire symphony orchestra and a wealth of fully-integrated music, giving ballet a new and higher form of musical unity. In this way Delibes' music pointed the way for Tchaikovsky in the future. But beyond these considerations was the sheer beauty and elegance of the music

Léo Delibes

itself. It was this which won him an initial following for *Coppélia*, and it was the energy and resourcefulness of his scoring which has helped retain that audience up to the present day. Listening to this ballet now only emphasizes what a skilful dramatic composer Delibes was.

From this point Delibes' life and career took an upward spiral, only halted by his death. The instant success of *Coppélia* led to a number of new commissions and projects. In 1872 a set of charming melodies, including the famous 'Les Filles de Cadix', was published, and Delibes married the comfortably-off daughter of an actress at the Comédie-Française. The following year a three-act comic opera, *Le Roi l'a dit*, appeared at the Opéra Comique. The next major occasion was another Opéra commission, the mythological ballet *Sylvia*. As with *Coppélia*, Delibes enjoyed wide and deserved success at the 1876 première, his ballet being the first such work accorded a complete evening's entertainment at the Opéra (up to then the first half of a theatrical programme

prior to intermission was usually filled by assorted excerpts from a well-known opera). Delibes was now perceived to be the foremost ballet composer of his day, and in 1877 he was appointed Chevalier of the Légion d'honneur.

Delibes was now a wealthy and successful man, but he still longed to write what he regarded as serious music—opera and religious music. In 1878 he fulfilled half of this ambition by seeing a performance of his cantata *La Mort d'Orphée*, but his 1880 opera *Jean de Nivelle* was not a success. Delibes had to wait until after his 1881 appointment to the Professorship of advanced composition at the Conservatoire before he finally wrote the work for which opera audiences today still revere him. This was *Lakmé*, an opera using the by then familiar theme of Eastern exoticism and cultural clashes intermingling with a good old-fashioned story of love and jealousy. Although the libretto was not exactly cliché-free, the first-night audience hardly cared, such was the exquisite nature of the musical invention, including the famous 'Flower Duet' and the 'Bell Song', both of which have won for this opera a permanent place on the opera stages of the world. In addition, the 'Bell Song' became one of the benchmarks upon which a coloratura's career stood or fell, with 20th-century

DON'T MISS

▶ **Les Filles de Cadiz**

▶ **Coppélia (1870)**

▶ **Lakmé (1883)**

▶ **Sylvia (1876)**

▶ **Le Roi l'a dit (1873)**

singers such as Lily Pons virtually basing their career on their ability to deal with its exotic leaps and cadences.

After this triumph Delibes took his time finding his next operatic subject.

Never a fast worker, he was still composing his last opera *Kassya* at the time of his unexpected and untimely death, aged 55, in 1891. The opera was completed by Massenet and premièred in 1893, but has since

failed to hold a place in the repertoire. But with three works of the standard of *Coppélia*, *Sylvia* and *Lakmé*, there is little chance of Delibes' music fading from the footlights.

GEORGES BIZET

1838–1875

The composer of perhaps the single most popular opera of all time—*Carmen*—Bizet was dogged throughout his life by bad luck and hampered by a temperament ill-suited to the insidious politics of theatrical productions; all his greatest successes came after his early death.

Bizet's family was immersed in music, his father a singing teacher and his mother a fine pianist. Georges showed musical talent when very young, and through the influence of his mother's brother François Delsart, a well-known singer, was accepted into the Paris Conservatoire at the age of nine where he was taught by Marmontel. Standards at the Conservatoire at that time were not universally high, and of all those who taught Bizet between 1848 and 1857 only Marmontel, Halévy and Gounod inspired him.

In 1855 Bizet, just 17 years old, wrote his first symphony, the Symphony in C, in six weeks: it bears the marks of his fascination with Gounod's music, but its vitality and sound palette are equally revealing of Bizet's own strong

musical personality. In 1857, in response to a competition organized by Offenbach who was looking for new material for his Bouffes-Parisiens theatre, Bizet completed his second operetta, *Le Docteur Miracle*. Bizet and Charles Lecocq shared first prize and *Miracle* was mounted at the theatre, helping to spread Bizet's name in the right circles. As a result, he was adopted by Rossini who invited him to his famous Saturday evening soirées. The same year the Académie de Musique awarded Bizet the Prix de Rome for his cantata *Clovis et Clotilde*, written to a turgid text by Amédée Burion. In late 1857 Bizet departed for Rome, armed with a glowing letter of recommendation from Rossini to many of his old contacts there. From the first Bizet enjoyed his time in the ancient city, writing to his mother: 'Life is too happy...we chat, we keep warm, we play cards...in short, we couldn't have a better time'.

During his time in Rome, Bizet completed *Don Procopio,* an *opera bouffe* in two acts written in a deliberately Italian style, which he delivered to the Académie towards the end of 1859. Their response was

encouraging: 'This work has a brilliant and easy touch, precious qualities for the comic genre for which the composer has shown a clear affinity'. Bizet's high spirits on receipt of this judgement were soon dissipated in a string of abandoned projects, including no less than two symphonies. Having proved his adeptness at light comedy, he was attempting more ambitious projects with the type of historical background beloved by his friend Gounod, but not suited to his own more quicksilver genius. His second composition for the Académie in Rome was an ode-symphony, *Vasco da Gama*, based on Luiz Vaz de Camoen's epic poem *The Lusiad*. This uninspired piece has rarely been heard. His last months in Rome were spent in the company of the 1859 winner, Ernest Guiraud, who was to remain a lifelong friend and a posthumous collaborator, preparing the grand-opera recitatives of Bizet's *Carmen* in place of the original dialogue.

Bizet arrived back in Paris in late 1860 to find his mother in poor health. As she lingered on, Bizet attempted to complete the *Rome* symphony. When his mother died in 1861, Bizet was plunged into agonies of regret; she had been the most important relationship in his life. Gounod, deep in preparations for the première of *La Reine de Saba*, deliberately involved Bizet in the opera's production to help him get over the loss. A rest cure in Baden-Baden left Bizet tense and irascible, his fiery temper to the fore. The major cause for his irascibility was the birth of a son, Jean, to a maid called Marie who had nursed his mother in Paris. Not until long after Georges was dead did Marie reveal that Georges was the child's father.

The greater part of 1863 was spent writing *Les Pêcheurs de Perles* to a commission from the Théatre-Lyrique. It is commonly accepted that the librettists Eugene Cormon and Michel Carré, unaware of Bizet's talents, made little effort to write a libretto for the opera; in fact Cormon later admitted that had they heard some of the music (they heard nothing until the final rehearsals), they would have tried at least to make the libretto make dramatic sense. As it is, the opera contains wonderful melodic invention from Bizet, and shows his instinct for exoticism (the opera is set in Ceylon). It also contains the famous duet, 'Au fond du temple saint'. It was a modest success, Bizet's music receiving just one positive review (from Berlioz), and had to wait until 1893 for its first Paris

revival, by which time the composer was long dead and *Carmen* had eclipsed all Bizet's other stage works.

In 1864 Bizet moved into a small cottage in Le Vésinet some 12 miles outside Paris, purchased by his father. There he concentrated on a score he had long failed to develop, *Ivan IV*, based on a libretto passed on to him by Gounod. The music was written in the grand opera style of Meyerbeer; unfortunately for Bizet, Meyerbeer had died the year before, his genre dying with him, and *Ivan IV* could not have been presented to the Paris opera companies at a worse time. The score had to wait until a German production in the middle of WWII for its première.

Bizet's career remained static for nearly a year, during which time he befriended influential women such as Princess Mathilde Bonaparte and Céleste Vénard, the former a great patroness of the arts, the latter a reformed courtesan and popular novelist who had a property adjacent to his in the country. In June 1866 the Théatre-Lyrique commissioned him to write the music to a libretto derived from a Walter Scott novel. By December 1867 *La Jolie Fille de Perth* was ready for its first performance. Like *Pêcheurs* before it, *Jolie Fille* was a failure, surviving for only a handful of performances. Once

again it was the libretto which was at fault, although the music is not Bizet's most distinguished either.

Money remained a constant worry as Bizet struggled to establish himself, though he continued to churn out a series of songs which he hoped to sell. Temporary optimism came in early 1869 when his symphony, *Rome*, finally received its première. He made light of the audience's reaction in a letter to a friend: 'My symphony went very well: first movement: a round of applause, then hisses, then a catcall. Andante: a round of applause. Finale: applause, three times repeated, hisses, three or four catcalls. In short, a success'.

In 1869 Bizet married Geneviève Halévy, daughter of the composer Fromental Halévy. This was not well received by Geneviève's family who felt she was marrying beneath her, but with her father dead and her period of mourning over, she felt a compulsion to renew life. Geneviève brought with her a dowry which alleviated any money worries for the time being, and the match was a happy one. But they had only a year to enjoy Paris before the outbreak of the Franco-Prussian War, followed by the occupation and the Commune of 1871. During the war Bizet was a member of the Paris National Guard, but with the onset of the Commune, Bizet felt that for Genevieve's sake they should move to his cottage at Le Vésinet. When order was restored, they returned to Paris.

Soon after, Bizet was commissioned by the Opéra-Comique to write the music to a libretto originally given to another composer, who had produced one aria in two years. Bizet rearranged the

---

DON'T MISS

▶ Carmen (1875)

▶ Les Pêcheurs de Perles (1863)

▶ L'Arlésienne – suite (1872)

▶ Jeux d'enfants (1871)

▶ Djamileh (1872)

libretto for what eventually became the one-act *Djamileh*. Delays and complications at the Opéra forced Bizet to shelve the project and take up others, including the delightful piano duet pieces, *Jeux d'enfants*, and the *Petite Suite*, which he extracted from the duet pieces and orchestrated.

Djamileh, though hindered by yet another feeble plot and indifferent libretto, was graced with luminescent scoring and memorable melodies, yet failed to make much of an impression at its opening in 1872. It was not helped by the mediocrity of the singers and poor casting. Bizet commented on opening night: "It's a total flop. You see what happens: you wear yourself out and do your best in vain. If you want to succeed today, you have to be dead—or German". Despite this failure, it is clear that, professionally at least, he had turned the corner.

Commissions from important clients were now frequent. The Opéra-Comique requested a new three-act opera, with Mehilac and Halévy as his collaborators. "They will do something jolly, which I will treat as lightly as possible", Bizet commented. This would later evolve into *Carmen*. From the Théâtre-Lyrique came a request for incidental music to a play by Alphonse Daudet, *L'Arlésienne*. In 1872 Geneviève was delivered of a son, Jacques. Still buoyed up by this happy event, Bizet completed the music for *L'Arlésienne* and it went into production. The score is one of Bizet's most subtle, intriguing and rewarding, though it is virtually never heard in its original context—as incidental music to a play which is where it works best. The two orchestral suites extracted from it (the first by Bizet, the second by

Georges Bizet

Guiraud), though shorn of theatrical context, deservedly remain popular with concert audiences. Predictably, the play was a flop, the critics pasted it, and only the approval of a number of his musician friends kept Bizet sanguine as to his prospects. It was Massenet who predicted a success for any suite drawn from the incidental music, and he was proved right: within months of the play having closed, a concert performance of the first suite drew ecstatic applause.

Bizet had begun considering Mérimée's story *Carmen* while *L'Arlésienne* was still in rehearsal, but did not begin serious work on it until after his involvement with Gounod's *Roméo et Juliette* was concluded by its

performance at the Opéra-Comique in 1873. He worked quickly on the music for *Carmen*, expecting an early production, but rehearsals were constantly delayed, partly because the theatre's management were nervous of having an opera at the Opéra-Comique in which the heroine dies at the end. The opera had been finished by autumn 1873, and only the hugely successful première of the overture, *Patrie*, Op. 19 (written 20 years earlier) in the meantime, served to calm Bizet's frazzled nerves. His state of mind had not been improved by a rift with Geneviève; from 1873 to early 1874 the couple had spent a good deal of time separated. Bizet was also suffering from angina of the throat.

Finally *Carmen* went into a production in September 1874 which was fraught with problems, especially with the chorus: they decided their part was physically impossible as they had to move and act as well as sing: a thing unheard of at the Opéra-Comique. On the morning of the opening night, 3 March 1875, it was announced that Bizet was nominated for the Légion d'honneur. It was the prelude to a disaster: the audience, prepared for a comic opera, was presented with Bizet's revolutionary work. Although the first

act was greeted warmly, by the end of the fourth the audience was stony and Bizet knew he had another flop on his hands. On the second night the audience was completely mesmerized, but this was negated by the swingeing reviews. The opera staggered on for 48 performances but never had a full house. *Carmen*, which should have been a triumph, had failed in Paris.

Yet the theatre commissioned another opera from him before he once again fell prey to an attack of throat angina,

complicated by muscular rheumatism in the legs. Bizet, depressed by *Carmen's* failure and long distressed by the failure of his marriage, was no longer able to fight such ailments with his usual vitality. On 3 June, after moving to Bougival by the Seine in an effort to revive his health, he died from heart failure. It would be another eight years before *Carmen* was a runaway success in Paris, although by the end of 1875 it had already been well received in Vienna and elsewhere. Success had come too late for Bizet to enjoy it.

MAX BRUCH
1838–1920

Bruch was a hugely gifted but deeply conservative composer; when at the height of his fame, he was often talked of in the same breath as Brahms and Mendelssohn by his contemporaries, but his subsequent reputation was eclipsed for decades by more radical musical events.

Bruch was born into a middle-class family in Cologne. His artistic and musical talent became obvious at an early age, which prompted his family to call him the 'new Raphael'. His father worked for the government; his mother was gifted musically and a fine singer. When Bruch was nine years old, some of his compositions were shown to the conductor Ferdinand Hiller, who was sufficiently impressed to take over his tuition and prepare him for an examination which secured him a scholarship to attend the Mozart

Foundation in Frankfurt-an-Main. Four years at the Foundation, allied to his continued studies with Hiller, gave Bruch a firm practical and theoretical foundation.

Between 1858–61 Bruch taught music in Cologne while pursuing his own compositions, which at this stage were concentrated mainly on the choral and operetta forms. His choral output at this time included the beautiful *Flucht der Heiligen Familie*, Op. 20, and the follow-up *Gesang der Heiligen drei Könige*, Op. 21. His first little operetta, *Scherz, List und Rache*, was performed to a muted response in 1858; he followed this in 1863 with a performance of his second stage work, *Die Loreley*, written to a text originally supplied to Mendelssohn.

By this time Bruch was based in Mannheim, where he gained valuable practical experience in opera staging

and the production of choral music, a form of composition he had loved as a child. It is fair to say that Bruch's reputation in the 19th century was founded more on his vocal output than his orchestral. His first real success came with *Frithjof-Scenen*, Op. 23, a work for soprano, male voices and orchestra. This brought Bruch fame beyond his part of Germany; he even travelled abroad to conduct performances of it. This naturally prompted follow-ups of a similar nature, which Bruch laced with military themes and touches of martial music with titles such as *Schön Ellen*, Op. 24, *Odysseus*, Op. 41 and *Achilleus*, Op. 50. Meanwhile, in 1865 Bruch had been appointed musical director of the Concert-Institution in Coblenz—a town he never liked, calling it a "damned, dark mousehole"—moving on two years later to become *Kapellmeister* for the Prince of Schwarzburg-Sondershausen.

Max Bruch

By this time Bruch had completed key orchestral works which would carry his fame up to the present day, while his choral works and operas are largely forgotten. Having completed two earlier symphonies (now lost), Bruch began his First Symphony, Op. 28 in Coblenz, revealing that his style in instrumental music, as in vocal, looked back to Mendelssohn, Schumann and their contemporaries, rather than forwards with Liszt and Wagner. In 1866 he produced his Concerto for Violin No. 1 in G minor, Op. 26, which was dedicated to the eminent violinist Joseph Joachim who gave the first concert performance in

1868, with Bruch conducting. At times the work bears an uncanny stylistic resemblance to Mendelssohn's own concerto, Bruch imbuing it with the emotional warmth and optimism of his great model.

The following year Bruch signed an important deal with the leading conservative publishing house of Simrock, thereby guaranteeing the wide dissemination of his music. By the summer of 1870, when he was completing his sombre Second Symphony, Op. 36, he felt it was time to leave Schwarzburg-Sondershausen. He moved to Berlin where he worked

as a freelance, conducting and composing to commission, moving on to Bonn in 1873 where he concentrated on composition. In 1878, the year of his beautiful and unjustly neglected Concerto for Violin No. 2, Op. 44, he was back in Berlin leading the Stern Singing Society before accepting an offer in 1880 to direct the Liverpool Philharmonic Society. This move turned out to be a mistake; after three largely unhappy years, he moved on, hoping to settle with his wife (Clara Tuczek, whom he had married in 1881) somewhere outside Germany. After a brief tour of America in 1883 he returned to run the Orchesterverein in Breslau, where he stayed until 1890, by which time he was in his early fifties and ready to move back to Berlin.

The period in Liverpool had been musically productive, with the *Scottish Fantasy*, Op. 46, second only to the first violin concerto in popularity, and the famous *Kol Nidrei*, Op 47, written to a set of Jewish melodies, appearing in 1881 to immediate acclaim. As the 1880s wore on, Bruch's tempo slowed, and his Third Symphony, Op 51 took nearly four years to find its final form. By then Bruch was one of the most famous living German composers, often mentioned in the same breath as Brahms. It was his misfortune to live on past the apotheosis of his own period to be confronted with what Mahler, Bruckner, Wolf and later Schöenberg and Strauss were doing with the Classical heritage in German-speaking countries. His subsequent relegation to the backwaters of Classical life must have been bitterly disappointing, although his *Romance* for viola and orchestra, Op. 85, appeared in 1911 and was popular at the time. It was only the advocacy of virtuosos such as Heifetz which gradually brought his key orchestral works back into common concert and recording usage and returned his name to something like its former eminence.

MODESTE MUSSORGSKY

1839–1881

Today, Mussorgsky is recognized as an original and influential Russian genius whose impact on modern music was crucial to the development of musical life after Wagner. His so-called barbarisms and his completely individual approach to form, melody and harmony aided the evolution of composers such as Debussy, Stravinsky, Ravel and virtually every Russian composer who followed.

Mussorgsky was born in his father's country house at Karev, in the region of Pskov. He became interested in music at an early age and his mother gave him piano lessons. He was so gifted that, despite his lack of discipline and endless quarrels with a string of tutors, he was capable of playing a recital at the age of nine, which included works by Liszt and John Field. When he was 10, the family moved to St Petersburg where Modeste was enrolled at the military academy. He continued with his music lessons, learning the piano with Herke and Orthodox Church music history from Father Krupsky.

Modeste Mussorgsky

At the age of 17, Mussorgsky entered a fashionable Guards regiment, the Preobrajensky, based in St Petersburg. So far his life had taken a conventional course; even though he showed outstanding musical ability, he only pursued his interest in music in a dilettante manner with no thought that it might one day become his career. Unfortunately, regimental life introduced Mussorgsky to the pleasures of alcohol: incapable of moderating his drinking habits, a pattern of heavy drinking was established which eventually led to alcoholism and an early death.

In 1857, soon after coming across Borodin at a party, came the meeting which changed the course of his life: he met the composer Alexander Dargomïzhsky who was already an accepted member of the New Russian school led by Balakirev. Dargomïzhsky introduced him to the leading members of the younger Russian generation, and through Balakirev's influence in particular he began to study composers such as Beethoven and Glinka. Balakirev initiated a period of organized study which widened and deepened Mussorgsky's knowledge of music. Again under Balakirev's guidance, Mussorgsky began to compose. With his commitment to music increasing, he found it increasingly hard to tolerate life in the army. By now he was convinced that it was his destiny to become a great composer.

One of the first products of his studies was the Scherzo in B flat for orchestra, completed with Balakirev's help in 1858 and premièred in 1860. By then he was arguing with his parents about his determination to leave the army, an argument which persisted while he attempted to write incidental music for the opera Oedipus in Athens, set as a task for him by Balakirev who had already noted his flair for drama. Mussorgsky eventually won the battle with his parents; resigning from the Guards in 1858, he took up the life of a full-time composer. While his family was able to

support him, all went well, but even at this early stage, his bizarre behaviour and his tendency to withdraw from society made him progressively more isolated, an isolation intensified by the long hours working alone at his music.

It is possible that his creative life would have been sustainable, and he would have completed many more of his unfinished and abandoned projects, if the emancipation of the serfs in 1863 had not ruined his landowning father and removed Mussorgsky's source of income. He now had to support himself and was eventually forced to take a lowly position in the civil service; his situation was now worse than it had been when he was in the army where at least his status had protected him. The company he kept at this time did not help matters; he was living in a bachelor apartment with five other young Russians who were all trying to live out their versions of de Musset's Scènes de la vie de Bohème.

Although Mussorgsky began composing a new opera based on Flaubert's highly-charged historical novel Salammbô (which, like so many other works, he was to leave unfinished), by 1865 he had reached such a low point in his life, exacerbated by his mother's death and his consumption of alcohol, that he suffered a complete mental breakdown.

He moved in to his brother's house where he quickly recovered and began the string of compositions which would bring him permanent fame. These included the initial version of A Night on the Bare Mountain, a work harshly dealt with by Balakirev for its startling modulations, rough-hewn chords and craggy orchestration. Mussorgsky reworked the score twice in an attempt to produce a work of which Balakirev would approve, each time robbing it of a little of its boldness and immediacy. It would remain his only major orchestral work fully completed by his own hand. Everything else would be arranged after his death by his colleagues from piano scores or opera sketches.

Mussorgsky also composed a string of songs which would place him on a par with any of his German-speaking contemporaries and far ahead of the field in Russia. The majority of his time, however, was now taken up with another opera, doomed to be abandoned, based on Gogol's story, The Marriage. In 1867 he resigned from his civil service position and returned to St Petersburg, hoping to make his way by teaching and piano accompaniment. This would not have been easy for an organized man to achieve, but for Mussorgsky it was tantamount to courting failure. Admitting defeat, in

---

DON'T MISS

▶ **A Night on the Bare Mountain (1867)**
▶ **Pictures at an Exhibition (1874)**
▶ **Songs and Dances of Death (1877)**
▶ **Sunless (1874)**
▶ **Boris Godunov (1874)**
▶ **Khovanshchina (1872–80)**

1868, he rejoined the civil service and resumed the daily drudgery which he so abhored, and moved in with his friend Alexander Opochinin. The major event of 1868 was his decision to begin work on *Boris Godunov*. Having begun, he made rapid progress, creating his own libretto from Pushkin's play. The entire work was completed in 14 months, ready for consideration by the board of the Maryinsky Imperial Theatre in early 1870. They rejected it, feeling it lacked a love interest and a prima donna, let alone a conventional method of story-telling or acceptably orthodox musical construction and scoring. It was deemed altogether too strange and savage, and would also probably run into trouble with the imperial censors.

As well as working on his first major song cycle, *The Nursery* (1870–72), Mussorgsky composed a second version of *Boris*, introducing a love interest (requiring a prima donna), but this was also rejected. Mussorgsky's friends, convinced that the opera deserved a chance in front of an audience, arranged for some excerpts to be performed at concerts in early 1872. The bass, Gennadi Kondratyev, even programmed three scenes from the opera into his benefit performance at the Maryinsky Theatre itself. The success of these

attempts, plus an acceptance for publication by the publisher Bessel, added to the pressure on the Maryinsky Theatre to which they finally capitulated, mounting a suitably bowdlerized revised version of *Boris* for its première in 1874. It was sufficiently successful to remain in the repertoire for the next 20 years, but was beginning to fade from public view when Rimsky-Korsakov undertook his extensive reworking of the opera which brought it such overwhelming international success.

Meanwhile Mussorgsky had moved in with Rimsky-Korsakov and was busy on his next operatic project, *Khovanshchina*, but the deterioration in his physical and mental health was accelerating, his frequent alcoholic binges leaving him debilitated for days afterwards. Throughout the 1870s Mussorgsky fought a losing battle with his health, but these years also saw the creation of *Pictures at an Exhibition* (1874), piano pieces inspired by the commemorative exhibition of 400 pictures by his artist friend, Viktor Hartmann, who had died that year. Mussorgsky decided to select 10 of the pictures and create his own musical response to them. The result was a unique piano work, but one which struggled to find an audience until after the success of the

orchestrated versions by Rimsky-Korsakov, Ravel and others. In the same year the song cycle *Sunless* appeared. This devastating examination of despair and ennui, which reaches harrowing depths, was one of his greatest latter-day achievements, together with the 1877 *Songs and Dances of Death*. They were also some of the few works Mussorgsky managed to complete in his final decade.

An 1879 tour of southern Russia accompanying the singer Daria Leonova earned him some money and was a respite from his squalid personal treadmill, but on his return to St Petersburg, he was dismissed from his civil service position for chronic unreliability. His friends, realizing that Mussorgsky was by now unable to support himself, provided funds to enable him to continue working on his operatic projects. But he continued his life of drunkeness and dissolution, and in February 1881 was finally ejected from his St Petersburg rooms, succumbing soon after to an epileptic fit. He died a month later in a military sanitarium, days after his forty-second birthday. In the following decades his friends, led by Rimsky-Korsakov, worked successfully to bring his music the international attention it deserved.

PYOTR TCHAIKOVSKY

1840–1893

A man cursed by the unhappiest and most tempestuous of lives, but also blessed with an ability to create music which has touched the

souls of millions, Tchaikovsky is not only Russia's most popular composer but one of the most universally loved musicians of all time.

Tchaikovsky was born into the family of a successful mining engineer who rose to the position of chief inspector of mines in Kamsko-Votkinsk. He was the second of six children, and one of three

Pyotr Tchaikovsky

the two eldest brothers were sent to Schmelling school, a boarding school of some distinction in St Petersburg, where Pyotr pined for the stability of his childhood in the country. Two years later, with his father now working in distant Siberia, Pyotr was sent to the School of Jurisprudence (where he was slightly less unhappy) until his family's final reunion in 1852 when his father retired and settled in St Petersburg.

This more stable period was shattered for Pyotr in 1854 by his mother's sudden death from cholera. His means of coping with this loss was to draw emotional succour from music, and by 1855 he was receiving occasional lessons in more than just piano technique. This encouraged him to write some songs which, though thoroughly derivative, demonstrated his passion for contemporary Italian opera. After leaving school he became a clerk in the Ministry of Justice and a veritable young man about town. By 1862 he was engaged in serious musical study at the newly-founded St Petersburg Conservatoire, where Anton Rubinstein was the inaugural director, taking lessons twice a week while keeping up his civil service job. This inevitable conflict of interests led to his resignation from the Ministry in 1863 and his adoption of a bohemian lifestyle. Within a short time he had produced some orchestral pieces not entirely devoid of merit, and when in 1865 Anton Rubinstein's brother Nicholas needed a new Professor of harmony for the Moscow Conservatoire, Anton suggested the newly-graduated Tchaikovsky, then just 25 years old.

At the beginning of 1866 Nicholas Rubinstein installed Tchaikovsky in his

brothers. His mother was of French Huguenot descent, and there was a neurotic dimension to her side of the family which does much to explain the origins of Pyotr's highly-strung personality. As a small child he was intensely attached to his mother, and when in 1844 the family engaged the Swiss governess Fanny Dürbach, he in turn became utterly devoted to her. She managed to guide and control his fragile temperament, dealing with his incessant tantrums with equanimity and warmth. At the age of five he began piano lessons, often becoming so obsessed by a piece of music that he was unable to dislodge it from his head, a state which upset and disturbed him.

However, it would appear that his first eight years were generally happy. Thus it was a personal disaster when in 1848 his father resigned from his post in anticipation of landing a similar position in Moscow. The domestic staff (including Fanny Dürbach) were dismissed and the family travelled to Moscow, only to find on their arrival that the position had been awarded to a local man. After a period of instability,

DON'T MISS

▶ **Capriccio Italien, Op. 45 (1880)**

▶ **Piano Concerto No. 1, Op. 23 (1875)**

▶ **Violin Concerto, Op. 35 (1878)**

▶ **Marche Slave, Op. 31 (1876)**

▶ **Romeo & Juliet—fantasy overture (1869)**

own house and introduced him to Moscow's artistic society. Initially, the young man was homesick, writing copious letters home, but gradually he settled down and even began work on his First Symphony in G minor, Op. 13 *Winter Daydreams.* In time, this work brought him to the point of mental collapse, yet he not only completed the symphony but took a holiday during which he enjoyed a harmless liaison with an opera diva before giving the completed manuscript to Rubinstein for comment. After considerable revisions and delays, the symphony was performed in Moscow 1868; Pyotr felt that the reception had been good.

This breakthrough led to him being welcomed by some of the composers of the New Russian school, notably Rimsky-Korsakov and Balakirev, and when he went to St Petersburg in spring 1868, he arrived armed with parts of the opera he was working on, *The Voyevoda* (excerpts of which would eventually surface in *Swan Lake* and elsewhere) which Balakirev had asked to see. During this visit he met the whole group of St Petersburg musicians, establishing cordial relations with Borodin and Rimsky-Korsakov in particular. It was Balakirev who suggested to Tchaikovsky the idea of an overture on the theme of *Romeo and*

Juliet. Balakirev entirely approved of the result, while Rimsky-Korsakov called the overture's second subject "one of the greatest themes in Russian music". He was right: Tchaikovsky had unquestionably found himself.

For the next few years Tchaikovsky moved easily between the opposite poles of the traditionalist Moscow Conservatoire and the forward-looking friends he had made in St Petersburg, and was as happy as he could ever hope to be, although he pined for a 'domestic life with a family' which would be denied him by his homosexuality. He composed a melodic and graceful string quartet in 1871 and his close friendship with Vladimir Shilovsky gave him an emotional anchor for nearly five years. In 1872 he finished his third opera, *Oprichnik*, but this was not performed until the Imperial Opera produced it in 1874; by then he had completed his Second Symphony, Op 17, *Little Russian*, the symphonic fantasia *The Tempest,* Op. 18 and was well advanced on his First Piano Concerto in B flat minor, Op. 23. The opera (and its successor *Vakula*) would prove infinitely less popular than this first attempt at the concerto form. The concerto was rejected by its first dedicatee, Nicholas Rubinstein, as 'unplayable', but its second dedicatee Hans von Bülow quickly accepted its

challenges and greatly helped its successful launch in 1875, giving the first performance while on tour in America.

In 1875 Tchaikovsky was not only attempting to smooth the path of his piano concerto, but also writing his Third Symphony (*Polish*) in D, Op. 29, in which he tried (largely unsuccessfully) to incorporate conventional developmental techniques into the work's architecture—a problem he also failed to overcome in the Fourth Symphony in F minor, Op. 36, written two years later. The following year he made trips to Paris, where he was completely seduced by *Carmen*, and Bayreuth, where he found *The Ring* cycle "incredible nonsense", commenting after making it through to the end of *Götterdämmerung:* "I felt as though I'd been set free from prison". Much more congenial was the commission from the Moscow Imperial Theatre in 1875 for a new ballet, *Swan Lake*. With this substantial work Tchaikovsky asserted his genius for rhythm and melodic line, as well as his total commitment to music which had real expressive meaning. The ballet was premièred in early 1877 but fared badly at the hands of an amateurish conductor and an audience unprepared for anything but the lightest balletic bon-bons. Just prior to that he had produced two works at opposite ends of the stylistic spectrum: the orchestral fantasia *Francesca da Rimini*, Op. 32, and *Variations on a Rococo Theme*, Op. 33 for 'cello and orchestra, in which Tchaikovsky paid extravagant but astonishingly poised and tasteful homage to Mozart, the composer who remained his ideal throughout his life.

In 1876 Tchaikovsky met Nadezhda von Meck, a recently widowed and enormously wealthy woman who was passionate about music. Indeed, their relationship was more about music than about personal love, however intimate they became, for it was conducted exclusively by letter. Von Meck had commissioned some personalized arrangements of his music, and from that time on their intimacy rapidly deepened. They never met, although on one occasion they caught sight of each other on different balconies while simultaneously but separately on holiday in Italy.

In the same year Tchaikovsky met Antonina Milyukova, a 28-year-old who had written a series of passionate letters to him, one of which he was unwise enough to answer. Overburdened with projects—he had just begun work on the libretto for his operatic setting of Pushkin's *Eugene Onegin*, and dedicated the Fourth Symphony, 'our symphony', to Mme von Meck—and acting from stress rather than clearheadedness, he decided that he was someone who needed to marry; after a few meetings with the decidedly unstable Antonina (she had already threatened suicide in her letters), he proposed to her. She accepted with gusto. Given that he was still unreconciled to his homosexuality and was perhaps looking for a

sympathetic and discreet partner and mother-substitute, he could hardly have made a worse choice. Antonina had little interest in music, was clearly as emotionally unbalanced as Tchaikovsky, and was unwilling or unable to confront the obvious—that Tchaikovsky had no physical interest in her whatever. With the composer obsessed with the idea of fate and seemingly living out the destinies of the characters in *Eugene Onegin*, he married Antonina in July 1876. Within days he was regretting his mistake and, after a disastrous visit to his new in-laws, he escaped alone to Kiev. A reunion of sorts and a half-hearted suicide attempt later, Tchaikovksy arranged through his friends to be sent a telegram demanding his immediate presence in St Petersburg. On his arrival he collapsed in a hotel and for 48 hours suffered a complete mental and emotional breakdown. Nicholas Rubinstein and Tchaikovsky's brother, Anatol, broke the news to Antonina, who calmly offered them more tea and vowed stoic endurance—for her husband's sake. Husband and wife never met again. Antonina was to spend her last two decades in a mental hospital.

The immediate aftermath of this disaster was a generous gesture by Mme von Meck: she granted Tchaikovsky an annuity which freed him

from the necessity of earning a living, thus enabling him to compose as he wished. He spent the winter and spring of 1877–78 in Florence finishing *Eugene Onegin*, his first indisputable operatic masterpiece. An additional bonus was his Concerto for Violin in D, Op. 35, which displays a remarkable optimism in the aftermath of what he had just experienced. As usual with Tchaikovsky, his original dedicatee (this time Leopold Auer) declared the piece virtually unplayable, and it languished unheard until 1881 when Adolph Brodsky made his Vienna debut with it.

As if entering a long period of recuperation, Tchaikovsky took years to approach this level of creativity again—with the Piano Trio, Op. 50, written to commemorate Nicholas Rubinstein's death in 1881, *Capriccio Italien* and the *Serenade for Strings* standing out from relative failures such as the Second Piano Concerto and the two operas, *Maid of Orleans* (1881) and *Mazeppa* (1884), both dealing with historical subjects and neither really catching fire. However, his old colleague Balakirev suggested a subject for a symphony which he thought would admirably suit Tchaikovsky's predilections; after some hesitation Tchaikovsky agreed, and in 1885 began writing the *Manfred Symphony*, Op. 58, modelled on the hero of Byron's famous poem and dedicated to Balakirev. It was premièred in Moscow in 1886, and it is not difficult to agree with the composer who thought it his finest symphony to date.

Even better was to come in 1888; in his Fifth Symphony, Op. 64, Tchaikovsky readdressed his favourite compositional subject of fate and the impossibility of

DON'T MISS

▶ Serenade for Strings, Op. 48 (1880)

▶ Symphony No. 5, Op. 64 (1888)

▶ Symphony No. 6 (Pathétique) Op. 74 (1893)

▶ Rococo Variations, Op. 33 (1876)

DON'T MISS

▶ **Souvenir de Florence,
   Op. 70 (1890)**

▶ **6 Songs, Op. 6 (1869)**

▶ **Eugene Onegin (1879)**

avoiding one's destiny. There is no doubt about the lessons learned from earlier works and applied here, for form and development is on a different plane to earlier symphonies, and even the controversial doomed struggle with fate in the finale makes its own logical points. The work is one of the great concert favourites, has the usual sumptuous melodies, and it is wholly appropriate that Tchaikovsky himself enjoyed conducting it. At the beginning of 1889 he set to work on his second great ballet, *Sleeping Beauty*, Op. 66, sandwiching its composition between two hectic tours of Western Europe. The ballet was given for the first time in 1890 in St Petersburg before the Tsar. Tchaikovsky was incensed when the monarch cut him dead, but happily this had little effect on the success of the ballet, his most subtle yet.

His next opera was again based on a Pushkin story, this time *The Queen of Spades* (Pique Dame). His brother

Modeste had prepared the basic libretto, which Pyotr altered, tightening it and highlighting the themes of fate, death and obsession which are at the heart of the opera. With the composition finished by mid-summer, Tchaikovsky left for Italy. That autumn he received a painful letter from his 'best friend', Mme von Meck, claiming that penury forced her to terminate her financial support. The money was no longer important as Tchaikovsky was now earning a comfortable living from his compositions, but the sense that he might have simply been an amusement to a rich woman drove him to distraction, and when she did not reply to his letters of remonstrance, a bitter silence fell between them. What Tchaikovsky did not know was that Mme von Meck was already suffering from the physical and mental deterioration which would end in her early death. Meanwhile, *The Queen of Spades* was a notable success in December 1890. A year later, after a gruelling tour of America which took its toll on the composer, the première was held for his last and most popular ballet, *The Nutcracker*, Op. 71, billed in the same programme as the opera *Iolanthe*, a success on the night but not his strongest stage work. Oddly enough, *The Nutcracker* failed to please, only

slowly becoming popular world-wide, with much of its advance in public esteem achieved by the suites prepared from the full ballet.

The year 1893 began well, with the short score of Symphony No. 6, (*Pathétique*), Op. 74, being completed by mid-spring. In May he went to England to accept an honorary Doctorate of Music from Cambridge University, then spent the summer orchestrating the *Pathétique*, the symphony he believed was his best yet. After its successful St Petersburg première in October, he remained in the city writing to friends of his plans. Within days he had been taken mortally ill, suffered appalling agonies before finally succumbing. The official reason for the death was cholera, but in recent years it has been surmised that Tchaikovsky had been ordered to commit suicide by a 'court of honour' of old school colleagues after an allegation had been made by Duke Stenbok-Fermor with regard to the composer's relationship with his son. The agonies had not been from cholera but from arsenic. A few days later there was a massive funeral in the city, with a large service in Kazin Cathedral, and Tchaikovsky was laid to rest near the graves of Borodin, Mussorgksy and Glinka.

E M M A N U E L   C H A B R I E R
1841–1894

Chabrier was important as one of the first French composers to grasp the substance and style of Spanish music and to translate it into compositions in such a way

that French audiences caught a glimpse of the exotic culture from which they had been separated both physically and culturally throughout the centuries.

Chabrier was born in Ambert in the Auvergne into a family long established in the region. His father was a prosperous lawyer, and Emmanuel grew up safe in the knowledge that a career in the legal profession awaited him. From the age of six he was given piano lessons, and soon exhibited a natural gift for music. His involvement, however, remained amateur throughout his education, including the four years he spent studying law at the Lycée St Louis in Paris. By the time he was 20 he had taken a post in the civil service which enabled him to support himself and pursue his interests. Apart from music, these included the fine arts and literature. During his first few years in Paris he discovered the Impressionists and became acquainted with Renoir, Monet and Manet, the latter becoming a close friend. At a time when these painters were derided, Chabrier supported them by buying their pictures, including Manet's famous *Un Bar aux Folies-Bergère*. Chabrier himself was painted by Manet, Fantin-Latour, Tissot, Degas and Desboutin. He also became friends with the poet Verlaine; indeed, his earliest attempts at a stage work were two short *opera bouffes* co-authored with Verlaine, *Fisch-Ton-Kan* and *Vaucochard et Fils Ier*.

The few works which have survived from Chabrier's first 30 years are relatively unambitious songs such as the Alfred de Musset and de Laprade settings of 1862, or salon-style piano pieces like *Souvenirs de Brunehaut* (1862), *Suite de valses* (1872) and the *Cortège burlesque* (1871). During the 1870s Chabrier, now married, moved slowly but unerringly into the orbit of a group of Parisians known—due to their unflinching admiration of Wagner and his music—as 'Le Petit Bayreuth'. This secondary influence was to prove decisive; in particular, it

---

DON'T MISS

▶ **España (1883)**

▶ **Suite pastorale (1888)**

▶ **10 Pièces pittoresques (1881)**

▶ **Le Roi malgré lui (1887)**

▶ **L'Etoile (1877)**

---

produced the exact balance of Chabrier's mature works for orchestra, although his first operetta, *L'Etoile* (Bouffes-Parisiens, 1877), shows nothing of this. *L'Etoile* was an immediate success and made Chabrier a name to reckon with for the first time at the age of 36.

Although *L'Etoile* has failed to sustain its place in operetta circles, it consistently drew extravagant praise from a succession of composers such as Debussy (who used to sing and play it for his own amusement), Koechlin and Poulenc. Virtually devoid of a coherent plot, it is full of charming and touching sequences, and is scored with a lightness and sureness of touch which belies Chabrier's relative inexperience in the theatre. *L'Etoile's* two librettists, Leterrier and Vanloo, once more collaborated with Chabrier on the follow-up, a one-act farce called *Une Education manquée*, which appeared in 1879; its success persuaded Chabrier that the time had come for him to resign his civil service post and concentrate exclusively on composition.

Chabrier quickly became immersed in many ideas for new theatrical works, and also accepted the responsibility of supervising rehearsals for the first Paris performance of Wagner's *Tristan und*

Isolde in 1881, but his first major composition after his liberation from his Ministry post was a set of piano pieces, *Ten Pièces pittoresques* (1881). Chabrier's love of the piano was total and his technique legendary; many observers wrote of his forcefulness at the instrument, and of his fascinating improvisations. Apparently, Renoir once remarked when Chabrier finished a recital on the piano: "I swore to myself that I would never touch the piano again. An amateur playing is really ridiculous. Like the people who, just because they like Renoir, want to take up painting. How can they? Besides, Chabrier had broken several strings and put the piano out of action!" There is no trace of Wagner in this astonishingly resourceful and imaginative set of piano pieces, which has been admired and imitated by many French composers, especially Ravel. In them Chabrier forged a new approach not dependent on Romanticism or Classicism, instead combining in a particularly subtle and brilliant way his own vibrant personality with the music of the salons and the countryside.

In 1882 Chabrier and his wife took a holiday in Spain which lasted all of five months and which took in virtually every province on the Iberian peninsula. His delight with the people, their culture, food and—above all—their music, was recorded in a series of perceptive letters written to friends. He became immersed in minute observation of the regional variations in the music he heard in the streets and restaurants, and of flamenco. The impact the music made upon him can be heard in the work he wrote on his return to Paris, the famous *España* which Chabrier thought of as a 'fantasia extraordinaire' for orchestra. The immediate and immense popularity of this work, premièred in 1883, was quickly transcribed into versions for various instrumental combinations, including one for two pianos.

Chabrier continued to compose for the piano, with the *Trois valses romantiques* being especially fine; he also completed a singularly lyrical setting of a portion of the 'Song of Songs' under the title *La Sulamite* (1885), but the next major undertaking was his first 'grand opera', *Gwendoline* (1886). It is often assumed that this was written wholly under Wagner's spell, but although the librettist, Catulle Mendes, was an ardent Wagnerite, the hackneyed story is pure grand opera histrionics, the battles, spectacle and love interest following each other in routine fashion, and while the music's adventurousness owes much to Wagner, Chabrier's models could easily include Berlioz. The work was well received in Brussels, but after just two performances the Brussels opera house owner was declared bankrupt, and the production lost. Only in 1893 did *Gwendoline* appear on a Parisian stage, by which time Chabrier was a very sick man.

The composer bounced back from this disappointment with an opera often described as his masterpiece, *Le Roi malgré lui*, a comic opera which received its first performance in Paris in 1887. Yet another improbable plot (taken from the life of Henri III), was ill-executed by no less than three librettists, but Chabrier's zestful, witty and always evocative music overcomes all such obstacles to deliver the audience a sparkling evening. The opera was a triumpant success on its opening, winning rave reviews from the critics, but then the Opéra-Comique building burned to the ground just one week into its run. A short run was cobbled together some months later in the company's temporary accomodation, but the impetus for fame had been lost.

The first years of the 1890s were largely taken up with having his works successfully staged in Germany as his reputation there began to take a firm hold. He also spent much time with his family, encouraging his two sons to study and tending his semi-invalid wife. A major choral piece, *Ode à la musique*, was completed in 1890, and was described by Debussy as Chabrier's own musical creed, and

can be seen as his farewell to music. By late 1891 he was suffering increasingly from a progressive paralysis of his nervous system which finally destroyed him. The nature of the disease suggests syphilis as its cause; as did many other sufferers, Chabrier experienced periods of respite and clarity. Now living in the country, he wrote the superb piano piece *Bourrée fantasque* (1891) and also worked on the uncompleted grand opera *Briséïs*, once again using the mediocre and dilatory Catulle Mendes as librettist. Chabrier completed the first act but realising that further composition was beyond him, in the spring of 1894 he called in his friend Vincent d'Indy to complete the work. D'Indy found not an opera needing minor work to complete it, but one which needed virtually recomposing from the beginning of Act II. *Briséïs*, premièred at a Chabrier memorial concert in 1897, has remained a fragment. Chabrier was now in a pathetic state, unable to recognize even his own music, and in September he was dead. His influence on subsequent generations was vast, especially on Ravel, and Debussy declared: "Chabrier, Mussorgsky, Palestrina, voilà ce que j'aime".

A N T O N Í N   D V O Ř Á K
1841–1904

Dvořák's musical achievements seem to grow with time as the qualities he held dearest become more central to the musical aesthetics of today. A humble man but a staunch believer in the

worth of folk and national music, and a composer blessed with a limitless supply of beautiful melody, he brought dignity and eloquence to every musical form he touched.

Dvořák was born in a small Bohemian village on the banks of the Vltava, the river which for generations of Czechs has given their land its special identity. He was the first-born child of Frantisek Dvořák, village innkeeper and butcher;

from an early age he showed musical prowess, allied to his keen appreciation of the world about him—an interest which matured into a deep love for his country. He quickly mastered the fiddle, playing at village festivals in his father's band, and sang in the church choir. At the age of 12 he was taught German by Antonin Liehmann, an excellent amateur musician with his own band. Dvořák was soon receiving music lessons in addition to his other studies, combining them with working in his father's butcher's shop. In 1857 he secured a position at the Prague Organ School where he was given a sound musical education, studied the Classical composers and played the violin in an orchestra. However, life was not easy for a country boy in cosmopolitan Prague, and when he finished school he was hard pressed to make a living. He joined a concert-band in the capital, playing the viola, then transferred to the Czech National Theatre Orchestra, conducted after 1866 by Bedřich Smetana.

Antonín Dvořák

This was a key meeting for Dvořák for it was Smetana who confirmed the young man's own inclinations towards nationalism in music as well as towards the romantic notions then espoused in Germany by composers such as Schumann, Liszt and Wagner. It also occurred when Dvořák was making his first serious attempts at composition, and although the young musician eventually consigned much of what he wrote to the fire, there were a number of works which he allowed into his official canon, including his first and second symphonies, in C minor and B flat respectively, both written in 1865. These two works show a number of influences mingling with his own

individual conception; they are not ones upon which to build a reputation—as Dvořák well knew—but he continued to make progress until he reached a point in the early 1870s when he felt artistically mature. Under the spell of Smetana and Wagner, he composed two operas, neither of which were produced, but in 1873 he enjoyed his first public success with his hymn, *The Heirs of the White Mountain*, an overtly nationalist poem to which Dvořák added lofty music which greatly appealed to his Prague audience.

This success convinced him that it was time to accelerate his growth as a composer; he resigned from the

orchestra and earned a living by playing the organ at St Adalbert's Church. Over the next three years he composed three more symphonies. In 1873 he married Anna Cermákova, a fine singer and a member of the National Opera chorus; it was to prove a happy match, producing six children. From this early period onwards, Dvořák consistently composed across a very wide range of genres. In 1875, the year of his Fifth Symphony, he wrote the utterly charming *Serenade for Strings*, Op. 22 as well as his *Piano Trio No.1*, while the period 1873–74 had seen three string quartets, the fifth, sixth and seventh, completed. He also continued to work at operatic ideas, rewriting an early effort, *King and Collier.*

Another important event took place in 1876 when Dvořák met Brahms, then in the first flush of international acceptance and putting the finishing touches to his own first symphony. Brahms was immediately impressed by Dvořák's immense melodic gifts. Noting the Czech's difficulty in finding a decent publisher for his music, Brahms wrote to the Berlin publisher Simrock, recommending his *Moravian Duets*, saying: 'Dvořák has written in all possible styles: operas, symphonies, quartets, pianoforte pieces. Decidedly he is a very talented man. Besides, he is poor. Please take this into consideration'. This did the trick, and Simrock published the duets, leading to a run of success which had other publishers approaching Dvořák for works. The bond of friendship between the two composers deepened, aided by their mutual admiration for each other's musical achievements and integrity. Now on a more secure financial footing and guaranteed access to a wider audience, Dvořák intensified his efforts to bring elements of his native country's music, which he so loved, into his works.

The most straightforward way to achieve this was to incorporate the key elements of Czech folk music into his compositions, especially the typical melodic shapes and characteristic dance rhythms. His publisher Simrock commissioned the first set of *Slavonic Dances*, Op. 46 (1878) as a follow-up to the *Moravian Duets*, and the successful dissemination of these pieces accelerated his burgeoning international reputation. The following year Dvořák produced the *Czech Suite*, while the *Serenade for Wind Instruments*, Op. 44 clearly reflected his experience in the concert band early in his career, playing dance music for festive gatherings. In 1879 the third *Slavonic Rhapsody* was performed in Vienna by Richter; after the performance, the conductor commissioned a new symphony from Dvořák. The result was Sixth Symphony in D, Op. 60, which Richter and the Vienna Symphony Orchestra premièred in 1880. The 1880s saw no let-up in either Dvořák's level of inspiration or in his expanding reputation; the collection of *Gypsy Melodies*, Op. 55 proved very popular, as did the *Ten Legends for Orchestra*, Op. 59, while the opera *Dimitrij* traced in epic style a historical Russian tale. His Violin Concerto, Op. 53 was written in 1880 and revised in 1882. After an 1883 performance of his *Stabat Mater* by the London Musical Society he was invited to England to conduct it in person. He led both this

and his Sixth Symphony at the Albert Hall and at Crystal Palace. This was the start of a long and close relationship with Britain, Dvořák visiting the country no less than five times between 1884 and 1886 alone, and premièring his Seventh Symphony there in 1885, while the oratorio *St Ludmilla* was written for the Leeds Festival.

Financially secure at last, and enjoying the benefits of his world-wide fame, in 1884 Dvořák decided to move back to his beloved Czech countryside and bought a small farmhouse called Vysoká. He now had the freedom to choose between his Prague and Vysoká bases, using the farm to do most of his creative work. By the end of the decade Dvořák had completed one of his most prolific periods as a composer, producing an opera, *The Jacobin*, a whole host of piano pieces, the Mass in D, Op. 86, the Eighth Symphony, Op. 88, the *Quintet for Piano*, Op. 81 and more collections of songs. Still more was to come, including his most popular music in the view of today's audience.

With the dawning of the 1890s Dvořák was becoming a much-honoured man, with honorary degrees from universities from Prague to Cambridge, and in 1891 he accepted the position of Professor of Composition at Prague Conservatoire. His Requiem was premièred in Birmingham in 1890, and within 12 months he had completed the concert overtures *Carnival*, Op. 92 and the charming *In Nature's Realm*, Op. 91. A third concert overture, *Othello*, Op. 93, was completed in 1892. In chamber music it was the time of the Piano Trio No. 4 *Dumky*, Op. 90 and the *Rondo in G minor*, Op. 94 for cello and piano.

DON'T MISS

▶ **Cello Concerto, Op. 104 (1894–5)**
▶ **Carnival Overture, Op. 92 (1891)**
▶ **Serenade for Strings, Op. 22 (1875)**
▶ **Slavonic Dances, Opp. 46 & 72 (1878–86)**
▶ **Symphony No. 8, Op. 88 (1889)**

In 1892 he received an invitation from the founder of the New York National Conservatory of Music, Mrs Thurber, to become its director. After obtaining leave of absence from Prague Conservatoire, Dvořák took up his new position in September of that year. Although relations with the Conservatory board were not always smooth, Dvořák was greatly stimulated by his three years in America, finding that absence from his beloved Czechoslovakia gave him creative impetus rather than the reverse. The torrent of works either completed or begun in America include the String Quartet *American*, Op. 96, the String Quintet *American*, Op 97, the *Biblical Songs*, Op. 99 and the great Cello Concerto, Op. 105 (1895). There were also the *Humoresques*, Op. 101 (1894), which subsequently became some of the most often heard piano music throughout America and Europe. But the crowning achievement of this period was his Ninth Symphony *'From the New World*, Op. 95, into which he wove both typically Czech motifs and

DON'T MISS
▶ Symphony No. 9, Op. 95 (1893)
▶ Piano Trio No. 4 (Dumky), Op. 90 (1890–91)
▶ String Quartet No. 12 (American), Op. 96 (1893)
▶ 8 Piano Humoresques, Op. 101 (1894)
▶ Kate and the Devil, Op. 112 (1899)
▶ Rusalka, Op. 114 (1901)

melodies from negro spirituals, the most famous being 'Going Home', which he used as the great theme in the symphony's *largo*.

At the end of his American tenure, Dvořák resumed his professorship in Prague. An unassuming and simple man, he was at his most contented when with his family, friends or in the countryside he loved so dearly. His music continued to reflect these priorities, and his last years were taken up with a series of operas and symphonic poems. Of the operas, *Kate and the Devil* (1899) is undoubtedly one of the most

successful to stage, while *Rusalka* (1901), set to an old Czech legend, has consistently been the most popular, partly because of the aria, 'O silver moon', which possesses an unearthly beauty when sung sympathetically. His remaining years produced works such as the symphonic poems *The Mid-Day Witch, The Golden Spinning-Wheel* and *The Water Goblin,* all pieces which reflected Czech and Bohemian folk-lore. Dvořák kept up a full schedule of work, composing right up to his death from heart failure. Recognized as one of the true greats of the 19th century, he was mourned the world over.

JULES MASSENET
1842–1912

Jules Massenet was the most important French opera composer between Meyerbeer and Debussy; his influence spread beyond the confines of French opera and affected developments in Italy towards the end of the century, as well as the instrumental music of Debussy's generation.

Jules was born into a musical family based in a village near St Etienne. His father ran a small foundry; his mother was an amateur pianist who gave lessons to supplement the family's income when her husband became too ill to work. The family moved to Paris when Jules was six years old, and over the next five years lessons with his mother brought him to a

level of expertise which gained him entry into the Paris Conservatoire. In 1860 the family moved to Chambéry; Jules, though tempted to remain with them, returned to the Conservatoire where he joined the harmony and composition classes under the direction of Ambroise Thomas. Massenet was a keen and disciplined student, and in 1863 he

Jules Massenet

Bizet, who recognized the 22-year-old's talent. The production led to concerts of his non-theatrical music in Paris, and before long he had concluded an important deal with the influential publisher, Hartmann, who published two of his song cycles in quick succession.

In 1865 he wrote his first suite for orchestra, and was to compose seven more before 1881, each with a descriptive title (for example, the third is *Scénes Dramatiques;* the seventh *Scénes Alsaciennes*) which reflects the contents. The fourth suite, *Scénes Pittoresques,* was written after Massenet, disgusted by what he had witnessed as an infantryman during the Paris Commune of 1871, moved his family to Fontainebleau; its dominant mood is resolute high spirits.

Massenet found post-Commune Paris a city looking for new heroes, and he was determined to become one of them. A production of his 'sacred drama in 3 acts and 4 parts', *Marie-Magdaleine* took place on Good Friday 1873 with the famous soprano Pauline Viardot emerging from retirement especially to sing the lead role. It was an immediate and massive triumph, with even his rival Saint-Saëns writing that it was 'the most audacious experiment made by any musician in Paris since Berlioz's *L'Enfance du Christ...*.' Repeating this success with a similar oratorio, *Eve,* in 1875, Massenet quickly assumed leadership of the group of young composers in Paris, quietly taking over Gounod's position while the older composer was in England. He achieved this with a

won the Prix de Rome for his cantata *David Rizzio.*

In Rome he met Liszt, who introduced him to a family whose daughter needed piano lessons; Mlle Sainte-Marie, his new pupil, was destined to become his wife before his three Prix years were over. During this period he also visited a number of European countries and studied their musical

traditions. While in Rome he finished his first opera, *Esmérelda*, which remained unperformed on his return to France. But by 1867, after supporting himself with various musical hack jobs, the influence of Ambroise Thomas landed a première at the Opéra-Comique for his second stage work, *La Grand' tante.* It attracted good reviews but poor attendance figures. However, from it came a friendship with Georges combination of real talent and the excessive flattery for which he had become notorious. Even a good friend like Bizet was occasionally unable to stomach Massenet's insincerity. At a party once, Massenet insisted on praising a very poor ballet by Ernest Guiraud, *Gretna Green*, which had failed at the Opéra. Bizet shouted "Shut up! You make me sick. All of us here love Guiraud as much as you do... Nevertheless *Gretna Green* is a failure. We are all miserable because Guiraud hasn't written a better work...and you, who don't admire it any more than we do, you call it a masterpiece!" Yet Bizet was railing against a flaw in someone he genuinely liked and admired, for the following year he dedicated his *Patrie* overture to Massenet. Massenet was one of very few people the following year to congratulate Bizet the day after his première of *Carmen*.

Massenet's unchallenged primacy in Paris, however, was assured in 1877 with the première of *Le Roi de Lahore* at the Paris Opéra. With this work Massenet established his own style, which eschewed the Meyerbeer concept of grand opera with its reliance on formal spectacle, but combined the dignified melodicism of Gounod with the lushness of Wagner, plus an altogether French penchant for pious eroticism. This latter quality was to remain a theme in his work for the rest of his music career. The combination appealed immensely to the French opera-going public—titillation without anything too vulgar to threaten its sense of self-worth. Massenet's decadence could be harmlessly enjoyed by every good burgher.

In 1878 he was appointed Professor of advanced composition at the Conservatoire, as well as being appointed a member of the Académie des Beaux-Arts; at the age of 36 he was the youngest ever to be appointed. A year previously he had been awarded the Légion d'honneur. All this came before his greatest triumph: *Manon*. To a libretto by Mehilac and Gille, he wrote an opera packed with incident, strong emotions, tragedy and a simmering, slightly risqué sensuousness. With this work, which was taken up rapidly throughout the operatic world, Massenet became not only the leading French opera composer of the late 19th century, but also a composer whose style could not be ignored by anyone seriously interested in the genre. His decisive step away from a historic treatment of his subjects (even though the subjects themselves were usually historic) opened the door to Italian *verismo* of the 1890s as much as to Debussy and Ravel, for without his concentration on the more venal and neurotic desires of his subjects, the world of Puccini, Mascagni and Debussy is hard to envisage. What Massenet also achieved time and again was to strike a fine balance between sentimentality and drama, allowing the audience to indulge in both excitement and bathos.

Later works such as *Werther* (1892), the infamous *Thaïs* (created largely for the American soprano Sibyl Sanderson, a discovery of Massenet's and an ex-mistress) and *Le Jongleur de Notre Dame* (1902), all struck this balance in varying degrees, and with very few of the heroines

managing to survive the last act. Another aspect of Massenet's dramatic talents was demonstrated in *Chérubin* (1903), an opera in an altogether lighter vein which lends itself to the composer's poised and elegant melodic lines and genuine wit. *Don Quichotte* (1910) was written with the great Russian bass Féodor Chaliapin in mind, but Massenet also ensured that Dulcinea—played by a late amour of his, Lucy Arbell—had plenty to do. The death of Don Quixote is suitably sentimental, but on the whole the opera holds up well as a piece of entertainment and, for a change, the man dies rather than the woman.

For his last completed opera, *Cléopâtre* (1912), Massenet reverted to type, creating a femme fatale who dies at the end of the opera. By this point in his career he was largely a forgotten man, creating his operas for the small but lavishly-equipped Monte Carlo opera house far from the mainstream in Paris. His last works have a clarity of line and a tartness which is not always present earlier, and his melodies are still not quite memorable enough, but as spectacle they always convince and entertain.

DON'T MISS

▶ **Elégie (1869)**
▶ **Le Cid (1885)**
▶ **Don Quichotte (1910)**
▶ **Manon (1884)**
▶ **Le Roi de Lahore (1877)**
▶ **Thaïs (1894)**

EDVARD GRIEG

1843–1907

As Grieg has long been recognized as Norway's greatest composer and the man who put that country on the musical map, it is ironic that his paternal ancestry was Scottish, his great-grandfather having abandoned Scotland in 1846 after the Battle of Culloden.

Grieg's musical abilities seem to have descended through the maternal side; his mother was a skilful pianist who performed at concerts in their home town of Bergen. It was she who gave him his first music lessons when he was no more than six years old, and within three years he was composing little sets of variations. In 1858, at the age of 15, he was accepted into Leipzig Conservatorium, where the shadows of the recently deceased Mendelssohn and Schumann still lay heavily on the musical activities.

Edvard Grieg

Leipzig remained Grieg's base until 1862. When it came to writing his own piano concerto in 1868, Grieg's vivid memories of his Leipzig years gave him the necessary impetus to create a Schumannesque extended work which nonetheless retains his characteristic melodic and rhythmic verve. If the four years in Leipzig gave Grieg the necessary technical and theoretical framework from which he could strike out on his own, it did not release him from the thrall of German stylistic ideas. This liberation had to wait until he moved to Copenhagen in 1863, where for the first time he came into contact with artists from every discipline who were attempting to formulate a specifically Scandinavian aesthetic. Thus while he was being tutored in conventional theory by the famous Danish composer Niels Gade, his interest in his own country's musical legacy was being awakened for the first time.

Grieg was constantly on the move, shuffling between Norway and Denmark. He spent the summer of 1865 in Rungsted, Denmark, where he wrote his First Sonata for Violin and Piano, Op. 8, with its mysterious two opening chords. He even travelled as far as Rome, where he met the great playwright and *Peer Gynt* author, Henrik Ibsen. Another friendly influence on Grieg was the sadly short-lived Richard Nordraak, whose interest in establishing a Nordic artistic tradition helped Grieg set his mind to forming a musical union which became the Norwegian Music Association, established in Christiana.

His ties to Norway were strengthened in a more personal way: in 1867 he married his cousin, Nina Hagerup, and the majority of his large output of songs were written with her in mind since she was a highly distinctive singer. As early as his Op. 5 songs, set to texts by the Dane Hans Christian Andersen, she was the object of his emotions and his ideal interpreter. Her own vocal career had been curtailed by damage done to her vocal cords when recovering from an illness; after her marriage they mounted tours throughout Europe where his songs, sung by her, were the focal point of the recitals. Grieg wrote in 1900: 'Why do songs play such a prominent role in my productions? Quite simply because I too, like other mortals, was (to use Goethe's phrase) once in my life touched with genius. The genius was Love. I loved a young girl with a marvellous voice and an equally marvellous gift as an interpreter. This girl has been my wife and life's companion until this day'. It is true to say that Grieg first found his true compositional voice in his songs, and that it was Norwegian in inspiration, although he did not 'lift' folk melodies and use them in his own works, preferring instead to utilize their general shape and accents to bring a folk inflection to his music. Only 'Solveig's Song', from *Peer Gynt* is a conscious borrowing.

The marriage was a true love match, both partners enjoying an unusually serene existence. Grieg's one weakness was his health, which was never good after an attack of pleurisy in his youth. From 1868 onwards Grieg's major works flowed without interruption: his piano concerto (mentioned above) was written in 1868, while his long-running series of piano pieces called *Lyric Pieces* began to appear in the year of his marriage. They would eventually number 10 volumes in all, and cover a period of some 34 years, from 1867 to 1901. These charming and wide-ranging miniatures almost took the form of a notebook delineating the composer's constant and changing reactions to the countryside around him, as well as his delight in using Norwegian folk sources for his characteristic dance rhythms and lilting melodies. The earlier books present few technical difficulties to a pianist and take a simple, but for the most part optimistic, viewpoint on life, while as Grieg enters middle age (he completed his last *Lyric Piece* when he was 58) the music becomes more introspective and nostalgic. As with so many of Grieg's orchestral works, the *Lyric Suite*, Op. 54 and *Two Lyric Pieces*, Op. 68 were arranged for string orchestra by Grieg from the piano originals.

Grieg made a second visit to Rome in the winter of 1870, meeting up with Liszt so that he could play the maestro his recent piano concerto. True to form, Liszt expressed admiration for the work, pointing out his favourite small turns and felicities to highlight his points. Grieg's international reputation was largely launched by this concerto, reaching Leipzig by 1879 and Britain by 1883, after which it has rarely been off concert programmes. Meanwhile Grieg had formed creatively rewarding partnerships with two key Norwegian writers, Bjørnstjerne Bjørnson and Henrik Ibsen. Between 1871 and 1874 he collaborated with Bjørnson on a series of settings of dramatic poems, including *Before a Southern Convent*, Op. 20, *The Mountain Thrall*, Op. 32 and *Bergloit*, Op 42, the last being a melodrama with music which Grieg did not complete until 1885. These works generally use Nordic subjects or passages from Norwegian history, and are consistent with the direction Grieg and his artistic colleagues wanted to pursue. They are also fine pieces in their own right and unjustly neglected. Equally rarely heard is Grieg's incidental music to Bjørnson's 1872 play *Sigurd Jorsalfar*. The music, written in 1876 for Ibsen's youthful theatrical setting of his poem *Peer Gynt*, is an altogether different matter; Grieg originally wrote 26 separate incidental musical items to accompany the play's wild, satirical and fantastical action, which extends as far as Africa and Arabia. Only later did Grieg form the best pieces into two orchestral suites, which today are regarded as quintessential musical depictions of Norwegian life, but originally

---

DON'T MISS

▶ **Piano Concerto, Op. 16 (1868)**
▶ **Holberg Suite, Op. 40 (1884)**
▶ **2 Elegaic Melodies, Op. 34 (1881)**
▶ **Lyric Pieces, Books 1–10 (1867–1901)**
▶ **Peer Gynt – Suites 1 & 2 Opp. 48/55**

accompanied outlandish cavortings in Bedouin tribes and darkest Africa.

By the mid-seventies Grieg was established as Norway's greatest living composer—indeed, the greatest composer the country had ever produced. His services as a conductor were often required, especially by the Norwegian Music Society, and it was only natural that during the 1884 bicentenary celebrations of the birth of the dramatist Ludvig Holberg, who was born in Bergen, Grieg was asked to write some music for the occasion. The composer wrote a suite for piano, *From*

Holberg's Time, commonly called the *Holberg Suite*, in which he shows himself entirely capable of using old musical forms in a fresh and stimulating way, just as Tchaikovsky had done with his *Rococo Variations*.

By this time Grieg and his wife had settled in a country house he had built near Bergen, and it was there that he composed his Third Violin and Piano Sonata, Op. 45 in response to a visit from the beautiful and sparkling young Italian violinist Teresina Tua, who played them dazzling virtuoso pieces and inspired

Grieg to write something specially for her. There is a rare drama and tension in the work, and it is Grieg's masterpiece in the field. Grieg and his wife continued their concert tours, albeit at a more modest pace, but in 1907 Grieg died suddenly while journeying form his house in Bergen to Christiana. His most popular works remain at the core of the modern concert repertoire, but his greatest and most characteristic achievements are perhaps to be found in his 100 or so songs, his piano music and his orchestral and choral settings of Nordic texts.

NICOLAI RIMSKY-KORSAKOV

1844–1908

Of all the great Russian nationalist composers of the latter part of the 19th century, Rimsky-Korsakov stands second only to Balakirev in his practical influence on the music created and preserved in that period. In so far as his own music is concerned, while some pieces have remained immensely popular, the bulk of his achievement is rarely heard today. Many people see him as the logical link between Mussorgsky and Stravinsky.

Rimsky-Korsakov was the second son of a substantial landowner who lived 'in his own house' (as Rimsky-Korsakov notes in his autobiography) on the outskirts of a small town, Tikhvin. Both his parents were musical and were

quick to perceive that their son was unusually gifted; he had perfect pitch and excellent time and by the age of six he was having music lessons, but was not sufficiently enamoured of music for it to supercede his love of books. In 1856 he was sent to the Naval College in St Petersburg where he spent the next four years. He also began to go to the opera in St Petersburg; struck first by Donizetti's *Lucia di Lammermoor* and *Robert le Diable*, he later discovered the joys of harmony through playing manuscripts of Glinka's *Ruslan and Lyudmila* and began making his own piano arrangements of excerpts from a range of favourite operas.

By 1861 the 17-year-old was becoming increasingly engrossed in musical studies and exploring the concert repertoire as well as opera. This same

year he was introduced by his tutor to Balakirev, then aged 24 and already the leader of a group of young composers, including Cui, Mussorgsky and Borodin. It was Balakirev who awoke in Rimsky-Korsakov the ambition to become a composer, approving of his tentative sketches for a symphony and demanding that he complete it; even Nicolai's posting abroad (1862–65) did not dampen his ardour; he took the unfinished manuscript with him on his tour of duty. On his return to St Petersburg he completed his symphony in time for its successful première under Balakirev's baton in 1865. Subsequent performances in 1866 confirmed his burgeoning reputation.

At this point he both idolized the domineering and opinionated Balakirev and was good friends with the younger and less musically trained Mussorgsky and Borodin. Still living what he termed the 'life of a dilettante', Rimsky-Korsakov was looked upon as a talented but unfocused musical amateur by his composer friends, but as a brilliant musical talent by his colleagues in the navy. He himself was only too aware of his own shortcomings, and his orchestral works at this time tended to be quite short—the *Overture on Russian Themes* (1866) was given a successful performance in the same year, while 1867's *Sadko*, taken over from Mussorgksy who had abandoned an earlier attempt to set the subject to music, was a short and brilliant exposition of memorable melodies, showing real flair in the orchestration—a talent for which he would later become world famous. His Second Symphony, sub-titled *Antar*, was completed in 1868.

At this time he began to realize his dreams of returning to his first musical love—opera. While on holiday with Borodin on his country estate, he resumed work on *Pskovitianka* (The Maid of Pskov). As he recalled: 'The picture of the impending trip to the dreary interior of Russia instantly brought an access of indefinable love for Russian folk life, for her past in general and for *Pskovitianka* in particular'. The opera engaged his attention intermittently for the next three years, while he also embarked on his second musical career—arranging and orchestrating the works of other composers. The recently deceased Darghomïzsky had entrusted the completion of his almost finished opera *The Stone Guest* to Cui and Rimsky-Korsakov; Nicolai did the orchestration, thus beginning a career as the realizer

---

---

of the works of deceased colleagues.

In 1871, in an extraordinary development, the 'amateur' Rimsky-Korsakov was offered the position of Professor of Composition and Instrumentation as well as leader of the St Petersburg Conservatoire orchestra. After consulting Balakirev, the composer made his decision. As he comments in his reminiscences: 'Had I ever studied at all, had I possessed a fraction more knowledge than I actually did, it would have been obvious to me that I could not and should not accept...that it was foolish and dishonest of me to become a professor. But I, the author of *Sadko*...was a dilettante and knew nothing'. He took the job. With it came the awful realization of the depths of his ignorance, and for a while his creativity evaporated while he tried to develop what he felt to be a mature style. At this point in his life he felt secure enough to resign his naval commission, but was persuaded by Grand Duke Constantine to become instead inspector of naval bands.

The following year, Rimsky-Korsakov, now 27, married Nadezhda Purgold: Mussorgsky was best man. In the same year he wrote his Third Symphony, a strangely formal affair which, in its

original incarnation, was too concerned with the counterpoint, correct modulations and other formal matters which Rimsky-Korsakov was desperately attempting to master for his professional peace of mind. As he consolidated his home and professional life, he found himself moving away from old colleagues: Balakirev, once a staunch atheist, had embraced religious mysticism and withdrawn almost entirely from his old circle of friends; Mussorgsky, in the first flush of success with *Boris Godunov*, had begun his slow physical and mental decline, brought on by alcohol.

In 1875, the year his daughter Sonia was born and his wife suffered a long illness, he began the editing and correction of Glinka's extant manuscripts, of which no definitive edition had been attempted since his death. By this time Rimsky-Korsakov, now fully at ease with his own musical knowledge and techniques, had renewed his mission to bring more nationalistic traits into his music. These are very noticeable in the two operas which appeared next, *May Night* (1878) and *The Snow Maiden,* both of which dealt with specifically Russian themes and used old modes, folk-like melodies and nationalistic rhythms and scoring. The death of Mussorgsky in 1881 found

Rimsky-Korsakov once more realizing another composer's scores, spending nearly two years deleting, rescoring and editing the musical fragments and completed works he found among Mussorgsky's effects. This work, today somewhat controversial due to the extent to which Rimsky-Korsakov departed from what Mussorgsky had composed, undoubtedly brought the composer's works into sharp focus in the public eye in the decades following his death. Without Rimsky-Korsakov's reworking of *Boris* for example, the opera would not have achieved its status as a national treasure by the turn of the century. Equally, it was Rimsky-Korsakov who made the first orchestral version of the piano work *Pictures at an Exhibition,* bringing it to the attention of concert-goers world-wide.

In 1883 the new Tsar, Alexander III, dismissed the old chapel musicians and appointed Balakirev as the new superintendant of the Court Chapel and Rimsky-Korsakov as his aide. This led both of them into utterly unfamiliar territory, preparing choral music for the coronation and other important occasions. A favourite new prodigy, Alexander ('Sasha') Glazunov, was the young composer-acolyte who came to Rimsky-Korsakov's aid in 1886 when the sudden death of Borodin left him with yet another disorganized heap of priceless unfinished compositions to put in order. Their major achievements were the performing version of *Prince Igor* and the realization of Borodin's unfinished Third Symphony, one movement of which Glazunov wrote down apparently from memory, having once heard Borodin play it on the piano.

Clearly all this work on other people's

music slowed Rimsky-Korsakov's own output considerably, and only by taking a break from his careful orchestration of *Prince Igor* during a summer holiday did he complete his sketches for *Capriccio Espagnol,* one of his most sparkling and delightful concert pieces. It is perhaps worth speculating whether the sublime melodies and scoring of the manuscipts he laboured on for so long had a subliminal effect on the 'editor' who was also a great composer, releasing a flood of ethnically-inspired music which, in the following year, would include his single most famous piece, the suite *Scheherazade* (musically illustrating characters and stories from the *Arabian Nights*) and the bouyant *Russian Easter Overture.*

This peak in his middle years was achieved—as he himself commented—'without Wagner's influence'. But Wagner's influence was brought to bear when Rimsky-Korsakov became involved in the production of *Der Ring des Nibelungen* in St Petersburg. The *Ring* made little impact on the audiences at the time, but Rimsky-Korsakov was impressed by the size and shape of the Wagnerian orchestra and used this in his next opera, *Mlada,* although he also incorporated the more exotic musical and dramatic devices he had witnessed in the Hungarian and Algerian cafés in Paris during the Universal Exhibition of that summer.

In the year after their return to St Petersburg his family was struck by illness: first his mother died, then his wife and three of his children fell seriously ill, one of them dying while a second, Masha, remained critical. In summer 1892, the composer suffered what seems to have been a nervous

breakdown, and was forced to take a prolonged break from music. In 1893 he had to deal with further illness, his son taking months to recover from a dangerous infection, while Masha continued to ail from consumption, dying that summer in Yalta.

Rimsky-Korsakov now retired. In spring 1894 his musical muse returned, and he began working on *Christmas Eve,* the first of a series of operas which would monopolize his creative interest until his death. This first manifestation was successfully premièred in 1895. With Tchaikovsky, Mussorgsky and Borodin all dead, Rimsky-Korsakov was unchallenged as the leading living Russian composer, and used his position both to promote his own operas and to forward the career of those composers, such as Glazunov, whose talents he firmly believed in. Bouyed by the relative ease of his composition of *Christmas Eve,* Rimsky-Korsakov next plunged into the legend of *Sadko,* completing an opera on it in 1896. It is in many ways his most accomplished opera and was very popular during his lifetime. After this, there was seldom a period when he was not devising, or working upon, his next opera, with *The Tsar's Bride* and *Mozart and Salieri* both completed before the end of the decade. With the opening of the new century *The Tale of Tsar Saltan* was produced privately in St Petersburg.

In the next decade operas such as *Pan Voyevoda* (1903), *Kastcheï the Immortal* (1902), the dramatic prologue, *Vera Sheloga* (starring the great bass Chaliapin), the mystical and extraordinary opera *The Legend of the Invisible City of Kitezh* (1905), and *The Golden Cockerel* all appeared. During these years Rimsky-Korsakov kept a high public profile, culminating in open discord with the St Petersburg Conservatory when students in 1905 rebelled against what they saw as an oppressive and conservative musical autocracy. The forthright Rimsky-Korsakov could not help but publicly agree with the students. As a result, his own works were banned from performance in St Petersburg and the school's classes were suspended indefinitely; instead Rimsky-Korsakov's students studied with him at his house. He was to remain at the hub of St Petersburg and Moscow musical affairs until his death three years later from a progressive throat and lung disease.

GABRIEL FAURÉ

1845–1924

A man as commited to what he perceived as the ineffable 'Frenchness' of what he created as he was to revealing aspects of his personal being through his music, the long-lived Fauré became a symbol for all that was subtle and lyrical in the music of his day.

Fauré was born in the village of Pamiers, near the Pyrenees. The sixth-born, he appears to have been an unwanted addition to a family whose resources were already overstretched, and he was packed off to a local nurse until he was four, growing up a reserved and withdrawn child. The family had no history of musical ability and it took some time for Gabriel's musical gifts to be noticed. Eventually, he was sent to the Ecole de musique religieuse et classique in Paris, run by the composer Louis Niedermeyer. Impressed by the boy and aware of the family's straightened circumstances, Niedermeyer agreed to waive his fees. Despite Niedermeyer's death in 1861, Fauré remained at the school (now known as the Ecole Niedermeyer), studying instrumentation, composition, piano

Gabriel Fauré

and the history of music. This last subject was of great importance for he came to appreciate the music of Palestrina, Lassus, Bach and Handel, as well as studying Gregorian chant, and developed a strong affinity with the music of the period. This was to prove of great value to him when he trod his own individualistic harmonic path, using the ancient modes as a basis from which to construct his techniques.

On Niedermeyer's death, Saint-Saëns took over the piano class, and the music of the newer Romantics—Schumann, Liszt and Wagner—was heard in the school for the first time. Fauré and Saint-Saëns became lifelong friends. In 1866, after winning the school's prize for his composition *Cantique de Jean Racine*, Fauré left the school to become organist in Rennes, taking up private tuition and composing in his spare time. In 1870 he became accompanying organist at St Sulpice in Paris and later principal organist at St Honoré. During the Franco-Prussian War and the Commune that followed, Fauré served in the National Guard. When peace was restored, Fauré drifted into Parisian musical circles via the salon of Saint-Saëns. In 1872 he returned to the Ecole Niedermeyer, this time as a member of staff.

At about this time Saint-Saëns introduced Fauré to the famous operatic singer, Pauline Viardot, a cultured woman who had helped to introduce Spanish music into Parisian musical circles. Fauré fell passionately in love with her daughter Marianne; she agreed in 1877 to an engagement, but then changed her mind. Fauré was devastated and took years to recover from the blow. Meanwhile he had slowly been trying to compose

orchestral music, abandoning a number of projects and patching together a 'symphony', or orchestral suite, which was performed in Paris in 1874. The work would remain unpublished and in time be used in other works. His violin concerto of 1878 was also unpublished, and the only works he composed were chamber music, songs and solo piano pieces—genres in which he would maintain a keen interest for the rest of his creative life. The First Sonata for Piano and Violin, Op. 13, was written in 1876–77, and reflects his early confidence and equanimity. His famous *Berceuse*, Op. 16 for violin and piano came in 1879, and was followed in 1880 by the *Elégie*, Op. 24 for cello and piano, and it is difficult not to read the emotional story of his dashed hopes into these short, melancholy works. The first significant piano piece, *Ballade*, Op. 19 also dates from 1880, and reflects a more serene and generally sanguine state of mind.

Trips to Germany between 1877 and 1879 took him to Weimar, Cologne and Bayreuth, and he met Liszt, who pronounced the *Ballade* "trop difficile"! Wagner's *Ring* he found interesting from the point of view of orchestral sonority, but he was one of the few composers of the period left untouched by Wagner's music and philosophies.

Fauré assuaged his disappointment in love by marrying Marie, the daughter of the eminent sculptor Emmanuel Fremier. Though not a passionate marriage, it seems to have been a source of strength and stability to both partners. The first child was born soon after, another son following some five years later. At this time Fauré was earning just enough for the family to subsist on. Fauré's major achievements in these years were a number of songs and a second symphony; the latter, though performed in 1885, was withdrawn by the composer. A third symphony was left incomplete and Fauré instead embarked on the first version of his famous Requiem, which was completed in 1888. Over the following two years Fauré, a passionate man of the theatre, wrote the incidental music for two dramas, the first for a production of Dumas's play *Caligula*, the second a French adaptation of Shakespeare called *Shylock*.

By this stage Fauré had written a couple of Barcarolles and four Nocturnes, while his song-writing still contained his most mature utterances at this stage of his career. By 1891 he was creating the *Cinq Mélodies*, Op. 58, set to poems by Paul Verlaine, writing them during a visit to Venice and catching the peculiar bittersweet passion of Verlaine's poetry. The following year he was swept off his feet by the vivacious Emma Bardac—the young wife of a wealthy but dull banker—and plunged into an affair with her. It was of relatively short duration; Bardac remained with her banker, but for Fauré it proved the catalyst for the symbolic outpouring of his love in the

---

DON'T MISS

▶ Élégie, Op. 24 (1896)

▶ Masques et bergamasques, Op. 112 (1920)

▶ Pavane, Op. 50 (1887)

▶ Dolly Suite, Op. 56 (1894–97)

▶ La Bonne chanson, Op. 61 (1892–94)

▶ Requiem, Op. 48 (1888)

---

beautiful form of *La Bonne Chanson*, Op. 61, the song-cycle composed to Verlaine's poems written after his own marriage. The set of songs was dedicated to Bardac, who was herself a fine amateur singer. This major work is one of the great 19th-century cycles, and shows that French song, in the hands of Fauré (and later Debussy) could stand comparison with the best of German *lied*. Fauré also created his piano work, the suite entitled *Dolly*, Op. 56, for Mme Bardac.

Fauré's marriage survived, and as the nineties progressed so his material circumstances improved. By late 1896 he succeeded Massenet as Professor of Composition at the Conservatoire and became principal organist at the Madeleine. By 1899 Fauré was once again composing incidental music for a play, this time Mrs Patrick Campbell's London production of Maeterlinck's symbolist masterpiece, *Pelléas et Mélisande*. In 1903 he became music critic for the newspaper *Le Figaro*, and two years later was appointed Director of the Conservatoire.

Between 1905 and 1921 Fauré composed his most deeply-felt and personal piano music, especially the last four nocturnes; passionate, declamatory yet strangely intimate—truly music from the deep well of life. He also managed a series of highly successful orchestral pieces as well as a triumphant revision of his Requiem. The beautiful and elegant *Masques et bergamasques*, Op. 112 appeared as late as 1919, perhaps a conscious reaction against the horrors of WWI. But the greatest achievements of Fauré's last years are probably his late flowering of utterly characteristic chamber music. The Second Piano Quintet, Op. 115, the Second Quartet, Op. 121, the Piano Trio, Op. 120, the Second Violin Sonata, Op. 108 and the two Cello Sonatas, Op. 109 & 117, all attest to Fauré's distillation of his musical message. This is also evident in his last great song-cycle, *L'Horizon chimérique*, Op. 118, where he sets the visionary poems of a young French writer killed in the first year of the War. By this time Fauré was virtually stone deaf, but he retained his total commitment to his composing. His opera, *Pénélope*, was a stunning example of French lyric opera on the grand scale when that genre seemed about to disappear; it was his only effort in that field, but it remains in glorious and beautiful isolation, both in his output and the history of this century's French opera.

Now nearly eighty, Fauré had outlived most of his generation; he had also continued to follow his own compositional path. In 1920 his deafness forced him to resign from the Conservatoire. Two years later a major benefit concert was organized for him by his colleagues and admirers at which many stars and old friends performed. He died of old age in his Paris home in 1924, leaving a uniquely valuable musical legacy.

PART VII

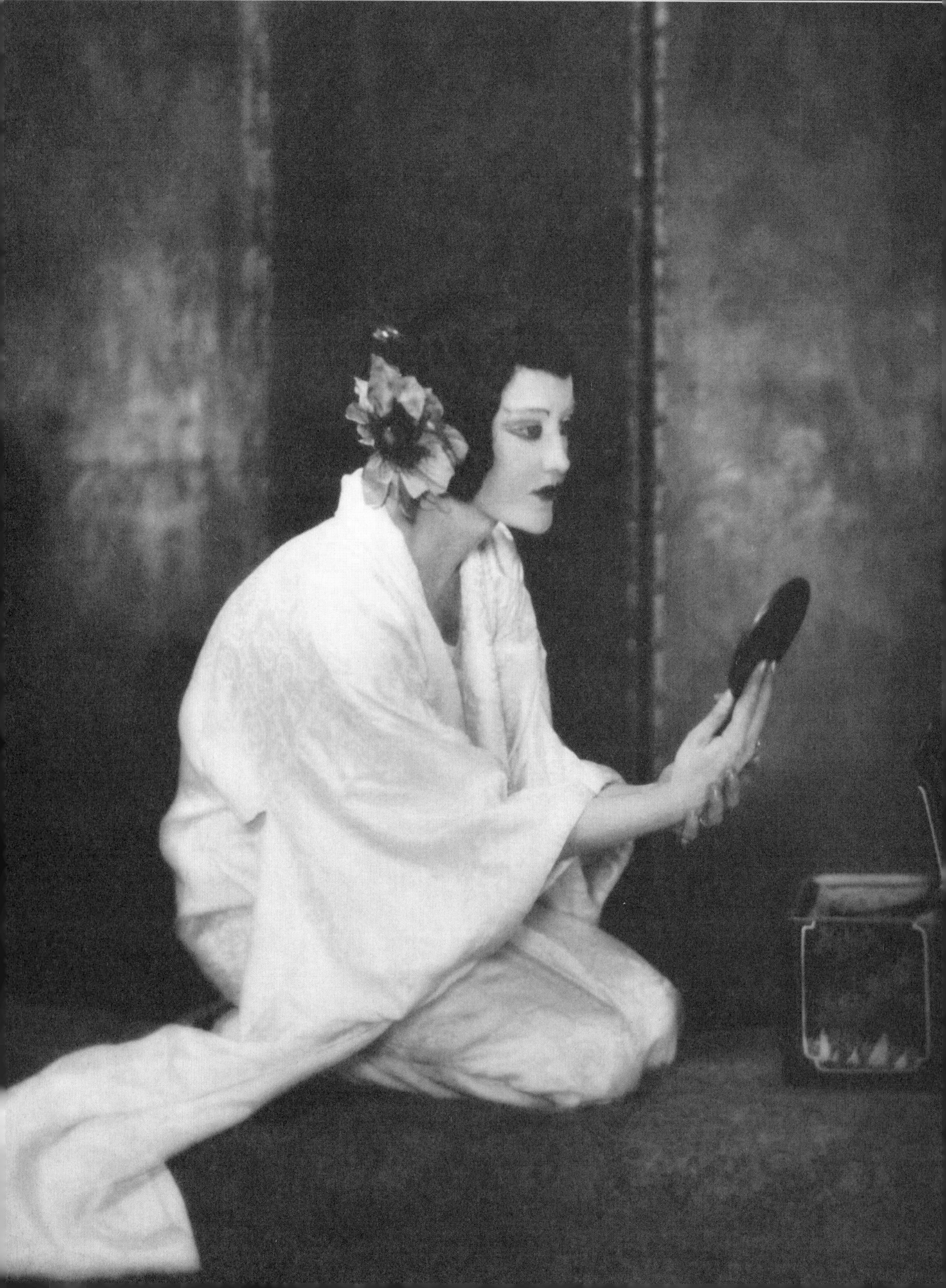

1850-1875

After finding their musical feet during the closing decades of the 19th century, this generation of composers went on to dominate the pre-World War I music scene in Europe and elsewhere. The longer-lived amongst them—Richard Strauss, Mascagni and Vaughan Williams—all saw the conclusion of World War II, while Strauss and Vaughan Williams survived long enough to reflect the new world order in their late works.

One of the period's major themes in music was the continuing proliferation of new cultural bases from which native composers derived their inspiration; Spaniards such as Albéniz and Granados, the American Charles Ives, the Czech Janáček, the Englishmen Vaughan Williams, Holst and Elgar, the Finn Sibelius and the Dane Carl Nielsen, all brought aspects of their indigenous cultures, musical and literary, into their work. Another major theme was the progressive extension of conventional harmony. After the work of masters such as Mahler and Strauss, Arnold Schoenberg took the next set of logical steps towards the disintegration of the concept of keys and tonality, followed by a slow, sometimes painful rebuilding of compositional foundations. These

would eventually be contained within the twelve-tone (also known as serialist and dodecaphonic) system of tonal organization. In an entirely separate and parallel development (and largely unrecognized at the time), Charles Ives was experimenting with composing music using quarter-tone intervals, complex and conflicting rhythms and polytonality. The Russian Scriabin went to different extremes, exploring both the spiritual dimension of music and its place in an overall artistic synthesis where notes and tones could represent colour, and the complete aesthetic experience would lead to something approaching catharsis for both composer and audience.

In the world of popular Classical music the arrival of the fashion for *verismo* in Italian opera (a preference for 'real life', mainly contemporary subjects, plainer, more everyday speech, and less emphasis on formal vocal set-pieces) delivered an astonishing array of new talent, including Mascagni, Leoncavallo and Puccini, the latter the last to arrive but undoubtedly the best of them all. In German-speaking territories, the operetta—through the delightful confections of Franz Lehár—proved that it was not yet a dead form.

A 1916 portrait of English opera singer Elizabeth Nelvi, costumed for Puccini's Madame Butterfly.

LEOŠ JANÁČEK
1854–1928

An older contemporary of Elgar and Mahler, Janáček reached an international audience much later than either, the extra-musical origin of much of his intense and carefully designed music being an initial hurdle to many listeners. Yet now that his speech-derived melodies and folk-derived rhythms sit as naturally on the ear as anything in Elgar's or Mahler's output, Janáček's importance is no longer in dispute.

The son of Jiri Janáček, an overworked village schoolmaster in Hukvaldy, Moravia, Leŏs grew up in relative poverty. By the age of 11, his father was sufficiently aware of his son's musicality to arrange for him to attend the Queen's Monastery School in Old Brno. Thus in September 1865 Janáček left home, his memories a mixture of his carefree country life, grating poverty and his father's excessive severity. Once at the school, where he came under the protective wing of Pavel Křižhovský, Janáček took advantage of the opportunities for a proper musical education. The boys were also trained to play a number of instruments and at school concerts they performed an impressively ambitious range of works, including Beethoven's *Eroica* Symphony and Cherubini's Requiem. In 1869, his last year at the Monastery School, Janáček prepared for his final examinations and also experienced a wave of religious and patriotic fervour which coincided

with the millenium of the death of St Cyril, the missionary who had translated the Bible into Old Slav. Janáček wore a Slav costume during the festivities, and this new awareness of his Slav roots was to remain with him all his life.

According to his deceased father's wishes (he had died in 1866), Leŏs spent the next three years at the Brno Imperial and Royal Teachers' Training Institute. His training included an additional two years' unpaid teaching at the Institute's school. He also gave organ and choral instruction at the Monastery School, and in 1872 was promoted to become Křižhovský's deputy choirmaster. This position gave him direct experience of conducting the music of composers such as Lassus, Palestrina and Victoria. It also led him to take the job of unpaid choirmaster to an amateur choral society, which gave him an outlet for his own early choral compositions, none of which were memorable in themselves but which helped teach him useful lessons about writing for choirs. In 1874 Janáček received his teacher's diploma, excelling in literary history and language, and through the good offices of Křižhovský, obtained a one-year leave of absence in order to study music at the Prague Organ School. He arrived in Prague, virtually penniless, knowing that he had to fit a three-year music course into one so as to abide by the conditions of his leave. Through the generosity of friends and teachers alike, and by dint of his own

iron self-discipline, Janáček survived the year.

After finishing his Organ School studies with an excellent report, which qualified him as an organist, he took a holiday in Moravia where he was struck by the beauty and romance of both the countryside and the girls. After studying to qualify as a teacher, in 1880 he became a member of staff at the Teachers' Training School in Brno. During this time he continued giving concerts and composing, although his small-scale orchestral music remained at this time heavily derivative of a great many sources, Handel and Dvořák among them. A further leave of absence, this time to study composition in Leipzig and Vienna, ended in a return to Brno in July 1880 with no further qualifications, but with a much greater sense of what he wanted to do in music.

He also returned to Brno to get married; in 1879, before he made his dash to Leipzig, he had discovered that he was in love with Zdenka Schulzova, one of his pupils. Not surprisingly, given their ages, (Zdenka was 14 and Janáček 25) Zdenka's parents were against the match and the engagement was deferred until Janáček's return from Vienna, the parents hoping the couple's feelings would change. But they held fast to their intentions and were married in 1881, two weeks before Zdenka's sixteenth birthday. On their honeymoon Janáček took Zdenka to meet Dvořák, who expressed surprise at the 'child' accompanying him.

Returning to Brno after the honeymoon, Janáček began organizing a school of music which would teach according to his own methods and theories. It opened in late 1882. For the next 20 years Janáček's life was divided between teaching, composition and giving concerts. His private life remained eventful: the birth of a daughter, Olga, in 1882 led to a separation from Zdenka (Janáček had longed for a son). After two years the couple were reconciled, and by 1888 Zdenka bore him a son, Vladimir. His intense happiness was short-lived, for in 1890 Olga contracted scarlet fever. Although she recovered, Vladimir caught the disease and died within days. This tipped the balance of the marriage, with husband and wife never regaining their former intimacy. They remained together, but there would be no more children.

Throughout this decade Janáček struggled to move beyond the Classical styles of his training to establish a personal style based on national music types which did not merely imitate Dvořák and Smetana. This irresolution is apparent in works like the Lachian Dances (1889–90) which came about as a result of Janáček's researches into folk songs and music, but which still retained a conventionality of rhythm and expression. As the 1890s progressed, however, he formed a friendship with the musicologist Frantisek Bartos and together they worked to make a collection of Moravian folk songs for eventual publication. Their massive joint work, Folk Songs of Moravia Newly Collected, contained over 2,000 songs and variants, plus a long introduction from Janáček in which he

expounded his theory of speech melodies. He was convinced that Moravian (as distinct from Bohemian) folk songs were initially derived from their own words, as demonstrated by the irregular rhythms of Czech. The opposite applied to dance pieces, where the rhythm came first and the melody for the most part was shaped by this. Moravian folk music also adhered more closely to the Slovakian, Asiatic and Hungarian influences, especially when it came to utilizing minor harmonies. These ideas were to form the core of his mature style. The important bridging work which connects together his pre- and post-research musical styles is the cantata Amarus, completed in early 1897 and (disastrously) performed in 1900, with the composer himself conducting a sub-standard orchestra and chorus. Janáček's efforts here prepared him for the drama of his great opera and first masterpiece, Jenůfa, begun in 1894 but not completed until 1903.

Jenůfa took so long partly because Janáček was still only composing part-time, partly because the concept took that long to become fully rounded in his imagination. He was also working out his approach to melodic curves of speech, developing his ideas so that they could be applied throughout the opera in a meaningful and coherent

way. The tragic story reflected Czech village life, its mores, obsessions, kindness and harshness. It had a tragic parallel in real life, for while Janáček worked on the final act in 1902, his daughter was dying from typhoid contracted while visiting her suitor in St Petersburg. She was brought back to the family apartment in Brno where, after a long and intensely painful struggle, she died, days after Janáček had finished his opera. Janáček later wrote: 'I would tie up Jenůfa with the black ribbon of the long illness, pain and cries of my daughter Olga and my little boy Vladimir'. At Olga's request, he played her the complete opera on the family piano just a few days before she died. The opera is dedicated to her memory.

Jenůfa was granted a production in Brno in 1904 and was an overwhelming success, but it was to be 12 years before Janáček would overcome the jealousies, enmities, politics and plain obstructiveness of the Prague operatic world and get his masterpiece staged at the Prague Opera House. During this time he continued as head of the Brno Organ School he had founded, all the while looking for ways of decreasing his commitments in order to allocate more time to composing. He next plunged into another opera, Destiny.

DON'T MISS

▶ Jenůfa (1904)

▶ Along an Overgrown Path (1910–8)

▶ Taras Bulba (1915–18)

▶ Káta Kabanová (1921)

This story of infidelity and desertion in upper middle-class circles is full of flashing and memorable music, but is let down by a poor libretto and a confused plot. Through a combination of mischance and intransigence, *Destiny* remained unperformed until 1934, six years after the composer's death. In 1908 he started on a further opera, the satirical *The Excursions of Mr Brouček*; this time the work was not completed until well into WWI with numerous long pauses and changes of direction before it took definitive shape. Meanwhile, however, a series of small masterpieces were written against the backdrop of tragedies which his personal life had become.

The first to be written was the deeply affecting set of 10 piano pieces, entitled *Along an Overgrown Path*. A good half of the pieces deal with the circumstances of his daughter Olga's death, each one given a title by Janáček which indicated a specific reminiscence, with some of them woundingly direct in their meaning: *Words fail*; *Such Infinite Anguish*; *In tears*. A second set of five pieces carried no titles, but were equally resonant in their emotional impact. At the time of his next work *Fairy Tale* (1910), for cello and piano, Janáček and his wife were preparing to move from their Brno apartment which

had been their home for 20 years. His Organ School had moved to elegant new premises, and he persuaded the board to erect a small house in the grounds. There he and Zdenka would spend the rest of their lives together. After a recuperative holiday by the Adriatic, in 1912 Janáček returned for the last time to the searing memories and anguished state of *Along an Overgrown Path* with the four-part piano suite *In the Mist*.

At last, on 26 May 1916, with Janáček now almost 62 years old, came the Prague première of *Jenůfa* at the National Theatre. It was a resounding success and led to its staging in 1918 in Vienna, with Maria Jeritza in the lead role. After hearing Jeritza, he wrote: 'I have at last heard and seen Jenůfa in my opera'. Janáček now had an international audience for his music, and *Taras Bulba*, his nationalistic response to the catastrophe of WWI, quickly won fame as his own country emerged from the ruins of the old Austrian empire into a new-found autonomy. But another life was now opening up for the composer, at least on a creative level, for he had met David Stössl and his wife Kamila in 1917, and had become increasingly infatuated with Kamila, who was just 25. Aware of what was happening, she did nothing either to terminate the

friendship or to pursue it. Janáček knew the infatuation was hopelessly one-sided, yet used the knowledge to inspire a stream of deeply-felt masterpieces, including the wonderful song-cycle *The Diary of one who disappeared*. On the operatic side, Kamila is ever-present in *Káta Kabanová*, and there are even echoes of her spirit in the next opera, that fascinating evocation of countryside and the cycle of life, *The Cunning Little Vixen* (1923). There is no doubting her presence in the two string quartets, from 1923 and 1928, the first being inspired by a reading of Tolstoy's story *The Kreutzer Sonata* and ending tragically, the second (subtitled *Intimate Letters*) from his last year and written after his confession to his wife of his passion for Kamila (which remained unconsummated), ending in optimism and warmth.

Other great works were to come from Janáček in his last decade, including two operas, the high-spirited *The Makropoulos Affair* and the bleak and compassionate Dostoyevsky adaptation, *From the House of the Dead* (premièred after his death). He would also create his choral masterpiece the *Glagolitic Mass*, as well as the charming *Capriccio* for chamber group, and perhaps his most famous orchestral piece, *Sinfonietta*. During the last 12 years of his life, Janáček produced masterpiece after masterpiece, with no falling-off of quality or inspiration. In the end, his demise was mercifully quick: catching pneumonia while walking during his summer holiday, Janáček succumbed to a heart attack. He was buried in Brno cemetery in the presence of numerous dignitaries and to the sound of horns.

DON'T MISS

▶ **String Quartet No. 1 (Kreutzer Sonata) (1923)**
▶ **The Cunning Little Vixen (1924)**
▶ **Sinfonietta (1926)**
▶ **Glagolitic Mass (1929)**

EDWARD ELGAR
1857-1934

If Elgar had died in 1897, the year of his fortieth birthday, he would be remembered today as a minor English composer of some fair to middling chamber and choral music. Within a year or so of his fortieth bithday he had experienced a creative emergence from this chrysalis which began with the *Enigma Variations*, kept up the pace with *Sea Pictures* and continued right through to the Cello Concerto of 1919.

Elgar was born in the Worcestershire village of Broadheath, the son of a music-shop proprieter and organist at St George's Catholic Church. His mother came from a monied farming background and prided herself on her cultural accomplishments. Both parents were ambitious, and this trait was passed on to their son Edward. With the early death of his two older brothers, Edward became even more the centre of his parents' ambitions. Aware of his musical talent, his parents encouraged him to learn the organ, but he taught himself the violin well enough to play in orchestral string sections. When he realised that his father was unable to afford further tuition, he also taught himself the rudiments of composition. Leaving school at the age of 15, Edward worked for a local solicitor, but after a year he returned to work in the family shop.

Elgar's life now revolved around the shop, playing the organ at St George's,

Edward Elgar

his early attempts at composition and his relationship with the Catholic faith which his mother had adopted but his father cordially detested. By the end of the decade he was appointed to conduct in a Worcester lunatic asylum (the appointment lasted five years), and began producing choral music for use in St George's. Little disturbed the course of his life until he took on a piano pupil, Alice Roberts. At 38 Alice was nearly 10 years his senior, yet a romance quickly developed and within two years they were engaged. This proved a turning

point of real importance for Elgar, and his spirited *Salut d'amour*, Op. 12 (1889), originally written for piano and later orchestrated by the composer, was a direct tribute to love's ability to bring out his hidden creativity. The couple were married in 1889, and Carice, their only child, was born the following year. A hint of Elgar's new happiness can also be found in the *Serenade for Strings*, Op. 20 of 1892.

In the next decade Elgar's main achievements were in choral music,

DON'T MISS

▶ **Serenade for Strings, Op. 20 (1892)**

▶ **Enigma Variations, Op. 36 (1898–99)**

▶ **Sea Pictures, Op. 37 (1899)**

▶ **The Dream of Gerontius, Op. 38 (1900)**

with *The Light of Life*, Op. 29 (1896), written for the Three Choirs Festival, and *Caractacus*, Op. 35 (1898), written for the Leeds Festival. In October 1898, after dismissing an idea for a symphony based on Gordon of Khartoum, he fell by chance on an entirely new line of approach. Extemporising on the piano one evening, Elgar came across a theme which promised such possibilities for development that he quickly began to devise a series of variations which he imagined represented the attempts his friends and family might make to come up with their own version of the original theme. The original, of course, Elgar never revealed, and to this day it remains a subject for conjecture, but the *Variations on an Original Theme*, Op. 36, later popularly known as the *'Enigma' Variations*, has been a resounding success since its first performance in London in June 1899, and quickly built Elgar a national reputation, making him one of the leading English composers of his generation.

Within a year the Birmingham première of *The Dream of Gerontius*, Op. 38, although a failure, had aroused sufficient interest for Elgar to achieve a major success with the work in

Düsseldorf in 1901, Richard Strauss commenting that its composer was undoubtedly a 'master'. Further confirmation of his rapid rise to international importance came with his knighthood in 1904. After *Gerontius*, his choral and orchestral works competed on a much more equal footing for the public's acclaim, and by the middle of the new decade Elgar had completed *The Apostles* (1903) and *The Kingdom* (1906), plus the orchestral work *In the South* (1904), four of the immensely popular *Pomp and Circumstance* marches, Op. 39, and also succeeded in his greatest ambition—to write a successful symphony.

By the time his eagerly awaited First Symphony in A flat, Op. 55 (1907–08) was premièred, its combination of rigorous development through the variation technique, used with incredible imagination and flexibility, plus the undeniable beauty of the material and its outstanding scoring, made it immensely popular from the outset. Equally popular was the passionate and tender Violin Concerto in B minor, Op. 61 (1910) which followed. Elgar himself was a reasonable violinist, and his writing had long exhibited his particular sensitivity to the tonal and expressive range of the instrument; in this work, Elgar perhaps hints at an affair he either regretted or regretted never happened.

With these two works it is arguable that Elgar reached a creative and popular height which he realized could not be sustained indefinitely. Certainly the Second Symphony, Op. 63 (1909–11) was given a more puzzled reception by the public, and this, combined with the ending of the

Edwardian era and the fact that he was now in his late fifties, gave him a sense that his time at the forefront of British music was coming to a close. A nostalgia which had always been part of his creative impulse became more pronounced, and his next major work, *The Music Makers*, Op. 69, actually quoted from some of his earlier works, making direct reference to the past he now felt was lost. This had always been an Elgarian theme (*Dream Children* of 1902 directly addressed the gulf between childhood and maturity), but now society itself was beginning to agree with him. The advent of WWI seemed to confirm his assessment, and his marvellous *The Spirit of England*, Op. 80 (premièred in 1917), a setting of three patriotic but compassionate poems by Laurence Binyon, gave him a chance to mourn the destruction of British youth and hopes in the carnage of the War, as well as the passing of the world in which he had grown up. Elgar's desire to retain this earlier world was winsomely expressed in the incidental music he wrote in 1915 (using extracts from an earlier work, *The Wand of Youth*) for Algernon Blackwood's fantasy play *The Starlight Express*, where the delights of a child's world, in which adults are pleasingly at sea, are eagerly embraced in music by the middle-aged composer.

Elgar was deeply affected by the War and the climate of suffering it imposed on the country, and in 1917 felt the need to rekindle his inner spirit and restore his now ailing wife by renting a cottage in the Sussex countryside. Here he succeeded in writing his superb late chamber music, including the Violin Sonata in E minor, Op. 82, the String Quartet in E minor, Op. 83 and the Piano Quintet in A minor, Op. 84. The use of minor keys throughout was certainly no accident, and this is music which consistently reached levels of inspiration which are profoundly moving. The String Quartet's dreamy second movement, the 'Piacevole', was to be played at Lady Elgar's funeral in 1920. The composition of the Piano Quintet ran into 1919, and soon after its completion Elgar was working on a Cello Concerto, a work which Lady Elgar described in a letter as containing music which 'should be in a war symphony'. Symphonies now seemed beyond him, but the Cello Concerto, although an initial failure in 1919 under his baton, was quickly recognized internationally as a work of the highest stature. As usual with Elgar, the

balance between soloist and orchestra is gained with extreme sensitivity, and the elegiac lines the 'cello describes are laden with regret, passion and loss in a way which strikes a deep chord in many listeners. This work was in many ways his swan-song, for although he lived another 15 years, with the death of his wife in 1920 and the evidence of social change all around him, the impetus for creation largely deserted him. The 1920s and 1930s found him making a

long string of historic recordings of his own works, often with the greatest talents of the age at his disposal, and most of these recordings are still available today. Elgar, ever a private man, withdrew from the world's bustle and confusion and lived among the pleasures of the countryside. A third symphony left uncompleted at his death has recently been 'realized' by Anthony Payne and given its world premier.

DON'T MISS

▶ **Pomp and Circumstance Marches 1–5, Op. 39 (1901–30)**
▶ **Introduction and Allegro, Op. 47 (1904–5)**
▶ **Symphony No. 1 (1907–8)**
▶ **Violin Concerto, Op. 61 (1909–10)**
▶ **Cello Concerto, Op. 85 (1919)**

RUGGIERO LEONCAVALLO
1858–1919

A composer who suffered more than most from the rising star of Puccini in the closing years of the 19th century, Leoncavallo had his first major operatic success prior to Puccini and in a long career even wrote his own version of *La Bohème*; today he is only remembered as the composer of the verismo favourite, *I Pagliacci*.

Leoncavallo was born in Naples, and as the son of a magistrate enjoyed a comfortable upbringing. His interest in

music was encouraged by his family and he was taught the piano as a boy, progressing to Naples Conservatory in his early teens. There he studied piano with Beniamino Cesi, composition with Lauro Rossi and harmony with Michele Ruta. At the age of 18 he plunged enthusiastically into the role of opera composer, using the tragic story of the English poet Thomas Chatterton as his starting point. The opera was completed while he was staying in Bologna and was immediately accepted for production. Unfortunately, before the opening night the promoter absconded

with what funds remained and Leoncavallo was left penniless. *Tommaso Chatterton* would not appear before the footlights until he was already famous.

Instead of returning abjectly to his home in Naples, he decided to support himself by taking on what accompanist's work he could find. This resulted in a peripatetic existence which eventually took him to countries as far distant as England and Egypt. He spent the best part of 10 years away from Italy, returning eventually not to Naples, but to Milan, where he

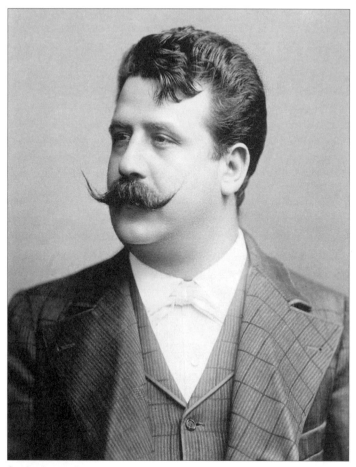

Ruggiero Leoncavallo

of the year Leoncavallo was being hailed throughout Italy as second only to Mascagni in the *verismo* school. Within a short time these two composers found their operas being given as a double-bill, and this practice has continued world-wide until the present day.

Convinced that his time had come, Leoncavallo resurrected his earlier work, *I Medici*, and it was produced in November 1893. It was a failure. Leoncavallo was so discouraged by its fate that he never revived the other two parts of his Renaissance trilogy. Failing to draw a lesson from this downturn in fortune, Leoncavallo revived the even older *Chatterton*. It was produced in 1896, but by then the style in which it had been written fully 20 years earlier had fallen out of favour. Once more Leoncavallo tasted rejection by the public, but he had already embarked on a new project which he was convinced would restore his reputation. He was working on a collection of stories of bohemian life in Paris written by Henri Mürger, turning it into an opera called *La Bohème*. To his intense chagrin he discovered that Puccini had begun work on precisely the same set of stories, and it became a race to see whose opera would appear first. Unfortunately for Leoncavallo, Puccini's opera won the race and all the kudos. It mattered little that Leoncavallo's version, applauded warmly in Venice in 1897, was a fine opera in its own right; the triumph of Puccini's *La Bohème* effectively buried Leoncavallo's work, which has only been revived and re-examined by the opera world in the last 20 years.

convinced the publisher Ricordi that his plan for an operatic trilogy covering the history of Renaissance Italy would be a sure-fire success. The libretto for the first part, *I Medici*, was accepted by the publisher as proof of quality, and Leoncavallo completed the music within 12 months. It took a further three years before he came to the reluctant conclusion that Ricordi, already deeply committed to their rising star Puccini, had no intention of promoting his epic.

Disgusted with the situation, he embarked on his next operatic project,

its story based on a court case which had once come before his father in Naples and which involved the *verismo* elements of low-life circus characters, love, jealousy and murder. Initially he wanted to enter the opera, entitled *I Pagliacci*, for the Sonzogno prize won by Mascagni with *Cavalleria Rusticana* in 1889, but the prize was for one-act operas only and his short piece was written for two. Sonzogno, however, was sufficiently impressed with the manuscript to mount a production of the work in the Teatro del Verme, Milan, in late sping 1892. It was an immediate success, and by the end

Leoncavallo was understandably bitter towards both Ricordi and Puccini and did everything in his power to assert his musical supremacy. With his next work, *Zazà* (Milan, 1900), he tasted success once more, the première lifted by the conducting of the young Arturo Toscanini and the audience's imagination fired by the story of a Parisian music hall artiste who returns to her one true love. Initially the opera made some progress overseas, but long before WWI it had been forgotten outside Italy. Yet Leoncavallo's name was still very much alive in Berlin, for the Kaiser, Wilhelm II, had attended a performance of *I Medici* there in 1894 and decided that Leoncavallo was the composer to write an opera celebrating the house of Hohenzollern. The result

was a curious and rather clumsy historical romance, *Der Roland von Berlin* (Berlin, 1904). Despite Hohenzollern enthusiasm for the work, *Der Roland* quickly vanished from the stages of Europe. Portentous subjects such as Friedrich II's subjugation of Berlin brought out the most unattractive side of Leoncavallo's talent, and he wisely returned to lighter subjects. His two light operas, *Maia* and *Malbruk*, were both produced in Rome in 1910. From then on he switched between operettas and more heavyweight themes.

In the last decade of his life Leoncavallo produced no less than 10 operettas, but none came close to rivalling *I Pagliacci* in the public's

affections. His more serious and ambitious works continued to come to grief, including his final work, premièred after his death in 1920, *Edipo Re*. Although a prolific opera composer, Leoncavallo—like the very different but equally unlucky Mascagni—never recovered his place in the public eye after his first great success, and died a disappointed man.

DON'T MISS

▶ I Pagliacci (1892)

▶ La Bohéme (1897)

▶ Mattinata, L'aurora di bianco vestita (1904)

GIACOMO PUCCINI
1858–1924

There is little doubt today that of all operatic music, Puccini's is the most universally known; more people know the famous arias from *La Bohème*, *Madame Butterfly* and *Turandot* than any others, with the single possible exception of those from *Carmen*. Considering Puccini's early artistic struggles, this is a remarkable achievement.

Puccini was a native of Lucca, born into a family which since the arrival there of a Giacomo Puccini in the 1730s had been involved in the music of the

ancient town for five generations. Each generation composed and played the organ for San Martino Cathedral in Lucca. Giacomo was the fifth child of Michele and Albina Puccini, but his father died in 1864 when Giacomo was nearly five years old. Contrary to the monotonous litany of childhood musical prodigies which litter history, Giacomo showed no early interest in music, although everyone in Lucca expected him to. Instead he was a lazy, shiftless boy, poor at schoolwork and apt to play truant. His mother, however, was convinced of his abilities and procured him a tutor at the Conservatorio Macini. This time he made modest progress,

becoming a choirboy at San Martino and playing the organ there from the age of 14. By his seventeenth year he had begun writing small compositions. While still 17, Puccini attended a performance of Verdi's *Aida* in Milan; it was this experience which concentrated all his ambitions, convincing him that a career as an opera composer was the only one to consider. For the next four years he studied hard, eventually writing a pleasing Mass in 1880 (later called *Messa di Gloria*).

Puccini spent the next three years at Milan Conservatoire, where he was taught by Bazzini and Ponchielli, and where he undoubtedly suffered privation due to a severe lack of funds, although this is not enough to explain the extraordinary meanness with money which he showed later in life, even when he was very rich. He submitted as his 'passing-out' piece the orchestral *Capriccio Sinfonico,* an attractive and colourful work which Puccini later cannibalized for operas, specifically *Edgar* and *La Bohème.*

Having left the Conservatoire, Puccini had to decide how to make a start in opera. An opportunity presented itself when the kindly Ponchielli drew his attention to a one-act opera prize announced by the publisher Sonzogno and arranged for a librettist by the name of Ferdinando Fontana. Puccini wrote *Le Villi* in such haste to meet the prize's deadline that the score was virtually unreadable, and this poor exhibit was ignored by the judges. Both Fontana and Ponchielli were convinced of its worth, however, and between them they engaged the sympathetic support of the great Verdi librettist and opera composer, Arriago Boito, as well as the enthusiasitc backing of Giulio Ricordi, owner of the Ricordi publishing house. A production was mounted in Milan in May 1884, proving an enormous success, with the *Corriere della Sera* critic commenting: 'We sincerely believe that Puccini may be the composer for whom Italy has been waiting a long time'.

His next opera, *Edgar*, though again given Ricordi's enthusiastic backing, just would not come right, its poorly-executed libretto, grand opera pretensions and melodramatic plot failing to inspire Puccini, despite much hard work. Even after its initial failure

in 1889, Puccini continued to revise it, determined not to waste five years of effort. But a failure *Edgar* has remained to this day. It is a measure of Ricordi's good judgement that he never wavered in his support for Puccini, although even he was unnerved by the composer's next choice of subject, the Abbé Prevost's novella *Manon Lescaut,* particularly in view of the fact that the story had been given successful operatic form by Massenet in his Paris production of *Manon* in 1884. Puccini remained unshakeable in his choice, knowing what type of subject most suited his abilities. When it came to establishing an acceptable libretto, Puccini showed that he had learnt from his experiences with *Edgar* and *Le Villi*; this time he engaged and dismissed three librettists before finally accepting Ricordi's suggested pairing, Luigi Illica and Giuseppi Giacosa. The result was a quantum leap forward from his previous efforts. It was premièred in Turin in 1893, receiving the unanimous praise for which Puccini had waited for nearly a decade. Before the year was out it had been successfully staged in St Petersburg, Rio de Janeiro, Buenos Aires and Munich. In one stroke the royalties enabled Puccini to repay his debts to Ricordi and begin living in his chosen village, Torre del Lago, a few miles outside Lucca, in some degree of style.

The 10 years since *Le Villi* had seen great changes take place in Puccini's private life: his beloved mother had died in 1884 and shortly afterwards he had eloped with 24-year-old Elvira Gemignani, the wife of a local businessman. Said to have been a beauty when young, Elvira was a woman of little gaiety or humour, and the marriage did not long remain a

happy one. Puccini, moreover, was a handsome man with a roving eye, and once he became famous he had endless poorly-concealed affairs.

After *Manon* came the first opera in the group later known as the 'Big Three'. *La Bohème*, taken from the Henri Mürger novel *Scènes de la vie de bohème*, was probably brought to Puccini's attention by his fellow-composer Ruggiero Leoncavallo, who was working on his own version of the tale. Puccini had a penchant for working on ideas first begun by others, as if their interest in the idea proved its worth. Needless to say, it became a race to see who could complete their opera first. Puccini, in league with his librettists, Illica and Giacosa, won; their treatment was ready for the Turin première in February 1896, conducted by the 28-year-old Arturo Toscanini. While the public was enthusiatic, only one of the critics present found good words to say for it, the rest seeing it as showing 'a deplorable decline' from the standards set by *Manon Lescaut.* They utterly failed to grasp its essentially different nature, rooted in lyric opera and a charming sense of the everyday.

The follow-up arrived four years later, in 1900; it was based on a shocking melodrama of the so-called 'realism' school of French drama, *Tosca* by Victorien Sardou, which had been a sensation in Paris, partly due to the presence of Sarah Bernhardt in the lead role. It was written with a minimum of problems with the libretto or the music, and was prepared meticuously for a Rome première, but this time the reception was not all that Puccini and Ricordi had hoped for. Few critics managed to see or hear the advances

Puccini had made in the work, or its incredible dynamism, preferring to stress only the tawdriness of the tale and the lack of any redeeming moral sense. In this sense Tosca was a truly modern opera, the closest to *verismo* which Puccini ever came.

The next subject for an opera took some time to find, even though Puccini was searching assiduously within a month of *Tosca's* première. After considering a good half-dozen ideas, in 1900 Puccini saw the London production of *Madam Butterfly* by the American playwright David Belasco. Although unable to understand English, Puccini was profoundly moved by its plot. Once a contract was signed with Belasco, Puccini began the work in earnest, including a painstaking search for background information on Japan and its culture. Work went smoothly until a major row developed between Puccini and Giacosa over whether the opera should be in three acts or two. In a rare theatrical misjudgement, Puccini wanted two: Giacosa three. The opening night's débacle at La Scala in 1904 was no doubt the result of an organized claque, but with only one interval, the two extra long acts were simply too much for a Milan audience unused to such demands being made on their concentration. At Brescia three months later the opera, now divided into three acts, was a stupendous success. *Butterfly* remained Puccini's favourite of his operas, and he spent the next few years travelling to far-flung productions to ensure that his wishes were honoured by the respective companies.

This was one of the factors contributing to the public's wait of seven years for

Giacomo Puccini

Puccini's next opera. Another factor was his fruitless search for operatic ideas. The subject of *La Fanciulla del West*, was only decided upon in the autumn of 1907, months after a trip with Elvira to New York where he had seen Belasco's play of the same title. There was a private reason for the hiatus, and it concerned his marriage; Puccini's propensity for affairs and Elvira's raging jealously had led to many quarrels over the years, and the relationship had now deteriorated into one of mutual exasperation. In late

1908 Elvira became convinced that Puccini had been unfaithful with their young maid, Doria Manfredi. Puccini, for once, was innocent, but Elvira began a vicious and systematic persecution of the girl, and in January 1909 Doria committed suicide. The whole village turned against Elvira while Puccini, horrified by the whole affair and disgusted with his wife, packed her off to Milan. Elvira was tried and sentenced to five months in prison. It was only after Puccini made a handsome settlement on the girl's family that the action was dropped. The rift between husband and wife took years to heal, and during the next decade Puccini embarked on a number of passionate and sustained affairs with younger women.

Under these circumstances, it is hardly surprising that *La Fanciulla* took until August 1910 to complete, or that the new opera, premièred at New York's Metropolitan Opera House with Caruso in the cast, would be a hit-and-miss affair. Though it demonstrated a convincing advance in musical styles for Puccini, it contained a surprising lack of set-piece arias or of sympathetic characters. For once Puccini enjoyed a rapturous first-night reception from the audience, but for the first time since *Edgar*, the welcome was not to sustain itself over the years to come.

During the following decade Puccini experienced many disappointments and partial successes. His next project, which was finally begun in 1913, was the trio of one-act operas called *Il Trittico*, made up of *Il Tabarro*, a bleak and violent piece of social realism; *Suor Angelica*, a delicate and lyrical tragedy with a suffering heroine; and *Gianni Schicchi*, a sparkling comedy. The idea for *Il Trittico* was one which his old publisher, Giulio Ricordi, had fought

DON'T MISS

▶ **Manon Lescaut (1893)**
▶ **La Bohème (1896)**
▶ **Tosca (1900)**
▶ **Madama Butterfly (1904)**
▶ **Gianni Schicchi (1918)**
▶ **Turandot (1926)**

against for years, but with his death in 1912 and the accession of his son Tito (who had little time for Puccini and his vacillations) as head of the firm, Puccini followed his own muse.

In 1913 Puccini was approached by two impresarios from the Theater an der Wien in Vienna to write 10 numbers for a new operetta, half of them to be sad, half gay, for which he was to be paid a fortune. The plan for *La Rondine* came together very rapidly, Puccini working hard on the project with his new librettist, Giuseppe Adami, but WWI intervened in 1915, putting Italy and Austria on opposite sides of the conflict. *La Rondine* was eventually premièred at Monte Carlo. Neither fish nor fowl, the work has never really secured a place on the world's stages, although it contains some glorious melodic moments.

Meanwhile, work on *Il Trittico* had slowly progressed and in December 1918 the three one-acters were premièred at the Metropolitan, New York; only *Gianni Schicchi* received unqualified approval. This pattern was repeated elsewhere, and although for years Puccini violently objected to the three works being parted from each other, when he finally saw a production in Lucca in 1921 he realized that its three hour duration was asking too much of the audience and stopped his objections—with the result that the first two operas virtually disappeared from public sight. In recent years, *Il Tabarro* at least has come to be recognized for the forward-looking masterpiece of mood and atmosphere which it undoubtedly is.

Now over 60, Puccini was determined to write an opera which was on a

higher plane than before and entirely different from all his others. Another long search for a subject led him to Gozzi's 18th-century play, *Turandotte*. Once Puccini had familiarized himself with the *commedia dell'arte* ideas of Gozzi and the ersatz Chinese setting, he commissioned a libretto and set to work in the spring of 1920. In many letters written at this time it is clear that he felt he was putting his soul into *Turandot*, and the work totally absorbed him. But it was delayed by problems with the libretto and Puccini moving house to Viareggio. By March 1924 the opera was complete bar the final two scenes, which Puccini, waiting for the right inspiration, shied away from completing. He was not to get the chance: a sore throat and cough which had begun to affect the lifelong smoker in the autumn of 1923 had not receded by the summer of the following year, and although doctors found nothing wrong with him, Puccini suspected the underlying seriousness of the malady. In October, the opera still not finished, he was told that he had throat cancer which was too advanced to be operable. Nevertheless, a treatment was attempted by surgeons in Brussels, but Puccini's heart was not strong enough to withstand the post-operative shock and he died on 24th November.

Turandot was given its première in April 1926; it had been completed by Franco Alfano, under Toscanini's sometimes irascible supervision. On the first night the music was stopped by the maestro at the point where Puccini's score broke off. After that, the completed version was given. It was a triumphant success, but one the composer would never enjoy.

ISAAC ALBÉNIZ

1860–1909

The Catalonian Albéniz was a vital figure in the evolution of late 19th-century Spanish composition, bringing to his great piano works the colours and flavours of the major musical traditions of his native land. As such, he laid the ground for much of what was to follow, particularly in Spanish instrumental music.

Albéniz was the tearaway son of a tax-collector from Camprodón in Catalonia. By the age of four he had taught himself to play the piano well enough to make his début at a concert in Barcelona where he improvised, to the delight of the Teatro Roman audience. By the age of seven, little Isaac (he remained very small in stature) had composed a *Pasodoble* which was adopted by the Barcelona brass bands. Just prior to his eighth birthday, he was taken to Paris where he easily passed the entrance exam to the Conservatoire, only to be thrown out when caught breaking classroom windows.

Back in Spain he was admitted to the Madrid Conservatoire and began his studies, but after a year he ran away from home and went on the road, supporting himself with an unending series of vaudeville engagements. By the early 1870s he had alternated between low-life escapades and periods of study in cities such as Brussels, Leipzig, Rome and Weimar, even spending some time under Liszt's

tutelage. After that, he stowed away on a steamer bound for the New World. By the time he returned to Europe at the close of the decade he had spent time in Cuba, Argentina and along both seaboards of America, supporting himself by his extraordinary ability at the keyboard.

By 1880 it seemed he was ready to modify his behaviour, for he settled in Barcelona where he tried to teach piano and also began serious attempts at composition. As with most Spanish composers of his generation, he was mainly attracted to two genres: solo piano music and music for the stage which, in Spain, usually meant *zarzuela*, Spain's equivalent to operetta. Albéniz would attempt no less than 30 theatrical projects during his lifetime, the vast majority of them in the *zarzuela* manner, and most of them not progressing beyond manuscript sketches, usually due to lack of a sponsor or a possible venue. With the piano music, however, Albéniz was not so restricted as he was by far his own best interpreter and a concert pianist with an international reputation. His earliest Barcelona pieces are in the salon style of the day, where classical and popular tastes frequently met. The *Pavana capricho* of 1883 is one of the earliest successful works to be published—there may have been others, but Albéniz destroyed much of his youthful material as 'worthless trifles'. Not so judged was his superb *Suite española No. 1* which contained some of his most popular pieces such as

'Granada', 'Sevilla' and 'Cádiz'. These show his style to be robustly mature and crammed full of the dash and flair he exhibited as a person.

Much of the piano music written after his move to Madrid in 1885 remains extant. Albéniz claimed to have written seven piano sonatas before the decade ended, although it is unlikely that sonatas two and six were ever more than schemes in his mind, and there is a possibility that the first sonata was left incomplete in the hands of a publisher who waited in vain for the last movements. Additionally, a sonata for violin and piano of 1887 is currently untraceable. Yet three sonatas were completed and published between 1886 and 1888, Nos. 3, 4 and 5. These are largely works given over to his predilection for the Classical style and form, and so reflect the other side of his musical personality from the one which has made his music world-famous. More typical are the two collections, the delightful *Recuerdos de viaje* and *12 Piezás Caracteristicas* (1888–89), where dance rhythms associated with both people and places make a vivacious collection.

That Albéniz would for the present continue to swing between the two sides of his compositional nature was shown in the two major works completed after his departure from Madrid, when he was alternating between living in London and Paris. *Suite española No. 2* appeared in 1889 and *España*, containing six vivid portraits of Spanish musical forms and rhythms (including his 'Malagueña'), was published in 1890, while the same year saw the composition of a long, melancholy and rather straight-laced waltz *L'Automne*, which shows the influence of both Massenet and Chabrier. Albéniz thought highly enough of this latter work to expend copious amounts of energy orchestrating it himself—a task he never undertook lightly, yet it has remained relatively unknown.

The same fate has befallen his theatrical efforts, although he achieved a staging of his early *zarzuela*, the comic *Catalanes de Gracia* (Madrid, 1883), and enjoyed a productive creative relationship with an English banker and amateur librettist, Francis Money-Coutts, in the first years of the 1890s. After two weak operas (set by Money-Coutts) which dealt with Arthurian subjects, the two managed something more lively with a comic opera *The Magic Opal* (1893), while *Enrico Clifford* (Barcelona, 1895), a three-acter based on an incident during the Wars of the Roses, only convinced

Albéniz that he was better off with a Spanish subject. He and Money-Coutts agreed on the choice of a fine novel by Juan Valera, *Pepita Jiménez*. Within a matter of months the libretto and music had been composed, and it opened in 1896. Although Money-Coutts failed in an attempt to bring it to Covent Garden, the work travelled well elsewhere, making it to Prague, Leipzig, Monaco, Nice and Madrid in the next six years.

By 1905 Albéniz had made his name internationally as a composer of characteristically Spanish piano music. Living mainly in Paris after 1893, he became part of the musical circles frequented by musicians such as Fauré, and his published works began to receive a wider audience; the deeply Spanish nature of this music often seems transcribed from guitar originals. He continued to compose successfully for the piano, gradually incorporating some of the French elements he heard around him in Paris, and in 1908 he published his *Catalonia—suite populaire* for orchestra. This work had been in gestation since 1899 and by the time of

its appearance Albéniz was no longer in good health. The following year saw both the publication of his most famous and brilliant set of piano pieces, *Iberia*, and his death. *Iberia* seemed to take his portraiture of his country to technical limits not attempted previously, and they mark a high point in his output. Albéniz's roots in Catalonia gave him an admirable sense of equanimity towards selecting the musical models from the rest of Spain which he would use in the 12 pieces which make up the suite, and allowed him to develop a beautifully and colourfully complete picture of his beloved country. It is our loss that he was allotted no more time to develop his passion further.

DON'T MISS

▶ **Suite española No. 1 Op. 47 (1886)**
▶ **Recuerdos de viaje, Op. 71 (1887)**
▶ **España, Op. 165 (1890)**
▶ **Pepita Jiménez (1896)**
▶ **Iberia (1906–8)**

GUSTAV MAHLER
1860–1911

Mahler's importance as a composer is based partly on his ability to bridge the styles of Wagnerism and of Schoenberg's dodecophany, but the sum of his work is more than that. Apart from the formal balance and

intricacy of his works, his sensibility remains utterly modern. His concerns lie with expressing the very limits of mankind's experience and understanding of life and its deepest mysteries through music.

Mahler commented about one of his symphonies that in writing it he had attempted to capture the entire world; in this he made no attempt to hide his Wagnerian roots. But to attempt to thus categorize Mahler would be to overlook the rich complexities of his inspiration and musical philosophy which have their origins in a multiplicity of artistic, cultural and emotional wellsprings.

Mahler may have been born in Kaliste, a village situated in the borderlands between Bohemia and Moravia, but his Jewish father was German-speaking with a peasant background; his mother, also Jewish, came from a middle-class family and possessed a 'sensitive' disposition which she evidently passed on to her son. Gustav's upbringing was relatively stable; at the age of nine his family moved to Iglau, where the following year the boy began his studies at the local Gymnasium. By the age of 10 he was a sufficiently accomplished pianist to give a local recital; by the age of 15 he was ready to enter Vienna Conservatoire where he spent three successful years. This is the public record of a gifted youth, but nothing in Mahler is straightforward and his childhood is no exception. His proud but ill-educated father poured all his ambitions into his children, insisting that they were well-educated. But his parents had a joyless marriage, and Gustav's memories of his early years included those of his father verbally and physically assaulting his beloved mother. They also included the death of a number of his siblings; death amidst the joys of life would remain a central Mahlerian theme.

From earliest youth Mahler associated different types of folk and popular music with particularly deep emotional responses in himself, and the ubiquity of popular airs, martial music and melodies played on a number of mechanical devices (including barrel-organs) meant that these simple

Gustav Mahler

musical types became raw material for brilliantly conceived later use in his symphonic works. Mahler could be equally literal when it came to representing his youthful love of the country: the cow-bells of the Sixth Symphony immediately come to mind.

Mahler's first major composition, the cantata *Das klagende Lied*, was begun while he was still a student at the Conservatoire. This work for soloists, chorus and orchestra combined many of his life-long themes, and also

demonstrates the pervasive influence of Wagner on his generation in Vienna. All Mahler's music, vocal or instrumental, tells a story of sorts, often from folk or legendary sources, all of it conceived on an epic scale, and much of it aspires to statements on the subjects of human life and its place in the cosmos. Another Wagnerian trait to which Mahler was to bring all his individualism in later years was the incredible lushness and detail of the orchestration, something for which he was singularly gifted and which would

DON'T MISS

▶ Symphony No. 1 (1888)
▶ Symphony No. 2 (1884-6)
▶ Symphony No. 3 (1893-6)
▶ Symphony No. 5 (1901-2)
▶ Symphony No. 6 (1904)

become one of his most readily identifiable traits—the characteristic Mahlerian sound.

Following a course at Vienna University in 1879 and a period of penury, Mahler realized that composition was not going to provide him with an income to live on and he took up his first conducting position in the small Austrian town of Bad Hall. This led to a string of engagements over the next few years, few of which were to give him much satisfaction. It was only his appointment as deputy to Anton Seidl in Prague in 1885 which began to steer him in the direction of interpretive fulfilment.

Meanwhile his creative and personal life had been vibrant, to say the least. He had written a series of songs, some of which would not be published until the 1990s, while others would be collected into the grouping *Lieder eines fahrenden Gesellen* (1883–85). By 1888 he had begun his settings of poems from the famous folk collection, *Des Knaben Wunderhorn* and had begun his passionate but doomed affair with Johanna Richter. The year before the move to Prague Mahler had also started on his first symphony, a work which he saw as the summation of all his earlier efforts as it was the symphonic form which he held to be

most precious of all. In the First Symphony Mahler begins as he means to continue, with the work lasting close to 50 minutes in its revised version (he dropped the so-called 'Blumine' movement prior to its première). The symphony was completed in 1888, by which time Mahler had moved on from Prague to become director of the Royal Hungarian Opera in Budapest.

His three years in Budapest witnessed a renaissance in playing standards and a revolution in performance repertoire, with Mahler introducing operas which he felt were imperishable classics, such as *Don Giovanni* and *Fidelio*, as well as Wagner's *Das Rheingold*—still a controversial work in the Budapest of 1889. During this period both his parents died, and Mahler took on the financial burden of the younger members of the family. After three years in Budapest, Mahler moved to Hamburg where he spent the best part of six years running the musical affairs of the Municipal Theatre (he was joined there by his sister Justine). Here he not only found a degree of satisfaction in his conducting, but he also had more time to compose, and he inaugurated the annual summer holidays in the mountains which were essential to the completion of his next three symphonies. Hamburg was also the setting for one of his more bizarre love affairs; a singer from the company by the name of Anna von Mildenberg attracted his attention and she responded. Ever protective of his 'freedom', Mahler's ardour quickly cooled, but Anna began a sustained campaign to get him to marry her, and this contributed to his decision to look for a position beyond Hamburg.

Anna was one of many adoring women whom Mahler seemed to attract effortlessly and who, together with his sister Justine, laboured to nurture his creative muse. One of the conditions he demanded on his summer holidays was unbroken silence while he composed; this required that his sister and friends should hover outside the summer-house where he worked, scaring away the birds in case their twittering brought the composer to the door in a paroxym of rage. Only later in life did he develop a sense of humour of sorts and any sense of humility; after his marriage he learned to allow the birds to sing, eventually taking inspiration from such facts of nature.

In 1895 Mahler became a Catholic, certainly an important step for his overall career as he would never have been appointed director of the Vienna Court Opera in 1897 if he had remained Jewish. As it was, he had to endure the determined opposition of Cosima Wagner to his appointment, and had Brahms—a great admirer of his conducting—to thank for smoothing his path. Mahler revolutionized both performance practice and performed repertoire at the Vienna Opera, raising its standards immeasurably; initially working in league with the newly-appointed conductor of the Vienna Philharmonic, Hans Richter, he brought it to a state of pre-eminence not experienced in the Austrian capital for nearly 100 years.

By 1901 Mahler was well advanced on his fourth symphony, the last to be inspired by the *Wunderhorn* texts and the last to be comprehensively concerned with the evocation or recreation through music of the entire natural world and man's place within it. From this point on, Mahler's music would become progressively more subjective as the muse he pursued became increasingly internalized. This process was hastened by a meeting, in November 1901, with his future wife, Alma Schindler, a 23-year-old composition student who had attended the Viennese première of his First Symphony in 1900, a work she maintained she 'had thoroughly disliked and even angrily rejected'. From the first Mahler seems to have decided that he wanted to marry her, and indeed talked about the wedding before even proposing. This, she later wrote, was typical of the man; he had made up his mind about it 'so why wait?'. The wedding took place in March 1902; by November of the same year their first child, Maria, was born.

The first musical fruit of his new life was displayed in the Fifth Symphony, his first symphony not to openly display an extra-musical programme or involve voices, but which nonetheless carried an *adagietto* which was a love song to his wife. Alma was important for him in a number of ways: younger than him, she knew many of the new generation of composers, introducing him into their circle as a sort of elder statesman. For Mahler, the focal point of Viennese cultural life and responsible for regenerating the Opera, this intercourse with young composers was of great significance. Through people such as Schoenberg and the Secessionists of the artistic world—Gustav Klimt and Egon Schiele—Mahler was kept in touch with artistic and philisophical developments, while his ties with his own generation—through people like Zemlinsky (at one time Alma's teacher), Gerhard

Hauptmann and Richard Strauss—were thus only part of a larger picture.

In 1904 his Fifth Symphony was premièred and published, his second daughter was born, and he completed his Sixth Symphony. This was his most personal symphonic work which, together with the *Kindertotenlieder*, not only dealt with his present but with his future. As his wife commented, 'he anticipated his own life in music. On him fell three blows of fate, and the last felled him'. *Kindertotenlieder*, Mahler's songs on the death of children, were premièred in January 1905. These beautiful but devastatingly sad songs terrified Alma, who felt they tempted fate, and in 1907, a year of great turmoil for the Mahlers, fate succumbed to the temptation. After 10 successful but highly controversial years, Mahler was manoeuvred into resigning from the Vienna Opera by a combination of the old guard and jealous colleagues; their elder daughter Maria contracted scarlet fever and diptheria, dying after days of suffering. Both parents were shattered, and Alma's mother, who was with them, suffered a heart attack in the immediate aftermath. The doctor brought in to treat her also checked Mahler and discovered the heart condition which was later to bring his life to a premature end. From that day on his life changed on almost every level.

During the previous few years Mahler had treated his family and colleagues virtually as servants, requiring them to remain at his beck and call while he composed and lived with complete freedom. As Alma noted: 'I lived his life. I had none of my own. He never noticed

this surrender of my existence... He was utterly self-centred by nature, and yet he never thought of himself. His work was all in all.... He saw in me only the comrade, the mother and the housewife, and was to learn too late what he had lost'. With the discovery of his heart condition, Mahler developed a new sense of urgency and a new set of priorities: he needed to set his family on a secure financial basis so that his own death would not render them penniless, and for this reason he accepted a lucrative offer from a New York impresario to go to America for the 1907–08 season. There he conducted at the Metropolitan and with the New York Philharmonic, garnering great success and adulation. Alma had accompanied him, and he attempted to bring a new softness to their relations, but the years of suffering and bitterness had decreased her expectations and formed an unbridgeable gulf between them.

On his return to Europe in 1908, Mahler began work on *Das Lied von der Erde*, unofficially his Ninth Symphony (the very different Seventh and Eighth had been written in the previous two summers), pouring all his grief and fears into the work, which used T'ang dynasty Chinese poetry (including Li Po and Wang Wei) selected by the composer, and

DON'T MISS

▶ **Symphony No. 9 (1909)**

▶ **Das Lied von der Erde (1908–09)**

▶ **Kindertotenlieder (1909–04)**

▶ **5 Rückert-Lieder (1902)**

which carries the refrain in the opening 'song': 'dark is life, dark is death'. Just how dark could be divined by his unceremonious replacement as conductor at the Metropolitan Opera that season by Arturo Toscanini. For the next two summers Mahler worked feverishly, completing his Ninth Symphony in 1909 and writing a first draft of the Tenth in 1910. While he was in the summer house at Toblach sketching his Tenth Symphony, the last of the farewell triptych of symphonies, Alma retired to a

sanitarium and had what she termed 'a complete breakdown'. While there she met the architect Walter Gropius, and they began an affair, soon discovered by a distraught Mahler. From then on he attempted to retrieve his marriage and the couple agreed to stay togther; Alma knew he was a dying man.

A last season in America—one which took him away from New York to other cities in the depths of winter—was not calculated to restore his health,

and he returned to Europe that spring a man clinging to what remained of his life. Debilitated by the time he landed in France, he made the journey to Vienna in the grip of a fever which left him helpless to combat any deterioration in his condition, and he died in May 1911. He was buried in Heitzing cemetery next to his daughter Maria, his grave marked with his surname only as he had requested; 'Any who come to look for me will know who I was, and the rest do not need to know'.

HUGO WOLF

1860–1903

Though Wolf himself would not have appreciated it, he is remembered as the pre-eminent German-language *lieder* composer of the latter 19th century, regardless of his other compositions. Today, little else of his music is either performed or remembered.

Wolf was born in the Styrian village of Windischgraz, at that time part of Austria but today in Slovenia. His father was German, his mother Slavic, and both temperaments can be clearly traced in Hugo's adult behaviour. His father, a man with a taste for music and a capable amateur pianist, ran a leather business which it was assumed his sons (of which Hugo was the fourth) would inherit. But in 1867 the business was detroyed by fire and from then on the family had to struggle to

make ends meet. From a relatively early age Hugo showed a strong interest in music and literature but little else, failing to make much progress at a succession of schools. He wanted to attend Vienna Conservatoire, and after a battle with his parents, who were unsure how to pay for it, he began his studies.

The same year Wolf met his idol Wagner, who was visiting Vienna, and from that day Wolf remained utterly unshakeable in his devotion to Wagner's music. One of the few friends Wolf made at the Conservatoire was Gustav Mahler. Wolf soon tired of the discipline of properly structured academic study, and after a series of confrontations with the Conservatoire staff he resigned just days before he was to be expelled. This precipitous action left him in a perilous situation;

he had no financial support from his family and was hostile to the idea of teaching music for a living. He often went hungry, and at one point almost emigrated to America to escape what he felt were his intolerable living conditions. His brusque manner and arrogance towards people he considered lacked musical talent added to his employment problems. Even when a kindly older composer obtained him an appointment as second *Kapellmeister* at Salzburg, within two months he was shown the door after quarelling with his superiors.

By this time Wolf had already contracted the syphilis which would eventually kill him. In 1879 he also fell out with Brahms; when Wolf showed him some early songs Brahms advised him that he should study more. Wolf never forgave him, and when he became music critic for Vienna's *Salonblatt* in 1884 he quickly made an enemy of Brahms together with anyone else who failed to support his rabidly pro-Wagner stance. Yet he still managed to preserve some friendships and take well-meant advice from august figures such as Franz Liszt, who in 1883 advised him to attempt works on a large scale rather than just songs. Wolf responded to this rare piece of encouragement by plunging into his only sustained orchestral work, *Penthesilea*, based on an Ancient Greek legend of amazons and bloody deeds. Wolf's two great loves remained literature and music, but he was yet to find his true milieu.

Although in 1886 he had begun an impressive but unjustly neglected choral piece, *Christnacht*, the following year marked the turning-point in his life and career. Firstly his father died, then a friend, Friedrich Eckstein, arranged for some of his early songs to be collected into two volumes and published. As with Liszt's praise four years earlier, this public recognition had a cathartic effect: he abandoned his position on the *Salonblatt*, moved into a house in a village called Perchtoldsdorf in the Wiener Wald just outside Vienna, and in 1888 began a sustained burst of music composition. What transpired must have shocked as well as exhilarated him, for in a torrent of creative invention he completed in three months close to 50 songs based on texts by the poet Mörike. What is so incredible (and Wolf was aware of this as he wrote) is that the songs, technique and ideas seemed to improve in quality rather than become imitative or stylized as time wore on. Wolf composed in a state approaching quiet

Hugo Wolf

frenzy, ignorant as to when the outpouring might cease. When it finally did, he returned to Vienna where he arranged to borrow his friend Eckstein's summer house. There he wrote the first of his famous Eichendorff settings before returning to the Mörike project and finishing the collection with a final spurt of 10 songs.

After a pause of some months, Wolf plunged into another bout of songwriting, this time picking Goethe as his literary source. Before three months were over he had completed over 50 *Goethe Lieder*, making a tally— for that calender year alone—of nearly 120 songs, all of the highest quality.

After this his inspiration was suspended while he attempted to gather his physical strength, taking a third trip to Bayreuth to drink in the intoxicating sounds of his favourite composer. Refreshed, he returned to Perchtoldsdorf in October of 1889, where his project was to set to music the translations by Paul Heyse and Emanuel Giebel of a body of poems into German from the original Spanish. Having chosen his preferred texts, Wolf set 28 by the end of the year, but was then laid low by a bout of influenza. Picking up the threads in spring after his health had improved, Wolf finished what became the *Spanisches Liederbuch* by the end of April 1890.

DON'T MISS

▶ Eichendorff Lieder
  (1880–88)

▶ Mörike Lieder (1888)

▶ Goethe Lieder (1888–9)

▶ Spanisches Liederbuch
  (1889–90)

▶ Italienisches Liederbuch
  (1890–6)

Following a break in May, he spent that June writing six fine songs to poems by Gottfried Keller. In the autumn he followed the example of the *Spanisches Liederbuch* by once again using Paul Heyse translations—this time of a disparate collection of Italian poetry—to produce the first songs of what eventually became the *Italienisches Liederbuch*. Wolf then took a rest from his composing to visit Schott, the Mainz publishers introduced to him by the composer Engelbert Humperdinck, arranging with them for his songs to be published. Following what had now become an unbreakable pattern, Wolf experienced a period of rest from composition which lasted until late 1891. At that point he picked up where he had left off, writing between November 29 and December 23 no less than 15 songs, completing the first 'book' of the *Italienisches Liederbuch*. After this incredible and unparalleled explosion of compositional activity, Wolf's *lieder* muse was utterly silent for over four years.

Instead, he turned his attention to opera, a genre in which he had long been desperate to succeed. After an extensive and frustrating search for a suitable libretto, he finally chose the Spanish novel *The Three Cornered Hat*

by Pedro de Alarcón. Starting work on *Der Dreispitz* in March 1895, Wolf completed the short score by July, then began to orchestrate it, a task which took him until December. A measure of his fast-developing reputation is the speed with which this first completed stage-work was adopted for its première, which took place in Mannheim in June 1896 under the title *Der Corregidor*. Unfortunately it soon became apparent that Wolf's genius for words and music did not extend to drama and a sense of theatre, and the opera was dropped after just two performances. In the meantime, no doubt inspired by the impending production, Wolf had in spring 1896 completed the second 'book' of the *Italienisches Liederbuch*, a set of 22 songs which sustained the standard of the first book.

The rest of 1896 passed uneventfully, with Wolf enjoying a gradually expanding reputation and an ever-widening circle of artistic and musical friends in and around Vienna. In the spring of 1897 he once again began work on a new set of songs, this time to sonnets by Michelangelo, as well as beginning to edit the libretto for a new opera, *Manuel Venegas*, based on another novel by Alarcón. In the fall of that year, although in deteriorating health, he approached his old colleague and student friend, Gustav Mahler, now music director at the Vienna Opera, to put on a production of *Der Corregidor*. Mahler, a stern and usually accurate judge, declined the offer. Offended, Wolf made a scene, refusing to leave Mahler's office. Excusing himself, Mahler withdrew. According to Alma Mahler, later that day Wolf tried to see Mahler at his Viennese

apartment, but the door was shut in his face.

Soon after this incident Wolf's mental condition became so precarious that he was admitted to an asylum. After nearly two years he appeared to have recovered his balance. This proved to be an illusion, and after a period of time living in rooms in Vienna working fitfully on *Manuel Venegas* (no music was ever written), Wolf's mind finally caved in; in October 1898 he attempted suicide by trying to drown himself in the Traunsee. He was taken back to the asylum, where a steady deterioration reduced him to a state of paralysis: tertiary syphilis had taken over. In February 1903 he died: he was only 43. In February 1904, a year later, in a gesture he regarded as a debt of honour, Mahler conducted the Viennese première of *Der Corregidor*. It was repeated in March, but after that it passed into obscurity.

Wolf's achievement was in the way he took the *lied* as developed by Schubert and Schumann and moved it successfully into an end-of-century sensibility. His equal love of words and music made his treatment of meaning through melody, rhythm and harmony uniquely sensitive, achieving a complete symbiosis between the two elements. He was also a great innovator in his writing for the piano accompaniment. His way of making melody and declamation merge into each other was a breathtaking stylistic breakthrough which would lead to many vocal music developments in later generations, and which enabled him to develop unique characters for each of his songs. This extreme elasticity of phrasing allowed Wolf to make the entire artefact as natural and unaffected an expression as the act of breathing or speaking. His determined accuracy when it came to printed instructions as to how his songs should be interpreted reflect his complete understanding of what he was achieving in each setting, and it is a courageous musician who departs a long way from the paths indicated by the composer.

CLAUDE DEBUSSY

1862–1918

Debussy was one of those key composers whose music represents a true break with the immediate past. He spent over a decade ridding himself of early influences, but then in the 1890s began the series of wholly original works which would provide an alternative approach to modernism for those unable or unwilling to embrace the Wagnerite philosophy.

Debussy was born into an impoverished Parisian family. His father, a philandering ex-soldier, was a junior clerk while his mother appears to have found children interfered with her activities. Consequently, Claude was more or less brought up by his father's sister, Clementine. His musical ability was recognized by the mother-in-law of the poet Verlaine, Madame Mauté, and it was she who prepared him for a successful sitting of the entrance examination to the Paris Conservatoire. In 1872, just 10 years old, Claude began formal music studies.

Debussy proved a brilliant and precocious student, but soon showed himself willing to apply himself only to what interested him; thus a career as a concert pianist was quickly abandoned. Studies in theory, harmony and composition kept him at the Conservatoire until 1882. In the summers between 1879 and 1882 he took private teaching positions with wealthy families and for three years he was the summer tutor to Tchaikovsky's patroness, Madame von Meck. That he came under the older composer's influence is indisputable; in 1880 there was even published a set of piano duet arrangements of the dances from Act III of *Swan Lake*, arranged by Debussy, then still in his teens. In 1884 he won the Grand Prix de Rome, entitling him to a year's study in Rome at the Conservatoire's expense. The two years spent there, interspersed by frequent dashes back to Paris, his bohemian friends and his paramour Mme Vasnier, were not happy; he called the Eternal City a town of 'fleas and boredom'. He did, however, meet Liszt in Rome who introduced him to the wonders of the music of Orlande de Lassus and Palestrina. Yet nothing would induce him to stay the Conservatoire course and by early 1887 he had abandoned Rome. Instead, he threw himself into the Parisian artistic milieu, and by 1888 he was attending the annual Wagnerian season at Bayreuth. For a man who was soon to become one of the most scathing critics of the Wagnerian cult and its pernicious effects on French musical life, he showed an intense interest in the German composer's music and ideas.

The World Exhibition in Paris in 1889 left an equally indelible impression. Its collating of ethnic musics from across the world—from black minstrels from America playing early forms of ragtime and syncopated music through to the magical, bewitching sounds of the Javanese *gamelan* orchestra—intoxicated and transfixed Debussy. The artistic exhibits from Japan in particular had a widespread impact, launching Orientalism on the *fin-de-siècle* world. Yet as the 1890s dawned Debussy remained an impecunious musician living a bohemian existence. His lot was made easier by the generosity of wealthy friends such as Ernest Chausson, and his circle of artistic acquaintances was immeasurably widened by his regular attendance at the soirées held at cabaret bars such as the Chat Noir, also frequented by his friend Erik Satie.

Although a string quartet and a number of songs of great beauty emerged, and in 1894 he completed the exquisite musical invocation of a Mallarmé poem, *Prélude à l'Après-midi d'un Faune*, Debussy was leaving a trail of unfinished projects in his wake as he searched for an operatic subject and form which conformed to his musical ideal. His long friendship with poet Pierre Louÿs helped concentrate his artistic endeavours, especially when it came to the protracted gestation of his one completed operatic masterpiece, *Pelléas et Mélisande*, which was completed in short score by late summer of 1895, but had to wait until 1901 and its acceptance by Albert Carré for production at the Opéra-Comique for the full orchestral score to be produced. Its première in 1902 lit the touchpaper of Debussy's international career.

During the long period of waiting, the Nocturnes (1900) had been completed, and on a personal level Debussy had progressed from his long, tempestuous affair with Gaby Dupont to a quick marriage to Rosalie (Lily) Texier in 1899. Pierre Louÿs and Erik Satie were the witnesses at the wedding. The marriage failed to survive Debussy's new life after the success of *Pelléas*, and in 1904, against a background of a failed suicide attempt by Lily (and a scandal), Debussy eloped with Emma Bardac, who was expecting their child.

His period of elopement with Emma in England led eventually to the inspiration for his greatest orchestral work, *La Mer* (1905). The following years saw the birth of his only child, the much-loved Claude-Emma (Chou-Chou) followed in 1908 by the marriage of Debussy to Emma Bardac. Debussy suffered a great deal from this marriage: although it was to last for the rest of his life, he lost many of his closest friends, including Pierre Louÿs, and *La Mer's* première drew great hostility from critics more concerned to teach him a moral lesson than to evaluate a new piece of music.

By 1908 Debussy's life had taken on the pattern which would last until his death: composition, regular conducting tours around Europe (including many visits to England), and endless plans for the follow-up to *Pelléas*, all of which were abandoned or left uncompleted at his death. A poor conductor, he found the rigours of touring debilitating in the extreme, but such concerts were a financial necessity. In 1910 Debussy met both Mahler and Stravinsky, but only the second meeting warmed into mutual admiration and friendship. His only other stage works performed during his lifetime were the ballet *Jeux* (1913), written for Serge Diaghilev to a slight but risqué plot involving Nijinsky and a game of tennis, and the strange

play-with-music in partnership with Gabriele D'Annunzio, *Le Martyre de Saint-Sébastien* (1911), starring Ida Rubinstein (Marcel Proust, attending the premiere, felt that Ida's legs were the most interesting thing about the event). At this stage Debussy's health was beginning to falter and he was often left exhausted, although the cancer which eventually killed him had not yet been diagnosed.

The onset of WWI initially halted all Debussy's creative ventures, but in 1915 he completed the last of his great piano cycles, the Etudes, as well as piano works for four hands and the late sonatas. Financial worries obliged him to continue touring until the end of 1915, but from then on he was virtually an invalid. Confined to bed during the winter of 1917–18, and while the Germans bombarded Paris, he succumbed to cancer in March 1918.

Debussy's music is such an intoxicating mix of timbre and colour that it is tempting to label him as a musical equivalent of the Impressionist art movement of the time. But Debussy himself felt his music to be closer to the Symbolist ideal of seeking the true meaning and nature of things beneath their surface, of attempting to get at the mystery which resides at the centre of all experience. His orchestral works were an attempt to delineate the precise qualities of nature, rather than record impressions of light and colour (the avowed aim of the Impressionists). His opera *Pelléas et Mélisande* is concerned with psychological reality and evoking mental and emotional states rather than dramatic action or conflicts between state and individual. His music for the most part avoids

---

DON'T MISS

▶ Fêtes galantes, Sets 1 & 2 (1891–1904)
▶ Prélude à l'après-midi d'un Faune (1892–94)
▶ String Quartet (1893)
▶ Nocturnes (1900)
▶ Pelléas et Mélisande (1903)

violent declamation and strident crescendos, and his rhythmic concepts are some of the most complex and subtle in the entire Western Classical canon. His is a music of exquisite mystery and extraordinary delicacy. His last works indicate a shift in style towards the Classicism of French 18th-century composers, but the music remains very much identifiable as his.

Many composers bring their influence to bear on just one genre of Classical music: Debussy is one of the few to have composed masterpieces across the disciplines which have had a profound influence on his contemporaries and subsequent generations. The opera *Pelléas et Mélisande* dispensed with both the Wagnerian and French Grand Opera models which had cast such long shadows over music for the stage in France and Germany, and forged a new relationship between singer and orchestra, where the whole work was deliberately undramatic, evolving more like a living organism. Debussy's great orchestral works *La Mer*, Nocturnes and *Images pour Orchestre* each attempt to depict both the inner and outer characters of natural phenomena—the sea, clouds, landscapes—while his exquisite tone-poem *Prélude à l'Après-midi d'un Faune* weaves an incandescent spell of lazy sensuality and unspoken yearning. In recent years, his late ballet *Jeux* has been named as an influential masterpiece by many composers and performers.

Yet if any of his music can be called definitive, it is perhaps his body of music for the piano. It was on this most impersonal of instruments that his most intimate and personal musical world

was conjured, from evoking Javanese *gamelan* music in 'Pagodes' from *Estampes* (1903) to depicting moonlight in the famous 'Clair de lune' from the *Suite Bergamasque* (1905) or executing an incisive and amusing sketch of vaudeville and low-life comic characters in 'Minstrels' from the first book of *Préludes* (1910). This merely touches on the vast range of his subjects. His *Children's Corner* (1906-08) is a suite of pieces, ostensibly for children, which resonate deeply in an adult sensibility. 'Jimbo's Lullaby', 'The Snowflakes are Dancing' and 'Golliwog's Cakewalk' all carry an air of magic and delight. Yet even here, the mystery at the core of Debussy's music is present in the form of the will-o-the-wisp arabesques and elusive melancholy of 'The Little Shepherd'. All of these tendencies can be traced at greater depth in the second book of *Préludes* (1913), both books of *Images* (1905 & 1908), and the enigmatic and abstract late work, Etudes (1915).

Debussy's chamber music is not plentiful, but is all worth studying; his early String Quartet (1893) takes a step back from current role models such as Fauré and Franck, looking for inspiration from pre-Baroque French music. His three late sonatas, for Violin and Piano (1916-17), Cello and Piano (1915) and Flute, Viola and Harp (1915), all written in a more severe and compact style, have latterly won a wider audience and been recognized as influential masterpieces. Lastly, it must be remembered that Debussy first found his mature style in songs (mélodies), and wrote a substantial body of works, many of them revolutionary in their own time and hauntingly beautiful.

Debussy was one of the key figures in showing that there was a way ahead in Western music which need not use the methods most favoured by German-speaking composers and theorists, whether they be Wagner, Brahms, Schoenberg or Strauss. He constructed a musical language which drew from hitherto neglected sources, including Palestrina, Mussorgsky, Couperin and the music of countries such as Spain and Bali. He was able to combine the most advanced study of harmony and musical construction with a sensitivity for sheer sound perhaps matched only by Ravel, and that in another context. He was also able to use the simplest of harmonic devices—such as the whole-tone scale—and invest it with such a personal identity that it could offer itself as a way out to later generations exhausted by the rigors of serialism. Debussy was also a master of rhythm: his use of silence and space, of *ostinato* patterns, of counter-rhythms and asymmetric phrasings foreshadowed much of the rhythmic freedom to be displayed by composers 50 years later. Debussy's contribution to the musical language of this century is an absolutely central one.

FREDERICK DELIUS

1862–1934

One of the true musical mavericks, Delius was also one of the most naturally gifted composers of his generation. A musician with an uncanny orchestral ear and a glorious gift for melody and modulation, he used his love of rich musical textures to illuminate an essentially dark and pagan view of the world at large.

Delius was born Fritz Albert Theodore, the second son of an immigrant German family who left Bielefeld in the late 1840s and settled first in Manchester then Bradford, becoming part of the burgeoning wool trade. The parents produced no less than 14 children, all of whom lived in fear of their Prussian father's temper and total inflexibility; emotional warmth was not on the agenda. High-sprited and gregarious, Frederick was an indifferent student but developed an early interest in music which he was left to pursue on his own. When his older brother emigrated to New Zealand, Fred became the heir to the business. Joining it as a clerk he was sent first to Stroud, then Chemnitz in Saxony, then spent periods in Norway and France.

Away from his father, Delius quickly decided that he no longer wanted to work in the family business, and on his return to England embarked upon a campaign to persuade his parents that money was to be made in America. Funds were made available for Frederick and a friend to buy a small orange

Frederick Delius

plantation at Jacksonville, Florida. Although growing oranges held little fascination for him, Delius was entranced by the opulent beauty of Florida and had the luck to meet a New York organist, Thomas Ward. Ward moved into Delius's house on the plantation and gave him lessons in counterpoint and harmony, "the only lessons from which I derived any benefit", Delius remarked many years later.

Leaving the plantation in the care of his older brother, Fred escaped to New York where he supported himself by playing and teaching music. When his father finally traced him, a deal was struck between father and son whereby Julius agreed to support him at Leipzig Conservatory for 18 months on condition that Fred then returned to

the New World and continued to make money from music. Delius started at Leipzig in late 1886 and although he later dismissed the training he gained there, he worked hard as well as making a start on an ambitious programme of composition of which the major achievement was the *Florida Suite*. In 1888 Delius wrote to Grieg, then in Leipzig, enclosing a selection of his manuscripts. Struck by their promise, Grieg made his acquaintence and eventually helped persuade Delius's father that his son had a great talent and should be allowed to develop it in Europe, not America. A compromise was reached whereby Fred took up residence with his uncle Theodore in Paris

From the first months in Paris Delius determined that he was going to be an opera composer, and indeed one of his chief interests throughout his time there (1888-97) was attending the theatres and opera houses, as well as less elevated entertainments (indeed, 1890 was the year he contracted syphilis). His first opera was begun in 1890 and completed during 1892: this was Irmelin, a personal favourite of Sir Thomas Beecham's. This was followed in 1895 by The Magic Fountain. For a time it seemed that the German Theatre in Prague would mount a production, but the arrangment fell through. However, 1896 was not entirely wasted, for in January he met the German artist Jelka Rosen. For the rest of the year, while Delius made a firm start on his third opera, Koanga, Fred and Jelka became regular companions, though Delius's eye continued to wander.

In 1897 Jelka bought a large house in Grez-sur-Loing in France and he moved in with her. A burst of creativity followed with Delius finishing Koanga, making progress on his piano concerto, writing a series of fine songs, and at last finishing the orchestral piece Over the Hills and Far Away. Delius now entered into his most sustained period of achievement, with the tone-poem Paris—the Song of a Great City appearing in 1899, and the plans for his finest opera, A Village Romeo and Juliet, being laid in 1900. This opera was completed in 1901, the year Paris received its German première, an event which established Delius beyond doubt as a force to reckon with in German music. With a string of unproduced operas behind him, however, he was determined to make his mark in the theatre, and entered a new one-acter for the famous Sonzogno Prize (once

won by Mascagni with Cavalleria Rusticana). This opera, Margot la Rouge, dealing with the Paris low life Delius knew so well, was not Delius at his best or most characteristic, and it failed to win the 1902 prize. But the year had better things to offer: he and Jelka were married, Koanga was accepted for production, and he completed his great orchestral remembrance of Appalachia.

Delius's inspiration did not flag: gripped by the words of Walt Whitman and Nietzsche, he produced the masterpiece Sea Drift in 1903 and the monumental oratorio A Mass of Life in 1905. Many of these new works received their premières in Germany, with A Village Romeo and Juliet being premièred in Berlin in 1907. For the first time in his career (he was now in his mid-forties) Delius had some prospect of making money from his music. Until now England had remained a closed book to him, but a London performance of Appalachia in 1907 struck the observer Thomas Beecham so forcefully that he determined to get to know the composer (who was present) and his works. A close friendship developed and Beecham rapidly became Delius's champion in Britain, together with Henry Wood who premièred Sea Drift in 1908, the same year that Brigg Fair gained its German première. Beecham gave the Covent Garden première of A Village Romeo and Juliet in 1910.

Delius continued to work steadily at Grez between visits to festivals and premières of his works, and in 1910 completed what was to be his last opera, Fennimore and Gerda. It was written to texts by his favourite author, the Dane Jens Peter Jacobsen, whose text was also used for Arabesk (for

chorus and orchestra) and whose poems had long been a source of inspiration for Delius's songs. Ignored in Britain, it gained its première as late as 1919 in Frankfurt. The year of the dark and intense Arabesk was also that of Summer Night on the River, No. 2 of Two Pieces for Small Orchestra, while No. 1, On Hearing the First Cuckoo in Spring, was written the following year. Begun at the same time as Fennimore were Songs of Sunset, settings of poems by Ernest Dowson, and the masterpiece In A Summer Garden, while North Country Sketches (1913-14) and A Song of the High Hills (1911) were completed as Delius began to suffer the first effects of the syphilis contracted 20 years earler.

The outbreak of WWII had a devastating effect on Delius's German reputation: he was reduced to a nonentity by the grim succession of events. The war also necessitated his retreat from France, initially to England, latterly to Norway. The quality of his inspiration suffered, as is shown by the patchwork Requiem of 1916, a complete failure at its première due to its bleak atheistic message in time of war, and the uneven series of chamber works and concertos written between then and 1920. From

---

DON'T MISS

▶ Sea Drift (1903-04)
▶ A Mass of Life (1904-5)
▶ Brigg Fair (1907)
▶ A Village Romeo and Juliet (1907)
▶ In a Summer Garden (1908)
▶ Two Pieces for Small Orchestra (1910/11)

this period only *A Song Before Sunrise* (1918) has held its place in the repertoire. Nevertheless, *Fennimore and Gerda* achieved its Frankfurt success in 1919, and in 1920 came a commission to write music for Flecker's play *Hassan*, which was finally produced in 1923 to good notices. A permanent return to Grez in 1921 was followed shortly after by a precipitous decline in Delius's physical condition: by mid-1922 his limbs were badly affected, and he had lost the use of his right hand. From now on Jelka wrote all his letters for him.

Delius's health fluctuated throughout 1923–24, but by the spring of 1925 he had lost the ability to walk and was almost completely blind. A virtual halt to all composing activity took place until one day in 1928 a letter from a 22-year-old Yorkshireman, Eric Fenby, arrived at Grez offering his services. Fenby had discovered an edition of *A Mass of Life* in a music shop and, on hearing of the composer's affliction, was determined to see if he could help; he could. After a tentative beginning, Fenby settled into the routine at Grez and became literally Delius's ears, eyes and hands. Working together (with Fenby often editing and collating masses of old, unfinished manuscripts before playing them to Delius), they completed a range of works, from *Cynara*, a setting of Ernest Dowson's disturbing poem (specially presented by Sir Thomas Beecham at the major festival of Delius's works in 1929 as a 'première'), to *Idyll, A Song of Summer*, the popular *Two Aquarelles* and the *Songs of Farewell*, set to words by Whitman. His exacting and exhausting work over, in 1933 Fenby returned to England. Once he and Fenby had completed all the manuscripts now worth keeping, Delius's health deteriorated rapidly. With his wife Jelka suffering from the onset of the cancer which was soon to kill her, Delius died in early summer, 1934. After a long battle with bureaucracy, he was buried in southern England. The following year his wife was laid alongside him.

PIETRO MASCAGNI
1863–1945

Like many other opera composers, Mascagni is remembered for one single work, in his case the stirring *verismo* one-acter *Cavalleria Rusticana*, when in fact he composed a great many works of surprising variety, some of which can stand comparison with his first and most popular stage work.

Mascagni was born in Livorno; his father was a baker who had high hopes for his son, wishing him to practise law. Pietro shared his father's ambition, but having discovered the seductive charm of music he channelled all his hopes into a profession abhorred by his parents. Banned by his father from pursuing musical studies, Mascagni secretly entered himself as a pupil at the Istituto Cherubini. When his father discovered what his errant son was up to, a major row ensued, the situation only resolved by Mascagni leaving home and going to live with an uncle, where he was able to continue his musical training.

Mascagni made such rapid progress with his studies that by 1879, when he was still 16, a symphony he had composed was performed locally; two years later a cantata entitled *In Filanda* received a favourable mention in a Milanese competition. Confronted by his son's obvious success, his father capitulated and allowed his son to continue with his chosen career. On the death of his uncle, Pietro returned home. Another work, a musical setting of an Italian translation of Schiller's *Ode to Joy,* was so successful that a rich aristocrat offered to pay Mascagni's tuition fees at the Milan Conservatory, where Pietro became a student of Ponchielli. However, he soon discovered that formal studies held little attraction for him, and he left the Conservatory to take up the career of an itinerant musician, playing in musical aggregations the length and breadth of Italy. He eventually came to rest in Foggia, where he supported himself by teaching the piano.

During this time his compositional career had languished, but with the establishment of the Sonzogno Prize in 1889 (offered by the Milanese publisher of that name in an effort to unearth

Pietro Mascagni

Strangely enough, the young composer was largely unmoved by talk of him leading a 'school'; he always considered himself an opera composer first and foremost, and one who wrote music to subjects which interested him, whatever genre or style they fell into.

This belief in his powers, and his determination to follow his own inclinations in the face of public expectation, led him to write *L'Amico Fritz* (1891), an opera of great charm and delicacy, wit and invention, but not in any way a companion-piece to *Cavalleria*. It enjoyed steady, though not runaway, success, and was taken up enthusiastically in foreign cities such as Vienna and London. The Italians, however, continued to regard it as a stop-gap work, and waited for the follow-up. They were to wait in vain, for the next two works were somewhat hyperbolic tragedies verging occasionally on melodrama, *I Rantzau* and *Guglielmo Ratcliffe*, the latter a revamped effort from his student days which received the condemnation it deserved. A return to the flashing drama and colour of *Cavalleria* was discernible in *Silvano* (Milan 1895), while *Zanetto* (1896) attempted a much more intimate drama by restricting the accompaniment to a chamber orchestra of strings and harp, a daring innovation for the period and one which did not wholly succeed—at least, not in the view of his contemporaries.

By now a major public figure, in 1896 Mascagni was invited to be present at the inauguration of a new Florentine tram system, and was on the maiden run of the first tram when he spotted his composer colleague and old friend, Umberto Giordano, in the crowd.

new operatic talent), Mascagni decided this was his chance to rediscover his creative muse. In accordance with the competition's rules, he entered a one-act piece called *Cavalleria Rusticana;* it was chosen by the judges to be one of three works to be produced in front of a Milan audience whose response would determine the winning entry. Mascagni's earthy tale of provincial love and revenge won outright, receiving tumultuous acclaim from the audience. Sonzogno took up his option in the work and within months Mascagni was the talk of the Italian operatic world, eclipsing every other composer who had been struggling for years to become Verdi's heir-apparent. Now a charismatic and forceful young man, with a shock of black hair and

rugged good looks, Mascagni was quickly embraced by the opera-goers of Italy and beyond.

With his fiery and brilliantly conceived opera of low-life love and morality, Mascagni is often praised (or condemned) for having launched the *verismo* school of Italian opera. The hunt for realistic treatments of common life subjects had been a vogue in literary and painterly circles for some time, but only in the closing years of the 1880s did such treatments seem at all applicable to the operatic stage. In one opera, Mascagni had not only showed that it was possible to compose such works, but that they could be an overwhelming dramatic experience. *Verismo* was suddenly in vogue.

Mascagni alighted from the tram and greeted his friend warmly; the tram, continuing on its journey, became involved in a major accident with grave loss of life. Mascagni swore that it was the intervention of his friend that had saved his life, and in turn intervened to insist on Giordano's one indisputably great opera, *Andrea Chénier*, being staged in Milan the following season.

In 1895 Mascagni had been appointed director of Pesaro Conservatoire, and his public standing continued unaffected by his relative lack of success in finding an adequate successor to *Cavalleria*, but his next effort, *Iris* (Rome, 1898), came closer than any other. It had a great deal in its favour, including some of Mascagni's most persuasive music and refined orchestration, as well as a fashionable Japanese subject and a libretto by the illustrious Luigi Illica. Unfortunately it was the libretto which proved to be the weakness which eventually led *Iris* into somewhat undeserved oblivion, for it was a squalid and somewhat hackneyed melodrama in which none of the characters were allowed to come to life by the clichéd and superficial text. Mascagni did not have the relentless eye for dramatic

efficacy which served Puccini so well when dealing with the same librettist, and *Iris* eventually faded.

Cavalleria continued to be produced on the world's stages, Mascagni using his fame to promote a conducting career which took him to most of the world's great opera houses, including those in the New World. However, with the débacle of his next major opera, *Le Maschere* (1901), he realized that things had gone badly wrong with the development of his career as a composer: tempting fate, he had allowed promoters to produce *Le Maschere* simultaneously in no less than seven Italian cities. Only in Rome was it given a faintly warm reception. This disaster shook even Mascagni's self-assurance, and while he continued to write for the stage, he never again had the confidence to follow his own instincts, constantly changing course and style in an effort to achieve success once more. By the outbreak of WWI he had begun to sense that he had peaked too early and would never reclaim his early pre-eminence.

This would have left him an interesting and uncontroversial figure for future

generations to analyse, but with the advent of Mussolini's Fascist government, Mascagni made the mistake of allowing himself to become closely identified with Fascist philosophy and social outlook, a thing Puccini and others carefully avoided. Honoured and pampered by the government for the 20 years of Mussolini's rule, he wrote a mass of undistinguished ceremonial music for official occasions, unable to see that the ceremony and pageant had a hollow centre. When Mussolini was driven from power, Mascagni was instantly plunged into disgrace, stripped of all his honours and deprived of the lavish lifestyle he had previously enjoyed. He died in obscurity and dishonour in Rome, outliving nearly all his old rivals but under the worst possible circumstances. His body of operatic work awaits a sympathetic reappraisal.

DON'T MISS

▶ **Cavalleria Rusticana (1890)**

▶ **L'Amico Fritz (1891)**

▶ **Iris (1898)**

RICHARD STRAUSS

1864–1949

Coming to prominence during the ascendancy of Wagner and Brahms, and dying soon after Germany's destruction during WWII, in many ways Strauss's long career perfectly

encapsulates both the climax and ultimate disintegration of German Romantic notions of music and its relationship to the society from which it came.

No relation to the Viennese Strausses, Richard was the son of Franz Strauss, a distinguished horn player in the Munich Opera Orchestra. Richard showed musical talent early and was encouraged by his father. By 1882 he was ready to enter Munich University, although even by this date he had composed a number of early pieces, utterly orthodox in approach, including the *Serenade*, Op. 7 (1871) for wind instruments.

In 1883 he left the University and went for a time to Berlin, where towards the end of the year he managed to interest the conductor Hans von Bülow in his music. Bülow clearly saw something exceptional in the 19-year-old, for by 1885 he had obtained a position for him at Meiningen as Assistant Music Director. By then Strauss had already completed two youthful symphonies, the second of which was performed in New York in 1884. Subsequently, he looked to Liszt, Berlioz and Wagner as his orchestral models. Strauss himself saw his orchestral fantasia *Aus Italien* (1886) as the work which bridged his two early styles. The *Burleske* for piano and orchestra from the same year contains similar hints of the future.

Richard Strauss

Strauss's conducting career began to take off; he succeeded von Bülow at Meiningen, then became sub-conductor at the Munich Opera until summer 1889, when he moved to Weimar to be Assistant Director. By then he had completed the tone poem *Don Juan,* Op. 20, which was premièred in 1889 and gave Strauss his first major popular success, as well as embroiling him in controversy—which did his career little harm. The energetic and colourful orchestral music of Strauss's youth is typified here, with its reliance on relentless modulation and large orchestral forces to keep up the momentum and the drama, plus the imaginative musical illustration of a work's theme—here the Byronic rake destined to eternal damnation.

Simultaneously he put the finishing touches to *Tod und Verklärung*, Op. 24. This became his pattern for the 1890s, writing spectacular and controversial orchestral pieces (together with a stream of high-quality *lieder*) and often conducting them together with older masterpieces in concert halls across Europe. A very ambitious man with a drive for material wealth, Strauss was always happy to accept guest appearances as a conductor, and he made prestigious appearances in many centres, including Bayreuth in 1891, where he gave the Bayreuth première of Wagner's *Tannhäuser*.

Strauss had a love of opera in general and of the soprano voice in particular, and was determined to make a success

in that field. He met soprano Pauline de Ahna in Munich at the beginning of the 1890s and they soon married (it was to prove a stormy but lasting relationship). Within a year he had begun his first opera, *Guntram*, which failed in both Weimar and Munich in 1894. His second opera, *Feuersnot* (Dresden 1901) also failed, although his orchestral music continued to be enthusiastically received. *Also Sprach Zarathustra*, Op. 30 (1895–96), inspired by Nietzsche, *Don Quixote*, Op. 35 in 1897 and *Ein Heldenleben*, Op. 40 (1898), Strauss's self-portrait, including a central portion which describes his recent bride and life's companion, all met with acclaim. His music and his career became part of the cultural scene in Berlin when he conducted there from the mid-1890s

DON'T MISS

▶ Don Juan, Op. 20 (1888)
▶ Till Eulenspiegels lustige Streiche, Op. 28 (1894–95)
▶ Also Sprach Zarathustra, Op. 30 (1895–96)
▶ Salome (1905)
▶ Der Rosenkavalier (1911)

onwards, and by the early 1900s it seemed that his career was mapped out, running along similar lines to that of his colleague and friend Gustav Mahler. The *Sinfonia Domestica* of 1904 seemingly confirmed it.

It was *Salome* which changed all that and began the second phase of Strauss's career. Strauss himself took Oscar Wilde's scandalous play and rendered it into an effective libretto; its amoral subject and sexually intoxicated heroine clearly inspired him, and while he adopted generally Wagnerian methodologies (the opera is called by Strauss a 'music-drama'), his usage of opera orthodoxies is wholly individual. One of the last of the truly great works inspired by exotic subject matter before all that was washed away in the carnage of WWI, its perfect drama, meticulous scoring, soaring melodies and headlong rush to its grisly resolution remain utterly convincing today. It is little wonder that *Salome*, despite the scandal, was an enormous success at its Dresden première in 1905. Its follow-up, *Elektra* (Dresden, 1909), took the hedonism of *Salome* to new extremes, not so much in terms of physical sensuality and excess, but in its fierce intoxication with sound. In giving the Greek tragedy a new, modern face, Strauss emphasized what he and his librettist Hugo von

Hofmannsthal saw as the 'ecstatic' and 'daemonic' elements to this powerful fratricidal drama.

After these two shattering triumphs, Strauss largely turned away from orchestral music; he had begun work on *Der Rosenkavalier* even before the Dresden première of *Elektra*. A man of astute perceptions when it came to his public, Strauss had decided that he needed to present a different aspect of his operatic abilities with his next effort, and *Der Rosenkavalier* could hardly have been more different, a stylish (and stylized) reinvoking of 18th-century amorous liaisons, even involving a so-called 'trouser-role' (a woman singing a man's part), whose only point of contact with his previous operas was its utter domination by female voices. The year of *Rosenkavalier*'s Dresden première (1911) saw the beginning of work on *Eine Alpensinfonie*, Strauss's last major orchestral composition prior to the series of pieces written in the last years of his life, but by the time of its 1915 première, he had not only completed *Ariadne auf Naxos*, but premièred it in 1912 in one guise, and was preparing its revised form for its 1916 Vienna première. *Ariadne* was another work lodged in the 18th century as it was originally designed as a pendant to a production of Molière's *Le Bourgeois*

gentilhomme, for which Strauss had written the incidental music. The shortcomings of this approach meant that the audience was never fully convinced, and Strauss's recasting— which has remained popular ever since—dispensed with the play and substituted a prologue which explained the presence of *commedia dell'arte* characters and the play-within-a-play idea which allowed Strauss another tribute to the Classical Greek culture he so loved.

Strauss and Hofmannsthal meanwhile knew the nature of their next enterprise, *Die Frau ohne Schatten* (Vienna 1919), and this metaphorical opera, calling for large orchestral forces and an expanded cast, was their major project during the war years. Reflecting Strauss's lack of interest in politics and world affairs, while the War raged across Europe, he and Hoffmannsthal wrote a beautiful opera set in no specific time and no specific place which reinterpreted old Persian fairy tales. A complex and haunting work, it is one of their finest.

By now the creative pattern for Strauss's middle period was well established: he and Hofmannsthal worked in close collaboration on a project or subject, Hofmannsthal being the slower, more deliberate partner, Strauss the more facile, urgent one. *Intermezzo*, a charming 'domestic comedy' (Dresden, 1924), was written exclusively by Strauss while he and his librettist made much slower and more laboured progress on their operatic treatment of Helen of Troy, *Die Aegyptische Helena* (Dresden 1928), a work which had been conceived as an operetta but which evolved into a romantic drama dealing with the nature of truth and deception in marriage. The follow-up, *Arabella* (Dresden 1933), was not only a more popular and genuinely lighthearted lyrical work, but it was also the last with Hofmannsthal, the great poet, dramatist and librettist, who died in early 1929, just six weeks after *Helena*'s opening night. Using Hofmannsthal's libretto, Strauss completed the work himself.

Strauss's next choice of partner was the Jewish Austrian writer Stefan Zweig, who managed just one opera with the composer, *Die schweigsame Frau* (Dresden 1935) before being forced by the Nazi government into exile in 1938. The history of Strauss's relationship with the Nazi government is not a proud one, and is dominated by Strauss's single-minded concentration on getting on with his own life regardless of what else was going on in the world. For two years, 1933–35, he allowed himself to be at the head of Hitler's council for music before resigning in protest at the Nazis' interference with his working relationship with Zweig. After that, there was an uneasy peace when the Nazis and Strauss gradually learned to

ignore each other. During this time Strauss wrote a series of operas with different collaborators (often with the unofficial aid of Zweig), none of which have held the stage and two of which, *Daphne* and *Die Liebe der Danae*, continued his fascination with Greek subjects.

His last opera, *Capriccio* (Munich 1942), completed in 1941 when he was 77 years old, is as equally removed from the horrors and destruction of WWII as was *Die Frau ohne Schatten* from WWI. Its subject, set once again in a tranquil and ordered past (18th-century France), dealt with the eternal question in opera—'the music or the words?' With a fine libretto by Clemens Krauss and a plot which involves a work within a work, it was a fitting and moving summation of Strauss's life in opera. Yet is was not to be his swan-song, for as he approached his eighties, Strauss turned seriously once again to other musical forms for the first time in 30 years. Although he had, like many other composers, composed songs throughout his creative life, Strauss crowned his career with a series of incandescent orchestral songs, presaged by his fine

Horn Concerto No. 2 of 1942, his Oboe Concerto of 1945 and the deeply-felt *Metamorphosen* for strings (1945), evolved from a 24-bar sketch he wrote after suffering what he perceived as the greatest disaster of his life—the bombing in April 1945 of the Munich Opera House. The work quickly assumed greater relevance, becoming Strauss's grieving for the destruction of an entire world within which he had existed and prospered. After that there was time and strength only for the autumnal *Vier letzte Lieder*, four songs (a fifth was left in sketch form only) dealing with valediction and approaching death, settings of poems by Hesse and Eichendorff. These achieved their 1950 première only after his own death in September 1949, at the age of 85.

DON'T MISS

▶ **Eine Alpensinfonie, Op. 64 (1911–15)**

▶ **Ariadne auf Naxos (1916)**

▶ **Capriccio (1942)**

▶ **Metamorphosen (1944–5)**

▶ **Vier letzte Lieder (1948)**

ALEXANDER GLAZUNOV
1865–1936

It may well be that now is not the ideal moment to assess Glazunov's achievements as a composer; at a time when most audiences demand an intensely subjective mode of expression from their favourite composers, **Glazunov rarely had such aims in mind. A man of great natural talent and an ability to employ it with deceptive ease, from the beginning he looked for balance, control and a concealment of the composer's craft.** Glazunov was born in St Petersburg at a time when the city was the centre of Russian artistic and musical endeavour, priding itself on its cultural sophistication. The son of comfortably-off middle class parents (his father was a publisher), by the age of nine

Alexander Glazunov

Glazunov had started piano and theory lessons, and soon showed that he had a natural aptitude for composition. This was nurtured by various private tutors until, in 1879, he met Balakirev, an enormously energetic and influential presence in Russian music at this time. Balakirev gave him a renewed sense of purpose and direction in his studies and introduced him to the 40-year-old Rimsky-Korsakov.

Glazunov and the music teacher Rimsky-Korsakov quickly developed a friendship, and before he was 16,

Glazunov had written a symphony which Rimsky-Korsakov and Balakirev ensured received its première in 1882. At the Free School concert in St Petersburg, Glazunov's music was listened to approvingly by the rich, cultured timber merchant Belayev, who proceeded to set up a publishing house expressly to propagate the works of the new Russian composers, especially Glazunov's. The patronage of such a distinguished group of men virtually guaranteed an audience for whatever music Glazunov composed, and his early efforts continued to receive

approbation. He also became involved with Rimsky-Korsakov in the completion of a number of Borodin's unfinished works after the composer's early death, especially the great opera *Prince Igor* and the Third Symphony. Glazunov was renowned for his ability to recall a piece of music once having heard it, and this enabled him to score sections of both works which Borodin had never committed to manuscript, but merely played to Glazunov shortly before his death.

Glazunov's early brilliance was universally acknowledged in his homeland; he even managed to appeal to practitioners on both sides of the great debate as to whether Russian music should draw on the Germanic or the native tradition for its model. The German-school conservative, Anton Rubinstein, was as happy to promote Glazunov's music as was Rimsky-Korsakov and Balakirev; as a result, within two years of the First Symphony's première, Glazunov's reputation had travelled west to Weimar, where in 1884, Franz Liszt gave its first German performance and spoke highly of the work. Glazunov himself conducted his Second Symphony (1886) in Paris in 1889.

His music quickly gained a foothold in most European countries, where his attention to matters of form and proportion in his music over those of subjective expression and self-glorification won him the respect of musicians and critics alike. During the 1890s he completed four more symphonies, the third to the sixth, before slowing his pace somewhat and turning his hand to works for the stage. One of his most popular compositions, the ballet *Raymonda*, was premièred in 1898 by the Imperial Theatre in Moscow; this has rarely left the repertoire of most Russian ballet companies since. Glazunov also pursued his interest in less formal structures initiated by his 1885 tone poem, *Stenka Razin,* with the two versions of the *Meditation,* for violin and piano or violin and orchestra from 1892.

In 1899 Glazunov scored another balletic success with *The Seasons,* in the same year joining the teaching staff of the St Petersburg Academy, where he was to remain until he left Russia for good in 1928. It is arguable that the following decade saw his creative powers at their peak, for during those years he completed his still popular Violin Concerto (1904) as well as the marvellous and curiously neglected suite *From the Middle Ages* (1902) in which he reveals both his concern to provide balance and colour in a work and to give a modern interpretation of old ideas. He also completed his outstanding two symphonies, No. 7 (1902) and No. 8 (1906), while a ninth was left unfinished. Smaller ensembles and soloists were catered for in 1899 by the magnificent Fifth String Quartet and the two Piano Sonatas, which stand as two of the greatest sonatas for the instrument by a Russian.

Glazunov's place among Russia's top composers seemed both apt and permanent, but in 1905 his very prominence and moderation proved a two-edged sword as violent student unrest at the Conservatory led to the gradual ousting of the old guard on the board and the appointment of Glazunov as Director. His administrative workload soared dramatically while his teaching

duties were hardly lighter than before. This resulted in the inevitable diminution of his creative energy and output, and in the following decade few works of great worth appeared. It was a critical time for Russian music as the younger men such as Stravinsky and Scriabin made their mark, and the hardworking Glazunov slowly found that he was being eased from the limelight by more spectacular music. He remained a great favourite with his students, who were well aware of his fondness for an occasional vodka or two as well as his tremendous powers of analysis and experience at dealing with composing and theory problems. Among his admirers in these years was the young Shostakovich, who would retain his affection for the older man's music and personality for life.

The 1917 Revolution distressed Glazunov as much as it did the majority of Russians, and he withdrew into his own world as the old order was dismantled around him. Increasingly dependent on alcohol, he composed progressively less music, and although in 1922 he was made People's Artist of the Republic in recognition of his four decades of composition, he refused the honours which went with the title, requesting instead that the Conservatory be granted fuel to heat it during the bitter winters. Glazunov's

disaffection grew to the extent that, when he attended the Schubert Centenary celebrations in Vienna as an official Soviet delegate, he opted not to return to what had now become Leningrad. In an effort to accommodate him and not lose their People's Artist, the Soviet government allowed him a role amounting to that of an informal roving ambassador of Russian music, but by 1930 Glazunov had settled in Paris (by then the major centre for Russian emigrés) and resigned his post at the Leningrad Conservatory.

This did not resolve his personal dilemmas, nor did it result in a last great outburst of creativity, although the Saxophone Concerto was completed in 1934, together with a Saxophone Quartet in 1930 and the final String Quartet, No. 7, in the same year. Glazunov was sufficiently secure financially to take up a peripatetic lifestyle, travelling to many countries in order to conduct his own works and that of other composers, but his last years were rarely happy. Since his death in 1936, Glazunov's reputation has never revived to its earlier level, though as that period of musical history assumes a less subjective and distorted shape, the virtues of his well-made and often inspired music will lead to a more balanced assessment.

DON'T MISS

▶ **Meditation, Op. 32**
▶ **The Seasons, Op. 87 (1899)**
▶ **Symphony No. 7 (Pastoral'naya), Op. 77 (1902)**
▶ **From the Middle Ages, Op. 79 (1903)**
▶ **Violin Concerto, Op. 82 (1904)**

CARL NIELSEN
1865-1931

Though he took longer than most to find his individual voice as a composer, Nielsen latterly became a towering figure in Danish culture, dominating both musical life and thought as his principles and ideas were expressed ever more authoritatively through his powerful cycle of six symphonies.

Carl Nielsen came from a peasant family living in the village of Nørre Lyndelse, on the Danish island of Fyn; he was one of 10 children. His early interest in music was fostered by his father, who taught him rudimentary violin. Interested in the music of the local military bands, Carl chose the trumpet as his instrument and played in the local band. A meeting with light music composer Olfert Jesperson helped focus his ambition on music, and his proficieny as a violinist gave him sufficient insight into stringed instruments to write some juvenilia for string quartet in the early 1880s. A similar grasp of the piano is also demonstrated by an unfinished piano sonata from the same period.

In 1884 his undoubted ability gained him a place at the Royal Conservatorium in Copenhagen, where he studied for four years. In 1885 he won a subsidy which enabled him to travel around the major European centres of culture, meeting his future wife, Anne Marie Broderson (a Danish sculptress), in Paris. At the end of this period he began work on a symphony in F (the opening movement was eventually transformed into the *Symphonic Rhapsody* of 1888), but his first notable orchestral work was the *Little Suite*, Op. 1 for strings (1888), in which he developed an essentially conservative style fostered by the Conservatorium's Niels Gade, but leavened with his own musical concerns—folk melodies, motivic melodic development and clarity of structure. This style, which was broadly in sympathy with the Romantic tradition of Brahms and composers such as Grieg and Johan Svendsen, informed all his music until shortly before WWI.

From 1889 to 1905 Nielsen was a member of the Royal Theatre Orchestra. During this time the major compositional achievements were his first two symphonies. The First Symphony, Op. 7 (1890–92), built on the foundations established by Brahms and Dvořák, is a thoroughly engaging work, written when the composer was in his late twenties and full of the optimism of youth. The work was premièred in 1894, with Nielsen conducting. The Second Symphony, Op. 16, subtitled *The Four Temperaments*, confirmed his Danish reputation as the foremost young composer of the day and would eventually help establish his name internationally. It is a major step forward from the first work, being more finely crafted and more imaginatively conceived. It is based on an idea Nielsen had after visiting a village pub which had paintings of the four temperaments of man in the bar-room. There is a strong undercurrent of self-identification in the work, especially in the two central movements depicting, according to the composer, firstly "a young fellow...with sky-blue eyes, confident and big...everything idyllic and heavenly in nature", and secondly "a heavy, melancholy man".

Between the second and third symphonies the outward circumstances of Nielsen's life changed: he achieved a successful première of his first opera, *Saul and David* in 1902, then began a superb programmatic work, the *Helios Overture*, while on holiday in Greece; 1906 brought the triumphant Copenhagen première of his light-hearted opera *Maskarade*, now regarded as the cornerstone of Danish national opera. Two years later he accepted the offer of the post of Musical Director for the Royal Opera, succeeding Svendsen. He retained this

DON'T MISS

▶ Symphony No. 2 (Four Temperaments), Op. 16 (1901–02)
▶ Maskarade (1908)
▶ Symphony No. 3 (Sinfonia espansiva), Op. 27 (1910–12)
▶ Symphony No. 4 (Inextinguishable), Op. 29 (1914–16)

position until 1914 when he resigned, wishing more than ever to devote his time to composing. He had managed to complete both the tone poem *Saga-drøm* (1907–08) and the Third Symphony, Op. 27 between 1910 and 1911, and it received a successful launch that year. This work showed his now complete mastery of form, individual melodic shapes and the clear orchestration which was to be at the core of his own special symphonic and orchestral identity, one which was closely allied to the Danish temperament and spirituality. The sub-title for this work is *Sinfonia espansiva*, and certainly there is a deal of intellectual, rather than emotional, inquiry and growth at the core of the work's character.

In 1915 he became musical director of the Copenhagen Music Society, a job which gave him more free time and even the opportunity to travel abroad for guest conducting appearances. The onset of WWI brought about a radical change in Nielsen's musical horizons and ambitions. His next symphony, about which he was thinking deeply when the War began, was an attempt to express the elemental life-force, the will to live, which he felt was 'inextinguishable' in nature. This raw energy needed a darker, more savage musical language, which in itself was encouraged into being by the appalling slaughter committed by all sides in the most brutal war in living memory. Nielsen would find that this sparer, more ambivalent and disturbing musical language would suit his intellectual and emotional needs more exactly than the harmonic and timbral palette he was wont to use. Even in the much less intense follow-up work *Pan and Syrinx*

(1917–18), its concerns revolving around the Greek myths loved by Nielsen, the programme does not deflect Nielsen from pursuing his new language, written with great sensitivity and a transparent orchestral scoring.

Sensitivity is also a keynote in the superbly evocative Suite, Op. 45 of piano pieces written in 1919–20, originally called *Den Luciferiske*, after Lucifer, the 'bringer of light' of Greek mythology. The six pieces which comprise the suite are admirably interrelated on many levels, not least emotionally, as a complex web of feelings and ambivalences become established and the listener is transported through the many transitory and illusory states Nielsen is relaying through the piano. The cohesion and intensity of this music is in direct contrast to the colourful but essentially playful incidental music written in 1918–19 for the 'exotic' five-act play *Aladdin* extracted from *The Arabian Nights* and rendered in Danish.

Nielsen's Fifth Symphony, Op. 50, composed between 1921 and 1922, is in many ways his most impressive and accomplished; it is certainly the work which did most to establish his international reputation. Its structure is a brilliant masterstroke by Nielsen; divided into just two movements, the symphony presents a mortal battle between order and brutal chaos, represented largely by strings (order) and drums (chaos). The music is immediately arresting, the drama of the struggle completely absorbing, but the work repays a detailed examination in terms of how Nielsen uses and reinterprets his material to give the work overall unity.

DON'T MISS

▶ **Wind Quintet, Op. 43 (1922)**

▶ **Symphony No. 6 (Semplice) (1924–25)**

▶ **Clarinet Concerto, Op. 57 (1928)**

The year 1924 to 1925 was spent mainly working on his Sixth (and last) symphony, tentatively called *Sinfonia Semplice*, although despite Nielsen's statement to his daughter that this time he would write a simple piece which would be 'completely idyllic', the work which emerged was anything but that. Cryptic, at times enigmatic, full of careful and subtle underminings of what at first seem straightforward musical ideas, the symphony which starts as a radiant and almost blissful statement becomes nervous, disquietened, even its humoresque section shot through with raucous uncertainties. By the end a sense of desolation has been exposed and remains unforgettable long after the music has ceased. Now in his late sixties, it is as if Nielsen had a foretaste of what was in store for him, for in 1926 he suffered the first of a series of heart attacks which were to rob him of vitality and finally kill him.

Yet Nielsen would complete two beautifully written Wind Concertos, his Flute Concerto of 1926 and Clarinet Concerto of 1928, both of them full of great intellectual suppleness and resource, revealing common ground between various schools of Classical music and Danish folk music, in particular in the realm of rhythm and melodic shape. Nielsen's pace of life slowed as the 1920s ended and the next decade began: he was already laden with honours, including a Danish knighthood. In 1931, in his 76th year, came the final heart attack, but by then his place in 20th-century European music had long been assured.

JEAN SIBELIUS

1865–1957

Prior to Sibelius, Finnish Classical music had made little impression internationally. By his sheer talent and through his fierce national pride and interest in his country's history, myths and culture, Sibelius brought to the world a considerable musical portrait of Finland.

Sibelius was born in Hämeenlinna, a few months later than the other great Scandinavian composer, Carl Nielsen. In 1809 Finland had been incorporated into the Tsarist Russian empire as a separate Grand Duchy, administered for the most part by the Swedes; for much of the 19th century a groundswell of nationalism grew apace until, by the time Sibelius reached manhood, it was the burning issue of the day.

Sibelius was born into a middle-class family, his father being the local doctor. Before he was three years old, Jean's father died in a cholera epidemic, and from then on was brought up by his mother and grandmother. At the age of eight Jean began piano studies, but soon decided in favour of the violin. A career as a violin virtuoso became his aim and throughout his adolescence he wrote prolifically for the instrument, mainly in chamber combinations. As a student at

Jean Sibelius

the Finnish Model Lyceum, Sibelius became aware of his need for formal music theory and took private lessons. At the age of 19 he entered Helsinki University as a law student, but after a year changed to music, later joining the Helsinki Institute of Music where one of his teachers was the composer virtuoso Ferruccio Busoni, a man with whom Sibelius was to enjoy a lasting friendship. While at the Institute his song 'Serenad', Op. 1, was published; songs would be a regular part of his output up until the last years of WWI. In 1889 he moved to Berlin to study counterpoint with Albert Becker, from there going to Vienna where studies with Goldmark and Robert Fuchs completed his education. He returned to Finland in 1891 and was immediately swept up in the fervour of nationalism. After studying the national epic, the *Kalevala*, and researching the traditions, legends and history of Finland, he commenced work on the symphonic poem *Kullervo*, Op. 7, for soloists, chorus and orchestra. This five-part work of epic proportions (it runs for over an hour) anticipates many 20th-century stylisitc devices with its use of *ostinato* rhythms, dramatic textural changes and coarse-grained mixing of instrumental sections, as well as short, insistent motifs. He also incorporated folk melody practices demonstrated to him by Finnish rune-singers upholding the oral traditions.

Kullervo achieved five performances in its first year, but then Sibelius abruptly withdrew permission for any further performances, only bringing it back into circulation in the early 1920s to meet a personal financial crisis. Despite *Kullervo*'s fate, for the rest of the 1890s Sibelius continued to work the seam of patriotic music to be played by large forces, supplying *En Saga,* Op. 9, two pieces called *Karelia*—an Overture, Op. 10 and a Suite, Op. 11 in 1893, and the *Four Lemminkäinen Legends,* Op. 22 in 1896. This consistent and impressive level of output masks a failure on the operatic front, for in 1893 Sibelius had begun work on a section of the *Kalevala* which he called *Veneen luominen*, driven by the belief (inherited

from Liszt, Berlioz and Wagner in particular) that 'music can only realize its full potential when directed by poetic ends'. A visit to a Munich production of Wagner's *Tristan* in 1894 left Sibelius's confidence in tatters, and the operatic project was abandoned. His private life, however, was proving to be more successful than his creative one, for he married Aino Järnfelt, daughter of a conductor, and became a composition teacher at Helsinki Music Institute in the same year. This post gave him financial stability until a government grant in 1897 allowed him to concentrate full-time on composing.

By 1899 the first fruits of this freedom appeared: the tone-poem *Finlandia*, Op. 26, which was to make his name throughout Europe. This was followed in the same year by his First Symphony in E minor, Op. 39, which was successful in both Finland and London. This was the beginning of his substantial English reputation, for which the reasons are not hard to find, his appreciation of models such as Tchaikovsky, Berlioz and Borodin evident in his compositional technique and construction, and even in some instances in his choice of orchestral sonorities. Encouraged by the success of the First Symphony, Sibelius completed his Second Symphony in D, Op. 43 and conducted its Helsinki première in 1902. This première was an event of national importance, demonstrating Sibelius's pre-eminent position in Finnish music. The increasing sophistication of his design and technique showed in the opening movement, a standard sonata form disguised by the elements Sibelius used and his unusual treatment of them in different sections of the movement. By

DON'T MISS

▶ Karelia Suite, Op. 11 (1893)

▶ Finlandia, Op. 26 (1899)

▶ Symphony No. 2, Op. 43 (1901)

▶ Valse triste, Op. 44/1 (1903)

▶ Violin Concerto, Op. 47 (1903-05)

now nearly forty, Sibelius was approaching not only complete mastery of the symphonic form, but also a long-awaited maturity of individual symphonic expression, giving him an instantly recognizable style and sound.

This made the timing of his next major composition, the Violin Concerto in D minor, Op. 47, absolutely perfect; first conceived in late 1902, it was worked on intermittently during 1903 with the intention that its original inspirer, the virtuoso Willy Burmester, would première it in Berlin in March 1904. However, Sibelius's unfortunate habit of amassing debts led to a financial crisis in late 1903 which in turn led to a poor and hurried première of the Concerto in Helsinki in February 1903 in the pursuit of some ready cash. A muted reception and Sibelius's own doubts led to its withdrawal; he did not rewrite it properly until the summer of 1905, when its final form was revealed. This is the version used by players to this day, although the original has recently been made available for study. The summer of 1904, however, was most notable for the triumph of his *Valse Triste,* Op. 44, originally conceived as part of some incidental music for the play *Kuolema* (Death) by his brother-in-law, but finally the only piece from it to achieve publication. Although not quintessential Sibelius, it has been massively popular ever since its Helsinki première.

The mid-1900s were a time of stylstic change for Sibelius, beginning with his retirement to the little town of Järvenpää, not far from Helsinki, and his concentration on more individual concerns. The symphonic fantasy *Pohjola's Daughter*, Op. 49 (1906), may have been inspired by the *Kalevala*, but it was moving from the programmatic to the symphonic, and by the time his Third Symphony in C, Op. 52 was completed in 1907, after three years of struggle, the transition had been safely accomplished. This work reveals a man not attempting to describe the universe in one work or to contain the entire history of his native land in a series of movements. His aim is more precise but at the same time more Apollonian: he is creating a work of balance, logic and clear proportions, written in an idiom which has become more personal, more emotionally contained, where the fire is not mellower but more finely applied.

Between the Third and Fourth Symphonies he produced his sole contribution to the string quartet genre, entitled *Voces Intimae* in D minor, Op. 58 (1909). He also experienced a serious illness which required hospitalization and a series of painful operations; for a time it seemed that Sibelius had contracted throat cancer (as a lifelong smoker and a long-term heavy drinker, this first physical collapse was perhaps overdue), and a cloud hung over the bare fact of existence for some considerable time afterwards. Under these circumstances it is not surprising to find in *Voces Intimae* an intimate communion with darker feelings and a modernity of expression not often encountered in Sibelius. It is a work from the soul of its author, and anticipates the inner depth and beauty at the core of the Fourth Symphony in A minor, Op. 62 (1911). This enigmatic work makes great use of such elements as the Lydian scale, the augmented fourth, even the diminished second, and a sparseness and clarity of scoring which is a world away from the congestion of late Romantic scores elsewhere. The two tone poems, *The Bard*, Op. 64 and *Luonnotar*, Op. 70 which followed this work, though different in aim, have a similar aura and working practice.

Prior to WWI Sibelius travelled extensively within Europe, appearing in many cities as guest conductor, and in 1912 Vienna offered him a position in the Imperial Academy, while Yale University bestowed on him an honorary doctorate during his visit to America. With the outbreak of war Sibelius found his pattern of life utterly disrupted: he was unable to travel or to accept overseas conducting offers, and it also froze his income from publishers' royalties in his main markets. Unused to financial abstinence, Sibelius quickly reached a point where he needed to generate income quickly, so work on the Fifth Symphony was interspersed with bouts of piano compositions suitable for domestic use, which had the advantage of generating quick income from sources within Finland. The Fifth Symphony in E-flat, Op. 82, was completed by 1915 and contained music which, for Sibelius, was remarkably optimistic, summarized by the famous brass fanfare which brings the last movement to its inexorable climax. The work was given at his fiftieth birthday celebrations in December of that year.

Following the Russian Revolution Finland declared its independence, but in the subsequent Russo/Finnish civil war, Sibelius—whose sentiments were on the side of the nationalists and the Russian White Guard—had to flee his home when it came under attack from the Bolsheviks. In 1918 he composed a patriotic choral work, *Oma Maa* (Homeland) Op. 92, set to an openly nationalistic text. It held a special place for the composer, who felt that it was in essence "a song of praise to nature and the white nights of Finland".

The Sixth Symphony in D minor, Op. 104 (1923), furthered Sibelius's increasingly subjective approach to his music. A remarkably restrained work considering the political climate in which it was conceived, it falls back on the traditional four-movement structure and makes intensive use of

---

DON'T MISS

▶ String Quartet (Voces intimae), Op. 56 (1908–09)
▶ Symphony No. 4, Op. 63 (1911)
▶ Symphony No. 5, Op. 82 (1915)
▶ Symphony No. 7, Op. 105 (1926)

---

polyphony to establish the fluency and flow of music which had become increasingly central to Sibelius's aesthetic as he approached his sixtieth year. This process became even more apparent in the Seventh Symphony in C, Op. 105. A quick check on the opus numbers of these two towering works reveals Sibelius's lack of interest in pursuing other compositional ends at this stage, and of his progressive slowing-down on the creative front. Neither work is particularly long, and the Seventh Symphony, although nominally given a number of tempo assignations which may suggest a number of movements, is in fact a one-movement work. The composer makes no pretence that any attempt has been made to follow conventional symphonic form, which no longer interests him.

Instead the listener is presented with a miraculously unified and flowing series of organically evolving segments and episodes in which concision is at a premium.

After these mighty achievements Sibelius had little more music to offer. In 1926 one more musical evocation of the world of *Kalevala* appeared, the tone poem *Tapiola*, Op. 112, which is a miracle of disciplined creativity, all the music in the score emanating from just one melodic fragment. After this and some further incidental music for dramas, Sibelius decided to hold his peace. Increasingly revered internationally and now entering his seventh decade, Sibelius had always been mercilessly self-critical and prepared to withdraw or destroy

works he deemed sub-standard. We can only speculate as to the shape of the Eighth Symphony which was completed prior to 1930 but subsequently destroyed by the composer in the 1940s while he was suffering a debilitating bout of self-criticism and depression.

Sibelius lived into his nineties and for the most part enjoyed a full and justly celebrated old age, but there was no more new music to emerge, although the occasional older manuscript was allowed to appear. He died of a cerebral haemorrhage, his reputation as one of the supreme symphonists of any age secure, while the nationalistic works of his earlier years continue to give delight and sustenance to listeners of every country.

ERIK SATIE

1866–1925

There is no doubt that for the first 50 years of his life, Erik Satie was somewhat undervalued as a composer and musical thinker. There is equally little doubt that for his last 10 years and during the subsequent revival of his music, his achievement and influence has been considerably overestimated.

Satie was born the son of a Scottish mother and a Norman shipping broker in the Channel port of Honfleur. An early interest in music was encouraged by the local organist, who introduced the boy to an unusually wide range of

musical history, including plainsong. When his family moved to Paris in 1879 Erik was accepted at the Paris Conservatoire. However, his years there were unhappy and unproductive, with Satie continually at loggerheads with the institutionalized approach to musical education that dominated every lesson. He was perceived as a not very gifted student and allowed to drift away. By his twentieth birthday he was earning a living by night playing in Parisian clubs and cabarets in order to finance his daylight hours spent creating his first piano works. After a brief period in the army fulfilling his national service duties, Satie engrossed

himself in further studies of Gregorian modes and plainchant and became increasingly involved in Catholic mysticism; his piano pieces of 1887 and 1888, the *Three Sarabandes* and *Three Gymnopédies*, reflect the results of his intense study. Both sets run counter to all prevailing pianistic tastes of the day; studies in harmonic stasis, they are of an extreme and delicate melodic and rhythmic simplicity.

After laying such promising foundations for his career, Satie showed the limitations of his compositional technique by following these works with a series of pedestrian

Erik Satie

Now at one remove from fashionable society, Satie for the most part restricted himself to short piano pieces which began to illuminate the other, more garrulous side of his divided personality. After a time at the Schola Cantorum studying with d'Indy and Roussel in order to overcome some of the compositional inadequacies which restricted his range, Satie become much more adventurous in his piano pieces. By the early 1920s he was writing a stream of eccentric and wild-eyed, often tongue-in-cheek pieces which amply demonstrated the distance between himself and Debussy by this stage. The *Préludes flasques* poked fun at so many targets that it became a forerunner of the Dadaists and Surrealists of a later generation. Similarly, *Descriptions automatiques* (1913) are deliberate distortions and desecrations of Classical form and practice hidden in innocuous nursery rhyme melodies. The *Embryons desséchés* (1923) serve a similar absurdist—and very mischievous—function.

It was his association wih Ravel, Cocteau and the younger generation during the war years, as well as his increased confidence in his own ability to compose for more than just piano, which led to the late blossoming of Satie's career. By the closing years of WWI he felt able to cope with extended forms such as ballet and his own individual version of the cantata form. Encouraged by the younger artists and musicians gathering around the flag of reform and the goad of Dadaism, Satie produced his one balletic masterpiece, the suite *Parade*, in 1917, brought to the stage by Diaghilev's Ballets Russe and immoderately applauded by the smart set intent on burying the pre-war aesthetic. Satie was uneasy about the

songs and a sequence of portentous piano works inspired by the confused mysticism of the Rose + Croix Temple presided over by Joséphin Péladan, a self-styled guru and man of letters whose literary incompetence was matched only by his intellectual pretensions. Satie soon became disaffected with the aims of Péladan's group, and although he continued to create medievally-inspired music until the mid-1890s, he publicly disassociated himself from them, setting up his own private church instead and appointing himself its head. By this time he had met Claude Debussy in the cafés of Montmartre,

both men discovering much in common in their musical thinking. This encouraged them to think about formulating a specifically 'French' musical aesthetic. There is little doubt that Debussy was much the better equipped to carry this impulse to a point of realisation, but Satie's intellectual input is undeniable. At the close of the 1890s, as this querulous man's circle of friends was disintegrating and he felt the need for a change, Satie moved away from the bohemian ambience of Montmartre to the austere suburb of Arcueil-Cachan, where he inhabited a spartan apartment until his death.

role he was being asked to assume by his younger colleagues, and often quarreled with them, but the opportunities he was being given were impossible for an artist such as himself to resist. In 1918 he completed the cantata *Socrate*, a well-meaning but terminally dull vocal work stripped of all artifice and ornament but with little in its place to recommend it.

After the *Cinq Nocturnes* for piano of 1919, Satie avoided a wholly serious expression of his artistic psyche, preferring slapstick theatrical events such as the ballets *Relâche* (meaning 'cancelled') which includes a football

rattle as one of its more provocative instruments, and *Les Aventures de Mercure* (1924), a work which could have come from the pen of Offenbach, and whose sets for the première were designed by Picasso. These works, and his latter-day evolution of the idea of *Furniture Music* (music to be played as pure background, not to be listened to closely) decisively split the public and his peers into two camps, mostly divided by age difference, but by late 1924 Satie was too ill to compose any more or take an active part in the lively debates which such ideas were provoking. After a six month illness he died,

just one year short of sixty. His ideas, many of them still in embryo, were left to be worked out in the decades to come by other more formally well-equipped composers, who in turn would credit him as being their chief inspiration.

DON'T MISS

▶ **3 Gymnopédies (1888)**
▶ **6 Gnossiennes (1890–7)**
▶ **Avant-dernières pensées (1915)**
▶ **Parade (1917)**

ENRIQUE GRANADOS
1867–1916

Granados was one of the first Spanish composers of the modern day to establish an international reputation; as with de Falla and Albéniz, he achieved this largely by transferring to the piano the musical idioms which he often heard played on the guitar in his native region of Spain.

Granados was born in Lérida in northern Spain, the son of a Cuban father serving in the Spanish army and a mother whose roots were in the city of Santander. Enrique's musical talent surfaced early and he was given his first piano lessons by a local bandmaster. When the family moved to Barcelona, Enrique began studies with Francisco Jurnet and Juan Pujol. After

winning a competition, he took private lessons with Felipe Pedrell, supporting himself by playing in cafés and salons around Barcelona.

By 1887 he felt ready to move to Paris, hoping to attend the Conservatoire, but his hopes were dashed by a bout of ill health and he turned instead to private tuition. After two years in Paris he returned to Barcelona in 1889, contriving to make a living as a concert pianist. This success enabled him to marry and take up composing in between his performing duties. For the 1892 Olympics, which were held in Barcelona, he composed his *12 Danzas españolas*, Op. 37. Less Catalan in his outlook than his fellow-composer Albéniz, in this collection Granados was aiming at creating a Spanish style of

piano music in much the same way as other composers earlier in the century had created an identity for the music of countries such as Poland, Hungary and Bohemia. Each piece in the set had as its inspiration a style and rhythm particularly associated with a separate region in Spain; in this way Granados hoped to construct a composite picture of variety and charm, stressing the urbane and refined nature of what he portrayed. Soon after the *Danzas* appeared Granados offered for publication the *Seis piezas sobre cantos populares españoles*, where his innate gifts for elegant line and phrasing bring the best out of the chosen melodies.

These and other similar works helped establish Granados's national reputation amongst musicians, but a wider acceptance had to wait until 1898 when Granados's first *zarzuela*, called *Maria del Carmen*, was given a Madrid production and proved irresistible. This indigenous form of light Spanish opera had been in vogue locally for 30 years and it was important for a new composer to make his mark in this way. Granados achieved this although he was to prove less successful in all his other theatrical ventures. But Granados's first love remained the piano, and during the opening years of the 20th century he not only founded his own piano school

DON'T MISS

▶ 15 Tonadillas al estilio antiguo

▶ 7 Valses poéticos (1887)

▶ 12 Danzas españolas, Op. 37 (1892–1900)

▶ Allegro de concierto (1904)

▶ Goyescas (1911)

in Barcelona, the Academia Granados, but also created one of his most refined set of piano pieces, the *Escenas románticas*, six exquisitely crafted pieces using elements of the Catalan style but laden with romantic languor and expressivity.

In 1911 came the suite for piano which more than any other work has guaranteed the preservation of Granados's reputation—the *Goyescas*. Like every educated Spaniard, Granados was appreciative of the great paintings of Goya, and as he matured he became increasingly fascinated with the great man's life and circumstances. From this fascination sprang the idea to set a range of his own impressions of Goya and his times to music, centred around two of Goya's most famous paintings, the clothed Maja and the naked Maja, both portraits of the Duchess of Alba. Granados himself gave the début recital of this music in Barcelona, and it was immediately recognized as an important and in many ways definitive suite of

Spanish piano music, crystallizing many of the basics characteristics of Spain's emerging Classical style.

The fame of the work quickly spread overseas and by 1914 Granados had prepared an operatic treatment of the same material. The Paris production for that year, however, was cancelled due to the onset of war, and it was not until 1916 that the opera was brought to life on the stage of New York's Metropolitan Opera House. Granados, although aware of a long-term presentiment that he would die at sea, was in attendance with his wife, having crossed the Atlantic on an ocean liner. Although the work met with only a qualified success, the composer was optimistic for its long-term future. Tragically, there was little time left for him to pursue further musical romances for on the return journey, after having safely reached Folkestone, their ship was torpedoed in the English Channel by a German submarine, and both Granados and his wife perished at sea.

FRANZ LEHÁR
1870–1948

Although Johann Strauss may be a better-known composer of operetta, Lehár's *Merry Widow* is undoubtedly the most well-known operetta of all time, its songs today being part of everyday life, long since detached from their original settings. In this sense at least, Lehár is one of the best-loved and most successful of all composers.

Lehár's family history is as typical a product of the Austro-Hungarian empire as is the music of his operettas prior to the Empire's dissolution in the carnage of WWI. Franz was born in Komárom in Hungary, into the family of a bandmaster in the Imperial Austrian Army. His father's family had roots in a part of Austria later swallowed up by Czechoslovakia, but his affair with a local Hungarian girl while billeted in

Komáron resulted in his son's Hungaro-Czech legacy—a legacy which he would make much of in his composing career.

Franz spent his early childhood on the move, the family trailing after his father's regiment, and his first 12 years were as polyglot as his genes. Some degree of stability was achieved in 1882 when he won a scholarship which allowed him to study at Prague's Music

Academy. During a stay of six years he became a highly accomplished violinist and made appreciable strides as a composer, completing a violin concertino which, although not particularly original, showed his hallmarks of grace and balance. His work attracted the attention and praise of both Dvořák and Brahms.

Lehár progressed to being first violin (later leader) of Elberfeld's municipal orchestra, a position he retained for a year before deciding to follow his father's example and become a military musician. Stationed in Hungary as a military bandmaster—the youngest-ever in the Austrian Army—he not only became widely experienced in the complex sonorities of every type of woodwind and brass combination, but he became increasingly convinced that the way forward was through composition. An opera, *Kukuschka,* was completed in the early 1890s, and Lehár found a publisher for it, followed by an acceptance for production in Leipzig. Following these key events in place, Lehár resigned his military commission and embraced the insecurities of being a full-time composer. *Kukuschka* was produced in Leipzig in 1896, and later in Budapest, but although it gained respectable results, by the beginning of the new century Lehár's interest in serious opera had waned.

A move to Vienna and a shift in emphasis brought him two modest successes with *Wiener Frauen* (Theater an der Wien, Vienna 1900) and *Der Rastelbinder* (Vienna 1902), which he followed with a production in Brünn of *Tatyana* (February 1905), which in reality was a reworking of *Kukuschka*.

Franz Lehár

During the previous year, however, Lehár had begun work with two librettists, Victor Léon and Leo Stein, on their own adaptation of Henri Mehilac's successful play from the 1860s, *L'Attaché d'ambassade*, into an operetta. Léon and Stein were experienced writers, having created the words for Johann Strauss's *Wiener Blut*, among other works, and after initial hesitancy, they opted for Lehár to write the music for *The Merry Widow*, much against the wishes of the management at Theater an der Wien.

What Lehár brought to this new venture was the desire and ability to go beyond normal operetta conventions when it

came to the size of the orchestra, the brilliance and precision of the scoring and the unending succession of dance numbers, set pieces and superbly pacy solos and duets. Lehár's choice of rhythms shows great judgement and taste, ranging from mazurkas, can-cans and gallops to the *valse lente* and even a selection of marches, each chosen to suit particular characters or dramatic situations. Thus the unusually fully-developed characters at the heart of the work—Hanna, Danilo and Baron Zeta—are given every possible opportunity to shine onstage and through the music. The other quality (also very much to the fore in the other sensation of 1905, Strauss's *Salome*) which sealed the

Widow's happy fate was the unaffected eroticism in the relationships between the principals, an eroticism which is considerably less strident than *Salome*'s, but present nevertheless. The Vienna première on New Year's Eve, 1905, was a success but not sensational, and it took a few weeks before the work really took off. Since then, *The Merry Widow* has never been out of production at least somewhere in the world. Strauss's most famous librettist, Hugo von Hofmannsthal, once remarked apropos of the *Widow* that *Der Rosenkavalier* would have been 'a really good opera' if Lehár had written the music!

Lehár responded to this success by producing a string of fine works with diverse subjects, though all of them revolved around love and intrigue. *Der Mann mit den drei Frauen* appeared in January 1908, then in late 1909 Lehár, in a burst of creativity almost unparalleled even in the fecund operetta world, had three new works staged in Vienna within three months: *Das Fürstenkind* (1909), *Der Graf von Luxembourg* (1909) and *Zigeunerliebe* (1910). Of these three it is *Der Graf* which has lasted with the public, it being the closest to the spirit and style of its distinguished predecessor. A return to more serious subjects, although still couched entirely within the now well-established Lehár

operetta tradition, was evident in *Eva* (1911). This continued the composer's remarkable run of success with both critics and public, and it tempted Lehár to think that he could take more chances. Thus an injudicious reworking of an older operetta, reaching the stage in 1913 as *Das Ideal Frau*, was a relative failure, and his last new work prior to WWI, *Endlich Allein* (1914) not only attracted a mixed reception but for the first time found Lehár accused of aspirations beyond operetta's ken. In the work he had devoted an entire act to a love duet between two singers, and this was regarded as ridiculous. Lehár demurred, but the operetta has rarely been sighted since. However, the composer felt little need for worry; he had recently married his Jewish fiancée Sophie, and together they had bought a beautiful villa in the Austrian resort of Bad Ischl, a location which took Lehár away from the small everyday concerns and battles of Viennese life.

WWI was a bad time for Lehár as it was for Vienna and Austria in general, and his new productions, hardly his greatest works, were given scant attention. Something of a return to form was evident in *Die Blaue Mazur* (1920), given as part of Lehár's fiftieth birthday celebrations and warmly received in the Austrian capital, but it seemed that Lehár was to be consigned to a distant past symbolized by the *Widow*. The means by which the composer escaped this fate were fortuitous, but he made the best of the chance meeting which in 1921 led the great tenor Richard Tauber to hear some melodies from the operetta *Frasquita* while Lehár was still writing it. Tauber's wholehearted endorsement of them led to his taking the lead role in *Frasquita*'s first

production (1922), and then forming a musical partnership with Lehár which was rare in its quality and longevity. From that time on Lehár wrote every new work to fit the exact characteristics of Tauber's voice, looks and stage personality, and Tauber was always given a special song to deliver at a key moment. These often became massive hits when recorded separately by Tauber, and took on a life of their own. After *Die Gelbe Jacke* (1923) and *Clo-Clo* (1924) (works already under way at the time of *Frasquita*'s première) were out of the way, both Lehár and Tauber made a major hit in German-speaking countries with *Paganini* (1925), which included the great aria 'Gern hab' ich die Frau'n geküsst', a sentiment not commonly associated with the great Italian composer and virtuoso.

A new Tauber-related success came Lehár's way every year between 1927 and 1930, *Der Zarewitsch* appearing in 1927, *Friedericke* in 1928, *Das Land des Lächelns* (The Land of Smiles) in 1929 and *Schön is die Welt* (another revision, this time of *Endlich Allein*) in 1930. Of these *The Land of Smiles* was undoubtedly the most popular, and remains the one Lehár operetta apart from *The Merry Widow* to enjoy regular revivals outside of German-speaking countries. However, the world around Lehár was changing quickly, even if his music was not. His last work—ironically an opera with a serious subject which carried Tauber's enthusiastic backing—was *Giuditta*, which saw its successful première in Vienna in January 1934. After this and for the final 14 years of his life he would maintain an artistic silence.

The year before had seen the rise to power in Germany of Adolf Hitler, and not long after *Giuditta*'s first night came the assassination of the Austrian Chancellor, Arnold Dollfuss. With the installation of a regime sympathetic to the Nazis, the cultural and political climate in Austria rapidly changed, with many prominent people, Richard Tauber among them, finding themselves suddenly not only out of favour, but under threat. Lehár himself experienced a period of intense personal upset,

involving both vexatious litigation and blackmail (the latter because of his inability to confine his libido to his wife). With the Anschluss of 1938, Lehár took himself and his wife permanently to Bad Ischl, and when the War came they kept out of the way and (they hoped) out of danger in their country retreat. They reckoned without the Gestapo, who decided that Lehár's wife Sophie had to be dealt with, and arrested her at the villa. Lehár's name and his subsequent

influence with the local Nazi gauleiters enabled him to repel this attempt, and the two elderly people survived the War, finally being 'liberated' by American troops. Sophie, however, had not long to live, dying after an illness in the bitter winter of 1947. Lehár, staggered by this blow and the subsequent loss in early 1948 of his friend Richard Tauber, succumbed to ailments associated with old age at his Bad Ischl villa in October 1948.

ALEXANDER ZEMLINSKY

1871–1942

Like Mahler, Zemlinsky was one of the great Austrian conductors of his generation and as well as a composer; similarly, he had to wait a long time for his compositions to be taken seriously, even though they included fine symphonies, operas and a substantial body of *lieder*.

Zemlinsky was born in Vienna and studied at the Conservatory between 1887 and 1892. His first musical inclinations were towards Brahms rather than Wagner, and as such he had a considerable influence on the musical developments of the early part of the 20th century since his brother-in-law, Arnold Schoenberg, held him and his views on music in great esteem. Schoenberg's own sincere appreciation of Brahms grew from this.

Encouraged by Brahms in his formative years, in 1893 Zemlinsky joined the

Society of Composers and his early works (mostly chamber in character) began to be performed. Before the 1890s were over Zemlinsky had moved on to larger forms, and his second opera, *Es war einmal,* was given by Mahler at the Vienna Hofoper in 1900. Zemlinsky's late-Romantic style would have appealed greatly to Mahler, who was grappling with many of the same musical questions as his colleague, although the subjects tackled by the two men in their symphonic and operatic works were a world apart, Mahler sticking to the high moral and philosophical ground, while Zemlinsky was willing to investigate both the murkier and more trivial aspects of mankind. His next opera, *Die Traumgörge* (1904) coincided with his appointment as opera conductor at the Vienna Volksoper, and with this appointment his extraordinary career as a conductor was launched. In this role Zemlinsky was a tireless advocate of

those composers whose music he admired. There is little doubt that this fact, as well as his historical position as a composer whose late-Romantic style was quickly overtaken by Strauss, Stravinsky, Schoenberg and his acolytes as the 20th century got under way, accounted for the obscurity which latterly engulfed his own music. Yet in 1911 he could produce a sparkling light operatic comedy with a serious undertow such as *Kleider machen Leute*, and be met with almost universal praise.

Zemlinsky's works include four outstanding string quartets written between 1896 and 1936, six operas and a series of vocal orchestral works, while his body of *lieder* are some of the most perfect representations of this form to be completed this century. One of his earliest successful orchestral pieces was *Die Seejungfrau* of 1903. His most strenuous efforts, however, lay in the direction of opera, and with the 1917 production of his setting of Oscar Wilde's *Eine Florentinische Tragödie*, it seemed as if his time as a composer had finally come. Critically acclaimed, it was performed often during the war years, but with the advent of peace and the gradual establishment of a different operatic aesthetic, the work dropped from the repertoire. A similar fate awaited Zemlinsky's next Wilde operatic setting (and last opera), *Der Geburtstag der Infantin* (also known as *Der Zwerg*), a one-act opera of great power and emotional depth. While it gathered praise and repeated performances in Austria and Germany during the 1920s, by the time Hitler's banning of his work had been nullified by WWII, Zemlinsky

DON'T MISS

▶ Die Seejungfrau (1903)
▶ Ein Florentinische Tragödie, Op. 16 (1917)
▶ Der Zwerg, Op. 17 (1922)
▶ Lyric Symphony, Op. 18 (1923)
▶ Symphonische Gesänge, Op. 20 (1929)

was first exiled and then dead, his work in obscurity and his compositional style regarded as hopelessly *passé*. It has taken until the 1980s for his work to be reassessed, given a proper context and recognized for the superior creation it undoubtedly is.

This is equally true of the masterpieces away from the stage, especially the rhapsodic and powerfully effective *Lyric Symphony* (1922-23), which interwove vocal lines from both soprano and baritone with luminescent passages from the orchestra which proved perfectly apposite for the sensual yet spiritual poetry of Rabindranath Tagore which Zemlinsky chose to illuminate by his musical settings. In this he was reaching back to Mahler's example in *Das Lied von der Erde*, yet the musical langauge, as well as the emotional and philosophical environment, were completely his own.

By 1927 Zemlinsky had moved from Prague (where he had lived since 1911), to Berlin, where he continued his conducting career at the Kroll Theatre and taught at the Berlin Hochschule für Musik, composing the *Symphonic Songs*

there in 1929, a short selection of pieces set to texts from a German translation of a book of Harlem Renaissance poets. By 1933 Zemlinsky, a Jew, was fleeing from the Nazis, returning to Vienna to conduct and compose. His *Sinfonietta* dates from these years, as does the last string quartet and his moving setting of Psalm 13. But he was living and conducting under a gathering cloud, and shortly before the Anschluss occurred, he removed himself and his family to America. There he eked out a living as a conductor, but his compositions were virtually forgotten. By the time of his death at the age of 71 he had sunk into what seemed like irrevocable obscurity. Only in the aftermath of the Mahler revival, and a general raising of public interest in the Viennese artistic milieu of the early 20th century, has his always beautifully crafted, sincere and resonant music been recovered from its undeserved oblivion—from the operas right through to the songs and chamber music. No longer is it necessary to see him only as a transition figure between Mahler and Berg; he can now be judged on his own aesthetic terms.

ALEXANDER SCRIABIN
1872-1915

Whether genius or madman, the Russian mystic and composer Scriabin created a kaleidoscopic series of ecstatic orchestral and piano works whose power and significance continue to resonate in the history of this century's music and artistic endeavours.

Scriabin was born into a Moscow diplomat's family, his mother dying within a short time of his birth. His education included piano lessons which soon confirmed an unusual talent; during his boyhood and adolescence he continued his musical studies privately with the composer Taneyev. At the age

of 14 he wrote his first piano sonata, although it waited until 1892 for publication. An Etude in C sharp minor dates from 1887. His lessons with Taneyev helped him gain entry to the Moscow Conservatoire in 1888, where he was under Safonov for piano and Arensky for composition. In his first year at the Conservatoire he completed his *10 Mazurkas,* Op. 3 (1889), combining Chopin's pianistic language with his own essentially Russian darkness and fire.

Like Robert Schumann, Scriabin suffered an injury caused by over-zealous practising in pursuit of a flawless technique. This led to a new approach to keyboard writing (for a time he composed pieces for left hand only). Due to a clash with Arensky, he left the Conservatoire without the requisite composing diploma, but this did not hinder his plunge into a career as a concert pianist. At his graduation recital for the piano class, he played Beethoven's Sonata, Op. 109, an unusual choice for that time, but typical of him, considering the intensity and difficulty of the music; he won the gold medal. He now needed a repertoire of his own to play, and within a short time some very considerable piano music appeared, including *2 Impromptus,* Op. 7 (1892) and the *12 Etudes,* Op. 8 (1894). These works show a significant development away from the rich romanticism of Chopin, although many of them display fierce technical difficulties on a par with Chopin's, combining a keen and rigorous sense of form with a strong chromaticism, a use of harmonies anticipatory of German composers of a decade later, and a blazing expressionism which would later become both erotic and metaphysical in inspiration.

His talents and charismatic stage persona encouraged the Russian publisher Belayev to sponsor a recital tour through Europe in 1895–96, during which Scriabin attracted admiration for his incredible keyboard skills, especially

Alexander Scriabin

his total command of dynamics. In December 1896 he set about completing a Piano Concerto (his only one) in F, Op. 20, which is laid out on traditional lines and carries echoes of Chopin, among others, although its deliberate and intricate interplay between soloist and orchestra was something contemporary observers took some time to assimilate. The short score was written in a matter of days. The pretty and romantic second movement is particularly affecting. His pianistic abilities remained deeply admired by the Moscow Conservatoire, and in 1898 Scriabin accepted their offer of a piano professorship, a position he held until

1903 by which time he had produced four piano sonatas, the *9 Mazurkas,* Op. 25 (1899), the second collection of Etudes, Op. 43 (1903), and his first two symphonies, in E major, Op. 26 (1900) and in C minor, Op. 29 (1901). Both symphonies had unusual forms, the First containing six movements (although the traditional four movements are traceable if one looks upon the first as an introduction and the last as a postscript to the fifth movement), the Second having five. The last movement of the First Symphony is the first clear statement of Scriabin's idiosyncratic aesthetic, and as such is more important than its intrinsic

DON'T MISS

▶ 22 Preludes, Op. 11 (1888–96)
▶ Symphony No. 3 (Divine Poem), Op. 43 (1902–4)
▶ Le Poème de l'extase, Op. 54 (1905–8)
▶ Prometheus, Le poème du feu, Op. 60 (1908–10)
▶ Piano Sonata No. 9 (Black Mass), Op. 68 (1912–13)
▶ Vers la flamme, Op. 72 (1914)

artistic worth. It carries a choir and solo voices singing a 'Hymn to the Arts' written by Scriabin himself which proclaims an exalted place in the scheme of things for the arts in general and music in particular, bestowing upon it powers which are little short of religious in their ecstasy. It would be a while before Scriabin's orchestral music matched these sentiments.

His Second Symphony has no self-avowed programme, and retains a traditional form within which to express its composer's aims. The work is closely argued and homogeneous, with a laudable economy of ideas and a great deal of work done on the material at hand. The salvation which comes at the end, and to which the whole work aspires, is not entirely convincing. The symphony which followed (1902–05) coincided with a move, together with his companion Tatiana Feodorovna, to Switzerland after his departure from the Conservatoire and a fuller development of his philosophy. He aspired to moulding every art form into a single mystical entity and experience by which the participant would become aware of the central religious governance of all existence. By this time his religious philosophy, or theosophy, embraced mystic notions of the ego and its place in the universe,

with art being the freeing agent in the ego's search for its proper fulfilment in the exterior world.

It is doubtful whether more than a tiny percentage of his audience, then or now, have come to terms with the philosophies upon which Scriabin increasingly relied and which inspired his own muse, and it is certain that the composer himself never objectively managed the total synthesis of all arts, visual, oral and musical, in a single work. He may well have experienced the ecstasy which he regarded as an essential state of mind with which to grasp his insights, but the means to bring about such a synthesis of art forms have only existed in the late 20th century with the advent of electronics and computers. Meanwhile, we still have his music, which in the Third and final symphony, *Divine Poem*, Op. 43, uses increasingly extended harmonic language (based around what he called his 'synthetic' chord, made up of a thirteenth, minor seventh and augmented ninth) to achieve its ends.

From this point Scriabin felt no need to continue with the conventional notions of the symphony; his next major orchestral work was *Le Poème de l'extase*, Op. 54, a single-movement piece of great Dionysian energy and

scope. Begun in Geneva, its composition ran parallel to the abortive Russian Revolution of 1905, and for a while Scriabin became convinced that the socialists shared his ideals. Later he decided that socialism was only a stage on the way to complete revelation for mankind, which could only be achieved through his art. As he explained it, complete synthesis "can only be obtained by a human consciousness, an individuality, of higher order, which will become the centre of global consciousness, which will...take everything with it in its divine creative flight". He naturally saw himself as this 'individuality'. It was entirely without irony that he noted in his diary in 1905: 'I am God'.

The final orchestral work embodying his certainties was *Prometheus 'Poème du feu'*, Op. 60. This was composed between 1908 and 1910, and presents for the first time his evolved musical theory, which abandons conventional major/minor tonality but takes a different route to the contemporaneous Second Viennese School of Schönberg. *Prometheus* is built from a six-tone chord made up of different fourths; from this he derives the chromatic stages which to him illustrate the different colours of the visual spectrum which he feels are equally as present as the music. A separate and parallel line of the *Prometheus* score is given over to an invention of his, a colour piano, every key of which was intended to trigger colours as well as tones. A manic and rapid shifting from one to another at the climax of the work resembles the fusing of all the colours of the spectrum to produce light.

After this monumental work, Scriabin chose to compose for the piano alone, and between 1911 and 1913 he completed a further five sonatas as well as the three Etudes, Op. 65. The piano music extends the surreal mystery of the orchestral pieces, its sonic range and individuality of timbre bringing both an increased intimacy and a heightened sense of the infinite to the music. The Sixth Sonata, Op. 62. was written in 1911 after *Prometheus* and its character frightened even Scriabin. He never played it in public, labelling it "dark and mysterious, impure, dangerous". The music borders at times on the maniacal, at other times on the visionary. Similarly the three Etudes, Op. 65 (1911–12) deal with ghostly, other-worldly, frightening visions. The first of the three Scriabin never performed in public, its technical difficulties defeating even him, his small hands unable to deal with the intervals demanded in the score. His last three sonatas were all composed on a country estate in Russia during the autumn and winter of 1912–13, and cover the extremes of his concerns, from a sense of total harmony with the world (Sonata No. 10, Op. 70) through the chaos and devilry of Sonata No. 9, Op. 68 ('Black Mass') to the inward and utterly other-worldly Sonata No. 8, Op. 66, in fact the last to be completed.

The year 1914 was given over to more piano pieces—the *Poèmes*, Op. 69 and 71, *Vers la flamme,* Op. 72 and two further *Preludes,* Op. 74, all of which Scriabin felt were, like the last three sonatas, at the beginning of a new stage of development for him. He noted in his diary that it was imperative he live 'as long as possible' so that his visions were fully realized. In fact, the shortest time possible remained. During a visit to England in the spring of 1914 observers noticed that he was suffering from a swollen lip of the type which indicated a blood disorder. Its disappearance was only a stage in the eventual development of full-blown septicaemia, from which he died in a particularly painful fashion in April 1915, at the age of 43.

RALPH VAUGHAN WILLIAMS
1872–1958

A late-starter, Vaughan Williams eventually developed into the most distinctive and influential British composer of the early 20th century, giving shape and impetus to the reflowering of British music and producing a stream of orchestral and vocal masterpieces.

Vaughan Williams was the son of the Rev. Arthur Vaughan Williams of Down Ampney in Gloucestershire. Arthur was the religious member of a well-off professional family, and his wife would claim such notable intellects as Charles Darwin in her family tree. Ralph's childhood in Gloucestershire was brought to an end in 1875 by the premature death of his father, and he moved with his mother to her parents' house near Dorking. By the beginning of the 1880s he was learning organ, violin and music theory. During his mid-teens Ralph began writing music, and by the time he went to Charterhouse School in 1887 he already had some pieces to show his masters. He left Charterhouse in 1890 determined to become a composer, arranging to attend the Royal College of Music in the autumn of that year. During the summer, he holidayed in Europe, making a pilgrimage to Bayreuth where he experienced *Die Walküre.*

The years 1890–92 were spent studying at the Royal College of Music under Parry, and in 1891 Vaughan Williams made his settings of two Shakespeare extracts, 'The Willow Song' and 'O Mistress Mine'. It was during his time at the College that he discovered, in a collection entitled *English Country Songs* published in 1893, the song 'Dives and Lazarus'; many years later he described his reaction to this find: "I had a sense of recognition—'here's something which I have known all my life—only I didn't know it!'" Vaughan Williams was one of many people to become aware of this rich legacy of folk music, perhaps inspired by the European researches (however superficial) of such influential figures as Grieg, Brahms and Liszt. This important shift in attitude eventually

Ralph Vaughan Williams

resulted in the founding in 1899 under Cecil Sharp of the Folk Song Society (Vaughan Williams joined in 1904).

Meanwhile Vaughan Williams progressed with his compositional studies, and in 1893 he entered Trinity College, Cambridge, studying history and obtaining his B. Mus. in 1894, although he maintained weekly lessons at the Royal College. Returning to the RCM in 1895, he continued studying under Stanford, and met Gustav Holst, who became a lifelong friend. At this time Vaughan Williams concentrated on small compositions, usually part-songs or voice and piano text settings.

Vaughan Williams' mature pattern of life was beginning to coalesce. Throughout his schooling he had been supported by his family, and once he had decided on a career as a composer, they continued to do so. He married Adeline Fisher in 1897, taking a working honeymoon in Germany where Vaughan Williams took musical instruction at Berlin's Akademie der Künste, studying composition under Max Bruch. Still unsatiated by study, he took his D. Mus. at Cambridge in 1901, and this, apart from a final burst, with Ravel in France studying orchestration in 1908, signalled the end of his long training.

It was the discovery of the oral tradition of English folk music in 1902–03 which finally pointed a way towards the capturing of his true musical self in pieces larger than song-forms. He wrote down his first folk song in Essex in 1903, at about the same time as Cecil Sharp was doing the same thing in Somerset. Both men in their different ways realized the need to preserve songs and variants which were rapidly disappearing. Sharp had no ulterior creative motive, but Vaughan Williams soon realized that the inexhaustible variety of folk music could be deployed in his own compositions. The first results are detectable in *In the Fen Country* (1904), an orchestral piece some 12 minutes long which eschews the fashionable chromaticism of the day. Although it quotes no folk song directly, its whole character derives from folk music. The three *Norfolk Rhapsodies* which followed, of which only the first was eventually published, utilized the rich musical catch he made from the fishing community in King's Lynn in 1905.

By this time Vaughan Williams had already begun work on his first symphonic work, set to words by the poet Walt Whitman, originally called *The Ocean* but which would transmogrify eventually into *A Sea Symphony*. It was natural to him to write this piece for choir and orchestra, having long been interested in the burgeoning choral festival scene in England. From 1905 he was directly involved in the annual Leith Hill (Dorking) Music Festival, and his *Toward the Unknown Region* for choir and orchestra was first produced at the 1907 Leeds Festival. Soon after he was involved in work (and compositions) for the Three Choirs Festival in Gloucester. Between 1904–06 Vaughan Williams worked diligently on the publication of the material collected in the *English Hymnal*, many of whose settings were his own. This experience, as well as his previous organ work, gave him a firm background for his later choral works.

If the 1890s had been the decade when Vaughan Williams had assiduously gathered the knowledge and experience to tackle his life's vocation, then the 1900s were the first flowering of that diligence, and by the end of the decade he was in the front rank of English composers. His song writing attained maturity in three remarkably different small cycles, written either side of his months in Paris with Ravel: *The House of Life* (settings from Dante Gabriel Rossetti's eponymous sonnet collection), *Songs of Travel* (settings of verse by Robert Louis Stevenson) and *On Wenlock Edge*, an unusual and imaginative rendering for voice, string quartet and piano of some of Housman's famous 'Shropshire Lad' poems. In 1909 he completed his first theatrical commission—the incidental music for a new production of Aristophanes' satirical play *The Wasps*. In 1910 he introduced two major works within weeks of each other: at the Three Choirs Festival that year, Vaughan Williams conducted the première of *Fantasia on a Theme by Thomas Tallis,* while the Leeds Festival witnessed the unveiling of the mighty *Sea Symphony,* six years in the making. The opening night caused the delighted composer/conductor to comment: "I nearly fell off the rostrum".

Vaughan Williams continued to compose in every genre available to him, finishing *Five Mystical Songs* and the *Fantasia on Christmas Carols*. He also spent much of 1912–13 composing his great tribute to his favourite city, *A London Symphony*. Living in a house on the Chelsea embankment, he blended into the music snatches of typical London sounds, woven into a formally elegant and satisfying whole. This work,

together with the virtually finished opera *Hugh the Drover*, was the last major undertaking to be completed prior to WWI. *The Lark Ascending* was written in August 1914 but had to sit out the War before Vaughan Williams completed his customary revisions.

With the outbreak of war, Vaughan Williams volunteered for active service. Although now 41 years old, he became a private in the 2/4th Field Ambulance in England, France and Salonika. He returned to England in 1917 to attend Officer Cadet School, becoming a 2nd Lieutenant and serving in France before being demobilized in 1919. Vaughan Williams had written to Holst during the war: 'I sometimes dread coming back to normal life with so many gaps—especially George Butterworth... I sometimes think now that it is wrong to have made friends with people much younger than oneself...'

Much of his war experience was to surface in his Third Symphony, called by him a *Pastoral Symphony*. As he recalled many years later: "It's really war-time music—a great deal of it incubated when I used to go up night after night with the ambulance waggon at Ecoivres...it's not really lambkins frisking as most people take for granted". The symphony was premièred in January 1922. Its quiet contemplation and lack of the spectacular has made it an infrequent concert hall visitor, but its emotional message is strong enough to overwhelm the listener who taps its deep rhapsody.

Post-war life for Vaughan Williams was materially untroubled; he was appointed a Professor at the Royal College of Music in 1918, and from

1921–28 was conductor of the Bach Choir. The only major cloud over his life was the increasing suffering of his wife, Adeline, who was subject to the crippling effects of arthritis. Major creative achivements of the 1920s included the *Concerto Accademico* for violin and orchestra, *Flos Campi* for viola, chorus and orchestra, the Mass in G minor and a series of songs. *Hugh the Drover* was finally produced in 1924, followed by *Sir John in Love* in 1928.

It was an interlude from this opera, Vaughan Williams's treatment of Shakespeare's *The Merry Wives of Windsor*, which was his next popular success; the interlude was based on the old Tudor song 'Greensleeves'. He now took this idea and devised a *Fantasia* on it, interpolating into it a central section based on a Norfolk folk song he had collected many years previously, 'Lovely John'. This beautiful and resourceful working of 'Greensleeves' was a world away from both the stage work *Job* (1931) and the symphony which emerged in 1935, conducted by Sir Adrian Boult, the passionate, violently explosive, severe Fourth Symphony in F minor. A work which even the composer was at pains to defend ("I don't know if I like it, but it is what I meant"), it may well have

DON'T MISS

▶ A Sea Symphony (1903–9)

▶ On Wenlock Edge (1908)

▶ Tallis Fantasia (1910)

▶ The Lark Ascending (1914)

▶ A Pastoral Symphony (1921)

been a different reaction to the War he had experienced, or some more canny presentiment of what would confront the world in the early 1930s. Written more or less in tandem with *Dona nobis pacem*, a choral work which attempts to resolve and place violence in this world, it remains an uncomfortable and challenging achievement. Other major works from the 1930s include two theatrical undertakings—the romantic extravaganza *The Poisoned Kiss*, and the one-act opera *Riders to the Sea*. One of the most arresting of his 1930s output was the *Serenade to Music*, written for Henry Wood's Golden Jubilee concert in 1938, a moving setting of Shakespeare, this time *The Merchant of Venice*, utilizing solo parts for 16 different singers. Meanwhile, Boult

commissioned Vaughan Williams to write some music for him to conduct at the 1939 World Fair. He took five variants on one of his first discoveries in folk song, 'Dives and Lazarus', and wove a new work for strings and harp.

By the time of the première of his Fifth Symphony in D (1943), Vaughan Williams was in his seventies, but his creative vitality was intact, and this remarkable, confident work, begun in 1938, seemed to suggest to war-torn Britain an optimism and a quest for formal beauty which the post-war world would need to treasure. This decade was also his most sustained period for concerto writing, the Oboe Concerto coming in 1944, the double Piano Concerto in 1946, and the Concerto Grosso in 1950. Of these, the enigmatic, at times searingly beautiful Oboe Concerto is perhaps the most impressive achievement. The Sixth Sympony in E minor also appeared before the end of the decade. This violent and fearful, almost Shostakovichian work, once again took its audiences by surprise with its utterly desolate *pianissimo* last movement. Vaughan Williams entered an equally

remote world, but one not so much of the spirit as of place, with his Seventh Symphony, the *Sinfonia Antartica* of 1952. This symphony grew from some of the film music he had begun writing in the 1940s, and he used the imagined white wastes of the Antarctic to develop a new fascination with the sonority of percussion.

In 1951 Vaughan Williams's wife Adeline died, the same year that his opera *The Pilgrim's Progress* first appeared; in 1953, at the age of 80, he married again, a younger woman by the name of Ursula Wood. They sold his house near Dorking and moved to Regent's Park in London. It was here that he wrote the great works of his last years—the Eighth and Ninth Symphonies (both of them distinguished by an eagerness to use new sound combinations by scoring for instruments such as gongs and saxophones), and the masterly *Ten Blake Songs* for voice and oboe (1957). Vaughan Williams remained superlatively creative until his death at the age of 86, as the last of his symphonies, dedicated to Sir John Barbirolli, attests.

SERGEI RACHMANINOV
1873-1943

A brilliant prodigy but a man cast adrift by the overwhelming events of the 1917 Revolution in Russia, Rachmaninov became both a musical and personal embodiment of Romantic melancholy.

Rachmaninov was born into a family of aristocratic landowners who owned the estate of Oneg in the province of Novrogrod. One of six children, he and his elder sister Helena shared the vein of musical talent which ran through his father's side of the family. By the time

Sergei was nine years old, his father had squandered the family fortune on ill-considered speculations and amorous pursuits. The compulsory sale of the Oneg estate led to the parents' separation and the family's removal, minus father, to St Petersburg. There

Sergei's mother, clearly a shrewd and capable woman, organized her reduced finances to ensure that all her children were properly educated. Despite a reluctance to study, Sergei's pianistic talents were encouraged by his mother and the piano teacher, and in 1883 he won a scholarship to St Petersburg Conservatoire. His studies there were by no means exacting, the professors assuming that a boy with perfect pitch and good keyboard technique needed little formal training, and it was only the intervention of his maternal grandmother which awoke in him the desire to progress.

The grandmother owned a country house on the banks of the river Volchov, a tributary of Lake Ilmen, and this became the family's annual summer retreat. These holidays rekindled in Sergei a love of the country which was to remain central to his life and creative impulses. Aware of Sergei's lack of progress at the Conservatoire, his mother placed him in the Moscow household of Nicholai Sverev, a composer and Professor of Piano at the Moscow Conservatoire. Sverev was a hard taskmaster but a dedicated teacher, and Rachmaninov studied hard to prove himself. In 1886 Rachmaninov passed the entrance exams for Arensky's class for advanced harmony and composition at the Conservatoire, thus at last finding teachers capable of dealing with his gifts both as a pianist (Sverev) and potential composer (Arensky). During 1887–88 he produced his first surviving piano pieces, Three Nocturnes, and later, Four Pieces, the latter originally designated the Opus 1 which was later given to his first piano concerto. An introduction by Sverev to Tchaikovsky,

Sergei Rachmaninov

accompanied by one of Rachmaninov's first compositions, a study in F, led to a friendship between the celebrated composer and the 13-year-old student. This proved invaluable when Tchaikovsky, a member of the board which decided which pupils entered Taneyev's advanced composition class, recommended Rachmaninov.

Rachmaninov's progress continued apace until 1889, when he rebelled against the restrictions of Sverev's austere household and moved out, first sharing with a friend and later with his father's sister. He continued his studies, in 1891 passing the final pianoforte exams with honours a year early. During

this year he also composed his First Piano Concerto in F sharp minor, published as Op. 1; as his first composition of any real substance, this was a considerable achievement. A bout of malaria left Rachmaninov weak and depressed at the prospect of a further two years of study. He approached Arensky for permission to conflate these two years into one, and secured it. The finishing requirement was for a symphony, some vocal compositions, and an opera written to a set text. It was the opera, *Aleko,* based on a Pushkin poem, which won Rachmaninov his Gold Medal in composition in the spring of 1892, and led to a reconciliation with his old teacher,

DON'T MISS

▶ Prelude in C sharp minor No. 2, Op. 3 (1893)

▶ Piano Concerto No. 2, Op. 18 (1900–1)

▶ Symphony No. 2, Op. 27 (1906–7)

▶ Piano Concerto No. 3, Op. 30 (1909)

Sverev, who presented him with his own gold watch, a gesture Rachmaninov treasured for the rest of his life.

Free of the Conservatoire after almost a decade, Rachmaninov looked for a viable way of sustaining a professional musical career. With the help of Tchaikovsky he secured a publisher, Gutheil; Tchaikovsky also arranged for *Aleko* to be premièred on the same bill as his own opera *Yolanthe* in April 1893. Prior to this, in late 1892, Rachmaninov had made his concert début as part of the Moscow Electrical Exposition, including in his programme a piece which was later to be published as No. 2 of his *Morceaux de Fantaisie*, Op. 3. This was the Prelude in C sharp minor. Published by Gutheil in February 1893, within a year the Prelude had made Rachmaninov internationally famous. However, as Russia was not a signatory to the international copyright agreement, Rachmaninov made precisely 40 roubles (the initial fee) from his most famous composition. He had to generate a living by other means, becoming pianoforte teacher at the Maryinsky Institute for Girls as well as developing his concertizing career. He also wrote the symphonic fantasy *The Rock*, Op. 7 as well as *Morceaux de Salon*, Op.10, the latter written during the winter of 1893–94. His first symphony was already begun when the deaths of Sverev and Tchaikovsky within two

months of each other left him devastated. The *Trio élégiaque* in D minor, Op. 9, was written in memory of Tchaikovsky.

The work on Rachmaninov's First Symphony in D minor, Op. 13 was done between the Op. 10 and the autumn of 1895, and there is evidence to suggest that its fiery, uncharacteristically tempestuous outpourings, allied to the dedication and the quotation from Romans XII: 'Vengeance is mine; I will repay, saith the Lord', points to a passionate but doomed affair. As with the affair, so with the music; the première of the symphony in St Petersburg in March 1897 was a complete disaster. It is possible that the old Moscow-St Petersburg cultural rivalry had much to do with the symphony's failure, for the work itself is by no means weak. Whatever the case, it had a catastrophic effect on Rachmaninov: the self-confident composer who had just completed the fine *Moments Musicaux*, Op. 16 found himself utterly unable to compose music of any significance until he had finished a course of psychotherapy in 1900. That the hurt was emotional as much as intellectual is borne out by the fact that during the intervening years Rachmaninov continued to pursue a highly successful concert career, in Russia and abroad. He suppressed the

First Symphony himself; the original orchestral performing parts were only found in 1945, annotated by Glazunov, the conductor for the première, in St Petersburg Conservatoire's archives. The original score has never been found.

Rachmaninov's confidence in his ability to write good music was eventually restored. His private life also revived as he began to fall in love with his cousin, Natalia Satin. Heartened by his progress on several fronts, Rachmaninov made a start on his Second Piano Concerto in C minor, Op. 18, which was finished in the spring of 1901 in time for a London première given by Basil Spellnikov. Rachmaninov's cousin, the pianist Alexandre Siloti, agreed to support him financially for two years, and during this time he composed his first extended piano work, the *Variations on a Theme of Chopin,* Op. 22, and then went on to write the famous set of Ten Preludes, Op. 23. This great cycle of creation was helped by the happiness engendered by his marriage, in May 1902, to Natalia. Their honeymoon in Bayreuth was blissful and set the tone for the marriage which produced a close family of children.

In 1904 Rachmaninov briefly became chief conductor of the Bolshoi Opera in Moscow, where his friend the great bass Chaliapin was the resident genius. He presided over productions of *Prince Igor* and *A Life for the Tsar* as well as his own two operas, *Francesca da Rimini* and *The Miserly Knight.* The latter were well received critically but proved only a moderate success with the public. Rachmaninov's tenure at the Bolshoi came to an end with the Revolution of 1905. As a public figure, Rachmaninov was fearful for his own and his family's safety during the disturbances; by late 1906 the family had moved to Dresden, where he wrote the first act of an opera, *Monna Vanna* within five months of their arrival (due to copyright problems the opera remained uncompleted). Meanwhile, Rachmaninov wrote his Second Symphony in E minor, Op. 27 and his First Piano Sonata in D minor, Op. 28. These were followed by the masterful tone poem *The Isle of the Dead*, in which Wagner's influence on Rachmaninov is at its most transparent.

During this time Rachmaninov did his utmost to remain in Dresden and refuse all concert engagements, but despite this resolution he found it impossible to abandon a busy schedule throughout Europe, and in late 1908 he accepted an invitation to tour America in the autumn of the following year. In order to have something new to play during what was to be an extensive tour—20 or so concerts—he began writing his Third Piano Concerto in D minor, Op. 30. While in Boston, Rachmaninov conducted the Boston Philharmonic several times and with such success that he was offered the regular conducting post, a position he declined as much due to homesickness as for any other reason. In New York he twice gave his Third Piano Concerto, conducted on one occasion by Mahler, who impressed Rachmaninov deeply with his insights into the music.

On his return to Russia in 1910 he was offered the vice-presidency of the Imperial Music Society; during his time there he concentrated on developing musical centres of excellence outside of Moscow and St Petersburg. This had an enormous impact on the development

of the next generation of musicians and composers. During 1910–14 his rate of composition slowed, although he completed the 13 Preludes, Op. 32. The 1911 appointment to the conductorship of the Moscow Philharmonic meant little time for composition—a repeat of the situation from which Rachmaninov had escaped by going to Dresden in 1906. Nevertheless, the superb set of six *Etudes-tableaux*, Op. 33 were published in 1911. The wonderful wordless piece for voice and orchestra, *Vocalese*, Op. 34, gained its first publication in 1912, although it was revised three years later. The choral symphony *The Bells*, Op. 35, inspired by a story by Edgar Allen Poe, was written during a family holiday in Rome, and given its première in Moscow in 1913. His Second Piano Sonata, Op. 36, was also premièred around this time; a less cohesive and disciplined work than his first, its more wayward character has over the years won for it a wide international audience.

The onset of WWI brought with it violent anti-German feelings in Russia and a beginning of the slaughter and deprivations which would lead to the 1917 Revolution. Rachmaninov continued in his official posts during the War and kept up his relentless concertizing schedule. In 1915 he was grieved by the death of his friend

Alexander Scriabin, and many subsequent concerts included works by the composer. Before the outbreak of the Revolution, Rachmaninov completed the beautiful and justly popular *Vespers 'All Night Vigil'*, Op. 37, and the *Nine Etudes-tableaux*, Op. 39— the latter being his final compositions completed in Russia. It was clear that people of his class would quickly fall from favour in revolutionary Russia, and when in November 1917 a Scandinavian tour presented itself, Rachmaninov and his family left the country, taking a few possessions and leaving the rest in storage. Rachmaninov was never to see his beloved Moscow again.

From this point on, Rachmaninov was to all intents and purposes an emigré, grieving over a Russia which he knew now only existed in his imagination. Yet he faced the practicalities of building a new life for himself and his family, and within a year of leaving Moscow he realized that the key to financial and domestic security was in America, with its limitless opportunities for public appearances and its generosity when it came to proper payment. In many ways Rachmaninov suited the Americans well, for by 1918 his music was already decidedly old-fashioned but retained enough of the authentic exoticism of the Russian sensibility for his audiences

---

DON'T MISS

▶ **Vocalise, Op. 34 (1912)**
▶ **Vespers, Op. 37 (1915)**
▶ **Rhapsody on a Theme of Paganini, Op. 43 (1934)**
▶ **Symphonic Dances, Op. 45 (1940)**

to be suitably beguiled. He was also a pianist of exceptional character and quality and his live performances kept his name before the public in the most vital way possible, as did the long series of recordings of his works which began shortly after his arrival in America and continued up to the year of his death.

The rigorous demands of this new mode of life—the tours expanded after the War to include most of Europe—are illustrated by the fact that his next major composition, the Fourth (and last) Piano Concerto in G minor, Op. 40, only appeared in 1927, a full 10 years after his flight from Russia. This was succeeded by a short burst of high-quality works, including the superbly constructed solo piano *Variations on a Theme of Corelli*, Op. 42 (1931) and the

equally artistically successful but enormously more popular *Rhapsody on a Theme of Paganini* for piano and orchestra, Op. 43 (1934). By this time Rachmaninov had established a bolt-hole in Europe, buying a house near Lucerne in 1931 (while still maintaining an apartment in New York's exclusive Riverside Drive), and though his touring schedule hardly relaxed, his own life now took on a little more balance. A slowing of the punishing concert schedules after 1936 enabled him to compose the scintillating orchestral piece *Symphonic Dances*, Op. 45 (1940), but by this time he was finding composition a considerably more fraught process. During this long period away from Russia he had never abandoned hope for his country, but Soviet Russia

certainly abandoned him, at one point banning his music from public performance. Only in 1939 did he once again find himself back in favour when his compositions were not only published in Russia but he was even invited to send them to Moscow for première performances.

But Rachmaninov, although rich and famous and awarded a string of honours and citations worldwide, was experiencing a considerable diminution of his energies. Now 70 years old, he had failed to detect the onset of cancer, and by the time his doctors were allowed to investigate, the cancer had become inoperable. He was buried in America in March 1943, while his beloved Russia remained embroiled in WWII.

GUSTAV HOLST

1874–1934

Due to the overwhelming success of *The Planets*, Holst was largely known as a one-work composer, although he was in fact the creator of many brilliant works. A man of keen intellect and shy of popular renown, he suffered from the exposure his late success gave him to the extent that it hastened his early death.

Of Swedish descent (von Holst became plain 'Holst' in 1918), Holst was born in Cheltenham, Gloucestershire, to parents who were both musical and

who actively encouraged his career as a pianist. Early experience with church organs, small orchestras and choirs was to prove fruitful in his later career, but from the first his main concern was with composition. In May 1893 he joined the Royal College of Music in London where he studied composition under Charles Stanford. It was in Stanford's class that he met Vaughan Williams, and the two students quickly struck up a friendship which was to survive until Holst's death.

At the Royal College Holst was obliged to switch from the piano to trombone

when he developed neuritis in his hands. When he left the College in 1898 he took up a position in the band of the Carl Rosa Opera Company. Between this date and 1903 he played for several seasons with the Scottish Orchestra and also played the organ at the Royal Opera House, Covent Garden, learning many valuable lessons during the course of his work about scoring and orchestral blending. His compositional activities centred largely on choral and operatic writing, and in 1901 he wrote one of his earliest published pieces, *Ave Maria*, in memory of his mother who had died two years previously. He worked on the unpublished opera *Sita* between 1898 and 1906 while writing the libretto and music for his unperformed opera *The Youth's Choice*.

A summer holiday in 1903 with his wife Isobel (they had married in 1901) in Germany was spent taking in the physical, cultural and musical delights of the country. But as Holst's letters show, he and his wife spent long hours discussing their current mode of life in England, concluding with the resolve that Holst would abandon his itinerant musician's profession. "I think it would be a great thing for me if I could always live in London and say goodbye to...seaside bands". On his return from Germany, Holst became a music teacher, first at the Edward Alleyn School in Dulwich (where he remained until 1920) and then in 1905 at St Paul's Girls' School in London. In 1907 he also took on the musical directorship of Morley College for Working Men and Women. This pattern of existence he found more congenial, particularly as he discovered himself to be a gifted teacher, and it left him the time and mental energy to tackle his own compositions. In 1908 the chamber opera *Sávitri* was completed, while in the same year he completed the choral hymns from the *Rig-Veda*, Op. 26.

Gustav Holst

He composed unceasingly, completing *The Cotswold Symphony*, Op. 8 (1900), *A Somerset Rhapsody*, Op. 21(1910), *The Mystic Trumpeter*, Op. 18 (1904), *The Cloud Messenger*, Op. 30 (1910), this last being an ode for chorus and orchestra, and a host of choral music. Many of the titles of his works testify to a strong interest in mysticism and the teachings of the East. While this music is worthy, none of it revealed a challenging and fully-formed musical entity ready to sweep the world off its feet. Even an attractive work such as the *St Paul's Suite* of 1913 for string orchestra, which has subsequently won a devoted audience, remained virtually unknown prior to Holst's surprise success with *The Planets*, Op. 32, a work he had long been contemplating. On his rejection for military service in 1914 due to his poor eyesight and neuritis, he continued his teaching career and settled to writing his orchestral suite. This was completed in 1916 (the same year as the rarely heard *Japanese Suite*, Op. 33), and premièred complete in February 1919. The *Japanese Suite* was given at a Queen's Hall Promenade concert that same summer, but today is virtually unknown.

DON'T MISS

▶ St Paul's Suite, Op. 29 (1912–13)

▶ The Planets, Op. 32 (1916)

▶ The Hymn of Jesus, Op. 37 (1917)

▶ The Perfect Fool, Op. 39 (1923)

▶ Egdon Heath, Op. 47 (1927)

Within a short time *The Planets* had become famous throughout North America and the Continent. All the drama of the music, which Holst had been trying unsuccessfully to impart through his stage-works, fired the imagination of a wide audience and has not lost its appeal to the present day. International fame does not appear to have impressed Holst, who wanted nothing more than to be left alone to continue his teaching and composing. From 1919 until 1924 he was a Professor of composition at the Royal College of Music, and also taught at Reading University until 1923. But as the invitations to conduct festivals and concerts flooded in, he found it increasingly difficult to answer the demands of his new celebrity. He did, however, manage to complete the opera/ballet *The Perfect Fool*, Op. 39 (1922), his most ambitious stage work to date, which was given its première at Covent Garden in 1923. In the same year, overworked and in poor health, Holst fell from the podium at a concert and suffered a mild concussion. Forced to rest for a while, he then suffered a physical and nervous collapse as the strain of the previous years caught up with him.

After a year of complete rest—although his previously robust health was never fully restored—he was fit enough to complete his one-act Shakespeare opera, *At the Boar's Head*, Op. 42. This was given a Manchester première in 1925, but was not a great success and has rarely been revived since. However, Holst's work away from the stage during the 1920s was consistently inspired: *A Fugal Overture* is a fine concert work and points to the highly successful *Fugal Concerto* for flute, oboe and strings of 1923, written for performance during a visit to America that year. In 1925 he premièred his First Choral Symphony, Op. 41 at the 1925 Leeds Triennial Festival, but this large scale work, using poems by Keats as texts for the music and lasting 50 minutes, failed to find favour either with audience or critics. Since then, the size of the forces needed for production has often deterred potential revivals.

Also from the 1920s came Holst's own favourite, *Egdon Heath*, Op. 47 (1927). The orchestral piece was inspired both by the writings of Thomas Hardy, who used the desolation of the Heath as a setting for his novels, and by the Heath itself which Holst knew well. Hardy had written of the Heath: 'The time seems near...when the chastened sublimity of a moor, a sea, or mountain will be all of nature that is absolutely in keeping with the moods of the more thinking among mankind'. Clearly Holst, now a refugee from celebrity and very much committed to expressing the hard won heights of human experience, found these words an irresistible lure and balm. Such an approach is also close to the surface in his 1929 Concerto for Two Violins, Op. 49 and his *12 Songs*, Op. 48, where the subtlety of his writing is a perfect match for the intensity of the emotions delineated.

By the turn of the decade Holst was visibly ailing, although he kept up a vigorous regime; 1930 had seen a commission from the Three Choirs Festival for a new choral work, and in 1931 Holst's *Choral Fantasia*, Op. 52 was premièred, although again its powerful presentation of the themes of time and mortality, wedded to its unusual meditative conclusion, meant another popular disappointment. In 1932 he became Lecturer in Composition at Harvard University for six months, but was taken ill during the course of that year; his remaining two years of life were spent as an invalid. During this time he managed to complete the charming *Brook Green Suite* for strings and woodwind (1933), a sort of companion piece to the 1930–31 *Hammersmith*, originally written for brass band but subsequently arranged by Holst for orchestra. An operation in May 1934 was undertaken in the hope that Holst might regain his former vitality, but two days later his exhausted body gave up the fight.

CHARLES IVES

1874-1954

Today it is difficult to conceive of the effort required by Ives to become such an original, distinctive and, above all, American musical voice. Raised in a country whose conservative musical culture was in thrall to what Ives called 'German rules', he was enough of a rebel to demand sound reasons why he could *not* do things. This refreshing iconoclasm, however, left barely a trace on his contemporaries and his achievements went unheeded for several generations.

Ives was born in Danbury, Connecticut, into an old New England family, and the county was to remain a key element in his creative make-up. His father, a successful businessman, was an enthusiastic amateur musician and leader of a local band. Ives adopted the democratic idealism of his family, allied to an intense interest in history, geography and culture (latterly manifested in his music in many remarkable ways). Charles's natural musical curiosity was encourged by his father, an inveterate experimenter. "Father used to say 'if you know how to write a fugue the right way, well, then I'm willing to let you try the wrong way... But you've got to know what you're doing and why you're doing it'".

Ives's early musical training has led to the notion that he was an incomplete musician, a 'modern primitive', but composer Lou Harrison refutes this,

claiming that 'his musical studies, begun in childhood, were authoritative and complete, as well as extensive'. Ives was writing small pieces as early as the late 1880s, but only with his arrival at Yale University in 1894, and his studies with the composer and teacher Horatio Parker, did he begin to take himself seriously as a composer. Ives consistently tried the patience of the conservative Parker, at one point demanding to know what was wrong with a fugue he had written in which each part was in a different key (indeed, in 1896 he wrote a work, *Fugue in 4 Keys, on 'The Shining Shore'*), but there is no doubt that Parker recognized Ives's natural musicality and gave him a strong theoretical basis. While at Yale, Ives was an enthusiastic sportsman and socializer, often extemporising on the piano at campus parties. He would later call these occasions 'piano stunts'.

Yet never for one moment did Ives consider pursuing a career as a composer. On his graduation from Yale in 1898 he went straight into the world of commerce, selling insurance policies in and around New York, and by 1906 had become so successful that he co-founded an insurance business of his own. However, he kept his hand in as a performing musician, firstly as organist/choirmaster in Bloomfield, New Jersey, then between 1900-02 at Central Presbyterian Church, New York. It was a performance of his major choral work, *The Celestial Country*, in the church in 1902 (with the composer leading from the organ) and the subsequent lack of

enthusiasm from the New York critics which led to him resign this position and withdraw his compositional activities from the public arena. Realizing that his music had absolutely no commercal potential at that time, henceforth he wrote purely for his own satisfaction and made little effort to have it published or publicly performed.

Most of his orchestral and chamber music dates from 1898–1918, while much of the 1920s was spent revising this body of work and writing a large number of outstanding songs. Ives suffered a major heart attack in 1918 which curtailed much of his more ambitious compositional activity. Some of the first surviving orchestral pieces emerged from the 'piano stunts' of his Yale years, and were written just prior to the end of the 19th century. Such short pieces as *Calcium Light Night* and *Yale-Princeton Football Game* were light-hearted but literal attempts at musical depiction which clearly signalled the direction he was soon to follow. Ives even picked up on the ragtime craze which swept the campus, writing a large number of his ragtime pieces, though by 1902 he had discarded the great majority of them. In 1904 he gathered four of the best into a *Set of 4 Ragtime Dances*, making his own orchestrations from the original piano versions.

One of the apparent paradoxes about Ives is that his music captures a vast array of humorous moments but that he is not being humorous about the scenes he depicts musically. His unique syntheses of outdoor events and celebrations attempt in all seriousness to capture the colour, excitement and, at times, chaos of outdoor festivities. This is precisely pictured in the *Country Band March* of 1903, where Ives carefully writes into his score the out-of-key playing, tempo fluctuations and ragged ensembles of amateur musicians out to enjoy themselves on a sunny parade day.

Ives was a determined symphonist, and though his First Symphony, written between 1895–98, was somewhat conventional in conception, by the time of the Second (completed in 1902) he had moved closer to his mature compositional style. In this work he used the traditional form of the symphony to undermine the selfsame tradition by interweaving European Classical themes (including the first theme from Beethoven's Fifth Symphony and a parody of Dvořák's Ninth) and motifs from popular American tunes of the day. In doing so he hoped to provoke and challenge the established mode of thinking about Classical music and suggest that other paths to the musical high ground were open to discovery. The Third Symphony, from 1904 and written for a chamber orchestra, moves closer to the concerns of the mature composer of orchestral portraits. Its subtitle, *The Camp Meeting*, immediately places it in

the group of New England works. The symphony is based on popular hymns and related music which Ives had played during his time as organist at the Baptist Church in New York. In 1911 Gustav Mahler had it copied at his own expense and took it back with him to Vienna with the intention of having it performed, but died before he reached the Austrian capital.

The range of Ives's musical exploration is quite extraordinary. During the time he was completing this symphony he began work on his *3 Quarter-tone pieces* (for two pianos) (1902–23), a uniquely disturbing trio of pieces in which Ives uses the quarter-tones (achieved by tuning the two pianos a quarter-tone apart) as accidentals in otherwise conventional compositional studies. The effect on the listener is akin to taking mind-altering drugs.

In 1906, the year he set up his own business, Ives completed two of his most famous short pieces, *Central Park in the Dark* and *The Unanswered Question*. These works, originally conceived as a contrasting pair, are both as far removed from contemporary European music of the Germanic tradition as can be imagined, and even today sound remarkably fresh and 'of the moment'. *The Unanswered Question* deals with his philosophical concerns

arising from Emerson's poem 'The Sphinx', dividing the orchestra into 'the silence of the Druids' (strings); 'the perennial question of Existence' (trumpet) and 'the invisible Answer' (woodwinds). *Central Park* was originally subtitled 'a contemplation of Nothing Serious', and depicts various small incidents 'in the Good Old Summer Time'.

Perhaps Ives's most famous orchestral work is the *Set No. 1, Three Places in New England*. This was composed between 1903 and 1914, and was one of the first works by Ives to be played in America and Europe, being championed from 1931 onwards by the conductor, Nicolas Slonimsky. The first movement depicts Ives's response to the statue of Col. Shaw in Boston Common, a statue which also features in Robert Lowell's famous poem 'For the Union Dead'; the second has the famous section where two bands playing in two different keys meet in a park and battle it out for aural supremacy. Ives's two piano sonatas were written between 1902 and 1915, the second, entitled *Concord, Mass.*, was to prove his masterpiece in the genre.

The lesser-known *Orchestral Set No. 2* was finished by 1913, and although it has no overall title, again the music is deliberately evocative, the titles resonating nostalgia and moments in time—'An Elegy to our Forefathers'; 'The Rockstrewn Hills'; 'Join in the People's Outdoor Meeting'; 'From Hanover Square North...'—and bringing rich tonal mixtures to the listener. *The Holidays Symphony*, completed from works written at various times and based on the theme of important American public holidays (Washington's Birthday; Decoration Day; Fourth of July; Thanksgiving and Forefathers' Day) again stresses the connection with the music of the people, the overriding importance of music for occasions and for people to do things by. Ives's music is often as much a celebration of American life as a recording in tones of his own thoughts and feelings.

Ives's last symphony, the Fourth, was created by using material from earlier works (up to 14 have been identified), as well as hymn tunes and old songs (there are over 30 in the symphony). Ives himself identified his aims in writing the work: 'the searching questions of What? and Why? which the spirit of man asks of life'. Within the vastness of this question, which also resides at the heart of his *Robert Browning Overture* of 1913 as well as many of his other works, Ives allows every conceivable response, from riot to calm solemnity to frivolity to peace. It was completed by 1916 (although subsequently revised), but the

work was never performed complete in Ives's lifetime, receiving its première in 1965. A 1927 New York performance by Leon Goosens of just two movements led to a near riot.

The heart attack of 1918 reduced Ives's physical capacities to a point where he could no longer stand the strain of composing and running a business, and much of the 1920s was spent revising and sharpening works or completing songs, another form in which the composer had been active since the 1890s. In 1930 another health crisis obliged him to retire at the age of 56; it is reported that by then he was a millionaire, but in his usual fashion he distributed the majority of his money to others, keeping only what he felt he needed to maintain a dignified existence in retirement. He and his wife moved to a Connecticut farm, and for the next 20 years Ives wrestled with a succession of

illnesses (including diabetes as well as the weak heart) which would have killed a man with less willpower.

The 1930s and 1940s saw a minor increase in the number of performances of his works. In 1947, after the New York première of his Third Symphony, he was shocked to hear that it had won a Pulitzer Prize. There now came a perceptible quickening of pace in the discovery of Ives's music, speeded up by Leonard Bernstein who became his champion during the following two decades. Ives died in May 1954, having survived for considerably longer than his doctors had expected, but just short of the explosion of interest which would have made him a very famous old man. Perhaps this was for the best, for he neither sought nor enjoyed public interest, and his music is an eloquent enough testimony to his life and obsessions.

ARNOLD SCHOENBERG
1874–1951

Schoenberg, who was born when Wagner and Liszt were in their prime, today remains a controversial and frequently fearsome musical figure to many. Yet his theories, which have now been influential for over 75 years, remain essential to an understanding of the position currently reached by modern art-music.

Schoenberg was born into a middle-class Jewish family (his father ran a shoe-shop) in Vienna. His family had

long shown an involvement in music and his parents both sang in local choral societies. Arnold was introduced to the violin at an early age, attending the Leopoldstadt District Volksschule from the age of six, graduating to the Realschule when he was 11. Over the next year he attempted his first composition, although at this stage he failed to show any outstanding musical talent or direction.

When his father died in 1890, the family was faced with financial hardship and Arnold, then 15, was

forced to work in a bank. During his four years there he joined a local choral society where he met the composer and conductor Alexander Zemlinsky. Zemlinksy not only became his friend but his teacher. He introduced Schoenberg, at that time an ardent fan of Brahms, to the hedonistic harmonic delights of Wagner. Fired by Zemlinksy, Schoenberg left his post at the bank, determined to make a living from music. This led to unlikely work such as scoring songs for the local cabaret, teaching composition to private students and scoring operettas for various ensembles.

Arnold Schoenberg

his most impressive achievements, *Gurrelieder*, a vastly ambitious work for soloists, narrator and orchestra which would take until 1911 to arrive at a satisfactory version. In 1901 he married Mathilde Zemlinksy, and they moved to Berlin to enable Schoenberg to fulfil a conducting commission at Ernst von Wolzogen's cabaret establishment, 'Uberbrettl', a well-known rendezvous for the Berlin *cognoscenti*. In Berlin Schoenberg met Richard Strauss who alerted him to the musical possibilities inherent in Maeterlinck's play *Pelléas et Mélisande*. The resulting tone poem is redolent with the overblown musical language of late Romanticism, carrying the emotional grandiloquence of both Strauss and Wagner, and suggests that the composer had little to add to an already fading genre.

After the birth of his first daughter in 1902, Schoenberg and his wife moved back to Vienna. There he returned to his previous work patterns, his teaching assuming a greater significance as his own musical theories developed. He took on two outstanding students who were to become his disciples and great composers in their own right, Anton Webern and Alban Berg. Schoenberg solved the immediate compositional problems posed by *Pelléas* by abandoning extended orchestral works based on extra-musical programmes. Returning to the concern with form he had first learned from Brahms, he combined it with the musical adventurousness of Liszt and Wagner, pushing tonality to its limits and abandoning traditional compositional building-blocks which, for him, had lost their meaning through slipshod

Meanwhile, he continued to compose. In 1897 a String Quartet in D, without an opus number, was completed.

A few days after its initial performance in 1898, Schoenberg took the step of leaving the Jewish faith and becoming a Protestant. The summer of 1899 was also momentous for Schoenberg, both as a man and as a composer: holidaying with Zemlinsky's family, he fell in love with Zemlinsky's sister Mathilde and the affection proved mutual. Equally decisive was the writing of a work initially scored for

string sextet but later arranged for string orchestra, *Verklärte Nacht*. The work's theme, based on a symbolist poem by Richard Dehmel, was risqué for the time: love and forgiveness between a man and a woman carrying another's child transfigures their own world, and they walk 'through a high, bright night'. The subject shocked the audience at the 1903 première more than the music, the work causing something of a scandal in Vienna.

By 1903 Schoenberg had already moved on, beginning work on one of use. In his First Chamber Symphony, Op. 9 (1906, the year of the birth of his son, Georg) the pared textures and rigorous working-through of his challenging material represented a considerable break with his own high-Romantic past. In these radical extensions of the lessons of his forebears he was generously supported by the director of the Vienna Opera, Gustav Mahler, into whose circle he was introduced by Mahler's young wife Alma. The First Chamber Symphony and its follow-up, the String Quartet No. 2, Op. 10 (1907-08) are transitional works on the way to stark expressionism encapsulated in what would become known as Schoenberg's 'atonal' compositions, although as the composer himself commented, 'atonal' literally meant the absence of tone, rather than the withdrawal from tonality; his compositions always had tones in them!

This Second String Quartet, however, carried another meaning, for while Schoenberg was working on it his wife Mathilde, tired of her supportive role as the wife of a composer, eloped with a mutual friend, the painter Richard Gerstl. Mathilde was soon prevailed upon to return, with Schoenberg's student Webern playing a leading role in pleading his mentor's case. The painter, distraught at the loss of Mathilde and unable to face his friend Arnold, committed suicide. Certain movements in the Quartet contain Schoenberg's reactions to these events, including the successful reconciliation of husband and wife. He also wrote a manifestly autobiographical 'drama with music', Die glückliche Hand, Op. 18 (1909-13), which sketched the drama of his life, ending in a form of

triumph where he is not only reunited with his wife but survives all manner of hostile activities from the 'non-elect' who fail to grasp what he, as an artist, is attempting to achieve through his music.

By now Schoenberg was on the brink of his most radical musical statements, compositions which would irrevocably change the course of European art-music. In the last years before WWI he created a string of very diverse masterpieces all linked by one thing—the potent emotional charge lying close to the surface and occasionally (and spectacularly) breaking through. This was perhaps most explicit in the works written to a text, such as the breakthrough music theatre piece from 1909, Erwartung, Op. 17. Written using a polyphonic approach and extreme expressionist techniques applied to a text which borders on existentialist hysteria, Schoenberg developed in it a vocalizing which, although its roots in Wagner and Strauss are clear, suggests a dialogue with the accompanying instruments rare in opera. Its semi-spoken rhythmic values suggest the ultimate breakdown into sprechstimme which was to be found in the thrilling, other-worldly Pierrot lunaire, Op. 21, another work conceived for the stage, this time for a reciter and chamber group. By this time Schoenberg was looking for a new way to organize his material which escaped the problems brought about by the disintegration of the 'old' tonality of key centres and modulation; a point reached, for example, by Strauss but at which he stopped, relying instead on obsessive and repeated harmonic modulations to give his melodic shapes continued refreshment. The text of this work, by

Albert Giraud, is forcefully erotic and full of striking symbolism. Pierrot lunaire scored something of a success at its Berlin première in 1912. Erwartung, on the other hand, had to wait until 1924 to be heard in public, when Zemlinsky directed it at a Prague concert. By then, Schoenberg had moved far beyond the expressionist approach its fabric had demanded.

By 1911 Schoenberg had come to an impasse in Vienna, where continued attacks on his works and theories had undermined his teaching income and had also affected his career prospects. The offer of a permanent position at the Vienna Academy of Music was withdrawn after protests—some of them blatantly anti-Semitic as well as musically reactionary—forced the board to back down. His great defender Mahler was now dead and he was almost entirely isolated; in the summer of 1911 he was even physically attacked by a mentally disturbed neighbour. Richard Strauss proffered valuable help, giving him a vote of confidence to the board of the Stern Conservatorium in Berlin, and he secured a teaching position at this institution. This move corresponded with a steady improvement in his living conditions and a gradual increase in

DON'T MISS

▶ Verklärte Nacht (1899)

▶ Chamber Symphony No. 1 Op. 9 (1906)

▶ 5 Orchestral Pieces Op. 16 (1909)

▶ Gurrelieder (1910–11)

▶ Pierrot Lunaire (1912)

the number of performances of his music, from London to St Petersburg. His Orchesterstücke, Op. 16 were given in London in 1912, while the monumental *Gurrelieder* received a Vienna performance under Franz Schreker in 1913.

Schoenberg was directly affected by the outbreak of WWI: returning to Vienna, he was called up, proving himself a patriot not only in his enthusiasm for the military cause but in his willingness to write occasional music for patriotic use. During an extended leave in 1916 he began the oratorio *Die Jakobsleiter* (1917–22), a paean to the ideas of pantheism and of obtaining release from the world's cares by an obliteration of individuality through the transforming power of divine intervention. The work, already well-progressed, became a victim of Schoenberg's recall to the Austrian army in September 1917. Within three months he had been discharged as physically unfit, but the continuity of composition had been broken and although Schoenberg repeatedly returned to the text, it was left unfinished at his death.

In the post-war years Schoenberg began to establish a working model of the dodecaphonic (twelve-tone) theory of composing which was to remain central to his output for the rest of his life. Already the author of *A Treatise on Harmony* (1911), a learned book on the development of Western harmony up to that time, Schoenberg now wrote a treatise on this new method which was to prove immensely influential. He did not claim to have invented the twelve-tone theory; that, he freely acknowledged, had been largely the

work of the composer/teacher Joseph Hauer (1883–1959), who had been composing according to his own dodecaphonic prionciples since about 1912. Hauer's first major treatise on the subject (he wrote over six), *Uber die Klangfarbe*, was published in 1920. Schoenberg's own treatise, *Komposition mit zwölf Tönen*, published soon after, mentions Hauer 'whose theories, even where I find them exaggerated, are deep and original'. Yet Schoenberg's own rigorous development of these ideas was to prove the decisive influence on subsequent generations. His ideas on serialism appealed to composers in virtually every country where Western music was written.

Schoenberg's works which first exhibited these principles were the *Five Piano Pieces*, Op. 23 and the *Serenade*, Op. 24, both completed by the opening of 1923. The *Suite for Piano*, Op. 25 and *Wind Quintet*, Op. 26 furthered these gains, and it is worth noting that all of these pieces are for a single instrument or small forces. In 1923, the year in which Schoenberg introduced his fully-formulated ideas to his students and professional companions, was also the year his first wife, Mathilde, died. After a period of intense mourning, in 1924 Schoenberg took action to radically alter his life, accepting Berlin's offer to take up a compositional master class at the Prussian Academy of Arts, then marrying a sister of Rudolf Kolisch, an old violinist friend. He and Gertrude Kolisch, a woman barely half his age, enjoyed a happy and productive marriage, producing a girl and two boys.

This was also a fruitful time on the compositional front; between 1926 and the rise of the Nazis to power in 1933, Schoenberg began (and almost completed) a series of major works, including the *Variations for Orchestra*, Op. 31 (1928–31), the Suite, Op. 29 for clarinets, strings and piano (1924–6), the further *Piano Pieces*, Op. 33 a & b, *Moses und Aron* (1928–32), his unfinished oratorio-opera (the single-scene third act was the stumbling block), and the one-act opera *Von Heute auf Morgen* (1928–29). He was as controversial a figure as ever, but his adherents were gaining in number as comprehension of his aims and musical advances widened and deepened. He was one of the first to feel the dead hand of Nazism on his shoulder, and within two months of Hitler's election, Schoenberg had not only been forced to resign from the Academy but had left Berlin for Paris.

His arrival there coincided with a reversion to Judaism, but a lack of work in the French capital paved the way for him to accept a teaching position in Boston. By October 1933 he and his family were living in America, and within three years he had made his final move—for reasons of health and financial security—to California. From then until 1944 (his seventieth birthday and the year of his retirement) he led a settled existence as a Professor at the Universty of California in Los Angeles. A sixteen-minute setting for string quartet, piano and reciter, of Lord Byron's *Ode to Napoleon Buonaparte*, Op. 41, completed in 1942, recorded his most personal reactions to Hitler's tyranny, and also showed that he had moved on from strict adherence to dodecaphony, now willing to marry all three previous approaches to music theory in a single piece. His feelings on once again embracing Judaism were expressed in his setting of the *Kol Nidre*, which became his Op. 39, written in 1938 in an entirely tonal manner in the (forlorn) hope of it being regularly performed in synagogues.

Having composed a Violin Concerto, Op. 36 in 1935–36, in 1942 Schoenberg used the unfolding drama of Nazi Germany to give an underlying narrative structure to his Piano Concerto, Op. 42. His String Trio, Op. 45 of 1946 was a return to absolute music, and found Schoenberg more daring than ever in his treatment of his material, allowing a new type of fragmentation to dominate the structure. This work was written immediately after a period in hospital in August 1946 after a near-fatal heart attack. Now 72, his health never fully recovered, but he completed the harrowing *A Survivor from Warsaw*, Op. 46 in 1947, movingly depicting the butchery of his people and anticipating a time when the Jewish nation could permanently escape such horrors. His last works, Op. 50 a, b and c, were choral in nature, being settings of contemporary texts and of Psalm 130. With his passing in July 1951 came the end of the beginning of modernism, and also the end of German 19th-century progessivism.

PART VIII

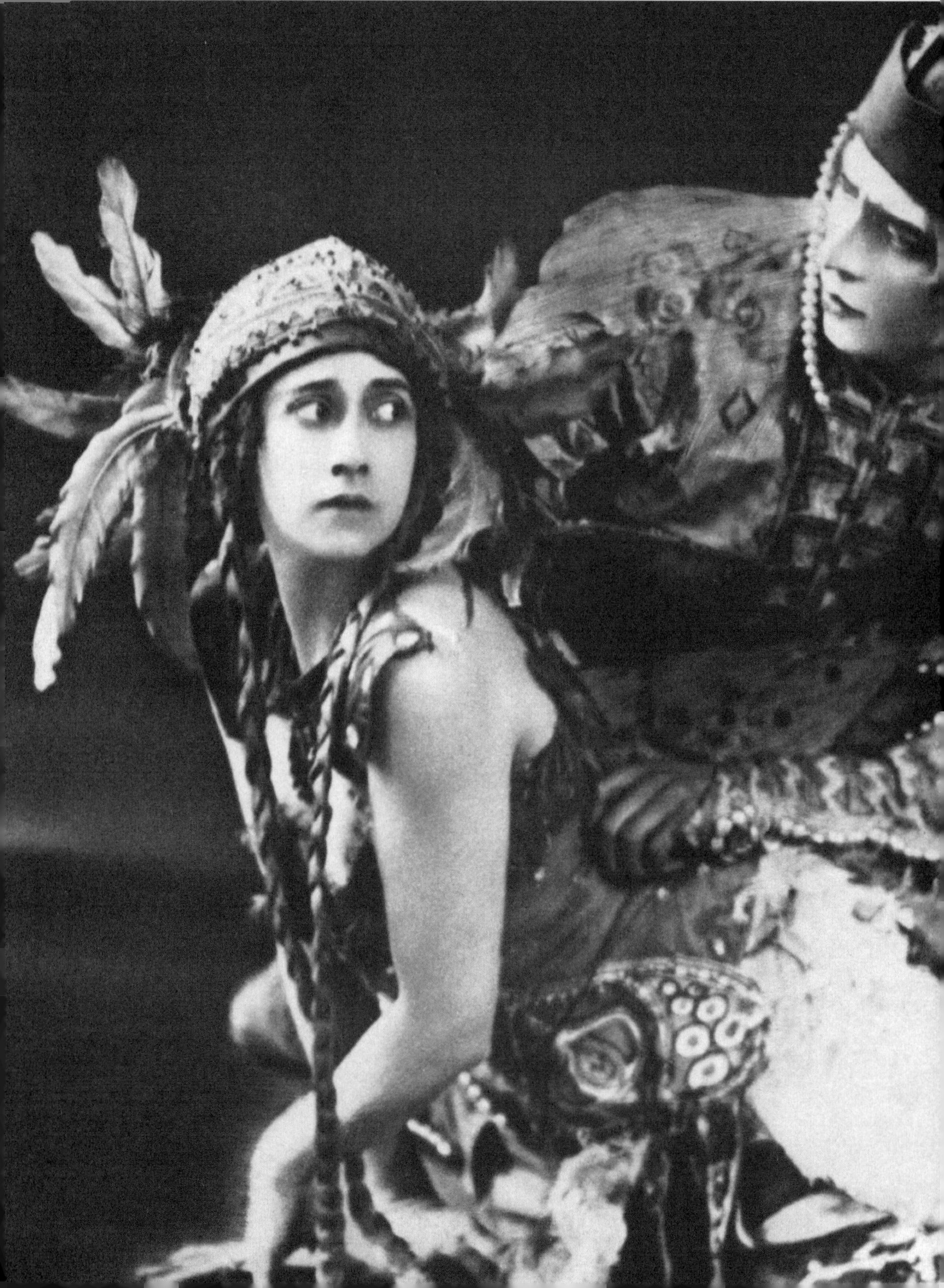

1875-1900

Composers during this period grew to maturity in time to experience the overwhelming impact of World War I on European and American life. They were the first group of composers able to use the new post-Romantic musical language with complete fluency and freedom, often finding the creative route into this new territory by studying the folk and native musics of their own countries.

While the previous half century had seen the birth of the first wave of great nationalist composers such as Dvořák, Mussorgsky, Grieg, Borodin and Smetana, this generation brought hitherto unsuspected musical treasures and experiences to the attention of the concert-goer and opera-lover. In the first decade of the new century central Europeans such as Kodály and Bartók began their systematic and rigorous study of peasant and folk music from Hungary, Transylvania, Romania, Turkey and Bulgaria. In Russia the legacy of Mussorgsky and Rimsky-Korsakov led the young

Stravinsky to use old Russian myths and folk tales to create a series of masterpieces, including *The Firebird* and *The Rite of Spring*. In America Gershwin delved into the rich folk traditions of the blues and related music while Ravel and de Falla explored very different Iberian traditions.

Meanwhile, in South America the first Brazilian composer to make an international impact, Heitor Villa-Lobos, was composing a plethora of works with differing degrees of direct input from the vernacular music of Brazil. Even followers of the Austro-Germanic traditions such as Berg, Webern and Hindemith exhibited a preoccupation with placing music in its proper contemporary context. Berg introduced an ultra-modern treatment to the subjects of his operas, while Hindemith was driven to make his music applicable to the needs of everyday life. The previous century's obsession with high Romanticism was fast receding.

Stravinsky's ballet, The Firebird, *with costumes by Léon Bakst, was premièred by Diaghilev's Ballets Russes at the Paris Opéra in 1910.*

MAURICE RAVEL

1875–1937

Often mistakenly labelled a musical Impressionist, Ravel was a fiercely intelligent and intensely private man whose most complete and perfect expressions of himself came through his uniquely imaginative music. He often referred to his Basque heritage, but the obsession with order and detail which enriches the realization of his vividly imagined music betrays the influence of his Savoyan father.

Maurice Ravel

Ravel was born in Ciboure on the Basque coast, the eldest son of Joseph Ravel who came originally from the Haute-Savoie, and Marie, a Basque native. It is important to stress the significance of this Basque inheritance to Ravel, who always maintained that his character and sensibilities were wholly Basque. At the age of seven, Maurice's father noticed his son's ear for music and decided he should have piano lessons. By then the family had left Ciboure and had been living in Paris for seven years. Ravel's first piano teacher, Henri Ghys, soon realised that the little boy (his height never exceeded just over 5ft) possessed a lively intelligence and a natural gift for music.

At the age of 12, Maurice became a student of the composer Charles-René, a former pupil of Delibes, who taught him harmony, counterpoint and, finally, the principles of composition using a method of teaching which allowed the student to regard his exercises as compositions. In 1889 Ravel entered

the piano class at the Paris Conservatoire. The same year was notable for the Exposition Universelle at which Debussy became entranced by Javanese music while Ravel acquired a taste for the exotic art of the East, both pictorially and musically. Two years later Ravel progressed to an advanced piano class, where he met the Catalan musician Ricardo Viñes who was to remain a friend and faithful interpreter of Ravel's music for many years. But Ravel's independence of thought and often ill-concealed contempt for his teachers' efforts to impose upon him a more conventional method of musical thinking made him unpopular. At the time, Ravel ignored the resentment he caused, but later in life it would come home to roost.

Ravel was one of those rare creative beings who achieves an early stylistic maturity in his profession, and thereafter composes consistently satisfying music at a very high artistic level. As in music, so in his artistic tastes: by the end of his teens he had discovered Poe, Mallarmé and Baudelaire, and the influence of these wildly imaginative and darkly inspirational writers remained with Ravel for life. Musically, he professed to be as impressed by Meyerbeer, Chabrier, Satie, Borodin and Rimsky-Korsakov as any of the German and French composers who were held up as good examples by his teachers.

This self-reliance and early stylstic perfection added to his frustrations with the Conservatoire, although relations with Gabriel Fauré, who taught him composition after 1897, were cordial enough. By then Ravel had published his first works, the *Menuet antique* and the *Pièce en forme de Habanera*, the latter designed to be part of a set called *Les Sites auriculaires* which Ravel, who already knew the value of self-criticism, had destroyed. These two early works point to Ravel's love of earlier forms of music and the Iberian legacy, both of which he would exploit so brilliantly in years to come.

Debussy was present at the 1898 première of the *Habanera* at the Société Nationale de Musique during which Ravel's bold music attracted audible protests. Debussy, however, was impressed, and asked for the loan of a manuscript copy of the *Habanera*. Debussy's use, conscious or unconscious, of the harmonic concept and rhythmic structure of this work in his 1903 *Soirée dans Grenade* was to lead later to a lawsuit between the two men, but at this point Debussy was a vocal supporter of the younger man.

Ravel decided that it was time he wrote an opera. Deeply under the thrall of the Russians, he made a start on one based on the story of Schéhérazade. Little was written as Ravel became bogged down in the rather gruesome story, although the overture was played by the orchestra of the Société Nationale in 1899, attracting loud whistling from a section of the audience. In terms of public scandals, at least, Ravel was doing nicely.

That same year he composed the work which was to make him a household name: the short piano piece *Pavane*

pour une Infante défunte (Pavane for a Deceased Infanta). Once again Ravel used his love for Spain and its history, as well as possibly paying tribute to his teacher Fauré whose own *Pavane* of 1887 had been one of his most popular pieces. Ravel used the pavane, the ancient courtly dance performed at the funeral bier of an Infanta, as a stately rhythmic basis, and over this wove a melody of entrancing melancholy. Within a short time the manuscript became hugely popular, despite its publisher referring to it sneeringly as being more suitable for 'young girls', although those eager amateurs made him and his composer a lot of money.

At this stage Ravel was leading a somewhat complex existence; he had been introduced into Parisian aristocratic circles through the famous soirées of Madame de Saint-Marceaux, while at the same time joining a loose-knit artistic and intellectual group of young rebels—centred around the artist Paul Sordes—called the Apaches. His musical friends included Riccardo Viñes, André Caplet and the eccentric Florent Schmitt, and later, de Falla and Stravinsky. This group had a rallying whistle, the first subject of Borodin's Second Symphony. They also had a penchant for rowdy late-night revels and spirited arguments over aesthetics in every field of art, and Ravel quickly became known as a stubborn debater. His appearance even then was singular; he sported a pointed goatee (à la Satie), dressed impeccably, and already had a highly developed taste in very loud cravats, scarves and other fashion accessories by which he would later become identified. The singer Jane Bathori, who premièred most of his

vocal works, remembered him at this age as possessing 'black, sparkling, imaginative eyes...[a] refined and equivocal smile', and speaking enthusiastically about Debussy's music. Everything about the man was elegant. Being shy, he tended to resort to irony and cryptic remarks when among those he did not know. He retained his inability to dissimulate in front of those he did not respect, even when they included critics whose favour he needed to advance his compositions.

This facet of Ravel's character went against him when he entered for the 1901 Prix de Rome. That year he gained second place, which under normal circumstances would have been quite acceptable. But that same year Ravel had enjoyed overwhelming critical and popular success with his short piano masterpiece *Jeux d'eaux*: the awarding of the prize to a nonentity instead of Ravel caused an uproar. A proud and intense man, Ravel tried again in 1902 with the cantata *Alcyone*, but again met with failure. In 1903 he failed yet again with *Alyssa*. Meanwhile, his musical career gathered momentum with the completion of the wonderful String Quartet in F in 1902–03. He also adapted much of the discarded music from the abandoned opera

DON'T MISS

▶ **Pavane pour une infante defunte (1899)**

▶ **String Quartet in F (1902–03)**

▶ **Schéhérazade (1903)**

▶ **Alborada del gracioso (1905)**

DON'T MISS

▶ **Introduction and allegro (1905)**

▶ **Rapsodie espagnole (1907)**

▶ **Gaspard de la nuit (1908)**

▶ **Ma mère l'oye (1908–11)**

Schéhérazade set to three poems by his Apache friend Tristan Klingsor on the same subject. These luscious and sensual works, full of beautiful melodies and luminous scoring, and redolent with sexual and emotional ambiguities as well as the most refined sensuality in the sung texts, were premièred in 1903 at a Société Nationale concert.

In 1905 Ravel decided to try one last time for a Prix de Rome. This time he was even refused permission to enter the competition. Considering his contemporary standing as a composer there seemed little sense in this decision, but some detective work by Ravel's friends, aided by a press campaign led by the distinguished author Romain Rolland, uncovered not only a predetermination on the part of the Conservatoire's board of directors to exact revenge upon Ravel, but also to allow only pupils of one of the directors to compete for the prize. Even in Paris this was too big a scandal to be ignored and the Director, Dubois, was forced to resign. His place was taken by Fauré, a man well disposed towards Ravel, but by then Ravel had lost all desire to pursue the prize any further.

While the scandal reached a climax Ravel was on a boating holiday in Holland with friends, including the millionaire Alfred Edwards and the painter Pierre Bonnard. During the trip Ravel wrote letters about what he saw which revealed his fascination with mechanics: 'In the fields, windmills, as far as the eye could see. In every direction we looked, we saw nothing but turning wheels. One finished up by thinking one had become an automaton oneself.' Ravel never lost his fascination for all things mechanical, but from that time on he developed a peculiar hatred for honours and distinctions. At the time of this yachting trip, people admired his apparently calm reaction to events in Paris, but it was during this voyage that his sleepless nights began, a problem which in later years proved insuperable.

This same year, 1905, saw the completion of the Classically-proportioned *Sonatine*, a work which again revealed Ravel's irony. He also perfected *Miroirs*, a set of five piano pieces of great rarification, along with the exquisitely scored *Introduction and Allegro* for harp, flute, clarinet and string quartet. *Miroirs* exhibited some startlingly new departures in harmonic language for Ravel, and contained two pieces, *Alborada del Gracioso* and *Une Barque sur l'Océan*, which would later, under his own luminous orchestration, become popular concert pieces. This set of five pieces were as bold and exciting as any piano music being produced at that time, and placed Ravel once more at the forefront of the avant-garde in musical circles.

His reputation increased during the next few years, with works such as the

remarkable set of songs describing various different animals, *Histoires naturelles*, which he completed in 1906. This was followed in 1907 by the rapturous *Rapsodie espagnole* and his imaginative, absurdist and sunnily comic one-act opera, *L'Heure espagnole*, where his love of clocks was given full expression. The opera was performed in 1911, and the other two works within a year of composition; the latter pieces both provoked a near-riot at their premières, with pro and con factions insulting each other throughout.

The year 1908 was a memorable one for Ravel as he composed two fantastical works which were at opposite poles to each other: the charming *Ma Mère l'Oye* for two pianos with its dreamy childhood fantasies, and the terror and grotesqueries of *Gaspard de la nuit*, a trio of piano pieces of formal beauty inspired by the macabre images of the poet Aloysius Bertrand, whose own inspirations were Brugnot, Goethe and Hoffmann. *Gaspard's* three constituent parts, *Ondine*, *Le Gibet* and *Scarbo*, contain passages of frightening complexity for any pianist, and the work remains one of the ultimate challenges to any keyboardist since it asks questions of the performer at every artistic level. The year 1908 was also memorable, however, for a deeply personal reason: his father died in October after a long illness. In a family as close as Ravel's, this was a hammer blow.

Yet his creativity did not falter: as well as the superb and extravagantly sensual ballet *Daphnis et Chloé*, commissioned by Diaghilev's Ballets Russes in 1911, the perennially popular piano pieces

Valses nobles et sentimentales appeared. Ravel was later to extract two concert suites from his ballet which would become concert favourites the world over. The Valses were also presented in ballet form by Diaghilev, with Ravel conducting. Around this time, with his fame steadily increasing, Ravel decided to shave off his beard, revealing a prominent nose and fine chin framing a large sensitive mouth, the image which is remembered by posterity.

Like everyone else Ravel was sucked into the vortex of WWI, serving first as an army hospital orderly and subsequently as a driver. Before he abandoned civilian life he finished his exquisite Piano Trio. After a year of training he left for the front, and spent a year amidst the hellish carnage of the front lines before falling ill in September 1916 with dysentery. This illness gave him leave to return to Paris, where he arrived in January 1917 in time to see his beloved mother die. On return to active duty, he was stationed in camp. Bored with routine, he wrote Le Tombeau de Couperin, ostensibly a tribute to 18th-century French music, but each piece was dedicated to a friend killed in the war. His service in the army, allied to his compositional prowess, no doubt led to his being nominated for a Légion d'honneur in 1920. He resolutely refused to accept it, commenting angrily that to accept such an award would be to condone the state's presumption that it had claims to assess his work. This did not prevent him from collecting an honorary music degree from Oxford University in 1928.

The first work completed after the war was one he had begun in 1914 and originally entitled Wien. Now retitled La Valse, it had become a delirious danse macabre. Ravel fully intended it to be choreographed by Diaghilev, who had originally been keen to mount a production. When the impresario turned it down in 1920, Ravel severed relations with the Russian. Still fascinated by the stage, however, he pressed on with an opera based on a children's story by the author Colette, in 1920 producing the opera L'Enfant et les sortilèges. In the same year Ravel also wrote a series of chamber works, including the sonatas for violin and cello and violin and piano, both of which demonstrated a change in style exhibiting a new severity in his approach to line and harmony. They also indicated a lively awareness of musical events in America, using syncopation and blue-note phrasings and harmonies previously unheard in his music.

L'Enfant was performed in 1926 at the Paris Opéra-Comique, and met with great critical acclaim, but it was not a success with its audience, who were unsettled by what was perceived as a distasteful love duet between the cats. Ravel distasteful? It seems impossible, but that was the perception. In 1928, a year after the eventual completion of his violin and piano sonata, he embarked on an extended tour of America. But while there Ravel over-taxed his already failing health. Since the war he had experienced debilitating insomnia, and with his move to a country house in the Ile de France, this had markedly increased. In 1928 he put the finishing touches to his most famous piece which he referred to as a work for orchestra without music. This of course was Boléro, a work which it

should be remembered was written as a ballet and composed for the dancer Ida Rubinstein who gave its first performance. It has long been thought that Ravel felt Boléro to be a kind of joke, but there is also evidence that in fact he was utterly serious about its creation. He remarked to a close friend in 1932 that it was not an amusement, but something terrible; that it was not just 'a dance', but life itself. He made a clear connection between this monolithic work and the timeless rituals utilizing the music of his beloved Basque people.

With Boléro Ravel reached unprecedented heights of popularity, although this fame held little interest for a man so intensely private. He maintained this privacy at all costs, hence the lack of any definite knowledge about much of his inner life, although he always claimed that his one true love affair was with music. The two great piano concertos were to follow in 1931, the Piano Concerto in G (with its charming echoes of L'Enfant and its beautiful adagio) and the D Major Concerto for Piano (left-hand) and Orchestra, commissioned by the virtuoso Paul Wittgenstein who had lost his right hand in an accident. Unfortunately, Wittgenstein did not like the work and refused to play it, and it

---

DON'T MISS

▶ **Daphnis et Chloé (1912)**

▶ **Piano Trio (1914)**

▶ **La Valse (1920)**

▶ **Boléro (1928)**

▶ **Piano Concerto in G (1931)**

is only relatively recently that it has become more popular.

In 1932 Ravel was involved in a minor traffic accident in a taxi in Paris, sustaining a mild concussion. Although he recovered quickly, he never wrote another note of music: the accident had precipitated a degenerative brain disease which gradually reduced him to a pathetic shadow of his former self. His memory began to fail and his powers of concentration gradually diminished. Every cure imaginable was tried, but without success. Finally in 1937 he underwent an operation from which he never regained consciousness, dying a few days later.

MANUEL DE FALLA
1876–1946

One of the second wave of Spanish composers to make an impression on the larger musical world as this century began, Falla was perhaps the first to translate his love of native Spanish musics into wholly convincing and idiomatic orchestral pieces.

Falla was born in the Andalusian city of Cadiz, the southernmost city in the Iberian peninsula and the one closest to the African continent. With a centuries-old seafaring tradition, Cadiz had been one of the last areas of Spain to be wrested from Moorish control, and much of the region's culture, including its music, still exhibits direct links with its Arabic past. The folk music of Andalusia was still very much part of daily life in the city itself, and readily accessible for entertainment or study. The richness and vitality of Falla's mature music, which is largely garnered from his study of Spanish folk musics, owes much to this heritage.

Falla was born into a comfortable middle-class family, the son of a local merchant who prided himself on giving his children a well-rounded education,

Manuel de Falla with singer Vera Jacanopulos

which included private music tuition. He made his first attempts (all of them later discarded) at composition as an adolescent and soon became acquainted with what musical and cultural circles existed at the time in Cadiz. Recognized as a boy with unusual abilities, he attended piano lessons in Madrid under José Tragó, a respected teacher at the Madrid Conservatory, and for several years regularly made the trip between Madrid and Cadiz. He quickly outgrew Cadiz's musical resources but by the time he was 18 a change in the family's fortunes led to his parents moving permanently to Madrid. This enabled Falla to concentrate fully on his private studies with Tragó, and two years later the young man passed the seven year Conservatory course in just two.

Now freed from his studies, the most obvious way for Falla to make a living from music was to become a composer of zarzuela operas, the Spanish equivalent of French operetta. It was light, lyrical and intensely rhythmic, its plots usually involving simple love stories and farcical situations. Falla duly tried his hand at this genre, writing five of them by the turn of the century, but only one gained a production, Los amores de la Inés in Madrid in 1902. Feeling zarzuela was not to be his natural compositional habitat, Falla began lessons with a composition teacher at Madrid Conservatory, Felipe Pedrell. Pedrell had an unusually comprehensive knowledge of Spanish musical history, including the rich heritage of the Spanish polyphonists as well as the huge variety of folk music from all the regions. These lessons, though lasting no more than a year, proved vital to Falla's discovery of his true musical direction.

DON'T MISS

▶ **4 Pièces espagnoles (1902–08)**
▶ **Noches en los jardines de España (1907–16)**
▶ **La Vida breve (1913)**
▶ **El Amor brujo (1915)**
▶ **El Sombrero de tres picos (1919)**

In 1904 the Royal Academy of Fine Arts of San Fernando in Madrid announced a competition (equivalent to the Sonzogno Prize in Italy) for various types of compositions, including one-act operas. Falla seized the opportunity; with his old Cadiz friend, zarzuela librettist Fernández Shaw, he quickly completed a one-act opera, La Vida breve; it won the prize. But Falla's dream of a Madrid production was not translated into reality, and in order to generate the income to escape from Spain and move to Paris, then the cultural centre of the world, in 1907 the composer joined a travelling dance troupe which eventually took him to Paris. There he found the musical world immersed in a series of Iberian evocations; Debussy and Ravel were both working on compositions with a Spanish theme, and Albéniz was working on his masterpiece Iberia.

Falla had already begun writing the Pièces espagnoles for piano while in Madrid, and on his arrival in Paris showed them, as well as La Vida breve, to Paul Dukas who immediately recognized their worth and effected Falla's introduction to Parisian musical circles. Together with Debussy, he also gently pressed the publisher Durand into publishing these piano pieces. For several years Falla eked out a living by giving lessons and undertaking musical hack-work. He also made a start on the famous Nights in the Gardens of Spain for piano and orchestra, but in 1912 the Nice Opera accepted La Vida breve for production in their 1913 season. This led directly to Albert Carré at the Opéra-Comique taking it for a January 1914 Paris production. Madrid's Teatro de la Zarzuela—until then disdainful of Falla's effort—gave a November 1914 première. Falla, back from Paris for the première, with the first draft of his beautiful Seven Spanish Folksongs in his bags, was given a torchlight escort home from the theatre.

As WWI began its destructive course in France, Falla opted to remain in Madrid. The stimulation of the Paris years sustained Falla between 1914 and 1919, and he wrote enduring masterpieces such as Nights in the Gardens of Spain, the ballets El Amor brujo and El Sombrero de tres picos (The Three-cornered Hat). Any one of these three wonderfully vivid and inventive masterpieces would have guaranteed Falla's international reputation; the three together made him an artist of the first rank in his own generation. Excerpts such as the 'Ritual fire dance' from El Amor brujo have since become independently famous in any number of arrangements, but this does not detract from the uniqueness and quality of Falla's achievement with these works, bringing together in a fiery and wholly convincing way the folk and art traditions of Spanish music through the medium of the dance. *El Amor brujo* in particular contains that peculiarly Spanish tradition of *cante hondo,* or deep song, the fierceness of which is burned into flamenco music as well as much of Federico Garcia Lorca's best poetry. *The Three-cornered Hat* was originally created for Diaghilev's Ballets Russes, which spent large periods of time during WWI in neutral Spain while the rest of Europe tore itself apart.

In 1919 Falla decided to leave Madrid and move to Granada, at which point the overt influence of Spanish folk music lessened. He was fond of saying "I feel like a Spaniard when I'm abroad and like a foreigner when I'm in Spain", and his slow distancing of his style from folk links was part of this process. The severity to be found in an otherwise typical piano work, *Fantasia baética* (1919), commissioned by Artur Rubinstein and dedicated to him, suggests a desire to compose music not necessarily so easily assimilable. Full of technical and musical difficulties and

not content to project merely a mellow face to the world, this remarkable work signalled the beginning of a new phase for Falla, and one in which he would attempt to reach the deeper core of Spain's identity. In this he was helped by his friend Lorca, who was also interested in the Spanish spirit and its many manifestations in words and music, and committed to what he called 'the poem of the deep song'. Out of this friendship grew the idea to set puppet plays—an old tradition in southern Spain—to music, and the two men collaborated on Falla's most famous puppet theatre piece, *Master Peter's Puppet Show,* which was extracted from *Don Quixote* and given its first performance at a private puppet theatre in Paris in 1923. The work had a role for harpsichord which perhaps hinted at what was to follow: Falla's own Harpsichord Concerto (1923–26), in which the keyboard instrument is accompanied by five others (flute, clarinet, oboe, violin and 'cello) each of which occasionally takes the soloist's role. The work was a conscious means of reinvestigating Spain's courtly past and the harpsichord

music which had arisen from the pre-Classical period.

Falla's latter years were not particularly fecund, and the added turbulence of the Civil War when it came made it impossible for him to remain in the country of his birth. On his doctor's advice, after serious illness had kept him virtually house-bound through the worst of the fighting, in 1939 Falla migrated to Argentina where he settled in a small town in the Sierra de Córdoba called Alta Gracia. Here he remained until his death in 1946. His final two decades were largely taken up with composing first the *Homenajes* (1920–38), a suite in four sections for orchestra, three of them dedicated to old mentors, including Debussy and Dukas, and latterly the ambitious scenic cantata *Atlántida*, a setting of a Catalan epic poem, which was left unfinished at his death. The work was finally brought to completion by one of Falla's erstwhile students, Ernesto Halffter, and premièred in Milan in 1961. Accorded a cautious welcome, *Atlántida* has since struggled to find a regular audience.

O T T O R I N O   R E S P I G H I

1879–1936

Respighi's gift for orchestral colour and flowing melodies would have made him a popular and respected figure in previous times, but he was composing traditionally-crafted music during a time of relentless exploration. Consequently, his popularity with

the public was never equalled by critical esteem.

Respighi was born in Bologna and studied at the Liceo Musicale where he was quickly recognized as an outstanding violinist and an equally accomplished viola player. When he

completed the Liceo course he accepted an appointment in St Petersburg as first viola player in the Russian Imperial Orchestra, a position which brought him into contact with Rimsky-Korsakov. During the three seasons he spent there, Respighi took private lessons from the great pedagogue, and his Russian mentor's gift for orchestration and exotic colour was by no means lost on the young Italian.

After a brief period in 1902 working in Berlin with Max Bruch, Respighi returned to Bologna and began composing in earnest. Some of the earliest pieces to have survived in today's repertoire are the Piano Concerto in A minor and the Suite for string orchestra, both from 1902 (the latter not to be confused with the Suite in G for organ and string orchestra, 1902–05), but it was as an opera composer that Respighi first tried to make his mark. His first, *Re Enzo*, was a full-length comic opera, reaching production in Bologna in 1905, but it failed to make a great impression. Similarly *Semirama* (Bologna, 1910) relied too heavily on lush orchestration and not enough on drama. Both operas disappeared after their initial production, and it seemed that Respighi, now married, would have to continue to make a living as a member of the Mugellini Quintet. But he was determined to succeed in composition, from around 1908 onwards working solely as a composer, teacher or as a conductor of his own works. In 1913 his burgeoning reputation led to his appointment as Professor of composition at the Santa Cecilia Conservatory in Rome.

By the end of 1914 he had written two more major orchestral pieces, the *Sinfonia drammatica* and *La Sensitiva* for voice and orchestra. By this time Respighi was well into his stride as an orchestral composer, his influences—such as Debussy, Richard Strauss and Rimsky-Korsakov—entirely subsumed by

---

DON'T MISS

▶ **Fontane di Roma (1914–16)**
▶ **Antiche danze ed arie par liuto 1–3 (1917–32)**
▶ **Pini di Roma (1924)**
▶ **Trittico botticelliano (1927)**
▶ **Gli uccelli (1927)**
▶ **Feste romane (1928)**

---

his own particular vision. In the following two years he wrote his first masterpiece, the symphonic poem, *Fontane di Roma* (Fountains of Rome) which brought him international fame. He followed this triumph in 1924 with *Pini di Roma* (Pines of Rome), delayed by the composition of two ballets, *La Pentola magica* and *Sèvres de la vieille France*, and another two operas, *La bella dormente nel bosco* and *Belfagor*. Respighi desperately wanted theatrical success, but it was his tone poems which were to keep his fame alive, and the *Pines of Rome* proved equal in popularity to the earlier Roman tone poem. His first serious attempt to utilize the music of past ages bore fruit with the 1917 first suite of *Antiche danze ed arie per liuto*, based on music by Molinaro and Galilei. The grace of his settings eventually led to two further suites, from 1924 and 1932. In 1919 Respighi enjoyed success when he took fragments of Rossini's canon and wove them into the ballet *La Boutique Fantasque*.

During the 1920s Respighi continued to compose music across a broad spectrum of genres (the *Concerto Gregoriano* for violin, a Toccata for Orchestra, his *Poema autunnale*, the major lyric poem *La Primavera*), but his most impressive results continued to

come from his tone poems. Now made financially independent by his royalties from *Fountains* and *Pines of Rome*, the middle-aged Respighi resigned from the Conservatorio in 1925, and after a long American tour accompanied by his wife (and where he was supported by his great champion Toscanini), he devoted himself entirely to composing. *Vetrate di chiesa* (Church Windows), a suite of four portraits, was the first result of this 'retirement', while 1927 (the year of his trip to Brazil which was to spawn *Impressioni brasiliane*) witnessed the creation of two of his most charming suites, the *Trittico Botticelliano* and *Gli uccelli*. In 1929 the last of the Roman tone poems, *Feste Romane*, appeared, but this rather garish and bombastic work has remained the least-known of the three.

By this time Puccini had died, leaving Respighi to succeed him as the premier Italian composer of the day. He still longed to enjoy unqualified success in the theatre, and to this end he wrote the ballet *Belkis, Queen of Sheba*, the opera *Maria Egiziaca* and the blood-curdling melodrama *La Fiamma*, first seen in Rome in 1934. None of them held its place on the stage, although the opera created a stir due to Respighi's use of a story which would have impressed even the young Verdi. By now he was perceived, even in Italy, as a purveyor of a style which was no longer up to date. Yet he had one more opera in him, inspired by a reading of Shakespeare's *The Rape of Lucrece*. He finished composition in the autumn of 1935. While orchestrating the finished short score Respighi was diagnosed as carrying the bacterial infection which was to kill him, and it was with the utmost difficulty that he came within 29 manuscript pages of completing *Lucrezia*. His widow Elsa scored these last pages after his death in the spring of 1936. A year later *Lucrezia* enjoyed its first performance, revealing a wholly beneficial simplification and clarification of Respighi's operatic style. The work has not survived as a regular visitor to the world's stages, but is a fitting testimony to Respighi's talent. Today he may be remembered primarily for his fantastic tone poems, but as this century closes, the real breadth of his musical achievement is finally revealing itself.

BÉLA BARTÓK
1881–1945

A committed nationalist and a musicologist with an endless fascination for native music generally, Bartók transcended academic constraints when it came to his own music. One of the towering composers of this or any other century, 50 years after his death he remains central to an understanding of the music of today.

Bartók's life shares so many characteristics with the disenfranchised and displaced inhabitants of central Europe during the first 50 years of this century as to be termed 'typical'. He was born in a town in eastern Hungary which was absorbed, together with vast tracts of Hungary, into Romania after 1920. He watched as the Austro-Hungarian empire imploded and the unstable political mix of post-1918 emerged. He finally became an exile when the shadow of Nazism fell over the Slav lands. The Magyars of Hungary were separate from every other Eastern European agglomeration, and Bartók's own nationalism was not one based on vague romantic notions of the beautiful countryside, but on the uniqueness of his nation's history and its people.

Bartok was born into a comfortable if not wealthy family; his father was a headmaster and his mother a talented amateur pianist. When Béla was only seven, his father died at the age of 33, leaving Béla to be brought up in an exclusively female household. Although a sickly child, Bartók's innate musical gifts greatly impressed his piano teacher, winning for his mother a year's sabbatical so that she could promote her son's career. Accordingly, his mother took the family to Pozsony (now Bratislava), a town with a respectable cultural tradition, where she obtained a job at the teacher training school. Béla took lessons with the son of the composer Ferenc Erkel, and fell under the influence of both Brahms and Dohnányi. Five years later this latter connection proved important when Dohnányi advised Bartók to chose Budapest Conservatoire rather than Vienna's.

The Budapest Conservatoire delivered Bartók into the hands of an old pupil of Liszt's, István Thomán, who taught him piano—a wholly beneficial influence, as Bartók later confirmed. His composition teacher was not so fortunate a choice; János Koessler saw little of merit in anything Bartók tried to compose. The end result was a creative silence between 1900–02 and a degree of misery for Bartók, who was also passing through another period of ill-health. Two events pulled him out of this trough, both of them discoveries: in 1902 "I was aroused as by a flash of lightning by the first Budapest performance of *Also Sprach Zarathustra*... Straightaway I threw myself into a study of Strauss's scores, and began again to compose..." (Nothing Bartók composed at this time, apart from the symphonic poem *Kossuth*, written along Straussian lines, has stood the test of time.) The second event was the discovery of native Hungarian folk music—as opposed to the gypsy and recruiting song traditions which previous composers had plundered. At about this time, Bartók also met the young composer and musicologist, Zoltán Kodaly, and the two became friends. In the summer of 1905 Kodaly made his first field trip to collect peasant music, and in 1906 Bartók went on his own mission deep into the Hungarian plains. That same year their joint booklet, 'Twenty Hungarian Folksongs', was published, and though the work it contained was quickly eclipsed by both men as their methods and research became more exacting, it remained a landmark publication.

The effect on Bartók's own compositional thinking, which anticipated so much of what was later to transpire in Western art-music, was profound. Later he wrote: 'From this music we may learn unique terseness of expression and inexorable rejection of all inessentials; that is exactly what we have been longing for after the prolixity of Romanticism'. The last piece of the picture in terms of Bartók's early influences followed when he was introduced by Kodaly to the music of Debussy.

With his way ahead now clear, Bartók was appointed Thomán's successor as Professor of piano at Budapest Academy. This gave him a stable income, a scholarly environment and plenty of free time to pursue his folk music studies. Unlike Kodály, who stuck mainly to Hungary, over the next few years Bartók travelled far and wide in his pursuit of various strands of song and style, making field trips to Transylvania, Romania, Turkey and even to Egypt. These early trips seem to have been some of Bartók's happiest times; moving among people who lived harsh, uncomplicated lives, often amongst countryside of arresting beauty, seemed

Béla Bartók (right) with violinist Rudolf Kolish

to produce a balance which Bartók greatly admired. Of their music he wrote that 'the melodies are examples of the highest artistic perfection'.

That same year, 1907, brought a romantic trauma which Bartók never forgot, and which penetrated his habitual icy, reserve: he fell for a 19-year-old violinist, Stefi Geyer. The relationship foundered on the question of religion—Bartók was a confirmed atheist—and Stefi broke off the liaison by letter. His replies indicated the

connection between the concentrated fire and wild expression of his music and the inner man, so rarely glimpsed elsewhere in his life. A natural corollary of his deepening understanding of folk music and his emotional devastation was his increased maturity as a composer. This was demonstrated in his piano and chamber music, with the First String Quartet being composed in 1908, the *Fourteen Bagatelles* the same year, and the early collection of folksongs and dance which, transcribed for piano, became *For Children*. Of the orchestral works, the *Two Portraits (One Ideal, One Grotesque)* were the most intriguing, being constructed on themes used in a suppressed violin concerto written for Stefi Geyer.

The First String Quartet Kodály once described as Bartók's "return to life". This was a literal as well as figurative return, for by the autumn of 1909 he was married to Marta Ziegler, a girl of 16 (he was 27). Their first child, Béla, was born just one year later. The externals of Bartók's life changed little in the years before the war; accompanied by his wife, he went on field trips, his teaching and research continued, and his music slowly gained more concert exposure. He gradually found himself in the same position as composers such as Schoenberg, Stravinsky and Berg as his new pieces aroused violently opposed reactions from his audiences. His exhilarating *Allegro barbaro* (1911) for piano became synonymous with his composer's personality. Unfortunately he was not the type of man who could deal confidently with this type of notoriety, his friends and colleagues noting his withdrawal from ordinary social intercourse. Bartók himself must have been aware of his own desperate

shortcomings, for his only opera, *Duke Bluebeard's Castle,* deals with a man whose profound loneliness is heightened by his inability to allow anyone, even his self-sacrificing wives, the intimacy for which his soul craves. The opera, superficially linked with *Pelléas,* is a strikingly original work which failed to find a production until 1918.

The outbreak of WWI had a minimal impact on him; anti-Hapsburg and increasingly aware through his studies of the richness of the folk cultures of nearby Romania and Slovakia, he was not called up due to his poor health and spent the first two years of the War collecting and ordering his folk materials, although the *Sonatina* (1915) was completed. With Romania's invasion of Transylvania in 1916, Bartók's feelings were expressed in the taut, urgent folk-inflected Suite, Op. 14 for piano, followed by the equal tension and passion of the Second String Quartet (1915–17). A return to the stage, however, came about due to the persuasiveness of a poet friend, Béla Balázs, who had been the librettist for *Bluebeard's Castle.* He and Bartók used Balázs' short story of *The Wooden Prince* as the basis for a ballet which was premièred in May 1917. It was Bartók's first unqualified success with the Hungarian public, its fairy tale light-heartedness clearly helping to smooth its path. This success triggered a production of the still unheard *Bluebeard's Castle* in 1918, and the work began its journey towards worldwide acceptance. Yet the turmoil of these years took their toll on Bartók's always precarious health.

The end of the war and the collapse of the Hapsburg empire led to political

turbulence in Hungary and the establishment of an oppressive right-wing government after a brief interim Communist regime. Bartók, Kodaly and Dohnányi had all helped create a new musical administration under the Communists and paid the price, remaining deeply out of favour until the 1923 celebrations of the union of Buda and Pest. During that time Bartók completed his third and last work for the stage, the ballet *The Miraculous Mandarin,* a work full of savagery and horror, murder and lust, all interwoven with a horror story usage of magic. Due to the lurid subject matter and the radical nature of the music, this work was not performed in Hungary until after the composer's death, although it reached the stage in Cologne (a single performance in 1926 before it was banned) and Prague.

The 1920s were the decade of Bartók's most extreme radicalism. As if attempting to purge himself of all outside influence, he retreated to works for piano alone or small chamber ensembles, with the extreme and complex Studies, Op. 18 of 1918 being followed by his two Sonatas for Violin and Piano, both dedicated to the brilliant emigré Hungarian violinist, Jelly d' Arányi. She and Bartók played the First Sonata together in Paris and London to great acclaim. After the folk-derived *Dance Suite* of 1923, written for the Buda and Pest celebrations, Bartók began his momentous set of piano studies, *Mikrokosmos,* in 1926, two years after the publication of his treatise on 'Hungarian Peasant Music'. This project would reach fruition in 1939. The Piano Sonata and the *Out of Doors* suite, with its vital, magical 'night music' movement, followed in

1926, both monumental keyboard achievements. With the arrival in 1927 of the revolutionary and epoch-making Third String Quartet, in which Bartók began his redefinition of the scope and musical language of the genre (furthered by the Fourth Quartet of 1928), his international status, aided by his frequent tours, became unassailable.

His personal life during this time had not been free from strife: a sudden divorce in 1923 followed by an almost immediate remarriage to Ditta Pástory, a 21-year-old student, led to a complete change in his domestic arrangments, and a break from his son. Yet the new marriage would bring him stablitiy and would last the rest of his life, as well as deliver him another son.

In 1927 Bartók made his first visit to America where he introduced his highly-charged, percussive First Piano Concerto. In Chicago he was taken to a speakeasy and heard 'real negro jazz' for the first time, finding that 'they frequently improvised and this was fascinating'. Yet he could see no reason to embrace jazz in his own music: 'We have beautiful folk music of our own', cultural hegemonies notwithstanding. The pattern of his life proceeded as before; he toured a great deal and appeared on various international cultural committees while the political and cultural situation in Europe gradually deteriorated. He was now more financially secure and in the novel position of being commissioned for new works. Among his major achievements in the early 1930s was the choral masterpiece the *Cantata Profana*, the Second Piano Concerto and the *Forty-four Duos* for violins. By 1934 his Fifth String Quartet was completed.

Shortly afterwards he left the Budapest Academy he had taught at for nearly 30 years and landed a research position at the Hungarian Academy of Sciences, a post which suited him perfectly. Yet the vicious cycle of Fascist thought and of tugging the forelock to Hitler drew Hungary ever closer into the Nazi orbit, and when the government began to pass anti-Semitic laws, Bartók could see what was coming. After the Austrian 'Anschluss' of 1938, Bartok wrote to a friend of 'the most terrible prospect. That is the imminent danger that Hungary will surrender to this regime of thieves and murderers. The only question is— when and how?' He speedily transferred his publishing rights from Universal Edition of Vienna to Boosey & Hawkes in London.

However, Bartók continued to write works of major importance. He also began extensive performance tours in tandem with his talented pianist wife. By the time he left Hungary in 1940 he had completed his last String Quartet No. 6, the Second Violin Concerto, the beautiful *Divertimento*, the *Music for Strings, Percussion and Celeste*, *Contrasts for Piano, Violin and Clarinet* and the thrilling *Sonata for Two Pianos and Percussion*. All these works show a total harmony of compositional method, content and style. The death of his mother in December 1939 freed him from the need to stay in Hungary, and he took his family to America in the summer of the following year.

Bartók's years in America were decidedly unhappy; he was dogged by illness, desperate homesickness, incomprehension by much of the musical establishment, and poverty brought about by the loss of royalties

frozen by the War in Europe. Only the constant kindness of friends kept the family afloat. By late 1942 Bartók's health had become precarious, and in early 1943 he was diagnosed as suffering from leukaemia. He was not told. In the summer of 1943 he received the first of the commissions which would alleviate his family's poverty and rekindle his creative spirit. In his last two years of life, though hampered by his progressive illness, he completed the luminous and optimistic *Concerto for Orchestra* as well as a masterful solo Violin Sonata (1944) for his great admirer and champion, Yehudi Menuhin. His Third Piano Concerto (written for his wife to perform) was completed—all but the last 17 bars of the orchestral score— and work on a viola concerto was sufficiently advanced for it to be completed from his sketches after his death. In September 1945, with his son Peter returned from the US army and the family reunited in New York, Bartók's condition suddenly worsened. He died before the month was out. There is little doubt that, but for his illness, Bartók would have continued at the peak of inspiration for many years to come.

DON'T MISS

▶ **Cantata Profana (1930)**

▶ **Piano Concerto No. 2 (1930–31)**

▶ **String Quartet No. 5 (1934)**

▶ **Sonata for Two Pianos and Percussion (1937)**

▶ **Concerto for Orchestra (1943)**

▶ **Piano Concerto No. 3 (1945)**

ZOLTÁN KODÁLY

1882–1967

As great a musical educator as a composer, Kodály split his career unequally between the demands of high academic positions in his native Hungary and the call of his creative muse. Although he perceived the voice as the foundation of his music, ironically his most famous music today is orchestral in nature.

Kodály was born in Kecskemét, a small town in southern Hungary. His father was a gifted amateur violinist, his mother a pianist, so music was present in the family home from the beginning. Zoltán began violin studies at the age of 10, and later taught himself 'cello so as to make up a family chamber group. His first experience of genuine Hungarian folk music came from a servant singing songs around the house; he became fascinated and spent a great deal of time listening to the songs and learning to differentiate the genuine article from that played by gypsy musicians in fashionable salons. By the age of 17 Kodály was ready to enter Budapest Academy of Music, where he began composing in the manner of Brahms; a short piece for violin and piano, *Adagio* (1902) has remained in the repertoire.

Zoltán Kodály

While at the Academy, he and Béla Bartók struck up a friendship. In 1905 Kodály was ready to take his interest in folk music to the point of field research, using cylinder recordings done 'on location' and on-the-spot transcriptions to record the music.

Bartók was to follow suit the next summer. In 1906 the earliest version of Kodály's first successful orchestral music, *Summer Evening*, was completed.

In 1907 he became a teacher at the Liszt Academy of Music in Budapest, a position he retained until his death.

More concerned with research than even the conscientious Bartók, Kodály was also a less prolific composer. In 1909 he wrote his First String Quartet, Op. 2, a work which contains folk-inspired elements, but in equal measure with music inspired by as diverse a set of composers as Debussy, Dvořák and Brahms. The fourth variation in the finale was written by Emma Sándor, who became Kodály's wife prior to the Quartet's première in 1910. That same year saw the completion of the Sonata for Cello and Piano, a work more important for what later emerged from it than for its own intrinsic merit; five years later, Kodály transformed the central material of this work into the masterpiece Sonata for Solo Cello, Op. 8 (premièred 1918), which used sonata form but was enormously inventive in the incorporation of modes, polytonality, slurs, speech-like inflections, harmonics and a range of expressive devices brought to the melodic line and heightening the instrument's eloquence.

His next significant work, written immediately after this, was his Second String Quartet, Op. 10. This work reflects the insecurity and tension of the times in which it was written, as well as the new angularity introduced into his music from his long study of folk music and his gradual weaning from his earliest stylistic influences. It was composed in 1916–18 and first performed in Vienna in 1919. Soon after, the Seven Pieces for Piano, Op. 11 were published. During the short-lived Communist regime of 1919, Kodály took on, together with Bartók and Ernö Dohnányi, the task of reforming Hungarian musical education. This alone was enough to damn him in the eyes of the right-wing successors to Communist government from 1920 onwards, and during the following decade Kodály experienced repeated difficulties in retaining his teaching position at the Academy, at one point having to accept a demotion from Deputy Director to mere Professor—this after nearly 20 years of service.

Nevertheless, his research activities, teaching and composing contnued unabated, and by the mid-1920s he had gathered nearly 3,000 folk melodies and their variants.

By this time Kodály had also determined that his specific compositional role lay chiefly with vocal music, and his offering for the 1923 celebrations of the joining of the towns of Buda and Pest was the major choral work, Psalmus Hungaricus, Op. 13. It was a very personal work, the text being drawn from Psalm 55, where David asks God to deliver him from the evil intentions of his adversaries, but its message was proved universal by the instant success it scored at its première. At a stroke Kodály was given an international profile as a composer. He was to continue setting choral texts for the rest of his life, but few attained that level of popular success, much of his choral writing being educational in intent.

The next major compositional achievement was the quasi-opera Háry János, a setting of a picaresque series of cameos reminiscent of the Czech anti-hero the Good Soldier Schwejk, and Kodály used a musical genre which he felt in keeping with the folk-like simplicity of the often comic and ironic situations in which the hero finds himself. It followed a similar musical treatment of the traditional Hungarian folk songs to be found in the stage work The Spinning Room (1924). The music is full of colour and melody, but the words are for the most part given in the singspiel tradition of acted dialogue, rather than sung, and it is significant that the première was given as a theatrical entertainment rather

than as an opera. After the work's initial success, Kodály rearranged the Háry János orchestral sections and edited them into a suite composed of six movements which remains possibly his most popular music worldwide. Two more direct results of his involvement with folk music were his Dances of Marosszék, written for piano in 1927 and orchestrated in 1930, based on music from the Transylvanian region of that name, and the Dances of Galánta, an orchestral working of gypsy-type music of the sort Kodály had heard when he lived there as a boy.

The 1930s brought Kodály more headaches as the Hungarian government became ever more closely identified with Hitler and his policies. The integrity of his work and his own international standing as both a scholar and a composer helped protect him from the worst excesses, and he continued to produce important new works, including the Budavári Te Deum (1936) and his Variations on a Hungarian folksong, 'The Peacock' (1938–9), the latter written on commission for the 50th anniversary of

DON'T MISS

▶ Sonata for Cello, Op. 8 (1915)

▶ Psalmus Hungaricus, Op. 13 (1923)

▶ Háry János, Op. 15 (1927)

▶ Dances from Galánta (1933)

▶ Peacock Variations (1938–39)

▶ Concerto for Orchestra (1939–40)

the foundation of the Amsterdam Concertgebouw Orchestra. In 1937 Kodály had given his fresh arrangement of the old tune new, politically incorrect, lyrics, and dedicated them to the Budapest Socialist Workers' Choir: after one Hungarian performance the song had, naturally, been banned. The *Variations* were like a public nose-thumbing to the authorities.

Kodály's Concerto for Orchestra was written in 1939–40 in response to a commission from Fritz Reiner's Chicago Symphony Orchestra. It was one of his most ambitious works and anticipates Bartók's eponymous piece by over three years. A cogently argued single-movement piece, its quality is insufficiently recognized. Unlike Bartók, Kodály remained in Hungary throughout the War resigning from the

Academy in 1941 and refusing to collaborate with the authorities. During the Russian siege of Budapest in 1944 he completed the moving *Missa brevis,* and with the coming of the Communist state after the end of the War, Kodály was universally acknowledged as the pre-eminent musician and music-historian in the country. His influence was complete, his system of teaching, based on the assimilation of sung music rather than instrumental, becoming ubiquitous throughout Hungary.

Kodály continued to divide his time unequally between his scholarly, administrative and creative vocations, often with the result that his own compositions took too long to produce, but many treatises and research papers were also written in the next 20 years

which were of great personal and national significance. His last major orchestral work was the Symphony in C, subtitled *In Memorium Arturo Toscanini,* in acknowledgement of the courage and good faith the Italian maestro had shown during the 1930s in particular when championing the works of composers of Kodály's generation, not least Kodály's own. The work skilfully blends folk elements with the Classical form of the symphony, showing Kodály's own complete mastery of his materials. The whimsy and lightness of the music—a feature of so much of his best work—is in direct contrast to the darkness and intensity in Bartók, and may give a clue to Kodály's manifestly more successful efforts to combine his life and life's passions into a satisfactory whole, living as well to a respectable and revered old age.

IGOR STRAVINSKY

1882–1971

Regarded by many as the most protean 20th century composer and a musical presence impossible to ignore, Russian-born Stravinsky repeatedly proved his brilliance at utilizing every musical style and genre in which he took an interest.

Born in Oranienburg, Stravinsky was the third of four sons. The well-off middle-class Stravinksy family spent the summer months in the country and the rest of the year in St Petersburg, where his father was a successful singer at the Royal Opera. From an

early age Igor showed great interest in music, finding the piano the most satisfying instrument. But a career in music—especially as a composer—was regarded as very insecure, and Igor was discouraged from pursuing formal lessons, although he was given private tuition in piano, theory and counterpoint before being compelled to attend law school. At St Petersburg University he encountered the sons of Rimsky-Korsakov, later meeting the composer himself who praised his earliest compositions. The death of Igor's father in 1902 removed one of the main barriers to his desire to

pursue a musical career, and from 1902 to 1908 (when Rimsky-Korsakov died), the older composer acted as Igor's personal tutor.

In 1906, now 23 and a university graduate, Stravinsky married his first cousin, Catherine Nossenko who bore him a son, Théodore, the following year. Stravinsky continued to compose with increasing confidence, and in 1909 one of his early orchestral works, *Fireworks,* so impressed Sergei Diaghilev—on a visit from Paris looking for new works for his Ballets Russes—that the great man commissioned

Igor Stravinsky

Stravinsky to supply a ballet based on a Russian folk theme. The result, *The Firebird*, premièred at the Paris Opéra in 1910, was a complete triumph. From then on, Stravinsky, now resident in Paris, was seen as a composer of international standing and at the forefront of the new generation of composers. For the next few years his destiny would be closely allied to Diaghilev and his Ballets Russes.

At Diaghilev's request Stravinsky began turning a piece of orchestral music featuring the piano into the disarming ballet *Petrushka*, a work which used the Russian folk tale of the puppet Petroushka who possesses seemingly magical qualities, only to suffer in love and death. The follow-up ballet, *The Rite of Spring*, again deals with Russian life and consciousness, but turns this time to prehistory where the coming of the new spring was welcomed by a pagan ritual ending in the death of a sacrificial victim. The enormously resourceful music, made up of simple elements but worked up to a degree of

unprecedented rhythmic complexity and stunning orchestral deployment, is full of the most barbaric and primaeval sounds, sounds moreover which are not in the least indulgent or comfortable but immensely threatening to the listener. The first-night Paris audience in 1913 was both terrified and outraged, and a near-riot ensued. From this time on Stravinsky, together with Schoenberg, was seen as the leading avant-garde composer of the day. In his last creative burst prior to the advent of WWI, Stravinsky offered *The Nightingale*. When the original plan for a Moscow production collapsed, Diaghilev again stepped into the breach and mounted successful productions in both Paris and London.

At the outbreak of War, Stravinsky was a successful man with a family of three children (one of whom later became a concert pianist), a landowner in Russia and a composer whose rich invention from Russian nationalist themes not only fitted into that age of rampant atavistic nationalism, but also echoed

the new primitivism of the visual arts. But the War, which gave rise to the Russian Revolution and the establishment of the Bolshevik dictatorship, led to the mass confiscation of private properties, and Stravinsky's family—like so many others—lost everything of value. He now had to work for a living. But he had already demonstrated his adaptability to external events by writing quasi-theatrical pieces such as *Renard* (1915) for voices and a much-reduced orchestra reflecting the economy required in times of war. He also suffered from a period of ill-health which took him to Switzerland in pursuit of a cure and interrupted his work on his next composition, an odd amalgam of ballet and cantata with strong rustic Russian ties, *Les Noces*. Although the vocal score was largely finished by 1917, another six years would pass before it was finally given an accompaniment which satisfied Stravinsky. By then his concerns had moved on; the wholesale nature of the War's slaughter is reflected in *The Soldier's Tale* (1918), another curious hybrid in which spoken declamation was equally as important as the music itself, and where for the first time Stravinsky stressed the universality of experience, rather than the peculiarly Russian angle he had previously pursued.

Stravinsky's movement away from folk and nationalist sources of inspiration is clearly documented by the music he composed during the 1920s, when he abandoned any hope of returning to Russia and took up residence in France. His interest in music and rhythms beyond Russia had been signalled by the short but effective *Ragtime* for 11 instruments (1918), where the music

DON'T MISS

▶ The Firebird (1910)

▶ Petrushka (1911)

▶ Le Chant du Rossignol (1917)

▶ The Rite of Spring (1913)

▶ Pulcinella (1920)

▶ Les Noces (1923)

which had been the rage of Europe before the War found its way into his creative system. His first major work of this period, the ballet *Pulcinella*, which was modelled on the old Italian *commedia dell'arte* characters and consciously built upon borrowings from the early 18th-century Italian composer Pergolesi, was premièred in 1920 by Diaghilev's Ballets Russes and showed a radical shift in musical emphasis. Within a few years Stravinsky was wholeheartedly embracing a neo-classicist approach to music-making which arose out of a twofold impetus. Firstly, he felt the need for a creative renewal away from Russian traditions, and that his new interest in earlier musical forms across Europe was profound and exciting for him. Secondly, Stravinsky had decided, not far short of his fortieth birthday, that it was time to change careers–from being a composer of staged material to a composer of concert music which he could also play and conduct. After 1925, when he recognized the value of mechanical recording during an American tour, he became an assiduous performer of his music in recording studios as well concert halls. Apart from leaving his interpretations for posterity, it also augmented his income.

The works which not only fit all these requirements but also exhibit a master operating at the peak of his powers in a new genre and style include the Concerto for Piano and Wind instruments (1923–24), the *Capriccio* for piano and orchestra (1929), the Octet (1923), *Symphonies of Wind Instruments* (1920, substantially revised in 1947), *The Fairy's Kiss* (1926) and the *Apollon musagète* (1928). In addition to these masterpieces were the one-act *opera buffa* called *Mavra* (1922) and the great opera-oratorio *Oedipus Rex* (1927), a setting of Sophocles' story with words by Jean Cocteau. During this extraordinary burst of sustained creativity Stravinsky reinvented himself as a musician and composer several times over. It is not surprising that many times in this decade he left his audiences a long way behind, and that works such as *Oedipus Rex* have taken decades to be assimilated into the mainstream of concert-going.

During the following decade, the plurality of Stravinsky's interests and influences, as well as the clarity of his methodology, became even more pronounced. An early indication of this came in the work delivered on commission to the Boston Symphony Orchestra in 1930, the *Symphony of Psalms*, composed 'to the glory of God'. In 1926 Stravinsky had experienced a profound rebirth of faith in the teachings of the Russian Orthodox Church, and the *Symphony* was only one of a continuing stream of religious works, major and minor, which Stravinsky would create during the remainder of his career. Combining musical elements found in the Slavic liturgy with such Western models as the fugue, complex rhythm and a

reduced timbral spectrum, this intense and uplifting work showed a deepening of his musical roots as well as a refinement of technical accomplishment and a previously unemphasized religiosity. A major landmark in Stravinsky's output and in this century's music, it is still somewhat undervalued. From just one year later came the Violin Concerto, written for the violinist Samuel Dushkin (who was the soloist at the Berlin première with Stravinsky conducting), followed by the Concerto for two solo pianos (completed 1935) and the *Duo concertant* for violin and piano.

True to his belief in sound recordings, by the mid-1930s Stravinsky had recorded the Octet, the *Capriccio* and the *Symphony of Psalms*, togther with smaller pieces such as *Ragtime*, the *Suite Italienne* and the *Duo concertant*. Stravinsky and his son also recorded the Concerto for Two Pianos. By 1934 his melodrama *Perséphone* had enjoyed a Paris première, the year he applied for and was granted French citizenship. The following year his autobiography, *Chroniques de ma Vie*, appeared and in 1936 he composed the three-act ballet *Jeux de Cartes*, commissioned by the American Ballet (New York), and a year later he began the marvellous *Dumbarton Oaks* chamber concerto.

The year 1938 saw the beginning of a series of personal disasters for Stravinsky when his daughter Ludmila died from consumption, followed by the death of his wife in 1939 of the same disease. Stravinsky retired to a sanatorium for a few months. Shortly after his re-emergence, his 85-year-old mother, a constant presence in the family since her flight from Russia in

1922, also died. This sequence of catastrophes, followed by Hitler's invasion of Poland and the onset of WWII, caused Stravinsky to take up an invitation to deliver a series of lectures at Harvard University as a method of removing himself from Europe and going to live in America. Settling initially in Boston and New York, by mid-1940 he had moved to Los Angeles where he applied for American citizenship and married his long-term amour Vera de Bosset (they had been lovers for over a decade), who had followed him from France earlier that same year.

With this second wholesale change in his circumstances accomplished, Stravinsky composed the five-minute *Tango*, a mordant, sensual piece of writing. His Symphony in C, which he had completed on commission from Chicago Symphony Orchestra soon after arriving in America, exhibited a simplicity and openness which linked it to Haydn, though Stravinsky himself was more concerned with the way the symphony fell into two halves— European and American. Just as *The Soldier's Tale* had evolved out of his impressions of WWI, five years after the Symphony in C, the Symphony in Three Movements—a radically different approach to symphonic structure—came from his reaction to what he called three 'specific cinematographic impression(s) of the war'.

Stravinsky, who had a long-time interest in certain aspects of jazz, had accepted a commission from Woody Herman for a chamber piece, and in 1945 supplied Herman with his *Ebony Concerto*, which was premièred by the First Herd at Carnegie Hall. This

followed the highly enjoyable *Scherzo á la Russe*, composed in 1944 for the Paul Whiteman Orchestra, a considerable aggregation with a foot in both the Classical and jazz genres.

Like Rachmaninov, for many years Stravinsky had suffered financially from the consequences of Soviet Russia's non-membership of the international copyright convention, except that in Stravinsky's case, it was his first and most popular works which remained in a financial limbo. After the War's end and his American citizenship was assured, Stravinsky signed an exclusive deal with the New York branch of Boosey & Hawkes for all future works, and helped them to buy the rights to music published by the Russian Music Publishing Company. Over the next few years he made new arrangements of older works with the twin aims of improving them for performance purposes and giving him a copyrighted and authorized performing version which would earn him legitimate income. By March 1948 he had also finished a religious work which had been ocupying him since 1944, *Cantata*. The ballet *Orpheus*, which sprang from a new interest in the music of Monteverdi and his contemporaries, was given its New York première in 1948, and its concentration on mimed song pointed to his major work begun in 1948 at the instigation of Boosey & Hawkes, the opera *The Rake's Progress*. The libretto was mapped out by W. H. Auden and Stravinsky, with assistance by Chester Kallman, and the work was premièred in Venice in the famous old Fenice Theatre in 1951. It has been the subject of controversy ever since, due mainly to its conscious use of what Stravinsky himself called 'clichés' of the

old operatic tradition of Mozart, Rossini and Gluck, especially the composer's insistence on writing a work which would be "told, enacted, contained entirely in song—as distinguished from so-called speech-song, and Wagnerian 'continuous melody' which consists, in effect, of orchestral commentary enveloping a continuous recitative". In a world still recovering from the shock of Berg's *Lulu* and *Wozzeck*, this was a radical departure.

Yet within a few years Stravinsky himself was to develop a previously dormant interest in serialism, spurred by his friendship with the young American musician and musicologist, Robert Craft, a devotee of the Second Viennese School. Stravinsky was too strong a musical personality to ever lose his own identity in another's, and his approach to dodecaphony was cautious and selective. The technique was noticeable in the ballet *Agon*, begun in 1953 but not completed until 1957, and consisting of 21 separate dance movements where serialism is an occasional presence. Two projects which interrupted work on the ballet were *Three Shakespeare Songs* (1954), his first song cycle since 1919, and *In memoriam Dylan Thomas*, a setting of

DON'T MISS

- ▶ **Piano Sonata (1924)**
- ▶ **Symphony of Psalms (1930)**
- ▶ **Symphony in 3 Movements (1942–45)**
- ▶ **Ebony Concerto (1945)**
- ▶ **The Rake's Progress (1951)**
- ▶ **Agon (1957)**

Thomas's own poem in memory of his father. Thomas and Stravinsky had planned to collaborate on an opera, and Thomas was en route to Hollywood for their first meeting when he died in New York.

Another reason for the delay in finishing *Agon* was the stroke Stravinsky suffered in 1956, but by 1958 he was putting the finishing touches to his third major sacred work of the decade, *Threni*, which was premièred at that year's Venice Festival. Similar to his 1955 Venice offering, *Canticum Sacrum,* in musical forces and forms but greatly dissimilar to that celebratory work in spirit (the texts are from the 'Lamentations of Jeremiah'), the series of settings are all composed within the bounds of serialism and the work is a fully-integrated artistic whole. This differs again from the *Cantata* of 1951—52, where medieval English words were used.

As with many of the greatest composers who manage to survive creatively into old age, Stravinsky's late works reveal a master who could compress his profoundest musical thoughts and expressions into miniatures of tremendous weight and authority. Both instrumental works (*Movements*, for piano and orchestra, 1960; *Variations, Aldous Huxley in Memoriam*, 1963–64) and vocal compositions (*The Flood*, 1961–62; *Abraham and Isaac*, 1962–63; *Requiem Canticles*, 1965–66) show utter mastery of musical colour and material with the sparest of ensembles. Stravinsky also avoids bombast and pretension, penetrating to deeper levels of human experience through the most economical of means. By this time Stravinsky had written many requiems for passing members of his generation and beyond, one of the most famous being the four-minute *Elegy for JFK*, with words by Auden,

but after the *Requiem Canticles* there was just *The Owl and the Pussycat*, then silence.

By then Stravinsky was in his mid-eighties and increasingly frail. His reconciliation with Russia had come in 1962 when he had been honoured in Moscow, Leningrad and his birthplace Oranienbaum, and had stepped onto Russian soil for the first time in nearly 50 years. The late 1960s was a time of illness and tidying-up, with various books of conversations, observations and reminiscences being prepared, invariably with the active participation of Robert Craft. A stroke and ulcer in 1967 presaged worse to come, and by 1970, having moved back to New York from Hollywood, Stravinsky was hospitalized for pneumonia. He enjoyed a reprieve that year, but died in April. He was buried according to his wishes in Venice, a city long associated with his artistic triumphs.

EDGARD VARÈSE
1883–1965

Varèse was one of the greatest musical mavericks of his time; so much so that half the current century had passed before critics and the public began to realize they had missed something of importance. By the 1960s his influence was making itself felt in virtually every area of modern compositional thinking.

Varèse, a native Parisian, was expected by his parents to become an engineer; to this end he was educated in science and mathematics at the Ecole Polytechnique. However, at the close of his teenage years, Varèse rebelled against his father's plans, abandoned the parental home and took up music studies at the Schola Cantorum where he was taught composition by d'Indy and counterpoint by Roussel. In 1907

he moved to the Conservatoire, joined Widor's masterclass and formed the Choeur de l'Université Populaire. At this point he was struggling to form his own compositional identity, convinced that he heard music in a different way to how it was taught but unable to articulate his visionary approach. He was attempting to combine an instinctive feeling for sheer sound with the influence of African percussion and the modernistic aesthetic tendencies of the Futurists. His greatest contemporary influences up to 1914 were Debussy and Busoni, both of whom he knew personally. He later destroyed all but a tiny handful of works written at this time.

Leaving Paris for Berlin in 1909, he continued to develop his theories until the outbreak of WWI, at which point he returned to France and enlisted in the French army. A near-fatal illness secured his release from further military duty in 1915, and at the end of that year Varèse decided to emigrate to America, setting up permanent residence in New York City. Once there he set about organizing the New Symphony Orchestra and the International Composers Guild in an attempt to get new works by contemporary composers onto the performing agenda. By 1920–21 he was writing music which would remain part of his official canon, including *Amériques* (premièred by Stokowski in 1926), a piece for over 140 instruments, and *Offrandes*, two songs for soprano and chamber orchestra. *Amériques* disappeared from the repertoire between 1929 and 1965, which is hardly surprising given the violent emphasis placed on sheer sound and the most brutal rhythmic thrust to be heard in Classical music apart from *The Rite of Spring*, still a deeply revolutionary work in 1920s America.

Hyperprism from 1922 contains a further step towards the mature Varèse, with its concision (just six minutes long) and its concentration on sound and percussion. By now Varèse

was decribing himself as a sculptor in sound and was dispensing with traditional methods of building musical form such as motific development, variation and even fragmentation. *Hyperprism* was also premièred by Leopold Stokowski in 1926. Following this were Varèse's two most famous scores, *Arcana* (1925–27), for orchestra, and *Ionisation* (1929) for percussion instruments and sirens. By this stage he was concentrating on sheer sound, and the monumentality of his creations was literally overwhelming to audiences, who felt as if they had been steamrollered by an elemental force. The 1933 première of *Ionisation* caused near-panic in certain sections of the audience.

Varèse was not to be deflected from his course, however, and broke new ground again in 1934 with *Ecuatorial* in which he combined his interest in Central American music with an early electrical instrument, the Thereminovox. This was combined with bass voice, bass chorus, various brass, organ and percussion. Such radical experiments virtually guaranteed Varèse's ostracism from the American mainstream, and with his own compositional process in a cul-de-sac, he withdrew from composing until the arrival in the 1940s of the magnetic tape recorder. After the birth in Paris of *musique concrète* and the subsequent development of pure electronic music in the 1950s, Varèse, excited by the possibilities, returned to composition. *Déserts* (1950–54) combined acoustic instruments with electronic sounds delivered by a tape recorder, and its

brilliant combination of percussive and tonal elements created a sensation at its Paris première. From this point onwards, although Varèse only had a decade left in which to write a handful of compositions such as *Poème électronique* and *Nocturnal*, his reputation burgeoned quickly as his early compositions were seen to exactly anticipate so many of the post-war concerns. His last works were typically ambitious, the *Poème* requiring no less than 425 loudspeakers and a battery of lighting effects to be adequately presented at its Brussels première in 1958. *Nocturnal*, incomplete at Varèse's death, came from a nightmare world of startling sounds and violent explosions, realizing his long-held belief in his role as a manipulator of sound, rather than as a formal composer.

Varèse remained a maverick until his death, and even today his music only fits awkwardly into the stream of this century's music, but many later composers have supped at his musical feasts and incorporated important lessons on the nature of organized sound and its relation to more orthodox musical practices.

DON'T MISS

▶ Arcana (1925–27)

▶ Ionisation (1929–31)

▶ Density (1936)

▶ Poème électronique (1957–58)

ANTON WEBERN

1883–1945

With the help of his artistic mentor Schoenberg, Webern worked through an early tendency to lush romanticism in his music to produce some of the most compressed, gem-like musical masterpieces of the century.

Anton von Webern (the 'von' was dropped in the chaotic aftermath of WWI) was born in Vienna into an ancient aristocratic family with an estate, Preglhof, in Lower Carinthia. His father, a highly-placed mining engineer, was transferred first to Graz, then to Klagenfurt in 1894, where Anton began to study the violin and 'cello. As a teenager he showed an interest in writing music rather than simply playing it (although some years later he would maintain that "quartet playing is the most glorious music making in existence"), and by the age of 15 had composed his first song, 'Vorfrühling'. Indeed, songwriting was to remain important throughout his career—more than half the opus numbers he ascribed were to vocal works, and a substantial number of the early works without opus number (like the piece above) were songs. Between 1899 and 1904 over 20 songs were composed, all of them containing a kernel of Webern's mature character as a composer, although the influences of composers such as Brahms, Mahler and Strauss is easily discernible. In 1902 he was allowed by his father to study music at Vienna University, a move facilitated by the family's return to Vienna for the father

to take up an appointment in the Ministry of Mines.

At the University Webern became a research assistant to the musicologist Guido Adler, but found little encouragement from his teachers for the type of forward-looking music he admired. Although he continued to write songs and, in 1904, an 'idyll for large orchestra', *Im Sommerwind*, which displayed a passionate fondness for Richard Strauss's tone poems, he felt frustrated at his lack of progress in the matter of theory, and applied to a number of composers to become their pupil. Only when he submitted some of his early songs to Arnold Schoenberg in late 1904 was he accepted by a teacher who could meet his compositional desires. Webern's formal lessons with Schoenberg lasted just four years, but during that time he became so closely identified with Schoenberg's approach to musical thinking that, like the younger Alban Berg, he remained intimately bound to the developments of Schoenberg's own theories for many years to come. In 1906, at the age of 23, Webern left university with a Ph.D in music.

During his years with Schoenberg he wrote a number of pieces, including a slow movement for string quartet, a *Rondo* for the same forces, a set of five songs to poems by Richard Dehmel, plus his first two works with opus numbers, *Passacaglia*, Op. 1 for large orchestra, and the piece *Entflieht auf leichten Kähnen*, Op. 2 for

unaccompanied choir. These latter pieces, although not fully mature in style, he regarded as a form of graduation from Schoenberg's intense tutorship, and by the summer of that year he was conducting in a theatre at Bad Ischl resort.

By this stage Schoenberg was investigating the implications of writing music without key centres, and Webern quickly followed suit. Earning enough to survive from conducting work at theatres in Vienna (even doing a brief spell at Danzig), Webern pressed ahead with consolidating his mature style. This process was evident in the 10 songs on poems by Stefan George in which Webern's style was marked by the use of extreme chromaticism, often mixed with large intervallic leaps in the melodic line and large pitch spans. His rhythmic flexibility and his concentration on small note values tended to differentiate his music from Schoenberg's, as well as their lower emotional and sensual content. Webern always preferred quiet to loud, and his crescendos, even in his works for full orchestra, tended to be brief to the point of short sharp shocks.

The next major work was the *Five Movements* for string quartet, Op. 5 of 1909, and this followed the lead taken by Schoenberg the previous summer in chamber music, as well as his own discoveries made in the George songs. Webern relished the widened timbral palette at his disposal as he utilized non-traditional bowing and percussive effects. This is immediately noticeable in the Six Pieces, Op. 6 for orchestra (1909), which carried an unstated programme (a Mahlerian echo, perhaps) dealing with a visit to his parents' graves in their Carinthian home town. His mother, to whom he was especially close, had died that year (his father had died earlier), and there is evidence from Webern himself that the more overt emotionalism in works from 1909 came from this event. These compressed movements, though identified by Webern as an informal arrangement, carry great emotional power in their lightning shifts from near silence to brief, shattering epiphanies.

In 1910 Webern's relationship with his cousin Wilhemina Mörtl resulted in marriage, and their first child, Amalie, was born soon after. The Rilke songs Op. 8 were closely connected with his feelings at this time, as were the *Bagatelles* for string quartet Op. 9, composed between 1911–13. When Schoenberg left for Berlin in search of a more sympatheitc working environment, Webern followed him in the autumn of 1911, but eventually returned with his wife to Vienna. He was rapidly reaching the conclusion— reinforced by a miserable period in Stettin—that he should dispense with his conducting career; certainly, the composition of the Five Pieces for orchestra, Op. 10 reinforced his desire to work solely as a creator.

Webern's life was interrupted by WWI; although his poor eyesight kept him from active service, he remained within the war machine until 1917, finding enough time to concentrate his compositional energies on the song-form: his Four Lieder, Op. 12 show a

wide diversity of poetic inspiration, from Chinese poetry to Goethe and Strindberg, though the thoroughness of their composition is paramount. From this period until 1926 Webern was almost exclusively concerned with composing songs accompanied by different types of chamber ensembles. The commonly given explanation for this was his need for a text to solve the structural problems posed by composing music without a key-based tonality (something Schoenberg also countenanced), but Webern's increasing abstraction of the vocal line, his growing determination to treat it as an instrument, suggests that he now regarded the vocal line as a convenient shape upon which to build his structures, regardless of the actual text being set.

After the War Webern had three children and a wife to support; a succession of uncongenial conducting jobs, plus the occasional student pushed his way by Schoenberg, kept the family barely solvent. As his compositions found wider international acceptance, the conducting work he was offered began to be both more to his taste and to be based in Vienna, where he could remain with his family. He also signed a publishing contract with Universal Edition in Vienna, and royalties, as

well as advances against future earnings, began to trickle in.

When Schoenberg adopted serialism and the twelve-tone theory in the early 1920s, Webern followed his example. Webern adhered more closely to the actual theory than did Berg, but this did not cramp his musical personality; indeed, in many ways it freed him to create his perfect miniatures within a system which offered him infinite choice alongside a reassuring musical architecture. His *Drei Volkstexte,* Op. 17, for soprano, clarinet and guitar— settings of simple, pious homilies—use the dodecaphonic system for the first time and are remarkable for their sophistication and complexity. His Lieder, Op. 18 find him using more developed serial techniques such as retrograde motion, inversion and retrograde inversion. By the time he returned to writing wholly instrumental works, such as Symphony, Op. 21, he had assimilated serial thinking completely. In this work the essence of his style was clear: the utter concision of his writing, the clarity of his textures, the extreme brevity of his statements, the obsession with leaving no inessential music on the page, the need to express himself musically in highly abstract, complex formulae and methods which continue to evolve for the entire length of a piece. These qualities are also demonstrated in his Trio Op. 20 and Quartet for violin, clarinet, tenor saxophone and piano, Op. 22 (1928–30).

By the end of the 1920s Webern was travelling throughout Europe to conduct his music and to attend performances of his works. From 1927 to 1934 he was a conductor for Austrian Radio and also worked as a transcriber for Universal Edition. He continually tried to use his influence to promote Schoenberg and his music, but with the rise to power of the Dollfuss government in 1934, his position was undermined as the political mood took a definite swing to the right. From 1936–38 he worked on his Variations for Piano, Op. 27 and his String Quartet, Op. 28 but again his family

faced hardship as the work began to dry up. With the Anschluss of 1938, Webern was declared *persona non grata* by the Nazis and his music banned in the fatherland (which now included Austria). Nevertheless, he continued composing, writing one of his greatest orchestral works, the Variations for Orchestra in 1940–41. This work, of great formal complexity and perfection, is in the same polyphonic tradition as that of Bach, although the elements of the polyphony are vastly changed.

Life in Austria during the war proved very difficult, and although Webern avoided imprisonment or any other direct oppression, he worked at menial jobs to keep his family afloat. His sons were pressed into the army, while in 1944 Webern, now over 60 years old,

became an air warden. All the members of his family, apart from one son who was killed on the Yugoslav front, survived the War, but Webern himself came to a tragic and senseless end. In September 1945, with Nazism defeated and a number of important peacetime appointments on offer, he travelled to the small Austrian town of Mittersill to visit two of his married daughters. Unfortunately, one of his sons-in-law was being pursued by the American military for trading on the vast black market which operated in post-war Austria. Outside his daughter's house on a dark night, Webern was quietly smoking an illicit cigar when confronted by a patrolling American soldier. The soldier shot first and asked questions later. By then, Webern was dead.

ALBAN BERG

1885–1935

Of the three great names assocated with the 'Second Viennese School' of the early 20th century, Berg is by far the most widely loved for the simple reason that he remained deeply devoted to melody, however radical his compositional techniques became. In his Violin Concerto he created one of the most luminous and beautiful violin works of the century.

Berg is one of the relatively few composers closely associated with

Vienna who was both born in the city and spent most of his life there. He was one of four children born to Konrad Berg, a self-made businessman, and Johanna. The family was sufficiently well off to afford a summer house, the Berghof, by Lake Ossiach. Though he did not excel at school, Alban was an energetic and happy enough boy, with a deeply romantic view of life. In adolescence his great passion was literature, not music. In 1900 his father died from heart disease at the age of 54, and shortly afterwards, Berg had his first attack of

the asthma from which he would suffer for the rest of his life. During the years 1900–1904, as the family's financial standing began to deteriorate, Berg tried to complete his education; although without any formal training, he made his first attempts at musical composition, writing a number of songs in the style of his favourite composers, Brahms, Wolf, Strauss and Schumann. The year 1903 was one of crisis and resolution for Berg: he sired an illegitimate daughter by a local girl, failed his final examinations and suffered from poor health and hypochondria. All this led to a failed suicide attempt, although it appears to have been more a cry for help than a serious attempt.

The help came a year later when he began working as a probationary accountant for the Austrian civil service; then, without his knowledge, his brother Charly took some of Alban's songs to Schoenberg. The composer was impressed; commenting that "music to him was a language", he took Alban on as a student. Years later, Schoenberg wrote that Alban was 'an extraordinarily gifted composer. But in the condition in which he first came to me, it was impossible for him to imagine composing anything other than *lieder*... He was absolutely incapable of writing an instrumental movement or even an instrumental theme'. So a rigorous diet of basic harmony and counterpoint set Berg on the road to adequate compositional techniques. The first signs of this evolution, *Seven Early Songs,* were written between 1906 and 1908 but not made public until their collation in 1928 by Berg himself. Still redolent of Brahms, Schumann and Strauss, the songs also exude the overpowering presence of Mahler, but nonetheless show signs of organization and symmetry which are so characteristic of the mature Berg.

The death in 1905 of a rich aunt brought unexpected financial relief. By 1906 Berg had left the civil service and become a friend of Anton Webern, another of Schoenberg's pupils. Webern, athough Berg's intellectual equal, did not follow the social and cultural pursuits which so fascinated Berg, who liked to spend his time with such

Alban Berg

luminaries as the artist Gustav Klimt, the architect Adolf Loos and critic Karl Kraus. Yet Webern, Berg and Schoenberg were bound together by their admiration for Viennese icons like Gustav Mahler and Richard Strauss. By November 1907 Schoenberg considered Berg and Webern's student efforts good enough to be heard in public, and a presentation concert was arranged

which was reasonably well received. A similar event took place in 1908, when Webern's *Passacaglia,* Op. 1 was presented, but Berg was still shy of his first opus number.

In the spring of 1907 Berg met Hélène Nahowski; a year later, after a long fight with Hélène's disapproving father, they were married. In the same year

DON'T MISS

▶ Altenberg Lieder, Op. 4 (1912)
▶ 3 Orchestral Pieces, Op. 6 (1914–15)
▶ Lyric Suite (1925–26)
▶ Wozzeck (1925)
▶ Violin Concerto (1935)
▶ Lulu (1937)

Berg wrote his Opus 1, his only piano sonata. This signalled the end of his formal period of training under Schoenberg who recognized that this deftly-constructed work marked Berg's transition into the world of mature composing, although Berg diligently continued until 1910 to show his works to Schoenberg for approval, submitting his Four Lieder, Op. 2 and String Quartet, Op. 3. Schoenberg's April 1911 concert under the aegis of the Society for Music and Culture included both Berg's piano sonata and his string quartet, but the concert was virulently attacked in the press and Berg was dismissed as a composer whose jokes were 'no longer funny'.

Berg's next completed composition was the breakthrough set of five orchestral songs set to picture postcard poems by Peter Altenberg, most commonly called the *Altenberg Lieder,* Op. 4. These extremely short songs (one lasts barely a minute) use a massive orchestra, but in the manner of a chamber ensemble. Altenberg's cryptic texts are given a passionate, overtly dramatic treatment (foreshadowing the dramatic genius Berg would bring to his operas) which, together with the general melancholy of the music, failed to please Schoenberg who was hoping Berg would shed his dreamy nature, and become more

worldly. In 1913, on a trip to Berlin to see Schoenberg, Berg received a severe reprimand from his old teacher, partly on aesthetic grounds and partly on grounds of disloyalty to him, which brought about a distinct coolness between them.

Berg made a genuine effort to write a lighter work, hoping that his *Drei Orchesterstücke,* Op. 6 (1914–15) would be 'happy music', but he could not gainsay his own creative nature, and one of the central motifs of the new work was a march in the final movement designed to honour a departed hero, Gustav Mahler, himself fond of both military and funeral marches in his symphonies. The touches of Debussy to be found in the orchestration would not have pleased Schoenberg either. This major orchestral composition had to wait until 1929 for its première. With the outbreak of WWI, the severely asthmatic Berg was enlisted in August 1915, but soon after the commencement of his training, he suffered a physical collapse which brought him back to Vienna and to a job in the War Ministry.

A further cause for the estrangement between Schoenberg and Berg was that in 1914 Berg had seen the Viennese première of Büchner's play *Woyzeck,* deciding at once that it was the perfect

vehicle for an opera. Schoenberg felt that a full opera was too much for Berg—that he was too timid to bring the savage and bitter tragedy of the poor soldier Woyzeck to the stage. Berg was determined to prove him wrong; his military service had given him first-hand experience of the life of a soldier and he was able to bring his own authentic angle to the drama. By the end of the war he had progressed sufficiently to be confident of finishing the music to *Wozzeck* (as the play and its operatic equivalent were known), and although he was characteristically slow in his compositional work, by early 1922 the work was ready for production.

Before reaching this stage Berg showed *Wozzeck* to Schoenberg, who immediately recognized the magnitude of his former student's achievement and wrote to Universal Edition in an attempt to get him a publisher. They refused, and Berg had the score printed privately. At this point Schoenberg again went cool on the whole project, and as opera house after opera house rejected the work, he poured scorn on Berg's hopes. It was Alma Mahler who was instrumental in charming the head of UE into publishing the opera, and after a great deal more effort from all concerned, the music director of the Berlin Opera, Erich Kleiber, resolved that he would bring about the opera's first production, which took place in December 1925.

From that point on Berg was famous, his opera an international talking-point in music circles. He had taken a series of dramatic fragments (Büchner had never finished the play) relating to the psychopathic study of a victimized army private who eventually kills his girlfriend, and turned it into a moving and compassionate elegy to all of life's victims. Its complex and ingenious formal organization was wholly subservient to the need to communicate. This latter quality even Berg seemed unsure of: his friend Adorno spent hours wandering the streets with Berg after the successful Berlin première trying to convince him that just because it was a success with the audience this did not mean there was something fundamentally flawed or facile about the work. Berg's drive to communicate artistically with the outside world was always stronger than either Schoenberg's or Webern's.

While Berg had been trying to find a producer for *Wozzeck*, he had managed to complete two new non-vocal works. The first one, Chamber Concerto for piano, violin and 13 wind instruments (1925), was intended as a present on Schoenberg's fiftieth birthday (it was 10 months late) and used a system of note identification which took the initials of Berg, Webern and Schoenberg, among others, to weave an entertaining concerted web of music. A work framed in good spirits (although the slow movement is a memorial to Schoenberg's recently deceased first wife Mathilde), it was his first composition after Schoenberg had announced his serialist theories to his colleagues, although Berg's work only refers to its methods occasionally. In its interweaving of initial-motifs, the Concerto also pointed to the method Berg would employ for telling the secret story of his passion for another woman, Hanna Fuchs-Robettin, in his Lyric Suite for string quartet (1926). This work, which has been termed an opera without

words, was by Berg's own admission 'a small monument to a great love', a love that lasted until Berg's death. The suite is a masterpiece of organization and inspired musicality, in which the severity of the musical logic does not for a moment restrict the music's humanity and powers of communication.

A similar judgement can be passed on all of Berg's later music, where the eloquence and intensity belies the rigorous musical logic holding the whole structure together. Berg's next opera, *Lulu*, begun in 1926 after some initial hesitation over choosing Wedekind's heroine from *Erdgeist* and *Die Büchse der Pandora* over Hauptmann's play *Und Pippa Tanze*, deals again with something he called in his Lyric Suite 'suffering destiny'. The heroine is an embodiment of pure female sexuality, aware of her power over men but not of its dangers. Berg constructs his entire opera as a palindrome, the apex of which is reached halfway through Act II, when Lulu's rise in society is finally halted and she begins her painful slide towards prostitution, destitution and finally death at the hands of Jack the Ripper. Berg is not telling a moral tale: he approves of Lulu's happy amorality, as his own identification with the love-stricken Alwa shows. Virtually every man who appears in the work stands condemned before its end. Yet the opera is nothing if not romantic, overflowing as well with Berg's characteristic compassion.

This is equally present in his last completed work, the Violin Concerto (1935) commissioned by Louis Krasner and dedicated 'to the memory of an angel', the angel being Manon Gropius, Alma Mahler and Walter Gropius's

daughter, who died suddenly that year, aged 18, from polio. Again the structure is binary, the first part depicting the life and achievements of Manon, the second describing the arc of her fall and death, with the chorale at the end drawing the concerto to a deeply sympathetic resolution. Berg's musical expression in this work is even more concentrated and lyrical, his creation of a true concerto, balanced between soloist and orchestra, an achievement equalled only by the eloquence with which he sublimates his grief.

Berg's own life while writing *Lulu* had not been easy; as his fame gathered pace and the expectations of his public and peers increased, his emotional life descended into a turmoil unsuspected at the time and, indeed, not revealed until after the death of his wife Helen in 1976. Berg also paid a high price for his principled stand against the drift of Austria towards totalitarianism; within months of Hitler's seizure of power in 1933, Berg's music was banned from live performances in Germany. Before his own death, he was distressed to be described by his own government in January 1935 as 'not a native Austrian composer', and to find his works unofficially blackballed in his own country. Yet it is clear that he would have continued doggedly along his own creative path had he not been struck down by a blood disorder in the autumn of the same year, leaving the orchestration of *Lulu*'s Act III incomplete. After several weeks of rapid deterioration, he died just before Christmas. It would be another 40 years before the world heard his *Lulu* as he had intended it, the missing orchestration completed by another hand.

HEITOR VILLA-LOBOS

1887–1959

An autodidact and a man essentially uninterested in music other than his own, over a period of time the prodigiously energetic and fecund Villa-Lobos came to symbolize the arrival of his native Brazil as a force in international music. He remains today one of the most popular of 20th-century composers.

Villa-Lobos was born into a large family in Rio de Janeiro, Brazil. His father, Raul, was a minor civil servant and an amateur musician. From an early age Raul taught his son the basics of playing his own instrument, the 'cello. Heitor also took up the guitar, teaching himself much of the popular repertoire of the day. At the age of 37 Raul died, leaving his wife with four children to bring up and no source of income. Aged 10, Heitor had to start earning what little he could from occasional jobs with his musician friends in the street bands of Rio.

In his early teens Villa-Lobos began to write music, concentrating for the most part on short compositions for piano, or voice and piano, many of which were unplayable as he had no knowledge of piano technique. By the early years of the new century, Villa-Lobos was making a modest living as a cellist with various travelling theatre companies. Between 1906 and 1909 he made a number of short tours into the Brazilian interior where he became interested in native folklore and music. His

Heitor Villa-Lobos

knowledge of such music was later rounded out by a friend, Edgard Pinto, who had travelled extensively and wrote books on folk music and whose published examples were invariably the source of most of Villa-Lobos's few borrowings from indigenous music. During his years with these travelling groups he met and married the pianist Luilia Guimaräes who was to become an important sounding-board for his musical ideas.

Feeling the need to expand his inadequate musical knowledge and technique, Villa-Lobos enrolled at the National Music Institute in Rio. Although quickly recognized as having outstanding talent, he was incapable of studying in a structured way and left within a year; from then on he was largely self-taught. It was only through

constant revision of his music that Villa-Lobos transformed himself from an occasional writer of short pieces into a serious composer. One of the first surviving compositions to demonstrate this was the *Suite populaire brésilienne* (1908–12), written for guitar. The following year a 'cello concerto appeared, followed in 1914 by the three *Danças caracteristicas africanas*. He also completed an opera, *Izath*.

With this burst of activity Villa-Lobos launched his compositional career, remaining from then on amazingly prolific, composing more than 2,000 works. For the rest of the decade he continued to write stirring and controversial music which spread his reputation nationally, with the *Dança frenética* of 1919 leading to the accusation that he had brought unbridled savagery to cultivated concert halls. In 1915 he also began the series of string quartets which would span the rest of his creative career and become one of his greatest compositional achievements, writing two in that year and completing four by 1917. Ever-ambitious, Villa-Lobos also completed four symphonies before the decade was out, and in 1920 he composed the first of his famous series of *Chôros*, the initial one for guitar.

In 1917 Diaghilev's Ballet Russes came to Brazil to escape the rigours of war-torn Europe, thereby exposing Villa-Lobos to the music of Stravinsky, Rimsky-Korsakov and Debussy. He also met the Ballet's conductor Ernest Ansermet, an astute judge of musical worth who suggested the piano virtuoso Artur Rubinstein should visit Villa-Lobos when he toured South America the following year. By this time the composer was becoming frustrated by his lack of critical recognition in Brazil, and Rubinstein's endorsement led indirectly to a government grant for him to visit Europe. In 1923, at the age of 32, he left for Paris where he only knew Darius Milhaud, whom he had met in Rio. His year in Paris produced little music, but opened his eyes and ears to the types of ideas which were then at the forefront of French music. He also discovered that what fascinated people most about his own work was its exoticism—its Brazilian-ness.

This led to an outpouring of more specifically nationalistic material; between 1924 and his return to Paris in 1927, Villa-Lobos wrote eight more in the *Chôros* series. This form was largely of his own concoction, modelled on the

type of rhythmic music played by Brazilian street bands. Europe's nearest equivalent to the *Chôros* is perhaps the serenade in its more formative years. Villa-Lobos wrote these works for many different instrumental and vocal combinations, including No. 2 for flute and clarinet (1924), No. 3 for male chorus and seven wind instruments, No. 5 (also known as *Alma brasileira*) for piano, No. 4 for three horns and trombone, and No. 10 for chorus and orchestra. This long series was completed during the two years he spent in Paris, a time when he was finally discovered by French and other European audiences. Other important pieces completed at this time included the beautiful piano sequence *Saudades das selvas brasileiras* and the remarkable 12 Etudes for guitar.

By now Villa-Lobos, for all his bluff, hyperbole and failure to deliver what he promised, was a respected figure in Europe and a grudgingly accepted composer in his own country, and was also in the full flood of stylistic maturity. On his return to Brazil he showed for the first time an interest in another composer: between 1930–32 he began his next important series of

compositions, the *Bachianas brasileiras* Nos. 1–9, in which he attempted to combine the counterpoint of Bach with the rhythmic and melodic grace of Brazilian music. He was also approached by the Brazilian government to establish a new organization for musical education in Rio. Like the *Chôros* series, the *Bachianas* group was written for differing combinations, including the voice. From the appearance in 1932 of No. 1 (for eight 'cellos) the series was a success, and in the fourth movement of No. 2 (for chamber orchestra) Villa-Lobos found he had an international success on his hands. This was subtitled 'The little train of Caipira', and is a wonderfully invigorating and affectionate portrait of a provincial steam train.

By 1939 Villa-Lobos had finished the first six *Bachianas brasileiras*, including perhaps his most famous single movement, the 'Aria' of No. 5 for soprano and eight cellos. After this masterpiece, his reputation was assured and his popularity grew apace, aided by the composition of the entrancing Five Preludes for Guitar, making him easily the most well-

---

DON'T MISS

▶ **Chôros No. 1 (1920)**
▶ **12 Etudes (1929)**
▶ **Bachianas Brasileiras No. 2 (1930)**
▶ **Bachianas Brasileiras No. 5 (1938–45)**
▶ **String Quartet No. 6 (1938)**
▶ **5 Preludes (1940)**
▶ **Guitar Concerto (1951)**

known South American composer of all time. By the time Villa-Lobos finished No. 9 in 1945, he was a firm favourite in America and had begun a sequence of annual visits there which he would sustain until his death.

That year saw the arrival of the first of an eventual five piano concertos, written betwen 1945–54, all dedicated to different South American pianists who had become friends, while in 1951 the great guitarist Andrés Segovia commissioned a Guitar Concerto which has remained in the repertoire to this day. Villa-Lobos suffered a health setback in 1948 when he was operated

on for bowel cancer, but during the 1950s, now an established international figure with bases in Paris, Rome and New York as well as his own school in Brazil, he continued to pour forth compositions at an astounding rate, eventually completing 12 symphonies and 17 string quartets, while a Second Cello Concerto also appeared in 1954. Works for the stage, film and for virtually every instrumental combination, let alone choral music (a greatly neglected area of his output), were written and performed, including a ballet of O'Neill's *The Emperor Jones,* and an opera of Lorca's *Yerma the Unfaithful.*

By now Villa-Lobos was almost 70 and his health fragile, although he kept up his formidable international itinerary of appearances and concerts, as well as his usual compositional output. In 1957 there were seventieth birthday celebrations in Brazil and other countries, but only two more years remained to the Brazilian in which, among other projects, he accepted a commission from Pope Paul VI to write a *Magnificat alleluia.* In 1959 he died, in Rio, from cancer. A year later the Brazilian government opened a Villa-Lobos Museum in memory of its most famous composer.

F R A N K   M A R T I N

1890–1974

Martin has taken longer than most of his contemporaries to reach a wider audience. This is not due to any inherent unattractiveness in his music, but more to the enigmatic, witty and measured qualities which make up its core characteristics. In recent decades, the special nature of his choral works in particular have begun to win him widespread acclaim.

Martin was born in Geneva the son of a Calvinist minister, and his reaction to his parentage was to govern much of his subsequent musical development. One of the European generation which included composers such as Poulenc, Honegger and

Milhaud, Martin is usually associated with a much later generation, mainly because his compositional style took an inordinately long time to settle and crystallize. He was nearly 50 before he gained a measure of international recognition with his *Ballade* for flute, piano and string orchestra.

Martin studied in Geneva as an adolescent with Josef Lauber and gained some local recognition in the years before WWI. After the War he went to Paris, remaining there from 1923 to 1925, a period when the city was awash with the exploits of 'Les Six', Stravinsky and early jazz. He assimilated what he could of these developments and then returned to Geneva, where he became an essential

component in Switzerland's musical world, heading organizations and teaching assiduously as well as promoting concerts and developing young talent. He became Director of the Dalcroze Institute in the 1930s, later becoming Director of the Technique Moderne Musique. Yet his own works gained little recognition beyond Switzerland's borders until the conclusion of WWII, when his 1942 cantata *Le Vin herbé* (based on the Tristan myth) was premièred at Salzburg in 1948. With this work it could be said that Martin had discovered his true compositional voice, one which always utilized the principles of tonality however far he might stretch or develop them. His brilliant gift for orchestration and the chamber music output demonstrates, and the 1949 Concerto is one of his most virtuosic.

Martin waited until 1955 before undertaking an opera, the first being *Der Sturm*, based on Shakespeare's *The Tempest*. Martin himself claimed that "the infinite psychological richness of the characters" had brought him to set this work to music; the nature of Shakespeare's late masterpiece also attracted him as it allowed him free reign to develop the idea of fantasy in his music, and indeed Martin incorporated both ballet (in the character of Ariel) and pantomime into his work. Martin's heterogeneous sources of inspiration come across also in his employment of jazz, tango and even Baroque pastiches at different stages of the action. Martin only wrote one further opera, although other stage works were undertaken and completed, his later works concentrating more on the contrasting areas of orchestral and choral music. Martin was not an originator, but he evolved into a highly original composer with a clearly defined method and patina of sound, and one with an unquestionable seriousness of purpose, however playful his theatre music might occasionally be.

Frank Martin

most transparent and delicate tonal colours, either with instruments or voices, makes his works a pleasure to hear, whatever the subject or forces.

One of Martin's most important works came in 1943; the *Sechs Monologe aus Jedermann*, (six excerpts from Hugo von Hoffmannstahl's morality play of 1911 based on the medieval English *Everyman*). The depth of his spiritual and moral questing is revealed in these wonderfully sustained monologues. This religious dimension was always of great importance to Martin, who was later to complete the oratorios *Golgotha* (1945–48), Requiem (1971–72) and *Pilate* (1964), addressing the personal and individual questions raised by these stories and

settings. This is not to say that he did not successfully compose for orchestra, as his Cello Concerto (1965–66), his Second Piano Concerto (1968–69) or his earlier Violin Concerto (1950–51) and Concerto for Seven Wind Instruments (1949) clearly show. He was particularly fond of writing for wind instruments, as his

---

DON'T MISS

▶ **Mass (1922–26)**
▶ **6 Monologues aus Jedermann (1943)**
▶ **Petite Symphonie Concertante (1945)**
▶ **Concerto for 7 wind instruments (1949)**
▶ **Violin Concerto (1950–51)**

B O H U S L A V   M A R T I N Ů

1890–1959

Even today Martinů is something of an enigma in the world of music, his considerable output largely unknown to the vast majority of music-lovers and academics. Yet he is responsible for a list of masterpieces across a range of genres, all of which deserve the widest possible audience.

Martinů was born in Bohemia, in the village of Polička. His father, in addition to being the village fire-watcher and cobbler, was the church clock-keeper. The family lived in the clock tower itself and Martinů spent his first 11 years reluctant to venture forth, content with his bird's eye view of the surrounding countryside. Interested from an early age in music, Martinů had to teach himself its rudiments as his parents could not afford a music tutor.

Martinů's chosen instrument was the violin, on which he demonstrated such prodigious ability that by his mid-teens he was something of a local celebrity. Impressed by the boy's talent, a group of prominent citizens subsidized him to attend Prague Conservatoire. His life there followed a familiar pattern: a bohemian existence by night, study by day interspersed by a series of confrontations with the teaching staff at the Conservatoire. Before long both Martinů and his teachers concluded that he was not cut out for the rigours of Conservatoire discipline, and in 1910 he was expelled. By then he had already begun composing chamber

music (the unpublished *Elegy* for violin and piano dates from 1909). After a brief period at Prague Organ School, he finished his scholastic career with no qualifications to show for it.

Yet he remained in Prague, playing in ensembles, attending the opera and theatre and composing at a considerable rate—a characteristic approach which would ensure that, by his death, Martinů had composed over 400 works across virtually the entire field of Classical genres. His war (1914–18) was relatively uneventful: unfit for the regular army (his health was never robust), he was relegated to the army reserve and allowed to return to his village where he continued to compose. His parents persuaded him to study to become a teacher, and in 1916 he eventually qualified to teach the violin. Back in Prague at the end of the War, he joined the second violins of the Prague Philharmonic under the great Vaclav Talich. He also spent another short (and unenlightening) period attempting serious academic study at the Conservatoire. Later in life he admitted that "I cannot *learn* anything. I must come to it intuitively".

Martinů continued to compose, and even had a ballet, *Istar,* produced in Prague in 1922. By this stage he knew that the only way for him to progress was to leave Czechoslovakia. As a devotee of modern French music, especially Debussy, Roussel and Ravel, Martinů had little doubt that he must move to Paris, which he did in 1923.

The Paris of the 1920s was no longer the city in which Debussy had held sway; 'Les Six', that irreverent and witty association of young French composers which included Poulenc, Honegger and Milhaud, and whose progenitors included Cocteau and Satie, currently dictated the artistic agenda. Within a few months of his arrival, Martinů was being tutored in composition by Roussel and had completed work on a ballet-comedy, *Who is the most powerful in the world?* (premièred in Prague in 1925). This light-hearted parable of a father mouse trying to establish the most powerful being in the world for his daughter to marry (the sun? a wall? a mouse Prince?) was his fifth ballet and is one of his first works to have remained in the regular repertoire. Martinů continued in a neo-classical vein, with the occasional eruption of popular American jazz-inflected rhythms and structures giving a characteristic flavour to works as diverse as the popular ballet *La Revue de cuisine* (1927), with a plot involving a love affair between kitchen utensils, and his *Cinq Esquisses de danses modernes* for piano (1927). His first major Parisian success was *La Bagarre* (1926), an orchestral piece celebrating

---

DON'T MISS

▶ **La Revue de Cuisine (1927)**

▶ **Trio for flute, cello & piano (1944)**

▶ **Symphony No. 5 (1946)**

DON'T MISS

▶ **Piano Concerto No. 4 (1947–48)**

▶ **Les Fresques de Piero della Francesca (1954)**

▶ **Oboe Concerto (1955)**

▶ **The Greek Passion (1961)**

Atlantic conqueror Charles Lindbergh. A later ballet, *The Amazing Fly* (1927), commemorated the deaths of two French pilots who had failed in their bid to cross the Atlantic by plane just weeks before Lindbergh's solo flight. By this time Martinů had also written two sonatas for violin and piano, and the first of an eventual five piano concertos.

At this time Martinů's music was perceived as being very modern and cosmopolitan (his ear for American popular music was by far the most acute of all the European composers), but his immersion in Czech music was also constantly revealed, especially in his rhythmic values, and in this way his lineage can easily be traced back to the great nationalist Czech composers— Dvořák, Smetana and Janáček. His attitude to creating music and stage works relevant to modern audiences is amply expressed in the preface to *Who is the most powerful in the world?*: 'We shall study the possibilities of the new ballet in the street, in circus rings and dance halls... We shall look for its direct expressions at football and boxing matches. In the same way in which the use of syncopations revolutionized contemporary music, modern reality will revolutionize ballet'. The orchestral work *Half-time* (1924) directly enforces this statement.

The following decade was spent mainly in Paris, where Martinů sustained his prolific output. His Second Piano Concerto (1934) showed the lucidity and freshness of his best writing in the neo-classical idiom he then preferred for concerted music. The multiplicity of stimuli is evident from the folk themes in the ballets *Spalíček* and *Borová* (seven Czech dances), to the provincial setting of the one-act opera *Comedy on the Bridge* (1935), the extraordinary Concertino for Piano Trio and Orchestra No. 2 (1933) and the String Quartets Nos. 4 and 5 (1937–38). The opera *Julietta* was produced in Prague in 1938, the same year as the *Tre Ricercari*, where his love of English madrigals and early polyphony was strongly evident. Another aspect of Martinů's output, which is all too rarely investigated, reached a peak in 1937 with the choral piece *Bouquet* for soloist and chorus. One of the greatest concertos from Martinů's pen appeared in 1938, the Double Concerto for two string orchestras, piano and timpani. During the same year his Concertino for piano and orchestra also made its début. These works are both clouded by emotions evoked by the Nazi annexation of his homeland, with the Double Concerto being finished the day after the infamous Munich Pact. The First Sonata for cello and piano was completed in 1939, by which time it had become clear to Martinů that the way back to Czechoslovakia was permanently barred by the War. Within a year, his expatriot's status in Paris was under direct threat from the invading German forces, and he and his wife fled to America.

Martinů had less difficulty dealing with the practicalities of living in America

than did such refugees as Schoenberg or Bartók, and his musical facility was not impaired after Serge Koussevitsky secured him a relatively undemanding position as teacher of composition in Boston. Perhaps trying to respond to the expectations of a new public which was willing to embrace his relatively comprehensible modern music, and eager to please his benefactor Koussevitsky, who commissioned an orchestral work from him in 1942, Martinů embarked on a series of symphonies, completing one per year between 1942 and 1946—a surprising development for a composer who as late as 1945 described himself as 'the Concerto Grosso type'. Martinů's love of Corelli is reflected in many of his works from the 1930s and 1940s; the Second Symphony shows clear traces of Corelli's artistry, filtered through Martinů's creative psyche. Yet the War remained inescapable, and the Nazi retaliation massacre of the population of Lidice in Bohemia led Martinů to compose his deeply-felt, dark *Memorial to Lidice* (1943). A similar mood grips much of the writing in the Third Symphony (1945), completed after a period of creative and emotional torpor brought about by a combination of homesickness and exhaustion.

Martinů's post-war output often deals with the difficulties inherent in resolving the incompatibilities of Classicism and Romanticism in a mid-century musical language. This at times makes him sound like a deeply conservative composer (much of his later 'cello sonatas would not have unduly disturbed Brahms) but, taken on Martinů's terms, the creative progression is a logical one. That Martinů continued to be interested in beauty as a major ingredient in music is evident from, for example, the exquisite adagio from the *Trio for Flute, Piano and Cello* (1944) and the entire Sonata for Flute and Piano (1945). In 1946 he noted about some of his contemporaries: "I often have the impression that despite the best of intentions there is a misunderstanding somewhere, that the beauty of music has been forgotten, and that music must be beautiful, or it would not be worth the effort". After the completion of his joyous and anticipatory Fifth Symphony, a serious injury resulting from a fall required Martinů to make a major effort to pull his health and creative thought back together. He suffered multiple skull injuries from the fall, and for months afterwards his hearing and balance were badly affected. The unaccustomed sombreness of much of his writing at this time—in the otherwise light-hearted 'Canzone' from the *Toccata e due Canzoni* (1946), for example—came from this shattering experience.

More disappointment came in the shape of Czechoslovakia's post-war

destiny: the advent of Communism meant the permanent barring of an anti-Communist such as Martinů from his homeland. The optimism of his Seventh (and last) String Quartet (1947) was dashed, and although he made a return to Europe in 1948, his Bohemian past was now gone forever. For the next five years Martinů hovered between America and Europe (he wrote his Sixth Symphony in America for his old friend, the conductor Charles Munch), continuing with his prolific output—for example, the delightful *Sinfonietta 'La Jolla'*. The Sixth Symphony, composed in 1951, is one of his most satisfying works, combining fantasy and delicacy with a strong emotional undercurrent. Originally conceived as a rather wild fantasia (with no less than three grand pianos onstage), it finally took more manageable proportions and has been his most popular symphony since its 1955 Boston début, under Munch's baton. By then Martinů was living once more in Europe, having returned permanently with his wife in 1953. The couple alternated between places in France and Switzerland (it is a curious

fact that Martinů never owned a house or apartment), and the composer continued to complete important works, including the massive oratorio *Epic of Gilgamesh* (1954–55) and the opera *The Greek Passion*, first produced in 1961.

Martinů continued in his habitually prolific way, with works such as *Les Fresques de Piero della Francesca* (1954) and the *Nonet* (1959) for wind quintet, violin, viola, cello and double-bass being outstanding and popular examples of his supreme craft, as well as carrying that desired balance between effortless buoyancy and emotional weight. The *Nonet*, written in Switzerland, betrayed the depth of his homesickness which persisted until the end of his life; as with his favourite Baroque composers, his inner longing and pain is revealed in the 'smiling while crying' lyricism of the adagio. By this time, Martinů was ill with what proved to be stomach cancer. He died in 1959, still an exile, but with the comforting thought that his tower in Polička was now a museum dedicated to his career.

SERGEI PROKOFIEV

1891–1953

Forced into exile by the 1917 Russian Revolution, but later swayed by personal beliefs and sentiment to return to his homeland then under Stalinist rule, Prokofiev today remains widely popular. His achievements, however, are commonly under-appreciated due to extra-musical considerations.

Born to successful middle-class parents in Sontzovka in the Ukraine, Sergei proved to be extraordinarily musical; his mother, a talented amateur pianist, began teaching him the piano while he was still an infant. By the age of five he had begun writing music (piano pieces), thus paralleling Mozart and Mendelssohn, and in 1900, at the ripe old age of nine, he composed his first opera, *The Giant*, to his own libretto. Prokofiev seems to have taken his

Sergei Prokofiev

shadows Scriabin, Medtner and Rachmaninov might have cast.

The Second Sonata, Op. 11 (1912) and the Second Piano Concerto, Op. 16 (1912–13) both reflect a more personal musical language and a more convincing emotional and intellectual substance. The concerto caused public dismay at its 1913 première, with the dominant voice of the piano being more strident, the dissonances keenly pressed home. The sonata was hardly better received, its combination of heightened lyricism and remorseless dexterity proving particularly indigestible to its St Petersburg audience. Prokofiev's *Scythian Suite* of 1914, commissioned by Diaghilev soon after the outbreak of war, had equal amounts of barbarism and riotous colour, but the orchestral context was different, its parameters regarded as imaginative invention in the context of programme music, and the work quickly became recognized as an important statement by a young and brilliant composer.

By this time WWI had erupted throughout Europe; as the only child of a widow, Prokofiev was not obliged to join up. Instead, he spent the War composing music, including a setting of Hans Christian Andersen's *The Ugly Duckling,* Op. 18 (1914). He continued with the series of *Five Akhmatova Poems,* Op. 27 (1916) and the Dostoyevsy opera *The Gambler,* Op. 24 before entering a period of 'neo-classicism' some time before his great countryman, Stravinsky, and composing three outstanding works utilizing classicist elements of form and style: his First Symphony, the *Classical,* Op. 25 (1916–17), the First Violin Concerto, Op. 19 (1916–17) and the Third Piano

talent in his stride, enjoying not only good health as a child but a varied and active life. By 1904, the year of his entrance examination for the St Petersburg Conservatoire, he had completed another two juvenile operas, *Desert Islands* and *The Feast during the Plague.* At the Conservatoire his teachers were Annette Essipov for piano, and Rimsky-Korsakov and Tcherepnin for composition.

From the outset Prokofiev's outstanding ability was recognized; his concert performance of his *Suggestion diabolique* (1908) was a particular

success, and it was with a certain amount of chagrin that his First Piano Sonata, Op. 1 (1910) and First Piano Concerto, Op. 10 (1911–12) were received, as it was the general view that such a talented young musician should not have to express himself so radically or so extravagantly. These assertions hardly stand up today; Prokofiev's early piano music bears the fire and élan of youth but little of the biting harmonic language which he was to use so successfully later in his career. Yet these works have sufficient pure Prokofievian elements to be pronounced mature compositions, whatever stylistic

DON'T MISS

▶ **Scythian Suite, Op. 20 (1915)**

▶ **Symphony No. 1 (Classical), Op. 25 (1916–17)**

▶ **Violin Concerto No. 1, Op. 19 (1916–17)**

▶ **Piano Concerto No. 3, Op. 26 (1917–21)**

▶ **Lieutenant Kijé, Op. 60 (1934)**

▶ **Peter and the Wolf, Op. 67 (1936)**

Concerto, Op. 26 (1917–21). In time, the *Classical* symphony became an international concert favourite, although its style remained something of an isolated experiment in terms of the composer's overall career, yet it points to the ability of Prokofiev's fertile musical imagination to mould itself to any given form.

On a more personal level was the series for solo piano: *Visions fugitives*, Op. 22 (1915–18), 20 diverse and poetic interior dialogues which, like late Brahms or Debussy, hardly hint at an intended audience. Short and often enigmatic, ranging from outbursts of joy and ecstatic dance to the gloomiest of meditations, these works seem a personal reflection of the chaos Russia was enduring at that time. Prokofiev remained in Russia throughout the two revolutions of 1917, successfully premièring his Third and Fourth Piano Sonatas in St Petersburg within days of each other in April 1918, but in May he began a world tour, terminating in November in America, only to find it impossible to return to his crisis-ridden homeland. America, however, was not particularly welcoming: his compositions were often misunderstood at best, denounced at worst, with some observers wondering aloud whether this Russian was a Bolshevik. Prokofiev's

stay in America was neither particularly productive nor successful, although his Third Piano Concerto, premièred in Chicago in 1921, was warmly received. His most important commission—from the Chicago Opera—was for the whimsical opera *The Love of Three Oranges*, Op. 33, which was disastrously received in Chicago in 1921 and later in New York.

Not everything connected with his American sojourn was stillborn: he met his first wife, Lina Llubera, in California in 1921, and they were married the following year. By 1922 Prokofiev was back in Europe, and after a period in Bavaria, where he composed his Fifth Piano Sonata and completed the piano score of an opera with a theme of religio-sexual possession, *The Fiery Angel*, he moved in 1923 to Paris which remained his base for the next 10 years. There he was taken up by the avant-garde set personified by Honegger with his *Pacific 231*, and found himself manoeuvred into a position of competition with Stravinksy, the other great Russian composer in Paris at that time, although the two men were operating from very different stylistic and inspirational bases and could hardly be compared. Prokofiev's music gained a noticeable edge and attack during this period, evident in his

Second Symphony, Op. 40 (1924–25)—very different in content and approach to his first—and the two ballets, *Le Pas d'acier*, Op. 41 (1927) and *The Prodigal Son*, Op. 46 (1929), the latter commissioned by Diaghilev.

Meanwhile, progress on *The Fiery Angel* had halted in the face of general indifference to the idea of a première. Frustrated beyond measure by this enforced silence, Prokofiev embarked on a reworking of the opera's music into a symphony which eventually saw the light of day as his Third Symphony, Op. 40 (1924–25). This was premièred in Paris with Pierre Monteux conducting, and its bewildering complexities made it few friends, one of them, oddly enough, being Stravinsky. Prokofiev was once again to base his following symphony, the Fourth, Op. 47 (1929–30), on material from a stage work, this time the failed ballet *The Prodigal Son*. Yet *The Fiery Angel*, a project which Prokofiev longed to bring to the stage, went unperformed in his lifetime, finally reaching the stage in Venice in 1955.

The composer's long exile from his homeland was coming to an end; during a tour of Soviet Russia in 1927, he was treated like a returning hero in the press and at concerts. His own music was beginning to veer away from the harshness of his initial years in Paris, and what he found in Russia made him want to contribute to the building of a new society. As he commented later: "I did not grasp the significance of what was happening in the USSR. I did not realize that events there demanded the collaboration of all citizens—not only men of politics, but men of art too". After his decision to return (the process itself took from 1932 to 1936, by which time he was permanently settled with his wife and two children in Moscow), he willingly bent his musical talents to suit the needs of socialist realism as defined by the Soviet government. It is a measure of the sincerity of his approach and the uncompromising nature of the projects in which he was involved that the music from his early years back in Russia was invariably of a very high standard. His first Soviet commission was for film music to the mildly satirical *Lieutenant Kijé*; by July 1934 Prokofiev had moulded the incidental music into a colourful and coherent five-movement suite full of his characteristic melodies. Prokofiev's run of piano concertos had been completed by the Fourth, Op. 53 (for left hand only) and Fifth, Op. 55 in the years 1931–32. Henceforth his concertos would be for stringed instruments. The first to arrive during his transition period was the Second Violin Concerto, Op. 63 (1935), quickly followed by the Cello Concerto, Op. 58, which was premièred in 1938. This première was a total disaster, the criticism of the work being so harsh that Prokofiev withdrew it; the concerto remained unperformed and forgotten in Russia until 1947, when Rostropovich played it to Prokofiev's approval. The composer then decided to completely recast the material as the *Sinfonia Concertante* for 'cello and orchestra, Op. 125. This has since remained the preferred version.

Just four days after the Cello Concerto's disastrous début came the triumphant opening night of the Eisenstein film *Alexander Nevsky*, with music by Prokofiev. The composer quickly recast the music from the film into cantata

form, and in this incarnation *Alexander Nevsky* has proved one of his most popular works. But by that date Prokofiev had triumphed with a creation whose melodies are still known worldwide by people who have never heard his name. This, of course, was *Peter and the Wolf*, Op. 67 (1936). Prokofiev had always been an enthusiastic composer of music for and about children, and in 1935 he had composed the piano pieces *Music for Children*, Op. 65 which in 1941 he orchestrated and named *Summer Day*. The piano pieces were originally written while he was putting the finishing touches to his great ballet *Romeo and Juliet*, Op. 64. *Peter and the Wolf* was inspired by a trip with his family to the Central Children's Theatre in Moscow. He eventually accepted a commission from the theatre's director, Natalie Satz, to write a piece of music which included speech and which children would enjoy. She and Prokofiev worked on the idea together, then he composed the music alone; in May 1936 it was premièred to the world's press at a Moscow Festival of Soviet Art. From that first success it spread like wildfire throughout the world, its simple but resonant words and story-line the perfect foil for the exquisite character sketches and dramatic punctuations Prokofiev supplied for the orchestra.

This success should have crowned his compositional career, but in December 1936 Prokofiev and every other notable Soviet musician came under direct attack from the Soviet authorities for creating art contrary to the spirit and letter of social realism. A direct consequence was the immediate banning of his dramatic recounting of Pushkin's *Eugene Onegin*, which was on the point of production at the Moscow Kamerny Theatre. The work went unheard and unpublished until the 1970s. From then until his death, Prokofiev was regularly denounced by spokesmen for Stalin's regime (his opera *Semyon Kotko*, mounted in Moscow in 1940, was greeted with outrage), and in 1948 he even had to defend himself in front of the Central Committee against accusations of formalism and anti-democratic musical inclinations. But, like Shostakovich, he was too important an international figure to be banished to Siberia or shot, and he slowly learned to bend with the political winds.

In 1939 Prokofiev divorced his first wife Lina and married the literary scholar Myra Mandelsson. He also embarked on a series of three piano sonatas the Sixth, Op. 82, Seventh, Op. 83 and Eighth, Op. 84, which he termed his 'war sonatas', all three of which differ

DON'T MISS

▶ **Romeo and Juliet, Op. 64 (1938)**
▶ **Violin Sonata No. 1, Op. 80 (1938–40)**
▶ **Alexander Nevsky, Op. 78 (1939)**
▶ **Piano Sonatas Nos. 6 & 7, Opp. 82/3 (1939–42)**
▶ **Symphony No. 5, Op. 100 (1944)**
▶ **Cinderella, Op. 87 (1945)**

greatly from each other in mood and technique. As the Patriotic War began and then ground on, Prokofiev's patriotism was not called into question; he had begun work on a major opera, *War and Peace*, in 1942, and as was his custom, he used some of this material to fashion a symphony, his Fifth, Op. 100 (1944). The symphony was one of the most complex and emotionally resonant works of his Soviet period. The opera, meanwhile—begun not long after the ballet *Cinderella*, Op. 87 and the music to Eisenstein's film *Ivan the Terrible* had been commenced—reached its first orchestrated completion in 1943, but was not performed. As a result, Prokofiev expanded it further and wrote new music. The project continued to grow and was on the point of production when in 1947 the whole work fell foul of the authorities, for reasons which defy logic. The full

opera only received its first performance in December 1959. In 1947 Prokofiev also completed his Sixth Symphony, Op. 111, which was roundly denounced in the 1948 artistic purges. Needless to say, it was his most completely satisfying symphonic work, both architecturally and emotionally.

The impact of the Zhdanov 1948 damnation of Prokofiev's career was profound, and the composer, like all his fellow-artists, had to bow to the pressure being applied simply to stay functioning. Prokofiev wrote an apology for perpetrating formalist errors which he had, he said, "picked up while abroad", and wrote an opera, *The Story of a Real Man*, which he hoped would fulfil every possible Communist stipulation. He was still unaware that in a climate of political terror such as the last years of Stalin, there are no

winners, only survivors. The opera, although it dealt with an approved subject in an exemplary manner, was still perceived as containing too much individuality and real content, and was roundly condemned. In this impossible artistic climate, Prokofiev wrote the popular *Winter Bonfire*, Op. 122, a work again for children, and found a means of escape by composing a symphony, his Seventh, Op. 131 (1952) and last, which again was conceived as one for children (it was commissioned by the Children's Radio Division) and was thus able to be simple, heartfelt and unabashedly nostalgic. He even supplied an alternative up-beat ending in order to win a Stalin Prize (later insisting that this ending should be suppressed). But by now his health was giving out; on the same day as Stalin in March 1953, and aged just 61, he died of a brain aneurism.

ARTHUR HONEGGER
1892–1955

Born in France but of Swiss parentage, Honegger combined in his music a seriousness of purpose with an ability to poke fun at a wide range of human activities. A member of 'Les Six', he quickly outgrew this arbitrary identification into a fully rounded composer.

Honegger was born in Le Havre and spent most of his life in France. His parents were both Swiss, and Honegger was to retain his Swiss nationality throughout his life, often taking

extended breaks in Switzerland to restoke the fires of creation. His mother was a keen amateur pianist and taught him piano from an early age. In 1910 he took up studies at Zurich Conservatoire, where his success in theory and piano allowed him to move to Paris Conservatoire; here he completed his musical training under d'Indy and Widor. His earliest mature compositions date from his years at the Conservatoire; they include an early Violin Sonata H3, *Four Poèmes* H7, *Six Poèmes d'Apollinaire*, H12, *Hommage à Ravel* (piano) and a *Toccata and Variations*, also for piano.

His studies in Paris were interrupted by a military call-up in Switzerland in 1914, but on his return to Paris he began to make a definite impression on the music scene, his First Violin Sonata, String Quartet and orchestral piece, *Aglavaine et Sélysette*, all receiving their début performances in 1916–17. His earlier style, as shown in his unpublished songs, was coloured by Debussy, but his own artistic temperament is discernible, highlighted by a starkness of harmony and angularity of melodic line alien to Debussy.

Arthur Honegger

In early 1918 he took part in a Paris concert organized by a group of young French composers calling themselves the Nouveaux Jeunes. This group recognized common artistic ancestry, professing admiration for the musical philosophy, if not the music, of Eric Satie, while most of them, perhaps influenced by Jean Cocteau, had a strong interest in music hall, circus music and ragtime. Co-ordinated projects soon began to appear. One of these was an album of piano pieces from composers Tailleferre, Honegger, Auric, Poulenc, Milhaud and Durey published in late 1919 which was reviewed by the critic Henri Collet. He identified certain common traits and dubbed the composers 'Les Six', after the famous Russian antecedents 'The Five'. Although the group in general, and Honegger in particular, would prove to share as many differences as commonalities, the name stuck and helped bring international attention to all six composers in the immediate post-war period.

Honegger, together with his amour, concert pianist Andrée Vaurabourg, was only a dilettante in the satiric, often frothy and humorous approach to music and musical events practised by other 'Les Six' members, and his essentially serious approach to his own music was firmly established by a string of sonatas written between 1919 and 1922, plus two Cocteau projects, the music for his play *Antigone* and *Six Poésies de Jean Cocteau* . Equally, the orchestral concert music *Pastorale d'été* and the music initially meant as a ballet, *Horace victorieux* but in fact premièred in the concert hall by Ernest Ansermet, show Honegger's intense commitment to what he called 'illustrative music' which nevertheless had a firm theoretical and structural base. In 1921 he was commissioned to write *Le Roi David*, originally incidental music for a play of the same name, then recast in 1923 as an oratorio.

In 1923 he had his first real success with a work, *Pacific 231*, which

identified him more firmly than ever with the Paris avant-garde, but which with hindsight fits just as comfortably into the progression of his own ideas about music written to describe objects from the everyday world. His choice, a locomotive, was what gave the music its modernistic, seemingly iconoclastic profile. Using an orchestra with a vast scale, he created a type of musical machine which speeded up and slowed down with inexorable logic, but it was the brilliance of the orchestral writing to which audiences most readily responded. Despite this popular success on a modernistic topic, Honegger averred: "I do not have the cult of the carnival and the music hall, but on the contrary that of chamber and symphonic music in all their most grave and austere aspects".

In 1926, after making a rare bow in the direction of irreverence with his Piano Concertino of 1925, the composer married Andrée Vaurabourg and also completed work on what he termed a 'biblical opera' which most closely resembles an oratorio in form, *Judith*. True to his own dictum, he remained active in serious music across a broad spectrum of initiatives, writing the soundtrack music for the epic silent film *Napoléon* in 1926, composing the second *Mouvement symphonique* (the first being *Pacific 231*), *Rugby* in 1928 and a charming and unjustly neglected Cello Concerto in 1929. Of the second *Mouvement symphonique* he commented: "I am indeed keen on football, and yet rugby means more to me... I feel myself more particularly attracted to the rhythm of rugby; untamed, abrupt, disordered, distressed". The musical means used to capture this empathy are appropriate.

By 1929 Honegger felt himself ready to tackle the symphonic form, in the next 20 years producing five completed symphonies. The first, commissioned by the Boston Symphony Orchestra, reflected his desire not to change the rules of symphonic composition, but to become the 'new player of the game'. Honegger jettisoned the traditional *scherzo* and ended the work on a quiet, tranquil note, on the way to this goal taking the listener through alternating violent, discordant passages and music of intense lyricism. The follow-up symphony did not arrive until two years into WWII, but the 1930s were a very important time for Honegger, with the two great oratorios, *Jeanne d'Arc au bûcher* and *La Danse des Morts* being completed. Both works demonstrate his deepening spiritualism and strengthening concern with traditional forms, and occupy a very different world from his old comrades in 'Les Six'. His final two String Quartets, Nos. 2 and 3, date from the early to mid-thirties, as does the last Violin Sonata, while his deep interest in chamber music is further reflected in the absorbing *Petite suite* for two flutes and piano and the *Prélude for Doublebass and Piano,* H79 (1932). His lifelong love of Bach's musical achievements is also revealed in 1932's *Prélude, arioso et fugue on BACH.* Throughout the 1930s Honegger also continued to concern himself with choral works (*Cris du Monde*; *Nicolas de Flue*) and film music, with over 10 film scores commissioned and completed during this decade, perhaps the most famous of which is the music to the 1934 version of Victor Hugo's *Les Misérables.* Honegger also wrote a comic opera or operetta, *Les aventures du roi Pausole,* based on a rather silly

Pierre Louÿs novel, which was given its Paris première in 1930.

Although as a Swiss national he had the option of moving to Switzerland for the duration of WWII, Honegger spent the war in occupied Paris. His feelings about the onset of this dark period are evident in the sombre, at times downright bleak Second Symphony, H153 (1941), commissioned by Basle Chamber Orchestra and written for strings, although a notable *obbligato* trumpet part arrives in the final movement to emphasize what Honegger felt was its choral nature. Although film scores and vocal works were also completed during the forties, the main emphasis continued to be the symphonies. The Third, H186, subtitled *Liturgique*, possesses the bleakness and despair of the Second, but is deprived of that symphony's positivist ending. The symphony carries an open programme, with each movement bearing a title from the Catholic liturgy; the longest of all his symphonies, its three movements paint a detailed and moving picture of suffering humanity, with the last, 'Dona nobis pacem', giving the listener only the hope of eternal rest in another world as a means of finding peace.

The Fourth Symphony, H191, subtitled *Deliciae basiliensis* (1946), is utterly different in character, full of light and warmth, reaching back for its inspiration to Mozart and Haydn, and perhaps reflecting the relief Honegger found in the countryside around Basle, where he had moved after the end of the War. The subtitle, added due to the usage of local Basle popular airs, confirms the beneficial nature of this restorative period in Switzerland. A

work which dates from 1949, the *Concerto da camera* for flute, cor anglais and strings, H196, also has more than its fair share of charm and beauty. However, by the time of the Fifth Symphony, H202, subtitled *Di tre re*, completed in 1951, Honegger was aware that his health was permanently impaired in the form of irreversible heart disease. This last symphony is every bit as dark and forbidding as the Third before it, its three movements being closely constructed evocations of a sometimes nightmarish nature. The middle *scherzo,* in particular, is an unnerving combination of gloom and dance rhythm. Honegger's mission, to deliver people, through the grace of music, from the evil in the world, here seems to be doomed.

Yet one of his last works, *Une Cantate de Noël* (1953), leads the listener from the darkness of this vale of tears and finds deliverance in the birth of the infant Jesus. The movement from music of unbearable tension and despair to that of deliverance and peace makes this one of Honegger's most unified and effective works, and an appropriate summation of his composing career. Two years later he succumbed to heart disease, dying in Paris in 1955.

DON'T MISS

▶ Le Roi David (1921)
▶ Pacific 231 (1923)
▶ Cello Concerto (1929)
▶ Jeanne d'Arc au bûcher (1934–35)
▶ Symphony No. 3 (Liturgique) (1948)

DARIUS MILHAUD

1892–1974

A self-declared 'happy man', but one who endured many hardships, including virtual physical incapacitation for much of his life, Milhaud's sunny nature is reflected in his early works in particular, though his later output reflects a deepening seriousness of purpose as he increasingly searched for ways of promoting peace between peoples.

Milhaud was born in Aix-en-Provence into an ancient Mediterranean Jewish family. His love of life and amiable personality, allied to his profound attachment to Provence, were to colour everything he wrote. Both his parents were musical, his mother a singer, and at the age of four Milhaud was already picking out melodies on the family piano, beginning violin lessons at seven. By his twelfth year he was playing in a local string quartet. His discovery in 1905 of Debussy's quartet galvanized him into studying the work of the reigning French composer. He also took his first clumsy steps in composition, when he was "quite unable to grasp the connection between the study of harmony and the music I wrote".

In 1909 Milhaud moved to Paris and began his studies at the Conservatoire. He also became an avid concert-goer, although a performance of *The Ring* proved a sobering experience: while the audience would burst into "wildly enthusiastic applause at the end of each act...I myself [was] bored to

Darius Milhaud

tears...unable as I was to share in the emotion". This was the start of a lifelong lack of interest in all German music. He found Diaghilev and his Ballets Russes far more to his taste. Before the summer of 1911, when he composed a violin sonata ("my first work worth preserving"), he wrote a full-scale opera, a ballet and various chamber music pieces, all of which he destroyed when he felt he had arrived at a mature style. By 1912 Milhaud was studying counterpoint and had reached a stage with his own compositions

where he no longer wanted to be a career violinist. Before the year was out he had been introduced to the writer Paul Claudel, who became a close friend and a major collaborator. At their first meeting, Claudel proposed that Milhaud should supply the music for his new translations of Aeschylus's great *Orestes* trilogy, and the composer's work on this major project kept him busy right up to the outbreak of WWI. Meanwhile, he continued his studies at the Conservatoire under Charles-Marie Widor, a kindly man who took fright at

Milhaud's experiments in dissonance, exclaiming on one occasion: "The worst of it is that you get used to them!"

In the summer of 1914, Milhaud met in Aix-en-Provence the composer/ musicologist Charles Koechlin whose wide-ranging ideas and enthusiasms were to have an impact on Milhaud's development. With mobilization for war under way, Milhaud was called up but rejected on medical grounds, and returned to Paris, where he helped with the civilian war effort and continued his composing. During his work in 1915 on the *Choéphores* section of the Claudel trilogy, Milhaud began systematically applying the results of his researches into bitonality and polytonality, to which he had become increasingly attracted—a major step towards the cementing of his musical personality.

The following year Milhaud, working at the Maison de Presse, found that the organization had been absorbed into the propaganda effort under the Ministry of Foreign Affairs. Claudel, a senior figure in this government department, had just been appointed Minister to Brazil, and accordingly asked his 'new employee' to go to Brazil as his 'secretary'. The pair left for South America in December of that year, arriving in Rio de Janeiro at Carnival time. Milhaud was immediately overwhelmed by the country, thrilling as much to the riot of tropical plants in Rio's Botanical Gardens as to the syncopated rhythms and fascinating melodies he heard in the city's streets. Milhaud continued to compose, and with *L'Enfant prodigue* and the first in his series of *Petites Symphonies* (symphonies in the Monteverdian sense,

not the Brucknerian, the first of which is just nine minutes long) he evolved his polytonality further until it was no longer a question of combining chords, but interweaving melodic lines into a polytonal polyphony. As he himself wrote: 'In composing this music I had recaptured the sounds I had dreamed of as a child when I closed my eyes for sleep and seemed to hear music I thought I should never be able to express'.

While still in Rio, Milhaud and Claudel had witnessed Nijinsky and the Ballets Russes when they were on tour there, and on Milhaud's return to Paris at the end of the War, he was inspired to begin work on the ballet *L'Homme et son désir*, one of his first completed works to reflect his new interest in Brazilian music. Milhaud's typical polyphony was used to depict the simultaneous dialogues of the insects and birds he had discovered in Brazil. 'My ears were still...full of the sumptuous sounds of the forest night and the subtle rhythms of the tango'.

Milhaud was soon swept up by the new vigour of post-war Paris, symbolized by Jean Cocteau's iconoclastic pronouncements and productions. He made friends with Poulenc, and as a long-standing colleague of the composers Honegger and Auric, he became—almost by default—a member of 'Les Six', the sextet of composers grouped together by critic Henri Collet. Each composer was well aware of how he differed from the others, but was happy to exploit the attention which 'Les Six' attracted from the press. Milhaud attracted attention of his own with his playful ballet, *Le Boeuf sur le toit,* which gathered together his

memories of 'Brazilian melodies, tangos, maxixes, sambas and even a Portuguese fado' into a succession of steps and sections, linked by a pretty little theme. Cocteau arranged the scenario, with sets by Raoul Dufy, and it was premièred in 1920 together with diverting pieces from Satie, Auric and Poulenc. The critics treated it as a deliberate joke, a mimicking of the *varieté,* and accused Milhaud of being a mere showground musician. His reputation was made. For the next three years Milhaud and his colleagues were never far from scandal and controversy, but the sheer diversity of Milhaud's composing was already apparent. From chamber works to orchestral suites, operas and songs, he was ceaselessly prolific.

Visiting London in 1920 Milhaud heard for the first time what he felt to be 'authentic jazz' in the shape of the Billy Arnold Band, who subsequently appeared in Paris to be greeted by both alarm and acclaim. Milhaud admired their combination of blues melodies and ragtime rhythms. Still under the spell of South America, while on a visit to Copenhagen in 1921 Milhaud wrote his Etudes for piano and orchestra, plus a dance suite entitled *Saudades do Brasil.* The same year he produced the two books of *Printemps* for piano, exquisite miniatures which employ bitonality in a wholly captivating, pastel way. By 1922 he was back in America, appearing in cities such as Philadelphia, Boston and New York where his concerts had a great impact. He visited Harlem, which 'had not yet been discovered by the snobs and aesthetes... The music I heard there was absolutely different from anything I had ever heard before, and was a revelation to me'.

DON'T MISS

▶ Le Boeuf sur le toit, Op. 58 (1920)

▶ Saudades do Brasil, Op. 67 (1920–21)

▶ La Création du Monde, Op. 81a (1923)

▶ Le Carnaval d'Aix, Op. 83b (1926)

▶ Scaramouche Suite, Op. 165b (1937)

He returned to France "resolved to use jazz for a chamber music work". Shortly after his arrival in France he agreed with Blaise Cendrars and Ferdinand Léger to collaborate on a ballet together. It was to describe the creation of the world using African folk-lore, and while Léger used the then-fashionable African art for his inspiration, Milhaud used jazz. The result, La Création du Monde (1923), was a sensation at its première, the brilliance of Léger's sets enhancing Milhaud's spectacular music. Critics felt that Milhaud had written music fit only for the music hall or restaurant, but the work has remained popular ever since. In 1924 two more ballets were mounted, a commedia dell'arte pastiche, Salade, and a frivolous Cocteau ballet-cum-operetta (without words), Le Train bleu. Before the year was out, Milhaud had also dashed off his first chamber opera, Les Malheurs d'Orphée, and in 1925 the comic opera in the Jewish dialect, Esther de Carpentras (given a radio performance in 1938). That same year he married his long-time amour, his cousin Madeleine, followed by a long honeymoon through the eastern end of the Mediterranean.

On his return to France in 1926 he began preparations for another American tour by quickly composing the charming Carnaval d'Aix, for piano

and orchestra, a piece which combined his waggish commedia dell'arte side with more reflective moments. On that tour he met Charles Ives and looked at some of his manuscripts, noting that therein lay 'an extremely original personality'. Back in Paris he again collaborated with Cocteau to produce his most widely-performed opera, Le Pauvre Matelot, which suffered from poor execution at its première but recovered to be performed relatively frequently over the next decade. In response to an idea suggested by his colleague Hindemith, Milhaud became interested in miniature operas, writing in 1927 a trilogy: L'Enlèvement d'Europe, Op. 94, L'Abandon d'Ariane, Op. 98 and La Déliverance de Thésée, Op. 99. The average length of each piece was just nine minutes; in that space of time a whole story-line, reduced to its essentials, was successfully negotiated and an audience educated and entertained by characters who, lacking the time to think and emote, reacted dynamically to each other.

The 1930s and 1940s were also extremely fertile years for Milhaud. He turned his attention to string quartets (Nos. 6–15 were written in these decades), while 1939 saw the completion of his 'official' First Symphony, Op. 210 (he was to write

over 12 more in the next 30 years). His interest was also revived in the concerto form, and by the end of WWII he had completed three piano concertos, a concerto for two pianos and orchestra, two violin concertos, two cello concertos, plus separate concertos for clarinet, percussion, viola, and chamber orchestra, among others. After the war his interest in this form would hardly wane, with more piano concertos, and even a concerto for marimba, vibraphone and orchestra (1949), appearing before the onset of the 1950s. But probably his best-known works from this time continued to be the occasional suites, such as Le Carnaval de Londres, Op. 172, composed in 1937 and based on his recent discovery of Gay's Beggar's Opera. The previous year he had completed his Suite Provençal, Op. 152, where the flavour of his native provence hangs heavy in the music, though the melodies are Milhaud's own and his exuberance is very much to the fore—as it was in one of his most famous pieces, written in 1937 for two pianos, the witty Scaramouche, Op. 165b.

By the outbreak of WWII, Milhaud was internationally recognized as one of the foremost living composers, but this did not save him from the prospect of persecution in occupied France. Although he had been seriously ill for a long time, after the allied failure of the Battle of France in 1940, his wife Madeleine made hurried arrangements for their departure via Spain and Portugal to America. The escape was hair-raising for Milhaud, still very ill, his wife and young son Daniel, but with help from American friends such as Kurt Weill, they finally arrived in New

York in mid-July 1940, and were met at the dock by Weill and Lotte Lenya. The first of his compositions to be premièred after his arrival was the *Cortège funèbre*, composed in 1935 for André Malraux's film *L'Espoir*, about the Spanish Civil War, and now played on the radio as a tribute to the fallen soldiers of a new war. Accepting an appointment to Mills College in Oakland, California, Milhaud lived a relatively settled existence, punctuated by dreadful news from occupied Europe, including the deaths of both his parents. Soon after his mother's death in 1943 he suffered the first of a debilitating series of physical collapses sparked off by arthritis which would eventually confine him to a wheelchair. His musical output, however, hardly faltered, and 1944 saw the arrival of the cheerful *Suite française*, Op. 248, based on folk songs collected from Normandy to Provence.

His symphonic output also began in earnest, with the Second, Third and Fourth symphonies all written between 1944 and 1947, the year Milhaud returned to France.

He celebrated his return by composing the joyous suite *Paris*, written for four pianos. That year he also finished yet another ballet, *'Adame Miroir*, and, back in America for the Tanglewood Festival, he finished *L'Apothéose de Molière*, Op. 286 in time for its first performance in Europe in Capri under Carlo Maria Giulini in 1947. Now in his sixties, Milhaud was revered as a teacher and composer on both sides of the Atlantic (he had tutored Dave Brubeck in California in the late 1940s), but his later work, no less ambitious, rigorous or colourful than his earlier work, has been largely ignored as musical fashions changed. That this neglect is undeserved is

shown by the vitality of his later symphonies and chamber music (the string quartets alone deserve much more attention), as well as his beloved choral works. The choral symphony *Pacem in Terris*, written in response to Pope John XXIII's encyclical of the same name, was a monumental undertaking lasting more than an hour. It was played at Notre Dame in Paris in December 1963 in the presence of a papal legate, and also premièred in America in the summer of 1964.

Milhaud's last decade was largely a story of the battle against gradual physical deterioration set against the stability of his family life and the undimmed creative vigour of his musical output. Sufficiently contented with his lot to name his autobiography *My Happy Life*, Milhaud finally succumbed to his ailments in Geneva at the age of 87.

PAUL HINDEMITH
1895–1963

Hindemith's approach to his music is very much that of the Baroque masters Bach and Telemann. His mastery of every form, his preoccupation with counterpoint and polyphony, and his desire to compose music which could be functional as well as artistically satisfying all bespeak an approach to creativity which is firmly rooted in pre-Romantic notions of the composer and his place in the world.

Born in Hanau in Germany, Hindemith's early interest in music was supported by his father who believed in furthering the aims and interests of his offspring. Paul was one of three musical children (his brother Rudolf was a 'cellist and his sister Toni a violinist) and rapidly became proficient on both the piano and violin. Taking advantage of his talented brood, the father arranged for them to play together in public under the name of the Frankfurter Kindertrio. This period of Paul's life ended at the

age of 13 when he became a student at Frankfurt's Conservatorium. An exceptional student, he joined the Frankfurt Opera Orchestra, co-founded the Amar String Quartet, performed Beethoven's Violin Concerto in public and commenced his composing career— all before his twentieth birthday.

The outbreak of WWI had little initial impact on him, but his father was called up and later killed in Flanders. Paul was also called up in 1917, but his

Paul Hindemith

place at the Frankfurt Opera was held open for him and he returned there in late 1918. He now felt sufficiently sure of his creative abilities to submit his String Quartet, Op. 10 to the publishers Schott, and it was this relatively conservative work which initiated a publishing agreement which continued throughout his life.

In the early twenties, Hindemith's own distinctive compositional voice began to emerge. Interested in developments in popular music, Hindemith wrote a series of ragtimes and foxtrots, although he refrained from having them published. Now in his late twenties, he was still looking for his first public breakthrough when the conductor, Fritz Busch, offered to produce two of the three expressionist one-act operas Hindemith had recently completed. Of these, *Sancta Susanna*, Op. 21, a peculiar work centred on a sex-obsessed nun, was a *succès de scandale* and gave Hindemith enough confidence to resign his position at the

Frankfurt Opera and concentrate on his composing. Another major event in 1921 was the foundation of the Donaueschingen Festival, an annual event planned for the most part by Hindemith and composer Joseph Haas with a clear emphasis on new music. Hindemith's first mature-style chamber works produced over the next few years all received their premières at Donaueschingen.

In 1922 Hindemith completed his Opus 24 (the first work in his *Kammermusik* series), and the piano piece, *Suite 1922*, Op. 26. Both works confirmed his populist music leanings, with portions of the Suite containing popular American dances of the day such as the shimmy and the fox-trot. This followed the success of his *Rag Time (well-tempered)* for orchestra of the year before. The following year, however, he wrote the song cycle from Rilke's poems, *Das Marienleben*, Op. 27 in which his admiration for—and command of—medieval idioms, married

to his own individual style, were demonstrated. The completion of his fourth set of *Kammermusik* pieces was followed in 1926 by the première of his first great opera, *Cardillac*, Op. 39. But by 1927 Hindemith and his wife (he had married Gertrude Rottenberg, the daughter of a Frankfurt Opera conductor, in 1924) had tired of the city's limitations and were prepared to move on. In that year Hindemith was appointed Composition Professor at Berlin High School for Music, and had soon struck out in a new and important creative direction. Not only did he respond to the challenges of his new position by writing *Schulwerk für Instrumental Zusammenspiel*, Op. 44 in 1927 (a series of four educational groupings demonstrating techniques of instrument and ensemble playing which would stand any student in good stead), but he also began elaborating a theory of *Gebrauchsmusik*—music to sing and play in an everyday setting as opposed to the concert hall. He wanted people to treat a series of his small compositions in this manner as something of a distraction from everyday cares, like reading a book or listening to the radio. The same year, 1927, saw the completion of the *Kammermusik* series, Nos. 5–7.

This was not Hindemith's only compositional activity as the twenties came to a close: another opera, *Neues vom Tage*, was produced in Berlin and set Hindemith's name before the public for an extended time. Although he now felt he had made his point with so-called 'utilitarian' music, written with the best of intentions and with a generous spirit, it took him many years to shake off the taunt that his generally undemonstrative, precise compositional

DON'T MISS

▶ Cardillac, Op. 39 (1926)

▶ Kammermusik No. 5, Op. 36/4 (1927)

▶ Mathis der Maler Symphony (1934)

▶ Mathis der Maler (opera) (1938)

▶ Cello Concerto (1940)

▶ Ludus tonalis (1942)

style contained more than simply uninspired 'everyday' music. But this phase had been very important to him from a theoretical point of view, allowing him to fully develop his ideas on counterpoint and musical form (which were later set down in an important treatise of the late 1930s, *The Craft of Musical Composition*) and brought him closer to the Baroque ideals of Bach and Bach's contemporaries.

Hindemith's Berlin career continued apace and his international reputation also blossomed, reflected in the number of recordings of his works. As an Aryan, he should not have been under any direct personal threat from the Nazi takeover of 1933, but not only was he a liberal social thinker and a modernist in music, but his wife was half-Jewish; the combination of all these elements made him vulnerable. The crisis in his relationship with Hitler's government was precipitated by his operatic masterpiece, *Mathis der Maler* of 1938. In 1933 Hindemith had begun work on this opera (which deals with the artist's relationship with society during dark and brutal times), and late that year conductor Wilhelm Furtwängler had

commissioned an orchestral work from him for the Berlin Philharmonic. Hindemith decided to use some of the orchestral material from the opera and mould it into a symphony. Premièred in March 1934, it was an overwhelming success, the public immediately recognizing it as a masterpiece. This success, allied to Furtwängler's impassioned pleas for Hindemith to be treated sympathetically, sealed the doom of both Hindemith and his opera. Although it was completed by 1935, it was never produced in Germany while the Nazis were in power, and all his works were banned as being decadent. Zurich became the beneficiary of Hitler's condemnation, receiving the composer and his wife in 1937 and premièring the opera in 1938.

By then Hindemith had been living outside Germany for two years, having spent some time in Turkey in 1935 helping the government to implement new educational methods into the schools. He also made a number of tours to America, where he found a relatively willing audience which admired his virtuosity as a string player. This would lead to his eventual emigration to America in 1940, but not before a number of other significant premières, two of them in Amsterdam, had taken place. The Concertgebouw Orchestra under Mengelberg gave the first performance of *Der Schwanendreher* (The Organ-Grinder) in 1935, a concerto for viola and orchestra which Hindemith composed using folk melodies as his principle source of motifs. The Concertgebouw also delivered the first performance of his important and unusually passionate Violin Concerto

from 1939. Two further works found a first performance in London: the *Symphonic Dances* of 1937 and the ballet *Nobilissima Visione*, given by the Ballets Russes in 1938.

Hindemith's life in America was not easy: he was homesick and found his teaching duties at Buffalo University too time-consuming. Nonetheless, he began to write new music which echoed, as did his late 1930s pieces, the emotional and moral turbulence of his experiences; the neo-classicism, which had for so long been a central identifying theme, was now leavened by a lyricism and harmonic movement which, couched in the more conservative musical language he evolved in his middle age, gave him a wider audience at the same time as displacing him from the forefront of musical events in the post-war period. The concert piece *The Four Temperaments* (1940) is a subtly worked four-movement set of variations which combines an interesting programme with rigorous musical logic, while his supreme piano achievement, *Ludus Tonalis* (1943) once again looks to Bach, specifically his *Art of the Fugue,* for its polyphonic inspiration. Using 12 three-voiced fugues, one for each key of the chromatic scale, it is topped and tailed with a praeludium and postludium and displays Hindemith's complete mastery of this form of composing. In the same year, his retrospective leanings gained further fulfilment through the masterful *Symphonic Metamorphosis on Themes of Weber.*

By the end of the War Hindemith was teaching at Yale, and in 1946 he became an American citizen as well as completing the engaging *Symphonia Serena*, commissioned by the Dallas Symphony Orchestra. But his hankering for Europe led to ever more frequent visits, tours and, in 1948, a Professorship at Zurich Univerity. He continued to compose more concertos and sinfoniettas, but the next major event was his opera *Die Harmonie der Welt* (1950). This massive, quasi-mystical vocal stage work was an investigation of the life of astronomer Johannes Kepler against the background of the Thirty Years' War. As

with so many of his stage works, Hindemith extracted some of the orchestral basis of the opera and fashioned it into a symphony bearing the same name as the opera. The symphony was premièred in Basle in January 1952.

In 1953 Hindemith decided to return permanently to Europe, moving to Zurich where he still held his university position. His health was no longer robust, and he began to curtail his activities so that he could concentrate more on composing. Another opera, *The*

Long Christmas Dinner, was premièred in Mannheim in 1961, while his last completed work was, surprisingly, a Mass (1963). Considering he had always held Protestant beliefs and felt that Palestrina had said everything worth saying on the subject, this was a novel turn, but the work itself is true to his search for clarity through angular polyphony. Hindemith conducted the first performance in Vienna in November 1963, entering hospital the following day, dying in late December of complications caused by pancreatitis.

CARL ORFF

1895–1982

The overwhelming popularity of Orff's realization of medieval German drinking and loving songs, *Carmina Burana*, has made him one of the most popular but least understood composers of any age. He spent much of his life creating music to be performed by amateurs and school groups, yet the bulk of this music is largely unknown outside the world of music education.

Orff was born into an aristocratic Munich family and became an early devotee of music in a house which was full of it, publishing a handful of his own songs by the age of 16. In 1913–14 he attended the Munich Academy, graduating before the onset of WWI, and for most of the War he worked in the Munich Kammerspiele as

a repetiteur and conductor. This experience proved of great importance later as his interest in theatrical music grew. Always prolific, by 1918 he had written a large amount of music, including an opera, but none of it in his mature style which he had yet to discover. After a period in the army in the War's closing months, he returned to Munich to further his studies. During this time he greatly increased his knowledge of earlier music, back to Monteverdi and beyond, at a time when such studies were regarded as mildly eccentric.

By 1924 he felt ready to begin educating others, and with Dorothee Günther he founded the Günther School of Music in Munich. This school aimed to educate children musically through gymnastic, verbal and musical exercises which were closely allied to earlier

theories regarding euthenics, which is the control of the educational environment on every level to achieve the maximum potential of every child. Orff's theories on learning through music gradually became codified and systematized under the title 'eurythmics', and in 1930 he published his treatise *Schulwerk*, a book which proved very influential amongst musical educationalists in many countries. Orff's ideas necessarily involved theatre, and were in part derived from Ancient Greek models. His own music, however, remained a source of dissatisfaction to him, his most rewarding effort up to the mid-1930s being his editing and production of Monteverdi stage works.

His research and theorising eventually had the desired effect, and in 1935 Orff began work on the first of what became his three *Trionfi* (Triumphs),

DON'T MISS

▶ Catulli Carmina (1930)
▶ Carmina Burana (1936)
▶ Die Kluge (1943)
▶ Trionfo di Afrodite (1953)

Carmina Burana. His attention had been drawn to a newly unearthed collection of 13th-century poems from Upper Bavaria, which had originally been accompanied by their own music, much of which was now lost. Orff seized the opportunity to create new music for them, forging a simpler, more ritualistic form of theatre which employed dancers onstage while the performers (including the singers) remained in the orchestra pit. The sheer zest of the music, its immediacy and

raciness, allied to the deliberate simplicity and repetitiousness of its construction, brought it a rapid international audience. Spurred by this success and the general acceptance of his musical and educational ideas, Orff completed in 1943 the second part of the Trionfi—Catulli Carmina, applying the same musical and theatrical principles to the amatory verses of the Roman poet, Catullus. In this work a reduction in scale perhaps accounts for the work's lesser reputation, although the actual music is equally effective as its antecedent, and its staging considerably more refined.

Trionfo di Afrodite completed the trilogy, and while this broke no new musical or theatrical ground, Orff's techniques in his chosen area of music

theatre were now highly sophisticated. He wrote many other works, but they are little known. Four operas, Der Mond (1939), Die Kluge (1943), Antigone (1949) and Prometheus (1966), testify to a steady and weighty continued commitment to his creative output, but the primitivism of much of this music, allied to a deliberately atavistic production technique, has made these sparse works somewhat intimidating for the average opera-goer, used to busy stages and fully-orchestrated musical settings for their vocal melodies. Antigone, for example, uses percussion instruments exclusively as the 'orchestral' backdrop for the singers. Orff may be one of the two or three most popular composers of the century, but that position was won by a small fragment of his overall output.

GEORGE GERSHWIN
1898–1937

Gershwin was the only American composer prior to the Second World War who successfully bridged the gap between the concert hall and Broadway. Although Irving Berlin is known as 'the father of American song', it was Gershwin who took the song form as it was used on Broadway, added to it blues and ragtime elements to forge a fresh melodic and harmonic hybrid, then took the huge imaginative leap required to convert this style into one which could sustain the larger forms of concert music, such as concertos and rhapsodies.

Gershwin was born into a Brooklyn family of Russian Jewish immigrants. His father Moishe contrived to keep the family in reasonable comfort through a variety of employments. In his sixth year George discovered music, enjoying the popular classics that could be heard being played around town on mechanical pianos and the ragtime pounded out on sideshows at Coney Island. Even at that age he was attracted to both art-music and popular forms. In 1908 the Gershwins acquired a piano, initially intended for George's elder brother (the lyricist Ira), but it was George who began to pick out tunes on it. His parents, impressed by

his innate talent, arranged for private lessons. George's digital facility quickly developed and in time he became a formidable pianist. His theoretical knowledge was acquired less systematically, learned from a series of tutors or picked up while attending concerts and performing with his peers. This method clearly suited his temperament as he was already inclining away from a career as a concert pianist and towards the lure of Broadway and Tin Pan Alley.

In 1914 he took the crucial step of leaving school and taking a job as a song plugger with Remick's (music publishers and sellers), playing the latest tunes on the shop piano to entice customers to buy the sheet music. It was only a matter of time before Gershwin decided he could write better tunes than the ones on sale, and in 1916 he proved it by publishing his first song, though not for Remick's. This was followed in 1919 by a complete musical, *La La Lucille*. Although not the hit Gershwin had hoped for, his song *Swannee*, featured in Al Jolson's musical *Sinbad*, became a nationwide sensation. This success led to his involvement in the annual revue, George White's *Scandals*, which brought him money, a high professional reputation and public acclaim.

Gershwin, however, had never lost sight of his early love of 'serious' music. In 1919 he composed a *Lullaby* for string quartet, followed a year later by a one-act opera, *135th Street* (later renamed *Blue Monday*), which was premièred in *Scandals* but dropped after one performance. Though the opera was little more than a string of songs held together by a fourth-rate plot, its importance lay in Gershwin's determination to weave the most exciting elements of the popular genres he loved into a more formal musical setting. This in itself set a precedent, and one that Gershwin was among the first to build on. His chance came when top bandleader Paul Whiteman, who was preparing for a major concert at New York's Aeolian Hall, commissioned Gershwin to write a piece of music to act as the centrepiece of a long and varied evening's entertainment which would range from light classics to corny ragtime pastiches. Using Whiteman's arranger Ferde Grofé to orchestrate his work (he had yet to acquire the

George Gershwin

confidence or expertise to do his own), Gershwin composed the *Rhapsody in Blue*. The work, with its inimitable Gershwin mix of blues inflections, rhythmic exuberance and utterly memorable melodies, washed down with a large dash of showmanship, was an immediate worldwide sensation. Gershwin became not only very rich, but achieved prominence as the first 'serious' writer to create a popular success from a hybrid of the new popular and Classical music cultures. This fusion of elements was new principally in its use of the blues idiom, its rhythms firmly embedded in ragtime. Gershwin's persuasive skill in using this new vernacular made this a deservedly popular piece of music.

From this time on Gershwin carefully maintained the twin careers of Broadway (and later, Hollywood) and the concert hall. It is arguable that his contribution to the song form is every bit as important as his concert works, although the musicals in which the songs appeared may be something of an acquired taste. Some of his biggest hit musicals were written with his brother Ira, who by this time had developed into one of the supreme Broadway lyricists, collaborating between 1924 and 1937 with virtually every great songsmith of the age. Such productions as *Lady, Be Good!* (1924), *Oh, Kay!* (1926), *Strike Up The Band* (1927–30), *Funny Face* (1927), *Show Girl* (1929), *Girl Crazy* (1930), *Of Thee I*

DON'T MISS

▶ Rhapsody in Blue (1924)
▶ Concerto in F (1925)
▶ Three Preludes for Piano (1926)
▶ An American in Paris (1928)
▶ Cuban Overture (1932)
▶ Porgy and Bess (1935)

Sing (1931), Pardon My English (1933) and Let 'Em Eat Cake (1933) not only kept Gershwin's name in the forefront of the world's theatre-going public, but provided an outlet for an inexhaustible supply of timeless songs. In the 1930s Gershwin began supplying music for Hollywood musicals, and some of his major successes (often starring Fred Astaire, an old ally from Broadway) included Delicious (1931), Shall We Dance (1936), A Damsel in Distress (1937) and Goldwyn Follies (1938).

Predictably, such popular success led to sniping from the critics and dismissal by snobbish members of the musical establishment. However, Gershwin's stock among his peers was high, with composers such as Ravel, Nadia Boulanger and Stravinsky openly expressing their admiration for his work. Gershwin managed to maintain a supply of quality concert music to parallel his Broadway output. In 1925 he produced the Concerto in F for piano and orchestra, commissioned by Walter Damrosch and the New York Symphony Society. Gershwin had bought himself a textbook on the concerto form in order to fulfil the commission, and this time managed the orchestration himself. Once again,

his use of vernacular and serious idioms was a popular success.

In the following year Gershwin produced one of the delights of modern-day miniaturists, the Three Preludes for piano, premièred by Gershwin at New York's Hotel Roosevelt. In 1928 Gershwin took a break in Europe, which included an extended stay in Paris. Visiting that city ostensibly to study music (Boulanger was one of the teachers approached), Gershwin instead produced the ebullient and instantly memorable tone poem, An American in Paris. The New York première, complete with car horn interpolations, was a wild success.

It was 1931 before a further work of substance in the concert idiom emerged: the Second Rhapsody was salvaged from music written for the film Delicious but dropped from the 'final cut'. Composed for a sequence describing the sounds of the city and based on a motif which echoed the noise of riveting, the rhythmic 'rivet' motif was woven through the fabric of the piece by various instrumental combinations. The rhythmic nature of Gershwin's interpretation appeared again in his Cuban Overture of 1932 which was inspired by the dance rhythms of Cuba. In 1934 he produced I Got Rhythm, a set of variations on his own theme, one of which he often improvized at society parties.

By this time, Gershwin was growing ever more ambitious in his plans for his 'serious' musical output, and in 1934 embarked upon his 'folk opera' Porgy and Bess. The opera was premièred in Boston in September 1935. It was a failure, criticized both for its episodic

nature and for Gershwin's penchant for composing set pieces for his singers rather than the style for seamless melody set by composers like Wagner and Strauss. Only the Italians wrote 'tunes' in operas, and they were not taken seriously. Porgy and Bess remained a failure for the rest of his life, although the songs were picked up by popular singers and instrumentalists and turned into hits. A song like Summertime— really a clever inversion of the spiritual Sometimes I Feel Like a Motherless Child—has subsequently become one of the world's most famous melodies.

The opera continued its chequered history for close on 50 years, with many observers believing that its dramatic and structural defects were such that it precluded a completely successful production, but revivals at the New York Metropolitan and Glyndebourne in the 1980s proved once and for all that it did indeed 'work' on stage if the conductor and performers took a properly sympathetic approach to its special idiom. Gershwin himself had few doubts about the opera's ultimate success, but he was not destined to enjoy it. In 1937, while in Hollywood with his brother working on the music for A Damsel in Distress, Gershwin consulted a doctor about the headaches from which he had been suffering for some time. An exploratory operation in July of that year established that he had a brain tumor, and he died shortly after the operation. His grief-stricken brother had to complete the lyrics to songs he and George had started for the follow-up film, Goldwyn Follies. In the song Love is Here To Stay Ira recorded with his customary understated eloquence his tender expression of love and resolution.

FRANCIS POULENC

1899–1963

**The popular image of Poulenc is
of an amiable eccentric addicted
to indulging his penchant for
farce, satire and spectacle. Yet
the deep religiosity of his latter
career and his unique
achievements in the field of
French *mélodie* show him to be a
considerably more complex
character than his famous
theatrical ventures would have us
believe. As he often commented
with regard to his own work:
"I have no principles, only
good taste".**

Francis Poulenc

Poulenc was born into a wealthy Parisian
family; his father, who owned an
industrial chemistry business, had
married a monied Parisienne with a lively
interest in music. This interest guided
Poulenc's early career, while his father's
devout Catholicism influenced his mature
output. Poulenc was taught the piano
from the age of five and proved a
responsive student; his favourite
composer was Mozart. In 1915 he began
more advanced piano lessons with
Debussy and Ravel's exponent, Ricardo
Viñes. Now moving in wider musical
circles, he met George Auric (also still a
teenager) and Erik Satie, by then aged 50
and beginning his second period as the
éminence grise behind the emerging
group of young French artists and
musicians. Satie's iconoclasm and lack of
formal disciplines appealed immensely to
the mischievous side of Poulenc's nature.

In 1917 Poulenc began composing his
own music, starting with a minor piano

piece and his tongue-in-cheek
Rhapsodie nègre, written for flute,
clarinet, string quartet and piano, with
two vocal interludes of almost
Dadaistic silliness, based around
pseudo-African dialect poems and
stressing the word 'Honolulu'. The piece
was given at a concert organized by
Poulenc's friend Jane Bathori, with the
composer himself delivering the 'lyrics'.
This Satie-esque touch made Poulenc a
popular figure in fashionable circles,
and although he was then inducted
into the French army (he was not
discharged until 1921), he spent the
majority of his service behind a desk in
the Ministry of Air, based in Paris,
which enabled him to continue his
burgeoning career. Between 1918 and
1919 he composed his first masterpiece,
Le Bestiaire ou Cortège d'Orphée—
imaginative and resourceful settings of
Apollinaire's witty 'animal' quatrains.

He followed the original setting for
voice and piano with a chamber
arrangement of these vocal pieces. His
friendship with Jean Cocteau led to
Cocardes in 1919, a setting of three of
Cocteau's fanciful versifications, which
was premièred at a concert organized
by Cocteau.

Aware that he lacked any formal
education in theory and harmony,
Poulenc elected to study for three
years with the composer and
musicologist Charles Koechlin.
Considering his circle of friends and
his compositions to date, it was no
surprise that Poulenc was included in
the group dubbed 'Les Six' by critic
Henri Collet when he identified the
new spirit of French music in an
article in 1920. Ever the impresario,
Cocteau took the opportunity afforded
by a ballet commission to involve not

DON'T MISS

▶ Le Bestiaire (1918–19)

▶ Aubade (1929)

▶ Concerto for Two Pianos (1932)

▶ Organ Concerto (1938)

▶ Sonata for Clarinet & Piano (1956)

▶ Les Dialogues des Carmelites (1957)

▶ Gloria (1959)

only his initial collaborator, Auric, but also Poulenc, Milhaud, Tailleferre and Honegger in writing the music for his absurdist scenario to *Les maries de la Tour Eiffel*, which involved a very odd cast and a hapless photographer who produced surprising results with his camera on the first level of the Eiffel Tower. Poulenc contributed music for two of the nine scenes. The June 1921 production caused a scandal, and although the ballet was quickly forgotten, the individual members of 'Les Six' remained very much in fashion.

Yet like most of the members of the group, Poulenc was not one-dimensional, either in art or in life, demonstrating this when he and Milhaud visited Vienna in 1923 in order to meet up with Schoenberg's circle, then in the throes of digesting the serial technique just adopted by their leader. On his return, Poulenc was asked by Diaghilev to compose a new ballet for his Ballets Russes. The response was *Les Biches*, a work originally in five scenes, with music for chorus and orchestra, set to a plot in which, according to Poulenc, "you may see nothing at all or into which you may read the worst".

By the mid-1920s, Poulenc had made considerable progress with the series of great chamber works which he would continue until his death: his Sonata for Clarinet and Bassoon was written in 1922 and qualifies as his first mature chamber work. This was followed in 1925 by the Trio for Oboe, Bassoon and Piano, another unusual instrumental combination, and revealed a close concern with form which Poulenc had been previously criticized for ignoring. His interest in older forms was indicated by the 1926 collation of anonymous 17th-century texts, *Chansons gaillardes*, which were notable for their risqué nature. The première of this collection was important for the singing of Pierre Bernac, who was to become the definitive Poulenc interpreter.

By 1928 the composer's enthusiasm for the concerto form was manifesting itself, with the *Concert champêtre* for harpsichord and orchestra (written for keyboardist Wanda Landowska) which fulfilled a dual purpose by giving Landowska something contemporary to play and creating a work with the same concerted values as that of the 17th and 18th centuries. This venture was followed four years later by the Concerto for Two Pianos and Orchestra,

a witty and sardonic work full of references to popular idioms and little musical jokes. Both works were commissioned by the wealthy music-lover, Princesse Edmond de Polignac, a great patroness of the arts.

In between these two works came the important development of the 'choreographic concerto', *Aubade* for piano and 18 instruments, in which Poulenc laid the ghost of motific development, finally abandoning any attempt to subvert his own natural compositional inclination. He commented at the time: "I know I am right. It is more courageous to grow just as one is than force feed one's flowers with the fertilizer of fashion".

His own growth was reinforced with the picture postcard atmosphere surrounding the 'cantata profane', *Le Bal masqué* (1932), written in a music hall style and full of jokes. But an even more courageous recognition of what he had become took place in 1936; on holiday near Rocamadour, he received the news of the death of a close friend in a car accident: immediately afterwards he visited the small chapel of St Amadour, carved from the Rocamadour rocks, and while in the chapel experienced a conversion back to the Catholic faith of his early adolescence. This had a profound effect on the subject and nature of many of his future compositions. That same evening Poulenc began the *Litanies à la vierge noire*, for voices and organ, using words from texts left in the shrine by pilgrims, the simplicity of the message intensifying the profundity of Poulenc's expressions of faith. The following year saw the production of the Mass in G major for unaccompanied choir, a remarkably human and unadorned composition eschewing the flamboyance of many previous incarnations by other composers.

From then on there was a new gravitas to the serious aspects of Poulenc's compositional career, aided by his passionate embrace of Paul Eluard's poetry and his decision to make Pierre Bernac the vocal ideal for all his songs. This led to the composition of a series of song cycles, such as *Tel jour, telle nuit* (1937) and *Banalités* (1940), which eclipsed his previous achievements in this genre, as well as scores of individual songs of the highest calibre, clearly making him the inheritor of the French tradition as sustained by Debussy and Fauré before him. Equally significant for Poulenc was the Concerto for Organ and Orchestra (1938), which has no specific religious subtext but which is filled with a religiosity of feeling and mood.

The outbreak of WWII did not deflect Poulenc from his course, and he continued to compose throughout the Occupation; it is claimed that he also worked with the French Resistance. Both in songs and religious vocal works this time was rich in music, with vocal works such as *Metamorphoses* (1943), *Montparnasse* (1941–45), two songs set to poems by Louis Aragon (1943), even the monologue/melodrama *L'Histoire de Babar* (1940–45), plus the religious settings *Un soir de neige* (1944), *Salve Regina* (1941), *Four Motets pour un temps de pénitence* (1938–39) and the *Figure Humaine* (1943), the last with

words by Eluard which reflect the suffering of his country under the Nazis. Poulenc also wrote instrumental works of great character, such as the ballet *Les Animaux modèles* (1942) and the Sonata for Violin and Piano (1942–43).

The general outburst of joy which greeted the end of War was best expressed by Poulenc in the farcical, high-spirited theatrical romp starring the Folies Bergère singer, Denise Duval, *Les Mamelles de Tirésias* (1947). A throwback to his heady 1920s style, even to the choice of text (a surrealistic play by Apollinaire, written before the advent of Surrealism) and the conscious pastiche of earlier musics, it was one in the eye for the bourgeoisie and a proof to Poulenc that, in these dark times, and in middle age, he could still cavort like a 20-year-old.

Other scintillating scores of the post-war period included the *Sinfonietta* (1947), full of wit and charm, and the Piano Concerto, commissioned by Charles Munch's Boston Symphony Orchestra and premièred in Boston by Poulenc himself during one of his numerous post-war American tours. As would be expected from Poulenc, he treats the piano as a concerted instrument among others, in the manner of his Baroque and Classical favourites, rather than as the dominant voice favoured by the Romantics.

The 1950s were a period of achievement in chamber music, with the *Capriccio* (1952) and *Elégie* (1959), both for two pianos, completed,

together with the Sonata for Flute and Piano (1956) and the Sonata for Two Pianos (1953–53). In terms of extended forms, the *Stabat Mater* (1950), first performed at Salzburg in 1951, must be placed among his greatest achievements, with 1959's *Gloria* not far behind, while in the song-form he continued to maintain his high standards with cycles such as *Le Travail du peintre* (1956) and *La Fraîcheur et le feu* (1950), both to words by Eluard. By this time Poulenc was universally recognized as one of the greatest living composers, his every new work greeted with international attention. His one serious stage work, *Les Dialogues des Carmélites* (1957), a three-act opera dealing with faith, death and routine within a nunnery, is a remarkable achievement but not entirely free of longueurs. Denise Duval, now in an entirely different role, was his choice for the leading role.

Duval also starred in Poulenc's last major work, *La Voix Humaine* (1959), a dramatic monologue written by Cocteau and sympathetically accompanied by full orchestra. This was followed by a fine Sonata for Clarinet (1962) and an equally admirable Sonata for Oboe (1962), each dedicated to a newly departed friend, Honegger and Prokofiev, and once again underlining Poulenc's total understanding of, and identification with, wind instruments, plus the *Sept Répons de ténèbres* (1961). But in the first month of 1963 Poulenc's time came to an end, his life abruptly ended by a heart attack in his favourite city of Paris.

PART IX

1900-1925

The generation of composers born at the time of World War I reflects a radically changing outlook on music and its place in society, as well as a seismic shift away from the old centres of power and influence as the chaos caused by Nazism and Stalinism forced the dispersal of German-speaking composers and stifled the creativity of most Russian composers other than Shostakovich, Prokofiev and Khachaturian. Only one German from this period—Kurt Weill—came to prominence, and he had fled from his homeland within months of Hitler's accession in 1933, eventually building a new career for himself in America.

Aerial view of lower New York and the Battery, 1922

Indeed, America became the beneficiary of many of the emigré artistic communities, in literature and fine art as well as music. This helped create a climate in which such home-grown talent as Copland and Bernstein could thrive and progress, while John Cage's iconoclasm was in part fed by the intellectual rigor of artists such as Duchamp. In South America, Argentina produced its first world-class composer, Alberto Ginastera. Of the Old World countries, only Britain and France continued to provide evidence of forward movement; Britain through the amazing precocity of Britten, Walton; France through the lone but crucial contribution of Messiaen. Italy and Spain, both labouring under Fascist regimes, produced the opposing talents of the conservative Rodrigo and the radical Luigi Nono. To the east of Germany and Austria, men such as Ligeti and Lutosławski persevered under intolerable political and social proscription until well after the end of World War II before they began to find an audience for their ideas. It was the Russians who perhaps had the longest and most courageous struggle for artistic freedom, with Shostakovich to the fore, not least because he was arguably the most gifted and substantial composer of his generation.

AARON COPLAND

1900–1990

Aaron Copland managed the rare and difficult feat of remaining true to his artistic and compositional principles throughout a long creative life while at the same time achieving real and lasting popularity in his own lifetime: a feat similarly achieved in America by only Gershwin and Bernstein.

Copland was born in New York of Russian Jewish emigré parents (the original family name being Kaplan). His father was a successful businessman which gave his family a comfortable buffer against material wants. Aaron began early with piano lessons and the piano was to remain his instrument. He later admitted to feeling "relieved when Stravinsky boasted that he always wrote at the piano... I need a piano to work at, as a writer would need a typewriter".

Aaron Copland

By the age of 14 he began lessons at Leopold Wolfstein's studio; by 1917 he took composition lessons from Rubin Goldmark, who had been a student of Dvořák. From Goldmark he gained "an excellent grasp on the fundamentals of music", although the witty little piano score, *Scherzo Humoristique: The Cat and the Mouse*, composed in 1920, was far too modern for Goldmark in its Francophile leanings. A further piano work, *Three Moods* (embittered, wistful, jazzy) was completed in 1920–21, hinting at what Copland would later attempt in *Statements for Orchestra*. The following year he convinced his parents

that Paris was the place he had to be, and Nadia Boulanger the teacher he needed. This was a most perspicacious choice, and in the course of the next three years Boulanger not only gave him a thorough theoretical grounding in composition, but also a marked taste for modern sounds. In 1921 he also became a published composer with the publication of the music for *The Cat and the Mouse*.

He returned to America in 1924 prepared for fame, but had to struggle for it. An idea implanted in him by

Boulanger for a ballet, combined with his first viewing of the silent expressionsist classic film, *Nosferatu*, led to the composition between 1922 and 1925 of a score which went unheard; it was eventually recycled in 1929 as the *Dance Symphony*, and won Copland the RCA Victor prize—a cool $5,000. By 1924, he had also composed *Symphony for Organ and Orchestra* which had been commissioned by Nadia Boulanger, an able organist in her own right; it was premièred at Aeolian Hall in New York in January 1925, with Boulanger in the soloist's seat, and

Walter Damrosch conducting the New York Philharmonic. (In 1928 Copland recast the work as his First Symphony, dropping the organ from the piece.)

The notoriety generated by this concert led to a generous society patroness taking up his cause. He also won Guggenheim Fellowships in 1925 and 1926, which gave him the time and space to concentrate exclusively on composing. In quick succession he wrote *Music for Theatre* (1925) and Concerto for Piano and Orchestra (1926), both pieces exhibiting his enthusiastic embrace of the jazz idiom which had emerged during the years he was away in Paris. The piano concerto, commissioned by Koussevitzky, shocked its initial audiences despite its considerable lyricism. Copland remarked: "Koussevitzky didn't mind. In fact, I think he rather enjoyed that aspect. It certainly got a shock reaction, especially from the old ladies on Friday afternoon". The follow-up *Symphonic Ode* eschewed the jazz influence and tightened the form, but was sufficiently abstract and dense for audiences to shy away from it in confusion. This confusion was compounded by what many regard as Copland's first masterpiece, his Piano Variations of 1930. Though just 10 minutes long, these variations are as severe, uncompromising and inexorable in their logic as anything in Bartók, though employing a musical idiom which, though harsh, is readily identifiable as Copland's own, both from a rhythmic and harmonic point of view.

Copland continued to follow this austere vein of development, completing such important works as the *Short Symphony (No. 2)* (1928–35), which

concentrated memorably on rhythm and showed a debt to Stravinsky, but which, in its harmonic idiom showed clear signs of the personal Copland orchestral sound which was soon to emerge. Copland followed this up with a key transitional work which is often overlooked: *Statements for Orchestra* (1934–35). In these six brief movements he creates music to illustrate titles such as 'militant', 'cryptic', 'subjective' and 'dogmatic' with great economy of means, signalling a move towards a simpler musical style with a broader appeal.

For some time Copland had been acutely aware of the gap between the contemporary composer and his audience, and ever more desirous of bridging it with music of undiluted integrity. At that time only Gershwin had achieved this dual aim in America. The first decisive steps came between 1933 and 1935 with his composition of the ten-minute travelogue of Mexican rhythms and exoticisms, *El salón México*, plus two small piano pieces for children. "I have always liked the idea of young people playing...my music. After all, they grow up and become our audiences". *The Young Pioneers* and *Sunday Afternoon Music* were clearly intended to be played often. *El salón México* only received its première in 1937 in Mexico City, but was his first popular hit and has remained a touchstone work in his *oeuvre* ever since. The following year Copland was commissioned to write a ballet and chose as his subject the Wild West legend of Billy the Kid. The ballet *Billy the Kid* was a major popular success and confirmed Copland's status as the leading serious American composer

(Gershwin had died the previous autumn). Copland quickly made a concert suite from the ballet, and this remains immensely popular.

Copland had now succeeded in his aim of creating artistically uncompromised music, instantly identifiable as being from his pen, which could reach a wide audience. He continued to write music of this kind for the rest of his life. This applied especially to his music for the stage, either in dance, drama or opera. In parallel, however, he continued to write music in his more severe vein. Thus, although *An Outdoor Overture* (1938) and *Quiet City* (1939) kept him at the forefront of popular opinion, and the children's opera *The Red Hurricane* (1937) renewed his commitment to supplying understandable music for young people, Copland worked through a more private aesthetic with his Sonata for Piano (1939–41) and Sonata for Violin and Piano (1942–43).

Despite this intensely serious, private work, Copland began to be accused of superficiality and of pandering to his audiences as he continued to use images of the American landscape and its folk legends to fashion works such as the wonderfully robust and evocative

DON'T MISS

▶ **Piano Variations (1930)**
▶ **El salón México (1933–36)**
▶ **Billy the Kid (1938)**
▶ **Piano Sonata (1939–41)**
▶ **Fanfare for the Common Man (1942)**

ballet *Rodeo* (1942). The four dance episodes are today the most commonly heard excerpts from this stage piece. With the ballet *Billy the Kid* there are liberal quotations from popular Wild West songs, such as 'Goodbye Old Paint' and 'Sis Joe', but these are beautifully integrated into the overall design. Such a fate did not attend the hugely popular *Fanfare for the Common Man*, originally commissioned by the Cincinatti Orchestra in 1942 as a patriotic gesture and subsequently positioned in the finale of Copland's ambitious Third Symphony (1944–46), written in time of war where it does not really serve a structural purpose or any musical function apart from stirring the emotions at an appropriate point.

More success in the theatre, firstly with music for the film *Our Town* (1940), from Thornton Wilder's play, and then the music for Martha Graham's ballet troupe, *Appalachian Spring* (1943/44), gave more fuel to his critics, although the music Copland had created was remarkable in its clarity and expressiveness, its unhackneyed use of folk material and its transparency of orchestral scoring (the opening of *Appalachian Spring*, in particular). Copland was here operating as a master of his profession at the peak of his powers. Even in something as risky as the *Lincoln Portrait* (1942), where a

DON'T MISS

▶ Rodeo (1942)
▶ Appalachian Spring (1945)
▶ Old American Songs (1950)
▶ Clarinet Concerto (1956)

speaker intones famous excerpts from Lincoln's speeches between portentous musical segments, his innate sense of drama won the day.

Copland's triumphs of the late forties came from quite different directions: the Clarinet Concerto (1947–48), commissioned by Benny Goodman, and the *Eight Poems of Emily Dickinson* (1949–50), the latter written alongside the Piano Quartet of 1950. The Emily Dickinson settings reveal a composer with an innate gift for setting words to music, as well as one sensitive to the minutest evocation of meaning from the poems themselves, whereas the concerto is by turns lyrical, moving, exciting and, finally ferociously difficult for the soloist (Goodman delayed the première for two years, uncertain of his ability to transcend the technical difficulties of the solo part). From 1948 also came the collation of the beguiling and jewel-like *Four Piano Blues*.

The end of the 1940s was a difficult time for Copland, as for so many creative spirits in America. He was one of many accused of being 'a fellow-traveller' of the Communists believed by Senator McCarthy to be secretly running (and ruining) America. But, like many others at the time, Copland continued to prove his partriotism through his art, and the two sets of *Old American Songs* (1950 and 1952) are utterly charming, occasionally heartwarming and utterly unpretentious demonstrations of his belief in the value of the common experience. His opera *The Tender Land* (1954) also attempted to prove a similar point, but it has to date failed to hold a regular place on the stages of the world. The challenging and abstruse work, *Piano Fantasy* (1956/57), an

extraordinary half-hour ramble which Copland hoped "would suggest...a spontaneous and unpremeditated sequence of 'events'...while at the same time exemplifying clear if somewhat unconventional structural principles", was from the first held in high esteem by musicians and critics alike.

By the end of the fifties Copland's compositional pace had slackened. The ballet *Dance Panels* was written in 1959 (revised in 1962) in six separate segments, and premièred in Munich in 1963. The work *Connotations*, Copland's public recognition of the uses of serialism, came from a 1961 commission from the Lincoln Center, and shocked its first-night audience (including the President's wife) with its aggressive dissonances. *Music for a Great City* (1963–64) was largely recomposed from a film score, *Something Wild*; Copland agreed with critics that the work had not entirely transcended its film origins.

The year 1967 saw the last major orchestral composition from Copland, *Inscape*, in which he managed a more satisfying personal combination of his typical style with serialist techniques. The work has remained relatively unknown, but is a late masterpiece. By the early 1970s Copland had begun to suffer the onset of the Alzheimer's disease which eventually killed him. His last extended composition was *Duo for Flute and Piano* (1971), although the two short piano pieces, (*Midday Thoughts* and *Proclamations*) of 1982, were his last works in any genre. By then, Copland was a much-honoured American citizen; among many other honours, he had in 1964 received America's highest civilian honour, the Presidential Medal of Freedom.

KURT WEILL

1900–1950

Kurt Weill has been important during the course of this century for two reasons: the quality of the music he wrote once he stepped outside the modernistic Germanic traditions in which he grew up, and the extent of continued influence these latter works exert on those maverick composers who attempt to combine popular and art-music traditions.

Weill was born into a humanist orthodox Jewish family in Dessau, near Berlin. His father, who composed choral music for the local synagogue, gave Kurt his first piano lessons. By the age of 10, young Kurt was already writing little one-act operas and other pieces, and proved a sufficiently adept musician to begin studying in his early teens with Albert Bing. He subsequently won a place at the Berlin Hochschule, where he commenced studies in 1918 with composer/teacher Engelbert Humperdinck. Even at this stage he was attracted by the music of Schoenberg, and his own early compositions—many of them purely instrumental or orchestral—reflect that passion. The parlous state of the German economy in the post-war period forced Weill to interrupt his education for two years and he worked as a repetiteur in Dessau until able to return in 1920 to his studies in Berlin.

After the usual flurry of songs and a sonata for cello (1920), Weill embarked on his modernist First Symphony in 1921, completing it just before he

Kurt Weill

joined Ferruccio Busoni's masterclass at the Prussian State Academy in Berlin. Weill remained part of Busoni's tutoring circle until the older man's death in 1924, and this experience was of prime importance in gradually turning Weill (who had continued the symphonic train of thought with a *Sinfonia Sacra* in 1922) away from the hyperbolic post-Romantic inheritance of the Mahler-Schoenberg school and towards a music which, while remaining true to this initial inspiration, sought restraint and a finer balance of forces and form.

By 1924 and his *Concerto for Violin and Wind Orchestra* (dedicated to Josef Szigeti), this new balance had most decidedly been struck, and the work has been for many years Weill's most popular concert piece.

The Berlin of the early 1920s held many intellectual and cultural attractions for a young alert composer such as Weill, and before the middle of the decade he had become a member of the November Group. Within this set of friends Weill continued to develop and refine his own cultural, political and artistic credo. His first attempt at opera was the one-act expressionist work *Der Protagonist* (1924–25) (with a libretto by Georg Kaiser), which was premièred in Dresden in 1926. By the time of the one-act ballet, *Royal Palace* (1925–26), Weill had begun introducing into his music the vernacular rhythmic, harmonic and melodic elements he was hearing in the Berlin clubs and cabarets. In this he was not abandoning his earlier compositonal bent, but reinforcing his natural musical inclinations with musical elements which gave him a tartness, a tautness and liveliness rare in the music of his day. His next theatrical venture, *The Czar has his Photograph Taken* (1927) has rarely seen the light of day, but by the time of its Leipzig première in 1928 this disappointment was easily put aside, as 1927 witnessed the beginning of Weill's short but artistically crucial collaboration with the left-wing poet, polemicist and playwright, Bertolt Brecht.

Brecht had a fully-formed theatrical aesthetic of his own, wholly dependent on his political and social objectives, and it was Weill (perhaps with Stravinsky's *Oedipus Rex* as a distant model for Brecht's idea of 'epic theatre') who had to construct a musical style which was fresh, unsentimental and immediate. Above all, Brecht wanted to make it impossible for his audiences to identify with the corrupt and debased characters he and Weill depicted. Fortunately, given the seductiveness of Weill's music, this ideal was never achieved.

They began two projects almost simultaneously: *Die Dreigroschenoper*

(based on Gay's *Beggar's Opera*) and the first version of the opera *Mahagonny*, called *Die kleine Mahagonny*, which at this point was just a series of songs yet to be set for the stage. *Die Dreigroschenoper* opened in Berlin in 1928 and was an immediate sensation, its adroit undercutting of emotion and style, either through Brecht's polemic or Weill's sardonic juxtapositions, adding immensely to its appeal. Yet even in this work, with which Brecht expressed his satisfaction, there were moments of declared and even tender emotion given fragile and moving expression by Weill. Such feelings were brought closer to the surface in the overtly political—and quietly suppressed—*Das Berliner Requiem*, in which a series of left-wing heroes and heroines were commemorated and celebrated, and which contained some deeply affecting and disturbing music from Weill. Disgusted by the successful suppression of the *Requiem*, Brecht and Weill turned once more to overtly popular theatrical works.

Mahagonny, which was completed and staged in 1930, was a full-blown contemporary opera. Its runaway success, in which the collapse of a terminally decadent society is lovingly invoked by Brecht and Weill, proved too much for Brecht who became exasperated with his success with the Berlin public: he, who had planned disruption and indignation as a necessary stage before public enlightenment, had suffered the ultimate indignity, that of being subsumed and disarmed by his own popular success. As is often the case, he blamed his partners, Weill in particular, and their collaboration on *Happy End*, which they had begun while

Mahoganny was being prepared for its premiere, was to be their last in this vein. In this shorter piece, Brecht (aided as ever by Elisabeth Hauptmann) attempted to prevent any chance of popular success by supplying the very opposite of what the work's title suggested: the end was anything but conventionally satisfying, and the work was deemed a failure by Berlin audiences who bayed instead for another *Dreigroschenoper*. Yet Weill and Brecht, in fashioning a work where the music came interspersed by longer stretches of spoken dialogue, were suggesting an entirely different tradition, closer to music hall than opera or music theatre, and Weill's own bitter-sweet music reached new levels of artistry in such ecstatic and disturbing pieces as 'Bilbao Song', 'Matrosen-Tango' and 'Surabaya-Johnny'.

With the broadcasting of the radio-musical *Der Jasager* (1930), a piece specifically written for children to perform, Brecht and Weill went their separate creative ways, but this meant little or no slacking of the pace for Weill, who was now the most famous and popular theatrical music composer in Europe. He plunged into work on *Die Bürgschaft* (1930–31) with Caspar Neher and *Der Silbersee* (1932—33) against a background of heightening political tension as the Nazis and Communists battled it out in the streets of Berlin. By the time of *Der Silbersee's* première, it was clear that Weill, as an internationally established leftist composer, would have to leave Germany. Weill and his wife, Lotte Lenya (they had met during rehearsals for *Die Dreigroschenoper*) left Germany the day after Hitler's infamous

Reichstag fire, reaching Paris and comparative safety. With all their German income impounded by the Nazis, they were close to poverty.

Once in Paris Weill was not idle for long; he was commissioned by Troupe 33 to supply them with a ballet, the choreography to be created by Balanchine. From this commission came *Die sieben Todsünden* (The Seven Deadly Sins), the last work in which the old Brecht-Weill team combined, Brecht supplying words for its seven dance sections. The work was successfully premièred in 1933. Weill also received a commission for a second symphony, and this, carrying unmistakable echoes of his stage music, duly appeared in late autumn of the same year. Yet the French theatrical sensibility was at least one remove from his essentially Germanic one, and Weill moved on, via London, to America, which he and Lenya reached in 1935. There he set about creating a Broadway career to rival his earlier Berlin years, but American theatrical tastes being what they were,

his forays onto the New York stage are notably less acerbic and pointed than his work with Brecht.

However, such productions as *Lady in the Dark* (1940) (lyrics by Ira Gershwin), *Knickerbocker Holiday* (lyrics by Maxwell Anderson), *One Touch of Venus* (1943) and *Street Scene* (1946) all had superior craftsmanship and a smattering of truly great songs, while *Street Scene* itself, together with *Lost in the Stars* in 1947 (again with Maxwell Anderson), would come to be recognized as a Broadway work only in name, and one of the first modern theatrical pieces which genuinely bridged the gap between popular and operatic music theatre. The same year saw the successful production of Weill's own American folk opera, *Down in the Valley*, a work written for amateurs to perform and which interpolated no less than five Kentucky mountain folk tunes.

All these late American works suggest that Weill had reached a point at which he was fully at ease with the

personal combination of vernacular and art-music traditions which he had fashioned on two continents, and would spend the rest of his creative life reaching further musical heights. Unfortunately this was not to be: in 1950, soon after the commencement of his latest collaboration with Maxwell Anderson—an adaptation of *Huckleberry Finn*—Weill suddenly died of a heart attack. His wife spent the rest of her long life staunchly promoting and defending Weill's posthumous reputation, making a series of definitive recordings of his most famous works, both German and American, by which all other performances must now be gauged.

JOAQUÍN RODRIGO
b. 1902

Rodrigo's position as arguably the 20th century's most popular instrumental composer is deeply resented by many observers who criticise him for writing in an unashamedly conservative style. The music is unmistakably Spanish in origin, but its warm harmonies and lilting melodies

cause few listeners any discomfort.

Born in the province of Valencia in Spain, Rodrigo suffered the fate of many children brought up in unsanitary conditions by succumbing to diphtheria at the age of three and permanently losing his sight. By the time he was

eight, however, he had shown such an unwavering interest in music that his parents allowed him to begin lessons. These were sufficiently successful for him to progress to Valencia Conservatoire in 1917, where he studied theory and composition until 1923. In that year he composed his first orchestral work, *Juglares*, as well

In 1947 Joaquín took up a professorship at Madrid Conservatoire. By the end of the decade *Aranjuez* had made him internationally famous. Its combination of intense orchestral warmth, melancholy, strikingly passionate melodies and a Moorish tinge of rhythm and melodic shapes, combined with a smattering of Spanish folk colour, proved irresistible. From then on Rodrigo wrote with the world watching; his next work for guitar and orchestra, *Fantasia para un gentilhombre* (1954) was commissioned by the greatest living Spanish guitarist, Andres Segovia. This serene and elegant work was written expressly for Segovia's exquisite artistry and to evoke an earlier age of Spanish music; it achieved its aim delightfully.

Joaquín Rodrigo

as a *Suite* for piano and *2 Esbozos* for violin and piano. Between then and 1927, when he moved to Paris, he completed further works such as *5 Piezas infantiles* (2 versions, for piano and for orchestra) (1924), a *Bagatela*, a *Pastorale* (1926) and a *Preludio ai gallo mananero* for piano (1926) and a *Zarabande* (1926) for guitar.

DON'T MISS

▶ **Concierto de Aranjuez (1939)**

▶ **Fantasia para un gentilhombre (1954)**

▶ **Invocacion y danza (1962)**

▶ **12 Cançiones populares españolas (1965)**

▶ **Concierto andaluz (1967)**

At the Ecole Normale in Paris, Rodrigo studied with Paul Dukas and became friends with another expatriate, Manuel de Falla. With the Spanish Civil War now raging in his native country, Rodrigo spent the 1930s in either France or Germany, working and composing, with the occasional return visit to Valencia and Madrid. With Franco in power, in 1939 Rodrigo and his wife Victoria decided to move back to Spain, thus fortuitously avoiding the even greater conflagration which was about to commence in France and Germany. During this time he had been steadily composing and expanding his reputation. Soon after his return to Spain, he produced the *Concierto de Aranjuez*, his first concerto and by far his most popular piece; named after a royal palace near Madrid it had, ironically, been composed in Paris.

That Rodrigo was also a successful composer of songs should come as no surprise, considering the quality of melody he brings to his 11 concertos. Throughout the 1930s and 1940s he wrote collections of songs, some from popular airs known to all Spaniards (*12 cançiones populares españolas* (1938); some more consciously crafted from his own imagination (*4 Madrigales amatorios* (1948). He also continued to write sparkling and vivacious piano music up until the 1980s, as well as a spattering of chamber music. But the pieces on which his reputation is based continue to be the concertos, which appeared regularly between 1939 and the close of the 1980s. His *Concierto de estio*, written for violin and orchestra, is a tribute to Vivaldi, while there are a number of other concerted pieces for guitar and orchestra, including the *Concierto madrigal* for two guitars and orchestra (1969) and the comparatively late *Concierto para una fiesta* (1982). There are also charming concertos for cello, flute, piano, harp (*Concierto serenata*, commissioned by the famous harpist Nicanor Zabaleta and completed in 1952) and the less frequently heard *Concierto andaluz* (1967) for 4 guitars and orchestra.

Rodrigo's style underwent no discernible development after 1939, though he became more expert and economical in his craft over the years, revelling in his expertise in orchestration and his sense of the perfect balance between rhythm and melody. Rodrigo avoided the many

pitfalls of relatively early fame, writing neither pompous nor vapid music to please either a misplaced vanity or a perceived popular audience. He stayed true to his inner voice, and the body of work he created—though couched in a highly approachable idiom—has the integrity of sincerity.

WILLIAM WALTON
1902–1983

Walton is most often noted as the link in English music between Elgar and Britten (although it is a moot point as to where that leaves Vaughan Williams), but this hardly does justice to a creative spirit every bit as identifiable and well-tempered as the two men he supposedly links, as the opening bars of his Violin Concerto attests.

Walton was born in Oldham, Lancashire. His father was involved in the local church choir and gave young William his first lessons in music. A keen and able student, Walton sang in the choir at the age of five, entering the Christ Church Cathedral Choir at Oxford five years later. His studies under the care of Sir Hugh Allen enabled him to matriculate at the age of 16, and he received a Music degree in 1918. His time at Oxford ended prematurely as he was sent down from Christ Church College for neglecting every form of study apart from music.

Clearly his time there was not entirely wasted as a string quartet written while still at Oxford (1919–22) was performed at the 1923 Salzburg International Contemporary Music Festival. This performance led to a cordial realtionship with the composer, Paul Hindemith.

While at Oxford he struck up a friendship with Sacheverell Sitwell, and on his arrival in London after the Oxford ejection, he lived in Chelsea with the Sitwell family. This connection was to prove decisive: within months he had started work on the music for the Sitwells' new venture, *Façade,* the 'entertainment' for speakers and ensemble. Aided and abetted by his friend (and the work's dedicatee) Constant Lambert, who was to prove very influential to the course of his career, Walton supplied music as witty and transparent as the words by Edith Sitwell. The first public performance at London's Aeolian Hall (where the curtain remained drawn and Edith

Sitwell spoke from behind it through a megaphone) caused shock and indignation. One newspaper headed its review 'Drivel They Paid To Hear', and even a sophisticate like Noel Coward walked out in disgust. But the critic Ernest Newman commented: 'As for Walton's music, nothing cleverer has been produced in this line by any composer in any country'. Walton revised the score several times (the definitive version was only published in 1951), and created two suites from the original score. From this early launch of his music in London there was little chance that his subsequent compositions would be ignored.

Only just 21, Walton had already reached an early mature style, a point emphasized by his brilliant overture, *Portsmouth Point* (1925), full of colour, rhythm and incident. A deepening of his expressive power is notable in *Sinfonia Concertante* (1927) for orchestra with piano obbligato, reworked from a ballet score rejected by Diaghilev, with each

William Walton

of lyricism and pre-Romantic, Classical compositional techniques.

Walton's ability to cover tremendous compositional ground was emphasized in his next major success, the cantata *Belshazzar's Feast* of 1931. With a text taken by Osbert Sitwell from the Bible, this immensely powerful work, conceived on a grand Handelian scale but couched in the harmonic and rhythmic ruggedness of its own age, produced a cathartic effect on its first audiences, and the work quickly assumed a place beside Elgar's *Dream of Gerontius* in the front line of English choral music.

During the 1930s Walton consolidated his already impressive career, as well as striking out in a new direction—film music—which steadily increased in importance for him. He had begun his first symphony in 1931, and by 1934 had completed three movements (such was the interest in the new work that these were played in 1934 by the LSO under Hamilton Harty). The following summer saw the completion of the fourth movement, and in November Harty conducted the première of the whole work. Again it enjoyed immediate success, and its individualistic design, allied to the typical Waltonian combination of verve and melodic beauty, deserved the commendation. The sheer intensity of the score is often explained as being a direct result of his new love for the rich and beautiful Alice Wimborne.

The year 1935 also saw the release of one of Walton's earliest film scores for *Escape Me Never*, and he soon discovered that his music's peculiar

of the three movements dedicated to one of the Sitwells: Osbert, Edith and Sacheverell. Walton's next notable work was a major success from its first performance, although the Viola Concerto (1929) had a problematic gestation, with its intended performer at the première, Lionel Tertis, rejecting it as 'too modern'. Happily, Paul

Hindemith, whose *Kammermusik, No. 5* was used as a partial model for the concerto, demonstrated his admiration of the work by performing the soloist's part at the Proms première. From the first, Walton's concerto was recognized as a great achievement, perhaps the greatest concerto for the viola in the 20th century, with its careful balancing combination of brilliance (and the occasional brashness) and lucidly tender melodicism was perfect for film. He was quick to repeat the experience, scoring *As You Like It* in 1936. For the next 12 years he returned regularly to this medium, with notable successes such as *Major Barbara* (1942), *Henry V* (1943–44) and *Hamlet* (1947). Indeed, he would continue to be associated with film music up to the beginning of the 1970s. He clearly enjoyed the challenge, once noting, "In films you don't have the time to be choosy". Having sampled the excitement of composing for celluloid drama, Walton was not averse to working in the theatre as well, and he provided incidental music for a 1941 production of *Macbeth*, as well as embarking on two ballets, both produced in London in 1943: *The Quest* and *The Wise Virgins*.

Major concert hall works were much less frequent after the first symphony, but the violin concerto of 1938-39 was a significant achievement, and again it reflected his relationship with Alice Wimborne, who in 1938 had introduced him to Italy, specifically the coast near Amalfi. The shimmering orchestration and the lightness of melody portrays a man secure in his love: after the rigours of the oncoming war, Walton would remember this time and return to Italy permanently. Walton's war was conducted from the propaganda department of the Ministry of Information, and he worked rapidly to turn out music for many filmic and radio broadcast occasions. By the end of the War, Walton was aware of time closing in on his relationship with Alice Wimborne as she was diagnosed as

suffering from cancer. His deeply-felt, elegaic String Quartet in A minor (1945–47), one of his few chamber works, carries his burden of impending grief. The composition of the Sonata for Violin and Piano, commissioned by Yehudi Menuhin and Louis Kentner in 1946 and dedicated to their wives, Diana and Griselda, spanned the death of Alice Wimborne in 1948, Walton's flight to Buenos Aires and his marriage there to Susana Gil, a woman a good 20 years younger than himself. It was completed in London in 1949, and premièred that year in Zurich by Menuhin and Kentner. As Walton remarked, "It's surprising that the piece has any continuity at all", but in fact it is a tightly constructed and musically satisfying two-movement work, written under pressure, which is often when Walton responded with his best music.

Walton and his wife moved to the Italian island of Ischia in 1949. The expatriate was knighted in 1951, by which time he had already worked for three years on his one 'major' opera, *Troilus and Cressida* (1954). The opera signalled a shift in his composing towards the human voice, with the *Coronation Te Deum* (1952-53) being composed contemporaneously, and other pieces—a *Gloria* of 1961, the song cycle *Anon in Love* (1959) and choral works such as *Jubilate Deo* (1971-72), the *Chichester Service* of 1966 and a *Missa brevis* (1965-66) following in its wake. Considering Walton's extreme melodic facility, it is interesting that he waited until his late middle age before addressing vocal music consistently, but these works are no less impressive for their tardiness.

Walton's Symphony No. 2 (1957–60) is heard less often than his first symphony; smaller in scale, it is still tautly and expertly written, the *passacaglia* finale being an especially impressive conclusion. The orchestral work written immediately prior to this was the Cello Concerto (1955–56), in turns lyrical and assertive. It was written for Piatigorsky who premièred it in Boston and well understood its broad melodic contours. By the early 1960s Walton's presence on the musical scene was fading; with his permanent removal to Ischia he gradually drifted further out of touch with post-war British developments. The occasional film score underlined his musical vitality (*Richard III* in 1955; *The Battle of Britain* in 1969), but also served to give people the impression that these less 'serious' commissions were his true milieu: a grave underestimation of his contribution. Since Walton's death there has been a slow, methodical re-assessment of his entire *oeuvre*, which is not particularly large, and it is conceivable that his reputation will continue to rise in the years to come.

DON'T MISS

▶ **Façade (1921–22)**

▶ **Symphony No. 1 (1931–35)**

▶ **Violin Concerto (1938–39)**

▶ **Henry V—film score (1947)**

▶ **Troilus and Cressida (1954)**

ARAM KHACHATURIAN

1903–1978

Khachaturian is one of the first Armenian composers to have established an international reputation, achieving it by using his country's folk traditions in his 'serious' compositions. The expert orchestration, colour and theatrical flair of ballets such as *Gayaneh* and *Spartacus* gained him world-wide appeal in the period following World War II.

Khachaturian was born in the Armenian capital, Tblisi, into a relatively comfortable middle-class family. Although he had always enjoyed the Armenian folk music, he showed no interest in pursuing a career in music until, at the age of 19, he approached the composer Gnesin to give him lessons in composition. This led to his attending the Gnesin School of Music in Moscow (then known as Moscow Conservatory) where he came under the influence of Miaskovsky. By then he was already writing his own music, mainly small pieces for piano, which showed a pronounced Asiatic tinge.

As he entered his fourth decade, he had gained sufficient confidence to attempt more ambitious music, moving from the rustic *Armenian Folksong and Dance* for wind orchestra of 1932 to his first full symphony in 1934. This work was a decided success—no mean feat in the critical climate of Soviet Russia at that time—and established him as a composer to be reckoned with. Its astute combination of folk-like elements and tidy musical development in relatively

Aram Khachaturian

conservative idioms made it difficult to criticize. More dramatic in impact was the Concerto for Piano and Orchestra of 1935-36 which won fulsome praise. The work uses every instrument of a large orchestra, making it a spectacular concert hall piece. Its popularity in the Soviet Union was immediate and

permanent, and when it was introduced to American audiences in 1942, it quickly became a staple part of the performing repertoire of a number of pianists, rapidly making the transition to records.

Khachaturian followed this concerto with another, Concerto for Violin and

DON'T MISS

▶ Piano Concerto (1936)

▶ Violin Concerto (1940)

▶ Masquerade (1941)

▶ Gayaneh (1942)

▶ Spartacus (1954)

Orchestra in D minor (1940) which was equally successful in the Soviet Union. It not only won him the Stalin Prize but the advocacy of the brilliant young violinist, David Oistrakh. Khachaturian had carefully balanced his folk-like elements with the type of virtuosity which appealed to top-flight violinists, and the work is still heard regularly in concert halls. The onset of what the Soviets called the Great Patriotic War did not find Khachaturian wanting, and his Second Symphony, subtitled *The Bell* (1943), contained a third movement which the composer felt conveyed "the superhuman sufferings caused to the Soviet people by the Nazi monsters". The Moscow première in 1943 was a great success, and within a year it was introduced to America by Leonard Bernstein.

By this time Khachaturian had become indissolubly linked with his Armenian roots, and his first ballet, *Gayaneh,* set great store by this heritage. Some of the dances are positively rustic, the rhythms violent and marked with clanging percussion, the melodies extremely vocal. Khachaturian made no bones about using as many kinds of Armenian dance as he could fit into the score, which runs for over an hour in its uncut version. The famous *Sabre Dance* has taken on a life of its own, played so often out of context that few who hear it are able to name its composer or the ballet from which it comes.

After this phenomenal world-wide success, Khachaturian found himself caught in the web of his own success, and though he wrote another symphony (1947), a cello concerto of distinction (1946) and various chamber works during his prolific career, he became typecast as a composer of folk ballets and theatre music. In 1943 he attempted to repeat his success with *Gayaneh* by mounting the ballet *Spartacus* (1943), which did enjoy a brief time in the sun,

but is now usually heard only in highlights, especially the overture. Throughout the 1940s and 1950s he wrote a number of excellent film scores, using his innate gift for music drama.

Like most Soviet composers of any worth, Khachaturian suffered in the attack launched in 1948 by the Central Committee of the Communist Party against so-called 'anti-popular trends' and the sin of 'formulism'. He was one of the few to criticize his critics publicly, winning for his colleagues some respite from the suffocating attentions of Stalin's cronies. In 1951 he was appointed Professor of composition at Moscow Conservatory and at his old college, the Gnesin School, retaining both posts until his retirement. Khachaturian's music did not benefit from a great latter-day wellspring of inner renewal, and long before his death he had become a man venerated for his early achievements rather than for the later repertoire. Yet even his least inspired scores were cleverly realized and had lessons to teach any student of modern composition.

MICHAEL TIPPETT
1905–1998

Though Tippett was of the same generation as Walton, his relatively late attainment of musical maturity, allied to his more angular musical style, places him in the public perception alongside Britten and **the post-war composers as one who directly shaped the course of British music between 1945 and the rise of minimalism.**

Tippett's family roots were Cornish, though he spent the majority of his childhood in Suffolk. Interested in music from an early age, he took piano lessons while still in Suffolk, moving to London in 1919 when his parents went to live in France. In 1922 he began lessons in composition and conducting at the Royal College of Music. Even at

DON'T MISS

▶ Concerto for Double String Orchestra (1938–39)
▶ A Child of Our Time (1939–41)
▶ Fantasia Concertante on a Theme of Corelli (1953)
▶ The Vision of St Augustine (1983)
▶ String Quartet No. 5 (1990–91)

this early stage he had discovered an affinity with Beethoven's music and muse. For the remainder of the decade he balanced composing (including a symphony) with teaching, but at the beginning of the 1930s, a concert which included his music revealed what he considered to be painful weaknesses in his compositional techniques, and he withdrew or destroyed everything written to that date. He went 'back to school', taking a course of counterpoint to correct his perceived deficiencies. Only one work from this period, his First String Quartet (1935), would remain in his canon, and this was recast some years later in order to render its form more acceptable to its composer. Unusually for a profession noted for the single-mindedness of its practitioners, Tippett had developed a strong social consciousness and a desire to do what he could to alleviate need. During the slow crawl out of the Depression, he conducted the South London Orchestra, an aggregation made up entirely of unemployed musicians, as well as undertaking other similar duties further afield.

Tippett's real 'arrival' on the music scene came with his *Concerto for Double String Orchestra* (1939). Long concerned with problems of form, Tippett gradually established a number of musical forms most suited to his musical imagination. In his symphonies the sonata form would be important; elsewhere he would be attracted to the 17th-century notion of the Fantasia. With this first fully mature work, it was the *concerto grosso* structure which was his ideal partner, using two sets of instruments to alternate in the presentation of his themes. Tippett himself conducted the 1940 première, but the advent of WWII postponed the implementation of a publishing agreement, thus delaying his arrival in the larger musical world until after the War. A pacifist by nature and conviction, he registered as a conscientious objector, and refused to comply with the Tribunal's findings that in his case the alternative to active service would be unskilled labouring work. Tippett believed himself to be a musician, and best able to serve his country in that capacity. He spent three months in prison for his beliefs.

The truth of his assertion, however, was soon borne out by the emergence of his oratorio *A Child of Our Time* (1939–41). Inspired by a 1938 newspaper report of the murder of a Nazi diplomat by a young Polish Jew in revenge for his people's persecution by Hitler, Tippett composed this passionate outcry against evil, inhumanity and oppression, writing both the music and the text. To convey the universality of the problem, Tippett included negro spirituals such as 'Deep River', using them in the role of chorales. The work's London première took place in the spring of 1944: it was his first notable public success.

Compositions written during the War include the *Fantasia on a Theme of Handel* (1939–41), composed for piano and orchestra and using as its main feature a fascinating series of variations resolving into a fugue; and the String Quartet No.2 (1941-42), a work Tippett himself felt to be "the most classically balanced, the closest to a 'standard' four-movement piece" of his earlier three quartets. Immediately after the end of the War, Tippett began his Third String Quartet (1945-46), which had five movements instead of the normal four and no longer relied on the sonata form to shape its content. He also completed work on his First Symphony which was premièred in 1945. In this work his contrapuntalism came to the fore, as well as his love of the Fantasia form.

Though his career had begun to take off, Tippett found it hard to distance himself from the individual and collective sufferings caused by the War, and this, exacerbated by the suicide in 1945 of a close friend, Francesca Allinson, delayed the process of renewal. The song cycle *The Heart's Assurance* (1950-51) was one of a very few projects allowed to interrupt his long gestation of the opera *The Midsummer Marriage* (1955), and dealt explicitly with the twin themes of love and death and the resolution of the two. Using verses by two poets killed in the War, he constructed a moving memorial to his lost friend and a hard-won victory for love over death itself.

In 1953 his *Fantasia Concertante on a Theme by Corelli* (1953) emerged and was to prove perhaps his most popular single composition. Written solely for · strings and—like the *Divertimento on 'Sellinger's Round'*—written for the 1953 Aldeburgh Festival, it was the result of a commission. The 1953 Edinburgh Festival wanted to celebrate the tercentenary of Corelli's birth (something guaranteed to attract Tippett's interest), and the première of this piece was conducted by Tippett himself. Using two quotations from Corelli, one dark and brooding, the other light and brilliant, he interweaves his development of the two motifs in to an ebullient Fantasia. The work was an immediate and deserved success. This happy result was not to be repeated with *The Midsummer Marriage*: the Covent Garden première was declared a grave disappointment, and the opera had to wait until the 1970s before it began to establish itself as a tenable theatrical production.

Yet the Concerto for Piano and Orchestra, begun in 1953 but shelved until after the opera's completion, carried within it elements of the opera's atmosphere and many of its stylistic traits, and was successful upon its 1955 première, with Louis Kentner as the soloist. Inspired by a Gieseking rehearsal of Beethoven's lyrical opening movement to his fourth piano concerto, Tippett concentrated on what he regarded as the piano's "poetic

Michael Tippett

capabilities". Although there are sections of wild and humorous music utilizing blues intervals and jazz-type syncopation, the lyrical mood predominates in one of Tippett's most attractive works.

A commission from the BBC led to the composition of Tippett's Second Symphony (1956-57), while a commission from the Kousevitzky Foundation gave him the impetus to write his next opera after the disappointments of *The Midsummer Marriage*. The opera *King Priam* was composed in three years (1958–61), less than half the time of the previous opera. Tippett again abstracted his own libretto, this time from Homer. A more dramatic style of music was evolved for a subject which by its nature held more drama than the previous stage work, and the Coventry Cathedral première

certainly led to Tippett being taken seriously as an operatic composer.

Another BBC commission led to one of his most beautiful works, the oratorio for baritone chorus and orchestra *The Vision of St Augustine* (1965). Tippett prepared his own text, mainly from *The Confessions of St Augustine*, and gave the work a three-sectioned structure. Concerned with the nature of visionary experience and the relation of mortality to eternity, the oratorio concludes with the realization, according to Tippett, "that the esctatic vision is now incomplete and incapable of being sustained, so that the human fallibility, in the last courageous choral statement 'I count myself not apprehended', has been prepared for".

By now Tippett's position in British music was assured. In 1965 festivals of his music were given on both sides of the Atlantic to mark his 60th birthday, and in 1966 he received a knighthood. His third opera, *The Knot Garden* (1966-69), was premièred in 1970 at Covent Garden, and where its predecessor had been compact and to the point—indeed almost brutally so— this opera returned to the diffuseness and subjectivity of his first opera. Music from *The Knot Garden* triggered a major piece: his *Symphony No.3 for Soprano and Orchestra* (1970–72) which carries a vocal movement derived in part directly from Act 1.

Tippett was now in his late sixties, but his creativity showed no sign of abandoning him: in fact, the 1970s saw a number of significant works completed, including his opera *The Ice Break* (1973–76), which dealt with his common theme of reconciliation, and

his Fourth Symphony (1976–77). The latter work is seen as the beginning of a phase in which Tippett was able to marry together the two dominant strands—the lyrical and the more hard-edged—in his musical thinking from his earlier periods. Again the sonata and fantasia forms are to be found in a single structure which can be divided into seven units, significant in that they can be seen as the 'seven phases of life'. An ambitious work on every level, it has come to be regarded as a late masterpiece.

In a development as unexpected by the composer as by his audience, Tippett then returned to the string quartet, composing his fourth in 1978, a work which, like the fourth symphony, is conceived in a single movement and can be interpreted as a 'life-cycle' composition. His *Triple*

Concerto for violin, viola, cello and orchestra (1979), which returned to the concerted forms with which he had been so at ease during his career, has proved to be perhaps his most popular concert work of the later period, full of brilliant contrapuntal writing and pleasing passages for soloists and orchestra alike. The late 1980s saw the completion of his opera *The New Year* (1985–88), while in 1991 a Fifth String Quartet was announced, bringing with it a return to lyricism also notable in other late scores such as *Byzantium*, for soprano and orchestra (1989–91) and the oratorio *The Mask of Time* (1980–82). Tippett remained creative up until his final years, a period in which he also reaped widespread recognition and countless awards and honours. He died in early 1998, his prominent position in British music assured.

DMITRI SHOSTAKOVICH
1906–1975

Together with Stravinsky and Prokofiev, Shostakovich has dominated 20th-century Russian music. Growing to maturity within the Soviet system which Stravinsky escaped, he remained a Soviet citizen throughout his life. His unceasing creativity, pursued in defiance of Stalin's harshest edicts, was an inspiration to all artists working under the totalitarian regime, and the integrity of his music speaks for itself.

Shostakovich was born in St Petersburg, the son of middle-class professionals. Both parents were musical, and Shostakovich's first piano lessons were with his mother, a Conservatoire-trained pianist. With an interim period at the Glasser Institute, he was ready at the age of 13 to attend St Petersburg (later Leningrad) Conservatoire. An outstanding pupil in every way, he completed his training by submitting as his graduation piece his first symphony, which made him internationally known. This early success helped him decide between a

career as a concert pianist (he had entered the 1927 Chopin Competition in Warsaw and received an 'honourable mention') or a composer, although he later commented: "If the truth be told I should have been both".

During the next few years Shostakovich took advantage of the latitude granted composers by the Soviet authorities—to be avant-garde in Russia at that time was both politically and socially correct—and experimented with the exciting ideas coming from composers such as Bartók, Berg,

Dmitri Shostakovich

Prokofiev and Stravinsky. Shostakovich's second and third symphonies, written in 1927 and 1929 respectively, reflect his keen interest in progressive musical ideas, and also show him to be a convinced and enthusiastic revolutionary in his politics, using simple choral settings at key moments to evoke the correct Soviet spirit of collective proletariat triumph. Shostakovich's overwhelming talent, his youth and ardour made him the favoured Soviet composer at that time, each new composition hailed as a triumph for the system as much as for the composer himself.

Yet in the maelstrom of evolving Communist politics, no reputation was carved in stone, and a work Shostakovich had written between his symphonic commitments—the satirical opera *The Nose* (1927/28)—marked something of a turning-point. It opened to enthusiatic audiences in 1930 and

enjoyed sustained success in cultured circles, but the Association of Proletarian Composers denounced it as being redolent with 'bourgeois decadence', the warning shot in what would eventually become a full-scale attack on Shostakovich's musical methods and outlook. Shostakovich, however, was too busy with new projects to pay much attention, completing the music for Mayakovsky's play *The Flea* (1929), writing a number of film scores—including *Alone* (1930) and *New Babylon* (1928)—and completing a major project with the ballet *The Golden Age* (1927–30). The ballet tells the story of a Russian football team which travels to the West to play a match, is arrested for dubious bourgeois reasons and is finally liberated in a battle between workers and capitalists. It gave Shostakovich the perfect excuse for incorporating a number of decadent musical forms into his score, whether for ironical reasons

or because he simply enjoyed fox-trots and syncopations, and also to employ some of the absurdist aspects of scenarios which had been so popular in Paris earlier in the 1920s when Jean Cocteau was outraging the French bourgeoisie. The ballet was only a muted success. The plot of his next ballet, *The Bolt* (1930–31), shows a narrowing of subject matter as the political mood darkened; at the time industrial sabotage aimed at damaging Soviet Russia's march to modernity was a burning issue, and Shostakovich could not have escaped composing music for a ballet on this theme, however inept the libretto. His compromise was to take a light-hearted approach—a recipe for disaster. The ballet was withdrawn after just one performance, with critics blustering that Shostakovich and his choreographer were 'not ready politically to stage a Soviet ballet'.

Shostakovich, recently married (1932) to the physicist Nina Varzar, brushed this setback aside as something best forgotten, and turned to his most ambitious work to date: the opera *Lady Macbeth of the Mtsensk district* (1930–32), after which he composed his first major works for the piano, the 24 Preludes, Op 34 (1932–33) and the Concerto for Piano, Trumpet and Strings Op. 35 (1933). Both compositions enjoyed satisfactory débuts, as had incidental music for the plays *Hamlet* (1932) and *The Human Comedy* (1933–34) by the time *Lady Macbeth* reached the stage in Leningrad in 1934. Written with a clear eye to the political situation in early 1930s Russia, the opera is a savage indictment of bourgeois Tsarist practices and provincial life, and is merciless in its depiction of bestiality and murderous lusts. Time and again Shostakovich forces the audience to distance themselves from the tragic and lurid action through music of cutting satire or unnerving coolness, and the public at its première was overwhelmed by the experience—as were the critics. For a period of two years it was hailed by all and sundry as a triumph of Soviet art. But in America its 1935 première caused consternation and revulsion, one critic commenting: 'Shostakovich is without doubt the foremost composer of pornographic music in the history of the art'.

Unfortunately for Shostakovich, comrade Stalin agreed. Having been shocked and disgusted when he attended a performance in 1936, he ensured that Shostakovich was made aware that he was violating the new Soviet aesthetic—as expounded for writers by Gorky in 1934 and then expanded to include composers. The core of this new aesthetic was that art had to stress 'all that is heroic, bright, and beautiful' and 'be embodied in musical images of beauty and strength'. Any lingering in the half-light of human motivation was tantamount to indulging in 'folk-negating modernistic directions...typical of decaying contemporary bourgeois art'.

DON'T MISS

▶ **Symphony No. 1 (1923–24)**

▶ **24 Preludes (1932–33)**

▶ **Lady Macbeth of Mtsensk district (1934)**

▶ **Symphony No. 5 (1937)**

▶ **Symphony No. 7 (1941)**

Shostakovich was guilty on all counts, as the infamous *Pravda* article of early 1936, 'Muddle instead of Music', made cruelly clear. Weeks later, the ballet *The Limpid Stream*, running successfully in Leningrad since June 1935, was forced to close after a visit by Stalin, and its previously praised music was labelled by *Pravda* as 'formalistic' and 'without character'.

Hoping to ride out the storm, Shostakovich pressed ahead with arrangements to give his nearly-completed Symphony No.4 its Leningrad première, but as the months passed and the attacks continued, and the rehearsals for the decidedly modernistic, complex and undeniably brilliant symphony became bogged down by musicians' incomprehension and fear, Shostakovich took the radical step of withdrawing the work before a note had been heard in public. It remained unplayed until 1961.

Realising that not only his artistic survival but his life were in peril, Shostakovich raised no public objection to the press vilification, and set about a painful re-evaluation of his own creative muse and what he could do to achieve both rehabilitation and a genuine creative renewal. If he was to be made an example of, then so be it. His "reply to justified criticism" was the famous Symphony No.5, Op. 47, premièred in Leningrad in 1937 and written from within the structure of tonality which Shostakovich knew was essential to political acceptance. A work full of tragic and intense emotions, its finale—full of near-jingoistic rhythms and melodies undercut by savage twists of harmony and juxtaposition—ends on a screaming

D major, seen by officialdom at the time as an affirmation of the Soviet artist's triumph over the odds, but later reinterpreted by commentators as an utterly hollow victory. Whatever interpretation is made, the sincerity of the music and the size of the achievement is unmistakeable and awesome.

Shostakovich's creative rebirth was confirmed in 1938 when, apart from experiencing the joy of seeing his first son born, he composed the first of what were to be 15 string quartets. These quartets, together with Bartók's, constitute the greatest single contribution to the genre this century. The first quartet was composed almost as a relaxing diversion from the struggle to complete the fifth symphony, but by the time he came to write the second in 1944, a subtle but fundamental shift had occurred in the way he presented his art to the world. In his Sixth Symphony (1939) he had moved away from direct emotionalism, relying more on enigmatic melodic suggestions, strong elements of burlesque and a continual undermining of so-called 'safe' sonorities. By the time of Symphony No.7 (*Leningrad*), in 1941, he was writing a public work, or 'music for the people', in this case a recognition of the unbearable suffering and loss the inhabitants of Leningrad suffered during its siege (1941–43) by German forces. At the time he made this connection explicit, although decades later, he also let it be known that the work was a requiem for Leningrad and its people which had suffered from Stalin's butchery prior to Hitler's arrival. It was a requiem for all victims. From now on, in one way or another, his symphonies would address public themes or ideas which reached out beyond himself and embraced others, even if his own secret programmes were hidden deep inside them for only the initiated to discover. Within the confines of the string quartet, however, his most intimate feelings and thoughts could be expressed in relative safety.

Shostakovich had a turbulent war, even though his physical infirmities (including poor eyesight) kept him from being called up. Forced to flee Leningrad by the German siege, he settled in Moscow in 1942 and began teaching at the Conservatoire. At the same time he pressed on with his Symphony No.8 (1943), a concentrated howl of anguish against the deprivations and degradations of the Russian people due to war and Stalinism. This unrelieved pessimism and his general inability to write 'uplifting' music (the so-called Symphony of Triumph No. 9, (1945), completely by-passed all thoughts of triumphalism by concentrating instead on classical poise and wit) led eventually to his notorious denunciation (together with Prokofiev) by the hated *apparatchik* Zhdanov at the 1948 Composers' Union Conference. Shostakovich made a brave defence of himself while admitting his deviation from strict Stalinist policy, but five years would pass before his next symphony was composed—in the year of Stalin's death. In the meantime, apart from lightweight works written to appease his critics, such as the cantata *The Sun Shines on Our Motherland* (1952), or the music for the film *The Fall of Berlin* (1949), Shostakovich continued to create deeply personal works such as the songs *From Jewish*

Folk Poetry (1949), the Fourth and Fifth String Quartets (1949 and 1952) and the memorable *24 Preludes and Fugues for Piano, Op. 87* (1950–51).

With the death of Stalin in 1953 there was a fundamental shift in Soviet life; Shostakovich could compose his Symphony No. 10, Op. 93, a work dedicated to the search for peace in "the aspirations of our contemporaries", without fear of recriminations. A relatively short work, its essence shines as brightly as those of its more complex predecessors. It is scintillatingly organized, and is one of his finest symphonic achievements. The following year he experienced personal sorrow with the death of his wife Nina, although two years later he was to remarry, settling into a new life with the young teacher Margarita Kainova. The rest of the decade was notable for the fine concertos completed at this time, as well as a thorough revision in 1955 (even to the extent of assigning a new opus number) of the First Violin Concerto, originally written in 1947/48. His Second Piano Concerto No.2 appeared in 1957, the First Cello Concerto in 1959. These were accompanied by the *Festive Overture* and Symphony No.11, (*The Year 1905*), Op. 103 of 1957. This work formed a duo with Symphony No.12 (*The Year 1917*), Op. 112 (1960–61) of openly programmatic symphonic compositions, an approach to music which Shostakovich happily traced back to Mussorgsky. 'Can music attack evil? Can it make man stop and think? Can it cry out and draw man's attention to various vile acts to which he has grown used?... All these questions began for me with Mussorgsky'.

Shostakovich, now into late middle age, wrote two more symphonies during the 1960s, the first of which, Symphony No. 13, (*Babi Yar*), came to be closely identified with the passionate poetic texts by Yevtushenko which Shostakovich had incorporated into the music's structure. Here his private feelings combined with a public statement—against the persecution of Jews everywhere—in a uniquely powerful way, so much so that the Soviet authorities as good as made the work a non-event, *Pravda* giving the 1962 première a one line report. In between this and Symphony No.14 (1969) came periods of bad health and an outburst of string quartet writing without modern parallel. Between 1960 and 1968 Shostakovich wrote six quartets, all of superlative quality. Quartet No.11 (1966) reaches levels of grief and loss rarely found, even in Shostakovich's canon, as it commemorates the recently departed musician and friend Vasili Shirinsky.

By now Shostakovich's health was beginning to fail, and his music, even the concertos (he wrote his second concertos for the violin and the cello in mid-decade) became increasingly dominated by the twin concerns of mortality and decline as he moved further into his sixties. Symphony No. 14 Op. 135 from 1969 used the voice in a similar way to Mahler in his *Das Lied von der Erde*, and was dedicated to another composer notable for his sensitivity to words—Benjamin Britten— except that Shostakovich's perception of death was unredeemed; for him death was final, and the overwhelming music of the work forcibly underlines this view. With his habitual use of irony, his Symphony No.15 (1971) rather qualifies that stance; he even uses brief quotations from Rossini's

William Tell and Wagner's *The Ring*, playing down the despair. But the final three string quartets, up to the fifteenth of 1974, remain overtly dark, oppressed by approaching death.

In 1973 he was diagnosed as suffering from lung cancer, reacting by saying "I'm not afraid of death; only of pain". Of his last three completed compositions, two were verse settings which revealed his obsession with approaching death and his concern with his place in the scheme of things. If his *Suite on Verses of Michelangelo Op.145* allowed him the freedom to

conjure lofty sentiments, then the *4 Verses of Captain Lebyadkin, Op. 146,* using the parodies of a Dostoyevkian character, allowed him to point once again to the blasted promise of so many Russian souls during his lifetime.

Although Shostakovich continued to appear in public, and sometimes even abroad, in the 1970s, his strength was ebbing and he finally succumbed to cancer in August 1975. By that time he was not only assured of his place as the greatest Soviet composer and last great symphonist, but also of his place among the greatest of this century's composers.

OLIVIER MESSIAEN
1908–1922

Messiaen is a crucial link between the anti-Wagnerian fancies of 'Les Six' and the post-war theories of Boulez and beyond. His highly original and very personal musical language, plus his admirable dedication to the expression of Catholic mysticism and extensive incorporation of birdsong, has led to him being wrongly perceived as a figure on the peripheries of general musical life. The sheer size alone of many of his best works militate against their easy public consumption.

Messiaen was born in Avignon. His father, Pierre, was a literature professor

Olivier Messiaen

and a noted translator of Shakespeare, while his mother, using the name Cécile Sauvage, wrote a number of books of poetry. Messiaen later acknowledged his debt to his mother's rich imagery, his authorship of the majority of his own songs a tribute to her and a continuation of the family tradition.

Messiaen showed musical promise from early childhood, teaching himself the rudiments of piano and composing little pieces from the age of eight. When he was 10 years old he was given a score of Debussy's *Pelléas et Mélisande*, which came as a revelation to him in terms of what could be done with harmony and orchestral colour. A year later, when still only 11, he entered the Paris Conservatoire at a time when the sudden arrival of a new musical aesthetic embodied by 'Les Six' was shaking the Parisian music world. Messiaen's teachers included the revered Paul Dukas and the organist Marcel Dupré. During his 11 years at the Conservatoire he became widely read, interesting himself particularly in Eastern religious and philosophical thought. He also took his first steps towards understanding birdsong, a form of musical sound he found utterly entrancing.

His first orchestral work of significance was *Les Offrandes oubliées* (1930). But it was with the organ, a constant companion after his appointment as organist at the church of La Trinité in Paris (a post he held for 50 years), that he created the first group of compositions which were to have a lasting effect. As early as 1928 he had composed *Le Banquet céleste*, and with *Diptyque* (1930) he began a

---

---

decade of organ works of the highest calibre. These included *Apparition de l'église éternelle* (1932) and *L'Ascension* (also for orchestra), as well as *La Nativité du Seigneur* (1935) and *Les Corps glorieux* (1939).

In 1936 Messiaen declared himself a member of the loose 'school' of new composers, Le Jeune France, (two of the members were Jolivet and Baudrier), all with widely differing styles but all with a core belief in the basic need for 'sincerity, generosity and artistic good faith' to be present before good music can be created. This may sound a rather vague aesthetic, but it was devoutly adhered to by Messiaen, a musician as natural and inspired as Delius, and equally incapable of writing music for mundane purposes or of adopting the then-fashionable neo-classicism.

Messiaen became a teacher at both the Ecole Normale de Musique and the Schola Cantorum in Paris, and began to appear at international festivals for new music, but his career path was severly interrupted by the War. He served in the French army, but in late 1939 was captured and sent to Stalag VIII-A camp in Görlitz, Germany. There, amidst the general cruelty and degradation, Messiaen found both

inspiration from the scriptures to write music and musicians to play it. By 1940 he had completed his most important chamber work, *Quatuor pour la fin du temps* for clarinet, piano, violin and cello, taking as his starting point a quotation from the Revelation of St John: 'There shall be time no more, but at the day of the trumpet of the seventh angel, the mystery of God will be consummated'. Messiaen once noted that "never was I listened to with such rapt attention and comprehension as that first time in the camp".

With the establishment of the Vichy government, French prisoners were repatriated, and Messiaen found himself not only back in Paris but also appointed Professor of harmony at the Conservatoire, becoming Professor of aesthetics and analysis in 1947. One of his pupils was the brilliant pianist Yvonne Loriod, and she became his partner in presenting a major new work for two pianos, *Visions de l'Amen* (1943), a seven-section composition full of the sound of heaven's bells as God creates the universe. Loriod was destined to become Messiaen's second wife and the foremost interpreter of his piano works. His next major work, *Vingt Regards sur l'enfant Jésus* (1944) for solo piano, describes the mystical state of the infant Jesus as he is contemplated by each member of the heavenly firmament. It is one of Messiaen's first compositions to reflect his growing fascination with birdsong, as well as his increasing sophistication in the use of the asymmetric rhythms he had encountered in musics from other cultures, especially those of the East. *Vingt Regards* received its première, with Loriod at the keyboard, in Paris in 1945.

Messiaen's reputation grew apace in the post-war period, furthered by such works as *Harawi* (1945), a set of 12 pieces for soprano and piano; the choral work *Trois Petites Liturgies de la Présence Divine* (1944); and the *Messe de la Pentecôte* for organ (1950). But his most significant work of this period was undoubtedly the *Turangalila Symphony* for piano, ondes martenot and orchestra (1946–48). This massive work, running for well over 70 minutes and requiring a very large orchestra as well as an augmented percussion section, is organized into 10 sections subdivided into three main groups: 'love', a darker, more sinister section, and a dance-like, scherzo-based group. This work was the result of a Koussevitzky commission, and was first played in Boston under Leonard Bernstein, with Loriod at the piano. To this day the music remains difficult to assimilate in one sitting.

Unconcerned with his growing international reputation, Messiaen continued teaching, a steady stream of brilliant young minds passing through his classes which included Stockhausen, Jean Barraqué and Boulez. He took care to nurture each one in such a way that their specific talents and inclinations

were developed.

The ritualistic, repetitive and timbral elements of Eastern music, which had so attracted him in the 1930s, can also be found in many different forms in the birdsong which became his most intense area of study in the 1950s. At the beginning of this decade he had undergone a period of self-doubt as he explored areas of creativity which turned out to be blind alleys. His *Réveil des oiseaux* (1953) for piano and orchestra was the breakthrough work, followed by *Oiseaux exotiques* (1955–56), a work for piano and chamber ensemble.

Encouraged by the other-worldly sounds and colours he was now skilled at creating, and convinced that birdsong was by far the most beautiful and mysterious melody which existed, Messiaen pressed on with his approach, completing his masterpiece *Catalogue d'oiseaux* in 1958. Thus within just five years he had created an entire new genre and an extensive library of music to represent it. It is fair to say that this music remains forbidding, even to those who have managed to conquer the mysteries of *Vingt Regards*, but once the meaning is penetrated, the sheer diversity and exultation to be found in the music can be overpowering.

Messiaen continued to pursue his interests in this direction, as well as his teaching and his writing for both voice and for orchestra. The death of his first wife in 1960 led to his marriage to Yvonne Loriod. On a visit to Japan they collected materials which would re-emerge later in the *Sept Haïkaï*, but in 1963 his first devotional work for orchestra since *L'Ascension* emerged.

This was *Couleurs de la cité céleste*; its title alone tells of his new obsession with expressing colour through music alone, equating the experience of colour with the experience of sound. He continued in this vein, creating *Chronochromie* (Colour of Time) for large orchestra in 1966, and the powerful *Des Canyons aux étoiles* for piano and orchestra in 1970–74. A break from personal concerns was realized through a commission from the French Minister for the Arts, André Malraux, for a work to commemorate the dead of two world wars: *Et exspecto resurrectionem mortuorum* (1964) was the result, a joyful celebration of the transmigration of suffering humanity to glorious heaven.

An opera, *Saint François d'Assise*, was performed in 1983, and after this last great work, Messiaen returned to more moderately scaled compositions such as *Un vitrail et des oiseaux* (1986) and *La ville d'en Haut* (1987), the latter realizing the colours and sounds of 'the city above us'. It is an amazing confraternity of sound and light, giving to massive slabs of sound a clear expression and elemental meaning. One of Messiaen's last works, commissioned by Zubin Mehta and the New York Philharmonic and composed between 1987 and 1991, was *Eclairs sur l'au-dela...* A choral work for large forces, including symphony orchestra, it quotes from a whole range of texts and combines most of Messiaen's lifetime musical obsessions, including birdsong and the capture of the divine spark of colour in music. In fact, the work could be summed up as being the homage of millions of birds to their creator, looking down from the infinite beyond. The fulfilling of this aim alone

SAMUEL BARBER
1910–1981

In a period of American musical history when modernism was everything, Barber was a great individualist. His conservative musical cast led him into both conflict and obscurity, but a rapid posthumous re-assessment of his work has led to the conclusion that he is one of America's most significant art-music composers.

Born in Westchester, Pennsylvania, Barber came from a famous musical family which included the American contralto Louise Homer, who gave her precocious young nephew singing lessons. By the age of 12 he was holding down a regular position as the local organist, and was already composing short pieces before entering the Curtis Institute in Philadelphia. There he was taught composition, piano and voice (by Emilio di Gorgoza), while classes in conducting were held by the legendary Fritz Reiner. By the age of 18 he was set on becoming a composer and after his graduation at the age of 23, he set about achieving his goal. Early on he wrote a great many songs of a very high quality (he was to return to the song form late in life). His first two works for orchestra, *The School for Scandal Overture, Op. 5* and *Music for a scene from Shelley, Op. 7*, from 1933 and 1935 respectively, not only reaped immediate success when first performed, but also demonstrated a fully-formed compositional style which had ample harmonic and instrumental interest, but whose crowning achievement was a rapturous lyricism allied to a natural

Samuel Barber

sense of musical drama—whether the work was entirely concert hall bound or written for theatre. By the mid 1930s, with his Symphony No.1, Op. 9 premièred in Rome by Artur Rodzinski, Barber at the age of 26 had become one of his country's most prominent composers. Between 1935 and 1937 he won the Pulitzer Fellowship and also the American Prix de Rome. The first symphony was also performed at the 1937 Salzburg Festival, the first work by an American composer to be so honoured.

On his return to America in 1937 Barber taught at his old college, the Curtis Institute, and during the next 12 months made an arrangement of the slow movement of his string quartet for Arturo Toscanini's NBC Orchestra to play over the airwaves in November 1938. This transcription was named

Adagio for Strings, Op. 11, and has since become Barber's most famous work. Yet Barber is by no means a one-work composer, as his *Essays for Orchestra, Nos. 1 and 2* (1937–42) and his beautiful lyric *Concerto for Violin and Orchestra* of 1940, amply demonstrate.

The years covering America's involvement in WWII found Barber serving in the Army Air Corps, where he was commissioned to compose his Symphony No. 2 (1944) and where he also completed his *Concerto for Cello and Orchestra* (1945). After the war Barber moved into a secluded house near Mount Kisko, where he was to stay for much of his remaining life, sharing it with his life's partner, the composer Gian Carlo Menotti. It was there that he did the majority of his subsequent composing. In 1946 he was commissioned to write a ballet by the

DON'T MISS

▶ The School for Scandal—
  Overture (1931–33)

▶ Adagio for Strings
  (1938)

▶ Knoxville: Summer of
  1915 (1947)

▶ Medea's Meditation and
  Dance of Vengeance
  (1955)

▶ Vanessa (1958)

legendary modern dance pioneer, Martha Graham. This was first performed as *Serpent of the Heart*, and later became *Medea (Cave of the Heart)*, from which the extracted *Medea's Meditation and Dance of Vengeance* is often given as a stunning virtuoso concert piece. By 1947 Barber, now approaching early middle age, was becoming an establishment figure, increasingly given to looking backwards at American culture. This gave rise to his sumptuous and nostalgic setting of James Agee's poem *Knoxville: Summer of 1915*, which features a soprano enveloped in waves of orchestral reverie unequalled since Mahler.

The appearance of *Knoxville* and *Medea* within the same decade signalled a shift in Barber's compositional preoccupations, possibly encouraged by Menotti, who was a talented composer of theatre music in his own right, as *Amahl and the Night Visitors* (1951) demonstrates. Thus the arrival of Barber's first fully-fledged opera, *Vanessa* (1958), with a libretto by Menotti, came as no great surprise to people in touch with his career. By this time, with the post-war generation engaged in such pursuits as total serialism and chance music, Barber was increasingly perceived as an anachronistic figure, and works such as the choral prelude *Die natali* (1960) and the 1962 Piano Concerto did little to dispel this impression. His position as the leading light of American Classical music reached its apotheosis on the first night of his second and last opera, *Antony and Cleopatra*, commissioned by Rudolf Bing, the general manager of the Metropolitan Opera, to be the first work staged at the Opera's new home in Lincoln Center. Franco Zeffirelli was hired to stage and design the production as well as shape the work's libretto from Shakespeare's original play. The first night was one of New York's most glittering occasions, with political and cultural leaders from all over America and elsewhere in attendance. Unfortunately, for the first time Barber failed to please his audience, giving them an unusually advanced musical context for Shakespeare's drama, and concentrating on psychological investigations rather than a continuous fount of melody.

Understandably, with a lukewarm critical reaction and a reluctance on the part of his audience to keep the work in repertoire for long, Barber saw this as the beginning of a period of eclipse, and in this he was right: for over 10 years he suffered from the vagaries of musical fashion and the rise of other favourites. Barber completed little music after this, although the attractive *Canzonetta, Op. 48* for oboe and strings dates from 1978, as does *Essay for Orchestra No. 3*. He died in 1981, largely forgotten by his previously large audience and in something of a critical limbo. In the years since his death his musical rehabilitation has grown apace, aided by the return to tonality by many contemporary composers, and by an embracing of spiritual and emotional values by a later generation of listeners as opposed to the remorseless intellectual progression in modern compositional music. Today his stock stands as high as at any time during his life.

JOHN CAGE
1912–1992

Cage was not so much a composer as a philosopher who used music as a means to further his enquiries about the nature of his world. He was often more concerned with sound and timbre, rhythm and space, and a search for music which had not been experienced before, than with any formal construction which relied on guidelines handed down from

the past. Cage perhaps was the first conceptual composer, the identification of the concept behind a given piece being of more worth than an appreciation of the piece itself. As Schoenberg once said of him: "Of course he's not a composer, but he's an inventor—of genius".

Cage was born in Los Angeles. His father was an inventor of sorts and a lay scientist. John began piano lessons in his ninth year, but quickly became more interested in the mechanics of his lessons than in the scales themselves. In his early teens he had the unique experience of running his own radio programme consisting of more or less disorganized readings, music playing and letter-answering; the show lasted two years, 1924-25. During Cage's time in college he decided that Europe rather than California would be a more useful training ground for a budding writer, so he went to Paris to study literature and continue his keyboard studies under Lazare Lévy. Paris had a liberating effect on Cage, making him realize that non-conformity could have its own code of honour.

Returning to America—then in the depths of the Depression—Cage dropped out of college and lived in Santa Monica. Shifting for himself, he sold lessons in modern music and painting, at the same time learning from the courses he was selling. By 1933 he had studied with Adolph Weiss for two years and was ready to be taught by an early hero, Arnold Schoenberg, then in America after fleeing from the Nazis. Lessons with others, such as Henry Cowell and

John Cage

Edgard Varèse, left him accomplished enough to become a member of the teaching staff at the Cornish School of Music in Seattle in 1936, leading his classes in all manner of musical experiments, especially in the field of percussion. His time with Schoenberg left an indelible impression on his creative process. "He told me", said Cage in 1976, "that without a feeling for harmony I would always encounter an obstacle, a wall through which I wouldn't be able to pass. My reply was that in that case I would devote my life to beating my head against that wall—and maybe that is what I've been doing ever since".

By the close of the decade Cage had progressed from his early interest in 12-tone and serial composition

(illustrated by *Metamorphosis* for piano, 1938), and was immersed in a wide variety of musical experimentation. During WWII he worked as an assistant to his inventor father. By the end of the War his early experimental concerts in New York had garnered enough reaction for him to feel that the city could sustain him in his career. Through the influence of his wife, Xenia, a talented painter, he was mixing with artists as well as musicians, and in 1942 a long series of *Imaginary Landscapes* began to emerge. Most of these works concern themselves with percussive sound in one incarnation or another, including sheer noise from 'non-instruments' such as buzzers and wastepaper baskets.

The experiments for which he is still best remembered began in 1946, when he started work on his *Sonatas and Interludes* for prepared piano. His early experience with Cowell had taught him the extended range of sound which could be extracted from a piano; Cage took this a stage further and began modifying the response of the strings, first attempting this in 1938 with his work *Bacchanale*. The mid-1940s works find him attaching a wide range of devices to alter the piano's characterstic sounds and timbres, inevitably stressing the instrument's naturally percussive nature even more strongly. The *Sonatas and Interludes* is a long work of many sections, lasting well over an hour, and it explores its subject fully. Cage, however, quickly moved on from these ideas. and by the 1950s was experimenting with natural sounds expressed in both random and formalized order, often with the help of magnetic tape: the *Williams Mix* of 1952 and *Fontana Mix* of 1958 are the apogee of this approach, which incorporates elements of *musique concrète* as well as other philosophies to achieve its indeterminate aims. Indeterminate is an important concept here, for in some of the pieces (including the *Williams Mix*), Cage is deliberately incorporating 'chance' into his music. With *Variations I* (1958) and *Variations II* (1961), Cage moves the element (or burden) of chance onto the performer, who is forced to make random choices between alternative notes, or even completely random choices of pitch, duration and speed.

This whole approach is naturally open to manipulation and even absurdist

exploitation, and Cage was not above introducing a strong dash of irony into his 'events'. His famous *Four-and-a-half minutes* (1964), consisting of a silence lasting that precise amount of time, may have made a serious point about the nature of a musical event, but it was also a simple joke at the expense of the audience's expectations. By 1965 he was creating multi-media events in theatre works such as *Variations V* and *Theatre Piece*, thus anticipating much of what artists such as Warhol would soon be applying to the popular end of art culture. This approach made the iconoclasm of his *Concert for Piano and Orchestra* of 1958 seem positively traditional, even though Cage had once again writ large into his score the concept of choice.

Cage's parallel with such an artist as Marcel Duchamp was now clear; the quality of the idea was more important than the perfect realization of it: the work itself could be of little or no value, as long as it communicated the concept. This concern for process, and its negation of the creator's role as a craftsman responsible for his own artefacts,

perhaps had its roots in Eastern thought, but its application was thoroughly Western.

By the early 1970s, Cage began to move into lecturing and writing papers more than composing, which in itself was a logical extension of what he had been doing. Towards the end of his life, he commented more than once that in living on Sixth Avenue in New York, he was blessed with "more sounds, and totally unpredictable sounds, than any place I've ever lived... I don't need a piano... I transfer the sounds into images, and so my dreams aren't disturbed".

By the 1980s the time for his musical events had passed, and he was seen more as a venerable theorist than as a composer at the cutting edge. Yet the work Cage did was essential in clearing the theoretical ground from which a valid new aesthetic could emerge. What Cage never reckoned with was the rise of popular culture to a place of creative supremacy which would make his theories and his metaphysical approach seem dated before their time.

DON'T MISS

▶ **The Wonderful widow of eighteen springs (1942)**

▶ **Sonatas and Interludes—prepared piano (1945–48)**

▶ **4'33' (1952)**

▶ **Concert for Piano and Orchestra (1957–58)**

▶ **Variations I–VII (1958–66)**

BENJAMIN BRITTEN

1913–1976

Britten is quite simply the most naturally gifted English composer since Purcell. A man with an utterly personal musical style, he is universally regarded as one of the most significant composers of the century.

Born in Suffolk, Britten was the fourth child of respectable middle-class parents: his father was a dentist, his mother a member of the Lowestoft Musical Society and a talented amateur singer. Piano lessons began at the age of seven; before his tenth birthday he was setting short poems to music, and within six months he was writing continuous reams of music. Between the age of nine and fourteen he wrote symphonies, oratorios, sonatas, tone poems and numerous songs. His father favoured a career in mathematics, but his mother was determined on music. In 1924 Britten saw Frank Bridge conduct *The Sea*, and was thrilled to meet the man himself in 1927. Bridge was the first person outside the family circle to detect something extraordinary about Ben's musical talent, and he proposed taking the boy as a house-guest in London and teaching him. As Ben was not yet 13, it was agreed that he would instead take regular lessons from Bridge, especially during his holidays from Gresham's School in Norfolk. This tuition was the turning point, forcing Britten to look critically at his own work and to correct his sloppy musical thinking. At the same time he heard

Benjamin Britten

music by Holst and Ravel, which encouraged him to develop a more contemporary musical language.

Britten obtained a composition scholarship to the Royal College of Music. During his three years at the College, he found what he termed the

'amateur' approach unduly dominant, even with John Ireland as one of his tutors, deriving more that was useful to him as a composer by attending concerts (he discovered Mahler in this way) and perusing manuscripts (Schoenberg's *Pierrot Lunaire*, for example). Britten's own thinking remained decidedly modern, and this did not lie easily with the College authorities, but with public concerts of some of his newer works, he was beginning to get noticed in the wider world. He finished his training at the RCM with a travelling scholarship of some £100, awarded to enable him to broaden his musical experience. Encouraged by Frank Bridge, he plumped for a summer of studying with Alban Berg, a composer he greatly admired, but his parents vetoed the idea after being advised by his teachers at the RCM that Berg's music was not altogether healthy.

In the first year outside formal studies, Britten's *Phantasy Quartet* was performed in Florence, and the BBC broadcast his choral piece, *A Boy was Born*. Oxford University Press also agreed to publish his new composition, *Simple Symphony* (1933–34). The same year saw the death of his father and his own 21st birthday. In need of an income, Britten accepted an offer by the GPO film unit and plunged headlong into the frantic world of writing music for film. This experience he found distasteful but useful: "I had to work quickly, to force myself to work when I didn't want to, and to get used to working in all kinds of circumstances... It was...

extremely good practice for me as a young composer".

At the GPO he met W. H. Auden who was writing occasional scripts for the film unit and soon joined it full-time. Seven years Britten's senior, Auden dazzled Britten with his intellect and capacity for verbal invention, and bullied him into adopting many of his political and social views. In turn, Britten educated Auden in contemporary music, encouraging him to dismiss all the British Renaissance school of composers symbolized by Vaughan Williams—a group Britten found unbearably inept as composers— and embrace instead the work of his heroes Mahler, Berg, Schoenberg and Stravinsky. While at the GPO Britten and Auden worked together on a number of projects, including the famous *Night Mail*. By 1936, they had grown sufficiently sure of each other's unique talents to attempt a collaboration which evolved into the orchestral song cycle, *Our Hunting Fathers*. Auden, an openly practising homosexual at a time when it was still illegal in Britain, also took pains to present Britten with the fact of the composer's own homosexuality, something Britten was as yet unwilling to accept. *Our Hunting Fathers*, an oblique but biting condemnation of

war, was premièred in Norwich that same year, and in April 1937 broadcast by the BBC, with Adrian Boult conducting. However, it was so badly received that it was left unplayed until 1960.

Britten's mother died in February 1937; in the aftermath of the shock he met Peter Pears and his friend Peter Burra (soon to die in an air accident), and was commissioned by the Boyd Neel String Orchestra to write a piece: the work he produced was *Variations on a Theme of Frank Bridge*. It was in the post to his publisher Boosey & Hawkes by the end of March, and premièred by Boyd Neel's aggregation at the Salzburg Festival that summer. By then Britten had discovered a mill in the Suffolk village of Snape which he decided to buy. As their common interests pulled them closer together, he also began to see more of Peter Pears. Britten moved into Snape in the spring of 1938, completing his piano concerto in time for it to be played at that year's Proms. The same year the *Bridge Variations* were recorded.

Britten's career was expanding rapidly, but with war clouds darkening over Europe, and a personal lifestyle which was anything but simple, Britten decided to go to North America with Peter Pears. It was during this period— initially intended to be temporary but which the outbreak of war turned into a three-year exile—that Britten and Pears cemented the personal and artistic relationship which was to remain unbroken until Britten's death.

In America Britten wrote some major works: firstly, the *Concerto for Violin and Orchestra* (1939), then the brilliant and

---

DON'T MISS

▶ **Variations on a Theme of Frank Bridge (1937)**
▶ **Les Illuminations (1939)**
▶ **A Ceremony of Carols (1942)**
▶ **Serenade (1943)**
▶ **Peter Grimes (1945)**

---

important Rimbaud cycle *Les Illuminations* (1940), followed that same year by the voice-and-piano settings of Michelangelo sonnets and the moving *Sinfonia da Requiem*. America also saw the genesis of another aspect of his composing career when Britten collaborated once more with Auden to create the operetta *Paul Bunyan* (1941), a work greeted with little enthusiam and promptly forgotten until after the composer's death. But the seed of theatrical music had been sown.

By now Britten's letters home were full of the desire to return; at one point he observed of America: "This country is dead because it hasn't been lived in, hasn't been worked on. It may come in several hundred years...but they have no standards, no culture". Now he was being made aware that his and Pears' absence from England during the darkest times of the war was being resented by both critics and public alike. Meanwhile, a reading of the 19th-century poet George Crabbe sparked off both nostalgia and a desire to write another opera. This desire, combined with a powerful performance of the *Sinfonia da Requiem* by Koussevitzky in Boston, led Britten to tell the conductor of his idea for an opera on Crabbe's poem *The Borough*. Koussevitzky commissioned Britten to write the opera. After the voyage back to Britain in March 1942, during which the beautiful *Hymn to St Cecilia* and *A Ceremony of Carols* were completed, Britten returned to Snape in March 1943, where he began work on the opera, as well as on other ideas such as the important song cycle *Serenade*, which dealt movingly with sin and redemption. Together with Montagu Slater, Britten worked on the libretto of

▶ **The Rape of Lucretia (1946)**
▶ **The Young Person's Guide to the Orchestra (1946)**
▶ **The Turn of the Screw (1954)**
▶ **War Requiem (1961)**
▶ **Symphony for Cello and Orchestra (1963)**

the opera, which took on the name *Peter Grimes*, the music being completed by February 1945. The opera's première in June of that year was not only a major watershed for Britten, but a key event in the history of British opera, not least because it gave the English language—to which Britten was extraordinarily finely attuned—an entirely credible theatrical setting for the first time since Purcell. As pacifists and homosexuals, Britten's theme—that of the idealist against the crowd—had a specific relevance for him and Pears. As Pears said later: "I think it was partly this feeling which led us to make Grimes, a character of vision and conflict, the tortured idealist he is rather than the villain he was in Crabbe".

The success of *Grimes* (soon to be repeated abroad) led to a splinter group of the Sadler Wells Opera Company forming itself with the purpose of performing Britten's works; he wrote the 'chamber opera' *The Rape of Lucretia* for them, which received its première at Glyndebourne in 1946. Although set in Ancient Rome, it again dealt with guilt, innocence and expiation, and had both dramatic and intensely lyrical passages which have kept it in the forefront of small-scale productions ever since. Prior to the completion of *Lucretia*, Britten finally

acted on an artistic impulse he had been ignoring for a while, and composed the nine settings for *The Holy Sonnets of John Donne*, again exclusively taken up with death, sin, the possibilities of redemption, and the likelihood of divine retribution. A short tour of war-ravaged Germany, playing recitals with Yehudi Menuhin, had taken him to Belsen; an experience he rarely mentioned, but which he told Pears many years later "coloured everything he had written subsequently".

The next opera, *Albert Herring* (1947), used a similar country town setting to *Peter Grimes*, but this time the action resolves into comedy and happy endings. Many observers felt this to be a lightweight production, although there was no doubting the quality of Britten's musical invention. The previous year, he had completed for a Ministry of Education film *The Young Person's Guide to the Orchestra (Variations & Fugue on a Theme by Purcell)*, Op. 34, one of his happiest and most popular orchestral compositions.

Increasingly well-established and successful, yet desirous of an artistic and expressive security, Britten hit upon the idea—together with Pears—of starting a music festival in Aldeburgh.

They had grown tired of the rows with other festival producers, and Britten in particular wanted direct control of his own output. Plans were drawn up, and by 1948 they were ready to present the first annual Aldeburgh Festival. Britten and Pears were always present at the festivals, donating their services free of charge, thus setting a pattern for other artists to follow. Many of Britten's new works were premièred at the festivals, and one of his greatest successes came in 1949, when *The Little Sweep* (*Let's Make an Opera*) was premièred to packed houses.

By the beginning of the 1950s Britten had established a pattern of living and working at Aldeburgh which was rarely disrupted and enabled him to compose at his best. In 1949 he finished the optimistic *Spring Symphony*, followed by the dark opera *Billy Budd* (1951), which was based on Herman Melville's tale and dramatized entirely with mens' voices. *Budd* was immediately hailed as a masterpiece of its kind. When Britten asked intermediaries to approach Princess Elizabeth in 1951 to ask her to bestow a quasi-official status on his setting of the Elizabeth and Essex story, it was confirmation of his undeniable importance in British artistic and cultural life that the royal approval was granted. From the first, *Gloriana* was conceived as part of the 1953 Coronation celebrations, but entirely passed over the heads of its first night audience. It has remained an under appreciated but wonderfully realized opera ever since.

After completing the evocative and witty settings of some Thomas Hardy poems, *Winter Words*, Britten plunged almost immediately into his next

operatic project. This time he chose the unsettling Henry James story, *The Turn of the Screw*, commissioned from him by the Venice Festival committee. This taut, perfectly conceived work preserved the menace and ambiguities of James's original story, without jettisoning the cast of characters or the novella's story line, and also returned Britten to the chamber-opera forces of *Lucretia*. Using his sixth librettist in as many operas, he once again dealt with the battle between innocence and corruption, good and evil, and their eternally twinned relationship.

The Venice première of *Turn of the Screw* in 1954 was a critical triumph. Writing to a friend, composer John Ireland commented: "I am now (perhaps *reluctantly*) compelled to regard Britten as possessing 10 times the musical talent, intuition and ability of all other living British composers put together". For Britten and Pears, the major event of late 1955 was their trip to the Far East, during which they encountered the music and cultures of India, Java, Bali, Japan, Thailand and Sri Lanka. Although Britten had earlier been introduced by Colin McPhee to Balinese *gamelan* music, it took first-hand experience to impress upon him its richness and complexity. As he himself commented: "It's about as complicated as Schöenberg". As a result, on his return to England in 1956, large sections of a ballet, *The Prince of the Pagodas* (already in progress before the journey), used *gamelan* music techniques and scales. It was premièred at Covent Garden on New Year's Day 1957.

A move to a larger house just outside Aldeburgh, plus the cycle *Songs from the Chinese* (for Pears and Julian

Bream) and the mystery play *Noye's Fludde* took up most of 1957, while 1958's works included the dream-like and disturbing *Nocturne* cycle of orchestral songs, dedicated to Alma Mahler, and his Hölderlin settings. Dreams—a Shakespearean one in particular—became the subject of his next opera, *A Midsummer Night's Dream*, completed in 1960, five years after his previous operatic success, the longest break in his compositions for opera since *Peter Grimes*. With Alfred Deller in the cast, it was successfully premièred at Aldeburgh, later transferring to Covent Garden.

By 1961 Britten had completed his first purely instrumental work for over 15 years, the cello sonata he wrote for his new friend, Mstislav Rostropovich, an ardent admirer of his music and a cellist nonpareil. He had also been commissioned to write a piece of music for the rebuilt Coventry Cathedral; this evolved into the choral masterpiece, *War Requiem* (1962). Rostropovich's wife, Galina Vishnevskaya, was one of three soloists on the studio recording, together with Pears and Dietrich Fisher-Dieskau. Taking the Latin mass and poems by the WWI poet Wilfred Owen, Britten fashioned a unique requiem for all those who have fallen in war. The work struck an unexpected chord with the larger music-loving public, and Britten's own recording of it quickly became a best-seller, exceeding 200,000 copies within a year of its release. This in turn made for intense public interest in his 50th birthday (1963) and his subsequent compositions, including a '*Cello Symphony* (1963) for Rostropovich; a *Nocturnal after John Dowland* (1963) for Julian Bream; *Curlew River* (1964), based on long-nurtured ideas of the Noh Theatre he had seen in Japan; *Songs and Proverbs of William Blake* (1965), written for Fischer-Dieskau; and *The Poet's Echo*, a series of Pushkin settings for Vishnevskaya. In 1965 Britten was awarded the Royal Order of Merit, a rare distinction in Britain, especially for a musician.

The next full-length opera was a long time in coming; the conversion of the Malt House at Snape into a concert hall and recording studio occupied much time and thought prior to its opening in 1967, while a television production in 1966 of *Billy Budd* encouraged Britten to consider writing specifically for the medium. The 1969 televised version of

Peter Grimes redoubled his determination to do so, and by the summer he was working on the libretto of what was to become the opera *Owen Wingrave*, based on another story by Henry James. The accidental razing by fire that year of The Maltings disrupted not only the Aldeburgh Festival, but also Britten's work schedule: *Owen Wingrave* was finally transmitted in the summer of 1971, and although it received good critical coverage, its ties to the TV screen have restricted its subsequent impact.

Despite numerous commitments and a slow decline in health (he had been diagnosed as having a weak heart), Britten was by this time well advanced in the shaping of his ideas for what

was to be his last opera, *Death in Venice*. Thomas Mann's short story—a stark delineation of the devastating effects of desire on a human being's dignity—presented an ailing Britten with one of his greatest challenges. After a first performance at the 1973 Aldeburgh Festival, the opera was premièred at Covent Garden. By now, Britten was visibly weakened, and although his mind was utterly intact— as demonstrated by the superb dramatic cantata *Phaedra* written for Janet Baker (premièred at Aldeburgh in 1976), he had only a short time to live. In December of that year, just six months after being made a peer of the realm, he died in the arms of Peter Pears in his bed at the Red House.

WITOLD LUTOSŁAWSKI
1913–1994

Lutosławski arrived at his mature style quite late in his career, having spent much time studying and emulating other composers, most of them distinguished by an adherence to tonality. It was not until the close of WWII, and the advent of Boulez and his contemporaries, that Lutosławski combined the elements he found personally relevant into a coherent compositional approach.

Born in Warsaw, Lutosławski took up both piano and violin before professing an interest in composition. In 1932 he enrolled at Warsaw Conservatory where he studied composition with Witold

Malisewski and piano with Jerzy Lefeld. By 1934 he had written a piano sonata which won approval. His *Symphonic Variations* of 1938 show that his compositional style at this stage was quite conservative and was to remain so throughout the War, during which he served in the Polish Army, escaping transportation to an extermination camp only by a combination of luck and sheer courage.

With the post-war Communist regime in Poland obeying Moscow's demands for folk-based compositions from its composers, Lutosławski towed the Party line by turning out finely-wrought works which displayed an unconcealed appreciation of Bartók's approach to

folk music. During the 1950s, while winning government approval and awards for works such as his *Concerto for Orchestra* (1954), Lutosławski came into contact with the newer ideas developing in Western Europe.

His international breakthrough came in 1958 with his *Funeral music in memoriam Béla Bartók*, in which for the first time, 12-tone techniques are given partial prominence in the structure and melodic development, combined as they are with conventional tonal thinking. The final steps towards his fully mature composing style took place after he heard John Cage's piano concerto at Darmstadt in 1961, which inspired him

Witold Lutosławski

was so titled because it was an orchestral piece 'in a large closed form'.

Lutosławski was also content to use the designation 'concerto' for two outstanding works combining soloist and orchestra, the Concerto for Cello of 1970 and the Concerto for Piano of 1987. The two are linked not so much by shared material as by the evolution of the composer's thinking, which is notably tonal and still concerned with the idea of chance, although he always stressed that his music contained not a jot of improvisation. This very personal compromise between modern trends and personal leanings is what gives his passionate and intricately formed music its weight and power, as can be heard in Symphony No. 3 (1983) and the often surprisingly lyrical Symphony No. 4 (1993), which many regard as his crowning musical statement. This lyricism is also a notable quality in the Berg-inflected *Chantefleurs et Chantefables* for soprano and orchestra of 1990. The self-contained nature of Lutosławski's achievement, and the long evolution of his personal style, has created a small but significant body of work which will continue to grow in stature as the perspective of the years lengthens.

DON'T MISS

▶ **Variations on a Theme of Paganini (1941)**

▶ **Concerto for Orchestra (1954)**

▶ **Funeral Music (1958)**

▶ **Cello Concerto (1970)**

▶ **Symphony No. 3 (1983)**

to consider employing aleatory practices in his own music. By the time of *Venetian games* (1962), he had evolved a way of using what he called 'aleatory counterpoint' within his given system, which gave him the added edge and tension from the juxtaposition of chance and formal organization.

The following year his *Trois Poèmes d'Henri Michaux* (1963) won the Koussevitzky International Award, confirming his growing international

stature. This work, one of his most cohesive and intricately balanced, keeps all his means of expression at optimum level and creates a marriage of musical languages which is utterly typical of the composer. For his second symphony he devised a highly successful way of limiting the element of chance within the overall form of the piece, thereby escaping what he regarded as the ossification of traditional forms evolved centuries before. This symphony, for example,

ALBERTO GINASTERA

1916–1983

Like Villa-Lobos, Ginastera is often referred to as a nationalist composer, but this is a misleading term to apply to a composer whose long career embraced so many different avenues of musical thought. Initially, Ginastera was unmistakably South American in his approach, and proud of his country's musical tradition. However, on reaching a mature compositional style, he was no more nationalist than his European contemporaries, all of whom have an identifiable style but eschewed wild-eyed nationalism as a musical stance.

Born in Buenos Aires, Ginastera studied music first at the Williams Conservatory (1928–35) in Buenos Aires and later at the National Conservatoire (1936–38). While still at the latter he wrote a number of works which immediately established his national reputation, including the *Danzas Argentinas*, Op. 2 for piano (1937) and, most importantly, the ballet *Panambi*, Op. 1 (1937), from which was extracted a concert suite (Op. 1a) ; its first performance marked him as a talent to watch. At this point Ginastera was taking inspiration from the folk music he had studied intensively during his years as a student. Between this date and his visit to America in 1945–47, Ginastera wrote prolifically in most musical mediums, including *Trez Piezas*, Op. 6 (1940) for piano, *Dos Canciones*, Op. 3 (1938), and the two contrasting sets of songs from

1943, *Cinco Canciones populares argentinas,* Op. 10 and *Las Horas de una estancia,* Op. 11, the latter setting poems by Silvina Ocampo to music. Even at this early point, however, his musical language included what he had learned and adapted from Bartók, Stravinsky and other modern composers.

In 1941 Ginastera became composition professor at the National Conservatoire. The same year he completed a major ballet score, *Estancia*, which had been commissioned by the American Ballet Caravan. Built around his concept of what constituted the Argentinean way of life in the pampas, the ballet allowed Ginastera to use themes from native Argentinean music, some depicted by spoken and sung excerpts from poetry, some evoked by native dance rhythms and melodic fragments— which became one of the major artistic and cultural statements of Ginastera's early career. The ballet suffered the slings of fortune, its commissioning group dissolving before the première, and although an extracted concert suite was successful in 1943, the ballet itself only received its première in 1952. The

vitality and colour of the music, as well as its brilliant scoring, begs the question as to why it is not better known internationally.

The sojourn in America, during which Ginastera became acquainted with both Aaron Copland's music and the man himself, was important in that it reaffirmed his inclination to move towards a more personal interpretation of what a national musical style had to offer. This is clear in the three *Pampeana* compositions written in the seven years after his return from America: No. 1 (1947), written for violin and piano, is a more subjective impression of Argentinean melodies and rhythms, and the 1950 composition *Pampeana,* No. 2, for cello and piano, extends this approach. By No. 3 (1954), Ginastera had included a whole symphony orchestra to deliver what he termed a 'symphonic pastorale', built around the open tuning of the guitar and incorporating elements of polytonality as well as driving rhythms. These rhythms were to become more central to Ginastera's music as the 1950s came to an end, and he entered his most modernistic phase.

DON'T MISS

▶ **Estancia (1943)**

▶ **Pampeana 1 & 2 (1947–50)**

▶ **Piano Sonata No. 1 (1952)**

▶ **Harp Concerto (1956)**

▶ **Beatrix Cenci (1971)**

The modernist argument is carried supremely well by his first two String Quartets, Op. 20 (1948) and Op. 26 (1958), both of which present an uncompromising development of jagged, fast-shifting and elusive thematic elements without sacrificing that ability for exquisite, shimmering rhapsody with which Ginastera was already identified. Dodecaphonic techniques have been identified in the second quartet, and indeed by the time of the Quintet for Piano and Strings, Op. 29 of 1963, Ginastera felt able to not only use serialism but also the aleatory techniques which had been promoted, particularly by the European avant-garde, towards the end of the previous decade. However, this did not mean a wholesale abandonment of Ginastera's earlier musical personality or the national source of much of his inspiration, as the subject of his first opera, *Don Rodrigo* (1963–64), demonstrated. This and his other completed operas, *Bomarzo* (1966–67) and *Beatrix Cenci* (1971), all deal with the complexities of sexuality and violence in people and society, and utilize most of Ginastera's vast panoply of compositional techniques. This is also observable in his final String Quartet, No 3 (1971), where he not only employs extreme distortions of tone and greatly plastic melody lines—in addition to his established notions of chance in compositions— but also adds a soprano voice for four of the five movements, thus placing the work in a specifically Latino-Spanish context.

By 1970 Ginastera had moved to Geneva in order to escape the worsening political situation in his homeland, but this exercised little direct influence on his compositional approach. For the last decade of his life he continued to personalize his use of modern techniques, as his piano sonatas No. 2 (1980) and No. 3 (1982) demonstrate, with their fantastic rhythms, harsh contours and brutal energy combined with a folk-like expressivity and outbursts of exuberance. By the time of his death, which left his fourth opera, *Barrabas*, unfinished, Ginastera had long combined the disparate elements of his compositional career into a highly distinctive personal style which, like his heroes Bartók and Stravinsky, was based on a thorough understanding of the folk music of his own part of the world.

LEONARD BERNSTEIN
1918–1990

Leonard Bernstein is as well known for his musical compositions as he is for his charismatic conducting, performing, books, television appearances, films and teaching. An influential and persuasive advocate of all good music, he is also one of a tiny handful of composers who are equally convincing in both art-music and the popular idiom.

Bernstein was born into a comfortably-off Massachusetts family, his parents having originally emigrated from Russia. From a very early age he demonstrated remarkable musical abilities. His parents, although initially hostile to the idea of their first-born pursuing a musical career, allowed him to study music while still a youth. At Harvard University he studied with the eminent Edward Burlingame Hill and Walter Piston, evolving a compositional style which accommodated the intellectual clarity of Stravinsky with the unabashed populism of Copland's most accessible pieces and the vitality of Gershwin. Bernstein's early embracing of jazz was also a key element in the rhythmic élan always present in his work.

Graduating from Harvard in 1939, he moved on to the Curtis Institute of Music in Philadelphia where he met composer/conductor Lukas Foss, who became a lifelong friend. He also studied conducting under the great Fritz Reiner, piano with Isabelle Vengerova and composition under Randall Thompson. With his voracious attitude to study, his progress was rapid, and he won scholarships to the Berkshire Music Centre at Tanglewood where he came to the attention of the

Leonard Bernstein

the Philharmonic (the first Amercian to hold the post), maintaining an active role with the orchestra until 1969 when he accepted the lifetime post of Laureate Conductor in order to free himself for more composing and freelance performing duties in Europe and America. He later developed close ties with both the Berlin Philharmonic and the Israel Philharmonic.

What lifted Bernstein out of the category of being just a great conductor was his instinctive musical theatricality and sense of melody. By early 1944 he was already at work on the ballet *Fancy Free*, which was to remain a definitive statement of Bernstein's mature compositional style for stage works. Focusing on his lifelong love affair with New York, the ballet's story revolves around the attempts by three sailors on leave to find girlfriends. The plot was reused later that year for the musical *On the Town* (also made into a successful film in 1949 with Gene Kelly and Frank Sinatra), but the music was kept separate, and was constructed in seven tightly-wrought episodes, opened by the blues song 'Big Stuff', which was recorded for the original show by Billie Holiday. The music from *On the Town* had as its principal theme a melody which has become synonymous with Bernstein's favourite city—New York— and was an immediate success. By the end of 1944 Bernstein was not only a famous conductor but an American composer of the first rank in the public eye.

Bernstein's second ballet, *Facsimile* (1946), was mounted—as the first had been—in collaboration with Jerome Robbins. A romantic, poetic work dealing with the flight from the inner

outstanding conductor and patron of new music, Serge Koussevitzsky. The great man was so impressed by Bernstein's potential that he made him his assistant at Tanglewood for 1942. During the year Bernstein resumed work on the sketches of an unfinished work for soprano and orchestra dating from 1939, and combined it with new ideas for a symphony. The two became fused, and from them emerged his *Jeremiah Symphony*. Always deeply aware of his Jewish cultural and spiritual legacy, he had taken his text from the 'Book of Lamentations'. The symphony enjoyed a successful Pittsburgh début in 1944, with Nan Merriman as the mezzo soloist. Before that, however, an even more sensational event would make

Bernstein a national figure and establish the dualism of his subsequent career.

Appointed assistant conductor in 1943 to Artur Rodzinski with the New York Philharmonic, Bernstein was called in as a last-minute replacement for the great Bruno Walter, who was taken ill just before a concert. Bernstein seized his opportunity with both hands, making a sensational impact with audience and critics alike. His relationship with the NYPO was to become legendary, and he took them on tours all over the world, becoming a fierce champion of modern masters such as Mahler and Shostakovich whose work he felt had not received the exposure it warranted. In 1958 he became Music Director of alienation of modern life, and revolving around just three characters, a woman and two men on a beach, *Facsimile* demonstrated that Bernstein had not lost his desire to write contemplative and downbeat works in the tradition of his first symphony. Indeed, the next major work was his second symphony. Given the title *The Age of Anxiety* (1949), it was inspired by an Auden poem of the same name. Written 'on the run' in hotel rooms around the world, the symphony exhibits Bernstein's penchant for using a wide range of musical styles. In contrast, he wrote the short, very jazzy *Prelude, Fugue and Riffs* (1949, revised 1955), a work often associated with Benny Goodman. Bernstein then returned to the stage, composing the satirical one-act opera *Trouble in Tahiti* in 1952, and the hit Broadway musical *Wonderful Town* in 1953, which in turn led to Hollywood's siren call. The result was a triumph: music for the film *On The Waterfront* (1954), starring Marlon Brando. This was followed in the same year by another notable work in Bernstein's more ascetic style, *Serenade*, which features a solo violin in dialogue with a string orchestra, harp and percussion.

In 1956 he experienced a rare setback when his witty and brilliantly scored revival of Voltaire's classic story *Candide*, with an acid libretto by Lillian Helman, was judged a somewhat leaden affair by contemporary observers, although the effervescent overture has been consistently popular in concert halls and on record. (He later revised *Candide*, producing two new versions in 1982 and 1988, and its rehabilitation has already begun.) He bounced back the following year with the biggest hit

of his career, *West Side Story*, with lyrics by Stephen Sondheim. This masterful retelling of the Romeo and Juliet story in modern-day New York had productions in virtually every country in the world which appreciated musicals, and was eventually made into a hit film starring Natalie Wood. In 1960 Bernstein made a suite of symphonic dances from the score. Many of its most famous melodies have since become part of everyday musical language.

Feeling a desire for creative contrast, Bernstein returned to the more solemn idiom of the symphony. His third such work, the *Kaddish Symphony* (1963), includes a singer and narrator, and uses a Jewish book of prayers as its intellectual and emotional backbone. Positive reviews notwithstanding, Bernstein was dissatisfied with his original effort, and in 1977 the symphony underwent a thorough revision and slimming-down. Though its theatricality was retained, the wordiness of the first version is made more palatable. This was followed by one of Bernstein's most beautiful works, *Chichester Psalms*, commissioned by the Dean of Chichester Cathedral and written and premièred during a year-long sabbatical in 1965. Appropriately enough, the language used is Hebrew, the selections emphasizing the need to 'make a joyful noise' (Psalm 100) and to find a way to coexist in peace (Psalm 133). Dismissed as simple-minded at the time, this work's stature has grown with every year.

After this, Bernstein's creative output receded. Although major works such as *Mass* (1971), an eclectic and somewhat polyglot musical *mélange,* and the more

coherent *Songfest* (1977), a cycle of settings from American poets, were completed and premièred, the more public aspect of Bernstein's life—his performing, lecturing and workshops—tended to take precedence. Much of his creative energy was now poured into meticulous reworkings of older material as well as attempts to make what he saw as 'definitive' recordings of his output. His 1989 recording of the revised *Candide* was one of the last and most typical of these afterthoughts. Two works from 1988 proved the durability of his creative muse, his *Missa brevis* succeeding where the less coherent *Mass* had perhaps failed, while the touching *Arias and Barcarolles* for two voices and two pianos demonstrate Bernstein's knack for the sweeping, emotional melody which can reveal the core of a set poem's message.

Bernstein continued to lead a hectic life right up until his abrupt retirement from conducting a week before his death, succumbing finally to the rigours of hard-living and a burning desire to complete every major project he undertook. His legacy, on record, film and in manuscript, is considerable and still awaits definitive assessment.

DON'T MISS

▶ **On The Town (1944)**

▶ **Prelude, Fugue and Riffs (1955)**

▶ **West Side Story (1957)**

▶ **Chichester Psalms (1965)**

▶ **Arias and Barcarolles (1988)**

GYÖRGY LIGETI

b. 1923

Ligeti is still regarded as a controversial composer, but his place in this century's music is given a proper perspective when it is remembered that he was 23 years old when his compatriot Bartók died in 1945, and that his gradual evolution of a distinctive compositional voice came about as a result of the great musical innovations in central Europe between the death of Mahler and the end of the War.

Ligeti was born into a comfortably-off family in a part of Hungary which was later ceded to Romania, near the town of Kolozsvár. His musical inclinations led to him being accepted at the local Conservatoire where he studied theory with Ferenc Farkas between 1941 and 1943. Having survived the horrors of WWII in Hungary, he moved on to the Liszt Academy in Budapest, where he combined a thorough knowledge of Classical techniques with a study of folk idioms as prescribed by Kodaly's educational programme. His compositions written for graduation hold no great surprises. However, once he was appointed as a teacher at the Liszt Academy, his composing began to diverge from the orthodoxy of post-war Hungarian music. During the brief period of liberalization which preceded the Revolution in 1956, Ligeti aligned himself with the European radicals operating on the other side of the Iron Curtain, producing a widely-read and influential paper on Boulez's *Structure*

1a in which he announced his rejection of Boulez's serialism. By now Ligeti was pursuing another technique in which many others, including John Cage, were involved—that of aleatory, or chance-derived music, and in the mid-1950s he wrote two works, *Artikulation* and *Glissandi*, which used the fashionable electronic medium. But electronic music soon lost its allure for him, and a third work planned for this medium, *Atmosphères* (1961), evolved into a composition for acoustic instruments. This work found Ligeti dispensing with theme and a recognizable harmonic structure or traditional notion of form, concentrating instead on dense, static masses of sound. The seemingly atavistic approach of this music was presaged by *Apparitions* (1958–9), in which Ligeti began exploring the basic musical assumptions behind modern composition.

By the time of his *Volumina* (1962) for organ, Ligeti had pushed the idea of chance and determinism in his music as far as he was prepared to go, and had realized that his concept of musical creation was fundamentally different to that of Cage, who was concerned to make art and life interchangeable. For Ligeti, the two things had to retain separate identities in order for a dialogue to take place. It is thus not altogether surprising to find Ligeti using traditional forms by the mid-60s, composing a Requiem (1963–5) and his First Concerto, for cello and orchestra (1966), both of which find him intensely

involved in such traditional elements as polyphony and harmonic movement, as well as the relationship between soloist and orchestra. Spurred on by the success of this piece, Ligeti returned to the concerto form four more times, fashioning the *Chamber Concerto for 13 Instruments* (1969–70), a double Concerto for Flute, Oboe and Strings (1971–2), a Concerto for Piano and Orchestra (1985–88) and, most recently, a Concerto for Violin and Orchestra (1992). In these works Ligeti is looking for new relationships between the massed and solo instruments, attempting to apply ideas which combine tempered and non-tempered pitch, tonality and atonality, and an assortment of different time durations. He is also acutely aware of instrumental timbre in all registers, and the way these timbres can combine. This makes for a remarkably attractive and transparent compositional style.

As the Requiem would suggest, Ligeti also became enamoured of the human voice, and one of his most influential and typical works, *Clocks and Clouds* (1972–73), used a vocal realization of a

DON'T MISS

▶ **Atmosphères (1961)**

▶ **Cello Concerto (1966)**

▶ **Lux Aeterna (1966)**

▶ **Le Grande Macabre (1978)**

▶ **Etudes (1985)**

written text which allowed Ligeti to write either in an entirely specific and articulated way (clocks) or in a way to create a blurring of elements, especially those of rhythm and harmony (clouds). This juxtaposition remains to this day an important one in Ligeti's works. Given the wide scope of his interests, the arrival of a full-length opera, *Le Grand Macabre* (1974–77) seemed logical, although the work itself, using a text written by an early exponent of theatre of the absurd, Michel de Ghelderode, guaranteed that operatic convention would be as undermined as it would be celebrated in the work. His second opera, *The Tempest,* has a more unified seriousness of intent, but the intoxication of timbral colour and the varieties of the human voice, allied to a fully-developed sense of musical drama, makes it as impressive an achievement as the earlier work.

LUIGI NONO
1924–1990

Nono was of the same generation as Boulez, Berio and Stockhausen. Like them, he came to the fore in the 1950s and helped to define what it was to be avant-garde during that period. Nono, however, was specifically inspired by political and humanist issues, and attempted repeatedly to give answers to pressing social and political dilemmas through the vehicle of his stage and concert works. This often gave his music—already difficult—a confrontational edge.

He was trained in the Conservatory of his home town of Venice by the unjustly neglected composer and pundit Gian Francesco Malipiero. In 1945 he left Venice for Switzerland to take lessons with Bruno Maderna. By 1948 he had moved on to Maderna's friend and champion, the conductor Hermann Scherchen, and closed the decade coming to terms with 12-tone composition. By then, Nono had long been a confirmed left-wing activist,

Luigi Nono

committed to airing his Marxist views while maintaining strong connections with the Communist cause in Italy. Many of his subsequent artistic creations would have as their central theme a deep concern for political,

moral and ethical problems and the possible means for their resolution.

Nono's *Variazioni canoniche* was conducted by Scherchen at the 1950 Darmstadt Summer Course, and by the following year he was being drawn into the avant-garde circles which were beginning to discover new post-war paths for art-music. During the remainder of the 1950s he forged an utterly personal mode of musical communication from the confluence of serialism, chance, electronic music, modified and altered instruments, noise and all the other new ideas which were currently swirling through modern music. Some of the results can be gleaned from such works as *Liebeslied* (1954) for chorus and orchestra, and *Il canto sospeso* (1955–56), for three soloists, narrator, chorus and orchestra, the texts of which also reveal the composer's concern with the victims of life. In 1959 Nono publicly declared himself to be against chance music and improvization in his own work, setting himself in exact opposition to the ideas of John Cage and his acolytes.

Nono's compositional progress came to its first peak in 1960 with *Intolleranza*, his first opera and a major milestone in his career. Not only did this work establish him in much wider circles than before, but it also pointed the way for his own creative effort, pushing it in the direction of theatre and the dramatic statement where he found himself completely at home and able to operate without any artistic constrictions. The subject of the work— a multi-layered attack on various forms of fascism and the oppression and exploitation of ordinary people—gave Nono both the inspiration and the dramatic setting to create a highly-charged and passionate theatrical piece calling for "a time when man will be a help to man". *Intolleranza* is composed in a fiercely individualistic style; it is divided into two sections, and even carries a scene with no music. The second half has echoes of an earlier orchestral work, *Incontri* (1955) (composed in the year he married Nuria, the daughter of Arnold Schoenberg), but here Nono is able to translate his intense style into ideal modern theatre music.

A prolific composer, Nono concentrated much of his post-*Intolleranza* efforts on either theatrical works or music incorporating the electronic medium, such as *La fabbrica illuminata* (1964) or *A floresta e jovem e cheja de vida* (1967). The operas included *Al gran sole carico d'amore* (1972–5), which he described as an *'azione scenica'* and dealt with the nature of revolutions which eventually fail, and the major late work *Prometeo, tragedia dell'ascolto*, first produced in Venice in 1984. This latter work attempted a non-traditional way of presenting a theatrical work by using electronic sound mixed with words— sung and spoken—which dispensed with visuals, causing an acoustic drama to be enacted instead. He himself saw it as a reinvention of his creative life, rethinking his "whole existence not only as a musician but as an intellectual in today's society in order to discover new ways of seeing things".

This new way had already included a rejection of old social and political certainties, and an embracing of doubt and irresolution, and it was this increasingly subjective vision which continued to inform this most individualistic and uncompromising composer until his untimely death in 1990.

DON'T MISS

▶ **Variazioni canoniche (1950)**

▶ **Intolleranza (1960)**

▶ **Omaggio a Emilio Vedova (1960)**

▶ **Prometeo (1984)**

▶ **No hay caminos, hay que caminar (1987)**

1925-PRESENT

From the composers who represent this generation we can see the gradual rebirth of creative diversity and the slow, painful healing of the scars of World War II as composers such as Stockhausen (who saw the horrors of war at first hand), Henze, Górecki and Boulez wrestled with what seemed a central question in the aftermath of such sustained carnage: what kind of music should serious composers be writing for post-war society?

For many, including Pierre Boulez and Theodore Adorno, the answer came in the form of increasingly rigorous applications of serialist theories, much of them derived from the later works of Webern, while others began investigating the laws of chance and random association which John Cage had been exploring, largely by himself, until the 1950s. While much of this activity could be said to be devoid of humour, a more human face appeared in the works of Luciano Berio, while the socially doctrinaire Hans Werner Henze was always at pains to stress the human aspects of music-making as opposed to the obsessive pursuit of intellectual purity. Meanwhile in Britain mavericks such as Birtwistle and Maxwell Davies developed along their own highly individual lines. By the mid-1960s the avant-garde, as represented by the serialists, had won such a complete

victory in contemporary music theory that they had become the new orthodoxy. Thus it was no surprise to find a reaction setting in against what had become something of an academic hegemony devoid of any discernible public support. From the late 1960s onwards, a parallel group of individuals pursued very different musical goals; based for the most part in America, and influenced by music from many lands, including their own (such as jazz and Broadway), young composers like Steve Reich and Phillip Glass began to follow their own instincts with regard to compositional form and tonality, and over the best part of a decade the so-called 'minimalist' movement emerged to claim its own dedicated followers.

In Europe similar techniques were investigated by composers such as Louis Andriessen and Otto Ketting, but a more profound impact on public consciousness was ventured by composers like Górecki, Pärt and Tavener, all of whom found inspiration for some of their finest works in the religious, spiritual and folk music of Europe. The transparent simplicity they brought to their structures came as a delightful shock to audiences who had found little to embrace in new music. It seemed that once again serious music could be popular, whether written by John Adams and Michael Torke or by Pärt and Tavener.

LUCIANO BERIO

b. 1925

Berio has been something of a modernist maverick throughout his long creative career. Despite being embraced by the post-war avant-garde establishment, and becoming a composition teacher on both sides of the Atlantic, Berio's natural expressionism and theatricality has led him to pursue direct communication with his audiences. His long collaboration with the extraordinary singer Cathy Berberian also gave his music a natural outlet and focus rarely found in other contemporary composers.

Luciano Berio

Berio was born in northern Italy. Early music lessons with his father led to the young Berio's acceptance at Milan's Verdi Conservatory where he was taught by Ghedini and Paribeni. Even at this stage, when his music was generally contained within a late-Romantic style, his intense interest in literature—especially non-Italian contemporaries such as Joyce and W. H. Auden—drew him towards ellipsis, fantasy and a sardonic humour in the intellectual and emotional concerns expressed in his music. By the end of the 1940s Berio had moved to New York to study under Luigi Dallapiccola, who encouraged him to make a close study of serialism. Before leaving Italy, Berio had met and married the young American singer Cathy Berberian. From then on Berio regularly composed provocative pieces for Berberian, a remarkable vocalist who was also

blessed with a highly developed sense of theatre, a vital element in so many of Berio's pieces. His differing approaches to her artistry are graphically displayed in *Recital 1 for Cathy*, compiled in 1971, but which has elements that were composed as far back as 1948 and were wholly tonal, while other parts sound like devilish parodies of serialism and beyond.

Berio demonstrated his continuing interest in poetry with *Nones* (1952), an orchestral piece which had originally been conceived as a setting of Auden's poem of the same name. However, Berio was quickly swept up by the general enthusiasm for the fast-evolving electronic music phenomenon. In 1954 he and Bruno Maderna founded and directed the Studio di

Fonologia Musicale, where many of his electronic pieces were first conceived. At the same time he was teaching at the Darmstadt and Dartington summer schools. In the mid-1950s there was a steady flow of electronic pieces, starting with *Mutazioni* (1955) and including *Thema (Omaggio a Joyce)* (1958)—which has Berberian reading extracts from *Ulysses*—and the remarkable *Visage* (1961), a 20-minute piece which combines electronic sound with Berberian singing syllables rather than words, which sound initially like something from a modern theatre of the absurd, but which build to a quasi-transcendental climax as unexpected as it is successful. This piece was later used as the soundtrack for the film, *La Prisonnière*.

By then Berio had abandoned any thought of writing exclusively electronic music. In 1958 he began to compose his long-running series of virtuoso pieces using acoustic instruments, *Sequenza*, which, by the end of the 1980s had reached *Sequenza X—trumpet in C and piano resonance*. Berio's natural theatricality has led inevitably to opera, just as his love of instrumental timbres drew him to writing a long string of orchestral pieces, especially during the 1970s, when works such as *Bewegung* (1971), *Still* (1973) and *Points on the Curve to find...* (1974)—the latter making a considerable impact. Operas such as *Opera* (1969–70) and *La vera storia* (1982) have been successfully staged, although they await their first commercial recordings. One of his most universally appreciated works is *Circles* (1960), written for voice, harp and two percussionists. Using settings of poems by e. e. cummings given a form which cleverly exploits minute musical arrangement, it also exploits occasional forays into much freer notation and

expressivity. In Berberian's practised hands, this balance became riveting. Yet perhaps his most well-known concert piece is one for large orchestra and eight amplified voices called *Sinfonia* (1968), which is built in five different movements and takes as its departure point the traditional notion that a symphony is a 'sounding together' of instruments. The voices in the original performance of this work were supplied by the well-known vocal group, the Swingle Singers, with whom Berio worked successfully for several years.

Berio and Berberian divorced in 1966, but continued to collaborate professionally, and she remained a definitive interpreter of Berio's vocal works until her death in 1983. Berio himself has maintained a prolific output, although he has occasionally come to grief when trying to incorporate of-the-moment elements into his scores (some of the vocal effects in *Laborinthus II* , for example). Berio's instinctive dramatic feel and his

natural ability to strike fine balances between chaos and structure, line and broken cadences, and his stylishness in the art of conscious pastiche, make him a continuously interesting member of the post-war avant-garde. Indeed, one of his more recent successes—a musical setting of a poem by Sanguinetti called *Canticum Novissimi Testamenti II* (1989)—is easily one of Berio's most eloquent and moving masterpieces, demonstrating that he remains creatively potent right up to the present day.

PIERRE BOULEZ
b. 1925

Boulez, like Mahler, is possibly better known as a conductor than as a composer. As he enters his eighth decade, his importance as a theorist and practitioner has perhaps begun to outweigh the significance of his compositions. As a young man he was a passionate advocate of the Second Viennese

School and the theories of Schoenberg, but his fierce intellect soon drove him to reinvent Schoenberg's own musical order to suit his more quixotic creative personality.

Boulez, born in the French town of Montbrison, was attracted in his youth as much by mathematics as by music.

For a time it seemed as if mathematics would claim his prime attention, and he even began classes in the subject at Lyon. But in 1944 he began musical studies at the Paris Conservatoire where one of his teachers was Olivier Messiaen, a man whose influence can be traced in Boulez's later musical thinking. His immediate interest in Schoenberg's theories led him to take private lessons

Pierre Boulez

with René Leibowitz in 1945–46. By the end of the 1940s Boulez had composed an impressive series of chamber works using his own personal combination of 12-tone techniques combined with other influences. His Sonata for Piano No. 2 (1948) was the key to realizing his own strict and intellectually remorseless idea of total serialism.

However, Boulez was not merely moving down a single musical channel; by the opening of the 1950s he was also intent on exploring the possibilities of what soon became known as *musique concrète*, an idea first disseminated by the Parisian Pierre Schaeffer. This was to take non-musical sounds from the natural world (non-electronically generated sounds) and subject them to a thorough redefinition by a variety of means of distortion—such as speeding-up, splicing and running the tape backwards—before combining these prearranged sounds with a prepared musical chart. Boulez made an impact

at the Donaueschingen Festival of 1951 with *Polyphonie X*, which, together with *2 Etudes*—a work equally concerned with such principles—became rallying points for the new European avant-garde as the world of *musique concrète* and, eventually, electronic music, became the front line in the battle to establish a new art-music world order. By the mid-1950s he had produced the work which was to stand as his most impressive achievement, and had also begun his extraordinary conducting career.

The work was *Le Marteau sans maître* (1953–55), a setting of three poems by René Char for soprano, xylorimba, vibraphone, flute, viola, guitar and 'little percussion instruments'. It was premièred at the Baden-Baden Festival for contemporary music in 1955, and its idiosyncratic use of serialist notions of form and order with its embracing of timbre and sound made it a sensation with Boulez's peers. Boulez commented that with this work he was attempting

to indicate the deep poetic roots in all music. This notion was carried a step further with *Pli selon pli* (1958), a work for soprano, piano, guitar, mandolin and orchestra, where words chosen from sonnets by Mallarmé are used as a basis for musical syntax, form and balance without regard for the actual verbal meaning; something Boulez saw as a secondary consideration.

Char and Mallarmé remained important creative catalysts for Boulez, with a series of other works evolving out of his constant study of their very different poetic and aesthetic worlds. In fact, it was sometimes the case that Boulez would reinvestigate parts of these works from the 1950s to spur him to another compositional step, as with *Eclat* (1964), a chamber work which builds upon the first movement of *Pli selon pli*. Other avenues Boulez explored in the 1950s were aleatory music, improvization, and music which was electronically generated. By the 1960s he was spending more time performing and teaching, most notably during the festival of the Domaine Musical in Paris of which he was the founder. His reputation as a composer was gradually eclipsed by his reputation as a performer. In the 1970s this process was completed by a series of brilliant concerts and recordings. In particular, his records of Debussy and Ravel were looked upon as revelatory, while his in-depth recorded survey of Schoenberg was unprecedented at the time.

In the next decade his performing and compositional careers tended to become more separate, and long periods of creative silence were filled by an ever more energetic professional career which embraced ground-breaking recordings and productions of works such as the first complete version of Berg's opera *Lulu* (1979) and, in a novel twist, a complete Bayreuth *Ring* cycle in the early 1980s. On the compositional side, Boulez poured most of his energies either into reinvestigations of old compositions and concerns, or into the implementation of his ideas of new musical order and form within the world of computerized music (*Domaines*

of 1970 was his first new work since *Pli selon pli*). To this end he helped found the Institut de Recherche et Coordination Acoustique/Musique in

Paris, which has been concerned with computerized generation of music along serialist lines, often in tandem with the use of acoustic instruments.

DON'T MISS

▶ **12 Notations (1945)**
▶ **Le Marteau sans maître (1952–54)**
▶ **Structures pour deux pianos, Books 1 & 2 (1952)**
▶ **Pli selon pli (1957–62)**
▶ **Domaines (1968)**

HANS WERNER HENZE

b. 1926

Although following no one musical creed and perceiving himself as something of a musical maverick, Henze comes from the European tradition of intense political radicalsim. His rejection of all types of fascism has led him into some particularly startling musical theatre, but the music itself has rarely approached the arid intellectualism of much post-war academic composing. Committed to man's basic freedoms, Henze has remained eager to embrace an audience, rather than the false comfort of isolation.

Henze was born in Westphalia, reaching adolescence just as WWII engulfed Europe. In 1942 he enrolled at the Brunswick State School, but in 1944 was conscripted into the army. After the war Henze became a répétiteur at

the Bielefeld State Theatre. In the following year he began music studies at the Heidelberg Institute for Church Music. By the time he progressed to summer courses at the 1948 Darmstadt School, Henze was already evolving a personal style with an unusually wide range of contributive parts: from ballet and opera music to Cocteau to Weill and Milhaud, as well as jazz and, most importantly, Stravinsky (then a deeply unfashionable source of inspiration for young composers). From the first, Henze was also a confirmed melodist, albeit in a contemporary manner, which made him something of a pariah in post-war New Music circles.

From 1948–50 Henze was employed at the Deutsches Theater in Konstanz. By then he had made notable strides as a composer, finishing three symphonies before the end of 1950, together with a First String Quartet and the First Violin

Concerto (both 1947). His gift for marrying the voice with melodic lines and attractive orchestral settings was evident as early as 1948 with *Whispers from Heavenly Death*, for soprano and chamber orchestra, and his first opera, *Das Wundertheater* (1949). Yet by 1953, after three years as composer and music director at the Wiesbaden State Theatre, Henze was sufficiently disenchanted with the post-war musical, political and cultural climate in Germany that he was ready to decamp to Italy. Before doing so he completed what he later called "the first of my works to fill a whole evening"—the opera *Boulevard Solitude*—in which he expressed his decidedly individual attitude towards serialism, using it especially in the love scenes "since my dodecaphony wanted to show, in those days, a free world, non-bourgeois, whilst the old corrupted world had to be presented in the usual

Hans Werner Henze

tonalities". This re-telling of the old Abbé Prévost story of *Manon Lescaut*, replete with lust, murder and prostitution, was premièred in Hannover in 1952 to a mixed reception, and presaged Henze's fascination in the later 1950s with earlier Italian operatic models, such as Verdi and Rossini.

Henze left Germany and settled on the island of Ischia. With this move came a transition into Henze's second composing period, characterized by much lighter and more vibrant musical colours and shapes and more melismatic melodic patterns. This is already glimpsed in *Ode to the West Wind* (1953), but is most gloriously displayed by the *Fünf Neapolitanische Lieder* (1956) and the opera, *König Hirsch* (1952–55). Both owe a debt to Stravinsky and Schoenberg, but these influences are now felt only through the powerful filter of Henze's mature

compositional style and Italianate flamboyance. Henze had completed his Symphony No. 4 in 1955, but the main thrust of his work in the 1950s remained vocal. Although his opera *Der Prinz von Homburg* (1958) was perhaps not entirely successful as a piece of drama, an undoubted masterwork arrived in 1961 with the first appearance of *Elegy for Young Lovers* (1959–61), the text written by W. H. Auden and Chester Kallman. This work combined thoughts on the nature of creativity with careful investigations into the role of the artist and the potentially destructive qualities of love, and was written in a newly-crafted Henze style which was notably harsher and more acerbic than before, while losing none of its lyricism and tenderness.

This gradual progress towards a leaner and more dynamic aesthetic continued during the 1960s, as is shown by *Der*

junge Lord (1965), although as always with Henze, there were glaring inconsistencies, such as the elegant but somewhat overly glossy Symphony No. 5 (1962). By 1966 *Die Bassariden*, another collaboration with Auden and Kallman, had arrived, announcing Henze's new preoccupation with violent blocks of sound, distorted vocal effects and a considerable toughening of his political and social stance. The heavy echoes of this work can still be heard rumbling through the equally uncompromising political satire *Versuch über Schweine* of 1969. By this time Henze had spent six years in Rome, but leaving Italy, he now divided his activities between Germany in the Old World and North and Central America in the new. His oratorio *Das Floss der Medusa* (1968) made no bones about his new political radicalism, with its regular use of Ho Chi Minh's name amounting to a declaration of left-wing flag-waving. Among other works, his two years of teaching music in Havana (1969–70) resulted in *El Cimarrón*, a chamber music piece based on the biography of a runaway slave. His *Der langwierige Weg in die Wohnung der Natascha Ungeheuer* (1971) was a blatant attempt to provoke his Berlin première audience into a frenzy of insult. Many see the apotheosis of this strain in Henze's work in the opera *We Come to the River* (1976), a Covent Garden collaboration with the English dramatist Edward Bond in which the bourgeoisie is ferociously attacked in the most strident manner by the actors.

Yet Henze's art had never remained wholly within one particular stream in the past, and it did not do so at this stage. His time in Havana also gave birth to Symphony No. 6, a work which Henze was happy to describe as revolutionary in intent (its première was attended by Cuban Revolutionary Army members), but which was at pains to evolve its argument from traditional European art-music forms. By the early 1970s Henze was based in Britain. By 1973 he was readdressing his musical heritage through a perceived similarity between one of his own musical themes and a motif from Wagner's *Tristan und Isolde*. Wagner had long been on Henze's hate-list, so *Tristan* (1973) was a remarkable *rapprochement*, although it takes the form of a virtual analytic deconstruction of parts of Wagner's original, using both acoustic instruments and taped sequences taken from a computer analysis.

During the late 1970s Henze became increasingly accepted by officialdom as a composer of rare stature, and a steady stream of awards, doctorates, honorary positions and the like have continued up to the present day on both sides of the Atlantic. More importantly, Henze has continued to compose, with Symphony No. 7 appearing in 1984, a year after his opera *The English Cat* (1983), while the ballets *Orpheus* and *Undine* also appeared at the closing of the previous

decade. He also continued to write instrumental music, such as the *Capriccio for cello* (1979–81) and *Royal Winter Music* (1975–76), the latter a guitar sonata based on Shakespearean characters commissioned by Julian Bream. Henze is a prolific composer who continues to lead a remarkably active musical life, becoming in 1991 the composer-in-residence for the Berlin Philharmonic and pursuing his musical interests world-wide.

DON'T MISS
▶ **Symphony No. 1 (1947)**
▶ **Boulevard Solitude (1952)**
▶ **Der junge Lord (1965)**
▶ **El Cimarrón (1969–70)**
▶ **Royal Winter Music—** sonata on Shakespeare's characters (1975–76)

KARLHEINZ STOCKHAUSEN
b. 1928

Stockhausen has not only been one of the most controversial of all 20th-century composers, but has exerted one of the most profound influences on all other serious music-making in the post-war period.

Born near Köln, Stockhausen's father was a schoolteacher, his mother an amateur pianist and singer. His father joined the Nazi party, untroubled by Nazism until Hitler began supplanting loyalty to the Catholic Church with

loyalty to himself. The young Stockhausen retained his religious outlook in secret, especially when he became a stretcher bearer in 1944 and saw the terrible human cost of war at first hand. In his mid-teens by 1945, Stockhausen's view of the world and of the place of art within it was profoundly influenced by his experience of the destructiveness of Nazi totalitarian political and cultural ideologies.

By the war's end his family had been obliterated: his father had vanished; his

mother, a long-term sufferer from mental problems, had been 'legally' killed in 1941 in accordance with Hitler's euthanasia policies. Stockhausen enrolled at Köln's High School for Music. Alone and penniless, he paid his way by playing the piano in bars and selling fag-ends remixed into cigarettes on the black market.

By the winter of 1949–50 Stockhausen's studies had brought him to the point where he could analyse and comprehend the music of modern

Karlheinz Stockhausen

masters such as Hindemith and Stravinsky, but when he discovered Schoenberg he came up against an attitude of total antipathy at the Köln school. Only when he moved to Frank Martin's composition class did he receive encouragement, which inspired him to write a thesis on Bartók. This breakthrough prepared him for a summer course in 1951 at the Darmstadt School, where he met the young composer Karel Goeyvaerts. At the time, Goeyvaerts was grappling with notions recently put forward by Messiaen, which made music a totally rational process, addressing the properties of each separate note (pitch, volume, timbre and duration) as basic structural building-blocks within a composition which is not attempting to obey the disciplines of old forms but represents a process governed, in some

cases, by numerology. This fearsomely logical process was soon to become an important part of the compositional philosophies of other composers such as Ligeti and Boulez.

This movement away from the bounds of 12-tone music as it had been formulated by Schoenberg and Webern marked a decisive point in the evolution of a genuinely new post-war musical aesthetic, and remained central to many of Stockhausen's own compositional concerns and procedures. The end of 1951 saw Stockhausen married to Doris Andreae, and finally completing a composition which satisfied him—the chamber work *Kreuzspiel*—which articulated his new approach to serialism. The year 1952 was a busy one, with Stockhausen travelling to Paris to receive tuition from Messiaen and

Milhaud, and the performance of *Kreuzspiel* at Darmstadt. His stay in Paris enabled him to meet Boulez and to become affiliated to Pierre Schaeffer's *musique concrète* studio, another crucial event as it led to Stockhausen's subsequent interest in working with electronic music. The immediate result was that during his studies in physics and acoustics at Bonn University (1952–54), he took up a position as co-director at the new Westdeutscher Rundfunk electronic music studios.

However, he did not neglect composing, as his *Kontra-punkte* (1953) and the initial *Klavierstücke* for solo piano demonstrated, but by the middle of the decade he had become sufficiently frustrated by the specifics of instrumental acoustics to look for more general answers in electronics instead. This did not prevent his continuing to try out ideas in acoustic settings, as the *Zeitmasse* (1956) for flute, oboe, English horn, clarinet and bassoon demonstrated. This composition, together with *Klavierstücke XI*, was one of his first which moved on from strictly proportioning everything within a given work in respect to the numbers 1–6. The work used the notions of improvization and infinite time, arrived at through fragmentation and specific forms of tempi disorder. Stockhausen was convinced that fragments of eternity—of some further removed state—could be glimpsed or established through following this quasi-spiritual approach to composition.

This sense of searching reached an unexpectedly lyrical apotheosis in the work *Gesang der Jünglinge* (1956), which combined electronically created sounds with a young boy's voice in a haunting and hitherto unknown sonic landscape. The touch of humanity brought to the piece by the fragmented vocalization was conspicuous by its absence in *Kontakte* (1960), a work combining electronically generated sound with piano and percussion in which the procedure of sound production becomes the focal point of the listener's attention.

In early 1961 Stockhausen met and fell in love with the artist Mary Bauermeister. Not only did he have a wife and family and his own guilt to contend with, but also the rage of a rejected former lover of Mary's, which came to ahead in 1962 when he confronted Stockhausen and a brawl ensued. For much of the 1960s Stockhausen remained 'on the run', only resolving his personal difficulties through divorce and remarriage to Bauermeister in 1967.

During this period Stockhausen was becoming more interested in describing structure and process than finalizing actual compositional detail, which he progressively left more and more to others. This fascination with process and the sparking-off of events is seen in *Aus den sieben Tagen* (1968), often performed live by Stockhausen and his performing group (formed in 1964 to give a realization of the work *Mikrophonie 1*), where there are a set of notated directions for change and overall architecture, but the musical detail is left to the players. Stockhausen's other growing passion in the late 1960s was a new unification of all the musics of the world, detailed in *Hymnen* (1968), a two-hour-long work

combining electronics and *musique concrète* which mainly consisted of national anthems from every corner of the world. The work aroused great controversy due to the perception that Stockhausen had not actually composed it, but for him this was important in itself. He regarded the gathering together of such disparate elements and procedures to be central to his new creative and intellectual beliefs. His piece *Stimmung* (for six vocalists intoning various phoneme sequences over a static chord) investigates the overtones and sound qualities of the resultant vocal patterns and timbres, and was received with howls of protest at some concerts where members of the audience imitated cats in an attempt to pour derision on Stockhausen's preoccupations.

By the beginning of the 1970s Stockhausen was by far the most famous avant-gardist in the world, a fame he had enjoyed for over a decade. He now embarked on a massively ambitious cycle named *Licht*, in which he created seven musical ceremonies linking every aspect of his musical concerns up to that point. This supreme ambition was proof to some that Stockhausen was now believing his own propaganda in a manner unheard of since Wagner, especially as he was now in the habit of demanding special venues to be built for performances of his music. Yet it is perhaps significant that during the 1970s and 1980s Stockhausen, though obsessed by his own musical world, began to embrace a vast range of musics from other cultures, especially those of the Far East. At the very heart of many of these musics lay ritual,

repetition, theatre and mysticism. As *Licht's* several segments—such as *Donnerstag aus Licht* and *Montag aus Licht*—evolved and were completed, these elements, transformed and personalized, became increasingly central to Stockhausen's music.

Stockhausen remains relevant today because so many of his concerns and so much of his musical output represents the beginnings of the music still regarded by the majority as contemporary. This is in spite of the fact that his own concerns are now possibly beyond most of his original audience. His preoccupation with a synthesis of world music sounds as fresh to today's audiences as it was startling to his 1970s audiences, while his attempts to penetrate to the core of musical sounds—to estimate accurately the meaning of their existence (within a given structure or even played seemingly for no overall purpose), has undoubtedly laid a bedrock for much of the music which has come forward in the last decade. As yet it is impossible to summarize his overall contribution to music in this century, especially as that contribution is still in the process of being made, but his stature in post-war art-music is second to none.

DON'T MISS

▶ **Kontra-punkte (1953)**
▶ **Gesang der Junglinge (1956)**
▶ **Stimmung (1967)**
▶ **Hymnen (1968)**
▶ **Tierkreis (1975)**

HENRYK GÓRECKI

b. 1933

Until 1992, when he was nearly 60, Górecki was just one of scores of obscure modern European composers dedicated to finding his own way in music and having his compositions performed at festivals which only fans of 'difficult' new music attended. Yet now his *Symphony of Sorrowful Songs* is perhaps the best-known symphony of the past 35 years.

Górecki was born and educated in the Polish Silesian town of Rybnik. A child during the war and occupation of Poland, he was constantly confronted with death and destruction. In 1953 he qualified as a teacher, teaching for two years before answering the urge to compose. Enrolling at the Katowice Conservatory, he studied composition with Szabelski. Even at this stage Górecki was wresting a personal language from the combination of earlier Polish and French traditions with the post-Webern Darmstadt School, whose music was heard virtually for the first time in Poland at the 1956 Warsaw Festival. By 1960, when Górecki left to study for a brief period in Paris under Messiaen, he had completed a First Symphony (1959) which reflected this marrying together of Polish/French traditions with the post-war serialism of Darmstadt and others. The orchestral work from 1960, *Scontri*, (Collisions), confirmed the radical, avant-garde side of this creative vision, and established Górecki as a leading 'difficult' composer in early 1960s Poland.

However, Górecki himself returned from Paris with a rapidly changing perception of what he wanted to achieve in his music. In 1963 he completed *Three Pieces in Old Style*, a work for string orchestra which reaches deep into Poland's musical past and combines a cultural and spiritual identity in a way which proved to be a fundamental characteristic of Górecki's music for the next 30 years. With this and other works such as *Old Polish Music*, Op. 24 (1969), *Genesis* (1962–63) for string trio, and *Refrain* (1965), Górecki pursued his own musical path to the detriment of his reputation, the radicals of the contemporary scene giving him up as a lost cause. Yet Górecki was anything but that, having discovered within his own country and culture the musical stimuli to produce works which were deeply felt and entirely in accord with the radical emotionalism of much earlier generations, all the way back to Chopin and beyond. The composer's own sense of himself in his environment was also affected by a life in which he rarely enjoyed good health, and has often been near death. By 1972 Górecki's second symphony, *Copernican*, Op. 31, had been completed, utilizing words from Copernicus and the 37th Psalm, this last idea being repeated in his first unaccompanied choral piece, *Euntes Ibant et Flebant*, Op. 32 (1972), which uses words from Psalms 126 and 95. This work, and the remarkable *Amen*, Op. 35 , (which is a setting of that single word alone), with their tight control and development of small

motifs and musical figures and intense musical insights into fragments or combinations of text, both look forward to Symphony No. 3, *Symphony of Sorrowful Songs*, Op. 36 (1976) . This symphony had been commissioned by South-West German Radio (then under the remarkable conductor Ernest Bour) and had its première at a festival in Royan conducted by Bour himself. At the time the work, with its combination of religious texts and the heartbreaking words taken from the wall of a Gestapo cell, had a considerable impact among the few who heard it as it seemed a large step by Górecki away from what was then regarded as the front line of radical composing. It was, however, entirely consistent with the direction his work was taking; there was no doubt of the itensity of vision he was bringing to his music as well as a straightforward musical discipline.

As if to reinforce his determination to continue in his own way, Górecki's next major work was another for choir, *Beatus vir* (1979), thus completing the decade as he had started it—with a

DON'T MISS

▶ **3 Pieces in Old Style (1963)**

▶ **Amen (1975)**

▶ **Symphony No. 3 (1976)**

▶ **Good Night (1990)**

▶ **Little Requiem for a Polka (1993)**

major choral piece (1971 had seen the publication of *Ad Matrem*, composed in memory of his recently deceased mother). The year 1981 also saw the appearance of the moving *Miserere*, Op. 44, a tribute to the courage of the protestors in Poland who were attempting to win some measure of freedom from Communist control. This type of consistency was thrown into relief by the appearance in the 1980s of a more out-going, exuberant music, such as the relentlessly driven piece, *Concerto for Harpsichord and String Orchestra* Op. 40 (1980), and sections of both *Lerchenmusik* (1984) and the later *Kleines Requiem für eine Polka*, Op. 66 (1993), in which Górecki's love

of folk music, especially its ecstatic and repetitive dance elements, comes to the fore.

Górecki has continued to write music across a broad spectrum of instrumental and vocal combinations, with two string quartets—*Already it is Dusk*, Op. 62 (1988) and *Quasi una Fantasia*, Op. 64 (1990–91)—creating a considerable impact with their typical intertwining of spirituality and wild dance rhythms. The integrity of Górecki's music has been sustained up to the present day with an extraordinary work, *Good Night, 'In Memoriam Michael Vyner,* (1989), proving to be a deeply moving experience, while his latest orchestral

work has been a carefully wrought *Concerto-Cantata* for flute and orchestra which eschews any attempt by listeners to see any form of follow-up to his greatest popular success— the *Symphony of Sorrowful Songs*. Górecki himself, like any true composer, is entirely taken up with the music he is writing today, and consumed by the need to express the concerns he lives with now, rather than those of his past. It is his unique ability to write music which touches the deepest wells of emotion in his listeners which will keep Górecki's name very much to the fore when the history of today's music is given its due perspective in decades to come.

KRZYSZTOF PENDERECKI

b. 1933

From the first, Penderecki showed intense interest in the most up-to-date compositional techniques and ideas, and his music shows an uncommon ability to bring the warm blast of humanity to the rarified theories and practices of composers such as Iannis Xenakis and Karlheinz Stockhausen. His musical world is passionate, extreme and demanding, but it gives much back to its audience.

Penderecki was born near Krakow in Poland and began studying the violin while still a child. He initially trained to be a performer and by his mid-teens had made his début playing Vivaldi. However, by the end of his teens he

had decided to pursue composition, and spent the years 1955–58 as a student at Krakow Academy of Music. While still at the Academy he wrote a series of outstanding student pieces, including a string quartet (1956–57) and his graduation exercise, *Emanationen* (1958) for two string orchestras. Penderecki graduated with top honours in 1958 and was immediately invited onto the staff of Krakow Academy, where he has taught ever since. The Academy's astuteness was borne out the following year when Penderecki entered three works (*Emanationen, From the Psalms of David* and *Strophes* for soprano, speaker and 10 instruments) for a Polish competition under the rules of anonymity demanded by the

competition's founders. He won the first three places, causing a sensation.

He has composed successfully for orchestra, as his long series of concertos (from 1963 to 1992 to date) demonstrate, but he has always perceived himself as a man of the theatre, exploring extreme technical and instrumental practices only as a means of addressing his audience in the most stark and unadorned way possible. His first opera, *The Devils of Loudon* (1968), was written to his own libretto and made an intense exploration of the relationship between extreme religious belief and sexuality; its musical language suits its subject-matter admirably, and it immediately established Penderecki internationally as an opera composer of prominence, gaining productions in Germany (two) and America in its first year.

Penderecki continued to paint vast operatic canvases with *Paradise Lost* (1978), *The Black Mask* (1986) and *Ubu Roi* (1991) all scoring remarkable successes. The inherently dramatic nature of his work has continued uninterrupted, while his musical language has slowly edged towards a more structured usage of motific material within large works. In his extensive catalogue of works for the church, such as *The Passion According to St Luke* (1963–65), *Te Deum* (1979), *Magnificat* (1974), *Agnus Dei* (1981) and *Polish Requiem* (1980–83), Penderecki has achieved a solemn spirituality which, while embryonic elsewhere in his work, has become an overwhelming concern for composer and listener alike, swept up as the latter must be by the vastness of Penderecki's canvas and the dignified musical materials he uses to illustrate his devotional portraits. In these works Penderecki has gradually simplified his musical elements and achieved an intense spirituality which is the direct counterpart of the dramatic atmosphere achieved in his operas.

DON'T MISS

▶ **String Quartet No. 1 (1960)**

▶ **Magnificat (1973–74)**

▶ **Polish Requiem (1980–84)**

▶ **Symphony No. 2 (1980)**

▶ **Viola Concerto (1983)**

HARRISON BIRTWISTLE
b. **1934**

Birtwistle, whose music is a highly personalized and intense form of communication, has gradually evolved a body of work which stands today as possibly the most substantive from a British composer since Britten and Tippett. That it remains enormously challenging to the listener goes without saying, although the rewards are great for those who come to terms with Birtwistle's musical language.

Birtwistle was born in the Lancashire town of Accrington. Even prior to secondary schooling he had decided he wanted to be a composer. His chosen instrument was the clarinet, which he studied at the Royal Manchester School of Music between 1952 and 1955. At this time he was still gathering his artistic credo together, and when he joined the Manchester New Music Group—then dominated by such powerful figures as Peter Maxwell Davies, Alexander Goehr and John Ogdon—he chose to watch and listen rather than enter the fray himself. Aware of the debates raging around total serialism, electronic music, aleatory music and other new developments, Birtwistle took what he needed from each idea and progressed towards his own individual synthesis, which was arrived at publicly for the first time in *Refrains and Choruses* for wind quartet (1957). This had enough of Birtwistle's mature style still to be called representative; it was dominated by severe disjunctive sound-blocks and a thorough involvement with repetition, whilst remaining devoid of serialist compositional techniques— something of a rarity in the contemporary music of the time.

After his schooling was completed, Birtwistle entered the teaching profession. The various demands on his time meant that nothing of great moment was completed until 1965, when the orchestral work *Tragoedia* was premièred. This work continued his concern with a methodology of fragmentation whereby the very deconstruction of a work's structure and content becomes its unity. With his next composition, the stage work *Punch and Judy* (1966–67), written during a year's respite on a scholarship to Princeton, Birtwistle's wider international reputation was quickly established. This was partly because composing for the theatre proved to be his natural musical *métier*, and partly because of the sheer impact of the deeply resonant theme as he and his librettist Stephen Pruslin interpreted it. The implicit (and explicit) cruelty and violence in this type of children's entertainment was effectively brought to the surface. By the time the two follow-up works, *Down by the Greenwood Side* and *Verses for Ensembles* (both 1969) arrived, the music world was in a tingle of anticipation to see what Birtwistle would come up with next. The success of these two meant that his first major work of the 1970s, *The Triumph of Time* (1971), found an appreciably wider audience than virtually any of his contemporaries could command. *Time* also had the advantage of being one of Birtwistle's more immediately palatable works, the music dealing less with violence and disintegration than with ritual and natural cycles, thus allowing a less fraught and aggressive atmosphere to prevail.

His next major stage work, *The Mask of Orpheus* (1973–83), had an unusually long gestation period during which Birtwistle continued to produce other music (most of it related in some way to the larger work), and also assumed the role (at the invitation of Sir Peter Hall) of Musical Director of the National Theatre in London. In this long and fascinating work Birtwistle managed to combine nearly all his main concerns and long-term themes, especially those closest to the production of theatre music for which he believed it imperative for action and speech to demand music, rather than for the music to be supplied for no apparent reason.

After the eventual (and highly successful) mounting of *Orpheus* in London, Birtwistle responded with a flood of new works, including *Secret Theatre* (1984), a work he claimed was "intended to bridge the gap between absolute music and theatre music. It contains a specific drama, but the drama is purely musical". In 1986 there also appeared the major orchestral piece *Earth Dances*. By 1991 Birtwistle's successor to *Orpheus* had been completed and performed at Covent Garden: this was *Gawain*, and many people, including the composer, believed it to be his first opera as opposed to music written for some form of theatre. *Gawain* has remained controversial in its reinterpretation of the Arthurian ideal and legend, as well as its stark and highly-charged musical atmosphere. It is clear even at this juncture that Birtwistle remains in a highly creative phase and that there will be more in the near future from this major British composer.

DON'T MISS

▶ **Secret Theatre (1964)**

▶ **Punch and Judy (1968)**

▶ **The Triumph of Time (1972)**

▶ **Antiphonies (1993)**

▶ **Gawain (1994)**

PETER MAXWELL DAVIES
b. 1934

Maxwell Davies has energetically pursued a long career of musical creativity which has seen him move through a number of stylistic and intellectual phases of development. Since the 1980s he has been perceived increasingly as one of the two or three most important post-Britten English composers.

Born in Lancashire, Maxwell Davies is a naturally gifted musician with a drive to compose. He attended the Royal Manchester School of Music at around the same time as Birtwistle and Alexander Goehr. As a member of the Manchester New Music Group, he was an energetic performer and composer. The group was one of the first in Europe to make meaningful contact with the music of India and to study medieval music, both areas which proved profound influences on Maxwell Davies's mature compositional voice. His propensity for slow, repetitive passages interspersed with sections of almost brutal violence gave him a compelling musical vision. Although his work contained the occasional reference to the twin mid-century

Peter Maxwell Davies

of a George Mackay Brown poem *Black Pentecost* but gradually grew into his First Symphony (1973–74). It was, as he himself recognized, the first of his major works to reflect his new environment, although he later pointed out that "possibly the creative artists I most admire are two 12th-century writers whose language, to my mind, builds the only sound structures parallel to the statement made by the mediaeval cathedrals—Dante and St Thomas Aquinas". This more extended architecture perhaps dovetails with the quasi-mystical religious schematics to be found in the literature from his favourite period of the past.

icons of Schoenberg and Stravinsky, it nonetheless had a distinctive flavour.

By 1957 Maxwell Davies had already created a series of works which would remain part of his mature canon: *St Michael* for wind ensemble, *Prolations*, *Five Motets*, *Alma redemptoris* and *Stedman Caters*. By the turn of the decade he was deeply immersed composing *O magnum misterium*, inspired by three years teaching music at Cirencester Grammar School. But the piece which established him internationally was the opera *Taverner*, begun while studying for a scholarship at Princeton under Roger Sessions and completed in 1968. The following year was a turning-point: Maxwell Davies produced his stage work, *Eight Songs for a Mad King*, originally performed by his own group, the Pierrot Ensemble. This violent, almost insanely visionary work was instantly successful. By the end of the 1960s Maxwell Davies was easily one of the best-known avant-garde composers in the world. His fame

reached such heights that he was embraced by the media and wrote two film scores for Ken Russell:*The Boy Friend* and *The Devils*. After this fleeting brush with the insubstantial world of media stardom, he took the radical step of moving to one of the most remote areas in Britain, the Orkney Islands.

Once established in his new location, Maxwell Davies kept up his prodigious rate of composition, but gradually modified the surface characteristics of his style. Within a short time he settled to writing his first extended composition, which began as a setting

The decade would end before Maxwell Davies returned to the symphonic form, but during the 1980s he wrote three more, while the Fifth Symphony (1994), established him among the very few major contemporary composers who could successfully build a body of such music. Yet it would be misleading to paint Maxwell Davies as a predominantly orchestral composer, for he has continued to work across many genres, with childrens' music remaining close to his heart. (Two short operas, *Cinderella* and *The Two Fiddlers*, were completed at the end of the 1970s and performed by local Orkney Islands childrens' groups.) Meanwhile, his

---

DON'T MISS

▶ **Eight Songs for a Mad King (1969)**
▶ **Black Pentecost (1979)**
▶ **The Lighthouse (1980)**
▶ **Symphony No. 2 (1980)**
▶ **Strathclyde Concerto No. 4 (1990)**

fascination with opera and music for the stage continued, and he produced three more works in the 1970s: *The Martyrdom of St Magnus* , *Kirkwall* and *The Lighthouse* .

Ballet has also repeatedly engaged Maxwell Davies's creative energies,

with *Salome* (1978) and *Caroline Mathilde* (1991) being outstanding examples. Maxwell Davies's traditional combination of plainsong with daringly off-centre harmonic displacement establishes the correlative musical tensions which display the uneasy balancing act so

many of his characters have to achieve. Maxwell Davies may often turn to the relatively remote past for his themes and models, but his music, and his keen sense of the theatrical, guarantees that his audience will always be dealing with timeless human and artistic issues.

ARVO PÄRT

b. 1935

Pärt is of the same generation as the American composers Steve Reich and Philip Glass, but while they were evolving a response to the rigours of serialism and a fresh musical language for late 20th-century music from a New World point of view, Pärt was making similar decisions about serialism but coming up with a wholly different set of answers.

Pärt was born in Estonia. After a period of National Service, he trained at the Tallinn Conservatory where his main teacher was Heino Eller. After graduation, Pärt worked as a recording engineer in the music division of Estonian Radio and also began to write film soundtracks, a source of work which was to prove financially and stylistically rewarding for him in the following decade. At the outset of his career, Pärt was under the influence of dodecaphony (the 12-tone system of serial music); by 1960 his *Necrology* for orchestra showed his absorption of this approach. During this decade works such as the Symphony No. 2 (1966), Concerto for Cello and Orchestra (1966), *Collage*

on the *Theme B-A-C-H* (1964) and *Credo* (1968), showed his ultimate rejection of serial techniques in favour of quotation and collage, an approach which, like serialism, was bound to land him in trouble with the Soviet authorities.

This conflict with the Soviet authorities, together with a sense of having failed to fully establish his own compositional voice, led Pärt into a period of silence and withdrawal from whence he determined to rebuild his compositional personality. For most of the early 1970s he studied the works of such earlier composers as Ockeghem, Obrecht, Machaut and Josquin Desprez, ultimately going further back—to the Gregorian and Orthodox liturgies. Within this music Pärt found the solution to his own aesthetic dilemmas, and one which was so utterly alien to his previous work as to make it sound like music by a different composer.

Central to this new style was a near-static harmony and rhythm, and a heightened spiritual and meditative element which could at times become

so powerful as to be overwhelming. The composer had discovered the truth of the paradox of applying great restraint and yet generating enormous emotional power. Pärt's first venture in this style, and his first composition for several years, was *Für Alina* (1976) for piano. This was followed by the popular and hypnotic set of variations called *Fratres*. Pärt took this set of violin variations and made different sets of transformations for different instrumental combinations, with one transformation, dating from 1980, involving a new set of variations on the original work. This group of works has remained his most oft-performed, but the body of work which has given Pärt such a huge international audience in the past half-decade has been his choral writing. Although Pärt continued to produce fine instrumental pieces (*Cantus in Memory of Benjamin Britten* for example), his delight in the human voice and his understanding of its qualities, is evident from his *Missa Sillabica* (1977) onwards.

The 1980s saw the completion of a series of major choral works, including a *Te Deum* (1984–86), *St John Passion* (1982), a *Stabat Mater* (1986) and a *Magnificat* (1989). This sequence

alone would confirm Pärt as the equal to any composer currently working with a religious theme.

During the 1990s Pärt has not slackened his compositional pace, with the *Berliner Messe* (1990–92) and *Silouans Song* (1991) setting a formidable standard in terms of both musicality and spirituality. This pattern is confirmed by his most recently completed works, *Litany* (1994), *Psalom* (1985–95) and *Trisagion* (1992–95), where the intensity of his vision is achieved through the most economical and restrained of musical means.

DON'T MISS

▶ **Symphony No. 2 (1966)**

▶ **Cantus in Memory of Benjamin Britten (1976)**

▶ **Fratres for violin and piano (1977)**

▶ **Te Deum (1984–85)**

▶ **Miserere (1989)**

STEVE REICH
b. 1936

Few who have heard Steve Reich's music come away unmoved: the strength of reaction from critics and audiences alike suggest that this founding father of the American movement away from the straightjacket of post-war serialism has produced a body of work which will continue to be both influential and music that is listened to by later generations.

Reich was born in New York. Due to his parents' divorce, he was brought up in the very different cultural atmospheres of New York and San Francisco. From a young age he showed an interest in a wide variety of intellectual and artistic pursuits, discovering jazz early in his musical development. His chosen instruments were drums and percussion (he studied them from the age of 14), but he graduated from Cornell University with a degree in philosophy.

During his time at Cornell, and later at Juilliard (1958–61), he was taught music theory by a variety of teachers, including Hall Overton, whom he later claimed to have had a greater influence on his evolution and technical competence as a composer than any of his teachers. It is perhaps significant that Overton, himself a skilled arranger, orchestrator and composer, had a foot in both the Classical and jazz camps during the 1950s and 1960s.

During his final years at the Juilliard, Reich came face to face with serialism, the all-dominating compositional orthodoxy of the period. Although he wrote studies in this style, by the time he reached Mills College (1962–63), he had realised that serialism was not the answer for him. When one of his teachers, the composer Luciano Berio (another teacher was Darius Milhaud), studied one of his pieces, he made the

comment: "If you want to write tonal music, then write tonal music". This had a liberating effect on Reich, although hours spent in New York night clubs listening to jazz saxophonist John Coltrane improvising proved a far more intoxicating demonstration of viable musical alternatives. Years later Reich commented that Coltrane was demonstrating that "you can stay in one key as a centre, and that will free you to make any sound you want, including noise".

By 1964 Reich was working at the Tape Music Centre in San Francisco where he produced the first work he still claims as part of his mature canon: *It's Gonna Rain* (1965), a piece for electric tape which took the end of the world as its subject. This was followed by *Come Out* (1966), where identical tape loops are played in parallel but at different speeds. These two works were his initial move into the area of music later known as minimalism. By the autumn of 1966 he was back in New York, setting up his own performing group in time to achieve a major breakthrough in instrumental composing with his piece *Piano phase* (1967). This, and every other work he wrote from then until 1971, (*Reed phase* and *Four organs* for example), employed the same technique of minute changes of speed in the execution of identically scored parts for different instruments. As a percussionist, it was natural for Reich to concentrate heavily on the rhythmic area of his compositions, exploring subtle shifts and combinations between the instruments as they went in and out of 'phase'.

In 1970, after a long period of preliminary research, Reich went to Ghana to study African drumming at first hand. Reich found his musical proclivities confirmed in Africa, not least the emphasis on percussion within his music. He also confirmed his belief in harmonic stasis and the artistic integrity of American musical forms which used this approach (rhythm and blues, soul and rock), where bass riffs and convoluted patterns remained in place for whole tunes.

Reich's work *Drumming* (1970–71), written for two voices, piccolo and percussion, was produced after his return to America and marked something of a full stop for Reich's period of phase compositions, although later works such as *Clapping music* (1972) still harked back to this technique. The turning-point, and a second blossoming of creative thought, came with *Music for Mallet Instruments, Voices and Organ* (1973), where his phasing technique was married with a more fully developed usage of time, metric shifts and juxtapositions. Reich's concern for a complete assimilation of instrumental timbre and a rendering of the inexhaustible number of sound variations possible with larger ensembles—such as the combination in *Music for Mallet*—was to become paramount. His work for the best part of the following decade—up to *Different Trains* (1983)—was in essence a further distillation and extension of the musical lessons and theories introduced in this work. Indeed, *Music for 18 Musicians* (1975) brought the timbral and ritualistic ecstasies of Balinese music within reach of Reich's audience as a new sound-world was opened up within its hour-long patterns of phrased variation.

Different Trains signalled Reich's first sustained attempt to marry his initial minimalist impulses with his fully-developed instrumental style of the early 1980s. In it he combined a string quartet with tape recordings of people talking, his old governess in particular. Reich's concerns with Jewish history surface in interviews with Holocaust survivors describing their appalling train journeys through Europe, interspersed with the other American excerpts. Although he continued to explore the intricacies of complex rhythmic displacement and intersecting patterns, as in *Sextet* and *New York Counterpoint*—the latter written for 11 clarinets and beautifully exploiting the whole clarinet range from soprano to contrabass—he focused increasingly on compositions with extra-musical themes. This culminated in his so-called opera, *The Cave* (1994). In this, his first-ever collaboration with his wife, Beryl Korot—an artist working in the video medium—Reich addressed the question of Jewish culture in Israel, the West Bank and America, and the way in which it affects the lives of the other cultures with which it comes into contact. Many critics found it difficult to define *The Cave* as an opera, preferring to describe it as a sort of multi-media theatrical event. Reich himself has little problem with the term 'opera', maintaining that it helps clarify what he is doing, provided it is understood that he is writing modern music theatre, not something conforming to a notion of musical theatre which predates electricity and the microphone.

It is clear from the course of Reich's development that he is, and will remain, a genuinely resourceful composer and a rarity among first-generation minimalists in that the music comes not from theory, but from an inner necessity. The music itself often contains a sort of ecstasy of tactile pleasure vividly expressed by timbral and rhythmic combinations which produce works of vibrant, shimmering beauty. Even now, as he moves into his seventh decade, Reich remains a central figure in contemporary music.

DON'T MISS

▶ **Drumming (1970–71)**
▶ **Music for 18 Musicians (1975)**
▶ **Tehillim (1981)**
▶ **Different Trains (1983)**
▶ **The Cave (1994)**

PHILIP GLASS

b. 1937

Glass has emerged in the past 10 years as the single most influential member of the minimalist movement in modern music, although it is arguable that his roles as a theoretician, publicist and performer have been at least as important as any of the actual music he has written.

Born in Baltimore, Maryland, Glass began learning violin at the age of six, but two years later switched to flute and percussion which he studied at Baltimore's Peabody Conservatory. An interest in composition in his mid-teens led him to Juilliard School in 1956 to study theory. At this point he began to realize there was more to modern music than Schoenberg and Webern. During his years at Chicago University he majored in philosophy and mathematics, but in his mid-twenties, with an MA in music to his credit, he decided to move to Paris to study with the legendary Nadia Boulanger—as had so many of his American predecessors. He claims Boulanger said: "Let's start from the beginning", and took him back through all the techniques he thought he knew. This, Glass admitted later, was essential in bringing him to a complete understanding of Western compositional techniques. By 1965 he had become deeply unhappy about following that tradition.

By chance, that year he met the Indian Classical music master Ravi Shankar in

Paris and assisted him on a number of projects, coming into contact with a radically different musical tradition and one which encouraged him to look further into non-European musics. Initially attracted to the scales and melodies these musics habitually used, Glass found himself back in New York in 1966 and becoming more enmeshed in the rhythmic complexities which were at the core of non-Western music's phenomenal expressivity and incandescence. By 1967 Glass was ready to begin incorporating his experiences into his own music, and formed the Philip Glass Ensemble in order to play what he composed. His early compositions, such as *Music in similar motion* (1969), *Music in Fifths* (1969) and *Two Pages* (1967–68) carried the essence of his development for the next decade: small motific cells, a careful control of tonality rather than an exploration of the outer reaches of extended harmony and serialism, and a constant, often hypnotic—even monotonous—rhythmic pattern or pulse, often aggressively stated. This last point was crucial to the finding of an audience for the music, as Glass's

Ensemble's early concerts, combining acoustic with electronic instruments, integrated amplification as one of its fundamental attributes. This made the music more visceral and exciting than the vast majority of serialist music being written for similar instrumental forces; it also made it easier to grasp for a generation brought up on the constant of a rock or blues drum beat.

This was not the first time that Eastern music had entered the consciousness of 20th-century Classical composers: both Colin McPhee and Britten had produced works under the spell of Balinese music, but the time was now right for a long-term marrying of techniques. Inevitably, Glass's music was dismissed with utter contempt by the Classical establishment, but by the early-to-mid 1970s he had exerted a profound influence on thinking musicians within the rock fraternity, such as Brian Eno and David Bowie, and their music on the albums *Low*, *Heroes*, *Another Green World* and *Before and After Science* show traces of Glass mixed with many other influences. This led new audiences

---

DON'T MISS

▶ **Music in Fifths (1969)**

▶ **Music in Twelve Parts (1974)**

▶ **Akhnaten (1984)**

▶ **Violin Concerto (1987)**

▶ **La Belle et la Bête (1994)**

Philip Glass

back to the Glass music which had helped motivate such albums, and musical fashion began to swing in Glass's direction.

Ironically, by this time Glass had moved away from the purely instrumental music which had provided him with his initial breakthrough, and was now entering a period where—apart from a few film soundtracks—he would concentrate exclusively on vocal theatre music and opera. Working in the previous decade as the music director of a theatre company, and being married to a performer, led to a singling out of the stage as his prime inspiration. His first stage work, *Einstein on the Beach* (1975), was premièred in Avignon and was an immediate sensation, leading to packed houses in Europe and America and a best-selling recording of it for Columbia by Glass himself. With this

and subsequent operas, Glass has proved that there is a new opera audience ready and willing to sit in a darkened theatre for two hours and immerse themselves in contemporary music—if that music is right for them. Works such as *Satyagraha* in 1980 (inspired by the life of Ghandi), *The Representative for Planet 8* (libretto by Doris Lessing), *Akhnaten* (1984) and *Hydrogen Jukebox* (1990) have all built on the foundations established by *Einstein on the Beach*, and have been singularly successful with theatre audiences and the record-buying public. The Philip Glass Ensemble remains a touring group and is consistently able to deliver the most inspired and accurate readings of Glass's music—a great challenge when the nature of the material and the degree of precision essential to its understanding is taken into consideration.

Glass has also been successful with film music, which again has pushed his name into the ambit of audiences entirely unused to other forms of modern Classical music. His latest opera production, *La Belle et la Bête* (1994), shows a subtle shift in his approach as more of his early background becomes slowly assimilated into his present creative processes. This backward-looking aspect of his creativity was also notable in the *'Low'* *Symphony* (1992), which took music from the albums by Bowie and Eno and created from them newly-scored and considerably reordered symphonic structures: a clear case of the disciples influencing the master! Glass is no longer writing music along the minimalist lines of 20 years ago, but his musical style is fixed, and even his Violin Concerto (1987) is deeply invested with the stylistic traits which brought him his initial fame.

JOHN TAVENER

b. 1944

Although Tavener first came to prominence through his dramatic cantata *The Whale* (1966), a rumbustuous retelling of the Jonah story which so impressed Ringo Starr that he recorded it for the Beatles' Apple label. His subsequent work has been almost entirely bound up in the beliefs of the Russian Orthodox Church which he has espoused since the mid-1970s.

Tavener was born in London in 1944. His love of music was awakened at an early age and while still a teenager he began his musical studies under Lennox Berkeley and David Lumsdaine at the Royal Academy of Music. His talent was appreciated, and it was as a prize-laden graduate that he left the Academy and began composing *The Whale* which was to bring him instant recognition. In the same year, commissioned to write a new work for the Proms, he composed the choral piece, *In Alium*.

John Tavener

Tavener's output became increasingly centred on spiritual matters, as the *Celtic Requiem* (1969) and *Ultimos Ritos* (1972) demonstrate. He was fast evolving his notions of music and its purpose in the modern world, centring around the idea of musical works being ikons which can shed spiritual light on mankind's existence. His opera *Thérèse* (1973–6) caused controversy over its handling of the crisis of faith of the nun St Thérèse of Lisieux. By the time he wrote the *Canticle of the Mother of God* (1977) Tavener was on the verge of being inducted into the Russian Orthodox faith, a crucial development in both his personal and artistic life as it confirmed his move eastwards in his creative thinking and his adoption of musical ikons as vehicles for his increasingly devotional compositions. Born into a Presbyterian family, from his early youth Tavener had been deeply religious, and his entry into the Orthodox faith finally gave complete expression to his spiritual needs.

In his desire to emphasize the spiritual and transcendental aspects of existence, and to evoke these sensations in his audience, Tavener concentrated on reducing his music to a state of utter simplicity. He openly embraced Byzantine modes and techniques to help him achieve this goal, which made him both a modern and a deeply traditional figure, and one entirely unaffected by musical fashions.

His output has remained prolific, although for the most part it has been choral or ritualistic in nature, *The Lamb* (1982), *Akathist of Thanksgiving* (1988), *Liturgy of St John Chrysostom* (1978), *Wedding Prayer* (1987), *Ikon of Light* (1984) and *Today the Virgin* (1989) being the most typical of his work up to 1990. Yet it was an instrumental work, arising from a commission suggested by cellist Steven Isserlis, which revitalized his contemporary reputation. Written for 'cello and orchestra, and premièred during the 1989 Proms season, *The Protecting Veil* is a musical evocation of a 12th-century visitation of the Mother of God in Constantinople. The work's transparent scoring, its deep and heartfelt message, and its simple lyricism made it an instant hit and a work of lasting significance. It has guaranteed Tavener an audience for any new work he premières.

DON'T MISS

▶ **The Whale (1966)**
▶ **Ikon of Light (1983)**
▶ **Hymn to the Mother of God (1985)**
▶ **Akathist of Thanksgiving (1988)**
▶ **The Protecting Veil (1989)**

Now married and a father, Tavener began the 1990s with renewed creative energy, producing vocal works such as *Thunder entered Her* (1990), the opera *Mary of Egypt* (words by Mother Thekla), *Innocence* (1995), *We shall see Him as He is* (1990) and *The Annunciation* (1992). His orchestral output is represented by *The Repentant Thief* (1991), while

the chamber work *The Last Sleep of the Virgin* (1991) demonstrates that his ability to write superbly for small groups is unimpaired. In January 1994 his *Akathist of Thanksgiving* was performed in Westminster Abbey and later broadcast on the BBC, confirming his unique position in British contemporary musical life.

JOHN ADAMS
b. 1947

Adams, often named as a leading light in the modern minimalist school of composition, sees himself more as someone wholly immersed in tonality and pulsation who, equipped with a complete education in composition and theory, is able to use any element of musical logic with which to construct his musical architecture. His mature works range far from the stripped down repetitions of his early explorations.

Adams was born in Massachusetts into a musical family—both parents were amateur jazz musicians—and from his early youth showed an interest in a wide range of music, especially music which had come to maturity in America. In the mid-1960s Adams became a student of Leon Kirchner at Harvard University. After graduation, he began teaching at the San Francisco Conservatory. By then he had discovered the writings of John Cage, whose theories of indeterminacy and open form—which demand a new

realization each time a work is performed—helped confirm Adams' own feeling that a further pursuit of the serialist ideal was not for him. Always interested in tonal music, he soon found the work of Terry Riley, Philip Glass and Steve Reich much closer to his own formative needs as a composer, and was quick to combine ideas of pulse, tonality and repetition in his music, together with the more usual influences of Stravinsky and Schoenberg. Being a second-generation minimalist, Adams had a wide range of

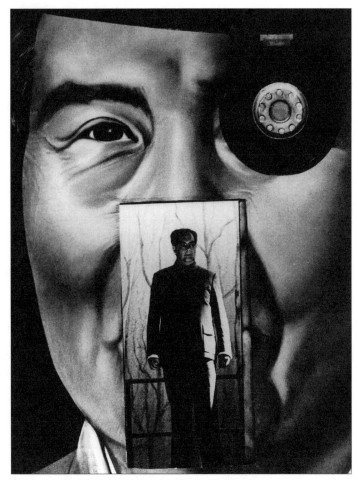

John Duykers plays Mao Tse-Tung in the opera Nixon in China *in 1988*

hearing, seem to have nothing to do with the minimalist aesthetic. Adams regards himself as a composer primarily for orchestra, rather than for electric or electronic sound generation. This, plus a gradual loosening of the ties to minimalist theory, makes for a natural progression to *Harmonium*, another large-scale orchestral work (with chorus). It was followed in 1986 by *Two Fanfares* which vividly displays the two faces of Adams' compositional psyche—the outgoing, colourful extrovert and the brooding introvert. Similarly, *Short Ride in a Fast Machine* (1986) has two faces, although both are manic in their celebration of an outdoor festival in Great Woods, Massachusetts, there being two performing versions of it. In *Fearful symmetries* (1989) a baritone was introduced into the musical equation, but this work appeared after the popular breakthrough Adams enjoyed with his widely-acclaimed first opera, *Nixon in China*, premièred in 1987 by the Houston Grand Opera.

Not an opera in the general sense, *Nixon in China* was a timely reinvestigation of two dominant figures in post-60s culture and politics: President Nixon and Chairman Mao. Adams again combined minimalist energy and rhythmic techniques with a rhapsodic sweep and attention to dramatic detail found in the work of a range of composers, including Britten and Berg. He used a similar combination in his second opera, *The Death of Klinghoffer* (1991). Due to its subject matter—the killing of a Jewish passenger by Palestinian terrorists during the 1985 hijacking of the liner *Achille Lauro*—this work

stylistic models to blend into his music. This is notable even in his earliest well-known piece, *Shaker Loops* (1978). This work was orginally written for string quartet, then septet. In it he combined his interest in minimalism with a fascination for wave forms and oscillations as well as a willingness to reinvent the Sixties notion of tape loops, this time applied to the septet itself. In 1983 Adams wrote an orchestral version of the piece, which is perhaps still his most frequently performed work. A section of it has

even been used as a soundtrack for the film *Barfly*.

Between 1979 and 1985 Adams was composer in residence to the San Francisco Symphony Orchestra. During this time he completed the major orchestral work *Harmonielehre*. The piece makes full use of minimalist energy and simplicity of form in a skilful and often moving marriage with the type of snaking melody and changes of mood which come from an earlier tradition and would, at first proved more controversial. It illustrates his recurrent desire to extract philosophical and moral lessons from the events portrayed; Adams is one of a small number of composers who remains convinced of the moral force of music.

In 1992–93 Adams produced a set of songs under the collective title *Hoodoo Zephyr*, which combine a raw energy and rhythmic vitality with a highly sophisticated sonic palette, including electronic sound production. His Concerto for Violin and Orchestra (1993) tackled a conventional form by

making it both a concert piece (with the violin constantly centre stage) and a dance work. It has since been choreographed by the New York City Ballet. Adams has long reached a point in his compositional career where he

can employ any number of musical tools from a great variety of music and disciplines. His recent interest in world music, especially from parts of Asia, suggests new developments in his work before the decade is out.

DON'T MISS

▶ Shaker Loops (1978)
▶ Harmonielehre (1984–85)
▶ Short Ride in a Fast Machine (1986)
▶ Nixon in China (1987)
▶ The Death of Klinghoffer 1991)

THE ORCHESTRA

The term 'orchestra' comes from the Latin, which had borrowed it from the Ancient Greek *orkhestra,* a circular space in front of a theatre proscenium used in Greek plays by the chorus of dancers; the Greek word comes from *orkheisthai,* the verb for dance. This combined meaning gradually became transferred to the musicians occupying the space in front of the proscenium in entertainments accompanied by music, and even as late as the 17th century the term could be used to describe any collection or combination of instruments. Only during the course of the 18th century, as composers became increasingly aware of the advantages of writing for larger

ensembles of a fixed nature, did any formal ordering of musical instruments and their numbers begin. This process was aided by the technical improvement and standardization of instruments such as the clarinet, trumpet, horn, guitar, piano and so on.

Even so, the orchestra in Beethoven's time—while considerably enlarged and standardized compared to those Haydn had been used to some 40 years earlier— were without harps, extended percussion and the cor anglais, while the woodwinds in his early orchestral works were normally represented by one musician for each instrument.

The massive growth in the size of an orchestra largely occurred in the mid-to-late 19th century, with composers such as Berlioz, Wagner, Strauss and Mahler calling for multiple representation of each woodwind and brass instrument, up to three percussionists and other permutations. At this time the instrumental division of the orchestra became standardized in the form shown. Most modern composers are adept at combining smaller sections of today's orchestras for new sonorities and are also practised at combining them with exotic instruments drawn from other cultures, as well as electrically generated sound.

1	First violins	8	Oboes	15	Horns
2	Second violins	9	Cor anglais	16	Trumpets
3	Violas	10	Clarinets	17	Percussion
4	Cellos	11	Bass clarinets	18	Timpani
5	Double basses	12	Bassoons	19	Trombones
6	Piccolos	13	Double bassoons	20	Tubas
7	Flutes	14	Harps		

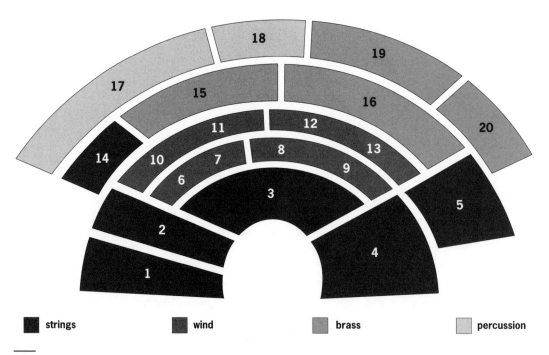

strings   wind   brass   percussion

GLOSSARY

a cappella – unaccompanied, usually singing but also solo passage in concerto or other instrumental work

aleatory music – music whose precise content and order has not been determined prior to performance, and where the final result is arrived at through the exercise of chance or through random procedures

allemande – dance type, usually moderate duple time, from Germany

anthem – derived from antiphon, and originally used to denote Anglican equivalent of Latin motet. Invariably written for whole choir to execute together

antiphon – originally a section of the Roman Catholic Divine Office in which verses or phrases are sung alternatively between two groups or choirs. Usually placed after the psalm or canticle. Latterly, a composition using the antiphon technique but divorced from plainsong origins

arpeggio – sounding the notes of a given chord in quick succession, usually ascending, although occasionally in descending order

atonal – literally, without tone. Usually used to denote music which is written without any tonal centre or key signature, as opposed to music written within the twelve-tone system, or using the notion of pan-tonality, where different tonal centres are implied in rapid succession

bel canto – (Italian, 'beautiful song'.) A distinct style and period of Italian operatic voice writing in the early 19th century in which lyrical, rather than declamatory melodic qualities are stressed. Later bel canto writing developed a distinct bravura aspect, where firm technique sometimes overrode pertinency to plot or character

binary – a piece of music comprised of two distinct sections

bitonality – the simultaneous use of two keys or scales

burden – recurring conclusion to verses or stanzas in ballad or song

cadence – (Italian for 'cadence') allied to speech patterns and sentence structure; a point in a harmonic progression or rhythmic pattern where the sequence comes to a natural pause or close

cadenza – (Italian, 'cadence') Latterly, a pause, usually at the end of a movement, whereby a soloist will ideally improvise unaccompanied through part of the movement's harmonic progression

canon – 1. The most basic type of polyphony or counterpoint, in which a line or 'part' is

begun, then an exact imitation of it is introduced after the passing of a number of beats so that a cycle of imitation is established. 2. A composer's entire output

cantabile – played or composed in a style imitating singing; lyrical, smooth

canticle – liturgical Bible song other than a psalm

cantilena – 1. Smooth lyrical vocal melodic writing. 2. In choral writing, the main melodic part

cantus – (Latin, 'song'). Used in Renaissance to identify top or 'lead' line in choral works

cantus firmus – (Latin, 'fixed song'.) Pre-existing melody used by Medieval and Renaissance composers as the basis for a new polyphonic work, usually sacred in nature, thereby supplying the basic structure or character for a composition

chaconne – French; originally a dance form closely related to the passacaglia; initially music in triple metre, constructed around a repeating ground bass melody. Later developments dispensed with the ground bass

chance music – 20th-century development adopted from fine art practitioners in the Dada and Surrealist movements where predetermined elements are then selected purely according to chance (the throw of a dice, the landing of torn pieces of paper) to determine the ultimate shape of a piece of music

chromatic – 1. Interval of a half-tone. 2. Type of scale comprising 12 ascending or descending half-tone steps within a given octave. 3. Chromatic chord; incorporates notes not falling in given key of passage

coloratura – elaborate, often spectacular embroidering of a melody, usually but not exclusively associated with bel canto opera

concerto – Italian; concerted performance, originally a quasi-antiphonal work contrasting and blending a solo instrument with a larger group, although Bach later wrote concertos for single instruments. Developed into a three-movement form

concerto grosso – orchestral music developed in Italy in 18th century in which the concerted dialogue takes place between different sized groupings of the orchestra

consort – alternative medieval spelling of concert; can refer to both a performance by a group or to the group itself, often one comprised of the same family of instruments, i.e. consort of viols

continuo – developed from basso continuo, or continuous accompanying bass figure, often doubling the lowest vocal part in a score

counterpoint – analogous to polyphony, counterpoint is the simultaneous playing of two or more parts which possess musical coherence both separately and combined

courante – lively French dance popular in 17th century

development – important compositional technique. The recasting or transforming of a previously heard musical motif or idea in a way that preserves the continuity and coherence of the overall composition. In traditional sonata or symphonic form the development usually follows the exposition

descant – 1. Type of organum or early church part-writing. 2. Extemporized melody sung in contrast to set part. 3. Soprano line or part in choral music. 4. Part-music itself

diatonic – type of scale which comprises eight notes made up of whole tone and half-tone steps through the octave. Each shift in the order of these steps results in a different scale or key

divertissement – French form of divertimento; originally an amusing collection of songs, dances and entertainments, often found within other theatrical or courtly works

dodecaphony – system of twelve-tone organization of music

exposition – the first appearance of the initial theme or subject; in sonata form most commonly falling in the first movement or at the outset of the piece.

fantasia – originally an instrumental imitation of the motet, the fantasia (also French 'fantasie' and German 'fantaisie') later became: 1. A work in which form takes second place to free-ranging expression of ideas and emotions. 2. A quasi-improvisatory development of a known theme or themes

fauxbourden – (French; English, 'faburden'); false bass. 1. fixed parts in plainsong melody accompaniment. 2. Later, any added parallel part. 3. Occasionally, such a part applied to a melody which is not plainsong. 4. Bass drone, similar to that produced by drone instruments. 5. Later, freely-written additional soprano part to hymn

figure – basic musical cell or theme used for musical development

form – the musical equivalent of a building's architectural structure; the overall shape and underlying design of a work

fugue - a type of contrapuntal composition where the separate voices (of any specified quantity) enter successively and complete the exposition before moving on to a variety of developmental techniques, all still in imitation, then perhaps moving on to further modulations, and so on until the end of the piece. A fugue is not so much a form as a compositional technique with any number of applications

galliard - medieval French in origin. Lively triple-time dance. Popular form for English Renaissance composers.

gamelan - type of Indonesian orchestra comprised of wooden percussion, woodwind, strings and brass chimes and gongs, formed to play traditional classical music of the region

gigue - (French 'jig'.) A lively dance style

grand opéra - French, originating in time of Lully. Epic, mythological or historical subject, treated in sumptuous style, incorporating a ballet and chorus

ground - also ground bass, A theme or short pattern which persists through the harmonic structure of a piece. Derived from cantus firmus

harmonics - as distinct from harmony, the harmonics are the upper or secondary resonations, often called 'overtones', which give each note an instrument plays its characteristic timbre

harmony - 1. The simultaneous playing or sounding of any two or more notes. 2. The study of the 'vertical' organization (also known as the tonal structure) of any given piece of music

homophony - literally, 'same sound'. Music where a single part or melody.is supported by other parts moving in the same melodic and rhythmic fashion

intermezzo - Italian; originally an entertainment inserted into a larger, more serious theatrical work. Later became a popular genre of its own. In 19th century became interchangeable with interlude, an instrumental insert into a larger work

interval - the distance in pitch between two given notes

inversion - literally, turning upside down—of chord, melody, motif or interval. Retrograde inversion is where a section of music is turned upside down and played backwards

key - successor to mode. The identifying name given to a particular scale used as the harmonic basis (tonality) for a work or a passage

legato - a type of playing. Opposite of staccato, a blending of one note into another in the execution of a phrase or passage

leitmotive - German; an ever-recurring theme in a work which in some way represents a leading characteristic of the work or, in opera, the character with which it is associated. Wagner, Berlioz and Richard Strauss all famously employed this device

lied(er) - associated with German-language song or songs from Middle Ages onwards, but most closely identified with post-Haydn compositions

madrigal - Italian; originally an unaccompanied secular composition for two or more voices. Later, instrumental accompaniment added, and form exported to many countries, especially 16th-century England.

maestro - 'master'. From Italian 'maestro di cappella', director of the chapel or courtly ensemble

marimba - percussive instrument made up of tuned wooden strips with resonators attached beneath, struck by mallets or sticks. African in origin; to West via Latin America

masque - Italian; developed by 17th-century English; a lavish private court entertainment using music, acting, dance, mime and elaborate dress. Reached a peak with Purcell, occasionally revived later

melisma - also melismatic. The using of a group of notes to sing a single syllable of text. Often associated with plainchant. Later with lieder and mélodie

mélodie - French equivalent of German lied

metre - a measure of recurring rhythmic succession or pulse. A further quantifying of rhythmic pattern

minstrel - (French, 'ménestrel'). Also jongleur. Professional medieval musicians, mostly recycling pre-existing melodies and lyrics, travelling from place to place

minuet - a dainty triple-time country dance which found wide popularity in 17th-century European courts, quickly becoming a standard movement in suites and later music forms

mode, modes, modal - 1. Scales of notes adopted by ancient Greeks and Romans from eastern practice for the ordering of their music, and which were the basis for all Western music until the end of the Middle Ages. Originally there were eight medieval modes, latterly twelve. 2. Description of the two methods of creating scales—major mode and minor mode

modulate - to move between one scale or key and another through harmonic progression during the course of a composition

monophony - literally, one sound. Music which has one single part or melody simultaneously played or sung by several people

motet - originally, brief unaccompanied sacred choral work, commonly using a cantus firmus and sacred text to which polyphonous melodies and words are added. Later, a wholly original work for between one and eight voices, even with accompaniment, and occasionally secular words

motif - type of musical theme. The shortest coherent musical figure.

motoric - description of mechanical or relentless rhythm, usually to be found in modern compositions

motto - a recurring theme, often in different contexts

musique concrète - music utilizing natural or man-made 'found' sounds. Idea evolved in post-war France and later taken up worldwide, often with electronic accompaniment

octave - interval of eight notes, measured according to Western (diatonic) scales. Starting note and finishing note share the same identifying letter

ondes martenot - early (1922) electrical instrument named after its French inventor, Maurice Martenot, capable only of a single note at a time. Used by a number of pre-war French composers

opera buffa - originally an opera dealing with everyday life and characters; quickly became identified as comic opera with its own formal properties

opéra comique - French comic opera arising from the success of opera buffa but not of the same lineage and also separate from operetta. Usually (but not invariably) dealing light-heartedly with a subject and often incorporating spoken dialogue

opera seria - (Italian, 'serious opera'.) A 17th-century genre of great formal complexity which aided development of elaborate set-piece arias, while its structure incorporated long stretches of recitative alternating with sung passages. After Mozart, the genre withered with the rise to popularity of opera buffa

ostinato - repeating and unchanging rhythm or phrase, e.g. basso continuo

part - (French, 'partie', 'voix'; German, 'stimme', 'part') 1. Single line of notes performed by any singer, instrument or grouping. 2. Section or division of larger work. 3. Assigned music from which a performer works in a score

passacagalia - music utilizing a ground bass (see chaconne)

pavane - (French; English, 'pavan'; Italian, 'pavana'.) Stately 16th–century Italian dance in duple time which was later adopted enthusiastically by English Renaissance composers and enjoyed revival in 19th–century French music.

plainsong - (Latin, 'cantus planus'.) An unaccompanied vocal melodic line delivered outside of metres, closely associated with traditional music of early Western Christian Church

polyphony - literally, several or many sounds. Used in music to describe a work in which any number of separate and simultaneous parts, vocal or instrumental, are combined

polyrhythm - the simultaneous employment of any number of different rhythms or metres

polytonality - the simultaneous usage of more than one key or scale

praeludium - Latin, 'prelude'

programme music - music written to an extra-musical story or theme, or illustrating a concept

quartertone - interval of half a semitone, uncatered for in traditional Western notation but found widely in other classical musics

recapitulation - restating, often in modified form, of work's or movement's initial themes

recitative - device used to advance the plot of early operas whereby expressive or declamatory spoken dialogue (and occasionally narrative) is delivered, usually with sparse accompaniment. Later elaborated to the point where it was absorbed into overall opera fabric

responsorio - a type of motet in which responsive singing between soloist and choir predominates

rondo - (Italian, 'round'.) A composition type whereby a section recurs at varying times, thereby establishing the work's form

sarabande - stately dance, originally in Latin America and much livelier; to Europe via Spain in 17th century

salon music - music suitable for playing in a 19th-century salon. Usually light, perhaps sentimental in nature

scherzo - literally, 'joke', 'fun'. The lighter movement of a work, often in 4/4 time, though the humour can often be dark in nature

scordatura - a novel or abnormal tuning arrangement of a stringed instrument

semitone - an interval of a half-tone. A single step of the chromatic scale

serial music - also serialism, serial technique. Term describing the musical practices which arose from the twelve-tone or dodecaphonic method of composition as espoused by Schoenberg. So named after the note series devised by him as a basic structural device. Later expanded into time and duration by Messiaen, Boulez and others

siciliano - a Sicilian country dance and song type in quadruple time

singspiel - (German, 'song-play'.) An 18th-century type of drama with music which usually had a light or comic subject and used spoken dialogue. Related to opéra comique

sonata - a composition, normally for no more than two instruments. Originally meant anything not sung. Later evolved typically into a three-movement work using different dance rhythms for each movement. More recent sonatas have often been formulated in sections rather than movements

sprechtstimme, sprechgesang - German; a type of vocal delivery using elements of both speech and song and hovering between the two

stimme - (German.) 1. Human voice. 2. Single part in composition

syncopation - a rhythmic device whereby the rhythmic stresses of a melody are moved from strong to weak beats, the accentuation falling at unexpected places and generally irregular, creating additional rhythmic interest

tarantella - Spanish; a fast dance in 5/8 metre

ternary - a piece of music comprised of three sections

third - an interval in the scale. Counting from first note, three steps upwards. Depending on the scale, the third will be major, minor or diminished

through-composed - originally a type of song where the music continually evolves, rather than repeats according to the stanza. Later applied to all types of composition as a term of approval

timbre - quality of tone, or colour, dictated by the specific harmonics given off by each instrument or voice

trio - 1. Any body of three performers. 2. The middle section of a march, minuet or scherzo, its name derived from the three part harmony originally used in such a section

tritone - the interval of the augmented fourth (occasionally called flatted fifth), made up of three whole tones. In medieval and Renaissance times its use was prohibited, being associated with the devil. Often used to suggest evil in film and theatre music today. Seen as a useful compositional building-block by serialists as it falls in the middle of the chromatic scale

troubadours - also trouvères. French medieval artists who composed or found songs, stories and poems which they then performed. Often aristocratic, troubadours were based in the south of France and used Provençal language. Trouvères lived further north, their language becoming modern French. Served as a model for the German variants, the Minnesinger and the latter Meistersinger

twelve-tone - also twelve note, or dodecaphony. System of tonal organization adapted by Schoenberg after dispensing with key signatures and atonality. Schoenberg advocated treating all twelve notes of the chromatic scale equally in harmonic terms, using a predetermined sequence in a strict order, with no repetition before the whole tone-row has been used. In practice, Schoenberg often broke his own rules

verismo - name given to Italian opera movement imitating the so-called 'realism' of the novel after Zola, and typified by Mascagni's *Cavalleria Rusticana*

vibraphone - in the family of the marimba and xylophone, it uses tuned metal bars which are sounded by mallets and electrically amplified

virelai - originally from Spanish but adopted and developed in France. A type of medieval French song, alternating stanza with refrain.

xylophone - instrument comprised of tuned wooden bars sounded when struck by mallets

zarzuela - Spanish operatic genre with origins in 17th-century Spanish courts. Revived in 19th century in a form not dissimilar to operetta, but imbued with Spanish character and musical style and often serious in subject

INDEX

Abandon d'Ariane, L', Op. 98
  (Milhaud) 323
Abendblätter (Offenbach) 175
Abraham and Isaac (Stravinsky) 300
Abu Hassan (Weber) 117
Academia Granados 256
Achilleus, Op. 50 (Bizet) 190
Aci, Galatea e Polifemo (Handel) 84
Acis et Galatée (Lully) 55
acoustics, instrumental 382
Ad Matrem (Gorecki) 385
Adagio
  for Strings, Op. 11 (Barber) 357
  in G minor (Att. Albinoni) 71
  Kodály 294
Adam, Adolphe: Delibes and 185
Adame Miroir (Milhaud) 324
Adams, John 375, **395–7**, *396*
Adelia (Donizetti) 126
Adelson e Salvini (Bellini) 134
Adieux, Les (Beethoven) 112
Adler, Guido 302
Adone (Monteverdi) 43
Adorno, Theodore 375
Adriano in Siria (Pergolesi) 93
Aegyptische Helena, Die
  (R. Strauss) 244–5
Aeneid (Virgil) 138
Africaine, L' 120–1
Age of Anxiety, The symphony
  (Bernstein) 370
Age of Enlightenment 91
Aglavaine et Sélysette (Honegger) 318
Agnus Dei (Penderecki) 386
Agon (Stravinsky) 299
Agoult, Countess Marie d' 151, 152
Agrippina (Handel) 84
Ahna, Pauline de 243
Aida (Verdi) 155, 223
airs 62, 64, 65
Akathist of Thanksgiving
  (Taverner) 395
Akhnaten (Glass) *374*, 393
Aladdin (Nielsen) 249
Alba, Duchess of 256
Albéniz, Isaac 215, 227–8, 287
Albert, Prince 143, 158, 162
Albert Herring (Britten) 363
Albinoni, Tomaso 51, **69–71**, *70*
Albrecht V of Bavaria, Duke 29
Album für die Jugend, Op. 66
  (Schumann) 149
Alcain, Hermine de 162
Alceste: Gluck 97
  Lully 55
Alcide (de la Motte/Marais) 61
Alcidiane (Lully) 54
Alcyone: Marais 61
  Ravel 283
Aldeburgh Festival 349, 363–5
aleatory music 371, 378
  counterpoint 366
Aleko (Rachmaninov) 267, 268
Alessandro (Handel) 85
Alexander III, Tsar 210
Alexander Nevsky
  (Prokofiev/Eisenstein) 317
Alexander VIII, Pope 58
Alexander's Feast (Handel) 85
Alfano, Franco 226
Alfonso und Estrella
  (Schubert) 129, 152
Alger (Delibes) 185
Alimelek (Meyerbeer) 120
Allegro barbaro (Bartók) 292
Allen, Sir Hugh 343
Allinson, Francesca 344
Alma brasileira (Villa-Lobos) 309
Alma redemptoris
  (Maxwell Davies) 388
Almira (Handel) 84
Alone (Shostakovich) 351
Along an Overgrown Path
  (Janáček) 218
Already it is Dusk, Op. 62 (Gorecki) 385
Also Sprach Zarathustra, Op. 30 (R.
  Strauss) 243, 290
Alt-Rhapsody, Op. 53 (Brahms) 181
Altenberg Lieder, Op. 4 (Berg) 306
Altenberg, Peter 306
Alyssa (Ravel) 283

Amahl and the Night Visitors
  (Menotti) 358
Amar String Quartet (Hindemith) 324
Amarus (Janáček) 217
Amazing Fly, The (Martinu) 313
Amelia, Princess 94
Amen, Op. 35 (Gorecki) 384
American Ballet (New York) 298
American in Paris, An (Gershwin) 330
Amériques (Varèse) 301
Amico Fritz, L' (Mascagni) 241
Amleto (D. Scarlatti) 87
Amor brujo, El (Falla) 287–8
Amores de la Inés, Las (Falla) 287
'An die Musik' (Schubert) 128
An der schönen, blauen Donau
  (Strauss II) 175, 182
Anacréon (Rameau) 78
Andersen, Hans Christian 207, 315
Andrea Chénier (Mascagni) 242
Andreae, Doris 382
Andriessen, Louis 375
Anglebert, Jean-Baptiste-Henri d' 68
Anglebert, Jean-Henri d' 68
Anna Bolena (Donizetti) 125, 127
Années de Pèlerinage (Liszt) 153
Annunciation, The (Taverenr) 395
Annunzio, Gabriele D' 236
Anon in Love (Walton) 345
Another Green World (album) 392
Ansault, Marie-Anne 61
Ansermet, Ernest 309, 319
anthems 32, 33, 46, 62, 85
Antiche danze ed arie per liuto
  (Respighi) 289
Antigone (Honegger/Cocteau) 319
Antony and Cleopatra (Barber) 358
Anzalone, Antonia 65
Apaches, the 283, 284
Apollinaire 318, 331, 333
Apollon musagète (Stravinsky) 298
Apostles, The (Elgar) 220
Apothéose de Molière, L',' Op. 286
  (Milhaud) 324
Appalachia (Delius) 239
Appalachian Spring (Copland) 338
Apparition de l'église éternell
  (Messiaen) 355
Apparitions (Ligeti) 371
Arabella (R. Strauss) 245
Arabesk (Delius) 239
Aragon, Louis 333
Arányi, Jelly 292
Arbell, Lucy 205
Arcana (Varèse) 301
Archbishop Parker's Metrical Psalter 24
Arensky 260, 267
'Aria' of No. 5 for soprano and eight
  cellos (Villa-Lobos) 309
Ariadne auf Naxos (R. Surauss) 244
Arianna (Monteverdi) 41, 43
arias 43
  da capo form 67
  set-piece 91
Arias and Barcarolles (Bernstein) 370
Arie musicali per cantari
  (Frescobaldi) 44–5
Arlésienne, L' (Bizet) 189
Armenian Folksong and Dance
  (Khachaturian) 346
Armida (Rossini) 123
Armide: Gluck 98
  Lully 55
Ars Nova movement 10, 15, 16
Art de toucher le clavecin, L'
  (Couperin) 68
art-songs 39, 40
  Monteverdi's influence 42
  see also madrigals; motets
Artaserse (Gluck) 96
Artikulation (Ligeti) 371
As You Like It (Walton) 345
Ascension, L' (Messiaen) 355
Aschenrödel (Strauss II) 176
Association of Proletarian
  Composers 351
Astaire, Fred 330
At the Boar's Head, Op. 42 (Holst) 272
Atlántida (Falla) 288
Atmosphères (Ligeti) 371

Attaché d'ambassade, L' (Mehilac) 257
Atys (Lully) 55
'Au fond du temple saint' (Bizet) 188
Aubade for piano and 18 instruments
  (Poulenc) 332
Auber, Daniel François 183
Auden, W. H. 299, 300, 362, 363, 370,
  376, 380
Auer, Leopold 197
augmented fourth, use of 252
Aureliano (Rossini) 123
Auric, George 319, 322
  Poulenc and 331–2
Aus den sieben Tagen
  (Stockhausen) 383
Aus Italien (R. Strauss) 243
autobiographies 298, 324
Avalos, Donna Maria d' 37
Automne, L' (Albéniz) 228
Ave Maria (Holst) 270–1
Ave regina celorum (Dufay) 16
Ave verum corpus (K618) (Mozart) 109
Avellino, Prince of 92
Aventures de Mercure, Les (Satie) 255
Aventures du roi Pausole, Les
  (Honegger) 320
Aveuglé Dieu, L' (Janequin) 20
'azione scenica' 373

B flat Sonata (Liszt) 152, 153
B Minor Mass, BWV 232 (J. S. Bach) 82
Ba-ta-Clan (Offenbach) 162
Babi Yar symphony (Shostakovich) 353
Bacchanale (Cage) 360
Bach, Ambrosius 60
Bach, Anna Magdalena 81
Bach, Carl Philipp Emanuel 81, 91,
  93–5, *94*
  Hayden's study of 99
Bach, Jakob 79
Bach, Johann Christian 93
Bach, Johann Christoph 79–80, 91
  Pachelbel and 60
Bach, Johann Sebastian 49, 51, 76,
  79–82, *80*, 94, 103, 140, 211
  Honegger and 320
  influence of Vivaldi 72
  Mendelssohn and   os. 1–9 (Villa-
  Lobos) 309
Bagarre, La (Martinu) 312–13
Bagatela (Rodrigo) 342
bagatelles
  and Impromptus (Smetana) 167
  for string quartet, Op. 9
  (Webern) 303
Bal masqué, Le (Poulenc) 332
Balakirev, Mily 173, 177, 193, 196,
  197, 203, 210
  Glazunov and 246
Balázs, Béla 292
ballades/ballade style 146
  for flute, piano and string orchestra
  (Martin) 310
  Machaut 14
  Op. 10 (Brahms) 180
  Op. 19 (Fauré) 212
  style 10
ballets: Delibes' output 185–7
  see also opera-ballets and
  specific ballets
Ballets Russes *see* Diaghilev, Serge
Ballo in maschera, Un (Verdi) 155
Banalitées (Poulenc) 333
Banquet céleste, Le (Messiaen) 355
Banquet Music of Tafelmusik
  (Telemann) *see* Musique de table
Bar aux Folies-Bergère, Un (Manet)
  199
Barbaia, Domenico 123, 125, 134
Barber, Samuel 357, 357–8
Barbiere di Siviglia, Il (Rossini) 123
Barbirolli, Sir John 266
barcarolles 212
Bard, The, Op. 64 (Sibelius) 252
Bardac, Emma 212–13, 236
Barezzi, Antonio 155
Barezzi, Margherita 153
Bärmann, Heinrich 119, 120
Baroque style 34, 35, 43, 51, 58, 65,
  67, 69
  apotheosis 82

concertos 72
Barrabas (Ginastera) 368
Barraque, Jean 356
Bartered Bride, The (Smetana) 168
Barthori, Jane 331
Bartók, Béla 281, **290–3**, *291*,
  350–1, 365
  Kodály and 294
Bartos, Frantisek 217
Basle Chamber Orchestra 320
Bassariden, Die (Henze) 380
basso continuo 36, 51
Bastien und Bastienne (Mozart) 105
Bataille, La (Mass; Janequin) 20
Bathori, Jane 283
Battaglia di Legnano, La (Verdi) 154
Battle of Britain (Walton) 345
Baudelaire 282
Bauermeister, Mary 383
Bauernfeld, Eduard 129
Bavards, Les (Offenbach) 163
Bavaria, Elector of 58
Bayreuth, Prince of 75
Bazzini 223
Bduets, piano 189
Béatitudes, Les (Franck) 165
Beatrice di Tenda (Bellini) 135
Béatrice et Bénédict (Berlioz) 138–9
Beatrix Cenci (Ginastera) 368
Beatus vir (Gorecki) 384–5
Becker, Albert 251
Beecham, Sir Thomas 239, 240
Beethoven, Johann van 110
Beethoven, Ludwig van 67, 91,
  110, **110–13**
  death and funeral 130
  lessons from Haydn 101
  Liszt and 150
  Schubert and 129
  theme from Fifth Symphony 274
  Wagner and 158
Before a Southern Convent, Op. 20
  (Grieg) 207
Before and After Science (album) 392
Beggar's Opera (Gay) 85, 323, 340
bel canto style 125, 133
Belasco, David 225
Belfago (Respighi) 289
Belkis, Queen of Sheba (Respighi) 289
'Bell Song' (Delibes) 186
Bella dormente nel bosco, La
  (Respighi) 289
Belle et la Bête, La (Glass) 393
Belle Hélène, La (Offenbach) 163
Bellini, Vincenzo 133, *134*, **134–5**
  Glinka and 139
Bells, The (choral symphony)
  (Rachmaninov) 269
Belshazzar's Feast (Walton) 344
Benavente, Marquis 104
Benedictus (Tallis) 25
Benvenuto Cellini (Berlioz) 138, 152
Berberian, Cathy 376
Berceuse, Op. 16 (Fauré) 212
Berg, Alban 276, 281, 302, **304–7**,
  305, 350–1, 362
Berger fidèle, Le (Rameau) 79
Bergloit, Op. 42 (Grieg) 207
Berio, Luciano 375, *376*, **376–7**, 390
Berkely, Lennox 394
Berliner Messe (Pärt) 390
Berliner Requiem, Das (Weill) 340
Berlioz, Hector 133, **136–9**, *137*
  commission from Paganini 115
  Glinka and 139
  influence on Chabrier 200
  Smetana and 167
  Wagner and 158
Bernac, Pierre 332, 333
Bernhardt, Sarah 224–5
Bernstein, Leonard 335, 347, 356,
  368–70, *369*
Berry, Duke de 14
Bertrand, Aloysius 284
Bestiaire ou Cortège d'Orphée, Le
  (Poulenc) 331
Bewegung (Berio) 377
Berry 377
Bianca e Fernando (Bellini) 134
Biancji, Antonia 115
Biblical Songs, Op. 99 (Dvořák) 203
Biches, Les (Poulenc) 332

'Big Stuff' (Bernstein) 369
'Bilbao Song' (Weill) 340
Billy Arnold Band 322
Billy Budd (Britten) 364, 365
Billy the Kid (Copland) 337, 338
Bing, Rudolf 358
Bingen, Hildegard von *see* Hildegard von Bingen
Binyon, laurence 220
Birthday Address to the King (Purcell) 62
Birtwistle, Harrison 375, **386-7**
Bismarck, Count von 163
bitonality 322
Biyd Neel String Orchestra 362
Bizet, Georges 173, **187-90**, *189*
   Massenet and 204, 205
Bjornson, Bjornstjerne 207
Black Mask, The (Penderecki) 386
Black Pentacost (Mackay Brown) 388
Blackwood, Algernon 220
Blaue Mazur, Die (Lehár) 258
Blow, John 46, 62
Blue Danube waltz (Strauss II) *see An der schönen, blauen Donau*
Blue Monday (Gershwin) 329
blues/blue-notes, use of 285, 322, 329, 338, 349, 369
'Blumine' movement *see* First Symphony (Mahler)
Boccherini, Luigi 91, **102-4**, *103*
Boeuf sur le toit, Le (Milhaud) 322
Bohème, La (Puccini) 222, 224
Böhm, Georg 80
Böhm, Theodore 139
Boléro (Ravel) 285
Bologna, Jacopo de 10
Bolt, The (Shostakovich) 351
Bomarzo (Ginastera) 368
Bonaparte, Lucien 104
Bonaparte, Princess Mathilde 188
Bonne Chanson, La, Op. 61 (Faurée) 212-13
Bononcini 85
Bontempi, G. A. 48
Bordes, Charles 166
Boris Godunov (Mussorgsky) 194, 210
Borodin, Alexander 173, **176-8**, *177*, 208-9, 281
   Glazunov and 246
   influence of Glinka 140
   Tchaikovsky and 196
Borough, The (Britten) 363
Borová (Martinu) 313
Bosset, Vera de 299
Boston Symphony Orchestra 320, 333
Bouffar, Zulma 163
Bouffes-Parisiens 162, 185
Boulevard Solitude (Henze) 379-80
Boulanger, Nadia 330, 336-7, 392
Boulez, Pierre 356, 375, **377-9**, *378*, 382
Boult, Sir Adrian 265, 266
Bouquet (Martinu) 313
Bour, Ernest 384
Bourgeois Gentilhomme, Le
   Lully/Molière 55
   R. Strauss/Molière 244
Bourrée fantasque (Chabrier) 200
Boutique Fantasque, La (Respighi) 289
Bowie, David 392, 393
Bowyer, Richard 24
Boy Friend, The (Maxwell Davies) 388
Boy was Born, A (Britten) 362
Brahms, Johannes 152, 173, 176, *179*, **179-82**
   and Mahler 230
   Dvorák and 202
   influence on Bartók 290
   Lehár and 257
   visit to Schumann 149
   Wolf and 232-3
   Zemlinsky and 259
Brandenburg Concertos (J. S. Bach) 81
Brandenburgers in Bohemia, The (Smetana) 168
Brandt, Caroline 117
Bream, Julian 364, 381
Brecht, Bertolt 340
Breville, Pierre de 165
Bride of Lammermoor, The (Scott) 127
Bridge, Frank 361, 362
Brigands (Les Offenbach) *132*
Brigg Fair (Delius) 239
Briséïs (Chabrier) 200

British Broadcasting Corporation (BBC) 349
Britten, Benjamin 335, *361*, **361-5**, 392
   interest in Tallis 24
   works dedicated to 354, 389
Brno Organ School 217, 218
Broderson, Anne Marie 248
Brook Green Suite (Holst) 272
Brubeck, Dave 324
Bruch, Max 173, **190-2**, *191*, 289
   Vaughan Williams and 264
Bruckner, Anton 133, **169-71**, *170*
Brunswick, Duke of 39
Büchse der Pandora, Die (Wedekind) 307
Buda and Pest celebrations, works for 292, 295
Budsvári Te Deum (Kodály) 295
Bülow, Cosima von 152, 159
   see also Wagner, Cosima
Bülow, Hans von 152, 196, 243
Bürgschaft, Die (Weill) 340
Burgundy, Duc de 67
Burleske (R. Strauss) 243
Burmester, Willy 251
Burney, Dr 87, 95
Busch, Fritz 325
Busoni, Ferruccio 250-1, 339
   influence on Varèse 301
Buxtehude, Dietrich 80, 84
Byrd, William 23, *31*, **31-3**
   friendship with Tallis 24-5
Byron, Lord 197
   Ode to Napoleon Buonaparte 278
Byzantium (Tippett) 350

C minor Mass *(Great)* (K427) (Mozart) 109
Caccia, La (Vivaldi) 73
Cäcilienmesse in C (Haydn) 100
'Cádiz' (Albéniz) *see Suite española No. I*
Cadmus et Hermione (Lully) 55
Caduta de' Giganti, La (Gluck) 96
Cage, John 335, **358-60**, *359*, 371, 373, 375, 395
Calcium Light Night (Ives) 273
Caletti-Bruni, Gian Battista 52
Caligula (Fauré/Dumas) 212
Calisto, La (Cavalli) 53
'Calm Sea and Prosperous Voyage' (Goethe) 142
Calzabigi, Ranieri 97
Cambefort, Jean de 55
Cambert, Robert 55
Cambiale di matrimonio, La (Rossini) 122
Cambise (A. Scarlatti) 66
can-cans 257
Candide (Bernstein) 370
Canon and Gigue in D (Pachelbel) 60, 61
canon, use of 17, 25
cantatas 65, 67, 71, 74, 76, 78, 80, 82, 84, 120, 123, 124, 160, 185, 186, 187, 204, 217, 229, 240, 254-5, 283, 310, 344, 353, 365
   'profane' 332
   Profana (Bartók) 293
   amalgamated with ballet 297
   see also chamber cantatas
Stravinsky 299
Cantate de Noël, Une (Honegger) 320
Canticle of the Mother of God (Taverner) 394
Cantico Canticorum Salomons (Palestrina) 28
Canticum Novissimi Testamenti II (Berio) 377
Canticum Sacrum (Stravinsky) 300
Cantiones Sacrae (Tallis/Byrd) 25
Cantiones Sacre (Lassus) 30
Canto sospeso, Il (Nono) 373
cantus firmus 10, 16, 25, 45
Cantus in Memory of Benjamin Britten (Pärt) 389
Canyons aux étoiles, Des (Messiaen) 356
'Canzone' (Martinu) *see Toccata e due Canzoni*
Canzonetta, Op. 48 (Barber) 358
Canzonette a tre voci (Monteverdi) 41

canzoni 23, 44-5, 89
Caplet, André 283
Capriccio
   for chamber group (Janácek) 218
   for piano and orchestra (Stravinsky) 298
   Poulenc 333
   R. Strauss 245
Capriccio Espagnol (Rimsky-Korsakov) 210
Capriccio for cello (Henze) 381
Capriccio Italien (Tchaikovsky) 197
Capriccio Sinfonico (Puccini) 224
Capuleti ed i Montecchi, I (Bellini) 135
Caractacus, Op. 35 (Elgar) 220
Cardillac, Op. 39 (Hindemith) 325
Carissimi, Giacomo 56-7, 65, 84
Carl Alexander, Grand Duke 151
Carmen (Bizet) *172-3*, 188, 189-90, 196
   recitatives 187
Carmina Burana (Orff) 328
Carnaval d'Aix (Milhaud) 323
Carnaval de Londres, Le, Op. 172 (Milhaud) 323
Carneval in Rom, Der (Strauss I) 175
Carnival
   Op. 9 (Schumann) 149
   Op. 92 (Dvorák) 202
Carnival des Animaux (Saint-Saëns) 173, 184
Caroline Mathilde (Maxwell Davies) 389
Caroline, Queen: funeral of 85
Carré, Albert 236, 287
Caruso 226
Castor et Pollux (Rameau) 78, 79
Catalanes de Gracia (Albéniz) 228
Catalogue d'oiseaux (Messiaen) 356
Catalonia-suite populaire (Albéniz) 228
Catarina Carnaro (Donizetti) 126
Cathedral Music (Boyce) 46
Catone in Utica (Vivaldi) 74
Cattaneo, Claudia 41-2
Catulli Carmina (Orff) 328
Cavalleria Rusticana (Mascagni) 222, 239, 241, 242
Cavalli, Federico 52
Cavalli, Pietro Francesco 51, **52-3**, 56
Cave, The (Reich) 391
Cecil, Sir Robert: letter from Dowland 39
Celestial Country, The (Ives) 273
Cello Concerto
   Honegger 319
   Martin 311
   Op. 105 (Dvorák) 203
   Op. 58 (Prokofiev) 317
   Op. 85 (Elgar) 221
   Walton 345
Cello Sonatas, Opp. 109/117 (Fauré) 213
Cello Symphony (Britten) 364
Celtic Requiem (Taverner) 394
Cendrars, Blaise 323
Cenerentola, La (Rossini) 123
Central Park in the Dark (Ives) 274
Ceremony of Carols, A (Britten) 363
Cermákova, Anna 201
Cervantes 163
Cesi, Beniamino 251
Cetra, La, Op. 9 (Vivaldi) 73
Chabrier, Emmanuel 173, **198-200**
   influence on Albéniz 228
Chaconne in F (Purcell) 63
Chaliapin, Féodor 205, 210, 268
Chalupetzky, Henrietta (Jetty) 175
Chamber Concerto
   for 13 Instruments (Ligeti) 371
   for piano, violin and 13 wind instruments (Berg) 307
chamber music 51, 59, 66, 102, 127, 182, 212, 213, 218, 237, 285, 291, 312, 325
   Boccherini's output 103
   cantatas 79
   concerto 298
   Poulenc's output 332, 333
   use of jazz 323
chamber opera 271
chance-derived music *see* aleatory music
Chandos, Duke of 85
Chandos Anthems (Handel) 85
chansons 16, 18, 19-20, 23, 30, 54

Chansons gaillardes (Poulenc) 332
Chant des oyseaux, Le (Janequin) 19-20
Chantefleurs et Chantefables (Lutoslawski) 366
Char, René 378
Charles I 40
Charles I of Bourbon, Duke 16
Charles II 62, 63
Charles IX 29
Charles V 14
Charles VI, Emperor 73, 74
Charles VII 17
Charles VIII 17
Charles X, King: coronation 124
Charles de Navarre 14
Charles-René 282
Charpentier, Marc-Antoine 51, **56-7**
Chasseur maudit, Le (Franck) 165
Chausson, Ernest 165, 235
Chérubin (Massenet) 205
Cherubini 101, 119, 135, 136, 142, 145
Chézy, Helmina von 118, 130
Chicago Opera 316
Chicago Symphony Orchestra 296, 299
Chichester Psalms (Bernstein) 370
Chichester Service (Walton) 345
Child of Our Time, A (Tippett) 348
Children's Corner (Debussy) 237
Children's Radio Division 318
children, works for 220, 237, 291, 317, 318, 337, 340, 388
Choéphores (Milhaud) 322
Choeur de l'Université Populaire 300
Chopin, Frédéric 133, 135, *144*, 144-6, 151
   Liszt and 151
   Schumann on 147
Choral Fantasia
   Beethoven 112
   Op. 52 (Holst) 272
choral works 57, 60, 140, 148, 182, 190, 200, 218, 233, 239, 252, 264, 266, 271-2, 273, 293, 295, 310, 313, 320, 356, 373, 384-5, 389-90, 394
   Elgar's output 219-20
   prelude 358
   unaccompanied 302, 332-3, 384
   see also motets; oratorios
chord inversions, principle of 78
chords
   six-tone 262
   'synthetic' 262
chori spezzati technique 36
Chôros series (Villa-Lobos) 309
Christ on the Mount of Olives (Beethoven) 112
Christian IV of Denmark 39, 48
Christian Ludwig of Brandenburg, Duke 81
Christina of Sweden, Queen 58, 65
Christmas Eve (Rimsky-Korsakov) 210
Christmas Oratorio (J. S. Bach) 82
Christmas Story, The (Schütz) 48
Christnacht (Wolf) 233
Christus (Liszt) 152
chromaticism 38, 264, 302
Chroniques de Ma Vie (Stravinsky) 298
Chronochromie (Messiaen) 356
Cimarrón, El (Henze) 380
Cimento dell'armonia e dell'inventione, Il (Vivaldi) 73
Cincinatti Orchestra 338
Cinco Canciones populares argentinas, Op. 10 (Ginastera) 367
Cinderella
   Maxwell Davies 388
   Op. 87 (Prokofiev) 318
Cinesi, Le (Gluck) 96
Cinq Esquisses de danses modernes (Martinu) 312
Cinq Mélodies, Op.58 (Fauré) 212
Cinq Nocturnes for piano (Satie) 255
Circles (Berio) 377
circus music 319
'Clair de lune' (Debussy) 237
Clapping music (Reich) 391
Clarinet Concerto
   Copland 338
   Nielsen 249
   Opp.73/74 (Weber) 119
Clarinet Quintet
   K581 (Mozart) 109
   Op. 34 (Weber) 119
Clarinet Sonatas, Op. 120 (Brahms) 182

Classical style 227, 237, 274
  early 51
  Satie's distortion of 254
Claudel, Paul 321
Clement XI, Pope 66
Clement XII, Pope 89
Clementina, La (Boccherini) 103
Clemenza di Tito, La (K621) (Mozart)
  108, 109
Cléopâtre (Massenet) 205
Clo-Clo (Lehár) 258
Clock Symphony (Haydn) 102
Clocks and Clouds (Ligeti) 371-2
Cloud Messenger, The, Op. 30 (Holst)
  271
Clovis et Clotilde (Bizet) 187
Cobham, Sir Henry 39
Cocteau, Jean 254, 298, 312, 319, 322,
  323, 351, 379
  Poulenc and 331-3
Colbran, Isabella 123, 124
Colette 285
Collage on the Theme B-A-C-H
  (Pärt) 389
Collet, Henri 319, 322, 331
Colloredo, Archbishop of Salzburg 106
colour, expressing through music 356
colour piano 262
Coltrane, John 359
*Combattimento di Tancredi e Clorinda,
  II* (Monteverdi) 42-3
'Combattimento fra Tancredi e
  Clorinda' (Tasso) 89
Come Out (Reich) 390-1
Come ye sons of art away (Purcell) 64
Comedy on the Bridge (Martinu) 313
commissioned works 115, 266, 285-6,
  288, 295-6, 298, 299, 307, 310, 316,
  318, 319, 320, 327, 329, 330, 331-2,
  333, 337, 338, 341, 343, 345, 349,
  356, 357, 362-3, 364, 370, 381, 384,
  395
  for the Ballets Russes *see* Diaghilev,
    Serge
composition
  'atonal' 277
  'life-cycle' 350
  numerology in 382
computerized music 379
Comte Ory, Le (Rossini) 124
Concert champêtre (Poulenc) 332
concertante form 59-60
Concertgebouw Orchestra, 50th
  anniversary work 295-6
concerti 36, 65, 69-70, 71, 72-4,
  76, 81
  a cinque (Albinoni) 70
concerti grossi 58, 59-60, 65, 348
Concertino
  for Clarinet, Op. 26 (Weber) 119
  for piano and orchestra
    (Martinu) 313
  for Piano Trio and Orchestra, Op. 2
    (Martinu) 313
Concerto Accademico (Vaughan
  Williams) 265
Concerto da camera H196
  (Honegger) 320
Concerto for Cello (Lutoslawski) 366
Concerto for Cello and Orchestra
  Barber 357
  Pärt 389
Concerto for Clarinet in A (K622)
  (Mozart) 109
Concerto for Double String Orchestra
  (Tippett) 348
Concerto for Flute and Harp (K299)
  (Mozart) 109
Concerto for Harpsichord and String
  Orchestra, Op. 40 (Gorecki) 385
Concerto for Orchestra
  Bartók 293
  Kodály 296
  Lutoslawski 365
Concerto for Organ and Orchestra
  (Poulenc) 333
Concerto for Piano (Lutoslawski) 366
Concerto for Piano and Orchestra
  Copland 337
  Ligeti 371
  No. 3 (Beethoven) 111
  Tippett 349
Concerto for Piano and Orchestra
  Khachaturian 346
Concerto for Piano and Orchetra
  Cage 360, 365-6

Concerto for Piano and Wind
  Instruments (Stravinsky) 298
Concerto for Piano in E flat (Liszt) 138
Concerto for Piano, Trumpet and
  Strings, Op. 35 (Shostakovich) 351
Concerto for Piano (left-hand) and
  Orchestra in D Major (Ravel) 285-6
Concerto for Seven Wind instruments
  (martin) 311
Concerto for Two Pianos and Orchestra
  (Poulenc) 332
Concerto for two solo pianos
  (Stravinsky) 298
Concerto for Two Violins, Op. 49
  (Holst) 272
Concerto for Violin
  in D, Op. 35 (Tchaikovsky) 197
  No. 1 in G minor (Bruch) 173, 191
  No. 1 in G minor, Op. 26 (Bizet) 191
  No. 2, Op. 44 (Bizet) 191
Concerto for Violin and Orchestra
  Adams 397
  Barber 357
  Britten 362
  in D minor (Khachaturian) 347
  Ligeti 371
Concerto for Violin and Wind
  Orchestra (Weill) 339
Concerto for Violin, Cello and
  Orchestra, Op. 102 (Brahms) 182
concerto form 51, 89, 91, 95
Concerto Gregoriano for violin
  (Respighi) 289
Concerto Grosso (Vaughan
  Williams) 266
Concerto in F for piano and orchestra
  (Gershwin) 330
Concerto No. 11 in F (K413)
  (Mozart) 109
Concerto-Cantata for flute and
  orchestra (Gorecki) 385
concertos
  'choreographic' 332
  cello 102, 103, 308
  flute/oboe 109
  Milhaud's output 323
  Penderecki's output 385
  piano 109, 112, 148, 149, 310, 313
    commissioned 333
  viola 293
  violin 115-16, 183
  see also specific names
Concierto (Rodrigo's)
  andaluz 343
  de Aranjuez 342
  de estio 342
  madrigal 342
  para una fiesta 343
  serenata 343
Concord, Mass. (Ives) 274
'Concordia' Ball waltzes 175
conductus 9
Connotations (Copland) 338
consort song 33
Constantine, Grand Duke 144, 209
Contes d'Hoffmann, Les
  (Offenbach) 164
contrapuntal polyphony 18, 36, 45
contrapuntal techniques 38, 48, 62-3
Contrasts for Piano, Violin and Clarinet
  (Bartók) 293
*Conversione di San Guglieme
  d'Aquitania, La* (Pergolesi) 92
Cooke, Captain Henry 62
Copland, Aaron 335, 336, 336-8, 367
Coppélia (Delibes) 173, 185-6, 187
Corelli, Arcangelo 51, 58-60, 59, 66,
  89, 313
  Couperin on 68
  Handel and 84
  Tartini and 88
  tercentenary celebrations 349
Cornaro, Cardinal Giorgio 88
Coronation Mass (K317) (Mozart) 109
Coronation Te Deum (Walton) 345
Corps glorieux, Les (Messiaen) 355
Corregidor, Der (Wolf) 234
Corsaire, Le (Adam) 185
Cortège burlesque (Chabrier) 199
Cortège funèbre (Milhaud) 324
Coryat, Thomas 36
Cosi fan tutte (K588) (Mozart) 108, 109
Costanzi, Giovanni Batista 102
Cotswold Symphony, The, Op. 8
  (Holst) 271
counterpoint 25, 42, 51

English tradition 20
  Villa-Lobos's use of 309
Country Band March (Ives) 274
Couperin, Charles 67
Couperin, François 51, 61, 67-9, 68
  Debussy and 237
  J. S. Bach and 80
Couperin, François (son) 67
Couperin, Louis 67
Couperin, Marguerite-Antoinette 67
Cowell, Henry 359
Crabbe, George 363
Craft of Musical Composition, The
  (treatise) (Hindemith) 326
Craft, Robert 299, 300
Création du Monde, La (Milhaud) 323
Creation, The (Haydn) *see
  Schöpfung, Die*
Credo (Pärt) 389
Crémieux, Henri 162
'Cries of London' (Gibbons) 46
Cris du Monde (Honegger) 320
Croce, Giovanni 39
Crociato in Egitto, II (Meyerbeer)
  120, 124
Cromwell, Thomas 21
Cunning Little Vixen, The (Janácek) 218
Curlew River (Britten) 364-5
Cygne, Le (Saint-Saëns) 184
Cynara (Delius) 240
Czar has his Photograph Taken, The
  (Weill) 340
Czech Suite (Dvorák) 202
Czerny, Karl 149-50

Dadaism 254
Dafne (Schütz) 47
Dalibor (Smetana) 168
Dallapiccola, Luigi 376
Dallas Symphony Orchestra 327
Damicourt, Catherine 61
Damnation de Faust, Le (Berlioz) 138
Damrosch, Walter 330, 337
Damsel in Distress, A (Gershwin) 330
Danaides, Les (Gluck) 95
Dança frenética (Villa-Lobos) 308-9
Danças caracteristicas africanas (Villa-
  Lobos) 308
dance music/dance suites 23, 39-40,
  44-5, 54, 65, 78, 76, 109, 174,
  270, 273, 283, 322, 326
  national styles 146, 295
    Armenian 347
  see also specific dances
Dance Panels (Copland) 338
Dance Suite (Bartók) 292
Dance Symphony (Copland) 336
Dances (Kodály's)
  of Galánta 295
  of Marosszék 295
Danse des Morts, La (Honegger) 320
Danse macabre (Saint-Saëns) 184
Dante symphony (Liszt) 153
Danzas Argentinas, Op. 2
  (Ginastera) 367
Danzi, Franz 117
Daphne (R. Strauss) 245
Daphnis et Chloé (Ravel) 284-5
Daquin, Louis Claude: on Couperin 68
Daudet, Alphonse 189
David et Jonathas (Charpentier) 57
David Rizzio (Massenet) 204
Death in Venice (Britten) 365
Death of Klinghoffer, The
  (Adams) 396-7
Debussy, Claude 173, 199, 235-7, 282,
  283, 287, 309
  Boulez' recordings 378
  influence of Couperin 69
  influence on Honegger 318
  influence on Varèse 301
  on Chabrier 200
  on Palestrina 25
  Saint-Saëns and 184
  Satie and 254
Dehmel, Richard 276, 302
Dehn, Siegfried 140
Delibes, Léo 173, 185-7, 186
Delicious (Gershwin) 330
Delius, Frederick 238, 238-40
Déliverance de Thésée, La, Op. 99

(Milhaud) 323
Deller, Alfred 364
Delsart, François 187
*Déploration sur le trépas de Jean
  Ockeghem* (Desprez) 17
Derr Herr ist König (Pachelbel) 60
Descente d'Orphée aux enfers, La
  (Charpentier) 57
Descriptions automatiques (Satie) 254
Desert Islands (Prokofiev) 315
Déserts (Varèse) 301
Desprez, Josquin *see* Josquin Desprez
Destiny (Janácek) 217-18
Detmold, Count of 180
Deutsch, Adele 176
Deutsches Requiem (Brahms) 181
Deux sous de charbon (Saint-Saëns)
  185
Devil's Trill sonata (Tartini) 88
Devil's Wall, The (Smetana) 169
Devils, The (Maxwell Davies) 388
Devils of Loudon, The (Penderecki)
  385-6
Diaghilev, Serge 236, 254, 284-5, 288,
  309, 321, 326
  Poulenc and 332
  Prokofiev and 315, 316
  rejected Walton score 343-4
  Stravinsky and 296-7, 298
Dialogues des Carmélites, Les
  (Poulenc) 333
Diary of one who disappeared, The
  (Janácek) 218
Dido and Aeneas (Purcell) 64
Dies Irae: Berlioz' use of 137
Dietrich, Angela (Lili) 175-6
Different Trains (Reich) 391
diminished second, use of 252
Dimitrij (Dvorák) 202
Dioclesian (Purcell/Fletcher/Dryden) 64
dissonance, Milhaud's experiments
  in 322
Divertimento
  Bartók 293
  on 'Sellinger's Round' (Tippett) 349
divertissements 78, 98
Dives and Lazarus (Vaughan Williams)
  263, 266
Djamileh (Bizet) 188-9
Djinns, Les (Franck) 165
Docteur Miracle, Le (Bizet) 187
dodecaphony/dodecaphonic theory
  215, 278-9, 303, 359, 365, 368, 379,
  382, 389
  treatises on 278
Dohnányi, Ernö 292, 295
  influence on Bartók 290
Dolly, Op. 56 (Fauré) 173
Dom Sebastien (Donizetti) 126
Domaines (Boulez) 379
Don Carlos (Verdi) 155
Don Giovanni (K527) (Mozart) 107,
  109, 230
Don Juan, Op. 20 (R. Strauss) 243
Don Pasquale (Donizetti) 126, 127
Don Procopio (Bizet) 187
Don Quichotte (Massenet) 205
Don Quixote
  Op. 35 (R. Strauss) 243
  Part III (Purcell) 64
Don Rodrigo (Ginastera) 368
Don Sanche (Liszt) 150
Dona nobis pacem (Vaughan
  Williams) 266
Donaueschingen Festival 325
Donizetti, Gaetano 124-7, 125, 133
  Glinka and 139
Donna del lago, La (Rossini) 123
Donnerstag aus Licht (Stockhausen)
  383
Dos Canciones, Op. 3 (Ginaster) 367
Double Concerto
  for Flute, Oboe and Strings
    (Ligeti) 371
  for two string orchestras, piano and
    timpani (Martinu) 313
Dowland, John 38-40
Dowland, Robert 40
Down by the Greenwood Side
  (Birtwistle) 387
Down in the Valley (Weill) 341
Dowson, Ernest 239
'drama with music' *see* 'music-drama'
Dream Children (Elgar) 220
Dream of Gerontius, The, Op.38 (Elgar)
  220, 344

Drei Orchesterstücke, Op. 6 (Berg) 306
Drei Pintos, Die (Weber) 118
Drei Volkstexte, Op. 17 (Webern) 303
Dreigroschenoper, Der (Weill) 340
Dreispitz, Der (Wolf) 234
Drum Roll Symphony (Haydn) 102
Drumming (Reich) 391
Dryden, John 64
Duboef, Estelle 139
Duchamp, Marcel 335, 360
Dufay, Guillaume 10, *15*, **15–16**, 28
Dufy, Raoul 322
Dukas, Paul 287, 342, 355
Duke Bluebeard's Castle (Bartók) 292
Dumbarton Oaks chamber concerto
  (Stravinsky) 298
Dunstable, John 15, 51
Duo concertante for violin and piano
  (Stravinsky) 298
Duo for Flute and Piano (Copland) 338
Duomo, Florence: dimensions 16
Dupont, Gaby 236
Dupré, Marcel 355
Durazzo, Count 97
Dürbach, Fanny 195
Durey (composer) 319
Dushkin, Samuel 298
Duval, Denise 333
Dvořák, Antonín **200–3**, *201*, 281, 313
  Janáček and 216
  Lehár and 257

Earth Dances (Birtwistle) 387
Easter Historia (Schütz) 47
Eastern music, influence of 356, 364,
  383, 392
  see also under orchestra
Eberst, Isaac Juda 161
Ebony Concerto (Stravinsky) 299
Echo et Narcisse (Gluck) 98
Eckstein, Friedrich 233
Eclairs sur l'au-dela... (Messiaen)
  356
Ecole amante, L' (Cavalli) 53, 54–5
Ecuatorial (Varèse) 301
Edgar (Puccini) 224
Edinburgh Festival 349
Edipo Re (Leoncavallo) 223
Education manquée, Une
  (Chabrier) 199
Edward VI 24
Egdon Heath, Op. 47 (Holst) 272
Egisto, L' (Cavalli) 53
Eichendorff settings (Wolf) 233
Eight Poems of Emily Dickinson
  (Copland) 338
Eight Songs for a Mad King (Maxwell
  Davies) 388
Eighth Symphony
  Op. 88 (Dvořák) 202
  Unfinished (Schubert) 129
  Vaughan Williams 266
Eine Alpensinfonie (R. Strauss) 244
Eine kliene Nachtmusik (K525)
  (Mozart) 109
Eine Nacht in Venedig (Strauss II) 176
Einstein on the Beach (Glass) 393
electronic music 371, 373, 376, 383
  aleatory 378
  tape recorder 301, 390, 396
  with boy's voice 382–3
Elégie
  Op. 24 (Fauré) 212
  Poulenc 333
Elektra (R. Strauss) 244
Elegy
  for JFK (Stravinsky) 300
  for violin and piano
    (Martinu) 312
  for Young Lovers (Henze) 380
  'to our Forefathers, An' 274
Elgar, Edward 215, *219*, **219–21**
Elijah (Mendelssohn) 143
Elisa of Lucca and Piombo, Princess
  114–15
Elisabetta, Regina d'Inghilterra
  (Rossini) 123
Elizabeth I 25
Elizabeth, Princess 364
Eller, Heino 389
Elsener, Joseph 144
Eluard, Paul 333
Emanationen (Penderecki) 385
Embryons desséchés (Satie) 254
Emperor Jones, The (Villa-Lobos) 310

Emperor piano concerto
  (Beethoven) 112
Endlich Allein (Lehár) 258
Enfance du Christ, L' (Berlioz) 204
Enfant et les sortilèges, L' (Ravel) 285
Enfant prodigue, L' (Milhaud) 322
English Cat, The (Henze) 381
English Country Songs (collection) 263
English Hymnal 264
Enigma Variations (Elgar) *see*
  Variations on an Original Theme
Enlèvement d'Europe, L', Op. 94
  (Milhaud) 323
Eno, Brian 392, 393
Enrico Clifford (Albéniz) 228
'entertainments' 78, 343
Entfliehit auf leichten Kähnen, Op. 2
  (Webern) 302
Entführung aus dem Serail, Die (K384)
  (Mozart) 107, 109
Epic of Gilgamesh (Martinu) 314
Ercole I 18
Erdgeist (Wedekind) 307
'Erlkönig, Der' (Schubert) 127–8, 129
Ermione (Rossini) 123
Ernani (Verdi) 152, 154
Ernst August, Duke 81
Erwartung, Op. 17 (Schoenberg) 277
Es war einmal (Zemlinsky) 259
Escape Me Never (Walton) 344
Escenas románticas (Granados) 256
Esmérelda (Massenet) 204
España
  Albéniz 227–8
  Chabrier 199–200
Essays for Orchestra (Barber) 357, 358
Essercizi per Gravicembalo
  (D. Scarlatti) 87
Essipov, Annette 315
Estampes (Debussy) 237
Estancia (Ginastera) 367
Este, Alfonso II d,' Duke of Ferrara
  27, 37
Este, Cardinal Ippolito d' 27
Este, Donna Eleonore d' 37–8
Esterházy, Count Johann 128
Esterházy, Nicholas 100–1
Esterházy, Prince Paul 100
Esther de Carpentras (Milhaud) 323
Estro armonico, L' Op. 3 (Albinoni) 70,
  72, 74
Etoile, L' (Chabrier) 173
Etoile du nord, L' (Meyerbeer) 121
Eton Choirbook 20
étude(s) 145
  d'exécution transcendante d'après
    Paganini (Liszt) 151, 153
  Debussy 236, 237
  for piano and orchestra
    (Milhaud) 322
  in C minor, Op. 10, No. 12
    (Chopin) 145
  in C sharp minor (Scriabin) 260
  Op. 43 (Scriabin) 261
  Op. 65 (Scriabin) 263
Etudes-tableaux, Op. 33
  (Rachmaninov) 269
Eugene Onegin (Pushkin)
  Prokofiev 317
  Tchaikovsky 197
Euntes Ibant et Flebant, Op. 32
  (Gorecki) 384
Euryanthe (Weber) 118
'eurythmics' 327
Eva (Lehár) 258
Eve (Massenet) 204
'events', multimedia 360
'everyday' music 325–6
Everyman (Hoffmannsthal) 311
Excursions of Mr Braucek, The
  (Janáček) 218
Expecto resurrectionem mortuorum, Et
  (Messiaen) 356
Exsultate, jubilate (K165) (Mozart) 109
extemporisations 82, 83, 95, 142

4 Madrigales amatorios (Rodrigos) 342
4 Verses of Captain Lebyadkin, Op. 146
  (Shostakovich) 354
44 Duos for violins (Bartók) 293
5 Piezas infantiles (Rodrigo) 342
F minor Piano Sonata, Op. 5
  (Brahms) 180
F sharp Sonata, Op. 2 (Brahms) 180
Fabbrica illuminata, La (Nono) 373
Façade (Walton) 343

Facsimile (Bernstein) 369–70
Fairfax, Robert 20
Fairy Queen, The (Purcell) 64
Fairy Tale (Janáček) 218
Fairy's Kiss, The (Stravinsky) 298
Fall of Berlin, The (Shostakovich) 353
Falla, Manuel de 281, 283, *286*,
  286–8, 322
Falstaff (Verdi) 156
Fanciulla del West, La (Puccini) 225–6
Fancy Free (Bernstein) 369
Fanfare for the Common Man
  (Copland) 338
Fantasia
  on 'Greensleeves' (Vaughan Williams)
    265
  on a Theme of Handel (Tippett) 348
  on a Theme of Thomas Tallis (Vaughan
    Williams) 24, 265
  on Christmas Carols (Vaughan
    Williams) 265
Fantasia and Fugue in G minor, BWV
  542 (J. S. Bach) 82
Fantasia bética (Falla) 288
*Fantasia Concertante on a Theme by
  Corelli* (Tippett) 349
'fantasia extraodinaire' for orchestra
  (Chabrier) *see España*
Fantasia para un gentilhombre
  (Rodrigo) 342
fantasias/fantasies 24, 46, 62–3, 65,
  191, 196, 243, 252, 348
  comic 173
Fantasias for Strings (Purcell) 62
Farewell to St Petersburg, A
  (Glinka) 140
Farkas, Ferenc 371
Fasch, C. F. C. 94
'Father of English Cathedral Music' *see*
  Tallis, Thomas
'Father of German music', the *see*
  Schütz, Heinrich
Fau, Lancelot du 19
Fauré, Gabriel *211*, **211–13**, 284
  Ravel and 283
  Saint-Saëns and 183, 212
Faust (Gounod) 160
Faust symphony (Liszt) 153
fauxbourdon 10, 25
Favorita, La (Donizetti) 126
Fearful symmetries (Adams) 396
Feast during the Plague, The
  (Prokofiev) 315
Feen, Die (Wagner) 157
Fenby, Eric 240
Fennimore and Gerda (Delius) 239, 240
Feodorovna, Tatiana 262
Ferdinandová, Bettina 168
Fermier, Marie 212
Feste romane (Respighi) 289
festival of the Domaine Musical 378
festivals *see specific festivals*
Festive Overture (Shostakovich) 353
Fêtes d'Hébé, Les (Rameau) 78
Fêtes de l'Amour et de Bacchus, Les
  (Lully) 55
Feuersnot (R. Strauss) 243
Fiamma, La (Respighi) 289–90
Fidelio (Beethoven) 112, 113, 118, 230
Field, John 139
Fierrabras (D796) (Schubert) 130
Fiery Angel, The (Prokofiev) 316
Fifth Piano Concerto, Op. 55
  (Prokofiev) 317
Fifth Piano Sonata (Prokofiev) 316
Fifth String Quartet
  Bartók 293
  Glazunov 247
Fifth Symphony
  H202 (*Di tre re*) (Honegger) 320
  in D (Vaughan Williams) 266
  in E flat, Op. 82 (Sibelius) 252
  Ives 274
  Mahler 231
  Martinu 314
  Maxwell Davies 388
  Op. 100 (Prokofiev) 318
  Op. 50 (Nielsen) 249
  Op. 64 (Tchaikovsky) 197–8
Figaro, Le: music critic 213
Figure humaine (Poulenc) 333
Fille du régiment, La (Donizetti) 126
Fille du tambour-major, La
  (Offenbach) 164
'Filles de Cadix, Les' (Delibes) 186
film (soundtrack) music 266, 310, 317,

  319, 320, 324, 338, 351, 353, 362,
  363, 370, 388, 389
  Barfly 396
  Espoir, L' 324
  La Prisonnière 376
  Our Town 338
  Walton's output 344–5
Fingal's Cave (Mendelssohn) 142
Finlandia, Op. 26 (Sibelius) 251
Finta giardiniera, La (Mozart) 106
Finta semplice, La (Mozart) 105
Fiori musicali (Frescobaldi) 44–5
Firebird, The (Stravinsky) 280, 281, 297
Fireworks (Stravinsky) 296
First Book of Selected Church Musick
  (Barnard) 46
First Cello Concerto
  Op. 33 (Saint-Saëns) 184
  Shostakovich 353
First Chamber Symphony, Op. 9
  (Schoenberg) 277
First Choral Symphony, Op. 41
  (Holst) 272
First Concerto, for cello and orchestra
  (Ligeti) 371
First Piano Concerto
  Bartók 293
  Beethoven 111
  in B flat minor, Op. 23 (Tchaikovsky)
    196
  in F sharp minor, Op. 1
    (Rachmaninov) 267
  Op. 10 (Prokofiev) 315
  Op. 17 (Saint-Saëns) 183
First Piano Sonata
  Bartók 292
  in D minor, Op. 28 (Rachmaninov) 269
  Op. 1 (Prokofiev) 315
First Sonata for cello and piano
  (Martinu) 313
First Sonata for Piano and Violin,
  Op. 13 (Fauré) 212
First Sonata for Violin and Piano, Op. 8
  (Grieg) 206
First String Quartet
  Bartók 291, 292
  Henze 379
  Op. 2 (Kodály) 294–5
  Tippett 348
First Symphony
  Classical, Op. 25 (Prokofiev) 315–16
  Gorecki 384
  in A flat, Op. 55 (Elgar) 220
  in C minor (Brahms) 181
  in D minor, Op. 13 (Rachmaninov) 268
  in E major, Op. 26 (Scriabin) 261–2
  in E minor, Op. 39 (Sibelius) 251
  in G minor, Op. 13 *Winter Dreams*
    (Tchaikovsky) 196
  Ives 274
  Mahler 230, 231
  Maxwell Davies 388
  Op. 210 (Milhaud) 323
  Op. 28 (Bizet) 191
  Op. 7 (Nielsen) 248
  Tippett 348
  Weill 339
First Violin Concerto
  Henze 379
  Op. 19 (Prokofiev) 315–16
  Shostakovich 353
First Violin Sonata (Honegger) 318
Firste Booke of Songes (Dowland) 39
Fisch-Ton-Kan (Chabrier/Verlaine) 199
Fisher, Adeline 264–6
Fisher-Dieskau, Dietrich 364, 365
Five Akhmatova Poems, Op. 27
  (Prokofiev) 315
Five Motets (Maxwell Davies) 388
Five Movements for string quartet, Op.
  5 (Webern) 302
Five Mystical Songs (Vaughan
  Williams) 265
Five Piano Pieces, Op. 23
  (Schoenberg) 278
Five Pieces for orchestra, Op. 10
  (Webern) 303
Five Preludes for Guitar (Villa-Lobos)
  309–10
flamenco 199–200
Flaminia, Il (Pergolesi) 93
Flaubert 193
Flea, The (Shostakovich) 351
Fledermaus, Die (Strauss II) 175, 176
Fliegende Holländer, Der (Wagner) 158
Flood, The (Stravinsky) 300

Florentinische tragödie, Eine (Zemlinsky) 260
Floresta e jovem e cheja de vida, A (Nono) 373
Florida Suite (Delius) 238
Floridante (Handel) 85
Flos Campi (Vaughan Williams) 265
Floss der Medusa, Das (Henze) 380
Flotow, Friedrich 162
'Flower Duet' (Delibes) 186
Flucht der Heiligen Familie, Op. 20 (Bruch) 190
Flute Concerto (Nielsen) 249
Foix, Jean de, Bishop of Bodeaux 19
Folk Songs of Moravia Newly Collected (Janáček) 217
folk/native music
  systematic studies of 281, 290–1
    see also Kodály, Zoltán; Bartók, Béla
  treatise on Hungarian 292
folk/native music, use of 18, 76, 89, 173, 199–200, 202, 203, 207, 287, 326, 338, 365, 385
  Armenian 346
  Brazilian 281, 308, 322
  Finnish 251
  French 324
  Moravian 217
  Vaughan Williams 263–5
Fontana Mix (Cage) 360
Fontane di Roma (Respighi) 289
For Children (Bartók) 291
'For the Union Dead' (Lowell) 274
'Forelle, Die' (Schubert) 128
Forkel: on Bach 72
Forza del destino, La (Verdi) 155
Foss, Lukas 368
Fountains of Rome (Respighi) *see* Fontane di Roma
Four Lemminkäinen Legends, Op. 22 (Sibelius) 251
Four Lieder
  Op. 12 (Webern) 303
  Op. 2 (Berg) 306
Four Motets pour un temps de pénitence (Poulenc) 333
Four organs (Reich) 391
Four Piano Blues (Copland) 338
Four Pieces (Rachmaninov) 267
Four Poèmes H7 (Honegger) 318
Four Seasons, The *see* Quattro stagione, Le
Four Temperaments, The (Hindemith) 326
Four-and-a-half minutes (Cage) 360
Fourteen Bagatelles (Bartók) 291
Fourth Piano Concerto
  in G minor, Op. 40 (Rachmaninov) 270
  Op. 53 (Prokofiev) 317
Fourth Symphony
  Deliciae basiliensis H191 (Honegger) 320
  in A minor, Op. 62 (Sibelius) 252
  in F minor (Vaughan Williams) 265–6
  in F minor, Op. 36 (Tchaikovsky) 196, 197
  Ives 275
  Mahler 230–1
  Op. 47 (Prokofiev) 316
  Op. 90 (Brahms) 182
  Tippett 350
fox-trots 325, 351
Fraîcheur et le feu, La (Poulenc) 333
Francesca da Rimini
  Op. 32 (Tchaikovsky) 196
  Rachmaninov 268
Francis I, Emperor 96
Franck, César 133, 164–6, 165
Franz Joseph, Emperor 171
Frasquita (Lehár) 258
Frate 'nnamorato, La (Pergolesi) 93
Fratres (Pärt) 389
Frau ohne Schatten, Die (R. Strauss) 244, 245
Frauenliebe und leben, Op. 42 (Schumann) 149
Frederick the Great of Prussia 81–2
Frederick William II 108
Frederick William IV 143
Freemasonry 107–8
Freischütz, Der (Weber) 118
Frescobaldi, Girolamo 23, 44, 44–5
Fresques de Piero della Francesca, Les (Martinů) 314
Fricken, Ernestine von 147–8

Friedericke (Lehár) 258
Friedrich Wilhelm I of Prussia 94, 104
Friedrich Wilhelm, Markgraf 94
Frithjof-Scenen, Op. 23 (Bruch) 190
From Bohemia's Woods and Fields (Smetana) 169
'From Hanover Square North' (Ives) 274
From Holberg's Time (Holberg Suite) (Grieg) 208
From Jewish Folk Poetry (songs) (Shostakovich) 353
From the House of the Dead (Janáček/Dostoyevsky) 218
From the Middle Ages (Glazunov) 247
From the Psalms of David (Penderecki) 385
Frühlingsstimmen (Strauss II) 176
Fuchs, Robert 251
Fuchs-Robettin, Hanna 307
Fugal Concerto for flute, oboe and strings (Holst) 272
Fugal Overture, A (Holst) 272
fugues 114, 273, 326
  in 4 Keys, on 'The Shining Shore' (Ives) 273
  see also preludes and fugues
Funeral Cantata (Beethoven) 111
Funeral Music in memoriam Béla Bartók (Lutosławski) 365
Fünf Neapolotanische Lieder (Henze) 380
Funny face (Gershwin) 329–30
Für Alina (Pärt) 389
Furniture Music 255
Fürstenkind, Das (Lehár) 258
Furtwängler, Wilhelm 326
Futurists 301

Gabrieli, Andrea 35, 65
Gabrieli, Giovanni 35–6
  Schütz and 47
Gade, Niels 206, 248
'gallant' style 106
Gallenberg, Count 145
galliard 23
galops/gallops 173, 257
Gambler, The (Prokofiev) 315
Garcia Lorca, Federico 288
Gaspard de la nuit (Ravel) 284
Gasparini, Francesco 70, 71, 72, 87
Gautier, Judith 159
Gawain (Birtwistle) 387
Gayaneh (Khachaturian) 347
Gazza ladra, La (Rossini) 123
Gazzetta, La (Rossini) 123
Gebrauchsmusik, theory of 325
Geburtstag der Infantin, Der (Zemlinsky) 260
Gedianishvili, Prince Luka Stepanovich 176
Geistliche Chormusik (Schütz) 47
Gelbe Jacke, Die (Lehár) 258
Geloso schernito, Il (Pergolesi) 92
Gemignani, Elvira 224, 225–6
Genesis (Górecki) 384
Genoveva (Schumann) 148, 152
Gentili, Maria Catalina 87
George II: coronation 85
George IV 150
George of Hannover
  Elector 84
  King 179–80
George White's *Scandals* 329
George, Stefan 302
'Gern hab' ich die Frau'n geküsst' (Lehár) 258
Gershwin, George 281, 328–30, 329, 337
Gershwin, Ira 329, 330, 341
Gerstl, Richard 277
Gerusaleme liberata (Tasso) *see* Combattimento di Tancredi e Clorinda, Il
'Gesang der Geister über den Wassern' (D714) (Schubert) 129
Gesang der Heiligen drei Könige, Op. 21 (Bruch) 190
Gesang der Jünglinge (Stockhausen) 382–3
Gesualdo, Carlo 23, 37–8
Gesualdo, Don Fabrizio 37
Getreue Music-Meister, Der (musical periodical) 76
Geyer, Ludwig 156
Geyer, Stefi 291, 292

Ghedini 376
Ghelderode, Michel de 372
Gheltretti, Gasparo 114
Ghys, Henri 282
Gianni Schicchi (Puccini) *see* Trittico, Il
Giant, The (Prokofiev) 314
Giasone (Cavalli) 53
Giazotto, Roberto 71
Gibbons, Ellis 45
Gibbons, Orlando 23, 45–6, *46*
Gibbons, William 45
Gibet, Le (Ravel) *see* Gaspard de la nuit
Giebel, Emanuel 233
Gigault, Nicholas 54
Gil, Susana 345
Ginastera, Alberto 335, 367–8
Giordano, Umberto 241–2
Giorno di regno, Un (Verdi) 153
Giovanna d'Arco (Verdi) 154
Gipsy Baron, The (Strauss II) *see* Zigeunerbaron, Der
Giraud, Albert 277
Giraud, Anna 72–3
Girl Crazy (Gershwin) 329–30
Giuditta (Lehár) 258–9
Giulini, Carlo Maria 324
Giulio Cesare (Handel) 85
  intermezzo for 77
Giusti, Chevalier 122
Gladkowa, Constantia 145
Glagolitic Mass (Janáček) 218
Glass, Philip 375, 392–3, *393*, 395
Glazunov, Alexander ('Sasha') 210, 245–7, *246*
  Borodin's unfinished works 178
  Rachmaninov's First Symphony 268
Gli Amori di Teolinda (Meyerbeer) 120
Gli uccelli (Respighi) 289
Glinka, Mikhail 133, 139–40, 151
Glissandi (Ligeti) 371
Gloria (Walton) 345
Gloriana (Britten) 364
Glorias, RV 589/588 (Vivaldi) 74
Gluck, Christoph Willibald 91, 96–8, 97, 107
  Wagner and 158
Glückliche Hand, Die, Op. 18 (Schoenberg) 277
Gnesin (composer) 346
Goehr, Alexander 386, 387
Goethe 127–8, 129, 142, 181
Goethe Lieder (Wolf) 233
Goeyvaerts, Karel 382
Gogol 193
'Going Home' 203
Goldberg Variations, BWV 988 (J. S. Bach) 82
Golden Age, The (Shostakovich) 351
Golden Cockerel, The (Rimsky-Korsakov) 210
Golden Spinning-Wheel, The (Dvořák) 203
Goldmark, Rubin 251, 336
Goldwyn Follies (Gershwin) 330
Golgotha (Martin) 311
'Golliwog's Cakewalk' (Debussy) 237
Gombert, Nicolas 19, 23
Gonzaga, Duke Giugliemo 27
Gonzaga, Duke Vincenzo I 41, 42
Gonzaga, Ferdinand, Viceroy of Sicily 28
Good Friday Improperia (Palestrina) 27
Good Night, 'In Memoriam Michael Vyner' (Górecki) 385
Good Soldier Schwejk (Kodály) 295
Goodman, Benny 338, 370
Górecki, Henryk 375, 384–5
Gorgoza, Emilio di 357
Gori, Lucrezia 26, 27
Götterdämmerung (Wagner) 159, 196
Gounod, Charles *160*, 160–1, 204–5
  Bizet and 187
Goyescas (Granados) 256
Graf von Luxembourg, Der (Lehár) 258
Graham, Martha 338, 358
Gran Partita (K361) (Mozart) 109
Gran sole carico d'amore, Al (Nono) 373
'Granada' (Albéniz) *see* Suite española No. 1
Granados, Enrique 215, 255–6
grand operas
  Chabrier's 200
  French 133, 173, 237
  birth of 127
  Verdian 155

Grand' tante, La (Massenet) 204
Grande Macabre, Le (Ligeti) 372
Grande-Duchesse de Gérolstein, La (Offenbach) 163
Graun, Carl Heinrich 94
Graupner, Christoph 75, 81
Great Service in F (Byrd) 32
Greek Passion, The (Martinů) 314
Gregorian chant *see* plainchant
Gregory I, Pope 9
Gregory XIII, Pope 29
'Gretchen am Spinnrade' (Schubert) 127
Gretna Green (Guiraud) 205
Grieg, Edvard 173, *206*, 206–8, 281
  Delius and 238
Griselda (A. Scarlatti) 66
Grofé, Ferde 329
Gropius, Manon 307
Gropius, Walter 232
Grosse Fugue, Op. 133 (Beethoven) 113
Guerre 'La battaile de Marignan, La' (Janequin) 19
Guglielmo Ratcliffe (Mascagni) 241
Guillaume Tell (Rossini) 120, 124
Guimarães, Luilia 308
Guiraud, Ernest 187, 205
Guise, Chevalier de 53–4
Guise, Duchesse de 57
Guitar Concerto (Villa-Lobos) 310
Günther, Dorothee 327
Günther School of Music 327
Guntram (R. Strauss) 243
Gurrelieder (Schoenberg) 276, 278
Gwendoline (Chabrier) 200
Gypsy Melodies, Op. 55 (Dvořák) 202

Haas, Joseph 325
Hagerup, Nina 207
Hail, bright Cecilia (Purcell) 64
Halévy, Fromental 182, 187, 188
Halévy, Geneviève 188, 189
Half-time (Martinů) 313
Halffter, Ernesto 288
Hamlet
  Shostakovich 351
  Walton 345
Hammersmith Suite (Holst) 272
Handel, Georg Frideric 49, 51, 82, *83*, 83–5, 211
  and Telemann 76
  Corelli and 59
  D. Scarlatti and 87
Hanslick, Eduard 170, 175
  and Brahms 181
  on Liszt 152
Happy End (Weill) 340
Harawi (Messiaen) 356
Hardy, Thomas 272, 364
Harlas, Hélène 120
Harlem Renaissance poets 260
Harmonia Sacra (Playford) 64
harmonic progression: Monteverdi and 41
Harmonie der Welt, Der (Hindemith) 327
Harmonielehre (Adams) 396
Harmonium (Adams) 396
harmony 18, 38, 43
  codification of 11
  Debussy's study of 237
  Janáček's use of minor 217
  Rameau's perception of 78
  treatise on 77–8, 88
Harold en Italie (Berlioz) 115, 133, 138
Harpsichord Concerto (Falla) 288
harpsichord music 68–9
Harrison, Lou, on Ives 273
Harty, Hamilton 344
Háry János (Kodály) 295
Hassan (Delius/Flecker) 240
Hatzfeld, Countess of 110–11
Hauer, Joseph 278
Hauptmann, Elisabeth 340
Hauptmann, Gerhard 231
Hausmusik (Telemann) 76
Havanaise, Op. 83 (Saint-Saëns) 184
Haydn, (Franz) Joseph 67, 91, *99*, 99–102, 103
  and C. P. E. Bach 95
  Beethoven and 110, 111
  influence on Mozart 106, 107
Haydn, Michael 116
Heart's Assurance, The (Tippett) 348
Heiligenstadt Testament (Beethoven) 112

Heirs of the White Mountain, The (Dvořák) 201
Heldenleben, Ein, Op. 40 (R. Strauss) 243
Helios Overture (Nielsen) 248
Henry V (Walton) 345
Henry VIII 21, 24
funeral 24
Henze, Hans Werner 375, **379–81**, *380*
'Here's that will challenge all the Fair' (Purcell) 62
Herman, Woody 299
Heroes (album) 392
Hérold 124
Heroum soboles (Lassus) 30
Herzogenberg, Heinrich von 181
Hesse, Landgrave of 75
Hessen, Landgrave of 39
Hessen, Philip von, Governor of Mantua 72, 73
Heure espagnole, L' (Ravel) 284
Heuschkel (Weber's teacher) 116
Hexachordum Apollinis (Pachelbel) 60
Heyse, Paul 233, 234
Hieremiae prophetae lamentationes (Lassus) 30
Hildburghausen, Prince 96
Hildegard von Bingen **12–13**
Hill, Edward Burlingame 368
Hiller, Ferdinand 190
Hiller, John Adam 93
Hindemith, Paul 281, **324–7**, *325*
Walton and 344
Hingston, John 63
Hippolyte et Aricie (Rameau) 78
'Hirt auf dem Felsen, Der' (Schubert) 131
Histoire de Babar, L' (Poulenc) 333
Histoires naturelles (Ravel) 284
Hochzeit, Die (Wagner) 157
Holberg, Ludvig 208
Holidays Symphony, The (Ives) 274–5
Holst, Gustav 215, 264, **270–2**, *271*, 361
Vaughan Williams and 265
Holst, Isabel 271
Holy Sonnete of John Donne, The (Britten) 363
Homenajes (Falla) 288
Hommage à Ravel (Honegger) 318
Homme et son désir, L' (Milhaud) 322
Honegger, Arthur 310, 312, **318–20**, *319*, 322, 332, 333
Hoodoo Zephyr (Adams) 397
Horace victorieux (Honegger) 319
Horas de una estancia, Las, Op. 11 (Ginastera) 367
Horn Concerto, No. 2 (R. Strauss) 245
House of Life, The (Vaughan Williams) 265
Hugh the Drover (Vaughan Williams) 265
Hugo, Victor 125
Huguenots, Les (Meyerbeer) 120, 152
Human Comedy, The (Shostakovich) 351
Humfrey, Pelham 62
Humoresques, Op. 101 (Dvořák) 203
Humperdinck, Engelbert 234, 339
'Hungarian Peasant Music', treatise on (Bartók) 292
Hunter, Anne 101
Hüttenbrunner, Anselm 129
Hydrogen Jukebox (Glass) 393
Hymn to St Cecilia (Britten) 363
'Hymn to the Arts' (Scriabin) 262
Hymnen (Stockhausen) 383
Hyperprism (Varèse) 301

I Got Rhythm (Gershwin) 330
Iberia (Albéniz) 228, 287
Ibsen, Henrik 206, 207
Ice Break, The (Tippett) 350
Ideal Frau, Das (Lehár) 258
Idée fixe, musical 137
Idomeneo, Rè di Creta (Mozart) 106, 109
'Idyll for large orchestra' (Webern) *see Im Sommerwind*
Idyll, A Song of Summer (Delius) 240
If ye love me (Tallis) 25
Ikon of Light (Taverner) 395
Illuminations, Les (Britten) 363
'illustrative music' 319
Im Sommerwind (Webern) 302

Images (Debussy) 237
Images pour Orchestra (Debussy) 237
Imaginary Landscapes (Cage) 359
imitation, use of 25, 27
Impressioni brasiliane (Respighi) 289
Impressionists 199, 236–7
impromptus 130
improvisation 77, 170, 293, 378, 390
In Alium (Taverner) 394
In Filanda (Mascagni) 240
In ieiunio et fletu (Tallis) 25
In memoriam Dylan Thomas (Stravinsky) 299–300
In Nature's Realm, Op. 91 (Dvořák) 202
In tears (Janáček) *see Along an Overgrown Path*
In the Fen Country (Vaughan Williams) 264
In the South (Elgar) 220
In the Steppes of Central Asia (Borodin) 178
In the Mist (Janáček) 218
incidental music 64, 118, 129, 130, 142, 143, 189, 193, 207, 213, 220, 244, 249, 265, 319, 345, 351
for *Kuoloma* 251–2
see also film music
Incontri (Nono) 373
Incoronazione di Poppea, L' (Monteverdi) 43
Indes galantes, Les (Rameau) 78
Indian Queen, The (Purcell/Dryden/Howard) 64
Indy, Vincent d' 165, 200, 300, 318
Ingegneri, Marc'Antonio 40–1
Innocence (Taverner) 395
Inscape (Copland) 338
Institut de Recherche et Coordination Acoustique/Musique 379
instrumental music 23, 33, 36, 44, 78, 92–3, 102, 156–7
as accompaniment 51
see also chamber music; consort dance music
intermezzi/intermezzo 74, 77, 92, 93
and rhapsodies, Opp. 116–119 (Brahms) 182
Intermezzo (R. Strauss) 244
International Composers Guild 301
Intimate Letters (string quartet/Janáček) 218
Intolleranza (Nono) 373
Invitation to the Dance (Weber) 118
Iolanthe (Tchaikovsky) 198
Ionisation (Varèse) 301
Iphigénie en Aulide (Gluck) 98
Iphigénie en Tauride (Gluck) 98
Ireland, John 361, 364
Irene (D. Scarlatti) 86
Iris (Mascagni) 242
Irmelin (Delius) 239
Isle of the Dead, The (Rachmaninov) 269
isorhythm (concept) 14
Israel in Egypt (Handel) 85
Isserlis, Steven 395
Istar (Martinů) 312
It's Gonna Rain (Reich) 390–1
Italian symphony (Mendelssohn) 142–3
Italiana in Algeri, L' (Rossini) 122
Italienisches Liederbuch (Wolf) 234
Ivan IV (Bizet) 188
Ivan the Terrible (Prokofiev/Eisenstein) 318
Ives, Charles 215, **273–5**, 323
Izath (Villa-Lobos) 308

Jacanopulos, Vera 286
Jacobin, The (Dvořák) 202
Jaconson, Jens Peter 239
Jahreszeiten, Die (Haydn) 101–2
Jakobsleiter, Die (Schoenberg) 278
James I 40
funeral 45
James II 58, 63
James, Henry 364, 365
Janáček, Leos 215, **216–18**, 313
Janequin, Clément **19–20**, 23
Janin, Jules 162
Japanese Suite, Op. 33 (Holst) 271
Järnefelt, Aino 251
Jasager, Der (Weill) 340
Jauner, Franz 175
jazz 299, 310, 311, 312, 337, 349, 375, 379, 390

'authentic' 322–3
'real negro' 293
Jean de Nivelle (Delibes) 186
Jeanne d'Arc au bûcher (Honegger) 320
Jeanrenaud, Cécile 143
Jeaune France, Le 355
Jenůfa (Janáček) 217, 218
Jephthas Gelübde (Meyerbeer) 119–120
Jeremiah Symphony (Bernstein) 369
Jeritza, Maria 218
Jeux (Debussy) 236, 237
Jeux d'eaux (Ravel) 283
Jeux d'enfants (Bizet) 189
Jeux de Cartes (Stravinsky) 298
'Jewishness in Music' (Wagner) 158
'Jimbo's Lullaby' (Debussy) 237
Joachim, Joseph 179–80, 182, 191
Job (Vaughan Williams) 265
Johann Georg I of Saxony 47
John William of the Rhine 59
John, King of Bohemia 14
'Join in the People's Outdoor Meeting" (Ives) 274
Jolie Fille de Perth, La (Bizet) 188
Jongleur de Notre Dame, Le (Massenet) 205
Joseph II, Emperor 110
Josquin Desprez 10, **13–19**, *18*, 28, 389
motet to Ockeghem 17
Jota aragonesa-Spanish overture No. 1 (Glinka) 140
Joyce, James 376
Jubilate Deo (Walton) 345
Judas Maccabaeus (Handel) 85
Judith (Honegger) 319
Juglares (Rodrigo) 341–2
Julietta (Martinů) 313
Julius Caesar (Handel) *see Giulio Cesare*
Julius III, Pope 26
Junge Lord, Der (Henze) 380
Jupiter Symphony (K551) (Mozart) 108
Jurnet, Francisco 255

Kaddish Symphony (Bernstein) 370
Kainova, Margarita 353
Kallman, Chester 299, 380
Kamarinskaya (Glinka) 140
Kammermusik series (Hindemith) 325, 326, 344
Karelia Overture, Op. 10 (Sibelius) 251
Karelia Suite, Op. 11 (Sibleius) 251
Kassya (Delibes) 187
Káta Kabanová (Janáček) 218
Kate and the Devil (Dvořák) 203
Keats, John 272
Keller, Gotfried 234
Keller, Maria Anna 100
Kemble, Charles 118
Kentner, Louis 345, 349
Kerll, Johann Kaspar 60
Ketting, Otto 375
Keverich, Maria Magdalena 110
Khachaturian, Aram 335, *346*, **346–7**
Khavanschina (Mussorgsky) 194
Kinderszenen, Op. 15 (Schumann) 149
Kindertotenlieder (Mahler) 231
King and Collier (Dvořák) 202
King Arthur (Purcell/Dryden) 64
King Lear overture (Berlioz) 137, 138
King Priam (Tippett) 349
Kingdom, The (Elgar) 220
Kinsky, Count, Chancellor of Bohemia 88, 112–13
Kirchner, Leon 395
Kirkwall (Maxwell Davies) 389
Kiss, The (Smetana) 168
Kitzler, Otto 169–70
Klagende Lied, Das (Mahler) 229
Klammer, Fräulein 139
Klavierstücke XI (Stockhausen) 382
Kleiber, Erich 306
Kleider machen Leute (Zemlinsky) 259

Kleines Requiem für eine Polka, Op. 66 (Gorecki) 385
Klimt, Gustav 305
Klingsor, Tristan 284
Kluge, Die (Orff) 328
Knaben Wunderhorn, Des (Mahler) 230
Knickerbocker Holiday (Weill) 341
Knot Garden, The (Tippett) 350
Knoxville: Summer of 1915 (Barber/Agee) 358
Koanga (Delius) 239
Kodály, Zoltán 281, 292, *294*, **294–6**
Bartók and 290–1, 292
Koechlin, Charles 322, 331
Koessler, János 290
Kol Nidre, Op. 39 (Schoenberg) 279
Kol Nidrei, Op. 47 (Bizet) 191
Kolár, Katerina 167, 168
Kolisch, Gertrude 278
Kolish, Rudolf *291*
Komposition mit zwölf Tönen (Schoenberg) 278
Kondratyev, Gennardi 194
König Hirsch (Henze) 380
Kontakte (Stockhausen) 383
Kontra-punkte (Stockhausen) 382
Körner, Phillip 127
Korot, Beryl 391
Kostcheï the Immortal (Rimsky-Korsakov) 210
Koussevitsky, Serge/Koussevitzky Foundation 313, 337, 349, 356, 363, 369
Koussevitzky International Award 366
Krasner, Louis 307
Kraus, Karl 305
Kreutzer Sonata, The (Janáček/Tolstoy) 218
Kreuzspiel (Stockhausen) 382
Krizhovsky, Pavel 216
Kukuschka (Lehár) 257
Kullervo, Op. 7 (Sibelius) 251
Kunst der Fuge, Der (J. S. Bach) 82

La La Lucille (Gershwin) 329
Lachian Dances (Janáček) 217
Lachrymae or Seven Teares (Dowland) 39–40
Lady in the Dark (Weill) 341
Lady Macbeth of the Mtsensk district (Shostakovich) 351
Lady, Be Good! (Gershwin) 329–30
Lagrime di San Pietro (Lassus) 30
Lakmé (Delibes) 186, 187
Lalande, Michel-Richard de 57
Lamb, The (Taverner) 395
Lambert, Constance 343
Lambert, Michel 55
Lamentations of Jeremiah
Palestrina 28
Tallis 25
Lamento d'Arianna (Monteverdi) 41–2
Land des Lächelns, Das (Lehár) 258
Landini, Francesco 10
Landowska, Wanda 332
Langwierige Weg in die Wohnung der Natascha Ungeheuer, Der (Henze) 380
Lark Ascending, The (Vaughan Williams) 265
Las, voulez vous (Lassus) 30
Lassus, Orlande de 23, **28–30**, *29*, 35, 40, 140, 211, 216, 235
source of texts 23
Last Sleep of the Virgin, The (Tavener) 395
Lauber, Josef 310
Lauda Sion Salvatoreum (Lassus) 30
Le Riche de la Pouplinière, Joseph 78
Lecocq, Charles 187
Leçons de Ténèbres (Couperin) 69
Leeds Festival 202, 265, 272
Lefeld, Jerzy 365
Legend of Saint Elizabeth, The (Liszt) 152
Legend of the Invisible City of Kitzeh, The (Rimsky-Korsakov) 210
Léger, Ferdinand 323
Lehár, Franz 215, **256–9**, *257*
Lehár, Sophie 258, 259
Leibowitz, René 378
Leipzig Conservatory, founding of 143, 148
Leith Hill (Dorking) Music Festival 264
leitmotifs: Glinka's use of 140

Lelio, ou le Retour à la Vie (Berlioz) 137
Leningrad symphony (Shostakovich) 352
Lenya, Lotte 324, 340-1
Leonardo da Vinci 18
Leoncavallo, Ruggiero 215, **221-3**, *222*, 224
Léonin 9
Leonova, Daria 194
Leopold II, Emperor 108
Leopold of Cöthen, Prince 81
Lerchenmusik (Gorecki) 385
Lescurel, Jehan de 14
Let 'Em Eat Cake (Gershwin) 330
Lévy, Lazare 359
Li Po 231
Liber divinorum operum (Hildegard) 13
librettists
  Adami, Giuseppe 226
  Boito, Arrigo 156, 224
  Burion, Amédée 187
  Carré 188
  Cormon, Eugene 188
  Fontana, Ferdinando 224
  Genée, Richard 175
  Giacosa, Giuseppe 224, 225
  Gille 205
  Halévy, Ludovic 162, 163, 189
  Helman, Lilian 370
  Hofmannsthal, Hugo von 244-5, 258, 311
  Illica, Luigi 224, 242
  Kind, Johann Friedrich 118
  Krauss, Clemens 245
  Léon, Victor 257
  Lessing, Doris 393
  Leterrier and Vanloo 199
  Meilhac, Henri 162, 163, 189, 205
  Mendes, Catulle 200
  Metastasio, Pietro 96, 97
  Money-Coutts, Francis 228
  Pepoli, Count Carlo 135
  Ponte, Lorenzo da 107, 108
  Pruslin, Stephen 387
  Puccini's approach to 224
  Romani, Felice 135
  Schnitzer, Ignatz 176
  Scribe, Eugène 120-1
  Sondheim, Stephen 370
  Stein, Leo 257
  Tchaikovsky, Modeste 198
  Zweig, Stefan 245
Libuse (Smetana) 168
Lichnowsky, Prince Karl 108, 111
Licht (Stockhausen) 383
Lieber der Danae, Die (R. Strauss) 245
Liebeslied (Nono) 373
Liebeslieder waltzer Op. 52 (Brahms) 181
Liebesverbot, Das (Wagner) 157
Liebmann Beer, Jakob *see* Meyerbeer, Giacomo
Lied von der Erde, Das (Mahler) 231-2, 260, 354
lieder 91, 243, 245, 259
  eines fahrenden Gesellen (Mahler) 230
  ohne Wörte (Mendelssohn) 142
  Op. 18 (Webern) 303
  Schubert's output 127-8, 129, 130-1
  Schumann's output 148, 149
  und Gesange (Schumann) 149
  Wolf's importance to 234-5
Liederkreis, Op. 24/39 (Schumann) 149
Liehmann, Antonin 201
Lieutenant Kijé (Prokofiev) 317
Life for the Tsar, A (Glinka) 140, 268
Ligeti, György 335, **371-2**
Light of Life, The, Op. 29 (Elgar) 220
Lighthouse, The (Maxwell Davies) 388
Limpid Stream, The (Shostakovich) 352
Lincoln Portrait (Copland) 338
Linda di Chamouniz (Donizetti) 126
Lingbergh, Charles 330
Liszt, Franz 133, 145, **149-53**, *150*, 178
  and Borodin 177, 178
  Brahms and 180
  Debussy and 235
  Fauré and 212
  Grieg and 207
  Massenet and 204
  Saint-Saëns and 182, 183
  Smetana and 167
  Wagner and 158
  Wolf and 233

Litanies à la vierge noire (Poulenc) 332
Litany (Pärt) 390
'Little Shepherd, The' (Debussy) 237
Little Suite, Op. 1 for strings (Nielsen) 248
'Little train of Caipira, The' (Villa-Lobos) 309
Liturgy of St John Chrysostom (Taverner) 395
Livietta (Pergolesi) 93
Livres de pièces de clavecin (4 vols./Couperin) 68
Llubera, Maria 316
Lobkowitz, Prince 96, 112, 113
Locatelli, Pietro 70-1, 114
Locke, Matthew 62
Lohengrin (Wagner) 152, 158
London Symphonies (Nos. 93-104) (Haydn) 102
London Symphony, A (Vaughan Williams) 265
Long Christmas Dinner (Hindemith) 327
Loos, Adolf 305
Loreley, Die (Bruch) 190
Lorenzo Colonna, Vittoria di 15
Loriod, Yvonne 355, 356
Lost in the Stars (Weill) 341
Louis XI 17
Louis XII 18, 19
Louis XIV 54-5, 57, 61
  marriage 53
Louis-Napoleon 162
Louys, Pierre 236
Love is Here To Stay (Gershwin) 330
Love of Three Oranges, The, Op. 33 (Prokofiev) 316
'Lovely John' (Vaughan Williams) 265
Low (album) 392
'*Low Symphony*' (Glass) 393
Lowe, Edward 63
Löwe, Ferdinand 171
Lucia di Lammermoor (Donizetti) 208
  'mad scene' 127
Luciferiske, Den (Nielsen) 249
Lucio Silla (K135) (Mozart) 105
Lucretia Borgia (Donizetti) 125
Lucretzia (Respighi) 290
Lucrezia Floriani (Sand) 146
Ludford, Nicholas 20
Ludus Tonalis (Hindemith) 326
Ludwig II of Bavaria 159
Ludwig of Württemburg, Duke 117
Luis, Infante Don 103
Luisa Miller (Verdi) 154
Lullaby for string quartet (Gershwin) 329
Lully, Jean-Baptiste 51, **53-6**, *54*, 57, 61, 79
  Couperin on 68
Lully, Louis de 61
Lulu (Berg) 299, 307
  Boulez' recording 379
Lumsdaine, David 394
Luonnotar, Op. 70 (Sibelius) 252
Lusiad, The (Camoen) 187
lute music 40
Luther, Martin 23
  on Desprez 18
Lutoslawski, Witold 335, **365-6**, *366*
Luzzaschi, Luzzasco 44
Lydian scale 252
Lyric Pieces (Grieg) 207
Lyric Suite
  for string quartet (Berg) 307
  Op. 54 (Grieg) 207
Lyric Symphony (Zemlinsky) 260

Má Vlast (Smetana) 168-9
Macbeth
  Verdi 154, 155
  Walton 345
Machaut, Guillaume de **14-15**, 489
Madam Butterfly (Puccini) 225
Madame Favart (Offenbach) 164
Maddalena (A. Scarlatti/Pamphili) 65
Maddaloni, Duke of 92, 93
Maderna, Bruno 372, 376
Madrigali spirituali (Monteverdi) 41
madrigals 10, 23, 27, 28, 36, 37-8, 41-3, 44, 45, 46, 47, 313
  and Mottets of 5 Parts: apt for Viols and Voyces (Gibbons) 46
  of Love and War (Monteverdi) 43
  spiritual 30
Maestro di musica, II (Pergolesi) 92

Magic Fountain, The (Delius) 239
Magic Opal, The (Albéniz) 228
magnetic tape, use of 360
Magnificat
  Cavalli 52
  Pärt 390
  Penderecki 386
  Victoria 34
Magnificat alleluia (Villa-Lobos) 310
Mahler, Gustav 215, **228-32**, *229*, 305, 306, 361, 362, 369
  Debussy and 236
  Ives' Third Symphony 274
  Schoenberg and 277
  Wolf and 232, 234
Maia (Leoncavallo) 223
Maid of Orleans (Tchaikovsky) 197
Major Barbara (Walton) 345
Makropoulos Affair, The (Janácek) 218
'Malagueña' (Albéniz) *see España*
Malarde imaginaire, Le (Charpentier/Molière) 57
Malatesta, Cleofe 15
Malatesti, Carlo 15
Malbruk (Leoncavallo) 223
Maledon, Pierre 182
Malheurs d'Orphée, Les (Milhaud) 323
Malisewski, Witold 365
Mallarmé 236, 282, 378
Malraux, André 356
Mamelles de Tirésias, Les (Poulenc) 333
Manchester New Music Group 386, 387
Mandelsson, Myra 317
Manfred Symphony, Op. 58 (Tchaikovsky) 197
Manfredi, Doria 225-6
Manfredi, Filippo 103
Mangot, Marie-Louise 78
Mann, Thomas 365
Mann mit den drei Frauen, Der (Lehár) 258
Manon (Massenet) 173, 205
Manon Lescaut
  Prévost 379
  Puccini 224
Manuel Venegas (Wolf) 234
marches/martial music 109, 144, 190, 220, 257, 274, 306
Marco Attila Regolo (A. Scarlatti) 66
Marenzio, Luca 39
Margot la Rouge (Delius) 239
Margot labourez les vignes (Lassus) 30
Maria Barbara, Queen of Spain 87
Maria del Carmen (Granados) 256
Maria di Rohan (Donizetti) 126
Maria Egiziaca (Respighi) 289
Maria of Austria, Dowager Empress 33, 34
Maria Padilla (Donizetti) 126
Maria Stuarda (Donizetti) 126
Maria Theresa, Empress 96, 100
Marie Antoinette 97
Marie Casimire, Queen of Poland 87
Marie Stuart et Rizzio (Gounod) 160
Marie-Magdaleine (Massenet) 204
Marienleben, Das, Op. 27 (Hindemith) 325
Maries de la Tour Eiffel, Les ('Les Six'/Cocteau) 332
Marmontel 187
Marriage, The (Mussorgsky) 193
Märschner: on Weber 118
Marteau sans maître, Le (Boulez) 378
Martin, Frank **310-11**, *311*, 382
Martinelli, Caterina 41-2
Martinu, Bohuslav **312-14**
Martyrdom of St Magnus, The (Maxwell Davies) 388
Martyre de Saint-Sébastien, Le (Debussy/D'Annunzio) 236
Martyrs, Les (Donizetti) 126
Marxsen, Edward 179, 182
Mary, Queen 64
  birthday odes for 64
  funeral music for 64, 65
Mary of Egypt (Taverner) 395
Mascagni, Pietro 215, **240-2**, *241*
Maschere, Le (Mascagni) 242
Mask of Orpheus, The (Birtwistle) 387
Mask of Time, The (Tippett) 350
Maskarade (Nielsen) 248
Mason, Charlotte 182

masques
  et bergamasques, Op. 112 (Fauré) 213
  music for 64
Massenet, Jules 173, **203-5**, *204*, 213
  Bizet's incidental music 189
  influence on Albéniz 228
Masses 26-7, 30, 31, 32, 34, 72, 93
  Bernstein 370
  Bruckner's 171
  development of 10
  Hindemith 327
  in D, Op. 86 (Dvorák) 202
  in G major for unaccompanied choir (poulenc) 332-3
  in G minor (Vaughan Williams) 265
  No. 1 in F (Schubert) 127
  of Life, A (Delius) 239, 240
  see also specific masses and *Messa/Messe; Missa; Missa brevis*
Master Peter's Puppet Show (Falla) 288
Mathis der Maler (Hindemith) 326
'Matrosen-Tango' (Weill) 340
Mattei, Padre Stanislao 122, 124-5
Mattheson, Johann 84
Maurice, Landgraf 47
Mauté, Madame 235
Max Franz, Elector 110
Max Friedrich, Elector 110
Maximilian II, Emperor 29
Maxwell Davies, Peter 375, 386, **387-9**, *388*
May Night (Rimsky-Korsakov) 209
Mayr, Johann 124
Mayrhofer (friend of Schubert) 128, 129
Mazarin, Cardinal 53
Mazeppa (Tchaikovsky) 197
mazurkas 145, 146, 257, 261
McPhee, Colin 364, 392
Meck, Madame Nadszhda von 196-7, 198, 235
Medea (Cave of the Heart) (Barber) 358
Medée (Charpentier) 57
Medici, Ferdinand de' 66, 84, 87
Medici, I (Leoncavallo) 222
Meditation (Glazunov) 247
Mehta, Zubin 356
melody
  cantilena 133
  Dowland's treatment of 40
  'sample' 18
Melzi, Prince 96
Memorial to Lidice (Martinu) 313
Mendelssohn, Fanny 141-2, 143, 160
Mendelssohn, Felix 82, 133, *141*, **141-4**, 148, 160
Menotti, Gian Carlo 357, 358
Menuet antique (Ravel) 283
Menuhin, Yehudi 293, 345, 363
Mer, La (Debussy) 236, 237
Mercy-Argentau, Comtesse Louise 178
Mère l'Oye, Ma (Ravel) 284
Merelli, Bartolomeo 153-4
Mérimée 189
Merriman, Nan 369
Merry Widow, The (Léhar) *214*, 215, 259-60
Messa/Messe
  Clementina II (A. Scarlatti) 66
  de Notre Dame (Machaut) 14
  di Gloria (Puccini) 223
  e la Pentecôte (Messiaen) 356
Messager 183
Messiaen, Olivier 166, 335, *354*, **354-6**, 377, 382, 384
Messiah (Handel) 85, 101
Metamorphosen for strings (R. Strauss) 245
Metamorphoses (Poulenc) 333
Metamorphosis for piano (Cage) 359
Metternich, Count 115
Meyer, Karl 139
Meyerbeer, Giacomo **119-21**, *121*, 124, 145, 188
  Wagner and 157-8
Miaskovsky 346
Michelangelo 234, 354, 363
Mid-Day Witch, The (Dvorák) 203
Midday Thoughts (Copland) 338
Midsummer Marriage, The (Tippett) 348-9
Midsummer Night's Dream (Britten) 364
Midsummer Night's Dream, A (Mendelssohn) 142, 143

'mighty handful/five' see Balakirev, Mily; Borodin, Alexander; Cui, César; Mussorgsky; Rimsky-Korsakov
Mikrokosmos (piano studies) (Bartók) 292
Mikrophonie 1 (Stockhausen) 383
Mildenberg, Anna von 230
Milhaud, Darius 309, 310, 312, 319, 321, 321-4, 332, 379, 382, 390
Military Symphony (Haydn) 102
Milyukova, Antonina 197
minimalism 375, 391, 396
Minkus 185
'Minstrels' (Debussy) 237
Miracle Symphony (Haydn) 102
Miraculous Mandarin, The (Bartók) 292
Mireille (Gounod) 160
Misérables, Les (Honegger/Hugo) 320
Miserere
Desprez 18
Op. 44 (Gorecki) 385
Tartini 89
Miserly Knight (Rachmaninov) 268
Missa
Aeterna Christi munera (Palestrina) 27-8
Assumpta est Maria (Palestrina) 28
Benedicta es (Palestrina) 28
cuisvis toni (Ockeghem) 17
Gaudeamus (Victoria) 34
in tempore belli (Haydn) 102
O Michael (Taverner) 21
Papae Marcelli (Palestrina) 27
pro Victoria (Victoria) 34
Puisque j'ay perdu (Lassus) 30
'Se la face ay pale' (Dufay) 16
Sillabica (Pärt) 389
sine nomine
Dufay 16
Taverner 21
Solemnis (Beethoven) 113
Trahe me post te (Victoria) 34
Missa brevis
Bernstein 370
Kodály 296
Palestrina 27
Walton 345
Missarum libri duo (Victoria) 34
Mlada (Rimsky-Korsakov) 210
Mocenigo, Girolamo 42
modal system, medieval 9
'modern primitive' see Ives, Charles
Moke, Camille 137
Molière 55, 57
Moments Musicaux, Op. 16 (Rachmaninov) 268
Mond, Der (Orff) 328
Monna Vanna (Rachmaninov) 269
monodic style 35, 36, 47, 67
monophonic style 13, 14
Montag aus Licht (Stockhausen) 383
Monteux, Pierre 316
Monteverdi, Claudio 23, 40-3, 42, 51, 299
Cavalli and 52, 55
Schütz and 47, 49
Montparnasse (Poulenc) 333
Montpensier, Mlle de 54
Moravian Duets (Dvořák) 202
Morceaux
de Fantasie No. 2, Op. 3 (Rachmaninov) 268
de Salon, Op. 10 (Rachmaninov) 268
Morgenblätter (Strauss II) 175
Mörike (poet) 233
Morley, Thomas 32
Mors et Vita (Gounod) 161
Mort d'Orphée, La (Delibes) 186
Mörtl, Wilhemina 303
Morzin, Count Wenzel von 73, 99-100
Moses und Aron (Schoenberg) 278
Mosson, Minna 120
motets 9-10, 16, 18-19, 25, 27, 28, 30, 31, 33-4, 38, 46, 52, 60, 66, 69, 72, 79, 93, 333, 388
see also 'occasional' motets
Mother Thekla 395
Mountain Thrall, The, Op. 32 (Grieg) 207
Mouvement symphonique (Honegger) 319
see also Pacific 231
Movements, for piano and orchestra (Stravinsky) 300
Mozart, Leopold 104-5

Mozart, Maria Anna (Nannerl) 105, 106
Mozart, Wolfgang Amadeus 91, 95, 104-9, 105, 331
Beethoven and 110
Haydn and 100, 101
Schubert and 127
Mozart and Salieri (Rimsky-Korsakov) 210
Mugellini Quintet 289
Munch, Charles 314, 333
Munich, Elector of 105
Mürgher, Henri 222, 224
Musette de Portici, La (Smetana) 166
Music for 18 Musicians (Reich) 391
Music for a Great City (Copland) 338
Music for a scene from Shelley, Op. 7 (Barber) 357
Music for Children, Op. 65 (Prokofiev) 317
Music for Mallet (Reich) 391
Music for Mallet Instruments, Voices and Organ (Reich) 391
Music for Strings, Percussion and Celeste (Bartók) 293
'music for the people' 352
Music for the Theatre (Copland) 337
music hall music 319
Music in Fifths (Glass) 392
Music in similar motion (Glass) 392
Music Makers, The, Op. 69 (Elgar) 220
'music-drama' see Glückliche Hand, Die; Salome
Musica Dei Donum (Lassus) 30
musical education, Hungarian 295, 371
Musical Offering, A (J. S. Bach) 82
Musicalia ad Chorum sacrum (Schütz) 48
Musicalische Ergötzung (Pachelbel) 60-1
Musiche Sacrae (Cavalli) 52
Musicien de l'avenir, Le (Offenbach) 163
Musick for the Royal Fireworks (Handel) 85
Musikalische Sterbens-Gedanken (pachelbel) 60
musique concrète 301, 360, 378, 382
electronics with 383
Musique de table (Telemann) 76-7
Mussorgsky, Modeste 173, 192, 192-4, 208-9, 281
Debussy and 237
influence of Glinka 140
Mutazioni (Berio) 376
Mutio scevola (Cavalli) 53
My Lady Nevell's Booke (Byrd) 33
Mystic Trumpeter, The, Op. 18 (Holst) 271

Nabucco (Verdi) 154
Nahowski, Hélène 305-6
Naissance d'Osiris, La (Rameau) 78
Naples, King of 58-9
Naples, Viceroy of 65, 66
Napoléon (Honegger) 319
'Napoléon Bonaparte' symphony see Symphony No. 3, Op. 55, Eroica
Narciso (D. Scarlatti) 87
Natali, Die (Barber) 357
national music 133, 144-5, 201, 217, 281 see also folk/native music
anthems 383
Argentinian 367
Debussy's use of 237
Javanese 235, 237
Polish 384
Sibelius's interest in 251, 252
Villa-Lobos's interest 309
Nations, Les (Couperin) 67-8
Nativité du Seigneur, La (Messiaen) 355
natural effects, use of 19, 68, 229, 322, 330, 355, 356
Neapolitan school 70
Necrology (Pärt) 389
Neefe, Christian 110
negro spirituals 203
'Deep River' 348
Sometimes I Feel Like a Motherless Child 330
Neher, Caspar 340
Nelsonmesse (Haydn) 102
'neo-classicism', Prokofiev's 315
Nerino e Nibbia (Pergolesi) 92
Nerone (Handel) 84

Neue Zeitschrift für Musik 147, 148, 149, 180
Neues vom Tage (Hindemith) 325
Nevell, Lady 32, 33
New Babylon (Shostakovich) 351
New German School 181
New Russian school 193, 196
New Symphony Orchestra 301
New Year, The (Tippett) 350
New York Counterpoint (Reich) 391
New York Symphony Society 330
Newman, Ernest 343
Nicolas de Flue (Honegger) 320
Niedermeyer, Louis 210
Nielson, Carl 215, 248-50
Night in Madrid, A (Glinka) 140
Night Mail (Britten) 362
Night on the Bare Mountain, A (Mussorgsky) 193
Nightingale, The (Stravinsky) 297
Nights in the Gardens of Spain (Falla) 287
Nikisch, Arthur 171
Nine Etudes-tableaux, Op. 39 (Rachmaninov) 269
Nine Mazurkas, Op. 25 (Scriabin) 261
Ninth Symphony
Choral (Beethoven) 113
From the New World, Op. 95 (Dvořák) 203
parody of 274
Mahler 232
Vaughan Williams 266
Nixon in China (Adams) 396, 396
Nobilissima Visione (Hindemith) 326
Nocent, Comte de 54
Noces, Les (Stravinsky) 297
Nocturen (Britten) 364
Nocturnal
after John Dowland (Britten) 364
Varèse 301
nocturnes 109, 212, 213
Debussy 236, 237
Nones (Berio) 376
Nonet (Martinu) 314
Nono, Luigi 335, 372, 372-3
Nordraak, Richard 206
Norfolk Rhapsodies (Vaughan Williams) 264
Norma (Bellini) 135
North Country Sketches (Delius) 239
Norwegian Music Association 206
Nose, The (Shostakovich) 351
Nossenko, Catherine 296
Nouveau système de musique théorique (Rameau) 78
Nouveaux Jeunes 319
Nouvelles suites de pièces de clavecin (Rameau) 78
November Group 339-40
Noye's Fludde (Britten) 364
Nozze di Figaro, Le (K492) (Mozart) 107, 109
Nozze di Teti e di Peleo, Le (Cavalli) 52
Nuits d'été, Les (Berlioz) 138
Nun danket alle Gott (Pachelbel) 60
Nuper rosarum flores (Dufay) 16
Nursery, The (Mussorgsky) 194
Nutcracker, The (Tchaikovsky) 198

'O clap your hands' (Gibbons) 46
O magnum misterium (Maxwell Davies) 388
'O Mistress Mine' (Vaughan Williams) 263
'O silver moon' (Dvořák) 203
Oberon (Weber) 118, 119
Oberto (Verdi) 153
Oboe Concerto
R. Strauss 245
Vaughan Williams 266
Obrecht 389
Ocampo, Silvina 367
'occasional' music 63, 64, 84-5, 168, 323
motets 15
Ocean, The (Vaughan Williams) 264
Ockeghem, Johannes 10, 16-17, 389
Octet
in F (D803) (Schubert) 130
Op. 20 (Mendelssohn) 142
Stravinsky 298
ode-symphonies 187, 271, 337
odes 63, 64
à la musique (Chabrier) 200

to Joy (Schiller) 113, 240
to Napoleon Buonaparte, Op. 41 (Schoenberg) 278
to the West Wind (Henze) 380
Odysseus, Op. 41 (Bizet) 190
Oedipus in Athens (Mussorgsky) 193
Oedipus Rex (Stravinsky) 298, 340
Of Thee I Sing (Gershwin) 329-30
Offenbach, Jacques 133, 161-4, 162, 173
Strauss II and 175
Officium defunctorum (Victoria) 34
Offrandes (Varèse) 301
Offrandes oubliées, Les (Messiaen) 355
Ogdon, John 386
Oh, Kay! (Gershwin) 329-30
Oiseaux exotiques (Messiaen) 356
Oistrakh, David 347
Old American Songs (Copland) 338
Old Hall manuscript 11
Old Polish Music, Op. 24 (Gorecki) 384
Olimpia vendicata (A. Scarlatti) 67
Olimpiade, L' (Pergolesi) 93
Olympic Games (1892), music for 255
Oma Maa (Homeland), Op. 92 (Sibelius) 253
'Ombra mai fu' (Handel) 85
On Hearing the Cuckoo in Spring (Delius) 239
'On the death of his worthy friend, Matthew Locke' (Purcell) 62
On the Town (Bernstein) 369
On the Waterfront (Bernstein) 370
On Wenlock Edge (Vaughan Williams) 265
Ondine (Ravel) see Gaspard de la nuit
135th Street (Gershwin) 329
One Touch of Venus (Weill) 341
Opera (Berio) 377
opera buffo/opera bouffe 74, 91, 92, 93, 112, 126, 132, 187, 199, 298
see also comic operas
opera seria 65, 74, 91, 93, 106, 108, 109, 123
interludes in see Intermezzo
opera-ballets 42, 53, 56, 78, 120, 272, 323
opéra-comiques see comic operas
opera-oratorio 298
operas see also opera buffo; opera seria; quasi-opera; tragédie-lyrique and specific operas
accompanied recitative 67
aversion to progressive 183
ballet music 53
'biblical' 319
'Big Three' see Boheme, La; Tosca; Turandot
castrato lead roles 97
chamber 177, 323, 363
comic 117, 118, 120, 153, 163, 169, 185, 186, 200, 228, 259, 284, 289, 320
development of 35, 40, 52
'domestic comedy' 244
Donizetti's output 125-7
first 42
German-language 47
'folk' 330, 341
for children 337
Gluck's reforming ideas 97
influences on Glinka 139
Liszt's staging of 152
lyric 213
miniature 323
one-act 188-9, 226, 241, 266, 278, 284, 313, 329, 340, 370
expressionist 325, 340
prize for see Sonzogno Prize
Prokofiev's output 315-18
televised 365
unfinished 177, 193, 200, 209, 226, 269, 278, 368
Verdi's output 154-6
verismo 205, 215, 222, 224-5
Mascagni's importance to 241
Wagner's output 157-9
operettas 162-3, 175, 176, 185, 187, 190, 199, 214, 215, 226, 320
Lehár's output 257-9
Spanish see zarzuela
Oprichnik (Tchaikovsky) 196
oratorios 57, 65, 72, 82, 83, 85, 103, 112, 143, 152, 161, 165, 202, 204, 239, 278, 311, 314, 319, 320, 348, 380

see also opera-oratorios
Orchesterstücke, Op. 16 (Schoenberg) 278
Orchestral Set No. 2 (Ives) 274
orchestras
  gamelan 235, 237, 282, 364
  Monteverdi's influence 43
  use of chamber orchestra 241, 306
  work for, without music 285
Ordo Virtutum (Hildegard) 13
Orestes trilogy (Milhaud/Claudel) 321
Orfée et Eurydice (Gluck) 98
Orfeo (Monteverdi) 42, 43
Orfeo ed Euridice (Gluck) 97
Orff, Carl 327–8
organ music
  Bach, Johann Sebastian 80
  Franck, César 166
  Messiaen 354
organum 9, 10
Orgel-Büchlein, BWV 599–644 (J. S. Bach) 80, 82
Orientalism 235
Orphée aux enfers (Offenbach) 162–3, 175
Orpheus
  Henze 381
  Stravinsky 299
ostinuto rhythms
  Debussy's 237
  Sibelius's 251
Otello (Rossini) 123
Othello
  Op. 93 (Dvořák) 202
  Verdi 156
Ottoboni, Cardinal Pietro 58, 59, 66, 84
  Accademie Poetico Musicali 87
Ottone in Villa (Vivaldi) 72
Our Hunting Fathers (Britten) 362
Out of Doors suite (Bartók) 292–3
Outdoor Overture, An (Copland) 337
Over the Hills and Far Away (Delius) 239
Overton, Hall 390
overtures/concert overtures 81, 137, 138, 142, 166, 189, 196, 202, 209, 275, 343, 353
  Gluck's reforming ideas 97
  'Italian' 67
  on Russian Themes (Rimsky-Korsakov) 209
  Op. 5 (Barber) 357
Owen, Wilfred 364
Owen Wingrave (Britten) 365
Owl and the Pussycat, The (Stravinsky) 300

Pachelbel, Johann 60–1
Pachem in Terris (choral symphony) (Milhaud) 324
Pacific 231 (Honegger) 316, 319
Paer, Ferdinando 150
Paganini (Lehár) 258
Paganini, Niccolò 91, 114–16, 115
  Berlioz and 138
  Liszt and 151
Paganini Caprices, Op. 3 (Schumann) 147
Pagliacci, I (Leoncavallo) 222, 223
'Pagodes' (Debussy) 237
Palestrina, Giovanni da 23, 25–8, 26, 160, 211, 216, 235, 327
  and Victoria 33
  Debussy and 237
Pampeana compositions (Ginastera) 367
Pamphili, Cardinal 65
Pan and Syrinx (Nielsen) 249
Pan Voyevoda (Rimsky-Korsakov) 210
Panambí, Op. 1 (Ginastera) 367
Panfili, Cardinal 58
Papillon, Le (Offenbach) 163
Papillons, Op. 2 (Schumann) 147
Parade (Satie) 254
Paradies und die Peri, Das (Schumann) 148
Paradise Lost (Penderecki) 386
Pardon de Ploermel, Le (meyerbeer) 121
Pardon My English (Gershwin) 330
Paribeni 376
Paride ed Elena (Gluck) 98
Paris (Milhaud) 324
Paris Quartets (Telemann) 76

Paris–the Song of a Great City (Delius) 239
Parker, Horatio 273
'parody' tradition 26, 27, 30
Parry 263
Parsifal (Wagner) 153, 159
Pärt, Arvo 375, 389–90
part-writing 25
Parthenia (Gibbons) 46
Pas d'acier, Le, Op. 41 (Prokofiev) 316
Pasadoble (Albéniz) 227
Pasquini 66, 84
Passacaglia
  and Fugue in C minor BWV 582 (J. S. Bach) 80, 82
  Op. 1 (Webern) 302, 305
Passion, The (Schütz) 48
Passion According to St Luke, The (Penderecki) 386
pasticcio/pastiches 96, 311, 323, 377
Pastoral Symphony (Vaughan Williams) 265
pastorales 66
  Rodrigo 342
Pástory, Ditta 293
Patrie, Op. 19 (Bizet) 189, 205
Pattern, Elizabeth 45
Paul Bunyan (Britten) 363
Paul IV, Pope 27
Paul VI, Pope 310
Paul Whiteman Orchestra 299
Pauvre Matelot, Le (Milhaud) 323
Pavana capricho (Albéniz) 227
pavane 25
  pour une Infante défunte (Ravel) 283
Pears, Peter 362–4
Pêcheurs de Perles, Les (Bizet) 188
Pedrell, Felipe 255, 287
Peer Gynt (Grieg) 207–8
Péladan, Joséphin 254
Pélissier, Olympe 124
Pelléas et Mélisande (Maeterlinck)
  Debussy 236, 237, 355
  Fauré 213
  Schoenberg 276
Pellegrin, Abbé 78
Penderecki, Krzysztof 385–6
Pénélope (Fauré) 173, 213
Penitential Psalms (Lassus) 30
Penthesilea (Wolf) 233
Pentola magica, La (Respighi) 289
Pepita Jiménez (Albéniz/Valera) 228
percussion
  African 300–1, 391
  'orchestral' backdrop 328
Perfect Fool, The, Op. 39 (Holst) 272
Pergin, Marianna 96
Pergolesi, Giovanni 91, 92, 92–3, 298
Peri, Jacopo 47
Pérotin 9
Perrin, Abbé Pierre 55
Persephone (Stravinsky) 298
Peter and the Wolf, Op. 67 (Prokofiev) 317
Peter Grimes (Britten) 363, 365
Peters, Frances 63
Petite Messe Solennelle (Rossini) 124
Petite Suite
  Bizet 189
  Borodin 178
  for two flutes and piano (Honegger) 320
Petites Symphonies (Milhaud) 322
Petrushka (Stravinsky) 297
Phaedra (Britten) 365
Phantasy Quartet (Britten) 362
Philemon und Baucis (Haydn) 100
Philip Glass Ensemble 392, 393
Philip le Bon, Duke of Burgundy son's tutor 16
Philipp II 34
Philippe of Orléans, Duke 57
'Piacevole' (Elgar) see String Quartet in E minor, Op. 83
piano, prepared 360
Piano Concertino (Honegger) 319
Piano Concerto
  Egyptian (Saint-Saëns) 184
  in A minor (Respighi) 289
  in F minor (No. 2) (Chopin) 145
  in F, Op. 20 (Scriabin) 261
  in G (Ravel) 285
  No. 1 (Brahms) 180–1
  Op. 16 (Grieg) 207
  Op. 42 (Schoenberg) 279
  Vaughan Williams 266

Piano Fantasy (Copland) 338
Piano phase (Reich) 391
Piano Pieces, Op. 33 a & b (Schoenberg) 278
Piano Quartet (Copland) 338
Piano Quintet in A minor, Op. 84 (Elgar) 221
Piano Sonata
  D958/959/960 (Schubert) 130–1
  in A minor (D784) (Schubert) 130
  Nos. 2 and 3 (Ginastera) 368
  Nos. 3 and 4 (Prokofiev) 316
  Op. 1 (Berg) 306
  Op. 1 (Brahms) 180
  Opp. 82/83/84 (Prokofiev) 317–18
'piano stunts' 273
Piano Trio
  No. 1 (Dvořák) 201
  No. 4 Dumky, Op. 90 (Dvořák) 202
  Op. 1 (Fauré) 213
  Op. 50 (Tchaikovsky) 197
  Ravel 285
Piano Variations (Copland) 337
Piatigorsky 345
Pictures at an Exhibition (Mussorgsky) 194, 210
Pièce forme de Habanera (Ravel) 283
Pièces de clavecin en concert avec un violon et une flûte (Rameau) 78
Pièces espagnoles (Falla) 287
Pierrot Ensemble 388
Pierrot lunaire, Op. 21 (Schoenberg) 277, 361
Pietra del paragone, La (Rossini) 122
Pilate (Martin) 311
Pilgrim's Progress, The (Vaughan Williams) 266
Pilgrimes Solace, A (Dowland) 40
Pimpinone (Telemann) 77
Pini di Roma (Respighi) 289
Pinto, Edgard 308
Pirata, Il (Bellini) 135
Piron, Alexis 78
Pisandel, J. G. 76
Piston, Walter 368
plagiarism 83, 283
  see also self-plagiarism
plainchant 13, 21, 25, 46, 211, 253, 389
  codification of 9
Planer, Minna 157, 159
Planets, The, Op. 32 (Holst) 271, 272
plays, music for see incidental music
Pleyel, Ignaz 137
Pli selon pli (Boulez) 378
Poe, Edgar Allen 269, 282
Poema autunnale (Respighi) 289
Poème de l'extase, Le, Op. 54 (Scriabin) 262
Poème électronique (Varèse) 301
Poèmes, Opp. 69/71 (Scriabin) 263
Poet's Echo, The (Britten) 365
Pohjola's Daughter, Op. 49 (Sibelius) 252
Points on the Curve to find... (Berio) 377
Poisoned Kiss, The (Vaughan Williams) 266
Poland-Saxony, King-Elector of 81
Polignac, Prince Edmond de 332
Polish Requiem (Penderecki) 386
Poliuto (Donizetti) 126
polkas 173, 175
polonaises 146
Polovtsian Dances (Borodin) 177
Polyphonie X (Boulez) 378
polyphony 9–10, 11, 16, 21, 25, 34, 45–6, 49, 57, 82, 253, 304, 313, 371
  English tradition 20
  polytonal 320
  see also contrapuntal polyphony
polytonality 322, 367
Pomone (Cambert) 55
Pomp and Circumstance marches, Op. 39 (Elgar) 220
Pompeo Magno (Cavalli) 53
Pompeo, Il (A. Scarlatti) 65
Ponchielli 223, 240
Pons, Lily 330
Porgy and Bess (Gershwin) 330
Portsmouth Point (Walton) 343
Poulenc, Francis 199, 310, 312, 319, 322, 331, 331–3
Praetorius, Michael 36
Preciosa (Weber) 118
preludes/préludes 145

à l'Après-midi d'un Faune (Debussy) 236, 237
and fugues 80, 82
arioso et fugue on BACH (Honegger) 320
Debussy 237
flasques (Satie) 254
for Doublebass and Piano, H79 (Honegger) 320
Fugue and Riffs (Bernstein) 370
in C sharp minor (Rachmaninov) 268
Liszt 152
Op. 74 (Scriabin) 263
Preludia ai gallo mananero (Rodrigo) 342
Premazone, Elizabetta 88
Premier Livre de pièces de clavecin (Rameau) 77
'Prete Rosso', Il see Vivaldi, Antonio
Prevost, Abbé 224
Prigionier, Il (Pergolesi) 93
prima prattica 51
Primavera, La (Respighi) 289
Primo libro di canzone a 1, 2, 3, 4 voci, Il (Frescobaldi) 44–5
Primo libro di Ricercari e canzoni francesci, Il (Frescobaldi) 44
Primo libro di toccata, partite, corrente, belletti, Il (Frescobaldi) 44–5
Prince Igor (Borodin) 177, 178, 210, 246, 268
Prince of the Pagodas, The (Britten) 364
Princesse de Navarre, La (Rameau) 78
Princesse jaune, La (Saint-Saëns) 183
Printemps for piano (Milhaud) 322
Prinz von Homburg, Der (Henze) 380
Prix de Rome 183, 187
  American 357
  first winner 160
Proclamations (Copland) 338
Prodigal Son, The (Prokofiev) 316
programme music 153, 168, 248, 249, 303, 353
Prokofiev, Sergei 314–18, 315, 333, 335, 351
Proksch, Josef 167
Prolations (Maxwell Davies) 388
prologue, dramatic 210
Prometeo, tragedia dell'ascolto (Nono) 373
Prometheus
  Beethoven 112
  Orff 328
'Poème du feu,' Op. 60 (Scriabin) 262
Promnitz, Count Erdman von 75
Prophète, Le (Meyerbeer) 121, 158
Proserpina rapita (Monteverdi) 42–3
Protagonist, Der (Weill) 340
Protecting Veil, The (Tavener) 395
Proust, Marcel: on Le Martyre de Saint-Sébastien 236
Provisional Theatre, Prague 168
Prussian Sonatas (C. P. E. Bach) 95
Psalmen Davids (Schütz) 47
Psalms of David 40, 46, 48 see also Symphony of Psalms
  dedicated to Palestrina 27
  settings of
    Gorecki's 384
    Palestrina 33
    Penderecki's setting 385
  Psalm 13 260
  Psalm 130 279
  Psalm 55 295
Psalmus Hungaricus, Op. 13 (Kodály) 295
Psalom (Pärt) 390
Pskovitianka (Rimsky-Korsakov) 209
Psyché (Franck) 165
publishers
  Attingnant, Pierre 19
  Belayev 246, 261
  Boosey & Hawkes 293, 299, 362
  Breitkopf & Härtel 180
  Calli & Diabelli 129
  Colombo, Professor 88
  Diabelli & Co 131, 150
  Durand 287
  Gutheil 268
  Hartmann, Viktor 194, 204
  Heseltine, Philip 62
  Paganini, Achillino 115
  Ricordi, Giulio 156, 222, 223, 224, 226

Russian Music Publishing
 Company 299
Schott 234, 325
Senff 180
Simrock 191, 202
Sonzogno 241
 see also Sonzogno Prize
Universal Edition 293, 303, 304, 306
publishing/printing 11, 23, 25, 31, 34,
 42, 100
 Ban on Boccherini 104
 Beethoven's problems 112
 musical periodicals 76, 147, 148,
 149, 180
Puccini, Giacomo 215, 223-6, 225
 Leoncavallo and 222-3
Pujol, Juan 255
Pulcinella (Stravinsky) 298
Punch and Judy (Birtwistle) 386-7
Purcell the elder, Henry 62
Purcell, Henry 46, 51, 62-5, 63, 84
Purcell, Thomas 63
Purgold, Nadezhda 209
Puritani, II (Bellini) 135
Pushkin 194, 197, 198, 368

Quantz, J. J. 94
Quartet
 for violin, clarinet, tenor saxophone
 and piano, Op. 22 (Webern) 304
 No. 11 (Shostakovich) 353
 see also string quartets
Quasi una Fantasia, Op. 64
 (Gorecki) 385
quasi-opera 295
Quattro stagione, Le (Vivaldi) 73, 74
Quatuor pour la fin du temps
 (Messiaen) 355
Queen of Spades (Tchaikovsky) 198
Quest, The (Walton) 345
Quickelberg, Samuel 28
Quiet City (Copland) 337
Quinault, Philippe 55
Quintet
 for Clarinet and Strings, Op. 115
 (Brahms) 182
 for Piano and Strings, Op. 29
 (Ginastera) 368
 for Piano, Op. 81 (Dvořák) 202

Rachmaninov, Sergei 266-70, 267
Radamisto (Handel) 85
radio-musical 340
Rag Time (well-tempered)
 (Hindemith) 325
ragtime 235, 273, 319, 322, 325
 Stravinsky 297-8
Rake's Progress, The (Stravinsky) 299
Rameau, Jean 77
Rameau, Jean-Philippe 51, 77-9, 78
 Gluck's study of operas 96
Rantzau, I (Mascagni) 241
Rape of Lucretia, The (Britten) 363
Rapsodie espagnole (Ravel) 284
Rastelbinder, Der (Lehár) 257
Ravel, Maurice 281, 282, 282-6, 287,
 330, 361
 Boulez' recordings 378
 Mussorgsky orchestrations 194
 Satie and 254
 Vaughan Williams and 264
Raymonda (Glazunov) 247
RCA Victor Prize 336
Re Enzo (Respighi) 289
Récio, Marie 138
Recital 1 for Cathy (Berio) 376
Recuerdos de viaje (Albéniz) 227
Red Hurricane, The (Copland) 337
Rédemption, La (Gounod) 161
Reed phase (Reich) 391
Reformation symphony (Mendelssohn)
 142
Refrain (Gorecki) 384
Refrains and Choruses for wind quartet
 (Birtwistle) 386
Reich, Steve 375, 390-1, 395
Reicha, Anton 111, 150
Reichart: on C. P. E. Bach 95
Reine de Saba, La (Bizet) 188
Reiner, Fritz 296, 357, 368
Relâche (Satie) 255
religious works see sacred music
Reményi, Edward 179
Renard (Stravinsky) 297
Repentant Thief, The (Taverner) 395
Representative for Planet 8 (Glass) 393

Requiem
 Berlioz 138
 Cavalli 52
 Cherubini 216
 Delius 239
 Dvořák 202
 Fauré 173, 212, 213
 Ligeti 371
 Martin 311
 Mozart (K626) 108, 109, 119, 146
 Vallotti 89
 Verdi 155
 see also specific requiems
Requiem Canticles (Stravinsky) 300
Respighi, Ottorino 288-90
Resurrezione di Nostro Signor Gesù
 Cristo, La (Handel) 84
Réveil des oiseaux (Messiaen) 356
Réveillon, Le (Strauss II) 175
Revolutionary symphony (Liszt) 150
Revue de cuisine, La (Martinu) 312
Rhapsodie nègre (Poulenc) 331
Rhapsody
 in Blue (Gershwin) 329
 on a Theme of Paganini, Op. 43
 (Rachmaninov) 116, 270
Rheingold, Das (Wagner) 159, 230
Richard III
 Smetana 168
 Walton 345
Richter, Hans 171, 181, 202, 230
Richter, Johanna 230
Ricimero (Pergolesi) 92
Riders to the Sea (Vaughan
 Williams) 266
Rienzi (Wagner) 157, 158
Rig-Veda, Op. 26 (Holst) 271
Rigoletto (Verdi) 154-5
Riley, Terry 395
Rilke
 poems set by Hindemith 325
 songs, Op. 8 (Webern) 303
Rimsky-Korsakov, Nicolai 173, 196,
 208-11, 309, 315
 Borodin's unfinished works 178, 246
 Glazunov and 246
 influence of Glinka 140
 Mussorgsky pieces reworked 194, 210
 Respighi and 288-9
 Tchaikovsky and 196
Rinaldo (Handel) 84
Ring das Nibelubgen, Der (Wagner)
 138, 152, 158, 159, 196, 210, 212,
 321, 354
 Boulez' recording 379
Rite of Spring, The (Stravinsky) 281,
 297, 301
Ritorno d'Ulisse in Patria, II
 (Monteverdi) 43
'Ritual fire dance' (Falla) 287
Robbins, Jerome 369
Robert Browning Overture (Ives) 275
Robert le Diable (Meyerbeer) 120,
 157, 208
Roberts, Alice 219
Rock, The, Op. 7 (Rachmaninov) 268
'Rockstrewn Hills', The (Ives) 274
Rodelinda (Handel) 85
Rodeo (Copland) 338
Rodrigo, Joaquín 335, 341-3, 342
Rodzinski, Artur 357, 369
Roi David, Le (Honegger) 319
Roi de Lahore, Le (Massenet) 204
Roi l'a dit, Le (Delibes) 173, 186
Roi malgré lui, Le (Chabrier) 204
Roland von Berlin, Der (Leoncavallo)
 223
Rolla, Alessandro 114
Rolland, Romain 284
Roman de Fauvel, La (Lescurel) 14
Romance for viola and orchestra, Op.
 85 (Bizet) 191-2
romantic extravaganza see Poisoned
 Kiss, The
Romantic movement 119, 133, 153
Rome Symphony (Bizet) 187, 188
Romeo and Juliet
 Op. 64 (Prokofiev) 317
 overture (Tchaikovsky) 196
Roméo et Juliette (Gounod) 160-1, 189
Rondine, La (Puccini) 226
Rondo (Webern) 302
Rondo in G minor, Op. 94 for cello and
 piano (Dvořák) 202
Rosamunde (Schubert) 129, 130
Rose + Croix Temple 254

Rose, La (Rameau) 78
Roseingrave, Thomas 87
Rosen, Jelka 239, 240
Rosenkavalier, Der (R. Strauss)
 244, 258
Rossetti, Dante Gabriel 265
Rossi, Lauro 221
Rossini, Gioacchino 91, 122, 122-4,
 133, 380
 and Paganini 115
 Bizet and 182
 Meyerbeer and 120
 requiem for 155
 Respighi's La Boutique Fantasque 289
 Saint-Saëns and 182
 'Rossini-fever' 113
Rostropovich, Mstislav 364
Rothschild family 145
Rottenberg, Gertrude 325
Roullet, Bailly du 98
Roussel 300, 312
Royal Academy of Music 85
Royal Winter Music (Henze) 381
Rubini (tenor) 135
Rubinstein, Artur 288, 309
Rubinstein, Ida 236, 285
Rubinstein, Nicholas 195-6
Rudolph, Archduke 112-13
Rugby (Honegger) 319
rune-singers 251
Rupertsberger Codex 12, 12-13
Ruslaka (Dvořák) 203
Ruslan and Lyudmila (Glinka) 140, 208
Ruta, Michele 221

Sabre Dance (Khachaturian) 347
Sacrae Cantiones (Gesualdo) 38
Sacrarum Cantionum (Gesualdo) 38
'sacred song' 92, 204
sacred music 40, 43, 46, 57, 74, 76,
 93, 102, 152, 161, 201, 299, 300,
 310, 332-3, 345, 389-90, 394-5 see
 also Masses
 Ives' use of hymn tunes 275
 Penderecki's 386
Sadko (Rimsky-Korsakov) 209, 210
Safonov 260
Saga, En, Op. 9 (Sibelius) 251
Saga-drom (Nielsen) 249
Saint François d'Assisi (Messiaen) 356
Saint-Marceaux, Madame de 283
Saint-Marie, Mlle 204
Saint-Saëns, Camille 173, 182-5, 183,
 211-12
Salade (Milhaud) 323
Salammbô (Mussorgsky) 193
Salieri, Antonio 120, 127
 Beethoven and 111
 Gluck and 98
 Liszt and 150
Sallustia, La (Pergolesi) 92
Salome
 Maxwell Davies 389
 R. Strauss 244, 257-8
Salomon, Johann Peter 101
Salón México, El (Copland) 337
salon music 174, 178, 199
Salonblatt, music critic of 233
Saltarello 23
Salud d'amour, Op. 12 (Elgar) 219
Salvator mundi (Tallis) 25
Salve Regina
 D. Scarlatti 87
 Haydn 100
 Pergolesi 93
 Poulenc 333
 Tartini 89
Sammartini, Giuseppi 96
Samson (Handel) 85, 143
Samson et Dalila (Saint-Saëns) 183
Sancta Susanna, Op. 21
 (Hindemith) 325
Sand, George 145-6
Sanderson, Sibyl 205
Sándor, Emma 295
Sapho (Gounod) 160
Satie, Erik 235, 236, 253-5, 254, 312,
 319, 322
 Poulenc and 331
Satin, Natalia 268
Satyagraha (Glass) 393
Satz, Natalie 317
Saudades
 das selvas brasileiras
 (Villa-Lobos) 309
 do Brasil (Milhaud) 322

Saul (Handel) 85
Saul and David (Nielsen) 248
Sávitri (Holst) 271
Savoy, Duke of 15, 16
Saxony
 Elector of 47
 King of 117
Saxophone Concerto (Glazunov) 247
Saxophone Quartet (Glazunov) 247
Sayn-Wittgenstein, Princess 138,
 151-2, 153, 180
Scandal, The School for (Barber) 357
Scandello, Antonio 47
Scaramouche, Op. 165b (Milhaud) 323
Scarbo (Ravel) see Gaspard de la nuit
Scarlatti, Alessandro 65-7, 66
 Corelli and 58-9
 Handel and 84
Scarlatti, Giuseppi Domenico 51, 66,
 86, 86-7
 Handel and 84
Scènes Alsaciennes (Massenet) 204
Scènes de la vie de bohème
 (Mürgher) 224
Scènes Dramatiques (Massenet) 204
Scènes Pittoresques (Massenet) 204
Schaeffer, Pierre 378, 382
Schéhérazade
 Ravel 283, 284
 Rimsky-Korsakov 210
Scherchen, Hermann 372
Scherz, List und Rache (Bruch) 190
Scherzo
 à la Russe (Stravinsky) 299
 Humoristique: The Cat and the Mouse
 (Copland) 336
 in B flat for orchestra (Mussorgsky)
 193
 in E flat minor, Op. 3 (Brahms) 180
Schikaneder, Emmanuel 108
Schindler (later Mahler), Alma 231,
 232, 234, 277, 306, 364
Schmallhausen, Lina 153
Schmitt, Florent 283
Schneider, Hortense 162
Schober, Franz von 128
Schoenberg, Arnold 215, 231, 275-9,
 276, 297, 339, 359, 362, 377-8, 380,
 387, 395
 Berg and 305, 306, 307
 Boulez' recordings 378
 Webern and 302
 Zemlinsky and 259
Schoenberg, Nuria 373
Schön Ellen, Op. 24 (Bizet) 190
Schön is die Welt (lehár) 258
Schöne Müllerin, Die (Schubert) 130
Schöpfung, Die (Haydn) 101-2
Schreker, Franz 278
Schubart, Christian: on Mozart 106
Schubert, Franz 91, 127-31, 128, 133
 Centenary celebrations 247
Schubert, Franz Theodor 127
Schubertiads 130
Schulwerk (treatise) (Orff) 327
Schulwerk für Instrumental
 Zuzammenspiel, Op. 44
 (Hindemith) 325
Schulzova, Zdenka 216-17
Schumann, Clara 143, 147-9
 and Liszt 151, 152
 Brahms and 180, 182
 Smetana and 167
Schumann, Robert 133, 146-9, 147,
 151, 152, 160
 Brahms and 180
 Mendelssohn and 143
 Schubert manuscripts 131
 Smetana and 167
Schütz, Heinrich 23, 47-9, 51
 teacher 36
Schwanendreher, Der (Hindemith) 326
Schwarzberg-Sonderhausen, Prince
 of 170
Schweigsame Frau, Die (R. Strauss) 245
Schwemmer, Heinrich 60
Schwind, Moritz von 129, 130
Scipione (Handel) 85
Scipione affricano (Cavalli) 53
Scivias (Hildegard) 12-13
Scott, Sir Walter 127, 133, 188
Scottish Fantasy, Op. 46 (Bruch) 191
Scottish symphony (Mendelssohn) 142
Scriabin, Alexander 215, 247, 260-3,
 261, 269
Scuola veneziana 69, 70

Scythian Suite (Prokofiev) 315
Sea, The (Bridge) 361
Sea Drift (Delius) 239
Sea Symphony, A (Vaughan Williams) 264, 265
Seasons, The
  Glazunov 247
  Haydn see Jahreszeiten, Die
Secessionists 231
Sechs Monologe aus Jedermann (Martin) 311
Sechter, Simon 169
Second Booke of Songes (Dowland) 39
Second Cello Concerto
  Villa-Lobos 310
Second Piano Concerto
  Bartók 293
  in C minor, Op. 18 (Rachmaninov) 268
  Martin 311
  Martinu 313
  Op. 16 (Prokofiev) 315
  Op. 83 (Brahms) 182
  Shostakovich 353
Second Piano Quintet, Op. 115 (Fauré) 213
Second Piano Sonata, Op. 36 (Rachmaninov) 269
Second Quartet, Op. 121 (Fauré) 213
Second Rhapsody (Gershwin) 330
Second Sonata, Op. 11 (Prokofiev) 315
Second String Quartet
  Bartók 292
  Op. 10 (Kodály) 295
Second Symphony
  Antar (Rimsky-Korsakov) 209
  Copernican, Op. 31 (Gorecki) 384
  The Bell (Khachaturian) 347
  Borodin 246, 283
  H153 (Honegger) 320
  in C minor, Op. 29 (Scriabin) 261, 262
  in D, Op. 43 (Sibelius) 251
  in E minor, Op. 27 (Rachmaninov) 269
  Ives 274
  Martinu 313
  Op, 17 Little Russian (Tchaikovsky) 196
  Op. 16 (The Four Temperaments) (Nielsen) 248
  Op. 36 (Bizet) 191
  Op. 40 (Prokofiev) 316
  Op. 63 (Elgar) 220
  Tippett 349
Second Violin Concerto, Op. 63 (Prokofiev) 317
Second Violin Sonata, Op. 108 (Fauré) 213
seconda prattica 44, 51
Secret, The (Smetana) 168
Secret Theatre (Birtwistle) 387
Seejungfrau, Die (Zemlinsky) 259
Segovia, Andrés 310, 342
Seidl, Anton 230
Seis piezas sobre cantos populares españoles (Granados) 255
self-plagiarism 123, 224
Selva morale e spiritual (Monteverdi) 43
Sémélé (Marais) 61
Semirama (Respighi) 289
Semiramide (Rossini) 123
Semyon Kotko (Prokofiev) 317
Senna Festeddiante, La (Vivaldi) 74
Sensitiva, La (Respighi) 289
Sept Haïkaï (Messiaen) 356
Sept Répons de tènebres (Poulenc) 333
Sequenza X-trumpet in C and piano resonance (Berio) 377
'Serenad', Op. 1 (Sibelius) 251
Serenade for Strings
  Op. 20 (Elgar) 219
  Op. 22 (Dvorák) 201
  Tchaikovsky 197
serenade(s) 109
  Bernstein 370
  Britten 363
  for Wind Instruments, Op. 44 (Dvorák) 202
  Op. 24 (Schoenberg) 278
  Op. 7 (R. Strauss) 243
  Opp. 11 & 16 (Brahms) 181
  to Music (Vaughan Williams) 266
Sergeyeva, Yekaterina 177
serialism 300, 303-4, 338, 359, 371, 392

see also dodecophany
Serpent of the Heart (Barber) 358
Serse (Handel) 85
Serva Padrona, La (Pergolesi) 93
Sessions, Roger 388
Set No. 1, Three Places in New England (Ives) 274
Set of 4 Ragtime Dances (Ives) 273
Seven early Songs (Berg) 305
Seven Last Words, The (Haydn) 102
Seven Last Words from the Cross, The (Schütz) 48
Seven Pieces for Piano, Op. 11 (Kodály) 295
Seven Spanish Folksongs (Falla) 287
Seventh String Quartet (Martinu) 314
Seventh Symphony
  Sinfonia antartica (Vaughan Williams) 266
  in C, Op. 105 (Sibelius) 253
  Op. 131 (Prokofiev) 318
'Sevilla' (Albéniz) see Suite española No. 1
Sèvres de la vieille France (Respighi) 289
Sextet (Reich) 391
Sforza, Ascanio 17
Sforza, Galeazzo 17
Shaker Loops (Adams) 396
Shakespeare, William 156, 160-1, 168, 169, 212, 263, 265, 266, 290, 311, 345, 358, 364
Shall We Dance (Gershwin) 330
Shankar, Ravi 392
Sharp, Cecil 264
Shaw, Fernández 287
Shelley, William 32
Sheppard, John 21
Shilovsky, Vladimir 196
shimmy (dance) 325
Shirinsky, Vasili 353
Short Ride in a Fast Machine (Adams) 396
Short Symphony (No. 2) (Copland) 337
Short Treatise on Lute-Playing, A (Dowland) 40
Shostakovich, Dmitri 247, 335, 350-4, 351, 369
Show Girl (Gershwin) 329-30
'Shropshire Lad' (Houseman) 265
Shylock (Fauré) 212
Sibelius, Jean 215, 250, 250-3
Sieben Todsünden, Die (Weill) 341
Siebold, Agathe von 180
Siege of Rhodes, The (Davenant) 62
Siegfried (Wagner) 158, 159
Sigurd Jorsalfar (Grieg) 207
silence, Debussy's use of 237
Siloti, Alexandre 268
Silouans Song (Pärt) 390
Silvano (Mascagni) 241
'Silver Swan, The' (Gibbons) 46
Simon Boccanegra (Verdi) 155
Simple Symphony (Britten) 362
Sinfonia (Berio) 377
Sinfonia Concertante
  for cello and orchestra, Op. 125 (Prokofiev) 317
  Walton 343-4
Sinfonia da Requiem (Britten) 363
Sinfonia Domestica (R. Strauss) 244
Sinfonia drammatica (Respighi) 289
sinfonia form 51
Sinfonia Sacra (Weill) 339
Sinfonietta
  Janácek 218
  'La Jolla' (Martinu) 314
  Poulenc 333
  Zemlinsky 260
single-line style see monophonic style
singspiel tradition 295
Sins of Old Age (Rossini) 124
Sir John in Love (Vaughan Williams) 265
Sita (Holst) 271
Sitwell, Edith 343, 344
Sitwell, Sacheverell 343, 344
Six Pieces
  Franck 166
  Op. 6 for orchestra (Webern) 303
Six Poèmes d'Apollinaire H12 (Honegger) 318
Six Poésies de Jean Cocteau (Honegger) 319

'Six, Les' 310, 312, 319, 320, 322, 331, 354, 355
Sixth Sonata, Op. 62 (Scriabin) 262
Sixth Symphony
  in D minor, Op. 104 (Sibelius) 252-3
  in D, Op. 60 (Dvorák) 202
  in E minor (Vaughan Williams) 266
  Mahler 229, 231
  Martinu 314
  Op. 111 (Prokofiev) 318
Sinfonia Semplice (Nielsen) 249
Slater, Montagu 363
Slavonic Dances, Op.46 (Dvorák) 202
Slavonic Rhapsody (Dvorák) 202
Sleeping Beauty, Op. 66 (Tchaikovsky) 198
Slominsky, Nicolas 274
Smetana, Bedrich 133, 166-9, 167, 201, 281, 313
Smithson, Harriet 136-7
Snow Maiden, The (Rimsky-Korsakov) 209
'Snowflakes are Dancing, The' (Debussy) 237
Socrate (Satie) 255
Soir de Neige, Un (Poulenc) 333
Soirée dans Grenade (Debussy) 283
Soldier's Tale, The (Stravinsky) 297, 299
solo instrument
  C. P. E. Bach and 95
  works for four hands 236
solo voice
  contrasting with accompaniment 36, 45-6
  juxtaposition with chorus 46, 49
'Solveig's Song' (Grieg) 207
Sombrero de tres picos, El (Falla) 287-8
Somerset Symphony, A, Op. 21 (Holst) 271
Something Wild (Copland) 338
Sonata for Clarinet (Poulenc) 333
Sonata for Clarinet and Bassoon (Poulenc) 332
Sonata for Flute, Viola and Harp (Debussy) 237
Sonata for Oboe (Poulenc) 333
Sonata for Solo Cello, Op. 8 (Kodály) 295
Sonata for Two Pianos (Poulenc) 333
Sonata for Two Pianos and Percussion (Bartók) 293
sonata(s) 58, 60, 69-70, 81, 87, 89, 91, 93, 95, 128, 227, 236, 261, 263, 274, 313, 319
  Beethoven's output 111, 112, 113
  Haydn's output 102
  in G minor (Tartini) see Devil's Trill
  No. 10, Op. 70 (Scriabin) 263
  No. 8, Op. 66 (Scriabin) 263
  No. 9, Op. 68 ('Black Mass') (Scriabin) 263
  Op. 109 (Beethoven) 261
  see also trio sonatas
Sonata(s) for Cello and Piano
  Debussy 237
  Kodály 295
  Op. 65 (Chopin) 146
Sonata(s) for Flute and Piano
  Martinu 314
  Poulenc 333
Sonata(s) for Piano
  Copland 337
  in E-flat, Op. 7 (Beethoven) 111
  No. 2 (Boulez) 378
  No. 2 in B flat minor (Chopin) 145
Sonata(s) for Violin and Piano
  Bartók 292
  Copland 337
  Debussy 237
  Poulenc 333
  Walton 345
Sonatas and Interludes (Cage) 360
Sonatas for Violin, Op. 5 (Corelli) 60
Sonatas of III Parts, for two violins and bass, to the harpsichord or organ (Purcell) 63
Sonate del Tasso (Tartini) 89
Sonatina (Bartók) 292
Sonatine (Ravel) 284
Song Before Sunrise, A (Delius) 240
'Song of Songs', setting of 200
Song of the High Hills, A (Delius) 239
Songfest (Bernstein) 370
Songs and Dances of Death (Mussorgsky) 194

Songs and Proverbs of William Blake (Britten) 364
Songs from the Chinese (Britten) 364
Songs of Farewell (Delius) 240
Songs of Sunset (Delius) 239
Songs of Travel (Vaughan Williams) 265
songs/song cycles and collections 63, 101, 113, 140, 180, 193, 194, 195, 199, 202, 212, 218, 230, 231, 235, 237, 265, 299-300, 301, 332-3, 340, 345, 348, 353, 357, 362-4, 367, 397
  see also lieder; art-songs
  Berg's output 304-6
  deep see cante hondo
  Delius' output 239, 240
  Fauré's
    Op. 118 213
    Op. 61 212-13
  Gershwin's output 329-30
  Grieg's Op. 5 207
  Ives' use of in Fourth Symphony 275
  orchestral 138
  Rodrigo's collections 342
  unpublished 318
  Webern's output 302-3
  Wild West 338
  Wolf's output 232-5
Songs Without Words (Mendelssohn) see Lieder ohne Wörte
Sonnambula, La (Bellini) 135
Sonzogno Prize 222, 224, 239, 240-1, 287
Sordes, Paul 283
Source, La (Delibes) 185
South-West German Radio 384
Souvenirs de Brunehaut (Chabrier) 199
Spalicek (Martinu) 313
Spanheim, Abbess Jutta von 12
Spanisches Liederbuch (Wolf) 233
Spartacus (Khachaturian) 347
Spellnikov, Basil 268
Spem in alium (Tallis) 25
Speziale, Lo (Haydn) 100
'Sphinx, The' (Emerson) 274
Spies, Hermine 182
Spinning Room, The (Kodály) 295
Spontini 145
sprechstimme (Schoenberg) 277
Spring Symphony
  Britten 364
  Schumann 148
St Cecilia's Day, odes for (Purcell) 63, 64
St John Passion
  J. S. Bach 82
  Pärt 390
St Luke Passion (C. P. E. Bach) 95
St Matthew Passion
  C. P. E. Bach 95
  J. S. Bach 82, 142
  Lassus 30
  Telemann 77
St Michael (Maxwell Davies) 388
St Paul (Mendelssohn) 143
St Paul's Suite (Holst) 271
St Ludmilla (Dvorák) 202
Stabat Mater
  Boccherini 104
  Donizetti 126
  Dvorák 202
  Haydn 100
  Pärt 390
  Pergolesi 93
  Poulenc 333
  RV 621 (Vivaldi) 74
staff, invention of 9
Stafford, Sir Edward 39
stage works 74, 75, 79, 204, 212, 240, 277, 295, 310, 319, 327, 328, 333, 386-7, 388-9, 393 see also 'entertainments; ballets; incidental music; opera-ballets; operas
  Broadway musicals 330, 369, 370, 375
  'epic theatre' 340
  farce 185, 199
  Gershwin's output 329-30
  non-traditional 373
  puppet theatre 288
  quasi-theatrical 297
  Spanish see zarzuela
Stalin Prize 347
Stamaty, Camille 182
Stanford, Charles 264, 270

Starlight Express, The
  (Elgar/Blackwood) 220
Statements for Orchestra (Copland)
  336, 337
Stedman Caters (Maxwell Davies) 388
Steiner, George 176
Stenbok-Fermor, Duke 198
Stenka Razin (Glazunov) 247
Stevenson, Robert Louis 265
Stigliano, Prince of 92, 93
stile antico/stile moderno 44
Still (Berio) 377
Stimmung (Stockhausen) 383
Stockhausen, Elisabeth von 181
Stockhausen, Karlheinz 356, 375, 381–
  3, 382
Stokowski, Leopold 301
Stolz, Teresa 156
Stone Guest, The (Darghomïnsky) 209
Story of a Real Man, The (Prokofiev)
  318
Stössl, David and Kamila 218
Straniera, La (Bellini) 135
Strauss II, Johann 164, 173, 174,
  174–6, 182
Strauss, Franz 242
Strauss, Johan Sr 174
Strauss, Josef 175
Strauss, Richard 215, 231, 242–5, 243,
  277, 305
  on Elgar 220
  Schoenberg and 276
Stravaganza, La Op. 4 (Vivaldi) 72
Stravinsky, Igor 173, 247, 281, 283,
  296–300, 299, 309, 310, 330, 351,
  362, 379, 380, 388, 395
  Debussy and 236
  on Gesualdo 38
  Prokofiev and 316
Street Scene (Weill) 341
Strepponi, Giuseppina 154, 155
Strike Up The Band (Gershwin) 329–30
string quartet(s) 91, 102, 103, 104,
  113, 114, 130, 178, 201, 218, 235,
  252, 302, 309, 310, 343, 350, 352–3
  American, Op. 96 (Dvořák) 203
  Debussy 237, 321
  dedicated to Haydn 100, 109
  Honegger 318
  in A minor (Walton) 345
  in D
    Franck 165
    Schoenberg 276
  in E minor, Op. 83 (Elgar) 221
  in F (Ravel) 283
  No. 2
    Op. 10 (Schoenberg) 277
    Tippett 348
  No. 3 (Ginastera) 368
  No. 6 (bartók) 293
  No. 7 (Glazunov) 247
  Nos. 2 and 3 (Honegger) 320
  Nos. 4 and 5 (Martinu) 313
  Nos. 6-15 (Milhaud) 323
  Op. 10 (Hindemith) 325
  Op. 28 (Webern) 304
  Op. 3 (Berg) 306
  Op. 51 (Brahms) 181
  Op. 80 (Mendelssohn) 143
  Opp. 20 and 26 (Ginastera) 368
String Quintet
  American, Op. 97 (Dvořák) 203
  K515 and 516 (Mozart) 109
String Symphonies (Mendelssohn) 141
String Trio, Op. 45 (Schoenberg) 279
Strophes for soprano and 10
  instruments (Penderecki) 385
strophic pieces 18
Structure 1a (Boulez): paper by
  Ligeti 371
Studies, Op. 18 (Bartók) 292
Studio di Fonologia Musicale 376
Study in F (Rachmaninov) 267
Sturm, Der (Martin) 311
Such Infinite Anguish (Janáček) see
  Along an Overgrown Path
Suggestion diabolique (Prokofiev) 315
Suite 1922, No. 2 (Hindemith) 325
Suite Bergamasque (Debussy) 237
Suite de valses (Chabrier) 199
Suite española (Nos. 1 and 2)
  (Albéniz) 227
Suite for Piano
  Op. 25 (Schoenberg) 278

Rodrigo 342
Suite for string orchestra
  (Respighi) 289
Suite française, Op. 248 (Milhaud) 324
Suite in G for organ and string
  orchestra (Respighi) 289
Suite Italienne (Stravinsky) 298
Suite on Verses of Michelangelo Op.
  145 (Shostakovich) 354
Suite populaire brésilienne
  (Villa-Lobos) 308
Suite Provençal, Op. 152 (Milhaud) 323
suites 76, 81, 189, 204, 207-8, 210,
  212, 213, 228, 237, 247, 251, 256,
  285, 288, 289, 295, 317, 323 see
  also dance music/dance suites
  for four pianos 324
  Op. 14 for piano (Bartók) 292
  Op. 29 for clarinets, strings and piano
    (Schoenberg) 278
  Op. 45 (Nielsen) 249
Suites (Sonatas) for Cello, BWV 1007-
  12 (J. S. Bach) 82
Sulamite, La (Chabrier) 200
Summer Day (Prokofiev) 317
Summer Evening (Kodály) 294
Summer Garden, In A (Delius) 239
Summer Night on the River
  (Delius) 239
Summertime (Gershwin) 330
Sun Quartets, Op. 20 (Haydn) 102, 106
Sun Shines on Our Motherland, The
  (Shostakovich) 353
Sunday Afternoon Music
  (Copland) 337
Sunless (Mussorgsky) 194
Suor Angelica (Puccini) see Trittico, II
'Surabaya-Johnny' (Weill) 340
Surge Debora et loquere canticum
  (Victoria) 34
Surprise Symphony (Haydn) 102
Survivor from Warsaw, A, Op. 46
  (Schoenberg) 279
Sverev, Nicholai 267-8
Swan Lake (Tchaikovsky) 196
  set for piano duet 235
Swannee (Gershwin) 329
Swingle Singers 377
Sylvia (Delibes) 173, 186, 187
Symbolist ideal 236
Symphonia Serena (Hindemith) 327
Symphoniae harmoniae a celestium
  revelationum (Hildegard) 13
Symphoniae sacrae (Gabrieli) 36
Symphonic Dances
  Hindemith 326
  Op. 45 (Rachmaninov) 270
Symphonic Metamorphosis on Themes
  of Weber (Hindemith) 326
Symphonic Ode (Copland) 337
'symphonic pastorale' 367
symphonic poems 140, 165, 168-9,
  203, 251, 289, 290
Symphonic Rhapsody (Nielsen) 248
Symphonic Songs (Zemlinsky) 260
Symphonic Variations
  Franck 133, 165, 166
  Lutoslawski 365
Symphonie Fantastique (Berlioz) 133,
  136-7, 151
Symphonie funèbre et triomphale
  (Berlioz) 138
Symphonie sacrae (Schütz) 48
symphonies 91, 119, 148, 149 see also
  ode-symphonies; String Symphonies
  Beethoven's 111-13
  Boccherini's output 103
  choral 113, 269, 272, 324
  Dvořák's output 201, 202
  five-movement 261
  Haydn's output 101, 102
  Henze's output 380-1
  Honegger's output 320
  interference with Bruckner's 171
  lost 131, 268
  Mendelssohn 142
  Milhaud's output 323, 324
  Nos. 38-41 (Mozart) 109
  Shostakovich's output 352-4
  unfinished 129, 178, 210, 212,
    246, 247
  Villa-Lobos's output 310
Symphonies of Wind Instruments
  (Stravinsky) 298

Symphony for Organ and Orchestra
  (Copland) 336-7
Symphony in C
  Bizet 187
  In Memorium Arturo Toscanini
    (Kodály) 296
  Stravinsky 299
Symphony in C minor (Bruckner) 170
Symphony in D minor (Franck) 165
Symphony in F minor (Bruckner) 170
Symphony in Three Movements
  (Stravinsky) 299
Symphony No. 0 (Nulte) in D
  (Bruckner) 170
Symphony No. 1, Op. 9 (Barber) 357
Symphony No. 2
  Barber 357
  in C minor (Bruckner) 170
  Pärt 389
  Walton 345
Symphony No. 3
  for Soprano and Orchestra
    (Tippett) 350
  Lutoslawski 366
  Op. 55, Eroica (Beethoven) 112, 216
  Organ, in C minor, Op. 78 (Saint-
    Saëns) 184
  Symphony of Sorrowful Songs, Op. 36
    (Gorecki) 384, 385
Symphony No. 4 (Lutoslawski) 366
Symphony No. 48, Maria Theresia
  (Haydn) 100, 102
Symphony No. 5 (Henze) 380
Symphony No. 6 (Pathétique), Op. 74
  (Tchaikovsy) 198
Symphony No. 7 in E (D729)
  (Schubert) 129
Symphony No. 9 (Great) in C
  (Schubert) 130
Symphony of Psalms (Stravinsky)
  298
Symphony Op. 21 (Webern) 303
syncopated music 235, 285, 349, 351
Szabelski 384

10 Mazurkas, Op. 3 (Scriabin) 261
12 canciones populares españolas
  (Rodrigo) 342
12 Danzas españolas, Op. 37
  (Granados) 255
12 Etudes, Op. 8 (Scriabin) 261
12 Piezás Caractericticas (Albéniz) 227
12 Songs, Op. 48 (Holst) 272
13 Preludes, Op. 32 (Rachmaninov) 269
2 Aquarelles (Delius) 240
2 Esbozos for violin and piano
  (Rodrigo) 342
2 Etudes (Boulez) 378
3 Impromptus, Op. 7 (Scriabin) 261
24 Caprices for Violin (Paganini) 116
24 Preludes and Fugues for Piano, Op.
  87 (Shostakovich) 353
3 Quarter-tone pieces (for two pianos)
  (Ives) 274
Tabarro, II (Puccini) see Trittico, II
Tafelmusik 61
Tagore, Rabindranath 260
Tailleferre (composer) 319, 332
Tale of Tsar Saltan, The (Rimsky-
  Korsakov) 210
Talich, Vaclav 312
Tallis, Thomas 24, 24-5
  and Byrd 31
Tamerlano (Handel) 85
Tancredi (Rossini) 122
Taneyev (composer) 260
tango 311, 322
  Stravinsky 299
Tannhäuser (Wagner) 158, 163, 243
tape recorder, use by Varèse 301
Tapiola, Op. 112 (Sibelius) 253
Taras Bulba
  Gogol 140
  Janácek 218
Tartini, Giuseppi 70-1, 88-9, 103
Tasso (Liszt) 152
Tate, Nahum 64
Tatyana (Lehár) 257
Tauber, Richard 258-9
Tavener, John (b. 1944) 375,
  394, 394–5
Taverner, John (c. 1490-1545) 20-1
Taverner, William 20

Tchaikovsky, Pyotr 173, 185,
  194–8, 195
  Rachmaninov and 267-8
Tcherepnin 315
Te Deum
  Bruckner 171
  Pärt 390
  Penderecki 386
  Purcell 65
Tel jour, telle nuit (Poulenc) 333
Telemaco (A. Scarlatti) 66
Telemann, Georg Philipp 51, 74-7, 75,
  81, 95, 103
  Handel and 84
Telemann, Maria Katherina 75
Tempest, The
  Ligeti 372
  Op. 18 (Tchaikovsky) 196
Tempesta di mare, La (Vivaldi) 73
Temps pent bien, Le (Lassus) 30
Ten Blake Songs (Vaughan
  Williams) 266
Ten Legends for Orchestra, Op. 59
  (Dvořák) 202
Ten Pièces pittoresques (Chabrier) 199
Ten Preludes, Op. 23 (Rachmaninov)
  268
Tender Land, The (Copland) 338
Tertis, Lionel 344
Terza, Marquis of 28
Texier, Rosalie (Lily) 236
texts
  Byrd's use of 33
  English language 25, 85
  Gesualdo's choice of 38
  motets by Lassus 30
  opera 52, 64
  Rameau's operas 79
  Schütz's theory 47, 49
  sources for madrigals 23
  Tartini's sources 89
  see also librettists
Thaïs (Massenet) 205
Theatre Piece (Cage) 360
Thema (Omaggio a Joyce) (Berio) 376
theme transformation 153
Thereminovox (electrical
  instrument) 301
Thérèse (Taverner) 394
Theresienmesse (Haydn) 102
Thieving Magpie, The (Rossini) see
  Gazza ladra, La
Third and Last Booke of Songes
  (Dowland) 39
Third Piano Concerto
  Bartók 293
  in D minor, Op. 30 (Rachmaninov) 269
  Op. 26 (Prokofiev) 316
  Prokofiev 316
Third String Quartet (Bartók) 292
Third Symphony
  Brahms 182
  Bruckner 170
  Copland 338
  in C, Op. 52 (Sibelius) 252
  Divine Poem, Op. 43 (Scriabin) 262
  Liturgique H186 (Honegger) 320
  Martinu 313
  Op. 27 (Sinfonia espansiva)
    (Nielsen) 249
  Op. 40 (Prokofiev) 316
  Op. 51 (Bizet) 191
  Polish in D, Op. 29 (Tchaikovsky) 196
  The Camp Meeting (Ives) 274
Third Violin and Piano Sonata, Op. 45
  (Grieg) 208
Thomán, István 290
Thomas, Ambroise 203, 204
Thomelin, Jacques-Denis 67
Thompson, Randall 368
Three Choirs Festival 220, 264,
  265, 272
Three Cornered Hat, The (Alarcón) 234
  see also Dreispitz, Der; Sombrero de
  tres picos, El
Three Gymnopédies (Satie) 253
Three Moods (Copland) 336
Three Nocturnes (Rachmaninov) 267
Three Organ Chorales (Franck) 166
Three Pieces (Franck) 166
Three Pieces in Old Style (Gorecki) 384
Three Preludes for piano
  (Gershwin) 330
Three Sarabandes (Satie) 253

Three Shakespeare Songs (Stravinsky) 299-300
Threni (Stravinsky) 300
Thun, Count Leopold 167
Thunder entered Her (Taverner) 395
Thurber, Mrs 203
Thurn und Taxis, Count, Canon of Salzburg 105
Tilge, Höchster, meine Sünden (J. S. Bach) 93
Tillet, Titon du: on Couperin 69
Timbre d'argent, Le (Saint-Saëns) 183
Timon of Athens (Purcell) 64
Tippett, Michael 335, **347-50**, *349*
toccata(s) **44-5**
  and Variations (Honegger) 318
  e due Canzoni (Martinu) 314
  and Adagio in C, BWV 564 (J. S. Bach) 82
  and Fugue in D minor, BWV 565 (J. S. Bach) 82
  for Orchestra (Respighi) 289
'Tod und das Mädchen, Der' (Schubert) 128, 130
Tod und Verklärung, Op. 24 (R. Strauss) 243
Today the Virgin (Taverner) 395
Tombeau de Couperin, Le (Ravel) 69, 285
Tommaso Chatterton (Leoncavallo) 221, 222
tonal system/tonality
  disintegration of 215
  Schoenberg and 276-7
  standardization of 67
tone poems 152, 153, 178, 236, 237, 239, 243, 247, 249, 269, 276, 289, 330
  Sibelius 251-3
Torke, Michael 373
Toscanini, Arturo 223, 224, 232, 289, 357
  work dedicated to 296
Toulouse, Comte de 67
Toward the Unknown Region (Vaughan Williams) 264
Toy Symphony (L. Mozart) 105
Tracollo (Pergolesi) 93
tragédie-lyrique genre 55, 56
Tragó, José 287
Tragoedia (Birtwistle) 386
Train Bleu, Le (Milhaud) 323
Traité de l'harmonie (Rameau) 77-8
Traumgörge, Die (Zemlinsky) 259
Travail du peintre, Le (Poulenc) 333
Traviata, La (Verdi) 154-5
Tre Ricercari (Martinu) 313
Treatise on Harmony, A (Schoenberg) 278
Trez Piezas, Op. 6 (ginastera) 367
trifles 124
Trio
  for Flute, Piano and Cello (Martinu) 314
  for Oboe, Bassoon and Piano (Poulenc) 332
  Op. 20 (Webern) 304
Trio élégiaque in D minor, Op. 9 (Rachmaninov) 268
trio sonatas 58, 61, 67-8, 69, 72
Trionfi (Orff) 327-8
Trionfo del Tempo e del Disinganno, Il (Handel) 84
Trionfo di Afrodite (Orff) 328
Triple Concerto (Tippett) 350
Trisagion (Pärt) 390
Tristan und Isolde (Wagner) 158-9, 170, 199, 251, 381
Trittico botticelliano (Respighi) 289
Trittico, Il (Puccini) 226
Triumph of Time, The (Birtwistle) 387
Triumphes of Oriana, The (Morley) 45
Triumphlied, Op. 55 (Brahms) 181
Troilus and Cressida (Walton) 345
Trois Petites liturgies de la Présence Divine (Messiaen) 356
Trois Poèmes d'Henri Michaux (Lutoslawski) 366
Trois valses romantiques (Chabrier) 200
Trouble in Tahiti (Bernstein) 370
Troupe 33 341
Trout quintet (Schubert) 128
trouvères 14
Trovatore, Il (Verdi) 154-5
Troyens, Les (Berlioz) 138
Truffot, Marie-Laure 184

Tsar's Bride, The
  Borodin 177
  Rimsky-Korsakov 210
Tua, Teresina 208
Tuczek, Clara 191
Turandot (Puccini) 226
Turandotte (Gozzi) 226
Turangalila Symphony (Messiaen) 356
Turco in Italia, Il (Rossini) 123
Turina, Giuditta 135
Turn of the Screw, The (Britten) 364
Turner, William 62
twelve-tone system of tonal organization *see* dodecaphonic theory
Twelves Etudes for guitar (Villa-Lobos) 309
'Twenty Hungarian Folksongs' (Bartók/Kodály) 291
Twenty-four Preludes, Op. 34 (Shostakovich) 351
Two Fanfares (Adams) 396
Two Fiddlers, The (Maxwell Davies) 388
Two Lyric Pieces, Op. 68 (Grieg) 207
Two Pages (Glass) 392
Two Pieces for Small Orchestra (Delius) 239
Two Portraits (One Ideal, One Grotesque) (Bartók) 292
Two Widows, The (Smetana) 168
Tye, Christopher 21, 23, 24

Uber die Klangfarbe (Hauer) 278
Ubu Roi (Penderecki) 386
Ugly Duckling, The (Prokofiev) 315
Ultimos Ritos (Taverner) 390
Unanswered Question, The (Ives) 274
Und Pippa Tanze (Hauptmann) 307
Undine (Henze) 381
'utilitarian' music 325

Vakula (Tchaikovsky) 196
Valiant Knights, The (Borodin) 177
Valse, La (Ravel) 285
valse lente 257
Valse Triste, Op. 44 (Sibelius) 251-2
Valses nobles et sentimentales (Ravel) 285
Vampyr, Der (Märschner) 118, 157
Vanessa (Barber) 358
Vannucci, Abbé 102
Varèse, Edgard **300-1**, 359
variations
  Diabelli waltz 150
  I, II and V (Cage) 360
  on 'La Carmagnole' 114
  on *Der Tod und das Mädchen* 130
  on *Venni Amorez* 110-11
  on a French Air, Op. 10 (Schubert) 129
  on a Hungarian folksong, 'The Peacock' (Kodály) 295-6
  on a Rococo Theme, Op. 33 (Tchaikovsky) 196, 208
  on a Theme of Chopin, Op. 22 (Rachmaninov) 268
  on a Theme of Corelli, Op, 42 (Rachmaninov) 268
  on a Theme of Frank Bridge (Britten) 362
  on an Original Theme, Op. 36 (Elgar) 220
  on themes of Paganini 116, 270
  resolving into fugue 348
  symphonic 80, 133, 326
  see also specific pieces
Variations & Fugue on a Theme by Purcell (Britten) 363
Variations, Aldous Huxley in Memoriam (Stravinsky) 300
Variations for Orchestra
  Op. 31 (Schoenberg) 278
  Webern 304
Variations for Piano, Op. 27 (Webern) 304
Variazioni canoniche (Nono) 372-3
Varietie of Lute-Lessons (R. Dowland) 45
Varzar, Nina 351
Vasco da Gama (Bizet) 187
Vasilissa, ergo gaude (Dufay) 15
Vasnier, Madame 235
Vasselli, Virginia 125
Vaucochard et Fils Ier (Chabrier/Verlaine) 199
Vaughan Williams, Ralph 215, **263-6**, *264*, 362

Holst and 270
  interest in Tallis 24
Vaurabourg, Andrée 319
Vénard, Céleste 188
Veneen Iouminen (Sibelius) 251
Venetian Games (Lutoslawski) 366
Venetian school 35
Venice Featival committee 364
Venni Amore (Righini)
  Beethoven's variations on 110-11
Venus and Adonis (Blow) 64
Vera storia, La (Berio) 377
Vergene bella (Dufay) 16
Verdi, Giuseppe 133, **153-6**, *154*, 380
  influence of Meyerbeer 121
Vergene bella (Dufay) 16
Verlaine, Paul 212-13
Vers la flamme, Op. 72 (Scriabin) 273
Verschworene, Die (Schubert) 130
verse anthems 33, 46
Verses for Ensembles (Birtwistle) 387
Versuch über die Wahre Art das Klavier zu Spielen (C. P. E. Bach) 94-5
Versuch über Schweine (Henze) 380
Vesperae solennes de confessore (K339) (Mozart) 109
Vespers
  'All Night Vigil,' Op. 37 (Rachmaninov) 269
  Cavalli 52
  Vivaldi 72
Vêspres Siciliennes, Les (Verdi) 154
*Vespro della Beata Vervine (Monteverdi) 42
Vetrate di chiesa (Respighi) 289
Viadot, Marianne 212
Viadot, Pauline 160, 204, 212
Viaggio a Reims, Il (Rossini) 124
Victoria, Queen 143, 158, 162
Victoria, Tomas Luis de 23, **33-4**, 216
Vida breve, La (Falla) 287
Vide homo quae pro te patior (Lassus) 30
Vie Parisienne, La (Offenbach) 163
Vier ernste Gesänge, Op. 121 (Brahms) 182
Vier Letzte Lieder (R. Strauss) 245
Villa-Lobos, Heitor 281, *308*, **308-10**
Village Romeo and Juliet, A (Delius) 239
villanelles 28
Ville d'en Haut, La (Messiaen) 356
Villi, La (Puccini) 224
Vin herbé, Le (Martin) 310
Viñes, Ricardo 282, 283, 331
Vingt Regards sur l'enfant Jésus (Messiaen) 355-6
viol music (Marais) 61
Viola (Smetana) 169
Viola Concerto (Walton) 344
Violin Concerto
  Beethoven 112, 324
  Berg 307
  BWV 1041/2 and 1064/5 (J. S. Bach) 81
  Glass 393
  Glazunov 247
  Hindemith 326
  in B minor, Op. 61 (Elgar) 220
  in D minor, Op. 47 (Sibelius) 251
  Martin 311
  Op. 36 (Schoenberg) 279
  Op. 53 (Dvořák) 202
  Op. 77 (Brahms) 182
  Stravinsky 298
  Walton 345
Violin Sonata
  Bartók 292
  H3 (Honegger) 318
  Honegger 320
  in A (Franck) 165
  in E minor, Op. 82 (Elgar) 220-1
  No. 1, Op. 75 (Saint-Saëns) 184
  Op. 2 (Vivaldi) 72
virelays (Machaut) 15
Visage (Berio) 376
Vision of St Augustine, The (Tippett) 349
Visions de l'Amen (Messiaen) 355
Visions fugitives, Op. 22 (Prokofiev) 316
Vitrail et des oiseaux, Un (Messiaen) 356
Vitry, Philippe de 14
Vivaldi, Antonio 51, **71-4**, *73*, 103

J. S. Bach and 81
  tribute to 342
Vltava (Smetana) 169
Vocalese, Op. 34 (Rachmaninov) 269
Voces Intimae in D minor, Op. 58 (Sibelius) 252
Vogl, Johann Michael 128, 130
Vogler, Abbé 116, 119
Voices of Spring waltz (Strauss II) *see* *Frühlingsstimmen*
Voix Humaine, La (Poulenc) 333
Volumina (Ligeti) 371
Von Heute auf Morgen (Schoenberg) 278
'Vorfrühling' (Webern) 302
Voyevoda, The (Tchaikovsky) 196

Wagner, Cosima: opposition to Mahler 230
Wagner, Richard 119, 133, **156-9**, *157*, 173
  Berlioz and 138
  Bruckner and 170, 171
  Debussy and 235
  influence of
    on Chabrier 200
    on Mahler 229-30
    on Rachmaninov 269
    on Rimsky-Korsakov 210
  influence of Meyerbeer 121
  Liszt and 151, 152-3
  Offenbach and 163
  Schumann and 148
  Wolf and 232
'waits', Cambridge 45
Walden, Lord 40
Waldmädchen, Das (Weber) 116
Waldstein, Count 110, 111, 166
Waldszenen, Op. 82 (Schumann) 149
Walküre, Die (Wagner) 159, 263
Wallenstein's Camp (Smetana) 168
Walter, Bruno 369
Walton, William 335, **343-5**, *344*
  waltzes 145, 150, 173, 175, 176, 181, 199, 200, 228, 285
Wand of Youth, The (Elgar) 220
Wang Wei 231
War and Peace (Prokofiev) 318
War Requiem (Britten) 364
'war sonatas' (Prokofiev) 317-18
Ward, Thomas 238
Wasps, The (Vaughan Williams/Aristophanes) 265
Water Goblin, The (Dvořák) 203
Water Music (Handel) 84-5
We Come to the River (Henze) 380
We shall see Him as He is (Taverner) 395
Weber family 101
Weber, Carl Maria von 91, **116-19**, *117*
Weber, Constanze 107, 116
Webern, Anton 276, 277, 281, **302-4**
  Berg and 305
Wecker, Georg Kaspar 60
Wecklinger, Regina 29
Wedding Prayer (Taverner) 395
Weill, Kurt 323-4, 335, *339*, **339-41**, *339*
Weinlig, Christian 156
Weiss, Adolph 359
welcome songs for the royal family 63, 64
Weldon, Augusta 161
Wert, Giaches de
  Monteverdi and 41
  source of texts 23
Werther (Massenet) 205
West Side Story (Bernstein) 370
Western Wind Mass (Taverner) 21
Whale, The (Taverner) 394
'What Is Our Life' (Gibbons) 46
Whispers from Heavenly Death (Henze) 379
Whiteman, Paul 329
Whitman, Walt 239, 264
Who can from joy refrain (Purcell) 64
Who is the most powerful in the world? (Martinu) 312, 313
whole-tone scale 237
'Why fumeth in flight?' (Tallis) 24
Widor, Charles-Marie 166, 300, 318, 321-2
Wieck, Clara *see* Schumann, Clara
Wieck, Friedrich 147, 148
Wien (Ravel) *see* *Valse, La*
Wiener Blut (Strauss II) 257

Wiener Frauen (Lehár) 257
Wilde, Oscar 244, 260
Wildeck, Magdalene 47
Wilhelm II, Kaiser 223
Wilhelm of Bavaria, Duke 29-30
William Ernst of Weimar, Duke 80
William Tell overture (Rossini) 354
Williams Mix (Cage) 360
'Willow Song, The' (Vaughan
    Williams) 263
Wimborne, Alice 345
Wind Quintet, Op. 26 (Schoenberg) 278
Winter Bonfire, Op. 122 (Prokofiev) 318
Winter Words (Britten) 364
Winterreise, Die (Schubert) 130
Wise Virgins, The (Walton) 345
Wittgenstein, Paul 285-6
Wodzinski, Marie 145
Wohltemperierte Klavier, Das
    (J. S. Bach) 82
Wolf, Hugo 171, 232-5, 233

Wolfstein, Leopold 336
Wolsey, Cardinal 21
Wolzogen, Ernst von 276
Wonderful Town (Bernstein) 370
Wood, Henry 239
    Golden Jubilee concert 266
Wood, Ursula 266
Wooden Prince, The (Bartók) 292
Words fail (Janácek) see Along an
    Overgrown Path
World Exhibition (1889) 235
World Fair (1939), commission for 266
Wozzeck (Berg) 299, 306-7
Wulf, Amalie 119
Wundertheater, Das (Henze) 379
Württemburg Sonatas (C. P. E. Bach) 95

Xerse (Cavalli) 53, 54

Yale-Princeton Football Game
    (Ives) 273

Year 1917, The symphony
    (Shostakovich) 353
Yerma the Unfaithful (Villa-Lobos) 310
Yolanthe (Rachmaninov) 268
Young Person's Guide to the Orchestra,
    The (Britten) 363
Young Pioneers, The (Copland) 337
Youth's Choice, The (Holst) 271

Zabaleta, Nicanor 343
Zachau, F. W. 83
Zadok the Priest (Handel) 85
Zaira (Bellini) 135
Zancia, Paolo 125
Zanetto (Mascagni) 241
Zarabande (Rodrigo) 342
Zarewitsch, Dar (Lehár) 258
zarzuela 227, 228, 256, 287-8
Zauberflöte, Die (K620)
    (Mozart) 108
Zauberharfe, Die (Schubert) 128-9

Zazà (Leoncavallo) 223
Zeffirelli, Franco 358
Zelenka, J. D. 76
Zelmira (Rossini) 123
Zelter, Carl Friedrich 141
Zemlinsky, Alexander 231, 259-60,
    275-6, 277
Zemlinsky, Mathilde 276, 277, 278
Zenobia, regina di Palmieri
    (Albinoni) 69
Ziegler, Marta 292
Zigeunerbaron, Der (Strauss II)
    176
Zigeunerliebe (Lehár) 258
Zingarelli, Niccolo 134
Zoraide di Granata (Donizetti) 125
Zoroastre (Rameau) 79
Zwerg, Der (Zemlinsky) 260
Zwillingsbrüder, Die
    (Schubert) 128
Zywny, Adalbert 144

PICTURE CREDITS

Page 8-9 Gianni Dagli Orti/Corbis; Page 10-11 The National Gallery, London/Corbis; Page 12 Gianni Dagli Orti/Corbis; Page 15 Lebrecht Collection; Page 22-23 Mimmo Jodice/Corbis; Page 24 Hulton Getty Collection; Page 26 Hulton Getty Collection; Page 29 Hulton Getty Collection; Page 31 Hulton Getty Collection; Page 35 Lebrecht Collection; Page 42 AKG Photo, London; Page 44 Hulton Deutsch Collection; Page 46 Hulton Deutsch Collection; Page 50-51 David Lees/Corbis; Page 54 Hulton Getty Collection; Page 59 AKG Photo, London; Page 63 Corbis-Bettmann; Page 66 Hulton Getty Collection; Page 68 Hulton Getty Collection; Page 70 Lebrecht Collection; Page 73 Library of Congress/Corbis; Page 75 Hulton Getty Collection; Page 78 Library ofCongress/Corbis; Page 80 Mike Nicholson; Page 83 Mike Nicholson; Page 86 Hulton Getty Collection; Page 90-91 Philip de Bay/Corbis; Page 92 Hulton Getty Collection; Page 94 Hulton Getty Collection; Page 97 Mike Nicholson; Page 99 Gianni Dagli Orti/Corbis; Page 103 Mike Nicholson; Page 105 Mike Nicholson; Page 110 Mike Nicholson; Page 115 Library of Congress/Corbis; Page 117 Mike Nicholson; Page 121 Library of Congress/Corbis; Page 122 Hulton Deutsch Collection/Corbis; Page 125 Mike Nicholson; Page 128 Corbis-Bettmann; Page 132-133 Gianni Dagli Orti/Corbis; Page 134 F. Bruckmann/Hulton Deutsch Collection/Corbis; Page 137 Hulton Deutsch Collection/Corbis; Page 141 Mike

Nicholson; Page 144 Mike Nicholson; Page 147 Mike Nicholson; Page 150 W. & D. Downey/Hulton Deutsch Collection/Corbis; Page 154 Mike Nicholson; Page 157 Mike Nicholson; Page 160 Nadar/Hulton Deutsch Collection/Corbis; Page 162 Mike Nicholson; Page 165 Corbis-Bettmann; Page 167 Mike Nicholson; Page 170 Corbis; Page 172-173 Robbie Jack/Corbis; Page 174 Mike Nicholson; Page 177 Corbis-Bettmann; Page 179 Mike Nicholson; Page 183 Mike Nicholson; Page 186 Corbis-Bettmann; Page 189 Mike Nicholson; Page 191 Hulton Deutsch Collection/Corbis; Page 192 Mike Nicholson; Page 194 Mike Nicholson; Page 201 Mike Nicholson; Page 204 Mike Nicholson; Page 206 Mike Nicholson; Page 211 Leonard de Selva/Corbis; Page 214-215 Ira Nowinski/Corbis; Page 219 Mike Nicholson; Page 222 Hulton Deutsch Collection/Corbis; Page 225 Library of Congress/Corbis; Page 229 Corbis-Bettmann; Page 233 Mike Nicholson; Page 238 Hulton Deutsch Collection/Corbis; Page 241 Mike Nicholson; Page 243 Mike Nicholson; Page 246 Il'ja Efimovic Repin/The State Russian Museum/Corbis; Page 250 Corbis-Bettmann; Page 254 Corbis-Bettmann; Page 257 Mike Nicholson; Page 261 Corbis-Bettmann; Page 264 Erich Auerbach/Hulton Deutsch Collection/Corbis; Page 267 Mike Nicholson; Page 271 Corbis-Bettmann; Page 276 Corbis-Bettmann; Page 280-281 E. O. Hoppé/Corbis; Page 282 Library of Congress/Corbis; Page 286 Hulton Getty Collection; Page 291 Corbis-Bettmann;

Page 294 Library of Congress/Corbis; Page 297 Erich Auerbach/Hulton Deutsch Collection/Corbis; Page 305 Corbis-Bettmann; Page 308 Erich Auerbach/Hulton Deutsch Collection/Corbis; Page 311 Corbis; Page 315 Hulton Getty Collection; Page 319 Corbis-Bettmann; Page 321 Ted Streshinsky/Corbis; Page 325 Hulton Deutsch Collection/Corbis; Page 329 Corbis-Bettmann; Page 331 UPI/Corbis-Bettmann; Page 334-335 UPI/Corbis-Bettmann; Page 336 Corbis-Bettmann; Page 339 Hulton Getty Collection; Page 342 Hulton Getty Collection; Page 344 Hulton Deutsch Collection/Corbis; Page 346 Dean Conger/Corbis; Page 349 Hulton Deutsch Collection/Corbis; Page 351 Erich Auerbach/Hulton Deutsch Collection/Corbis; Page 354 John Wildgoose/Hulton Getty Collection; Page 357 Corbis-Bettmann; Page 359 Hulton Deutsch Collection/Corbis; Page 361 Hulton Deutsch Collection/Corbis; Page 366 Hulton Getty Collection; Page 369 Hulton Deutsch Collection/Corbis; Page 372 Hulton Deutsch Collection/Corbis; Page 374-375 Donald Cooper/Photostage; Page 376 Richard Mildenhall/Hulton Getty Collection; Page 378 Hulton Deutsch Collection/Corbis; Page 380 Erich Auerbach/Hulton Getty Collection; Page 382 Hulton Deutsch Collection/Corbis; Page 388 Hulton Deutsch Collection/Corbis; Page 393 Richard Mildenhall/Hulton Getty Collection; Page 394 Erich Auerbach/Hulton Deutsch Collection/Corbis; Page 396 Richard Mildenhall/Hulton Getty Collection

BIBLIOGRAPHY

Anderson, James: Dictionary of Opera & Operetta (Bloomsbury, 1989)

Anderson, Nicholas: Baroque Music from Monteverdi to Handel (Thames & Hudson, 1994)

Arnold, Denis & Fortune, Nigel (Ed): The New Monteverdi Companion (Faber, 1985)

Ashbrook, William: The Operas of Puccini (Cassell, 1968)

Becker, H & G: Meyerbeer – A Life in Letters (Christopher Helm, 1983)

Beecham, Sir Thomas: Delius (Hutchinson, 1959)

Bélague, Gerard: Music in Latin America – An Introduction (Prentice-Hall, 1979)

Biancolli, Louis & Mann, William: The Analytical Concert Guide (Cassell, 1957)

Bird, John: Percy Grainger (Faber, 1982)

Blom, Eric (Ed): Grove's Dictionary of Music and Musicians (Macmillan, 1975)

Blom, Eric (Ed): Mozart's Letters (Pelican, 1968)

Brown, David: Tchaikovsky Remembered (Faber, 1993)

Brown, M.H. & Wiley, R.J. (Ed): Slavonic & Western Music (Oxford, 1985)

Campbell, M: Henry Purcell – Glory of His Age (Oxford, 1993)

Carner, Mosco: Alban Berg (Duckworth, 1975)

Carner, Mosco: Puccini (Duckworth, 1992)

Carpenter, Humphrey: Benjamin Britten (Faber, 1982)

Carter, Tim: Music in Late Renaissance & Early Baroque Italy (Batsford, 1992)

Conrad, Peter: A Song of Love & Death – The Meaning of Opera (Chatto & Windus, 1987)

Craft, Robert: Stravinsky in Conversation (Pelican, 1960)

Culshaw, John: Sergei Rachmaninov (Dennis Dobson, 1949)

Curtiss, Mina: Bizet & His World (Secker & Warburg, 1959)

Dale, Katherine: Brahms – A Concertgoer's Companion (Bingley, 1970)

de Marliave, Joseph: Beethoven's Quartets (Oxford, 1928)

Demuth, Norman: Ravel (Dent, 1947)

Dent, E.J.: Ferruccio Busoni (Ernst Eulenberg Ltd, 1974)

Einstein, Alfred: Music in the Romantic Era (Norton, 1947)

Evans, Edwin: Tchaikovsky (Dent, 1957)

Ewen, David: The World of 20th Century Music (Robert Hale, 1968)

Fenby, Eric: Delius As I Knew Him (Bell, 1937)

Garden, Edward: Tchaikovsky (Dent, 1984)

Gershwin, Ira: Lyrics on Several Occasions (Omnibus, 1978)

Gillies, Malcom: Bartók Remembered (Faber, 1990)

Girdlestone, G.M.: Mozart's Piano Concertos (Cassell, 1958)

Gray, Cecil: A Survey of Contemporary Music (Oxford, 1947)

Griffith, Paul: Encyclopaedia of 20th Century Music (Thames & Hudson, 1986)

Grout, Ronald Jay & Palisca, Claude V: A History of Western Music (Dent, 1993)

Grun, Bernard (Ed): Alban Berg – Letters to His Wife (Faber, 1971)

Hall, Eric (Ed): The Concerto (Pelican, 1958)

Hanslick, Eduard: Music Criticisms 1946-99 (Peregrine, 1971)

Harding, James: Jaques Offenbach – A Biography (Calder, 1980)

Harewood (Ed): Kobbé's Complete Opera Book (Bodley Head, 1987)

Hodgson, Julian: Music Titles in Translation (Bingley, 1976)

Holmes, John L.: Conductors on Record (Gollancz, 1982)

Hoppin, Richard H: Mediaeval Music (Norton, 1978)

Horton, John: Some 19th Century Composers (Oxford, 1950)

Howe, Marie (Ed): The Intimate Journal of George Sand (Williams & Norgate, 1929)

Hussey, Dynesley: Verdi (Dent, 1973)

Hutchings, Arthur: Mozart The Man, The Musician (Phonogram, 1976)

Isaacs, Alan & Martin, Elizabeth (Ed): Dictionary of Music (Hamlyn, 1982)

Jablonski, Edward: Gershwin Remembered (Faber, 1992)

Josephson, David: John Taverner – Tudor Composer (UMI Research Press, 1979)

Kemp, Peter: The Strauss Family (Omnibus, 1989)

Kennedy, Michael: The Oxford Dictionary of Music (Oxford, 1985)

Kerst, F & Krehbiel, H (Ed): Beethoven – The Man & The Artist (Dover, 1964)

Kostelanetz, Richard (Ed): Conversations with Cage (Omnibus, 1988)

Kurtz, Michael: Stockhausen – A Biography (Faber, 1988)

Layton, Robert (Ed): A Companion to the Symphony (Simon & Shuster, 1993)

Leach, Robert: Berlioz (Omnibus, 1983)

Lesure, F & Nichols, R: Debussy Letters (Faber, 1987)

Lockspieser, E: Debussy – His Life & His Mind (Oxford, 1978)

Lockwood, Lewis: Music in Renaissance Ferrara (Oxford, 1984)

MacDonald, Malcom: Schoenberg (Dent, 1976)

Mahler, Alma & Mitchell, Donald (Ed): Gustav Mahler – Memories & Letters (John Murray, 1973)

Martinů: Catalogue of Works (Panton, 1980)

Mellers, W: Vaughan Williams & The Vision of Albion (Barrie & Jenkins, 1989)

Mertens, Wim: American Minimal Music (Kahn & Averill, 1980)

Milhaud, Darius: My Happy Life (Marion Boyars, 1994)

Millington, Barry: Wagner (Dent, 1984)

Milne, Hamish: Bartók – His Life & Times (Midas, 1982)

Monson, Karen: Alban Berg (MacDonald & Jane's, 1979)

Myers, Rollo: Erik Satie (Dobson, 1948)

Myers, Rollo: Chabrier & His Circle (Dent, 1969)

Orga, Ates: Beethoven (Omnibus, 1978)

Orledge, Robert: Debussy & The Theatre (Oxford, 1982)

Orledge, Robert: Satie Remembered (Faber, 1995)

Osborne, Charles (Ed): The Dictionary of Composers (Macmillan, 1981)

Osborne, Charles: Verdi – A Life in the Theatre (Michael O'Mara, 1987)

Peppercorn, Lisa: Villa Lobos (Omnibus, 1989)

Poulton, Diana: John Dowland (Faber, 1982)

Prawer, S.S.: The Penguin Book of Lieder (Penguin, 1968)

Raynor, Henry: A Social History of Music, From the Middle Ages to Beethoven (Barrie & Jenkins, 1972)

Reese, Gustav: Music in the Renaissance (Norton, 1959)

Reich, Nancy: Clara Schumann – The Artist & The Woman (Oxford, 1985)

Reich, Willi: Alban Berg (Thames & Hudson, 1963)

Rimsky-Korsakov, Nicolai: My Musical Life (Faber, 1942)

Robinson, Michael F: Opera Before Mozart (Hutchinson, 1966)

Sachs, Kurt: Music in the Ancient World (Norton, 1943)

Sadie, Stanley (Ed): The New Grove Dictionary of Music & Musicians (Macmillan, 1980)

Schumann, Euginie: Memoirs (Eulenberg, 1985)

Scott, Michael: The Great Caruso (Hamish Hamilton, 1988)

Seligman, Vincent: Puccini Among Friends (Macmillan, 1938)

Shaw, George Bernard: On Music (Pelican, 1962)

Shead, Richard: Constant Lambert (Simon, 1973)

Slonimsky, Nicholas: Lexicon of Musical Invective (Univ. of Washington Press, 1981)

Smith, Geoff & Nicola Walker: American Originals (Faber, 1994)

Sorrell, N: A Guide to the Gamelan (Faber, 1990)

Southern, Eileen: The Music of Black Americans (Norton, 1971)

Stein, Erwin: Orpheus in New Guises (Rockliff, 1953)

Stevens, Dennis: The Letters of Claudio Monteverdi (Faber, 1980)

Stevens, Halsey: The Life & Music of Béla Bartók (Oxford, 1964)

Stuckenschmidt: Ravel – Variations on His Life & Work (Calder & Boyars, 1969)

Talbot, Michael: Vivaldi (Dent, 1984)

Taylor, Ronald: Franz Liszt – Man and Musician (Grafton, 1986)

Tovey, D.F.: Essays in Music Analysis (Oxford, 1972)

Vaughan Williams, Ursula: RVW – A Biography (Oxford, 1964)

Vaughan Williams, U & Holst, Imogen: Vaughan Willams and Holst – Heirs and Rebels (Oxford, 1959)

Vogel, Jaroslav: Leos Janáček (Orbis, 1981)

Volkov, Solomon: Testimony – The Memoirs of Shostakovich (Hamish Hamilton, 1979)

Whittall, Arnold: Music Since the First World War (Dent, 1977)

Young, Percy M.: Schubert (Benn, 1970)